CW01594673

MARK! MY WORDS

How to Discover the Joy of Music, the Delight of Language, and the Pride of Achievement

In The Age of Trash Talk and Cultural Chaos

MARK! MY WORDS

How to Discover the Joy of Music, the Delight of Language, and the Pride of Achievement

In The Age of Trash Talk and Cultural Chaos

MARK EVANS

Published by Basset Books
An Imprint of Cultural Conservation

Mark! My Words © 2023 by Mark Evans. All rights reserved. Printed in the United States of America. No part of this book May be used or reproduced in any manner whatsoever without written permission except in the case of brief quotations embodied in critical articles and reviews. For information address Cultural Conservation, P. O. Box 3785, Pinehurst, NC 28374, or visit the publisher's website for this book:

www.culturalconservation.org

Third Edition © 2023

ISBN 978-0-9847679-8-4

Library of Congress Control Number: 2022934779

In memory of my parents, who inspired me for a lifetime, my mother, Rea Evans, and my father Yale B. Evans, who would have said, "Dedicate it to your mother."

CONTENTS

ACKNOWLEDGMENTS

BOOKS DO NOT WRITE THEMSELVES. As an author, I always find it a pleasure to thank those who aided this book's journey from idea to publication. My parents, in whose memory this book is dedicated, are always first on such a list.

Much has happened in the several years since this book was first published. Many developments especially in the worlds of education, history, language, and the arts in general and music in particular, have indicated that our cultural crisis is more severe than ever. Nor is this just a challenge for Americans; friends in the United Kingdom, Australia, and Canada concur that the need for cultural conservation is universal.

Sadly, several friends acknowledged and thanked in the earlier edition of this book have passed away, but their friendship, support, and encouragement remains eternally in my memory.

I would also like to express my appreciation to: Sondra Nelson, friend and proofreader *extraordinaire*, with whom I have shared many a spirited discussion regarding some subjects of great mutual interest, the profound implications of the period, comma, colon, and apostrophe.

Carol Ann Johnson, not only for bringing her considerable designing skills to this book, but also for her patience in seeing me through an assortment of crises caused by a computer which is often cooperative, but also has ideas of its own and feels compelled like most digital devices to express itself. Brendan and Christine Walsh, my wonderful Irish friends in Sydney. As Australia's leading radio presenter of classical music, and one recently honored on the Queen's Birthday List with the Order of Australia Medal (O.A.M.) for his contributions to broadcasting, Brendan has been a constant advocate for Cultural Conservation and my belief that our cause will strike a responsive chord across the oceans. My colleagues, board members, and supporters of Cultural Conservation, the foundation dedicated to the principles espoused in this book, especially James Williford II for his continued enthusiasm and support, and the Holbrooks, Charles and Jewell, with a special hat tip to Charlie for his welcome advice and counsel. We continue to miss our former director and my good friend, the late J. Raymond Watson, and as I've often told his wife Bruny, no one was a greater advocate for the survival of grand operas and great music than Ray. Also a tremendous thank you to a great attorney, Donnel G. "Buck" Adams, and my incredible accountant, Howard Gartman, and his team, with the patience to teach mathematics to a musician.

Also missed greatly are the late Robert B. Bronec, whose friendship and constant encouragement remain appreciated beyond words, along with his devoted support for my books and their message, and his family, his late wife Dagmar, and the DeRoses, Ellen, Rodger, Steven, and Kimberly, the late Ted Dawes and his late wife Pat, whose friendship (and Ted's many years of experience as a publisher) have always made challenging decisions easier, the late Trish Samson, who made such splendid artistic contributions to our web site, and my late friends, Mohsin Ali and his wife Dolores Gregory. As I always told Dolores, Mohsin was a cultural conservationist every time he put words to paper.

Finally, there are dozens of musicians, writers, artists, historians, and teachers whose ideas have contributed greatly to the best of our past, present, and future culture, and in the process, have given us all a legacy worthy of conservation, providing the reason I wrote the book you are about to read. It would be impossible to list them all.

However, a life devoted to words and music is not nearly so serene as many imagine. It is rather like seeking the perfect word or sound in the middle of a thunderstorm; you hope for inspiration, but what you really need is a good umbrella. Several very special and extraordinary friends have helped turn chaos into order in too many ways to mention here. But I thank them.

The columnist Walter Winchell said, "A real friend is one who walks in when the rest of the world walks out." This is a perfect description of my always loyal friend for years, Johnnie Drakeford and his late wife Sharon, especially during days of trouble and challenge as well as those when the sun is shining. It applies as well to Judith Greer Bender, the epitome of generosity and kindness at all times, not to mention the surprises that delight all fortunate to be her friends.

And speaking of crises, it is hard to conserve our culture if our broadcast television equipment is misbehaving or the roof is leaking, so a heartfelt thank you to those who always come to the rescue, Terry Johnson, whose faith, friendship, and generous guidance is always inspiring in the tumultuous world of broadcast television and Jim Ransdell, ever present in weather foul as well as a fair.

A special thank you to my wonderful neighbors, including the; The Buecheles, Dr. Walter and Frances, Maureen Hunt, the Littlefields, Karen and John, and my former neighbor but always friend, Virginia Nickel. And of course, thanks as well to those nearby and faraway who remain loyal and faithful readers of my books, listeners to my music, but most important of all, the best of friends: Charlie (Mrs. Lou) Thesz, Barbara Covino, Susan and Fred Powell, Orriel and Bertha Smith, Michelle McNally, Paulette Drakeford, Harry Murchison, Ava and Bill Hubble, David Reeves, Helen Thomas, Dorita de Lemos Down, the late Christopher Hinkel and his wife Debbie, Karin Rodgers, Trudy McNair, James Stuart Davis, Jr. , Sir Bernard Ingham, Donald Armour, Gerry and Joanne Dryansky, Sissy and Joseph Kern, Jon and Jackie Henschen, John and Nancy Lambert, the late Dr. Aurelio de la Vega and his wife Anne Marie de la Vega, Dr. Christopher Armitage, and Susan Peterson.

My distinguished friend, the legendary pianist Ruth Slenczynska, has said that it is not what you can take from the world, but what you can give to it. One's goal, she says wisely, should be to make someone smile or think a happy thought. Not all the ideas expressed in this book will make you smile. But smiling doesn't mean that we don't take the mission of Cultural Conservation seriously. I invite you, dear reader, to join us with a smile and with determination to achieve a mission that can only benefit everyone in preserving our cultural legacy.

INTRODUCTION

In 1963, Stewart L. Udall, then Secretary of the Interior, wrote in The Quiet Crisis[1] that our nation must recognize the need for conservation. He said that "We stand today poised on a pinnacle of wealth and power, yet we live in a land of vanishing beauty, of increasing ugliness, of shrinking open space, and of an overall environment that is diminished daily by pollution, noise, and blight." Udall was talking about the need for conservation of natural resources, but today his words ring true in a description of a popular culture that often achieves goals of the marketplace while reflecting a spiritual bankruptcy. A hollow crown of gross profits is a poor excuse for a paucity of inspiration.

Turn on your television or radio, go see the latest multi-million dollar masterpiece at the neighborhood theater, visit the local museum, and check the best-seller list. You will likely discover the work of geniuses of little talent, imagination, or creativity. What you will find is the work of geniuses of self-promotion.

This is especially true in the world of music. In the world of popular music, we are treated daily to a parade of "superstars" whose voices and musical skills are an embarrassment. In the era of vaudeville, their caterwauling would have earned them the jeers of a scornful crowd and calls for a hook to pull them off the stage. Today, they earn millions of dollars, win awards, and enjoy the adulation of the crowd. Nor is the situation more encouraging in the world of classical music. The tortured dissonances of the self-proclaimed avant-garde are manifested in the assorted beeps and squeaks, which proclaim the future but make one long instantly for the past.

While adoring critics praise today's talentless wonders as the voices of tomorrow, our society gradually loses interest (and awareness) of the most talented contributors to our culture. Today's colleges are likely to produce graduates who may be blissfully unaware of the identities of most major American musical figures, including those key pioneers of jazz, musical theater, motion picture scores, and the concert repertoire.

William F. Buckley, Jr. wrote of a poll of students unable to identify a single 20th century composer. (Among their answers were Beethoven, the famed operatic tenor Luciano Pavarotti, and a rock star.) Buckley observed, "It requires dogged resolution to avoid coming across the name of Gershwin."

In 1975, the New York City Department of Education abandoned all instruction in the arts. Classes in music, dance, and art were dropped from the curriculum. Students could no longer play in school orchestras or be introduced to classical music or jazz, even though they lived in a city in which the arts thrived. In 1997, under the leadership of Mayor Rudolph Giuliani (and with the encouragement of Schuyler Chapin, his Cultural Commissioner), New York City finally resumed musical instruction in the public schools after twenty-two years of absence. What are we to expect from several generations of students who have been liberated from any knowledge of real music? They are like the clerk in a store selling compact discs, who responded to a request for Cole Porter recordings with a puzzled inquiry, "Is he new?" Nor is the problem limited to music or those outside the worlds of the arts, or even popular culture. Frequently, those most ignorant of our culture are those who spend their lives and careers determining what will be commercially distributed and critically and financially supported.

Steve Allen, in his book *Dumbth,*[2] tells of a young disc jockey who spent his life immersed in recordings, but failed to recognize a photograph of the most famous jazz clarinetist, Benny Goodman. Allen also writes of a story conference in which a television producer responds to a proposed tribute to legendary comedian Sid Caesar by asking, "Who's he?" An equally befuddled television producer, this time, a young woman, tried to conceal her ignorance of the prominent male television writer Paddy Chayefsky by declaring, "Patty Chayefsky, she was great, wasn't she?" Writer Harlan Ellison suggested to one of his publishers a cover design for a comic book he was creating. Ellison envisioned a parody of James Hilton's novel and its film adaptation starring Ronald Colman. The publisher had never heard of *Lost Horizon* or the motion picture, and clearly had never heard of Ronald Colman, a British actor with perhaps the finest speaking voice ever heard on the silver screen. After this episode, Ellison wrote, "It's impossible, almost impossible, to write anything today that an audience today knows anything about if the audience is under 20." Ellison added that the new audiences don't know and don't care. He wrote, ". . . we live in a time in which cultural illiteracy is at its peak. People aren't reading anymore. They're watching this tube. They're doing some movies. They're spending endless hours playing video games and getting their brains fried by what they call the Infobahn, which is one of the great hypes of the world."[3]

A freelance writer revealed his enthusiasm when offered a chance to interview the distinguished actor-playwright Peter Ustinov, only to discover his editors had no interest in buying an interview with anyone who isn't "young and with it," whatever "it" is supposed to represent. Their confusing "new" with "improved" reflects an attitude described by Ken Jowitt, Senior Fellow at the Hoover Institution, when he says, "We live in a world with no sense of boundaries, no distinction between past, present, and future. We have no memory, no discipline of the past, no comparative reference. Everything is now."

André Previn had a similar experience when a powerful Hollywood producer, Jeffrey Katzenberg, told him the only music that would survive the twentieth century was composed by the Beatles. Katzenberg added that he had never heard a piece of twentieth century classical music that would "knock my socks off."

(Previn turned down the opportunity to work as a composer- conductor with Katzenberg, who wanted to remake the Disney classic *Fantasia*. Katzenberg had decided to replace the music of Beethoven, Schubert, and Ponchielli with arrangements of songs by the Beatles. But the typical 21st century academician is likelier to agree with Katzenberg than with Previn.)

In 2011, Mary-Lu Zahalan-Kennedy, a former Miss Canada finalist, became the first student at England's Liverpool Hope University to receive a master's degree in Beatles Studies. Mike

Brocken, founder of the Master of Arts program in Beatles, Popular Music and Society, declared her to be part of "an internationally recognized group of scholars of Popular Music Studies who are able to offer fresh and thought-provoking insights into the discipline of musicology." There is a litany of such stories. The significance of such tales is more than anecdotal. The student who is blissfully unaware of anything but the latest television shows, recordings, and video games grows up to be the executive who determines the very content of popular culture. One day, the ignorant teenager will be an adult asked to support the opera, the symphony, the ballet, a major jazz ensemble, the legitimate Broadway musical theater, not to mention the local library or museum. What support can be expected from someone who has evolved from a culturally illiterate student into a mature ignoramus?

For too long we have taken the best of our culture for granted. Now as we witness the transfer of cultural judgments to a second (and coming third) generation raised on rock music, can we be surprised that musical ignorance is not only bliss, it is ever present? No one has expressed outrage over the neglect of the arts (especially those of serious and noble purpose) more than Norman Corwin. Corwin, who along with Orson Welles was one of the two great figures of radio drama, wrote for stage, screen, television, and published everything from opera librettos to poetry. In his book, *Holes in a Stained Glass Window,*[4] Corwin related tales of two distinguished composer friends who devoted years to their art. One, whose violin concerto was performed by Jascha Heifetz with both the New York Philharmonic and Dallas Symphony, received payments of $50 and $75 for these performances. The other composer spent part of a lifetime devoted to an opera, spent thousands of dollars of his own money copying and binding the score, won the praise of some of the world's greatest conductors for his work, but was unable to secure a performance of the work during the last thirty years of his life. It was finally performed in its entirety after his death. (Sadly, the experience of Corwin's friends, both of whom were very famous and prominent men, was not unique. I once asked the eminent American composer Aaron Copland what advice he could offer a young composer thinking about writing an American opera. Copland went straight to the point: "Plan on never hearing it performed.") Corwin bristled, "So what incentive is there for a practicing composer to write serious new works? He may wait thirty years for a performance, or have none at all. The appreciation of posterity makes mighty thin soup, assuming posterity will ever be interested at all." Corwin continued, "I believe a man who has and exercises a rare, but not especially marketable talent is a national treasure, and should be treated as such." National treasures? That is hardly the way our most creative artists are treated, especially if they eschew revolutionary and rebellious approaches to their art.

A few years ago, only one article, my own, followed the untimely death of Calvin Jackson, a brilliant pianist, composer, conductor, and (to use an overworked word, which is justified in this case) an absolute genius. The article, which ran in a high quality but little known magazine on African-American culture, was the only tribute paid to a man who was one of the most remarkable musicians of his generation. In contrast, the death of Michael Jackson, always described in the media as "the King of Pop," was treated by the press as a national tragedy worthy of coverage and mourning normally reserved for heads of state or historical heroes. Millions of people (including those often protesting the neglect of African-American achievers) have heard of Michael Jackson; very few have heard of Calvin Jackson, and that is the problem in a nutshell.

The challenge to preserve and conserve good music might as easily be issued on the subjects of literature or art. The novelist who ignores the fashions and fads of the moment is likely to be dismissed as a dreamer who does not acknowledge the harsh realities of the contemporary world. (Robert Nathan, a master of satiric fantasy who wrote such wonderful books as *Portrait of Jennie* and *The Bishop's Wife* dismissed the champions of realism by observing that an open sewer is real, but so is an April meadow.

It's all a matter of where you choose to focus your attention.) An artist who produces paintings of objects you can recognize (or people who do not appear to be in the middle of horrendous nightmares) will probably be dismissed with a casual wave of the hand by those who insist, "representational painting" is "too traditional." When "traditional" becomes pejorative, our culture is in trouble. Within a few years, these writers and painters will also suffer the fate of the forgotten composers, while ignorant throngs cheer the latest four chord virtuoso of rock music, the most recent master of the foul-mouthed screenplay, or the most contemporary painter of ugliness on canvas.

Like all crises, this one is not predestined. There is an alternative. It is time for those who value art, who take culture seriously, to recognize that Corwin was right when he spoke of artistic genius as a national treasure. Our society is full of people who have come to recognize that it is important to preserve our natural resources. But just as preserving our rivers and forests is important, so is preservation of our cultural treasures (and support and encouragement of those who created them in the past and continue to create them today). "Culture" and "Conservation" are words that are not often used together. This should change. A society that preserves its natural resources should preserve its cultural resources; it will be a far better society in the long run.

Many would recognize that our society is in crisis, offering a multiplicity of diagnoses as the cause. Taxes are too high. (They are.) Government is too big, intruding its bureaucratic nose into even the most private activities. (It is.) Politicians disappoint and deceive. (They do.) Financial markets go up and down. (They will.) Dictators and fanatics represent a serious threat to peace and prosperity. (Is there any doubt?) Children drive their parents to distraction. (It was ever thus.) Therefore, the natural tendency is to think that most problems facing us are political or economic in origin and solution.

Culture in general and the arts in particular are often regarded as the icing on the cake, the cherry on the sundae. In effect, cultural questions are regarded as decorative and ephemeral. If a list of people and things that matter in society were to be made, there is little doubt that musicians, writers, and artists would not be anywhere near the top. Yet it is often the musicians, writers, and artists of an age who are remembered, and even if their work is forgotten, their legacy for good or ill remains. However, we often fail to recognize that many of our most serious problems are actually cultural in origin and therefore cultural in solution.

In the 21st century, despite incredible technological advances, we live in an age of cultural confusion. Our sense of history is vanishing faster than anyone could ever have predicted. Our ability to master our own language is declining in a sea of jargon, bureaucracy, and commercial profanity. Music, art, and the written word are devalued by some and declared irrelevant by others. Classical music appears to be a dinosaur unready to assume its place among the fossils, while popular music has become an appalling circus of amplified vulgarity. Art has become an arena for prosperous charlatans while gifted artists struggle to survive. All the while, a superficial celebrity culture thrives and occupies our attention.

Every era has its Chicken Littles, convinced that the sky is falling. You will not find one here. No one should imply that recognizing the existence of a problem is a suggestion that the sky is falling. Nevertheless, becoming aware of the problem is actually the first step to finding a solution. The answer to this problem cannot be found in the places usually expected to represent beacons of light in our cultural confusion: academia, the entertainment industry, or government. These institutions are frequently part of the problem, not the solution. Nor should these pages be regarded as a critique of the free market system. You will find no argument here for a culture controlled by self-styled intellectual wise men or government bureaucrats. But we cannot succeed if we remain a society that, in the words of Oscar Wilde, knows the price of everything and the value of nothing. Only we ourselves can discover, develop, and empower our culture.

In the age of trash talk and cultural chaos, we need not despair or surrender. As a society, we can take positive steps toward the ideal of cultural conservation. As an individual, you can discover the joy of words and music and the pride of achievement. This book is about that alternative. It seeks to invite you, dear reader, on a journey. With a bow to Charles Dickens's classic *A Christmas Carol,* you are invited to explore our past, our present, and our future. Together, we can discover how we reached this sorry state of affairs and what we can do to change it. Let the journey begin.

DO THE ARTS MATTER?

MEANING AND MESSAGE

DO THE BOOKS, MUSIC, AND ART we choose matter? Are our choices more important than selecting hotdogs or hamburgers, vanilla or chocolate, Coke or Pepsi? The arts have a unique ability to communicate beyond themselves. The choice of a sandwich, ice cream, or soft drink will probably not have consequences, save an occasional case of indigestion. But when we choose the books we read or the music we hear, we are choosing the way in which our culture (or lack of it) may influence us.

Some regard books or recordings as simply objects—a book or compact disc on a shelf. Others may study the techniques required to write books, compose music, or paint pictures. The aspiring writer may attend classes to study grammar and even analyze the style of famous authors. The student painter can learn about the chemical content of paints and the technique of applying them to canvas. The apprentice composer may learn the rudiments of harmony, counterpoint, rhythm, melody, and orchestration. However, absorbing the technical aspects of these subjects does not guarantee inspiration, creativity, or imagination. It says nothing about the artist's message. All great art (and bad art) sends a message to readers, listeners, and viewers. These messages can accomplish great good or prove to be destructive beyond our wildest imagination.

From the earliest days of childhood, what we choose to read affects our outlook, our values, and our ideals. Dr. John Silber, former President of Boston University, said that moral lessons can be learned as early as a child memorizes the Mother Goose rhymes. Silber recalled that small children were once taught, "If wishes were horses, then beggars would ride." He said, "The child was warned to remember the reality principle and not to be misled by the attractions of wishful thinking."

Russell Kirk, an eminent philosophical historian, reminded us, "The person who reads bad books instead of good may be subtly corrupted, the person who reads nothing at all may be forever adrift in life." Kirk said, "If a small boy does not read *Treasure Island*, the odds are that he will read *Mad Ghoul Comics*." What is most important, however, is that bad books are not bad only because they are badly written. A book may also send a bad message, faulty reasoning, and encourage certain kinds of behavior. John Locke wisely declared, "The reading of bad books is not only standing still, but going backwards, and he that has his head filled with wrong notions is much more at a distance from the truth than he that is perfectly ignorant." Henry David Thoreau said, "A truly good book teaches me better than to read it. I must soon lay it down and commence living on its hint. What I begin by reading, I must finish by acting." Today, we have not only books, but also films, television programs, magazines, music videos, the Internet, all of which ask us subtly or demand with the vigor of a sledgehammer that we "commence living on their hint." There is an old saying, "You are what you eat." You are also, what you read. Meghan Cox Gurdon, Children's Book Reviewer for *The Wall Street Journal*, made the case for good taste in children's books in a speech at Hillsdale College. She observed quite correctly that "Books tell children what to expect, what life is, what culture is, how we are expected to behave--what the spectrum is. Books just don't cater to tastes. They form tastes." She also quoted the English writer Roger Scruton who perceived that artists, directors, musicians, among others, are not only in a flight from beauty, but have a desire to spoil beauty, because beauty calls upon us to renounce narcissism. Meghan Cox Gurdon concluded her remarks with a reference to Saint Paul the Apostle in Philippians 4:8 "Whatever is true, whatever is noble, whatever is right, whatever is pure, whatever is lovely, whatever is admirable—if anything is excellent or praise-worthy—think about such things." She advises us to think about these words when we go shopping for books for our children. This is indeed admirable advice, applied not just to books, but to music, art, and all elements of the best of our culture if we seek to conserve it.

The messages of art and music are subtler than those of books. If an author says, "Bake a cake," "Vote for Jones for President," or "Jump out the Window," the message is obvious. But what messages do painters and composers send? Do they send any messages at all? Some would reply no, insisting that painting and music are abstract arts that offer little meaning beyond light, color, or sound. (Igor Stravinsky once created controversy by dismissing those who liked to imagine plots or story lines in the sounds he created. Stravinsky once insisted, "music means nothing outside of itself.") Certainly many composers write music in absolute forms.

Beethoven composed a *Sonata quasi una fantasia in C# minor.* Perhaps because it was dedicated to an Italian countess, the piece engendered numerous tales and legends. It became known as the *Moonlight Sonata,* with poets, painters, and people who had overactive imaginations supplying all sorts of subtexts, which undoubtedly never occurred to Beethoven. On the other hand, we may never know what occurred to Beethoven at the moment he actually created the sonata we play.

Composers have freely admitted that all kinds of emotions and events inspire them. Since music is their language, they express their message in sound rather than in words. But the message is there. Composer George Antheil wrote, "I believe in music. When I am true to it, music is my friend. It consoles me in my hours of consternation and gives me added flight in my hours of luck. Music is, mostly, faith: but after that, it is something that makes life, always beautiful, doubly worth living." Like Antheil, Henry Cowell also declared, "I believe in music: its spirituality, its exaltation, its ecstatic nobility, its humor, its power to penetrate to the basic fineness of every human being." Cowell said that as a composer, he contributed his religious, philosophical, and ethical beliefs in terms of the world of creative sound.

Antheil and Cowell were both expressing something known to all good composers: music is not just a collection of notes or sounds, but the expression of a message, often too personal to be put into words by its creator. Beethoven's *Fifth Symphony* became the sound of resistance to tyranny during World War II. There was a reason why this magnificent symphony inspired people, and a reason why a cacophony of banging pots and pans did not. The inspired artist delivers a gift to his audience—what the English painter Dame Laura Knight called "a sunset in your hand."

We should not assume that such gifts only come from classical music. Duke Ellington used the jazz idiom to express his deepest religious beliefs. Oscar Hammerstein II chose the idiom of musical comedy lyrics to denounce racial prejudice and to convey to listeners his self-proclaimed "cockeyed optimism" about the human condition. Clearly, these artists were sending messages to us. This does not mean that music should not be amusing, entertaining, or even uproariously funny. It does not mean that art is undeserving if it does not deliver an academic or philosophical message. However, the music we hear, the art we see, and the books we read, send us messages whether or not we recognize them. It should be obvious that to reject the finest books, art, and music of the past is also to reject their messages. If we engage in such rejection, we do not do so in a vacuum.

Nancy Pearcey, in her book *Saving Leonardo*,[5] writes that the arts affect our minds, morals, and meaning. She correctly observes, "The common stereotype is that art is merely a matter of personal expression. But the truth is that artists interact deeply with the thought of their day. They translate worldviews into stories and images, creating a picture language that people often absorb without even thinking about it. Learning to 'read' that language is a crucial skill for understanding the forces that are dramatically altered our world." She calls artists "society's barometers, sensitive to new ideas as they percolate through the cultural stratosphere."

Similarly, the distinguished historian David McCullough, in "Knowing History and Knowing Who We Are,"[6] recognized the influence of our cultural heritage. He said, "They have shaped us too—the people who composed the symphonies that move us, the painters, the poets, those who have written the great literature in our language. We walk around every day, every one of us, quoting Shakespeare, Cervantes, Pope. We don't know it, but we are, all the time. We think this is our way of speaking. It isn't our way of speaking—it's what we have been given."

Today's popular culture is sent with lightning speed over the airwaves and the Internet. The ubiquitous rock videos and television commercials often define our ambitions and inspirations. Some would suggest that today's pop culture has not only a right, but an obligation to replace yesterday's pop culture. Those who criticize today's pop culture or its messages are likely to be dismissed as prudes, censors, elitists, intellectual snobs, or worst of all, people who are too old fashioned to be "with it." What "it" signifies is never defined in precise terms, but the meaning is clear enough: today's pop culture delivers messages that are relevant today. The messages that were delivered yesterday (let alone last year or a hundred years ago) have little to tell us today. This is absurd, of course, but it is appealing to those who don't want to bother opening a book, listening to a piece of music, or thinking about the messages they deliver.

For the most gifted creators in the arts, the message they communicate is often what matters most. The words, the notes, the colors are a means to an end. When we read a book, fiction or non-fiction, there are two elements on the page: a collection of words and what those words teach us when they are put together. *Alice in Wonderland*, for instance, is on one level, a delightful story for children about a little girl who pursues the White Rabbit and finds herself having a series of adventures. But on another level, Lewis Carroll is delivering a scathing satire on the people and ideas he found ridiculous. The same can be said for Jonathan Swift in *Gulliver's Travels* or the operettas of Gilbert and Sullivan. Satire and ridicule enable the author to send us a message about behavior he finds absurd and outrageous.

The novels of Charles Dickens are filled with a rich collection of characters whose behavior often stays with us long after we have forgotten the details of his plots. The obsequious, oleaginous Uriah Heep, in *David Copperfield*, always protesting that he is "'umble" while secretly plotting and scheming, is unforgettable. Why? Because many of us have known people who behave like Heep, and there is a lesson to be learned from what Heep does to others and from what life ultimately does to him. So we can read a book in two ways: for enjoyment and for what we take away from it.

Not everything we read must be instructional. There's certainly nothing wrong with a good western or a good murder mystery. However, everything we read, often unconsciously, sends us messages. Dr. William J. Bennett culled the stories, letters, poems, and speeches of America's founders to produce a book, *Our Sacred Honor*.[7] He found their words reflected a host of virtues: patriotism, courage, civility, frugality, justice, industry, and piety.

It is harder to identify the messages found in music and art, because they are often non-verbal. Yet music represents a language all its own. Helena Lewyn was an internationally distinguished pianist and teacher. In her essay, "Must Music Be Edited?"[8] she wrote, "Music has a grammar; clauses, phrases, sentences and paragraphs. Its punctuation includes periods, commas, as well as exclamation points, as purposeful as in any spoken language. The observance of phrasing is as important as taking a breath in speaking or singing." When a great pianist or violinist plays or when a great singer performs, they are at their best when they move beyond mere notes on the page to convey a whole cornucopia of emotions. Johann Sebastian Bach said that the primary purpose of music was "to praise and glorify God."

Many of Bach's compositions were signed by the composer with the initials S.D.G. (Soli Deo Gloria) or "To God Alone the Glory." Masaaki Suzuki, founder of the Bach Collegium in Japan, has directed performances of Bach's *Christmas Oratorio* and *Passion According to St. Matthew* each year. Suzuki credits Bach as a missionary among the Japanese people, inspiring thousands to convert to Christianity. Beethoven tried to reflect what he saw as the heroic spirit of Napoleon, a man he admired, in his *Eroica* symphony. When Napoleon crowned himself Emperor, a furious Beethoven ripped his name from the dedication page.

Beethoven's music can deliver a powerful message, as the first movement of his *Fifth Symphony* seemed to be the epitome of resistance and defiance during World War II. The distinguished

Australian conductor, Patrick Thomas, has written, "Above all, perhaps it was Beethoven's faith in Man's inextinguishable Brotherhood and his hatred of tyranny that remain the finest examples of this man's unique and lasting inspiration."[9]

Paul Creston, a prominent twentieth century composer, said that the most important quality to be found in his own music was spiritual. Composers have found ways to express a host of emotions and ideas through notes. At some point, individual notes disappear and blend into harmonies, melodies, and rhythms, which in turn reach the listener on an emotional level. Frederick Delius managed somehow to translate the tranquility of the English countryside into sound. Tchaikovsky conveyed his personal pathos and tragedy to audiences through his music. Listen to a performance by a great jazz musician and you may encounter a wide variety of emotional experiences, ranging from the sadness of the blues to the exuberant joy of a piano virtuoso like Art Tatum.

Like a great musician, a great painter uses color, light, proportion, and design as the technical means to an artistic end. Does an artist choose to paint that which is beautiful or that which is ugly? There are those who suggest that nothing is intrinsically beautiful, that beauty is only in the eye of the beholder. Gertrude Stein once declared that great art was an irritation. Perhaps some great art may be irritating, but should we conclude, that if art doesn't irritate us, it is not really the work of a master?

Today's pop culture sends messages too, many of them destructive and debilitating. Too often, these messages provide children and young adults with a rationale for behaving irrationally. "If it feels good do it" and "Decide for yourself what's right and wrong" are examples of these messages. Of course there are constructive messages to be found in modern music, art, books, and even motion pictures and television programs. But it isn't easy for most people to separate the wheat from the chaff. Too many absorb the messages rejected by Russell Kirk: that the world is purposeless, that life is meaningless, and that a writer should only express a vagrant ego.

In today's world, two generations of students have grown up to be increasingly ignorant of the facts, names, places, and events we assumed were common knowledge. However, these same students are intimately familiar with the names and faces of personalities who are depicted on television, in the movies, and in pop music. We shouldn't be surprised if today's teenagers are more familiar with the names of rock groups or tabloid celebrities than great figures in the arts. These people are declared "important" by virtue of their exposure in the media. But we should ask ourselves what will happen if this situation doesn't change. A professor at a Midwestern college described his son's taste in music in these words: "If I want to get him out of the house," said that hapless professor, "all I have to do is play a recording of Luciano Pavarotti singing opera. He can't stand it, and he leaves immediately." The young man in question, undoubtedly familiar with all the icons of pop culture, is likely convinced that his father has odd taste in music, and worse, that he is "old-fashioned" and not "with it." If nothing is done, the future of our museums, libraries, opera, ballet, musical theater companies, symphony orchestras, jazz bands, and the all-powerful media will

Now this professor's son may be a perfectly well-behaved teenager who will go on to be a solid citizen. But an amiable ignoramus is still an ignoramus, and the rest of us will pay a price for the legacy the ignoramuses have wrought. Still, what can be done? A child offered a choice between junk food and spinach is not likely to choose the spinach, even though it is healthy. (Popeye the sailor, hero of many a cartoon, persuaded a multitude of children to eat their spinach. We have to find the Popeyes who can persuade them to open their eyes and their ears to all that our culture has to offer.) This isn't an easy task. Men and women of all ages, not just children, are bombarded with the constant messages of the pop culture, a continuous assertion that taste and talent are defined by commercial success and the blessings of the media.

Finally, we must ask of necessity the question, "Do the arts matter?" Henry James said, "It is art that makes life, makes interest, makes importance and I know of no substitute whatever for the beauty of its process." Years later, John F. Kennedy expressed a similar sentiment when he said, "A nation may be moved by a statesman, defended by its military, but it will be remembered for its art." However, radio, television, and films focus much of their attention on people who contribute little to our culture. The vaunted social media are also dominated by a group of individuals who may accomplish nothing more tangible than capturing public attention. In the age of trash talk and cultural chaos, talent and the pride of achievement are considered far less important than a highly marketable commodity: celebrity.

THE CULTURE OF CELEBRITY

THE ADDICTION TO FAME

In the 21st century, fame and achievement have become synonymous. The greatest accomplishment is to be noticed. Given the choice between the perception of achievement in public and the reality of achievement in private, which would you choose? In our culture, image is everything.

Have you kept up with the Kardashians? If you haven't, you're likely in the minority. The Kardashians are the first family of the celebrity culture. Not everyone is a fan or a follower.

Ellis Cashmore declares, "In terms of influence, it's tough to think of any other family in history that's defined an era quite like the Kardashians. The Borgias, maybe. Neither Kim nor the other Kardashians are Hollywood movie stars, singers, or artists of any note. They are propelled into our lives by nothing but trash—and I mean this in the nicest possible way: cultural items, ideas and objects of no noticeable quality that might, at another time in history, be regarded as waste material. At the start of the century, the name Kim could have referred to a member of the North Korean Defense Committee. Now, we know it's the name of the most recognizable, ubiquitous, inescapable celeb of all time."

It was not always thus; the ubiquitous celebrity culture, sustained and supported on social media by millions of fans with stars in their eyes, is notoriously fickle. Today's celebrity may only be memory tomorrow; today's nonentity may be the subject of obsessive idolatry tomorrow.

Only a few years ago, the most widely discussed celebrity was pop singer Britney Spears. The world in general and her fans in particular wanted to know everything about Britney Spears. For instance, they responded breathlessly to the news that Britney Spears didn't like to eat fish. We know this because she said, "I've never really wanted to go to Japan. Simply because I don't like eating fish. And I know that's very popular out there in Africa." If Britney Spears somehow thought that Japan is part of the African continent, her admiring public didn't hold it against her. Perhaps it is because the pop star expressed enthusiasm for travel, "especially to overseas places like Canada."

We know these things because the smallest detail, the tiniest iota of information pertaining to Britney Spears was reported, discussed, analyzed, digested, debated, dissected, and above all, marketed. This occurred in newspapers, magazines, television, radio, the Internet, and an assortment of tabloid publications that defy classification. In 2008, "Britney Spears" was the most popular annual search term on the search engine, Yahoo, for four years in a row. She fell to number five in 2009, and in 2010, she dropped to number ten, upstaged by the BP Oil Spill, the World Cup, and several other objects of public attention. By 2021, Britney Spears was still a celebrity, but her fans and followers were now aware that her life was in turmoil as she took legal action to end a conservatorship that controlled her daily living and the millions of dollars she had earned. The fickle spotlight of the celebrity culture had moved on.

While the names at the top of the list may change daily, the principle remains. Why should we care about celebrities whose daily activities are similarly reported, discussed, analyzed, digested, debated, dissected, and above all, marketed? What are their accomplishments? Paris Hilton, the great-granddaughter of hotel magnate Conrad Hilton and the blonde heiress has been quoted as saying, "I'm very intelligent. I'm capable of doing everything put to me. I've launched a perfume and want my own hotel chain. I'm living proof blondes are not stupid."

Of course, this is the same Paris Hilton who asked if Walmart "sells wall stuff." There is no question that she displays brilliance in the field of self-promotion. But the crown of celebrity lies uneasily on the head. The popular search engine, Yahoo, reported gleefully that Paris Hilton had been displaced in the public sweepstakes by her friend and former stylist, reality television personality Kim Kardashian.

(Because of the incredible success of their reality show, *Keeping Up with the Kardashians,* the Kardashian family and the sisters in particular have parlayed their fame into a plethora of products ranging from perfume to a personalized credit card.) Yahoo posted its verdict in 2009 by declaring, "Two years ago, you might have said 'Kim who?'" (Yahoo went on to announce that "the celebutante Kim Kardashian swiped the 'famous for being famous' crown from Paris Hilton and placed it squarely on her own long locked head." As the tabloid queen says in one of the show's earlier episodes, 'There's a lot of baggage that comes with us, but it's like Louis Vuitton baggage. You always want it.")

The term "celebutante" is a portmanteau of "celebrity" and "debutante." A celebutante is famous, primarily for just being famous. It was apparently coined in 1939 by columnist Walter Winchell. Being a celebutante can be profitable. Kim Kardashian came to prominence after a sex tape featuring her with her then boyfriend, *Kim Kardashian Superstar*, became public in 2002. Soon she was starring (along with other members of her family) in the reality television series, "Keeping Up with the Kardashians." The series enjoyed a fourteen-year run, but television stardom was only the beginning of the story. Kim Kardashian acquired hundreds of millions of followers on Twitter and Instagram. She launched her own lines of beauty and fragrance products. By 2015, *Time* magazine named her one of the world's hundred most influential people. Kardashian knew how to get attention by posing nude and also releasing a book filled with hundreds of pictures of herself. All of this led to a net worth reportedly in the hundreds of millions of dollars.

By 2021, various members of the Kardashian family had a total of over seven hundred million followers on Instagram. The most followed celebrities on Instagram (between one hundred and three hundred million followers) included pop stars Katy Perry, Miley Cyrus, Nicki Minaj, the latter known as "the Queen of Rap," Taylor Swift, Justin Bieber, Beyoncé, Selena Gomez, and Ariana Grande. Athletes like Dwayne Johnson and Cristiano Ronaldo were on the top of the list. The actual lists are unimportant, and the names and numbers change daily. What is important is the realization that these are the people who matter to hundreds of millions of individuals who follow every detail of their lives and consider everything from their political opinions to their product endorsements as Gospel. At the height of its popularity, more people watched the television program "American Idol" than watched the nightly news on all three television networks combined. With vast wealth and fame as the ultimate prizes, it matters not to the celebrity what you have to do for attention as long as you get it. There are no rules or standards. Publicity is all that counts. Ellis Cashmore writes that for a celebrity of any rank, indifference is the equivalent of lethal injection.

Especially for boys and girls growing up, are these influences to be applauded? Hardly. Not everyone has jumped aboard the celebrity bandwagon. All the way back in 1967, decades before personal computers, cell phones, and social media, British writer Malcolm Muggeridge anticipated what was coming. He concluded, "In the past if someone was famous or notorious, it was for something—as a writer or an actor or a criminal; for some talent or distinction or abomination. Today one is famous for being famous. People who come up to one in the street or in public places to claim recognition nearly always say: 'I've seen you on the telly!'"

A more recent observer of contemporary celebrities, writer P. J. O' Rourke, observed, "If you say a modern celebrity is an adulterer, a pervert and a drug addict, all it means is that you've read his autobiography."

Once upon a time, an individual arrested and charged with a crime would demand a phone call to contact his or her attorney; today, the demand for the phone is the same, but it is more than likely placed to a publicist. The Internet and untold fame and fortune await.

The celebrity culture presents a daunting challenge to any parent or grandparent trying to explain to a boy or girl why certain values are important. Why should a student work hard in school, study history, read great literature, discover musical masterpieces, view fine art, or devote hours to important ideas expressed by philosophers and minds of consequence when a well-planned campaign on You Tube, Facebook, Instagram, Twitter, and whatever burgeoning social platform of the moment offers the deceptive appeal of instant celebrity? One could, of course, present to the skeptical boy or girl a host of arguments grounded in intellect, principles, and logic. But faced with the chance to acquire millions of followers, having one's face splashed and plastered on digital sites around the world, and the prospect of earning "big bucks," making these arguments becomes increasingly more difficult. But it is a challenge we must face or lose all that is truly important in our society and our culture.

MOSQUITOS AND REFLECTED GLORY

The exploits, scandals, misadventures, and trivial pursuits of celebrities are chronicled in detail by tabloid publications, often with pictures taken by paparazzi. In Federico Fellini's 1960 film, *La Dolce Vita*, Walter Santesso portrayed a news photographer called "Paparazzo." Screenwriter Ennio Flaiano said that Fellini took the name from the name of a hotel proprietor, "Signor Paparazzo," in George Gissing's 1901 travel book, *By the Ionian Sea*. Robert Hendrickson, suggests in his book, *Facts on File Dictionary of Words and Phrase Origins,*[10] that Fellini used nickname, "paparazzo," slang for "mosquito," that had been applied to a schoolmate who constantly talked, since the word implies a buzzing sound. Wherever the word originated, its plural, "paparazzi," is now used to describe freelance photographers who specialize in surprise photos of celebrities who don't plan to have their pictures taken. Photos of celebrities eating, shopping, or doing anything unscripted can be worth substantial amounts of money. A photo of a celebrity cheating on a spouse, getting intoxicated, or being arrested is worth even more. Major celebrities are pursued by paparazzi who will stop at nothing to get their pictures. Ironically, some publicists cooperate with paparazzi, letting them know the whereabouts of their clients, facilitating the "unauthorized photos," all in the name of publicity. There are even reports of so-called "faux-paparazzi," actors who are hired to act like the pursuing photographers, to impress clients that they are important enough to be pursued. Astronomical fees for celebrity photos are only paid because their publication will boost sales of the tabloids. People buy publications featuring photos of the celebrities about whom they care the most. The public, it appears, is addicted to fame.

Our familiarity and occasional obsession with celebrity should be obvious to anyone who explores anecdotal evidence, which forms a dubious mosaic of popular taste. Radio and television talk show host Sean Hannity frequently presents "man in the street" interviews in which people selected at random on the streets of New York are asked to name the Vice President of the United States. Many fail. Comedian Jay Leno elicited startling answers in his hilarious "Jaywalking" interviews and the results are telling. A young woman was asked to name the second winner of the television singing competition, *American Idol,* and she immediately replied, "Rueben Studdard." But when asked to name the second President of the United States, the name of the most obscure John Adams didn't occur to her. One participant in Leno's impromptu quiz couldn't recall the Presidents on Mt. Rushmore, but easily knew the names and nicknames of Nicole "Snooki" Polizzi, Michael "The Situation" Sorrentino, and Jenni "Jwoww" Farley, stars of the MTV reality television show *Jersey Shore.* Another had no idea how many justices sit on the United States Supreme Court but could identify the number of children in the Gosselin family, featured on reality TV. The identities of three explorers who are of importance in United States history remain a mystery, but the names of the Kardashian sisters are as familiar as their reality television show, *Keeping Up with the Kardashians.* What is the name of a Supreme Court Justice who left the Court? Leno's question got a blank stare; but the same person was quick to identify Paula Abdul as the judge who left *American Idol.* As for famous couples, "Antony and Cleopatra" remained unknown, but "Spencer and Heidi" were easily recognized as Spencer Pratt and Heidi Montag, stars of the MTV reality show, *The Hills.* There are hundreds of such examples, but critics will be irate that such anecdotes are unscientific and don't really prove anything.

Jake Halpern explored the idea of celebrity in his book, *Fame Junkies: The Hidden Truth Behind America's Favorite Addiction.*[11] In association with the Newhouse School of Public Communications at Syracuse University, Halpern polled 650 children in Rochester, New York, on their attitudes toward fame and pop culture. The results were troubling. When asked if they would like to be stronger, smarter, famous, or better looking, boys chose fame almost as often as intelligence. Girls chose fame more often. Forty-three and four-tenths percent of teenage girls wanted to become celebrity personal assistants, choosing that option twice as often as that of "the president of a great university like Harvard or Yale," three times as often as "U.S. Senator," and four times as often as that of "the chief of a major company like General Motors." Teenage girls were given a chance to choose someone they would most like to meet for dinner. Those girls who said they were appreciated by their parents, friends, and teachers, often chose Jesus Christ. Those who felt underappreciated were likely to choose Paris Hilton.

Halpern writes about aspiring child actors and teenagers who are convinced that fame is a solution to all of life's problems. Psychologists have actually developed a term, "BIRGING," to describe the phenomenon of "basking in reflected glory." If associating with celebrities seems like an odd career ambition, think again. Incredibly, there is even an Association of Celebrity Personal Assistants. Halpern became acquainted with one assistant who had worked for Oliver Stone, Sharon Stone, and Dennis Hopper, and who teaches classes for aspiring celebrity personal assistants.

Joseph Epstein, writing in *The Weekly Standard,* turned caustic wit on the familiar names and faces that seem to populate our daily lives. "The Culture of Celebrity: Let Us Now Praise Famous Airheads"[12] sums up the phenomenon. Epstein observes that the greatest celebrities are instantly recognized by their first names alone. Imagine a headline with the latest news on Liz, Liza, Oprah, Kobe, Britney, Shaq, J-Lo, O.J., or the latest gossip about celebrity couples like "Tomkat" and "Brangelina." Marilyn Monroe passed away years ago, but "Marilyn" is unmistakable in the headlines. Epstein cites the example of Boston Red Sox baseball legend Ted Williams to distinguish between fame and celebrity. Williams wanted to be famous, to be remembered as the greatest pure hitter in the history of baseball. He did not want anyone to think that the description applied to his greatest rival, Joe DiMaggio of the New York Yankees. But Williams had no interest in being a celebrity. During his playing days, he gave no autographs to fans and avoided interviews with the press more than called third strikes. Williams drew a distinction between his fame as a ballplayer and his celebrity because of that fame.

All kinds of people become famous. Some receive recognition for their ability; great composers, writers, and artists, for instance, can become known to the public for their achievements. But public recognition also comes from publicity, and there are those who become better known for their efforts at self-promotion than their actual talents.

There are also those who become famous through a single sensational occurrence, usually a scandal or a crime. Without the single scandal that makes them famous, they might go through their lives without a moment of public attention. Sometimes their fame lasts only a few minutes, and they are discarded, replaced by another instant and equally fleeting celebrity. Their scandal, their moment, however, may propel them into continued fame that can be exploited for years. An army of publicists, lecture agents, promoters, managers, and hustlers is always ready to seize upon the outrage of the moment in order to turn a profit. The more salacious the scandal, the worse the outrage, the better for the army who feast like vultures off the whims and failings of a celebrity conscious public.

The problem is not exclusively American by any means. In 2008, the Association of Teachers and Lecturers of the United Kingdom conducted a survey of over 300 British teachers and found that the most admired celebrities were soccer star David Beckham and his wife, former "Spice Girl" Victoria Beckham. The survey concluded the celebrity culture persuades children they can become rich and famous without working hard in school. Schoolchildren who are imitating the language, behavior, and dress styles of their idols are busy dreaming of becoming pop stars and professional athletes. They have little time for school and display minimal interest in their studies. The Beckhams were the most popular celebrities. Others on the list included, not surprisingly, Paris Hilton. Heather Wagner, writing in *Vanity Fair*, observes, "In the past, you usually had to do something significant to become famous, like act or sing or play a professional sport. But this decade, thanks to TMZ and *US Weekly*, the barrier to entry became absurdly low, as witnessed by the glut of "celebutards": the young, wealthy, spray-tanned, multiple-D.U.I-receiving, brawling-outside-L.A.-nightclubs, underwear- shunning set. The world changed the day we all clicked to view Lindsey Lohan's lady business with our morning coffee, and not, one suspects, for the better."

Does it matter that more Americans seem to be interested in the hard-drinking, foul-mouthed personalities appearing on *The Jersey Shore* than in people of true accomplishment? (In 2011, the Rutgers University Student Association hired Nicole "Snooki" Polizzi, *Jersey Shore* star, to speak to 1,000 undergraduates. Her $32,000 fee, paid from mandatory student activity fees, exceeded the $30,000 the university paid Nobel laureate Toni Morrison to appear as commencement speaker. Her topics ranged from hair styling to lessons for life. Presumably, the Student Association thought it important for members to follow "Snooki's" advice when she said, "Study hard, but party harder.") Meanwhile, "Snooki's" co-star, Mike "The Situation" Sorrentino, was reportedly paid $400,000 to endorse "Devotion," a brand of vodka, while publishers allegedly were offering him a six-figure book deal. The public may assume Sorrentino thinks life is just a big party, but he knows what needs to be taken seriously. He consulted billionaire entrepreneur Mark Cuban about how to invest some of his presumed $5 million income; Cuban was impressed by Sorrentino's ideas to "market his brand." In the celebrity culture, the notion of a brand is what seems to count.

On Nov. 24, 2009, Michaele and Tareq Salahi, a married couple from Virginia, attended a White House reception for the Prime Minister of India, Manmohan Singh. They were photographed shaking hands with President Obama; the episode was regarded as a major breach of security when it was revealed that the Salahis apparently had no invitation and still managed to gain access to a major White House event. While the arrival of the Salahis may have been a fiasco for those in charge of Presidential security, it proved a publicity bonanza for the two party-crashers.

While preparing to crash the President's party, the Salahis had been filmed by a camera crew for the reality television series *Real Housewives of D.C.* After multiple investigations by politicians, lawyers, and a small army of reporters, the Salahis insisted that they were targets of a public flogging. But the Salahis became full-fledged celebrities. *New York Times* columnist Maureen Dowd opined, "Even the outrage over the fakers is fake. The capital has turned up its nose at the tacky trompe l'oeil Virginia horse-country socialites: a faux Redskins cheerleader and a faux successful businessman auditioning for a 'reality' show by feigning a White House invitation. Yet Washington has always been a town full of poseurs, arrivistes, fame-seekers, cheaters and camera hogs." The *Washington Post* gossip column *Reliable Sources* declared, "The Salahis took what could have been an enjoyably seedy little horse-country melodrama and catapulted it into the gossip stratosphere with one fateful night at the White House that exposed the dark secrets of our decade's major growth industries: national security and reality television." The *Washington Post* might have added "celebrity" to its list of major growth industries. For today, a significant portion of society values fame for its own sake; how fame is achieved is entirely irrelevant.

On both sides of the Atlantic, celebrities take up far more than their share of public attention, but is this just the triumph of superficiality? Unfortunately, our international obsession with celebrities has serious consequences. Sir Bernard Ingham is a noted author, columnist, and veteran British journalist who served for eleven years as Press Secretary for Prime Minister Margaret

Thatcher. He observes quite correctly in the *Yorkshire Post*, "We are so dumbed down we cannot educate our young properly, partly because discipline has gone out of the window. Television has reduced our attention span to that of a gnat and our concept of worth to 'celebrities' who behave badly on the box." The distortion of our concept of worth on either side of the Atlantic is at the heart of the problem.

Take a hard and dispassionate look at the people who become celebrities. Certainly, there may be a few heroes among them, for example, Chesley Sullenberger, the airline pilot who safely landed his plane in the Hudson River and saved the lives of hundreds of passengers. Occasionally, public recognition may be directed at a volunteer who sacrifices a life of privilege to help those in need. But by and large, people become celebrities simply because they receive public attention. The historian Daniel Boorstin once defined celebrities as people who were well known for their "well-knowness," what he termed, "human pseudo-events." The public attention they receive may be divorced from any real accomplishment. It is likely to be unrelated to any qualities of moral strength or character.

Notoriety can increase the level of celebrity. Outrageous behavior usually increases the degree of public interest and attention. We live in a society that has become obsessed with being "non-judgmental." The virtue of an open mind has been distorted and carried to extremes. Being tolerant doesn't mean we should tolerate anything and everything. Too many people today are afraid that even the most basic standards or values will result in their being labeled biased, bigoted, or narrow-minded. So the non-judgmental among us look the other way while celebrity is often bestowed upon those least deserving of its rewards.

Children are likely to choose their heroes from among those who receive a vast amount of public attention. This inevitably means figures from the worlds of sports and entertainment. There is nothing new about people admiring athletes, movie stars, or famous musicians. Fan magazines of the 1930s were full of admiring stories about such figures. But something has changed.

Many heroes of the past, especially those in the entertainment industry, led highly flawed private lives that were concealed from their adoring public, often by skilled press agents. Nevertheless, underlying their efforts of public relations was an assumption that bad behavior would be detrimental to their careers. There is a fine line between fame and notoriety. Hollywood stars, professional athletes, and even gangsters tend to glory in publicity, any publicity, good or bad. The important thing to these people is to get attention. Sometimes they cross the line and their private behavior is professionally damaging.

The tabloids devote barrels of ink to the private travails of actors like Charlie Sheen, Lindsay Lohan, Johnny Depp, and Amber Heard. or sports figures like boxer Mike Tyson, football star Michael Vick, and golfer Tiger Woods. Today, private behavior that would have once destroyed the career of a Hollywood star or highly paid athlete merely whets the public's appetite for more. Those actors, musicians, and sports figures who lead exemplary private lives are often regarded as uninteresting by the media, while their scandalous counterparts are simply considered colorful.

What would today's athletic stars, with agents, publicists, money managers, and sports psychologists, think of Hobey Baker? Baker was considered the first great American hockey player. He excelled at any sport he tried, including not just hockey, but football, baseball, tennis, swimming, and track. He played golf brilliantly the first time he tried, performed one-legged stunts on roller skates after trying on his first pair of skates, and once entered a highly competitive track event for fun and defeated some of the finest runners. His athletic exploits at St. Paul's School and Princeton, where he captained the hockey and football teams, were legendary. F. Scott Fitzgerald met him only once, but admired him so much that he used him as a character in his novel, *This Side of Paradise*. Baker turned down a chance to become a professional athlete, because he considered it inappropriate to make money through his athletic skills. He remained an amateur, instead, volunteering to serve as a fighter pilot in World War I. So many of his Princeton classmates followed him into the military that the school had to cancel its 1917 hockey season. Baker eschewed publicity, asked that a sign promoting his appearances be taken down, and said he hoped no one would write anything about him. He was cited for exceptional bravery during World War I and was due to return home a hero when he died testing a plane in what was to be his final flight in France. He was only twenty-six years old. Today, the best NCAA hockey player each year receives an award named in his honor. In recent times, the sports world was puzzled by Pat Tillman, an NFL football star who turned down a multimillion-dollar contract to join the St. Louis Rams out of loyalty to the Arizona Cardinals. After the terrorist attack on the World Trade Center on September 11, 2001, he gave up his football career to serve in the military in Afghanistan, where he was killed in a "friendly fire" episode. Despite his heroism, athletes who turn away from untold riches out of a sense of duty or principle are regarded as oddities.

Certainly, they are exceptions to the rule. In 2011, St. Louis Cardinal baseball legend Stan Musial was awarded the Medal of Freedom by President Barack Obama. Musial's career in baseball speaks for itself. When he retired in 1963, he held seventeen Major League records and twenty-nine National League Records; he was elected to the Baseball Hall of Fame. But what is interesting about Musial is his personal behavior. In 3000 games, Musial was never ejected by an umpire. He was a devoted family man, married to his wife Lillian for more than seventy years, known for playing the harmonica, and had a reputation for being gracious in signing autographs. Missouri Sen. Claire McCaskill had written to the White House praising Musial's devotion to the USO, Boy Scouts, Senior Olympics, President's Council on Physical Fitness, Crippled Children's Society of St. Louis, and other groups and charities. She described Musial as "the kind of role model that America longs for. He has always cared about his community, his country, his fans and his teammates much more than he cared about his own glory." When he died in 2013 at age 92, he was described as "baseball's perfect knight." How many of today's sports or entertainment stars could fit such a description? Of those who do, how many are likely to receive attention in the media, always in search of bad behavior that generates tabloid headlines?

One 21st century athlete who does receive recognition for his good works is Tim Tebow. In recent months, even people who don't follow professional football have become aware of Tebow, The home-schooled winner of the coveted Heisman Trophy in college, Tebow's extraordinary behavior off the field is even more meritorious than his athletic triumphs. During his time as quarterback of the Denver Broncos, Tim Tebow invited the disabled and the terminally ill to be his guests at NFL games. He flew them to Denver, arranged for their dinner and accommodations, provided them with pre-game passes and 30-yard tickets to the game, visited with them before kick-off and after the game, and sent them home with gifts to remember the experience. He brightens the lives of people like a girl who had endured multiple surgeries or a high-school quarterback whose leg had been amputated. (Tebow encouraged him to get a prosthetic leg and to attempt to return to football.) Tebow explained, "Here you are, about to play a game that the world says is the most important thing in the world. Win and they praise you. Lose and they crush you. And here I have a chance to talk to the coolest, most courageous people. It puts it all into perspective. The game doesn't really matter. I mean, I'll give 100 percent of my heart to win it, but in the end, the thing I most want to do is not win championships or make a lot of money, it's to invest in people's lives, to make a difference." Tebow devotes much of his time to charitable works. Tebow is regarded as a hero by legions of fans and would seem to be totally removed from controversy. But because he is an outspoken Evangelical Christian, he has drawn ridicule, scorn, and abuse from those who are more comfortable with athletes who display the worst, not the best, behavior. For a segment of our society, heroic behavior becomes something to tear down, not admire.

WHAT'S IN A NAME?

Public attention—in the print press, on radio and television, and on the Internet—can make someone into an instant celebrity. Daniel Boorstin rightly drew the distinction between heroes, who were men and women of great stature, and celebrities, who had "big names." People become heroes because of their deeds, but they become celebrities because of their fame. More often than not, that fame is the result of marketing and promotion. Boorstin also said that a sign of celebrity is that his name is often worth more than his services. Some celebrities are well aware of the importance of their names. Igor Stravinsky, at the time the world's most famous composer of concert music, was asked to score a motion picture. The famed composer offered to do the music, but insisted on a substantial fee. The studio demurred. Stravinsky then offered to cut his fee if the studio used his music but left his name off the screen credits. "The music is cheap," said Stravinsky. "It's the name that's expensive." He wasn't wrong. The studio turned down his offer and his film-scoring career ended before it started.

The people who promote celebrities usually are quick to display their lack of taste and their lack of conscience. Consider the case of O.J. Simpson. Simpson became a celebrity as a football star and after he retired, as a sometime actor and television pitchman. But his name was etched in infamy at his trial for the double murder of his wife Nicole and her friend, Ron Goldman. As everyone in the world knows, Simpson was acquitted in the criminal trial, but found to be liable in a civil trial that persuaded the public that Simpson was guilty. After thirteen years of freedom, he was convicted in Las Vegas for a bungled attempt at robbery involving what he claimed was his own property. Incredibly, there were people in Las Vegas still trying to get Simpson's autograph. Autographs of history's most evil men and women do bring a good price on the collector's market. (There are collectors willing to pay top dollar for signatures of anyone ranging from Adolf Hitler to Al Capone.) But were the autograph seekers looking for a financial gain or just seeking Simpson's signature because he was a celebrity, regardless of the reason?

On the day Simpson was sentenced, a company called Xtreme Entertainment Group (XEG) announced that it was releasing a comedy video starring Simpson. This masterpiece, called *Juiced,* featured Simpson performing a "gangsta rap," entitled *Get Juiced.* Simpson also appears in what are supposed to be comedy sketches, including one in which he pretends to be a car salesman promoting a White Bronco like the one in which he nearly fled after his wife's murder, a car described as containing a bullet hole to symbolize its "escapability." A press release from XEG promised a sketch in which Simpson brandishes a golf club and nearly decapitates one of the paparazzi. The company marketing this video had no scruples about using domestic violence, race, and murder as subjects for comedy. Rick Mahr, the founder of the company, was also behind such tasteful entertainment as *World's Wildest Brawls, Brawling Broads,* and *Ghetto Brawls.*

With the advent of reality television, anyone can become world famous because of exposure on the small screen. In 1968, artist Andy Warhol made his famous comment that "in the future, everyone will be world-famous for fifteen minutes." In the 21st century, the prediction in some ways has come true. Anyone appearing on a reality television program can be instantly recognized by millions of people. An amateur performer can gain greater fame after a few weeks on television than artists who have worked all their lives to develop their talents and perfect their art. In recent years, "reality television" has become a major contributor to the celebrity culture. In 2000, sixteen men and women became competitors and instant stars on *Survivor,* a television program photographed on the island of Borneo. The finale drew fifty million viewers, eager to see which cast member would collect a million dollar prize. Members of the cast became instant celebrities, as famous and recognizable as actors who were the stars of scripted dramas and comedies.

The success of *Survivor* produced a predictable reaction in the entertainment industry. Reality shows, allegedly unscripted and featuring "real" people instead of actors or performers, became all the rage. Some programs were contests requiring competitors to demonstrate their talents: aspiring singers appeared on *American Idol*; well-known personalities tried their hand (or feet) at ballroom dancing with gifted professional partners on *Dancing with the Stars*; chefs battled for the title of *Top Chef*. But the most remarkable trend was identified by CBS television commentator Jeff Greenfield, who observed that "Producers also discovered a different audience appetite—a hunger to watch people with no discernible talent, no discernible insights, but who are willing, eager to be seen and heard doing . . . nothing." Some shows, like *The Bachelor*, offer the hope of a marriage proposal at the end of the season. But others simply provide the public an opportunity to eavesdrop on the daily lives and relationships of a group of people, obviously chosen by producers for the ability to generate controversy, get attention, and guarantee high ratings; the more outrageous the behavior, the likelier that audiences will pay attention.

The rise of the untalented and frequently uninhibited television star was a new element in entertainment. From its early days, television had on occasion featured non-professional people on the air. There were talent competitions like *Ted Mack's Amateur Hour*, game shows on which contestants won prizes, and comedy programs like Allen Funt's *Candid Camera*, in which participants were caught unaware of a hidden camera presenting their hilarious and often embarrassing behavior. But people who appeared on these programs almost never became "stars"; after a few minutes of fame, they usually returned to lives of relative anonymity.

Today's reality shows are different. Appearances on successful reality shows provide the same level of public recognition previously enjoyed by actors who held lead roles on the most popular programs on television. Not everyone on reality television becomes a celebrity, but the opportunity is there. Jeff Greenfield interviewed Omarosa Manigault, who became a celebrity icon when she competed unsuccessfully on Donald Trump's reality program, *The Apprentice*. Although she didn't win the competition to become an apprentice to the future U.S. President, she established an identity for herself in the mind of the public. She told Greenfield, "A friend of mine said, 'The fabric of reality TV is conflict, so make sure that you're either in the fight, breaking the fight up, or starting the fight.'" Greenfield concludes that "the sheer volume, as well as the often jaw-dropping behavior of today's reality shows has opened another chapter in a very old debate: can what we see and hear on television affect us for the worse?"

Why have reality shows become so popular? In the entertainment industry, the answer is money. Advertisers will spend as much as a million dollars for a 30-second advertising spot on *American Idol.* But reality shows, especially those involving contestants eager for a chance to achieve fame and fortune, cost only a fraction of the production budget for more traditional dramas and comedies. Network executives and cable syndicators can dispense with high salaries for actors, and the reality shows (with some exceptions) do not require highly skilled writers and composers. At one time, the chance to become a star seemed limited to people who professed to have talent, the ability to act, sing, dance, or do something extraordinary. Now anyone can be a reality star. Once established as a celebrity, a reality star can move from one show to another and enjoy all the benefits of being famous. The public now follows the intimate lives of "celebrities" in the same way they follow every detail relating to their favorite movie or television stars. Persons of great accomplishment and achievement may toil in anonymity, while an untalented reality star achieves his or her life's ambition, and the ambition of a multitude of aspirants to be noticed, at all costs.

Some people who should become celebrities do not. In 2007, President George W. Bush awarded the Medal of Honor to Lt. Michael Murphy, a Navy SEAL who sacrificed his life in Afghanistan. Lt. Murphy was part of a four-man reconnaissance team, surrounded by fifty Taliban fighters. Although he was already wounded, Lt. Murphy crawled into open space to radio for help. One of Lt. Murphy's men was rescued as a result, but he was killed by enemy fire. Although Lt. Michael Murphy was from Long

Island, his receipt of the first award of the Medal of Honor for Operation Enduring Freedom was ignored by the *New York Times.*

Celebrities are regarded by many people as heroes, but sadly, real heroes often do not become celebrities.

How many Americans today would recognize the names of Jared C. Monti, Salvatore Giunta, Robert James Miller, Leroy Petry, Clinton Romesha, Dakota Meyer, or William Swenson? Like Michael Murphy, they were all awarded the Medal of Honor. Despite being wounded in the neck, arms, and shoulder, Romesha provided suppressive fire that allowed three other wounded American soldiers to reach an aid station and directed air support in the twelve hour Battle of Kamdesh that enabled his fellow soldiers to regroup and fight off a much larger enemy force. Meyer defied orders from his superiors, in the process, rescuing twenty-three Afghan Allies and thirteen Americans in combat in Afghanistan. In the same battle, Swenson repeatedly exposed himself to deadly enemy fire to recover fallen comrades and save fellow soldiers. A medevac crew's helmet cameras captured Swenson delivering a severely wounded soldier to a helicopter. For the first time, the public could actually watch video of actions resulting in a Medal of Honor award. Giunta was the first living recipient of the Medal of Honor since the Vietnam War. Romesha, Meyer, and Swenson also survived, while Monti, Miller and Petry, like Murphy, gave their lives in service of their country. Similarly, the names of Paul R. Smith, Ross A. McGinnis, Jason Dunham, Travis Atkins, Michael A. Monsoor, David Bellavia, would not likely be familiar to most Americans. McGinnis, Atkins, Dunham, and Monsour sacrificed their lives earning the posthumous Medal of Honor Award for service in Iraq. We know the names of the most trivial celebrities, yet what celebrity would make the choice made by Atkins, McGinnis, Dunham, and Monsoor, who, in separate combat events, threw themselves on grenades to save the life of their fellow countrymen?

Do those college students who could easily recite every detail of the lives of various pop culture celebrities known the name of Sgt. Major Thomas "Patrick" Payne. Inspired by the a desire to respond to the September 11 terrorist attacks, Payne enlisted and in 2020 was presented with the Medal of Honor by President Donald J. Trump for liberating over seventy hostages from an ISIS prison in Iraq.

On May 21, 2021, President Joseph Biden awarded the Medal of Honor to Col. Ralph Puckett, Jr., U.S. Army Retired, for conspicuous gallantry during the Korean War. How many people today could explain in even a simple way why Americans fought in the Korean War or know how many lives were lost in that conflict?

Much has been written about the overemphasis on celebrities in our public discourse. Students who are totally ignorant regarding the greatest figures in American history can supply every detail about talentless celebrities they have seen on television. Large segments of the public are oblivious to the skills and struggles of the truly talented artists in our society, all the while heaping honors and attention upon entertainers who are treated as if they had achieved fame through the ability they lack. In the process, we forget what happens to the truly talented.

Why are great composers, writers, and artists neglected? Sometimes it is because they create works of art in styles that are out of fashion. It is fashionable to talk about modernists and revolutionaries who are neglected because they are "ahead of the times." But what about those who are unfairly dismissed as being "behind the times" and forgotten? Some are neglected because they simply lack the gift of self-promotion. Others are cast aside in history because they run afoul of a political system, which doesn't tolerate them. Sometimes the political system is simply an established group of artists or business executives who simply choose to ignore them. In other cases, they conflict with political dictators who don't tolerate dissent. Some of the greatest figures in the arts have gone through periods of neglect and rediscovery. Consider the fate of a German organist whose Baroque masterpieces were forgotten by the early nineteenth century. The music of Johann Sebastian Bach is revered today, but Bach's music might have withered on the historical vine were it not for Felix Mendelssohn who discovered and championed Bach's works long after his death. We all know the stories of Vincent van Gogh, whose paintings today sell for millions of dollars, but who only sold one painting in his lifetime.

WE THE PEOPLE, WE THE PROBLEM

Whenever we discuss the great creators and performing artists of the past, someone is bound to ask, "What about the great performers of today?" Many people in our society will be quick to assert that we have just as many fine writers, composers, and artists today as in past years. Does this argument hold up under scrutiny? The answer is more complex than it might first appear. Among those making this argument are a variety of men and women whose motives are obviously commercial. A record company executive, for instance, insists that the products he markets today are merely "contemporary" for "today's audience," or, at its lowest common denominator, "what the kids want." The owner of an art gallery promotes a bizarre exhibit of avant-garde art as "the wave of the future" and declares, "Art is worthless if it isn't provocative." A book publisher spends millions promoting the latest literary potboiler while its author tells interviewers his view that "we can't be prudes" and that his book "simply reflects real life."

None of these assertions should come as particularly surprising. What do we expect an executive of a recording company to say? Is it likely that he will say, "I know I'm marketing trash, but I want to make a lot of money?" What do we expect the owner of a gallery to say? Should we anticipate her declaring, "I know these paintings could just as easily be done by a chimpanzee throwing paint at a canvas, but they bring high prices and critical acclaim?" What do we expect a book publisher to say? Is it likely that he will declare a preference for best-selling junk than for volumes of great literature that are about to be sold to a remainder house which markets books at deep discounts? (Coincidentally, an author receives no royalties from the sale of a book after it has been remaindered.) So the assertions of these individuals should be taken for what they're worth: campaign speeches by candidates in search of profit. It isn't always complicated to discern motivation.

(One is reminded of director Alfred Hitchcock's response to a skeptical actor who asked him, "What is my motivation in this scene?" To which Hitchcock responded, "Your salary.") On the other hand, this argument is also advanced by a number of critics and self-styled intellectuals. Some may be self-serving, but others truly believe that music, art, literature, and our culture in general have improved over the years. They espouse a type of "evolutionary" theory about culture.

We might call it "cultural Darwinism, the survival of the fittest music and art." In effect, they are saying that the best always survives. Does it? Not really.

There are several factors that proponents of this theory always neglect. One was developed brilliantly by Peter Reilly, writing in a 1979 article in *Stereo Review*. Reilly turned his focus on a subject rarely addressed by critics, the changing nature of the audience. Reilly said, "Time was, when you could point out undisputed excellence on all sides of the entertainment business. Where have you gone, Joe DiMaggio? Where are you now, Cary Grant, Audrey Hepburn, Peggy Lee, Lena Horne, Julie Harris, Rex Harrison, George Shearing, and all the rest? Oh, they're there all right, but the public appetite for them has noticeably cooled." (With laser-like accuracy, Reilly turned his attention to today's audiences.) He continued, "We want to 'identify' not with symbols of what we possibly could be, but with avatars of our own let-it-all-hang-out amateurism. We want to turn the whole world into the Arthur Godfrey Show. I could—you could—fake a Travolta, for example, but never an Astaire. And to sing like any number of today's chart heavyweights would hardly tax the resources of a high school sophomore. But to sing, that is . . . to perform would not only require an interesting musical voice to begin with, but also that its own cared enough about expressing the emotional meaning of song lyrics to labor long and lovingly until that became clear."

Many years have passed since Reilly's observations. What has happened? Some of the talented individuals he described are, sadly, no longer there, having passed away or retired. In today's pop music, some "superstars" are delighted that the demands of stardom do not exceed the talents of high school sophomores, since they are high school sophomores. Audiences today, more than ever, seem to admire performers whose abilities to a great degree do not exceed their own. (At the height of the rock music revolution, composer-pianist Mel Powell described "the empathy of the talentless kid in his living room, plunking away on his guitar for the equally talentless kid on the tube, plunking away on his guitar." Powell assumed this should be obvious to anyone with "minimal musical awareness.") Unfortunately, minimal musical awareness is frequently in short supply. Reilly's point, as valid today as when he made it originally, is that past audiences watched Fred Astaire and Ginger Rogers whirling around the black and white art-deco sets of their movies and knew in their hearts that they would never dance with such elegance and abandon. But they could hope, dream, and imagine the possibility of dancing like that. (The same could be said for any of the performers Reilly cites, the on-screen elegance of Grant and Hepburn, the lyrical expressiveness of Shearing at the keyboard.) But many of today's audiences are content, even thrilled, to cheer for performers whose limited abilities are obvious to those with even a modicum of common sense. One should not require the discerning eye of an artist or the alert ear of a musician to recognize this fact. Do today's audiences know what they like or do they simply like what they know?

An obvious problem arises in speaking critically of audiences. People do not like to be told they are gullible, ignorant, or just plain stupid. So telling an audience that it is part of the problem, not part of the solution, isn't always helpful. It may come as a shock (although it shouldn't) to learn that audiences think they're really quite intelligent. They know when to applaud. If you suggest that the cheers of the crowd are directed at mediocrities, the crowd will cheer louder. It will also laugh loudly at the silly person making the suggestion.

Those who suggest that our culture is evolving and improving miss a second and equally disturbing fact. They assume that writers, composers, or artists whose work reflects traditional styles or standards are probably passé: elderly, frustrated, untalented individuals. They ignore the best-kept secret in our culture. There are numerous writers, composers, and artists of all ages who find energy, vigor, beauty, vitality, elegance, and an intense sense of personal expression in styles and standards that have evolved over hundreds of year. But consider the fate of these talented individuals. The representational painter is one who paints scenes and objects people can recognize. He may display brilliant skill with his sense of color or design. But critics will dismiss him as merely "copying reality." The composer who writes melodies that people can remember is likely to find an audience that will not walk out of the auditorium when his name appears on a program. But he, too, will incite the critics who insist that only music devoid of melody, harmony, and rhythm should be considered "contemporary."

The writer who chooses to focus on the better angels of our nature rather than the misfits and malcontents of our world will meet a similar fate. Readers may welcome his work, but critics will be quick to suggest that his focus is upon people and ideas that lack "relevance" in a contemporary world. Some of these "critics" will not just be firing verbal bullets from the pages of a newspaper. They will be producers, publishers, executives, and people whose control over funding sources gives them the power to determine which artists are given a forum. The artist dismissed as a "traditionalist" may be facing a career of frustration and anonymity, earning the recognition of genuine admirers, but the guaranteed contempt of the cognoscenti. It is, therefore, an all too neglected fact that the gifted and talented people admired by Peter Reilly are not necessarily extinct; they are too often ignored. Those who should know better frequently tip their hats to the exponents of what Reilly calls "gimmickry, faddishness, and narcissism." Those who neither know better nor care will make up an audience delighted with its own blissful ignorance.

When today's audiences are confronted by genuine artistic brilliance, a great pianist, for instance, or operatic tenor, they will often respond with astonishment and adulation. But such instances are rare, and too often, dependent more upon the celebrity of the performer than a real curiosity about the music being performed. If audiences are not exposed to the good, the true, and the beautiful, why should we be surprised if they are all too eager to cheer the not very good, the untrue, and the ugly?

It is sad, but true, that today's audiences are generous with their applause to performers on television, on record, in films, and on stage, not because of their ability, but because they are on television, on record, in films, or on stage. In effect, the audience assumes that the performer is talented because he is in the public eye, not that he is in the public eye because he is talented. This raises the question of celebrity and how it affects our view of culture.

Though some of the world's most accomplished people are artists, few of these individuals appear on a list of people regarded as heroes by the American public. In cooperation with *U.S. News & World Report*, the Harris Interactive poll asked over 1000 Americans who their heroes were. More than 50 percent responded that they did not regard any living public figure as a hero. The individual receiving the most votes (6 percent) of those polled was Jesus Christ. Others often mentioned included Martin Luther King, Jr., Colin Powell, John F. Kennedy, Mother Teresa, Ronald Reagan, Abraham Lincoln, John Wayne, and Michael Jordan.

What is a hero? Whom should young people admire? The question is an important one, and the heroes—musical, artistic, and otherwise—admired by young students may affect them for the rest of their lives. Ed Colina, Principal of Immaculate Heart of Mary School in Burlington, Kentucky, expressed the important classroom choices well. He said, "When I taught and was feeling particularly unappreciated I would call to mind some of the great people in our history. We tend to forget that these great ones attended elementary and high school and were taught in classrooms like ours. The point is that the president didn't know he was destined to be president when he was a fifth grader. St. Augustine didn't know he was 'Saint' Augustine. Heart surgeons, Supreme Court justices, advocates for the homeless, sports figures and movie stars were all, at some time, first graders seated in some underpaid teacher's classroom."

If young students learn early to develop an enthusiasm for the artists of great accomplishment, they can develop a sense of values that may transcend the bombardment of commercial media. Stephanie Perrin, Head of the Walnut Hill School in Massachusetts, has stressed the positive self-identification that results when a young girl studies the violin. She says, "At the time in her life when she is developing a sense of her own identity, in the world, the young violinist has the gift of seeing herself as a 'musician,' as a member of a larger community of accomplished people. She isn't a 'nerd,' a 'prep,' a 'jock;' she is a musician. In a time when Madonna tops the list of people most admired by teenagers, to have a student wish to emulate Itzhak Perlman is much to be desired."

The pop culture sends most young people a deadly message, predictably confusing notoriety with achievement, commercial success with accomplishment, public recognition with ability. The student who develops a true sense of values will not be fooled by this. But it isn't easy, and both teachers and students are faced with an apparently overwhelming challenge: a commercial entertainment industry that determines who and what are important. Such determinations are made by only one factor: who made the most money yesterday.

LOST ALONG THE WAY

Why are some figures abandoned by history, at least for a time? Often the answer is one of style, politics, misfortune, or a combination of all three. Consider the stories of four distinguished musicians, each of whom, through no fault of his own, suffered periods of great neglect.

In 1932, Berthold Goldschmidt was considered one of Germany's leading composers, with a brilliant future ahead. His opera, *The Magnificent Cuckold*, was performed in Manheim and scheduled for a 1933 performance in Berlin. Germany's leading conductors, Otto Klemperer and Erich Kleiber, competed for the right to conduct his music. However, Adolf Hitler and the Nazis ended all that. Goldschmidt found himself a refugee in England, where he remained musically neglected for nearly the rest of his life. Writer and critic Norman Lebrecht found him living in the same one bedroom flat he rented on his arrival in England seven decades earlier, with hot water only recently installed. One of his operas won a major prize in England, but it was rejected for a performance because it was "not British enough." Goldschmidt acquired some powerful enemies when he protested. According to Lebrecht, an atonalist writ imposed on the B.B.C. by William Glock in 1959 closed Goldschmidt's last outlet in Britain. He was a confirmed melodist and simply stopped composing for twenty-five years.

The Goldschmidt story had an unusual twist. Goldschmidt was rediscovered by the public near the end of his life. A performance of *The Magnificent Cuckold* at Trinity College sparked the interest of a publisher and Decca Records decided to record his works as part of an effort to restore works suppressed by the Nazis. Nearly ninety, Berthold Goldschmidt found himself in demand in Europe and America, and even lived to see the performance of *The Magnificent Cuckold* in Berlin, sixty-one years late. Goldschmidt found fame before his death in 1996. He treated his newfound fame without bitterness and with some amusement, speculating that it would be nice for his enemies to see what finally happened to his neglected music. But we shouldn't be misled by the happy ending. Goldschmidt endured a lifetime of musical neglect, while a multitude of pretentious classical composers and talentless pop musicians were basking in the public spotlight.

Erich Wolfgang Korngold had a career, which proved very different from that of Berthold Goldschmidt. In his native Vienna, Korngold was considered one of the greatest child prodigies since Mozart. Gustav Mahler called him a genius, Richard Strauss said that he was astonishing, and Giacomo Puccini declared him "the greatest hope of German music." His operas, *Die Tote Stadt* and *Das Wunder der Heliane*, won him critical acclaim and it appeared that Korngold was on his way to becoming one of the most important composers of the century.

But when the Nazis took over Austria, Korngold and his family found themselves refugees in America. Unlike Berthold Goldschmidt, Korngold was able to find steady work in Hollywood. He worked primarily at Warner Brothers, scoring the great swashbuckling films of Errol Flynn, notably *The Adventures of Robin Hood.* But Korngold eventually decided to devote himself entirely to concert music again. After World War II, composers who didn't follow in the path of Arnold Schoenberg or Igor Stravinsky were often neglected. A caustic critic dubbed Korngold's music "more corn than gold." By the time of his death in 1956, Korngold's fame was a memory. His biographer, Brendan Carroll, wrote, "Korngold's passing merited only small mention in the obituary columns; most described him as a famous film composer, a label he would have hated." A memorial concert was held in Los Angeles, but it did not launch a resurgence of interest in his music and the works of Erich Korngold disappeared from the repertory for at least two decades. Happily, Korngold's music has been rediscovered and much of his music is now available through many new recordings. His magnificent *Violin Concerto,* written for Jascha Heifetz, is now regularly played and recorded, and his reputation is now as high as it ever has been. But Korngold died thinking that he would be forgotten.

Dr. Aurelio de la Vega was one of Cuba's most distinguished musicians in the years before the Castro revolution. He was a prominent composer, Vice President of the Havana Philharmonic, and director of the school of music he founded at the University of Oriente, the first at the university level in Cuba, the second in all Latin America. Cuba had enjoyed a proud musical history. José Martí, the great 19th century Cuban poet and advocate of independence, said, "The rhythm of poetry, the echoes of music, the beatific ecstasy that the contemplation of a beautiful painting brings to the soul, and the soft melancholy that overtakes the spirit after these superhuman contacts, are mystical raiments, gentle prophecies of a time when all will be light." Martí warned that tyranny could dress in handsome names and grand deeds.

This was a lesson sadly learned by Cubans with the rise of Fidel Castro.

Like thousands of his countrymen, Aurelio de la Vega fled the tyranny in his homeland and settled in the United States. Happily, he enjoyed a distinguished career in his new home, including a thirty-three-year teaching career at California State University, Northridge, where he was named the most outstanding teacher in the whole university system. He expressed his musical philosophy with the declaration, "The composer of art music is a crusader whose goal is not to kill or conquer, but to elevate beauty to such lofty heights that it shines like a gigantic beacon for all humanity." His works have been played throughout the world by major orchestras, ensembles, and soloists in Europe, Asia, and Latin America. He is also widely remembered as a distinguished writer on both the music and art of Latin America. However, works from his extensive catalogue were not performed in Cuba for political reasons. The Castro regime simply decided to erase the contributions of Cuba's musical pioneers from the Republican era. Aurelio de la Vega explained in a cogent essay, "The Age They Wanted to Erase."[13] "After 1959, in the anti-historic ardor of Castroism, my existence was erased from Cuba's musical world and my name disappeared as founder of this university school of music, to be replaced by that of two of the professors whom I had brought to the University. My biographical ostracism joined that of others who had also contributed to the development of Cuban classical music in the Republican era."

Despite neglect in his original homeland, Aurelio de la Vega refused to compromise his integrity or artistic standards. He wrote, "Faced with an evil person, I shrug my shoulders; faced with a doctrinary and furious Marxist, I keep silent; faced with an imbecile, I leave to drink a good wine. The real facts, dear one, remain, based on books, memories, essays, articles, magazines, dictionaries, publications of international economic agencies and, above all, in the truth proclaimed by those of us who were witnesses and participants of a magnificent era, in which Cuba came to occupy, in spite of the prevailing political corruption and damage to the civic society, an enviable economic position and to have a truly astonishing intellectual and artistic life. It is moving to remember such times."

Calvin Jackson was a remarkable Renaissance man whose musical brilliance was expressed as a composer, conductor, arranger, concert pianist, and jazz virtuoso. Despite a lifetime of musical accomplishments and the respect and admiration of some of the world's most eminent musicians, his name remains relatively unknown to the general public. An African American born in Philadelphia, Jackson emerged from the Juilliard School of Music as a master of both the European classical tradition and American jazz. He developed a unique style of piano performance, combining the best of both worlds. It wasn't unusual to hear him dash off a fugue based on *My Funny Valentine* or to quote dozens of classical works in a jazz improvisation. He spent five years at MGM as assistant musical director, scoring classic musical films, and then moved to Toronto at the suggestion of Oscar Peterson. During his five years in Canada, he performed Rachmaninoff's *Fourth Piano Concerto* with the Toronto Symphony, introduced two of his own ballets, *Maria Chapdelaine* and *The Loon's Necklace* to an enthusiastic public, and led his own jazz combo and orchestra as the star of his own television show. But genius isn't always easily classified or marketed. Although he was greatly respected and regarded in awe by his more famous musical colleagues, since he passed away in 1985, only one major magazine article (by the author of this book) was written about this amazing musician.

Some neglected achievers like Berthold Goldschmidt live long enough to achieve vindication after a lifetime of being ignored. Others, like Erich Wolfgang Korngold, receive their just recognition only after they are gone. Some, like Aurelio de la Vega, are honored and respected throughout the musical world, but simply ignored in the countries of their birth because of political bias. Still others, like Calvin Jackson, remain relatively undiscovered. Skeptics will be quick to observe that classical and jazz musicians are, by the nature of their art, likely to be overshadowed by performers with mass media appeal. Then there are those classical musicians, Leonard Bernstein and Luciano Pavarotti for instance, whose fame transcends their musical accomplishments and emerge as full-fledged celebrities. But these are exceptions. Ask a teenager anywhere in the world to name the important political figures in his or her country. Ask about the major historical events that shaped our world. Ask for a selection of heroes. In most cases, the best musicians, writers, and artists will not be on their lists. But you will find plenty of celebrities, especially those of the unaccomplished variety.

For a time, even the best-known Hollywood celebrities were upstaged by the saga of Anna Nicole Smith. In 1993, Anna Nicole Smith was *Playboy's* "Playmate of the Year," and the following year she married J. Howard Marshall II, an eighty-nine-year-old oil tycoon with a fortune worth a half-billion dollars. Marshall died in 1995, and Anna Nicole Smith began an extended legal battle with his son over the family fortune. She found time to star in her own reality television show and then died of a drug overdose in 2007. The tabloids and cable networks followed every detail of the saga of Anna Nicole Smith. In 2011, the Royal Opera of Britain produced *Anna Nicole*, an opera written by composer Mark-Anthony Turnage and librettist Richard Thomas. The opera, produced at prestigious Covent Garden, was publicized as "a celebrity story of our times that includes extreme language, drug abuse and sexual content, provocative in its themes, exciting in its bravura style and thrilling with its sheer contemporary nerve."

Richard Thomas is not a novice in the world of celebrities. He was co-creator with Stewart Lee of *Jerry Springer: The Opera*, a work based on the outrageous television show hosted by Jerry Springer, which provoked huge protests in 2005 when it was broadcast over the BBC. The network itself declared, "It was reported the show contained a total of 8,000 obscenities—a total reached by adding every swear word sung by each member of the 27-strong chorus." But a BBC spokesperson said the number was less than 300 and was arrived at "even using the broadest definition of an offensive word." The BBC received 45,000 calls from listeners, including many Christians, outraged by the portrayal of Jesus Christ as a homosexual, and the repeated use of obscenities and mockery of religion.

We can admit that the operatic plots are full of outrageous characters that seem larger than life. But what does it say about our celebrity culture that at a time when opera companies are struggling worldwide to raise money and stay afloat, two major operas are produced about celebrities? With Jerry Springer and Anna Nicole Smith as the subjects of operas, will works inspired by the Kardashians be replacing *The Magic Flute* or *Mme. Butterfly* any time soon?

IN SEARCH OF HEROES

We should ask ourselves, whom do we admire as a society and why do we admire them? Who really deserves our attention? Russell Kirk, in his book, *The Wise Men Know What Wicked Things Are Written in the Sky*,[14] declared, "Boys and girls will model themselves, if they can, upon exemplars. But what sort of exemplars? Rock stars, and the fancied personalities of the heroes and heroines of the soap operas, have become the exemplars for a multitude of American young people in the most formative years. Rarely are such persons, or pseudo persons, admirable mentors."

What makes a true hero?

The British journalist and historian Paul Johnson explored this question in his trilogy devoted to many figures, past and present, who receive much public attention: intellectuals, creators, and heroes. In *Heroes: From Alexander the Great and Julius Caesar to Churchill and De Gaulle*,[15] he considers the criteria for modern heroism. He suggests four principal marks of heroism today: absolute independence of mind and the ability to treat the current consensus with skepticism; the capacity to act resolutely and consistently; to ignore or reject the reaction of the media; and to act with personal courage regardless of the consequences to you. There are heroes today who meet these criteria, but few if any will ever be found on the list of celebrities. Johnson describes five keys to democratic statesmanship: ideas and beliefs, willpower, pertinacity, the ability to communicate, and magnanimity—greatness of soul.

Says Johnson, "All history teaches and my personal experience confirms that there is no substitute for courage. It is the noblest and best of all qualities and the one indispensable element in heroism in all its different manifestations." Again, these are the qualities we should find in the people we admire. Some celebrities, if they are entertainers, may be capable communicators. But since there are so many great communicators who do not become celebrities, it is clear that other qualities are far more significant in receiving public attention. Too often, celebrities receive attention for no other reason than the fact that they somehow end up in the public eye.

Johnson also explored the nature of creativity in his book, *Creators*,[16] with attention to the achievements of artists such as Dürer, composers, including Bach and Verdi, and writers like Shakespeare, Charles Dickens, Jane Austen, Mark Twain, and T.S. Eliot. Johnson found that while creative people are highly individual, original, and do not fit any pattern, many display what he calls "the anatomy of creative courage." Johnson writes, "What strikes me, surveying the history of creativity, is how little fertile and productive people often received in the way of honors, money, or anything else." For Johnson, much creativity is pursued under daunting conditions. He declares that creative originality often reflects huge resources of courage, especially when an artist will not bow to age or debility. We might add that truly creative people often function under lifetime pressures not to be creative—to bow to fads and fashions. Contrary to what many people believe, these fads and fashions are often tied to the notion of "change," and artists who try to maintain their integrity when urged to be "modern" often face the greatest neglect. Again, how many of our current celebrities display true creative greatness at all, let alone, creative courage?

We often overlook the fact that a society's choice of celebrities says much about the society's values. Following the death of pop star Michael Jackson, television, radio, and the Internet were full of wall-to-wall, frame-to-frame, 24-hour coverage. Every detail of the life and death of Jackson, invariably described as "The King of Pop," was considered important beyond belief. The news media reacted as if a president had been assassinated or a great leader had suffered an untimely death. News and entertainment reporters alike were literally tripping over their own feet in dithyrambic praise of Michael Jackson. When celebrities die at an improbably young age, the lost years of their later lives become a *tabula rasa*, an empty slate. People can project their greatest hopes and desires onto the legacy of their imaginary heroes. Some have dreamed of the unfulfilled second term of John F. Kennedy, in which all the nation's problems were solved. Others speculate that the greatest performances in the history of film would have been delivered by an aging James Dean or Marilyn Monroe. Then there are those who think of the good works of Princess Diana if she had remained married to Prince Charles and lived long enough to become Queen. All of these speculations offer writers opportunities for literary flights of fancy, but they bear little relationship to the likely realities of what would have occurred in the lives of these people had they lived.

The sycophantic fans of Michael Jackson were perfectly willing to overlook his bizarre personal life, insisting that "talent" is more important than "morality." Certainly if we apply a high moral standard to great artists, many genuine artists can be found lacking: Beethoven was a misanthrope, Liszt a philanderer, Wagner an adulterer and egocentric bigot. The list of 20th century writers, artists, and musicians who drowned their sorrows in drugs, drink, and strange sexual behavior is long and sad. Would you really want to depend on the emotional stability of Vincent van Gogh, with or without his ear? Michael Jackson's admirers include a strange patchwork quilt of characters: the teenagers rushing to buy the recordings, which Hollywood promoters rushed to put back on the market or the academicians pontificating about his "cultural legacy." Jackson's most vocal adulator turned out to be Sheila Jackson Lee, a member of the House of Representatives from Houston, who introduced a resolution proclaiming Jackson to be an American legend, a musical icon, and a world humanitarian. The resolution wasn't passed by her colleagues, aware that, despite Jackson's acquittal on charges of child molestation, his personal behavior hardly made him a role model.

While Jackson's personal behavior remained a source of controversy, only a few commentators addressed the question of his talent as an entertainer. One, Dr. Victor Davis Hanson, wrote, "Jackson always wanted to be seen as a Peter Pan–like innocent. Yet again, his performance videos were sexually charged, as he often grabbed his crotch or strutted about in other lascivious dance moves before legions of under-age fans." Hanson concluded with an observation that rings true to anyone who understands the truth about the Hollywood publicity machine, the stars who are the beneficiaries of its marketing engine, and the truly gifted and talented artists it ignores. Hanson says, "In the end, Jackson will be known mostly as a path-breaking marketing genius. His extravagant stage shows and music videos—replete with fireworks, celebrity cameos, animation, and special effects—finally overshadowed the music itself. And largely for that reason, he captivated millions of concert-goers, in an electronic and video age." Victor Davis Hanson identifies the true legacy of Michael Jackson. He says, "Jackson's quasi-military uniforms, gloved hand, pet chimp, and weird habits added to the Hollywood hype. His legacy includes the similar, though lesser, careers of Britney Spears and Madonna—superstars who put on spectacular, sexually charged performances, with elaborate outfits and props, but who cannot compose, sing, or act in any memorable fashion. In the end, Michael Jackson taught other superstars that in today's America, they too could continue to remain famous—for being famous."

A few journalists and commentators (very few) responded to the Jackson spectacle with integrity. Roger Kimball, editor of *The New Criterion*, summed up Jackson's life as "a monument to voracious commercial exploitation, on the one hand, and artistic nullity fired by unstopped narcissism, on the other." But the

Hansons and Kimballs of the world are in the tasteful minority. Most of the media coverage devoted to Michael Jackson was typified by perennial celebrity interviewer Larry King. *Chicago Tribune* writer James Rainey has chronicled the journalistic obsessions with Michael Jackson, practicing a new form of journalism, described by Jon Stewart as "obitutainment."

Apparently, no detail is too bizarre for some members of the press. Rainey goes on to cite a telephone call to the *Tribune* from an anonymous Scandinavian journalist asking for the name of "an expert on Debbie Rowe's womb" (Rowe is the mother of two of the Jackson children). Rainey declared that the "gravel-voiced" television host Larry King was leading the pack in coverage of Jackson. He observed that "the suspendered one" told his audience, "We don't know the facts yet, all of these are assumptions." King offered a panel discussion featuring former Jackson lawyer Mark Geragos and observed, "We don't know what we're talking about, no one knows what we're talking about." Geragos responded, "That hasn't stopped us any night for the past three weeks." Geragos, probably secure that King didn't have the power to hold him in contempt of court, was skeptical about a video clip of Jackson's hair catching fire while filming a Pepsi commercial, and said, "I don't understand why we keep playing it. I guess it's good for ratings." The King of Talk said, "Rather gripping, isn't it?" Geragos responded, "So are car accidents and beheadings." So the relentless publicity machine goes on, and Michael Jackson assumes his place along with other alleged musical icons Elvis Presley and Beatle John Lennon.

Compare the public perceptions of so-called legends and kings of pop with the life and work of a truly accomplished musician. No one could have been less like the over-publicized, overrated stars of music than Hugo Friedhofer. Although Friedhofer won an Oscar for his score for the 1940 classic film, *The Best Years of Our Lives*, and orchestrated Max Steiner's scores for such legendary films as *Gone With the Wind* and *Casablanca*, his was not a name well-known to a large musical public. Friedhofer was praised by his colleagues. Henry Mancini said of Friedhofer, "An affirmative nod from the man is worth more than all of the trinkets bestowed by the film industry." While musical stars of all kinds are quick to sound their own trumpets and proclaim their own greatness, Friedhofer was modest to a fault. With self-deprecating humor, he described himself as more of a plumber than an artist and advised his colleagues, "no matter how much you know, it isn't enough." David Raksin, the distinguished composer and a lifelong friend, said that Friedhofer was "the most learned of us all and the most subtle." Once during his long career, Friedhofer agreed to work with a publicist who could provide him "name value" with the public at large. After a short time, he dismissed the publicist, declaring, "I much preferred the relative obscurity I had been assiduously cultivating to the unlikely image they were trying to perpetrate." After Friedhofer's death, Gene Lees, a close friend and noted writer, called the *Arts & Leisure* editor of the *New York Times*, offering help, anecdotes, and information about the highly quotable composer. In the response, the *Arts & Leisure* editor of the *New York Times*, the self-proclaimed paper of record, inquired, "Who's he? I've never heard of him." As Shakespeare said, there's the rub.

Pop stars and tabloid celebrities are always going to engender more publicity than self-effacing men and women of accomplishment. Scandal will always sell more newspapers or increase broadcast ratings more than mere accomplishment or even true genius. But when our whole society becomes collectively obsessed with the wrong people and the wrong things, we lose our capacity to even recognize real achievement. Even as these words are being committed to paper, a brilliant composer, a gifted artist, or an inspiring writer is struggling against the odds for recognition. Simultaneously, the massive media machine that directs our attention is focused upon a new celebrity. The crowds are gathering, delighted to be part of what is "really important" in our society. Sadly, through their cheers and tears, they haven't a clue.

THE DECLINE OF LANGUAGE

THE INARTICULATE AMERICAN

WHAT HAS HAPPENED TO OUR LANGUAGE? Hamlet's soliloquy is probably the most famous speech ever delivered on stage. The phrase "To be or not to be, that is the question," has been uttered by the greatest and worst actors throughout history. Winston Churchill could recite long excerpts from memory. But times change. A modern day American Shakespeare would likely offer us an up-to-date version of Hamlet, with the gloomy Danish prince saying, "To be or not to be . . . y'know. Like, that is the question." When it came time for Hamlet to direct the speaking habits of others, our newly liberated hero would say, "Speak the speech, I pray you, y' know, as I pronounced it to you, like, trippingly on the tongue." Romeo and Juliet could be similarly modernized, with the winsome Juliet calling from her balcony, "Romeo, Romeo, y'know, wherefore art thou Romeo? Or if thou wilt not, y'know, be but sworn my love and I'll no longer be, like, a Capulet." The 21st century Romeo, dazzled by Juliet's beauty, would gaze up at her on the balcony, reach into the inner depths of his soul, and proclaim his devotion by declaring, "AWESOME!"

While our British friends may enjoy a laugh or two at the expense of American English, the United States has produced eloquent writers and speakers. In a country that began with the matchless prose of the Declaration of Independence, how did "Y'know" get into the picture? And unfortunately, "Y'know" doesn't sound better with a British accent. On both sides of the Atlantic, "Y'know" is ubiquitous. Edwin Newman spent many years as a news anchor and bureau chief with NBC, and was known as the "house grammarian." So it wasn't surprising that his 1974 book, *Strictly Speaking,*[17] was subtitled, *Will America be the Death of English*? Newman posed an intriguing question when heasked, "Can a phrase be repealed?" He explained, "I have in mind, Y'know. The prevalence of Y'know is one of the most far reaching and depressing developments of our time, disfiguring conversation wherever you go. I attend meetings at NBC and elsewhere at which people of high rank and station, with salaries to match, say almost nothing else." Newman tried asking people who kept saying "Y'know," why, if he knew, were they telling him? This lunchtime query didn't stop "Y'know," but it did result in Newman dining alone more often. In 1969, the "National Society for Suppression of Y'know, Y'know, Y'know in the Diction of Broadcasters" was organized. The offending broadcasters were made aware of how many times they said, "Y'know." They went right on saying it. Newman suggested that the reason people insist on saying "Y'know" is that they are embarrassed by silence in their conversation, or afraid of appearing to think about what they are saying. Newman said he could hear "Y'know" as often as eight times a minute. Over three decades after Newman wrote these words, "Y'know" is still very much with us.

"Y'know" and "Like" are hardly the only interpolations derailing contemporary speech. Listen to any major newscast, and you are likely to hear well-groomed, well-coiffed, but sadly, inarticulate newscasters refer to everyone, including their colleagues and their audience, as "you guys." "It's been great working with you guys," says the departing news anchor. "I couldn't of done it without all of you guys out there in the audience either." (The ungrammatical anchor meant to say "couldn't have" done whatever he is congratulating himself for doing, but we'll get to that in an upcoming paragraph.)

When Frank Loesser wrote his classic musical, *Guys and Dolls*, there was little question as to the difference between the guys and the dolls. (The great piano virtuoso Vladimir Horowitz attended a performance of *Guys and Dolls* when it ran on Broadway. He was accompanied by the pianist and pedagogue Constance Keene. The two found that their seats had been given to someone else, and they had to sit in the aisle. During intermission, Horowitz, whose first language was Russian, looked perplexed; he turned to his friend and said, "What is a guy? What is a doll?") Now, however, everyone is apparently a "guy." Female interviewers have even referred to a group of contestants in the Miss America pageant as "you guys." There is something disconcerting about seeing a very attractive female television newscaster address a group composed entirely of beautiful women as "you guys." There are those who will read the preceding paragraphs and be quick to say, "What are you guys worried about? Who cares if the chair of a committee is a guy?" The problem, of course, is that a "chair" is actually a piece of furniture, not the person in charge of a committee. (If the chairman of a committee is female, she will improbably be addressed as "Mme. Chair.")

When searching for a word of praise, we should remember that "awesome," perhaps the most overused word in our limited contemporary vocabulary, isn't awesome at all. The Urban Dictionary, a Web site, defines "awesome" as "something Americans use to describe everything, a 'sticking plaster' word used by Americans to cover over the huge gaps in their vocabulary." Do you find something or someone to be "awe inspiring?" How about using "astonishing," "astounding," "breathtaking," "formidable, "impressive," "incredible," "magnificent," "outstanding," "spectacular," "splendid," "striking," or "wondrous?"

"Amazing" is a perfectly fine word, but it has been turned into the dullest of clichés. Reality television programs often feature encounters between bachelors and bachelorettes. Nearly every such encounter will feature one telling the other, "You look amazing." In response, the only appropriate reply is "awesome." In *Sonnets from the Portuguese*, the poet Elizabeth Barrett Browning asked famously "How do I love thee?" and elaborated, "Let me count the ways. I Love thee to the depth and breadth and height my soul can reach, when feeling out of sight." Today's hip, cool, phrase master, however, would find Browning's query intimidating. Count the ways? He has only one.

"It rocks" and "rock star" are rapidly achieving dubious distinction as major clichés. Both are derived from the mistaken notion that success in rock music implies quality. We hear about political "rock stars" who have charisma and an ability to mesmerize voters with their rhetorical skills. But real "rock stars" are usually untalented and unskilled performers whose lack of ability is masked by incredible promotion. Many adults think using such terms and phrases identifies them with the young. They would do well to recall the definition of "it rocks" found in one online dictionary. "It rocks," we are told, is another way of saying "Awesome!"

Still, we have to answer the question: are expectations of clarity in language important or is the whole discussion simply a teapot tempest?

SING A SONG OF CONFUSION

When is a song not a song? A curious question, you may say. The answer is deceptively simple. *The Oxford Dictionary of Music* defines a song as a vocal composition based on a text, accompanied or unaccompanied. But in today's 21st century digital world of pop culture, every piece of music has suddenly become "a song." For years, most of us thought of songs as popular melodies with words. They were written by composers like George Gershwin or they were folk songs of imprecise origin, passed down as a legacy from one generation to another. In 1940, a remarkable series of concerts celebrating American music was presented in San Francisco under the auspices of the American Society of Composers, Authors, and Publishers (ASCAP.) A group of major symphonic works was played, along with a substantial number of songs from Broadway and films, the latter performed or accompanied by the composers themselves. ASCAP's President, Gene Buck, the master of ceremonies for the event, had the odd habit of referring to popular songs as "folk tunes," although they were clearly no such thing, since the composers or lyricists of these "folk tunes" were actually present.

If you were to ask a symphony or operatic conductor about his favorite songs, he would likely respond by choosing excerpts from lieder by Schubert, Schumann, or Brahms. All these pieces are still songs. Today, however, in an age of digital downloads, everything is suddenly a "song." This includes symphonies, operas or musical shows containing many songs, string quartets, or even long jazz improvisations on no melody in particular. Since most of the computer programs and services enabling downloads cater to very young audiences whose whole musical awareness is limited to rock, rap, and pop, downloads of music have become "downloads of songs." When the spokesman for a software company responded to a protest that the movement of a Beethoven symphony wasn't a song, he responded, "In our software, we call everything a song." Does this matter? Does anyone care or is it just an example of much ado about nothing? It matters because gradually, the whole vocabulary and attitudes of the rock-rap-pop world of music are suddenly imposed on everything and everyone. An instrumental piece with no lyrics and longer than the standard length of a rock hit is suddenly deficient in meeting the requirements for a "song."

In 2013, a video of a Georgia Tech student making a fiery speech went viral on the Internet, in part because he used a piece of incredibly stirring music to build up audience emotion. The music was an excerpt from *Also Sprach Zarathustra*, a symphonic tone poem by Richard Strauss. The opening of the work is one of the two most popular orchestral fanfares invoking a sense of strength, power, majesty, and destiny. (The other is Aaron Copland's *Fanfare for the Common Man.*) Strauss's work has been used in many contexts that would have startled the composer, including its use as entrance music for a famous professional wrestler. In the film *2001,* director Stanley Kubrick inserted Strauss's music into the musical soundtrack, replacing a commissioned score by the noted composer Alex North, and without bothering to inform North that his music had been replaced. The *Daily Telegraph* dutifully reported on the success of the student's speech, declaring that his words had been delivered to "the tune from *2001: A Space Odyssey.*" So much for Richard Strauss's tone poem. Now, everything is a song and no song is better than another.

CLICHÉGATE

In 1972, five men were arrested on charges of breaking into Democratic National Committee headquarters located in the Watergate, a hotel-office complex in Washington, D.C. The press initially talked about the "Watergate Caper," which sounded like the title of a lighthearted British spy movie. But the episode soon evolved into the Watergate Scandal, complete with congressional hearings, the resignation of President Richard M. Nixon, and the elevation of investigative reporters to full-fledged media stardom. One dubious legacy of "Watergate" (the scandal, not the hotel) was the now common practice of attaching the word "gate" to anything, serious or trivial, being investigated by anyone from a Pulitzer Prize winning reporter to a high school sophomore trying to raise his grade in journalism class from D+ to C-.The use of the word "gate," attached to nearly everything written by everybody, accomplishes two things: it suggests that a scandal of earth-shattering proportions may exist when there may be none, and it elevates the importance of the person using the word "gate." In 1986, the attention of the media was focused upon revelations that the U.S. had secretly sold arms to Iran and that the profits had been diverted to support the U.S.-backed, anti- communist Contras in Nicaragua. While the episode was generally characterized as "The Iran-Contra Affair," some in the media, eager to force another presidential resignation, were quick to try to attach the label "Irangate,"while others pressed for "Contragate." By the 21st century, the use of the word "gate" had become ubiquitous. Reporters demanded to know if Alaska Governor Sarah Palin had used undue influence in the firing of a state trooper who happened to be her brother-in-law. Although the affair came to naught and no scandal was revealed, headlines were suddenly full of "Troopergate." In 2009, a white police sergeant, James Crowley, arrested a black Harvard professor, Henry Louis Gates, for disorderly conduct. When the episode burst into the national press and President Barack Obama invited both men to the White House for a beer, headline writers were quick to dub this matter "Gatesgate."

The use of "gate" as the suffix of choice has now unfortunately crossed the Atlantic. Sarah Lyall, in her book, *The Anglo Files: A Field Guide to the British*,[18] reports that the mother of Kate Middleton, prior to the announcement of her daughter's engagement to Britain's Prince William, received unwanted attention because of her vocabulary. It seems that Mrs. Middleton, who worked as a flight attendant in her youth, had been overheard referring to bathroom facilities as the "toilet." Sarah Lyall writes, "It was reported that whenever they saw Kate, William's friends muttered, 'Doors to manual,' a point that whether true or not, played right into the anxieties of the class conscious public." This phrase wouldn't raise egalitarian American eyebrows an iota. But in class-conscious Britain, the word related to the British notion of upper and lower class expressions. Lyall concludes, "The papers had a field day with 'Toiletgate,' as they were soon happily calling it." No doubt. Now that Kate Middleton has become the Princess of Wales and she is happily married to her prince, this expression will undoubtedly be jettisoned. But British journalists, like their American counterparts, are likely to be busily searching for another "gate" to open.

In recent years, the number of real and alleged scandals labeled with the "gate" suffix has increased, not declined. Wikipedia, the online encyclopedia, reports over 250 such "gate" scandals, traveling around the world, from the sublime to the ridiculous. "Gate" has been attached to controversies and scandals in politics, entertainment, sports, technology, academia, and journalism. This is not an exclusively American phenomenon; examples have been found everywhere including the UK, Ireland, Australia, New Zealand, South Africa, the Philippines, Mauritius, Malawi, Pakistan, Poland, and Peru. While some episodes earning a "gate" from journalists are serious and involve scandals or crimes, the absurd occurrences are never exempt. A classic example was what happened when a South Korean airlines executive ordered a plane to return to the gate before takeoff because she was unhappy with the way a flight attendant served her nuts. This episode actually involved a real "gate" at the airport and was quickly dubbed by the press "nutgate."

In 2022, British Prime Minister Boris Johnson and his colleagues and staff received criticism for having unmasked social events at a time when Britain was under a severe lockdown because of the Covid Pandemic. The episode was quickly dubbed "Partygate" by the press.

No one expects journalists to be stuffy or stodgy. One can be irreverent and even impertinent, and still be witty or clever. (Read the lyrics of Noël Coward and Cole Porter, if you are skeptical.) A Hollywood trade paper reported the ghastly news of the stock market crash, which announced the financial collapse that began The Great Depression on October 29, 1929 with the headline, "Wall Street Lays an Egg." Mercifully, journalists of past times didn't call the "Teapot Dome" scandal "Domegate" or the treachery of Benedict Arnold "Traitorgate." But is the day far off when historians will begin applying the word "gate" retroactively? Should they do so, they deserve to be implicated in "Gategate," and hopefully, put this matter to rest once and for all.

The overuse of the word "gate" is hardly our only popular cliché. Researchers at Oxford University compiled a list of the most irritating and annoying phrases. "Couldn't of," used instead of the correct "Couldn't have," made the list, along with improbable clichés, "At the end of the day" and "At this moment in time." We can fill whole books with clichés and over used phrases. But before we have reached the second page, someone is bound to scream, "Who cares?" Does it matter if our speech is increasingly peppered with meaningless phrases, clichés, and grammatical mistakes?

GOOD GRAMMAR, BAD GRAMMAR

In 1934, Jay Hanna Dean, known in baseball as "Dizzy," made a startling prediction. "Dizzy" Dean was a star pitcher for the St. Louis Cardinals. Joined by his brother Paul, who had never pitched in the major leagues before, he confidently announced to the astonished press, "Me 'n' Paul will win about forty games this season." Dizzy was being modest. He and Paul combined to win forty-nine games for the legendary "Gas House Gang" team that won the 1934 World Series against the Detroit Tigers. While Dizzy could pitch like a magician, he had his problems with the English language. After he retired from baseball, he became a radio and television announcer, speaking what he called "plain pinto bean English." With gusto, Dizzy informed his listeners, "The runner slud into third base." He declared that the pitcher just "throwed" the ball to the catcher, that a batter shouldn't have "swang" at a bad pitch, and that runners had returned to their "respectable" bases. When Baseball Commissioner Kennesaw Mountain Landis said that Dean's diction was "unfit for a national broadcaster," Dean shot back, "How can that Commissar say I ain't eligible to talk?" English teachers were taken aback that boys across the country didn't just want to pitch like Dizzy; they wanted to talk like him as well. In 1946, a story began circulating that the English Teachers Association of Missouri was going to file a complaint with the Federal Communications Commission maintaining that Dean's assault on English was a bad influence on children. There has been speculation that the story may have been started by a clever publicist, as a variety of sports and literary figures, including the prestigious *Saturday Review of Literature*, came to Dean's defense.

Today, Dizzy's "Me 'n' Paul" wouldn't raise any eyebrows. Listen to today's "reality television" stars, college athletes, or virtually anyone who appears in a public forum. You are likely to hear "him and me" do this or that, "her and I" think this or that, all in a way that would have made Dizzy Dean proud. Nor should we assume that only those lacking in education make such mistakes. In 1979, *Esquire* magazine published Harry Stein's interview with Tennessee Williams, one of America's most honored playwrights. Williams compared himself to a character in his own play, *The Glass Menagerie.* He said, "The principal difference between he and I is stamina." (Williams should have said "between him and me.")

Does it matter? Should we care if someone doesn't say "he and I" or "she and I"? Those of us who raise such objections are likely to be dismissed as "frustrated English teachers" or "grammar police." We need to recognize a simple fact: there is such a thing as good English, best expressed through correct grammar. The dissenters immediately snap, "Who decides what is correct?" It is true that language evolves, that language changes. But the notion of language evolution assumes that all change in usage is progress. Of course, we adopt new words and sometimes old ones acquire new meanings. But we can make a strong case that the trend we are observing is not language evolution but linguistic decline. The rules of grammar do not exist because a cantankerous, hatchet-faced English teacher imposed them on a group of free-spirited students by rapping their knuckles with a ruler in some ancient classroom. Those who suggest that such rules are out of date invariably invoke the image of a changing language. John Simon describes these people as believing that language cannot be pressed forever, like a dead flower, between the pages of a dictionary, but is instead a living organism that, like a live plant, sprouts new leaves and flowers. Simon is right to reject this argument. In *Paradigms Lost*, he says, "Alas, this lovely albeit trite image is—as as I have said before and wish to say now with even greater emphasis—largely nonsense. Language, for the most part, changes out of ignorance."

At one time, students were expected to master the rules of grammar as a condition of being promoted or graduated. A student who couldn't tell the difference between a noun and a verb was clearly a student in trouble. Such a student would not only miss an opportunity to understand the best books ever written, he would have great difficulty in finding a job. Today, however, the techniques used to teach grammar are regarded as simply quaint. Ask a twelfth-grade student today if he has learned to diagram sentences. Ask a college student majoring in English if she is familiar with the technique. You will probably receive a blank stare in reply. A sentence diagram is a pictorial representation of the structure of a sentence. The student who truly learns about sentence structure learns more than a few old-fashioned rules. The student learns to think logically about the words he uses.

Kitty Burns Florey wrote a delightful book, *Sister Bernadette's Barking Dog: The Quirky History and Lost Art of Diagramming Sentences.*[19] Diagramming was once the mainstay of every English teacher. Florey describes diagramming sentences as "one of those lost skills, like darning socks or playing the sackbut, that no one seems to miss." But Florey does miss the techniques she learned in the sixth grade at Brooklyn Polytechnic from her teacher, Sister Bernadette. The most popular method of diagramming sentences was introduced in the nineteenth century by Alonzo Reed and Brainerd Kellogg. Florey says that the Reed-Kellogg method swept through American public schools like the measles, as teachers attempted to reform students engaged in the cold-blooded murder of the English tongue. She writes, "By promoting the beautifully logical rules of syntax, diagramming would root out evils like 'him and me went' and 'I ain't got none,' until everyone wrote like Ralph Waldo Emerson, or at least James Fenimore Cooper."

Today's students are likely to ask if "syntax" is a rock group or inquire as to which sin is being taxed. Grammar is the rock on which a language stands. If we maintain our language on a pile of sand, we shouldn't be surprised if it collapses. Good grammar yields clarity. Linguistic clarity, like moral and musical clarity, is desirable. Linguistic chaos is not. Those who suggest that such errors do not matter usually come in two varieties: those who don't care about the language and those who do, but throw up their hands in despair.

Not surprisingly, the "woke" academicians who want to politicize everything in the curriculum, have launched an assault on traditional English grammar. Rebecca Walkowitz, chairman of the English Department at Rutgers University, a public institution in New Jersey, announced that the school would respond to the demands of the Marxist group, Black Lives Matter, by emphasizing "social justice and critical grammar." Walkowitz declared proudly, "This approach challenges the familiar dogma that writing instruction should limit emphasis on grammar/sentence-level issues so as to not put students from multilingual, non-standard 'academic' English backgrounds at a disadvantage." So graduate students at Rutgers can make grammatical mistakes with confidence; linguistic accuracy will not be a hallmark of their studies. Instead, Walkowitz announced, the students could explore reading and writing about "racism, sexism, homophobia, and related forms of "systemic discrimination." Happily, not everyone was impressed with this new curriculum. Leonydus Johnson, a speech pathologist, told the *Washington Free Beacon* that it was "insulting, patronizing, and in itself, extremely racist." Johnson correctly observed, "The idea that expecting a student to write in grammatically correct sentences is indicative of racial bias is asinine. It's like these people believe that being non-white is an inherent handicap or learning disability . . . that's racism. It has become very clear to me that those who claim to be 'anti-racist' are often the most racist people in this country."

Johnson's sentiments were echoed in the UK by Katharine Birbalsingh, the outspoken educator at the Michaela Community School in London, who ridiculed the notion that proper English is racist. She asked, "What is our world coming to? I have a school full of black and brown kids who are taught proper English and doing well at it, thanks very much. To deny children the opportunity to write and speak well is a SCANDAL! How dare you all behave like this?"

But unfortunately, advocates of true education and equal opportunity such as Johnson and Birbalsingh must contend with countless educrats on both sides of the Atlantic who think they can advance their careers or prevent their institutions from being criticized by militant ideologies by caving to their demands. The English language, a pillar of western culture, indeed of all civilization, can only suffer the consequences.

BUREAUCRATS OF THE WORLD, ARISE

While the inarticulate in our society express themselves through a tiny repertoire of limited words and phrases, the rest of us may be drowning in too many words, not too few. In the worlds of business, diplomacy, the military, academia, the law, and especially government, words can frequently conceal the meaning of what is written or said. Big words, or even simple words rearranged in a confusing way, can often convey the opposite meaning of a statement or label. They can impress readers or listeners, while meaning nothing at all. William Lutz, an author and English professor, defines "doublespeak" as a language that pretends to communicate, but really doesn't. In his book, *Doublespeak*,[20] Lutz identified four kinds of doublespeak: (1) euphemisms, inoffensive or positive words used instead of accurate, but negative words; (2) jargon, the often pretentious and obscure technical language adored by doctors, lawyers, educators, and computer experts, which makes simple ideas hard to understand for all but the uninitiated; (3) gobbledygook or bureaucratese, a veritable verbal landslide that seeks to overwhelm the reader or listener, obscuring the fact that the mountain of words makes no sense; and (4) inflated language designed to make the simple seem complex, the undistinguished extraordinary.

All of these forms of doublespeak turn up constantly in our daily lives. Used cars are sold as "previously owned." Black and white televisions have been marketed as "televisions with non-multicolor capabilities." The death of a patient has been described as "a negative patient care outcome." Lawyers refer to your stolen car as "an involuntary property conversion." The Pentagon once dubbed the neutron bomb a "radiation enhancement device." Tax increases become "revenue enhancements" when passed by Congress. The U.S. Department of Homeland Security, under the Obama administration, changed "terrorism" to "man-made disasters." In 2011, Secretary of Transportation Ray LaHood evidently was uncomfortable reporting that the National Highway Traffic Safety Administration determined that the sudden and inexplicable acceleration of Toyotas was the result of driver error: the drivers mistook the accelerator for the brake. LaHood's solution? He simply did away with the term "driver error" and attributed the problem to "pedal misapplications." Finally, humorist Dale Ervin quipped, "We talk about 'migratory transients' or 'transitory migrants.' We used to call them 'bums.'"

Doublespeak is not an exclusively American phenomenon, nor is it limited to the English language. Soviet Russian publishers redefined English words when they published their own version of a student's dictionary. Capitalism was redefined as "an economic and social system based on private ownership of the means of production operated for private profit, and on the exploitation of man by man, replacing feudalism and preceding communism."

Many examples of doublespeak are amusing. What are we to think of a hospital which bills patients an "oral administration fee," when this term is used to describe a nurse handing the patient a pill? It is hard to keep a straight face when someone describes a racketeer belonging to the Mafia as "a member of a career-offender cartel." William Lutz writes, "We laugh and dismiss doublespeak as empty or meaningless words at our own peril, for, as George Orwell saw so clearly, the great weapon of power, exploitation, manipulation, and oppression is language. It is only by being aware of the pervasiveness of doublespeak and its function as a tool of social, economic, and political control that we can begin to fight those who would use language against us."

Sometimes masters of doublespeak admit that their efforts are meant to obscure the true meaning of their remarks. Alan Greenspan, some years before he became Chairman of the Federal Reserve Board, told an audience, "I guess I should warn you, if I turn out to be particularly clear, you've probably misunderstood what I've said." In 1982, Dr. Herman Kahn appeared on the television program, *Nightline*, hosted by Ted Koppel. When Koppel asked him to put his ideas into a straightforward sentence, Professor Kahn declined. "Absolutely not," he said. "And, let me spend a minute on that. The attempt to put these in straightforward sentences simply confuses."

Among the most confusing writers and speakers currently using the English language are Professors of Education. It is ironic that those who are supposed to teach others how to teach often need instruction themselves. They need to learn the virtues of simplicity in language. Richard Armour was an eminent humorist and teacher. He earned his Ph.D. at Harvard, where he began his career as a serious scholar with expertise in English literature and philology, combining literary studies, history, and linguistics. But he subsequently emerged as one of America's most prominent humorists. Dr. Armour wrote over sixty books and six thousand verses and articles. He was also a lifetime educator. In his book, *Educated Guesses*,[21] he took up the subject of educational jargon. The word "jargon," he told us, comes from the Old French word meaning to chatter or warble, and is related to the word "gargle." The purpose of educational jargon (called by Dr. Armour "educationese") is to express ideas in ways that are hard to understand, and therefore, by implication, profound. He offered an example, a direct quotation from a dictionary of education edited by a school administrator, a definition of "dynamic substrata-factor theory of reading." If you don't know what this theory is, check the dictionary:

A theory proposing that reading is a dynamic and complex act compounding and recompounding for each new and/or different reading task an appropriate integration of a multiplicity of related and underlying subabilites; some key concepts postulated are an integrating principle, a functional equipotentiality, cognitive working systems of subabilities, predominant use of preferred modes (tactile-kinesthetic, motor, auditory, and visual) of functioning in different learning situations, maturational gradient-shifts, and the constant interaction of the whole and its parts.

Is this definition helpful? Are you still awake after reading it? Or does it simply sound important while confusing the reader? Richard Armour observed that the intention of such a definition is more to impress than to communicate. The impression actually left by the editor of this dictionary is one of elitist, obscure jargon. Richard Armour wisely suggested that teachers who teach others how to teach should also learn how to express themselves in simple, understandable English. Simplicity is not necessarily a virtue in itself. A football coach in Florida once gave his team what he thought were simple instructions by announcing, "You guys line up alphabetically by height." But clarity matters and clarity is far likelier to be the result of plain English than academic jargon.

On occasion, the advocates of incomprehensible language reveal their own ineptitude. In 1996, *Social Text*, a self-described academic journal of postmodern cultural studies, published an article by Alan Sokal, a physics professor at New York University. Sokal titled his article "Transgressing the Boundaries: Towards a Transformative Hermeneutics of Quantum Gravity."[22] Readers learned that Sokol was suggesting that quantum gravity is a social and linguistic construct. On the same day the article was published, Sokol revealed that he had written "a pastiche of Left-wing cant, fawning references, grandiose quotations, and outright nonsense." Sokol used absurd quotations on physics and mathematics made by so-called post-modernist academics. His carefully crafted hoax proved his point: a scholarly journal would publish an article consisting entirely of twaddle, if it were concealed by jargon and appeared to reflect the ideological biases of the editors. *Social Text* subsequently developed a plan for peer review of articles before publication, but Sokol had proven his point. Four-syllable words impress people even if they mean nothing.

Inspired by the Sokal affair, beginning in 2017, three authors, Peter Boghossian, an American philosophy professor at Portland State University, James A. Lindsay, an American mathematician and cultural critic, and Helen Pluckrose, a British writer and editor, launched what has become known as the "Grievance Studies Affair." The trio believed that in modern academia, so-called "scholarly journals" had become dominated by a culture in which grievances were valued more than objective truth and only conclusions deemed politically correct were allowed or encouraged. To prove their point, they submitted papers to academic journals that focus on gender, race, cultural, queer, fat, sexuality, and various cultural studies. The journals were known to take seriously such new academic disciplines as critical race theory, intersectional feminism, and postcolonial theory.

The articles submitted by the three writers were a carefully crafted hoax in which fashionable left-wing jargon was used to advocate complete nonsense and the most absurd notions the trio could imagine. A number went through peer review and were put approvingly into print by such journals as *Fat Studies*, which published their article suggesting that bodybuilding was “fat exclusionary” and proposed a brand new classification to be called “fat bodybuilding.” Another journal, *Gender, Place, and Culture*, published “Rape Culture and Queer Performativity at Urban Dog Parks.” The article warned against the shocking display of gender bias on the part of human owners in responding to sexually aggressive canines. A half-dozen articles, generated by algorithm, made it through peer review and were published by the *Journal of Poetry Therapy* along with a description of monthly “feminist spirituality meetings.” But the most embarrassing article had to be "Our Struggle Is My Struggle: Solidarity Feminism as an Intersectional Reply to Neoliberal and Choice Feminism." This literary masterpiece was published by *Affilia*, a journal of women and social work; the editors failed to recognize that the feminist jargon used in the article concealed its origins; one section was adapted and rewritten from perhaps the most infamous book of the 20th century, *Mein Kompf* by Adolf Hitler.

Of course, academics were outraged by the hoax which clearly proved the authors’ point: today’s “scholars” and “editors” can be easily fooled into accepting complete poppycock as long as it is wrapped in current ideological slogans and invokes the required buzzwords.

Unfortunately, while the efforts of Boghossian, Lindsay, and Pluckrose proved their point, the widespread prevalence of “grievance studies” continues in colleges, universities, and think tanks where such “academic disciplines” continue to thrive. We can all laugh at the foolishness intentionally presented in these clever hoax articles, but there is nothing amusing in the realization that significant amounts of money, time, and prestige are given to those writers and pseudo-scholars who aren’t creating outrageously amusing hoaxes. The individuals who write such articles for real reap financial and professional rewards at the expense of those who are true scholars, cultural critics, and discerning observers of both cultural decline and the achievements of those who truly merit recognition. Nor is it particularly funny to realize that students everywhere are taught such nonsense at universities charging a king's ransom in tuition, leading them intellectually astray and wasting both their time and substantial sums of their parents' money.

Why is jargon so popular among academics? Unfortunately, jargon impresses people, especially outside the academic establishment. Vassar College, for instance, offers a course in "the sociology of sociability." The course title will sound far more impressive in a catalogue than an actual description of the course, the study of parties. The catalogue, of course, doesn't give details as to how students do research on parties. Presumably, there are always students willing to volunteer to have parties in order to do the required research. Dennis Prager is a prolific author and columnist who has hosted his own radio program for many years. He offers a clear explanation of the reasons why academicians are notorious for their incomprehensible language. He says, "One of the things colleges have taught is that complexity equals depth. The reason that your professors write in such complex, opaque prose is that they are not clear about what they wish to say in their own minds, and therefore it comes across that way in most academic writing—not all—most. They believe that making it impenetrable will make you think how deep the writer is."

Dr. Laurence Peter was the discoverer of The Peter Principle, which establishes that in hierarchies, people rise to their maximum positions of incompetence. An academician who was also a brilliant satirist, Laurence Peter was skeptical of those who often profess expertise through longwinded jargon that is difficult to understand. He observed that explanations and solutions to problems provided by real experts are often concise, direct, and much easier to understand. Dr. Peter's observation can also apply to the spoken word. Many people, ranging from lawyers to computer technicians, and especially politicians, will avoid answering a direct question because they want to avoid giving a direct answer. So they indulge in long-winded, periphrastic responses that leave the listener confused and perhaps impressed with the speaker's wisdom.

Eric Hoffer was a self-educated philosopher who developed his own ideas about research and scholarship. He wrote, "Sometimes a man writes a thin book and a thick book. Usually in the thin book he tells you what he knows. And in the thick book he tries to cover up what he doesn't know. The thin one is clear and interesting, the thick one is dull. In general, the thin books give you as much as you want to know on the subject." Since the book you are reading is rather a thick one, the author hopes the reader will make an exception in this case.

Even at its worst, the language of bureaucrats can be hilariously funny. Dr. James H. Boren had a distinguished career in academia, government, and diplomacy. But he was startled and frustrated by the inability of bureaucrats to use plain English, and especially by members of Congress praising the testimony of witnesses who said nothing, but said it with style. Politicians are especially notorious for lapsing into rodomontade, a pompous, boastful style of speaking in which they sing their own praises and bore the living daylights out of everyone listening. Dr. Boren responded by changing careers and emerging as the liveliest and funniest Oklahoma humorist since Will Rogers.

In numerous books (including the classic *When in Doubt, Mumble*[23]) and in countless speeches around the world, James Boren used the deadliest weapon of all against an incompetent and intransigent bureaucracy: laughter. He formed INATAPROBU (The International Association of Professional Bureaucrats), and, with mock solemnity, presented his annual award, "The Order of the Bird," to bureaucrats who did the most to foster what he called "dynamic inaction."

In his book, *Fuzzify*,[24] James Boren published a long table of "wordational fuzzifiers," which he said were invented by a forgotten Royal Canadian Air Force officer and rediscovered by Philip Broughton of the U.S. Public Health Service in 1968. The words (or "fuzzifiers") can be chosen from three column groups and strung together at random, producing incredibly impressive and thoroughly meaningless sentences.

A skilled fuzzifier can talk for hours and say nothing, but those ignorant of the technique can be persuaded that they have heard the orator of the century. Policy can be explained as "retroanalytical procedural methodology." College courses can be described as offering "randomized historo-cultural dynamics." Critics can be accused of engaging in "contrived counterproductive intervoidance." Your tax returns can be analyzed in terms of "recapitalized compensatory retropuntality." Anyone who is uncomfortable using big words should not feel excluded from the techniques of causing verbal confusion. The inarticulate speaker can refer to a special table of words for use by athletes on radio and television talk shows. "Anduh," "Welluh," or just plain "Uuhh" can keep sentences separated. An occasional word or phrase like "great fans" can be uttered. When truly in trouble, the speaker can always fall back on "Y'know," which is very popular in a variety of sports. While James Boren originally identified this style of speaking with athletes, he may have underestimated its appeal. Since the publication of "Fuzzify," the latter technique has been widely adopted by an assortment of Hollywood personalities, rock stars, and other celebrities whose reason for being famous defies classification.

For good measure, Dr. Boren appointed himself lexicographer of bureaucracy, producing his own dictionary of Borenwords. If stringing together real words doesn't confuse the issue enough, James Boren developed an astonishing list of new ones. He reminds us, "the spirit of creative nonresponsiveness, the beauty of orbital dialogues, and the expression of dynamic inaction can be enriched by the appropriate use of the Borenwords." He offers us "abstruct," a new verb, "to destroy an idea, policy, or concept by making it so abstract that no one, including the abstructor, can understand what is being abstructed." To abstruct, he tells us, one combines the essential qualities of abstraction and destruction. Another new verb, "blockstone," can describe the actions of numerous public officials, lawyers, and college professors, who "bring things to a halt by combining the skills of blockheads and stone-wallers." When required to commit ideas to paper, the bureaucrat may be required to "memostraddle," straddling an issue by a carefully written memorandum that profundifies, fuzzifies, and trashifies. Dr. Boren also produced a word that ideally describes a technique perfected by governmental task forces, study committees, and fixed-address law offices. They are masterful "yesbutters," agreeing with something and then negating the agreement in a single sentence. A master satirist can heap ridicule on foolish and ponderous distortions of language; but the subject ceases to be funny when we examine the real titles of doctoral dissertations, government reports, and actual laws. Linguistic confusion generates real confusion, and we pay the price in terms of dollars and sense (yes, not just the loss of "cents" but "common sense").

Richard Lederer has written extensively about the pervasive influence of "gobbledygook," a word coined by Texas Congressman Maury Maverick, who compared incomprehensible talk to the gobbling of turkeys. Lederer writes, "Gobbledygook is alive and well and multiplying in the parlance of press releases, official reports, and government and corporate regulations." Sometimes even the users of gobbledygook are aware of what they are doing. Lederer cites Malcolm Baldrige, former Secretary of Commerce, who described a government official rejecting a subordinate's request for a pay raise when he said, "Because of the fluctuational predisposition of your position's productive capacity as juxtaposed to governmental statistics, it would be momentarily injudicious to advocate an incremental increase." The puzzled employee said, "I don't get it." His boss said, "That's right."

Lawyers are among the worst offenders in the use of confusing language. Do lawyers speak and write differently than the rest of us on their own, or are they taught to do so in school? *The Paper Chase* was a popular film and television series, due in part to the acting skills of John Houseman, who portrayed the autocratic and thoroughly intimidating legal scholar, Professor Charles Kingsfield. At the opening of each class, he thundered to his pupils, "You teach *yourselves* the law. I train your minds. You come in here with a skull full of mush, and if you survive, you'll leave thinking like a lawyer." Indeed. "Professor Kingsfield" was a fictional character apparently based on a real professor at Harvard Law School. Unfortunately, the students of the real Professor Kingsfields of the world may also leave law school writing like lawyers and society must deal with the consequences.

Dr. Rudolf Flesch was a lifelong critic of the way reading and writing are taught. In his book, *How to Write Plain English*, he correctly identified the incomprehensible language that warms the hearts of attorneys everywhere: constant use of double-negatives instead of positive statements, meaningless cross-references understood only by other lawyers, and broken sentences. Flesch declared that lawyers drown in "oceans of verbiage," shredding the English language in the process. Professors Layman Allen of Michigan State University and Reed Dickerson of Indiana University coined a term to describe what lawyers do to the language, "systematic pulverization." Dr. Harry G. Nickles, writer, editor, scholar, and teacher, wrote *The Dictionary of Do's and Don'ts,"*[25] a guide for writers and speakers. Like Dr. Flesch, Dr. Nickles has little tolerance for the legal massacre of English. He says, "Only lawyers can compose a fifty page document and call it a 'brief.' They bewilder the layman with references to the said, aforesaid, and aforementioned, or to what may be sought hereinbefore or hereinafter. They cling to archaic, pleonastic phrases (any and all, part and parcel, unless and until, when, as, and if) and to redundancies (cease and desist, false pretenses, one and the same, will and testament), many of which escape from the courtroom to encumber our daily speech."

The proclivity of lawyers for writing tortured prose and verbose volumes of legalese can be amusing, but it has serious consequences. Thousand-page laws are passed unread by the United States Congress. Congressman John Conyers of Michigan responded to critics who protested members of Congress voting on bills they had never even read. He said, "'Read the bill'. . . What good is reading the bill if it's a thousand pages and you don't have two days and two lawyers to find out what it means after you read the bill?" The problem gets worse after the unread bills are passed. Dr. Larry P. Arnn, President of Hillsdale College, writes in *Imprimis*, "After these laws are passed, they are enhanced, expanded, interpreted, and complicated by regulatory agencies." Then these government agencies fill volumes of fine print with regulations that have profound consequences. James Madison anticipated this problem when he warned against laws that are so voluminous that they cannot be read or so incoherent that they cannot be understood. For Madison, incoherent laws produce not just inefficiency, but injustice, since the will of the people can be frustrated by ambivalent and confusing language. Why are laws and regulations incomprehensible? Because the people who write them are either incompetent or intentionally using language to advance their own agendas while avoiding public scrutiny.

Occasionally, government and private bureaucrats try to simplify language. But they are often motivated by a desire for political correctness, assuming that anything but the most ordinary words will be offensive to someone or make poor readers feel guilty about themselves. In England, regional councils have banned their employees from using "elitist phrases" derived from Latin. The *Daily Telegraph* reports that The Bournemouth Council, which has the Latin motto "Pulchritudo et Salubritas," meaning "beauty and health," has listed nineteen terms it no longer considers acceptable for use. Included are bona fide, e.g. or exempli gratia, prima facie, ad lib or ad libitum, etc. or et cetera, i.e. or id est., inter alia, NB or nota bene, per, per se, pro rata, quid pro quo, vis-a-vis, vice versa, and even via. Its list of more verbose alternatives includes "for this special purpose," in place of "ad hoc" and "existing condition" or "state of things," instead of "status quo."

Eugene Ehrlich, a writer and editor of many books on language, wrote, *Amo, Amas, Amat and More: How to Use Latin to Your Own Advantage and to the Astonishment of Others.*[26] Ehrlich recognized the problem. He said, "There is no doubt that readers are plagued by writers and speakers who blithely drop 'Latin phrases into their English sentences with no hint of translation.'" William F. Buckley, Jr., a frequent "Latin dropper," wrote the introduction to Ehrlich's book and addressed the very question raised by the British bureaucrats. He said, "There is no English substitute, really, for 'He faced the problem ad hoc,' which is much easier than the cumbersome alternative in English ('He faced the problem with exclusive concern given to the circumstances that particularly surrounded it.')"

Words derived from Latin can be found in many languages, including our own, so those who have studied it learn not only a language but many of the origins of our own speech. Brander Matthews was the first U.S. professor of dramatic literature. He was so influential in the 19th and early 20th centuries that generations of students were said to have been "brandered by the same Matthews." It was Matthews who declared mischievously, "A gentleman need not know Latin, but he should at least have forgotten it." Today, however, most students will be far more familiar with the terms of cyberspace and will have little Latin to remember or forget.

In the marketplace, people often try to make themselves or their work sound important. A company selling consumer electronics always called its sales personnel "consultants." The company still filed for bankruptcy. Presumably, the enterprise required more sales and less consultation. No harm may be done by upgrading someone's title. Jackie Gleason and Art Carney starred in the classic television series, *The Honeymooners*. In one episode, Carney, portraying the master of malapropisms, Ed Norton, described himself as a "sanitation engineer." Gleason, as the blustery bus driver Ralph Kramden, bellowed, "Sanitation engineer? You work in a sewer!" If someone who works in a sewer wants to call himself a "sanitation engineer," we may find it amusing. Mangled syntax and inflated definitions can be hilarious and we can have great fun enjoying them. William Makepeace Thackeray said, "A good laugh is sunshine in the house." Brendan Walsh is an internationally known Irish humorist, author, and speaker. For many years, he has been one of the most popular radio presenters of music in Australia. He wisely reminds us, "Humor is to life what shock absorbers are to the car." But after we stop laughing, we realize that there is nothing funny about the use of inflated, verbose language in an environment with serious consequences.

Lewis Carroll wrote the great 19th century classics, *Alice in Wonderland*[27] and *Through the Looking Glass and What Alice Found There.*[28] While Carroll's books are usually identified as books for children, they are filled with satirical lessons for adults. *Through the Looking Glass* contains Carroll's immortal nonsense poem, "Jabberwocky," filled with original words entirely made up by the author. The verse begins:

> *'Twas brillig, and the slithy toves, Did gyre and gimble in the wabe; All mimsy were the borogoves, And the mome raths outgrabe.*
> *The reader is advised:*
> *Beware the Jabberwock, my son!*
> *The jaws that bite, the claws that catch! Beware the Jubjub bird, and shun The frumious Bandersnatch!*

Carroll was skilled at satirizing pretentious poetry of the day. But read a binding legal contract, a law passed by Congress or your state legislature, a scholarly journal, or a textbook used by education professors to train teachers. They are filled with real jargon that sounds like the language ridiculed so skillfully by Richard Armour, Laurence Peter, and James Boren. If the jargon adversely affects our nation's financial wellbeing or security, no one will be laughing for long. When language is used to defraud, intimidate, or just provide reams of useless paperwork, you may be next on the list. The frumious Bandersnatch awaits!

BIG WORDS: FRIENDS OR FOES?

Big words can be funny. Walt Disney's 1964 film, *Mary Poppins,* was based on the classic writing of P.L.Travers and featured Julie Andrews as the nanny with magical powers. The film contained a song by the Sherman Brothers, Robert B. and Richard M.,

Supercalifragilisticexpialidocious. The invented 34 letter word was soon on the lips of millions of children who might never have remembered such a word if it had been uttered in a real classroom. During the song, the irrepressible nanny says, "You know, you can say it backwards, which is 'dociousaliexpilisticfragicalirupus', but that's going a bit too far, don't you think?"

Even in politics, where big words can cause the worst kinds of mischief, there are causes to smile. In 1950, Sen. Claude Pepper, a Florida Democrat, was locked in a bitter primary battle with challenger George Smathers. An item in *The Washington Post,* picked up by *Time and Life* magazines, both at the height of their influence, set the stage for one of the most hilarious and controversial political quotes of all time. Smathers was quoted as using innocuous big words in a blatant attempt to persuade unsophisticated rural voters that Pepper was a nefarious character. The publications quoted Smathers as saying to Florida voters, "Are you aware that Claude Pepper is known all over Washington as a shameless extrovert? Not only that, but this man is reliably reported to practice nepotism with his sister-in-law and he has a sister who was once a thespian in wicked New York. Worst of all, it is an established fact that Mr. Pepper, before his marriage, habitually practiced celibacy." Although Smathers denied making the remarks, they were widely circulated and passed into the pantheon of political legends. Smathers won the election, but the comments followed him throughout his senatorial career.

Smathers' biographer determined that the quotations may have originated as a joke initiated by Washington and Miami reporters, tired of hearing Smathers deliver the same stump speech. In later years, Pepper, who ended his career as a long serving member of the House of Representatives, admitted that he never heard Smathers repeat the alleged comments. After Smathers left the Senate, he offered a $10,000 reward to anyone who could produce a recording proving that the quotes were legitimate. At the time of his death in 2007, fifty-seven years after the original stories in *Time and Life,* the reward remained unclaimed. But the quotes still live today, turning up on the Internet as an example of dirty politics and deceptive rhetoric.

Reed Irvine was Oxford-educated, a Fulbright scholar, and an economist with the Federal Reserve Board. For three decades, he was a conservative gadfly and critic who fought what he perceived to be a liberal bias in the national news media. Irvine's criticisms finally became too much for *Washington Post* editor Benjamin Bradlee, who called him "a miserable, carping, retromingent vigilante." Irvine was curious about the unusual word "retromingent," which turned out to be a reference to an animal urinating backwards. Bradlee offered no proof that this word was accurately applied to Irvine, or even if this description had been true, that such an assertion invalidated Irvine's media critique. Irvine responded by sending Bradlee a trophy from the "Miserable, Carping, Retromingent Vigilante Society," which an un-amused Bradlee promptly returned. The word "retromingent" failed to pass into general usage among journalists.

Not all political figures use language deceptively. Abraham Lincoln once asked, "How many legs would a horse have if you called his tail a leg?" Lincoln provided the answer, "Four, calling a tail a leg doesn't make it a leg." Lincoln also asked, "If I were two faced, would I show this one?" Early in his administration, Ronald Reagan was asked by an advisor to explain his strategy in approaching the Cold War. Reagan said, "We win, they lose." But for every statesman who speaks in plain English, there are dozens of political figures who make statements that are either deceptive or confusing and unintentionally amusing. For example, former California Governor Gray Davis enthusiastically declared his desire to make California the most diverse state on earth and then proudly concluded by explaining, "We have people from every planet on the earth in this state."

Today, a writer or speaker who draws upon the full resources of the dictionary may create the impression he is simply trying to impress people. Robert L. Green, long time men's fashion director for *Playboy*, adopted a flowery style of speaking; when television star Johnny Carson interviewed him, Carson asked, "Are you

British?" "No," said Green, "just affected." Big words are not always confusing. Unusual and apparently exotic words can, when properly used, establish clarity. Consider the view of William F. Buckley, Jr. No one had a more colorful vocabulary or a greater mastery of words than Buckley. In numerous works of fiction and non-fiction, thousands of newspaper columns, debates, speeches, and television programs, William F. Buckley, Jr. displayed prodigious knowledge of the English language with casual ease. But a well-developed vocabulary makes the user an easy target for critics. Most such critics echo the words of Henry Evans (no relation to the author of the book you are reading), a columnist for the *Maries County* (Missouri) *Gazette.* Henry Evans accused William F. Buckley, Jr. of being a lexicographical snob, a show-off who used obscure and unfamiliar words known only to him. The purpose of this verbal virtuosity, according to Henry Evans, was to remind the reader of his intellectual inferiority and send him scurrying off to the nearest dictionary.

Jesse Sheidlower, writing the introduction to *The Lexicon,*[29] the Buckley cornucopia of wonderful words for the inquisitive word lover, responds. He says, "We have any number of authors who revel in arcane vocabulary, but Mr. Buckley surpasses them all, for the simple reason that when he uses a hard word, he knows what it means." He adds, "Mr. Buckley uses them in context, without calling special attention to them, because he knows them, not because he scribbled them in a notebook after finding them in the Oxford English Dictionary. He uses them because they are right."

Russell Kirk, an eminent author, teacher, and philosopher, wrote the introduction to another Buckley volume, *Rumbles Left and Right,*[30] and used the word "energumen" to describe the book's critics. ("Energumen" means "someone possessed by an evil spirit.") The critics howled, and Buckley came to his friend's defense, advising those unfamiliar with the word not to pout, but to open a dictionary and decide for themselves if they should learn a new word. Should writers and speakers who have a thoroughly developed vocabulary avoid using unfamiliar words? The question, of course, must be asked: unfamiliar to whom?

A beginning pianist or aspiring composer may have a limited musical vocabulary. Would anyone expect a great composer to restrict his creativity by discarding the sounds that are not instantly familiar? André Previn was one of those rare musicians equally comfortable in the classical and jazz worlds. He once compared the orchestrations of a major figure in jazz to those of Duke Ellington. The first composer could score a passage for a hundred instruments and Previn said that every studio arranger could say, "Oh, yes, that's done like this." Then he said that Duke Ellington could raise a finger and two horns would make a sound, and he wouldn't know what it was. Should Duke Ellington have limited his musical vocabulary to sounds or ideas recognized only by the least sophisticated ears in his audience? Not everyone writes music, but everyone speaks and writes using words. But the principle is the same.

Big words are unnecessary if they are an affectation. Unfamiliar words are a delight if they add a new dimension to what is being written or said. Today the words most often used by writers and speakers of all ages seem limited. Listen to the average teenager. Slang can be colorful and colloquialisms are sometimes more descriptive than words chosen from a textbook on grammar. But the range of descriptive words in popular speech today is narrow. Today someone worthy of praise is likely to be either "awesome" or "amazing." Someone unworthy of praise is likely to be described in the same few coarse and vulgar words. Listen to the dialogue in most contemporary films. With a few exceptions, you are likely to hear everyone indulging in the same profanities, sometimes every few words. Are the creators of such characters unimaginative or do they think they are merely writing dialogue as it is spoken in the real world? Either way, they are producing bad scripts and even worse films. To say their range is limited is an understatement. Dorothy Parker once dismissed a stage performance by Katharine Hepburn by declaring, "She runs the gamut from A to B." Many of today's speakers have miles to go before they even reach the letter A.

The Lexicon, William F. Buckley, Jr.'s collection of favored words, is filled with nouns, verbs, adjectives, and adverbs that shouldn't be banished from the language because someone has to look them up in a dictionary. Why? Because they clarify meaning, they bring to a sentence a precision and a specificity that would be otherwise lacking. Do you know a politician who always tells the crowd what it wants to hear? You could say, "He's a jerk." You clearly don't like him, although no one may know why this is the case. But if you say "he's a demagogue," you define his behavior precisely. Does he pretend to be humble, like Uriah Heep, the character Charles Dickens etched into our collective memory in *David Copperfield*? Does he appear to be artificially smooth and express himself in a perpetually oily manner? What better word exists to describe him than "oleaginous"? Is he small-minded and overly concerned with petty details? How can his behavior be better characterized than as "pettifoggery"? Is he an idealist who always pursues hopeless causes fighting villains who aren't really there? Then he's "quixotic," a word derived from the character of Don Quixote who tilted at windmills courtesy of Miguel de Cervantes. Does he constantly take positions and then reverse them? He is known for his "tergiversations." But if you use these words instead of saying "he's a jerk," someone will accuse you of being a linguistic snob.

There is more than one type of snobbery. Some snobs are indeed intent upon reminding you of their superiority. But there are also the inverse snobs, those who resent anything or anyone who challenges them to learn something new or answer the unfamiliar. During World War II, CBS Radio correspondent Edward R. Murrow said of Winston Churchill, "He mobilized the English language and sent it into battle to steady his fellow countrymen and hearten those Europeans upon whom the long dark night of tyranny had descended." Murrow's remark became a favorite quotation used by and often attributed to President John F. Kennedy. A modern day Churchill would be denounced as a linguistic elitist, who should quit trying to impress people.

THE SPOKEN WORD

Peggy Noonan wrote speeches for President Ronald Reagan. As an imaginative writer with a flair for poetic phrases, she found herself in conflict with the "White House staffing process," in which a speech was circulated among and edited by an assortment of staffers and bureaucrats, often with questionable writing skills. In her memoir, *What I Saw at the Revolution,*[31] she recalled writing one of Ronald Reagan's most moving addresses, delivered after the space shuttle "Challenger" exploded. The President had to speak to a nation in shock over the deaths of the seven-member crew, including Christa McAuliffe, the schoolteacher whose journey into space had captured the country's imagination. Peggy Noonan included a quotation from John Magee's celebrated poem, *High Flight.* The President said, "The crew of the space shuttle Challenger honored us by the manner in which they lived their lives. We will never forget them, nor the last time we saw them, this morning, as they prepared for the journey, and waved good- bye, and 'slipped the surly bonds of earth' to 'touch the face of God.'" According to Peggy Noonan, a pudgy young staff member from the National Security Council told her to change the quote from "Touch the face of God" to "reach out and touch someone, touch the face of God." He had heard what he thought was an eloquent phrase, "reach out and touch someone" in a television commercial for the telephone company. Peggy Noonan said she would resign if the Madison Avenue phraseology were inserted in the speech. This time the original quote survived, without preposterous editing.

Could the greatest orations of history survive editing by committee? Not likely, says Peggy Noonan, who circulated a copy of "The Gettysburg Address" as it might be edited today. Lincoln's powerful opening, "Fourscore and seven years ago" would be excised, and the speech would have to include feminist references. "Our fathers created here a new nation," would be changed to "Our fathers and mothers." The phrase, "conceived in liberty," would have to go ("too much sexual imagery, sounds like we're talking about teenage pregnancy"). Lincoln's declaration, "We cannot dedicate, we cannot consecrate, we cannot hallow this ground" would be deleted as "too negative." Word by word, line by line, Lincoln's majestic prose would be altered by committee to express the dull, neutral, colorless style of speech pleasing to bureaucrats, but boring the life out of audiences. The New York State Education Department issued bias and sensitivity guidelines, and then in 2002, acknowledged bowdlerizing readings on its own examinations to comply with the guidelines. Dale McFeatters suggested in the *New York Post* that 'The Gettysburg Address" couldn't survive the guidelines for a moment. Lincoln quoting the Declaration of Independence and declaring, "All men are created equal" was "clearly sexist." The speech today would be dismissed as full of images that reflected positively on religion and the military, and that talking about "Gettysburg" produced images of violence. McFeatters concluded that the only phrase to remain from the original speech would be "The Biglerville Address, by Abraham Lincoln: We have a really cool country, and we should keep it that way."

SHOULD JOHNNY SPELL CORRECTLY?

Is it too much to expect students to learn to spell correctly? Yes, according to advocates of an "approved, optional alternative phonetic spelling." It is hard to quarrel with the legacy of a man who remained active and devoted to his causes until his death at 104.

But quarrel we must! Dr. Edward Rondthaler founded companies that developed typefaces and provided headlines to major magazines. He credited his longevity to following his morning hot shower with an ice-cold one. For much of his life, Edward Rondthaler campaigned to change the way the English language is spelled. He went so far as to suggest that putting winners of the National Spelling Bee on a pedestal is a bad idea, and blamed a course of study that is partly to blame for illiteracy and its byproducts: dropouts, juvenile delinquency, crime in the streets, hard-core unemployment, and poverty. Dr. Rondthaler and his followers advocated a new form of spelling, a language to be called "American," which eliminates confusing or difficult spellings of words. Members of what he calls the "literate elite" could continue to spell conventionally, while those who couldn't read, write, or spell well, could adopt the optional system, spelling words in ways which would be regarded as incorrect by anyone else's standards. Advocates of this system insist that literate elites shouldn't look down upon those who are illiterate. They are right. We should encourage them to learn to read. Dumbing down our language (or "dumming down" as Dr. Rondthaler would have it) and creating a two-tier system of spelling accomplishes exactly the opposite of what society needs. With this system, we assume that if Johnny can't read, he shouldn't spell either.

If academicians have found "oppression" in requirements that students spell correctly, by 2021, a new and even more absurd example of oppression has been found: capitalization!

Consider the announcement of Canada's Mount Royal University in 2021 that Dr. Linda ManyGuns had been named Associate Vice-President of Indigenization and Decolonization. Her credentials include a law degree from the University of Ottawa and a doctorate from Trent University. Dr. ManyGuns is a true warrior and she is determined to rid our world of that appalling manifestation of oppression and discrimination, *capital letters*. She explains, "We resist acknowledging the power structures that oppress and join the movement that does not capitalize." She declared herself a follower of "leaders like e.e. cummings, bell hooks, and peter kulchyski, who reject the symbols of hierarchy wherever they are found and do not use capital letters except to acknowledge the Indigenous struggle for recognition." So ManyGuns does, however, capitalize the word "Indigenous" as it represents the oppressed.

Does this mean that all who write only in lower case type will be given equal literary status to Edward Estlin Cummings, the contemporary poet who allegedly signed his name "e.e. cummings"? Actually, the use of two small letters in his name was the result of an experiment in style by one of his publishers. In fact, Cummings signed his name using his initials as "E.E. Cummings." While he played with punctuation in his poems, he didn't eschew capital letters entirely; the rumor that he'd legally changed his name to "e.e. cummings" was started by a critic, Harry T. Moore, and described by Cummings' widow as "stupid and churlish."

The truth is that there are pseudo-intellectuals looking for oppressors hiding under every bed (or on every printed page they can find). The notion that one is fighting "domination" by getting rid of capital letters is as foolish as the nonsense spread by music professors that the idea of a weak to strong musical cadence is somehow a secret plot against feminists.

Are we to believe that writers are all oppressing someone when they check the *Chicago Manual of Style* to be sure they are not incorrectly capitalizing a word? Now however, Dr. ManyGuns is clearly going to be the trailblazer of what she calls "The lower case movement." ManyGuns' ideas about "inclusion to all forms of life and all people" may not extend to including capital letters, but what about her students? One can only wonder what will happen to alumni of Mount Royal University in the real world when their employers wonder why they seem unable to use capitalization in their writing? Of course, they will be highly employable at assorted colleges and universities so that the protest can continue. We should not be startled to hear that the woke want to foolishly overthrow capitalism, but to launch a struggle against capitalization is both foolish and absurd.

IS IT WRONG TO WRITE?

Even if students are properly taught to read and spell correctly, they may be unable to put thoughts together in a coherent way on paper. In 2008, New Dorp High School on Staten Island in New York had a reputation as a poor school in danger of being closed. The school's principal, Deirdre DeAngelis, began an investigation that produced surprising results. Writing in *The Atlantic,* Peg Tyre explains DeAngelis's conclusions. She says, "By 2008, she and her faculty had come to a singular answer: bad writing. Students' inability to translate thoughts into coherent, well-argued sentences, paragraphs, and essays was severely impeding intellectual growth in many subjects. Consistently, one of the largest differences between failing and successful students was that only the latter could express their thoughts on the page." DeAngelis instituted a writing program based on the teaching of Judith Hochman, former head of the Windward School in White Plains, New York. Hochman had become legendary for her ability to teach writing skills. Peg Tyre writes, "The Hochman Program, as it is sometimes called, would not be unfamiliar to nuns who taught in Catholic schools circa 1950. Students don't have to "catch" a single thing. They are explicitly taught how to turn ideas into simple sentences, and how to construct complex sentences from simple ones by supplying the answers to three prompts, but, because, and so." New Dorp has now become a model for other high schools by recognizing that the inability to write and express thoughts clearly on paper affects a student's performance in every other subject.

But while certain schools are moving in the right direction, too many are moving in the wrong direction. Incredibly, many academicians support abandoning the teaching of cursive writing. So while students may need new and demanding instruction in organizing their thoughts on paper, in the future, they may not even be able to write their own names. Christina Hoag writes, "Whether it's required or not, cursive is fast becoming a lost art as schools increasingly replace pen and paper with classroom computers and instruction is increasingly geared to academic subjects that are tested on standardized exams." Young teachers who are proving unable to teach cursive writing to young pupils and self-styled experts both insist that a student who can type messages quickly is fully prepared to communicate through texting. There are numerous reasons to continue to learn cursive writing skills. Students should be familiar with longhand writing used by the parents, grandparents, and historical figures in letters and documents. Handwriting reflects the personality of the individual in a way that typing e-mails cannot. Students who write can do so with much greater speed than those who print. Of course, students should develop typing skills on a computer keyboard to facilitate using high-tech devices. Students who use cursive writing are going to be able to organize their thoughts more coherently than those who do not. Can we imagine a time when those with graduate degrees such as the M.A. or Ph.D. will not even be able to sign their own names?

One casualty of abandoning cursive writing is the handwritten note. A note in the author's handwriting is personal in a way that an e-mail message is not. Even a letter composed on the now extinct typewriter with a handwritten signature carries a sense of the writer that an electronic note cannot. High technology encourages brevity; while brevity may be a good thing and "the soul of wit" according to Lord Polonius in *Hamlet,* brevity in all communications may be superficial and ultimately meaningless. Consider the published letters of great writers and statesmen of the past. Future generations may one day be reading only the superficial "Famous Tweets of Famous People" and "Awesome E-Mails of Celebrities." Writing a real letter requires the writer to collect., organize, and even edit his thoughts. In today's instant communications, the flowery forms of address used in the past have disappeared. But again, too much informality may be worse than too little. It implies a lack of respect by the sender for the recipient. In recent months, I have received an abundance of e-mails from perfect strangers all beginning with the greeting "Hey!" Now no one will regret the passing of the greeting, "Dear Sir or Madam," an opening revealing that the writer clearly knows nothing about the person to whom he is writing. I often receive messages from friends beginning, "Hi, Mark." It doesn't bother me and if the writer happens to be a pretty girl, I am in fact quite pleased. But "Hey" from strangers sounds like something you would say to a person who abruptly stepped in front of you while standing in line. "Hey" as in "HEY, YOU!" is not the way to begin writing to strangers. Hay is for horses, not the openings of letters. But in an age when profanities are dropped by students in classrooms like snowflakes in a storm, should we be surprised at bad manners?

POLITICAL CORRECTNESS

The march toward political correctness has become a plague upon our language. Anything considered controversial or offensive can be targeted by someone for revision or deletion. Diane Ravitch made the case against such behavior in her book, *The Language Police.*[32] Who are the language police? For Diane Ravitch, an education professor and historian, they are textbook publishers, writers of academic tests, school boards, and federal and state bureaucrats. According to Professor Ravitch, they combine forces to engage in a beneficent censorship designed to purge instruction and textbooks of words, pictures, and subjects that someone may find offensive. The problem, of course, is determining who gets to decide what is offensive and whose sensibilities are to be considered. Censorship, with the best of intentions, has not led to greater learning or literacy. It has encouraged authors and teachers to be boring and dull. The extremes to which the language police will go defy the imagination. One publisher's guideline insists that textbooks must not portray women as caregivers, that men must not be lawyers, doctors, or plumbers, but must be nurturing helpmates, that cake is not nutritious and must be excluded from stories, and that setting a tale in the mountains "discriminates" against students who come from the flatlands. *The Language Police* is filled with examples of such foolishness, hundreds of attempts to impose a rigid framework of rules, regulations, and ideology on the way we write and speak. Diane Ravitch compiled a long list of words that are culled from bias guidelines used by editors, writers, and illustrators. Among the banned words: "actress" (sexist), "Adam and Eve" (to be replaced with Eve and Adam to demonstrate that females are not inferior), "confined to a wheelchair" (to be replaced by "person who is mobility impaired"), "cowboy" (sexist, to be replaced by "cowhand"), "housewife" (sexist, to be replaced by "head of the household" or "homemaker"), manhunt (sexist, to be replaced by "hunt for a person"). The list goes on and on and on, ad infinitum. There are pages and volumes of such foolishness, phrases, images, and topics that might offend someone who is a member of a group or category that must not be offended. There are even lists of foods that must not be mentioned." Diane Ravitch concludes, "I, for one, want to be free to refer to 'the brotherhood of man' without being corrected by the language police. I want to decide for myself whether I should be called a chairman, a chairwoman, or a chairperson (I am not a chair). I want to see 'My Fair Lady' and laugh when Professor Higgins sings, 'Why can't a woman be more like a man?' As a grandmother, I want to feel sure that my grandchildren can read works of literature and history that have not been cleansed, sanitized, expurgated, and bowdlerized."

The march toward political correctness and verbal foolishness is hardly an American phenomenon. While some Americans think of Europeans as culturally enlightened and far more sophisticated, many of the worst excesses in this brand of linguistic pettifoggery can be found in Europe. Bureaucrats in charge of such matters in the European Union have banned the use of "Miss." and "Mrs.," or any words referring to a woman's marital status. This includes such well-known international terms as "Mademoiselle" and "Madame," "Fräulein" and "Frau," "Señorita" and "Señora." The headmaster or headmistress of a school must be called "head" or "head teacher," while sportsmen and statesmen are now to be dubbed "athletes" and "political leaders." The Brussels bureaucrats ignore the fact that many women want to be called "Miss" or "Mrs." and do not wish to be addressed by their first or last name, or by the term "Ms.," now imposed on everyone. Nor do they realize that there is a difference between a headmaster and a "head." Not all athletes are sportsmen; all political leaders are hardly statesmen. In fact, there are very few statesmen to be found in international affairs today and the European Union clearly can boast a paucity of statesmen of any gender. Stamping out sexism? To use a fine old English word, balderdash!

Not all Europeans are tolerating the arrival of the speech police. The *Daily Mail* reported that Scottish Tory MEP Struan Stevenson said the guidelines were "political correctness gone mad." He called them ludicrous, comparing the guidelines to efforts by the EU to ban bagpipes and dictate the shape of bananas. Stevenson said, "Gender-neutrality is really the last straw. The Thought Police are now on the rampage in the European Parliament. We will soon be told that the use of the words 'man' or 'woman' will be banned in case it causes offense to those who consider gender neutrality an essential part of life."

The level of political correctness has reached the point of absurdity. Nicole Mamo is director of Devonwood Recruitment, a British firm that supplies hundreds of cleaners, caterers, and porters to hospitals. When she published an advertisement seeking applicants for a job as a domestic cleaner, she included the words "reliable and hard-working." She was then informed by a government agency, the Job Centre in Thetford, Norfolk, that the ad was inappropriate because it discriminated against people who were unreliable and might be offended. The astonished Mamo told the *Daily Mail*, "Unfortunately it's extremely alarming. I need people who are hardworking and reliable—and I am pleased to discriminate in that way. If they're not then I really can't use them. The reputation of my business is on the line. Even the woman at the Job Centre agreed it was ridiculous but explained it was policy because they could get sued for being discriminatory against unreliable people." Camilla, Queen Consort, married to King Charles, offered a cogent British view of the problem, which seems to know no national boundaries. Although declaring enormous pride in the ability to question, debate, and criticize all aspects of our society, she said, "Please let us not become too politically correct, because surely political correctness is as severe a form of censorship as any."

The great classics of literature are full of words, phrases, and images that someone might find offensive. But in the name of sensitivity, those who turn a blue pencil on the original classic texts are also directing their blue pencils at thought, imagination, and creativity. Poor reading instruction renders the best literature "hard" and the finest writers "difficult." Educational theorists worried about correcting a child's "miscues" insure that he or she will read poorly, thereby never being exposed to much of our cultural heritage. Rodney Atkinson, who spent thirty years as a California public school teacher, administrator, and specialist in children's literature, and Diane Ravitch state the case on behalf of classic literature: "It is both amusing and disheartening to meet adults today who express regret that they never read (or heard) works like *Aesop's Fables* or *Heidi;* or to hear a recent high school graduate complain that she spent nearly four years in English class without reading a classic English novel; or to hear of classrooms where popular teen literature is required reading, but the literary classics are not; or to hear of a library that discards *Little Women* because it is too hard for children to read and its place on the shelf could be better used by books with higher circulation rates." The notion that big words, colorful language, and a rich, well-developed vocabulary will make some children feel inferior is pernicious nonsense.

As a proponent of cultural conservation, you are likely to meet a variety of challenges, some from unlikely sources. One of the most vigorous and inevitable challenges comes from those who question your right to judge or evaluate what they do. In their eyes, being judgmental is the ultimate sin. We must never (they tell us) try to impose our standards, values, or ideas on others. But while insisting they are open-minded about everything and everybody, they reveal a curious and constant bias of their own.

THE TRIUMPH OF THE VULGARIANS

If students are not learning the best of language in school, they are exposed to the worst of language on the streets and the screens of television, film, and computers. It is impossible to spend more than a few moments in our popular culture without hearing a deluge of foul language. In 1939, movie audiences were shocked to hear Clark Gable (as Rhett Butler in *Gone With the Wind)* utter the famous exit line, "Frankly, my dear, I don't give a damn." A single profanity was the cause of controversy. In the 1960s, the self-proclaimed "Free Speech Movement" on the campus of the University of California devolved into the so-called "Filthy Speech Movement," demanding the "rights" of students on campus to use obscene language in public. People were shocked by what they regarded as inappropriate language. Today's hit movies and recordings abound in obscenities, spoken proudly by men, women, and children of all ages.

Consider the MTV Movie Awards, broadcast over cable television to an audience of adults and children. The Culture and Media Institute counted 100 swearwords in the 122-minute special. Network censors bleeped seventy words, but at least thirty obscenities went past the censors. In describing what he called a "piñata of profanity," L. Brent Bozell III wrote, "One of the most egregious offenders was actor Peter Facinelli, who accepted the 'Best Picture' award for the teen vampire drama *Twilight: New Moon.* He cooed, 'I've never heard the word "f***" used so many times in one evening.' He then went on to use it eight times himself, four of which made it past the censors. He only skipped cursing as he honored Stephenie Meyer, the author of the *Twilight* books, because he explained, "She's a Mormon." Bozell added, "That's consideration, Hollywood style." MTV apologized after the inevitable protests by describing the event as featuring "irreverent comedy" and a "party atmosphere" in which guests speak freely. The episode revealed what anyone watching MTV would already know: that MTV welcomes and encourages the vulgarians because it boosts ratings and makes money. The consequences are of no importance.

The late George Carlin was a comedian who began his career doing standard, stand-up comedy. But he became famous (and some would say infamous) for challenging acceptable standards for the use of language. When it was still shocking to hear comedians peppering their acts with four-letter words, Carlin uttered "The Seven Words You Can't Say on Television." Today, young comedians not only use all of these words freely, they are emulated by children who hear such language in movies that are allegedly available only to adult audiences. Carlin had declared that it is the job of the comedian to "determine where the line is drawn and then cross it." In a television interview with Bill O'Reilly, Carlin presented a clever, but flawed, defense of the profane language used freely in his comedic material and that of his many imitators. Words, Carlin suggested, are merely symbols. They mean nothing in themselves. Those who agree with Carlin say, "So as long as you respond to certain words differently than I do, no one can say that the use of such words is really offensive. It's all relative, all a matter of opinion." For Carlin, ideas and conditions in the world that offended him were truly objectionable. (For the record, Carlin listed traditional religious values and private property as concepts that bothered him.) His objections to the idea of private property clearly did not extend to his own. Carlin and his admirers prided themselves on being "challengers to tradition," implying that tradition ought to be abandoned for its own sake.

Like Carlin, comedian Lenny Bruce became best known for breaking rules. In Bruce's case, the rules he broke related to his use of language considered to be obscene. In the 1960s, audiences were shocked by Bruce's typically profane comments on sexual behavior, religion, and politics. Today Bruce's language wouldn't shock anyone; acts seen in comedy clubs and on cable networks are filled with obscenities. Bruce wrote a book entitled, *How to Talk Dirty and Influence People.* He unfortunately succeeded in doing both. Comedians who followed Bruce and Carlin became more interested in offering shocking commentary than in making people laugh. But not everyone applauded this legacy, including Steve Allen, on whose television show Bruce achieved early recognition.

Scrapping rules and standards provokes consequences. Steve Allen, one of television's legendary funny men, recognized this in his last book, *Vulgarians at the Gate.*[33] He wrote, "The consequences of rearing millions of initially innocent children in a social atmosphere characterized by vulgarity, violence, brutish manners, the collapse of the family, and general disrespect for traditional codes of conduct is to chill the blood of even the most tolerant of observers."

The indiscriminate use of foul language has been popularized by rap music stars and comedians. The great comedians of vaudeville, who became popular through radio, films, and later television, were hardly prudes. One cannot imagine strings of profanities coming from George Burns, Jack Benny, or Bob Hope, for instance. Lucille Ball, whose classic television series, *I Love*

Lucy, is still delighting audience more than a half-century after episodes first aired, would often turn off her television in response to the crude vulgarity in today's comedy.

Comedians would often have "roasts" in their private clubs, in which jokes and language would have shocked their audiences. (But at these private events, the audiences were all adults and composed of friends.) These masters of comedy understood that one didn't have to use obscene language or incredibly vulgar material in their public performances in order to be funny. Their material could be broadcast to family audiences without incident. Today, a significant number of successful male and female comedians have earned their stripes in the entertainment industry through foul-mouthed comedy acts laced with profanity and explicit language of every type. Comedian Tom Dreesen observes that many young audiences and young comedians have never heard a comedian make an audience laugh without using what used to be called "X-rated" language. Anyone objecting to such performances will be quickly labeled a prude, a censor, and finally, the ultimate term of derogation, "old-fashioned." Dreesen, a successful comedian for many years, notes that he has been described as a practitioner of the old school. While performing at a comedy club, Dreesen overheard a pair of newer, younger comedians discussing him. In particular, they were puzzled by his avoidance of a familiar obscenity repeated ad nauseum in their routines. One comedian asked the other, "If he doesn't use the 'f-word', what does he use?" Dreesen couldn't resist answering. He said, "Adjectives!" It is doubtful that they will follow this advice George Carlin's arguments about obscene language also represented a slippery slope. If no words are obscene, then anything anyone chooses to write or say must be accepted without criticism. This same argument has been used by artists and musicians. Just as Carlin said words are merely symbols, contemporary composers suggest that no sounds are truly dissonant. It's all relative, all a matter of opinion. A piece of music can consist of 100 percent dissonance and its creator can demand that it be treated as a work of beauty. The same can be said for a hideous piece of artwork. Nothing is intrinsically beautiful, the artist insists; definitions of "beautiful" and "ugly" are entirely arbitrary. The idea that everything is relative and subjective is dangerous. The Declaration of Independence says nothing about all opinions being created equal. Some ideas are brilliant, others foolish. Some people are geniuses; others seem bent on advertising their stupidity in public. In this topsy-turvy world, every artist, every critic becomes a lexicographer with his or her own set of definitions. A chef can declare that Tabasco sauce isn't actually spicy and pour it over vanilla ice cream. But the patrons of his restaurant wouldn't be amused or accept the idea that he had simply "redefined taste." So why do we accept similar foolishness in talking about artistic and cultural subjects? What's the difference between music and noise—between eloquence and a string of four-letter words—between the beautiful and the hideously ugly? Some would have us believe that the answer is "Absolutely nothing."

A small army of academicians has become skilled at a process called "deconstruction," in which all kinds of hidden meanings are found in works formerly thought to be great masterpieces. But if everything means nothing, then nothing means anything. This is an argument for artistic and cultural anarchy. A foul-mouthed comedian can claim to be pushing the envelope while his critics are expected to apologize for objecting to his language. A musical charlatan can sell recorded noise, while his critics are expected to apologize for observing that he has no talent. An artist can throw paint at a canvas, declare that his work expresses a philosophy too profound for the public to understand, and cry all the way to the bank. His critics are expected to apologize for recognizing that a five-year-old could paint just as well.

All of these people will be quick to talk about their rights to do what they do. They may have the right to demonstrate their ignorance, incompetence, lack of talent, imagination, or creativity to the rest of us. But we also have a right to respond to their message, without accusations that merely being judgmental about their work disqualifies our opinions from being taken seriously. In fact, the time and attention often given to these individuals means that others with different standards and values are disenfranchised. Words mean what they mean. Musical sounds and visual images are intrinsically beautiful, dissonant, lyrical, or repulsive. We have a right to say so. When someone accuses you of being judgmental, he is trying to avoid the harsh reality of criticism.

Critics of foul language are invariably accused of intolerance. Advocates of such language are quick to wrap themselves in the mantle of free speech and the rights of "artists" to self-expression. They want to confine the discussion to "rights," because they don't want to deal with the issue of "responsibility." Anyone has the right to make a fool of himself in public, but that doesn't mean it's a good idea. The writer of pages of four-letter words is quick to compare himself to Ernest Hemingway or James Joyce. The vulgar "shock jock" on radio pontificates about the First Amendment. The rap star whose recordings are full of racial epithets and violent obscenities tries to portray himself as an "artist." All of these people are following their chosen road for one reason: to make more money than their competitors. An increase in shock value is considered to relate directly to an increase in profit. As nearly nothing today is regarded as shocking, there is a constant temptation to find a new and extreme way to shock people. In the process, these people cover their own lack of talent and originality, and reduce the level of verbal communication to its lowest common denominator. They portray their critics as censors and cry all the way to the bank.

Does it matter? Geoffrey Hughes, author of *Swearing: A Social History of Foul Language, Oaths and Profanity in English,*[34] declares that "The influence of Hollywood has become a dominant factor, initially for restraint, but subsequently for license." It doesn't take much imagination for a screenwriter to write a string of obscenities or to pepper his dialogue with a four-letter word in every other sentence. The writer gets credit for "pushing the envelope" while eloquence goes out the window. Dr. Robert Thompson, founding director of the Bleier Center for Television and Popular Culture at Syracuse University, has studied the impact of television on society. He observes that language, fashions, and behavior frequently enter the cultural mainstream through television. He says, "Once prime-time television decides to absorb something, it becomes a stamp of normalcy. It's no longer controversial. It's no longer a big deal. It makes it a casual, accepted sort of thing." Language once characterized as "making a sailor blush" now is used freely by women and even children in films, television, and on stage.

"Shock jocks" on radio can boost their ratings by competing to see who can shock his audience the most. The vulgarian Howard Stern, the highest paid and most popular of the "shock jocks," is unapologetic. In 2003 he said, "Foul language is all around us; porn is rampant, and you know what? The country's running fine." Really? Dr. Megan Fitzgerald wrote her doctoral dissertation at Florida State University on the state of offensive language in popular morning radio programs. She concluded that the bulk of such language occurred on stations with "formats such as Rock and Popular that target a young audience."

Vulgarity is hardly new. So anyone criticizing today's pop culture is met with a predictable response. "Every generation rejects yesterday's standards," scoff the skeptics. "What's different about today?" James B. Twitchell addresses this question in his book, *Carnival Culture: The Trashing of Taste in America.*[35] Acknowledging that every era produces its own special brand of vulgarity, Twitchell argues a difference in degree and kind. He says quite accurately, "We live in an age distinct from all other ages that have been called 'vulgar' because we are so vulgarized that we have even lost the word in common use and, in a sense, the aesthetic category. It is not that we think it bad manners to criticize someone else's taste, as much as it is that we have lost the concept of taste as a measure of criticism. While the vulgar is usually pleasurable to those experiencing it, the greatest pleasure intellectuals used to have was to call someone else's behavior or taste 'vulgar.' No more." Twitchell observes that the one place the word "vulgarity" seldom appears (with the rare exception of critics like John Simon, Miss Manners, Jonathan Yardley, William Buckley, and Allan Bloom) is where it used to belong: in cultural criticism.

We have become so accustomed to vulgarity that when it is challenged or criticized, people often react with astonishment. Late night television comedian David Letterman told a crude sexual joke about the fourteen-year-old daughter of Alaska Governor Sarah Palin, who had accompanied her mother to a New York baseball game. When a firestorm of protest erupted, at least among those who care about such things, Letterman defended himself by explaining that he thought he was telling the joke about the Governor's eighteen-year-old daughter, who had not accompanied her to New York. The idea that such humor might be offensive, appalling, and inappropriate with reference to a girl of any age never seemed to enter his mind.

Charlton Heston is best remembered for his portrayals of heroic figures in the movies, including Moses, John the Baptist, Ben-Hur, Michelangelo, and Andrew Jackson, among others. He was politically active, marching with Martin Luther King, Jr. to advance the cause of civil rights and later, campaigning for Second Amendment rights as President of the National Rifle Association. Heston was outraged when he heard the lyrics to *Cop Killer*, a hit by a rap music performer who called himself "Ice T" and released under the auspices of Time-Warner. Heston owned some Time-Warner stock. Against the advice of family and friends, he attended the stockholders' annual meeting and read the lyrics out loud, word for word, before a hushed audience of 1,000 stockholders. The company had promoted the CD by "Ice T," called *Body Count*, by sending advance copies to radio stations in miniature black body bags. Protests from the President of the United States, police groups, religious leaders, and others led nowhere. But when Heston read the actual lyrics performed by "Ice T," celebrating the killing of policemen and an imaginary violent act performed against the twelve-year-old niece of the Vice-President's wife, executives were horrified and embarrassed. The press covering the event couldn't print the lyrics in their newspapers, and when Heston was interviewed on television by Tony Snow, the lyrics couldn't be broadcast. Heston succeeded in embarrassing the executives into firing "Ice T," and pulling the recording off the market. Heston's critics were quick to scream about censorship, but this completely begs the question: why was such a recording released in the first place by the nation's largest entertainment conglomerate—to make money, regardless of the consequences.

Today's films, plays, television programs, books, and song lyrics are filled with nearly constant profanity, all justified because such speech reflects "reality." But whose reality? Donald O'Connor, when he wasn't dancing up the sides of walls in classic movie musicals, was an entertainer with a serious side. He once said, "You don't talk that way, I don't talk that way, but producers and movie executives do. Since they talk to each other, they think everyone else sounds the same way." Allan Jeffreys, a veteran theater critic, suggested that an overabundance of four-letter words reflects anything but maturity. In "Adult Language Is Anything But,"[36] he wrote, "We keep lowering our standards—in speech and dress and manners and morals. We sneer at those who try to raise the bar as we slouch our way through life in droopy, baggy pants—in need of a shave, a haircut, and a bath." Jeffreys said that he was "sad for those too young to remember beauty and romance and songs sung by people who took pride in their appearance and pride in their respect for the lyrics." He concluded that such language, once the property of the barracks and frat houses, should go back where it belongs. Unfortunately, there are many other critics, commentators, and academicians who apparently disagree. These people will offer glib excuses, usually in the name of free speech or realism. However, upon close analysis, their excuses usually reflect a desire to stay in fashion or to make a fast profit.

Arguments on behalf of vulgar speech and foul language are specious. The argument most often advanced is that the speaker or writer is "pushing the envelope" or "challenging the old restrictions and taboos." Such persons invariably project an attitude of self-satisfaction based on the assertion that they are daring to risk the opprobrium of "the establishment." But this is ridiculous. In fact, these people are following the easy path. The film producer who releases a motion picture rated "G" that is directed to family audiences is far more daring than one who simply fills the screen with four-letter words and pretends he is taking a risk. Do not be fooled. There is no risk in marching in the parade of vulgarians.

The last word on the assault and triumph of the vulgarians must belong to Victor Buono, a gifted actor of Falstaffian proportions. Buono spent his career dividing his time between playing Shakespeare on stage and portraying dastardly television villains with a twinkle in his eye worthy of the great Sidney Greenstreet. He also wrote a collection of light-hearted poems, *It Could Be Verse.*[37] The concluding lines of his poem, *O Tempora, O Calcutta,* sum up the situation. Buono described today's plays and films by declaring,

> *The language is crude, the characters rude, Their actions I can't bear to mention.*
> *The emotions are raw as the ones that we saw at the last Democratic convention.*

As for aspiring thespians, he advised,

> *So don't bother gaining professional training. And don't even bother rehearsing.*
> *Be a star overnight and the critics' delight. Just take off your pants and start cursing.*

Does it all matter? Is the state of the language or our ability to use it really important? Or is the whole subject, as some would have us believe, of interest only to old fogies, a few English professors, eccentric linguistic purists, and people too stuffy or conservative to change with the times? Each of these arguments in its own way, helps to corrupt the language. People who cannot read, write, or spell are denied access to the best of our culture.

Their ability to make intelligent decisions as citizens is called into question. The fate of the arts at the hands of these people is dubious. Bureaucratic language can be used by those in government, business, and the law to hide the truth and to shield incompetence. Political correctness becomes an excuse to stifle free expression, often in the hands of those who are the first to mouth slogans about free speech while trying to shut down the speech and thought of those with whom they disagree. Rampant vulgarity cheapens our language, our culture, and our standards. Our glorious language should be learned, used, and enjoyed. It does not belong only in museums and textbooks.

John McWhorter, a linguistics professor at the University of California at Berkeley and a prolific author, addressed the issue in his book, *Doing Our Own Thing: The Degradation of Language and Music and Why We Should, Like, Care.*[38] McWhorter makes a solid argument that the countercultural revolution of the 1960s produced a major change in the ability of Americans to express themselves formally through writing, rather than through casual verbal communication. He writes that "Peter Fonda and Dennis Hopper, mumbling their way through *Easy Rider* in 1969, can be thought of as the totemic inauguration of this new linguistic order, the film being the first major release to celebrate the countercultural ethos in all of its grimy vitality." McWhorter believes that the situation has turned into a crisis in which a significant number of citizens cannot convey ideas and arguments effectively.

In a world without standards, anyone can get away with anything. Every self-proclaimed artist is as talented as every other self-proclaimed artist. But when everyone is a winner, everyone a champion, in truth, success loses its value. As a cultural conservationist, you are certain to be greeted with the challenge, "Who are you to make judgments about culture? What right do you have to impose your values on society?" Ironically, that is exactly what the person speaking is trying to do. George Carlin, for example, was trying to impose his own standards on the entertainment industry. When someone says, "Anything goes," they're not promoting freedom, they're promoting anarchy. When the rules in society (or in the arts) are "no rules," the result isn't freedom, but chaos. Seeking order in place of chaos is a noble calling, but one that will result in inevitable criticisms. Are we going to be judgmental? Of course we are, but judgmental based on principles and ideas that we believe are valid. Can critics of cultural conservation make the same claim?

Advocates of the "no standards" approach to art invariably suggest that their critics are opposed to progress, imagination, innovation, and creativity. They insist proudly that they are going to continue "pushing the envelope," challenging accepted ideas about what kind of art, music, books, and entertainment a society will not only tolerate, but applaud. They depict themselves as daring non-conformists who are challenging old-fashioned notions that will ultimately be left behind in a cloud of artistic dust. But in reality, these people are anything but non- conformists. They are totally conforming to today's version of "no rules" art. The philosophical basis of such "art" is simple, and right out of the counterculture of the 1960s: "Do your own thing, and if anybody criticizes what you do, attack them as a censor, a prude, a pedantic egghead, an intellectual snob, and worst of all, someone with the temerity to be judgmental." Writing noisier music, creating uglier paintings, increasing the level of profanity and violence in entertainment is always easy and requires little courage. Of course, a small army of self-styled critics, eager to appear progressive and open-minded, will always herald the new art as "experimental," "daring," and challenging. In the 21st century, it is hard to write good melodies, paint fine pictures, turn out well-crafted dialogue, or master the art of comedy. It is easy to use material that would once have made a whole navy of sailors blush. Yet artists who pursue the former avenue of creativity are apt to be dismissed casually as "old-fashioned." Their work is likely to be described as relevant only to a world of families derived from wholesome television programs such as *Leave It To Beaver, Ozzie and Harriet,* or *Mayberry, RFD.* "We can't be old-fashioned," say these critics. "We can't be judgmental." So the gifted composer is sent packing because "the kids won't understand his music." The brilliant painter is told his work is merely "representational art," not worthy of serious criticism. The articulate, literate writer's books and scripts remain unsold or they are rewritten by professional hacks who can assure their commerciality. While the truly talented and creative are dismissed, the purveyors of clichés in every form receive adulation and attention. Usually they are praised (again) for "pushing the envelope."

The key to standards is language. What we say and write about the world in general and the arts in particular have a profound effect on what kind a world will be inherited by future generations. Clarity in language is the foundation of standards and values. Language can be used to enlighten or corrupt, to empower or debase a culture. Which road will we choose?

A WAR OF WORDS

In the 1960s, a literary battle erupted over the publication not of a book of politics or a salacious novel, but of a dictionary, "Webster's Third," to be specific. The controversy stemmed from the dictionary's inclusion of slang or non-standard words such as "ain't" and the underlying assumption of its editors that a dictionary should reflect a changing language and common, rather than "correct," usage. The debate was entirely civilized, with respected experts on the English language such as Wilson Follett, critic for *The Atlantic*, calling the volume "a calamity." Bergen Evans, equally respected as a broadcaster, professor, and lexicographer, was far more approving.

The debate reflected two distinct points of view: those of the "descriptivists" who thought dictionaries should report how language is used, and "prescriptivists" who thought they should report how language *should* be used.

Decades later, the civilized and genteel arguments among scholars are but a memory; in the 21st century, the civil society is faced with a most uncivil debate over the use of words. A movement has erupted on both sides of the Atlantic demanding that certain newly invented words be forced into common usage, and words with long histories be summarily banned and banished from polite conversation forever.

Lest anyone think this is a battle over issues appealing mostly to intellectuals sporting bow-ties and thick glasses, happily ensconced in their ivory towers, think again. In the new war over words, anyone caught using the wrong word may be subject to cancellation: the offender may lose his job, his friends, his social standing, and he (or she) may be subjected to a public shaming by the social media mobs who seem to regret that the guillotine went out of fashion with the French Revolution.

The reason for this verbal debacle is that the offending individual, whether intentionally or accidentally, will have used a word that might result in the speaker being branded "racist," "sexist," or one of a long list of words ending in "ist," and the label may stick to a reputation longer than burned scrambled eggs stick to a non-Teflon pan.

Consider the word "Latinx," invented to apply to persons of Latin-American origin who do not "identify" as male or female. There are differences of opinion as to the origins of the term; the most likely origin may be traced to Puerto Rican academics. But scrutiny does not bode well for "Latinx." Linguistics professor John McWhorter has said that the word has failed to achieve widespread use because it reflects the concerns of the intelligentsia rather than the proverbial man in the street.

No one is quite sure how to pronounce the word. Some say "Latin-ex" while others say "Latinx" rhyming with "jinx." Spanish is a gendered language, with masculine words ending in "o" and feminine words ending in "a." Dario Villanueva, director of the Royal Spanish Academy, explained the Academy's rejection of "Latinx" as a word more concerned with machismo than grammar. Hector Luis Alamo, in his article "The X-ing of Language: The Case AGAINST Latinx," wrote, "If we dump *Latino* for *Latinx* because it offends some people, then we should go on dumping words forever since there will always be some people who find some words offensive."[39] A 2019 poll by Pew Research revealed that "Latinx" was used by only three percent of Latinos. It is far more popular among white academics and self-styled intellectuals. You are likelier to hear "Latinx" on the campuses of Princeton or the University of California at Berkeley than in Mexico City or Buenos Aires. "Latinx" is clearly virtue-signaling by non-Latinos to describe people who clearly dislike the term, disapprove of its use by others, and don't use it themselves.

Can you imagine being accused of racism because you'd like to take your family on a picnic? Brandeis University, a liberal arts college in Waltham, Massachusetts, defended a list of terms in the spring of 2021, providing students with words that should be avoided because they are linked to "violent language." The list is laughable, but what should be understood is the highly flawed rationale used by Brandeis's modern day speech police. These aspiring censors research a commonly used term, trace its long-forgotten and discontinued origin, and then try to banish the word from contemporary usage today by ignoring the fact that no one but a Brandeis censor would possibly identify the word with its checkered history.

"Rule of thumb" is a term implying a commonly accepted principle. "Its origin," sniff the haughty word police at Brandeis, "comes from an old British law which allowed men to beat their wives with a stick no wider than their thumbs." The bland "general rule" is offered as a replacement. Are we expected to believe that anyone saying "rule of thumb" is conjuring up vile images of wife-beating?

"Picnic," declare the Brandeis bullies, "refers to white crowds eating while watching the lynchings of black people. "So forget your picnic basket and just say 'outdoor eating.'" The sages in Waltham don't tell us what to do about William Inge's classic play *Picnic,* about a Midwestern family and how their lives change at a picnic, the popular film based on the play, or its wonderful film score by composer George Duning. Are they all to be banned as well?

This is all twaddle, of course, a word that like all others, may be subject to an origin search by the word police on campuses throughout the country. Elimination of colorful language shouldn't be the goal of a university, but it seems to have joined the curriculum at Brandeis. As for telling someone he is doing a splendid job by "killing it," this expression is clearly forbidden as it implies violence. The suggested substitute? "Awesome," the verbal cliché of our age.

Joyce Carol Oates, an award-winning novelist and visiting professor at the University of California at Berkeley, ridiculed the list, asking, "What sort of punishment is doled out for a faculty member who utters the word 'picnic' at Brandeis or the phrase 'trigger warning'—loss of tenure, public flogging, self-flagellation?"

But Brandeis offered a defense, explaining that the list was compiled by students and that the university didn't require such usage. It was only a resource to encourage campus behavior.

Ironically, Brandeis University is named for Louis D. Brandeis, a Supreme Court Justice famed for his militant defense of freedom of speech. What would Justice Brandeis think of the political correction of our national vocabulary? Especially when instigated by the school that bears his name?

In truth, the entire English language has been targeted and those who are "woke" but not awake want the language remade to their specifications. At England's University of East Anglia, the School of Literature, Drama, and Creative Writing has declared it will "decolonise" its curriculum; students expecting to be taught about great books and plays and how to write them will instead be instructed that "English was the language of the coloniser." The decision was made by "woke" administrators who caved to student demands and protests that the curriculum had too many "white, male, cis-gendered authors." The students, who presumably went to East Anglia to learn from, not instruct the faculty, declared the university "complicit in upholding exclusionary, erasive, patriarchal, heteronormative and white supremacist standards." As usual, the racial or gender identity of the authors was the only criterion of importance, not the quality of their work. Not all professors are on board.

Frank Furedi, emeritus professor of sociology at Kent University, summed up the situation when he explained, "The project of decolonising the English language has nothing to do with genuine academic concerns. Associating the evils of colonialism with English literature is more about turning the subject into a political dogma than studying the merits of different writing and authors. None of this is about English literature. It is using English literature as a medium to make a statement about how morally superior these students are."[40]

Former Soviet dissident Vladimir Bukovsky explained the improbable popularity of censorship and linguistic control among academics. In a 2001 interview with Derek Turner in *Right Now* magazine, Bukovsky recalled, "I was at Stanford in the mid-1980s and watched with amazement how political correctness erupted. I had always blamed people like Stalin or Beria for censorship, but now I realized that many intellectuals want it too! Such people will always want censorship; they will always want to be oppressors because they always pretend to be oppressed." [41]

As usual, George Orwell anticipated the manipulation of language and the war of words in his classic book, *1984*. He described the ultimate control of human beings by the state through language, by allowing one of his characters to declare, "It's a beautiful thing, the destruction of words. Don't you see that the whole aim of Newspeak is to narrow the range of thought? In the end we shall make thoughtcrime literally impossible, because there will be no words in which to express it." Orwell's only error was assuming that verbal tyranny would come earlier than it did. In 1984, American voters re-elected Ronald Reagan, a staunch anti-communist, as President; the Berlin Wall soon fell and the Soviet Union collapsed. But in the 21st century, the war of words is in full swing not only in the United States, but in Canada, the U.K., Australia, New Zealand, and much of the European Union. Anna Krylov, born in the Soviet Union and now a prominent Professor of Chemistry at the University of Southern California, understands what has happened. In an article, "The Peril of Politicizing Science," she wrote, "Whereas in 1950, the greater good was advancing the World Revolution (in the USSR; in the USA the greater good meant fighting Communism), in 2021 the greater good is 'Social Justice' (the capitalization is important: 'Social Justice' is a specific ideology, with goals that have little in common with what lower-case 'social justice' means in plain English.)"[42]

A 21ST CENTURY RENAISSANCE OF ENGLISH

What shall we do? We have a pop-culture abounding in inarticulate heroes. Television, radio, and the Internet often highlight the worst, not the best, of our language. Advertising is riddled with clichés. Professors with overblown titles advise us that it isn't important if children can't read or spell as long as they have self-esteem and feel good about themselves. Bureaucrats corrupt the language with meaningless phrases and generate mountains of paper that should be sent to the shredder before they see the light of day. Inarticulate and semi-literate celebrities are publicized and analyzed as if their words are important. But we *can* take action.

1. *Limit the use of jargon.* We must make a concerted effort to eliminate jargon in public discourse, including a national effort to require legal documents to be written in plain English. Similarly, we should create a culture of public criticism directed at so-called scholarly publications that are written in incomprehensible language. Know in advance that defenders of jargon will insist that only they, the specialists and experts, are qualified to understand their writing. This argument must be dismissed. One way to restrain private and public bureaucracy is to limit the ability of bureaucrats to create mountains of paper through misuse of the English language.

2. *Support the teaching of traditional grammar, phonics, and spelling.* Most of our problems with language are the result of a lack of proper education. Again, the experts (in this case, education professors) will howl, but we should ignore them.

3. *Rediscover the idea of appropriate language in public discourse and private behavior.* We must again establish the principle that vulgarity is not an old-fashioned notion that disappeared in the days of the horse and buggy. We must be far

less tolerant of coarse and vulgar language on television and radio, in film, on the Internet, and in general. This is not a call for increased censorship. We must promulgate the principle that just because you can say or write something doesn't mean that you should.

4. *Challenge the inarticulate, especially those in the teenage pop culture that has such a deleterious influence.* Teenagers are particularly prone to inarticulate expression, emulating the speech patterns and slang they hear on television and in the movies. It is essential that poor grammar, confusing jargon, and bad writing be challenged. Actress Emma Thompson observed, "It does hamper people's intelligence because they simply just copy others rather than thinking for themselves and, of course, a lot of that today comes from TV, which promotes abrasive pretentious teenagers. Real teens, being impressionable, just soak these phrases up like sponges from TV, films and the Internet and then they are out there. But if, when a teenager says something like, 'You know what I mean' or 'Whatever,' you ask them, 'No, what do you mean?' or 'Whatever what?', they start thinking for themselves again and generally come back saying something far more articulate." Thompson concluded, "We have to reinvest, I think, in the idea of articulacy as a form of personal freedom and power."

5. *Encourage the development of a rich, creative vocabulary.* We should use big words when they are the right words and simple ones when we can. Clarity in language should become a goal in our daily living.

6. *Approach the battle to recapture our language with humor.* Many of those who are responsible for the decline of our language cause serious problems, but in the final analysis, they are as absurd as they are dangerous.

Clearly, a decline in our language is accompanied by a decline in thought, a decline in our ability to reason clearly and communicate with each other. Certainly, we must take action. Otherwise, we'll be . . . like . . . confused. Y'know?

OUR VANISHING HISTORY

DO YOU CARE ABOUT WHAT HAPPENED YESTERDAY? If you received good news, a Christmas bonus, a marriage proposal, or a long awaited promotion, you probably want to remember every detail of what occurred. If yesterday's news wasn't good—a tax increase, a tornado, or several hours in the dentist's chair—you may want to forget about yesterday. But in either instance, what happened yesterday is likely to affect what happens today. What about those things that happened many yesterdays ago? Do you still have fond memories of your childhood or things you would like to forget? Life is made up of small episodes that sometimes seem unrelated to one another. When these small episodes are stitched together, they make up the patchwork quilt known as history.

Some of the most gifted minds of all time were steeped in the memory of history. In 1953, the prolific author and speechwriter James C. Humes, then a student at Stowe School, met Winston Churchill, who advised him, "Young man, study, study history, in history lie all the secrets of statecraft." Does history matter? Should we care today about what happened yesterday? It depends entirely on the person to whom you ask such questions. History can be regarded with wit. (Dr. Samuel Johnson defined a second marriage as "the triumph of hope over experience.") It can be regarded with reverence. (Historian David McCullough declared, "History is who we are and why we are the way we are.") It can be regarded with hostility. (George Bernard Shaw, in *The Devil's Disciple,* suggested that "History will tell lies as usual.") Abraham Lincoln (who made history as well as writing it) speaking about it, said "History is not history unless it is the truth." But today, in the real world, in our daily lives, history is typically regarded with boredom. If you pose the question of history's importance to a typical high school sophomore, a likely response will be somewhere between laughter and puzzlement. "Who cares about a war fought two hundred years ago?" the sophomore will declare, "and besides, my history teacher is boring."

Unfortunately, the sophomore may be right on both counts. He doesn't know or care about what happened two centuries ago; his history teacher may well be boring as can be. Schools are full of boring teachers and not all of them teach history. But our intrepid sophomore is busy thinking about girls, sports, cars, and in some cases, getting a job. The idea that what happened in Philadelphia in 1776 or at Pearl Harbor in 1941 should be important today seems strange to him. (A survivor of the "Day of Infamy," December 7, 1941, recently spoke to a group of students. When told the visitor to their class would speak about Pearl Harbor, a girl in the class promptly asked, "Who's she?") This troubling issue is raised again with regard to the arts. Why should a child living in the inner city in the 21st century care about music written by an 18th century organist in Germany, an opera composed by 19th century Italian, or a musical show, which lit up the lights of Broadway in the 1920s?

Of course, there are history buffs that follow the events and characters of yesterday with great interest. One can still find men and women trying to prove that the South should have won the Civil War. Others may insist the United States should have stayed out of World War I or that William Shakespeare didn't really write the plays that are attributed to William Shakespeare. However, they are likely to be found on college campuses, at meetings of little-known literary societies, or debating the merits of their positions at parties devoted to wine and cheese. They affect our high school sophomore not at all.

OUR DISAPPEARING PAST

In recent years, Americans have become increasing oblivious to our own history. Stephen Bertman, Professor of Languages, Literature, and Culture at Canada's Windsor University, wrote a provocative book, *Cultural Amnesia,*[43] addressing what he termed "America's Future and the Crisis of Memory." In Bertman's view (and mine), America's loss of collective memory is one of our most serious problems. To put it bluntly, if we don't know where we've been as a nation, a society, and as a culture, we haven't a clue as to where we are going. Bertman poses some diagnostic questions to

Americans. They are the kinds of questions a physician might ask a patient facing a memory crisis. When posed to us as a society, the results are disturbing. Bertman asks, "Do you know what day it is? Do you remember what happened before we got here?" Our collective knowledge of our own history (or the history of the world) is appalling. In 1992, the National Association of Educational Progress concluded that half of all adult Americans lacked the basic skills to read or write basic written English. Stephen Bertman also likes to pose the question, "Do you know where you are?" For many Americans, the answer unfortunately is "no."

The National Geographic Society commissioned a survey of over 10,000 adults in nine industrialized nations. In knowledge of geography, the U.S. finished dead last. So when asked if we know where we are, the answer is "no." (Nearly half couldn't find England on a map of Europe and 14 percent couldn't find the U.S. on a map of the world.) A candidate for the United States Senate was unable to correctly name the current Prime Minister of Canada or find Bosnia on a map. (He said he didn't have his glasses and won the election anyway.) A local politician in Wisconsin was complaining about an immigration law passed in Arizona and said she objected because it wasn't as if Arizona were a border state. Sen. Jon Kyl of Arizona sent her a map assuring her that Arizona did indeed share a border with Mexico. This woman had obviously never studied basic geography, but she has been elected to public office.

When a public official makes mistakes regarding geography, it is particularly embarrassing. In "Don't Know Much About Geography," classics professor Victor Davis Hanson presents a whole list of geographical errors made by President Barack Obama.[44] Obama talked about deepening ports along the Gulf, including Charleston, South Carolina, or Savannah, Georgia, or Jacksonville, Florida. Hanson observes, "The problem is that all the examples he cited are cities on the East Coast, not the Gulf of Mexico. If Obama does not know where these ports are, how can he deepen them?" The President also discussed the Falkland

Islands, attempting to use the name preferred by Argentina, "The Malvinas." Unfortunately, the President instead dubbed the islands "The Maldives," actually located southwest of India. In reference to residents of Austria, the President talked about their speaking "Austrian" instead of German.

On occasion, errors in geography or history may seem amusing as when Barack Obama talked about visiting "all 57 states" or then-Vice-President Joseph Biden talked about Franklin Roosevelt addressing the nation on television in 1929, as Hanson observes, at a time "when there was neither a President Roosevelt nor televisions available for purchase." But the subject becomes less amusing when one reads the Obama claim that Ho Chi Minh, communist dictator of North Vietnam, was inspired by the U.S. Declaration of Independence and Constitution and the words of Thomas Jefferson. Hanson declares, "That pop assertion is improbable, given that Ho systematically liquidated his opponents, slaughtered thousands in land-redistribution schemes, and brooked no dissent."

Geographical and historical ignorance are not limited to a single political figure, administration, or party. We have stopped teaching these subjects as they should be taught in school, so why should we be surprised if graduates of the "best" colleges are lost in the past or present? Hanson wisely concludes, "Both disciplines are the building blocks of learning. Without awareness of natural and human geography, we are reduced to a sort of self-contained void without accurate awareness of the space around us. An ignorance of history also creates the same sort of self-imposed exile, leaving ignorant of both what came before us and what is likely to follow."

Roger Kimball also addressed the question of "cultural amnesia" in describing the goals of *The New Criterion*, the magazine of cultural criticism he edits. Kimball said, "The great enemies here are forgetfulness and what Richard Weaver called 'presentism,' the belief or assumption that our little moment of time somehow represents the pinnacle of existence. Allen Tate once wrote about those who begin each day as if there were no yesterdays: part of what *The New Criterion* endeavors to do is repopulate the vista of our yesterdays, showing how what once mattered still matters." Hilton Kramer, co-founder of *The New Criterion* with the late concert pianist and cultural critic Samuel Lipman, observed, "Every day grows more amnesiac about its recent past." However, *The New Criterion* is an exception to the rule. Most popular publications today are obsessed with trends and fads of the day. This is even true of self-styled scholarly and cultural publications. These periodicals may use a vocabulary designed for intellectuals, but their cultural frame of reference is not different from that of reality television or supermarket tabloids.

We may well ask how our educators could discard our past cultural heritage in favor of trends and fads. Yet we shouldn't be surprised if the arts are neglected by an educational system, which has discarded basic history. John Pyne, a New Jersey educator and historian, told the *Washington Post* that the architects of curriculum standards for students from grades K-12 "tend to view history as a mostly irrelevant 'pastology' that is useful only when it can enhance lessons on current events." The Gallup Youth Survey, revealed that only four in ten teenagers knew what happened in 1492, the discovery of America by Christopher Columbus.

Colonial Williamsburg is an entire Virginia town, which functions as a living museum, restored to 18th century glory. It has as its motto, "That the future may learn from the past." In 2001, the Colonial Williamsburg Foundation commissioned a survey of over 1000 teenagers in a national poll to determine what students were learning about American history. The results were startling. The survey concluded that more than 5 million teenagers couldn't answer basic questions about the meaning of Independence Day, our national holiday on July 4. The students couldn't answer basic fourth grade questions on U.S. history. Nine percent of the teenagers didn't know that George Washington was the first President of the U.S. Fifteen percent didn't know that the Declaration of Independence was the document adopted on July 4,

1776. Fourteen percent thought that the U.S. won its independence during the Revolutionary War from France. Nearly a quarter had no idea who fought in the Civil War. Thirteen percent thought the Civil War was fought between the U.S. and Great Britain. Though the test was conducted after the election of George W. Bush to the Presidency, 4 percent improbably believed that the President was Bill Clinton or Albert Gore. One in five believed that John Adams or Betsy Ross wrote the words for "The Star Spangled Banner" while almost a third couldn't correctly identify Francis Scott Key as the author. Does this matter?

AMNESIA ON CAMPUS

A friend of mine decided to attend a lecture on environmentalism by Robert F. Kennedy, Jr. and asked a friend to accompany her. She was startled when her friend had no idea who Kennedy was, even when told he was the son of Robert F. Kennedy, the late Attorney General and assassinated presidential candidate, and not coincidentally, the brother of President John F. Kennedy. But her friend's eyes brightened with recognition when she found out that Robert F. Kennedy, Jr. was the father of Connor Kennedy, a former boyfriend of singer and celebrity Taylor Swift. Michael Reagan, the son of President Ronald Reagan, had a similar experience while playing golf. One of the four golfers in his group was a young Los Angeles restaurateur who was surprised to hear that Reagan was going to Normandy, France, the next day, to raise a flag at the American cemetery there. He asked Reagan why there would be an American cemetery at Normandy. The bewildered restaurateur had no notion of D-Day, presumably because he had never seen any movies depicting the historic liberation of Europe. Michael Reagan concluded, "History is one of our greatest teachers. It's just too bad so many of our young people think history started with the death of Princess Di or the birth of the iPhone." Reagan was sadly reminded of America's historical illiteracy and the failure of our educational system. Meghan McCain, daughter of Arizona Senator and 2008 Presidential candidate John McCain, appeared on a television program with Democratic political strategist Paul Begala. When Begala insisted that Ronald Reagan had blamed Jimmy Carter for problems that existed during his administration, McCain found herself unable to defend the Republican president and responded, "You know I wasn't born yet, so I wouldn't know." Begala said, "I wasn't born during the French Revolution but I know about it."

In today's celebrity-driven pop culture, a reference to a famous historical disaster may seem deceptively familiar. In 1912, the White Star liner, "Titanic," sank on its maiden voyage after hitting an iceberg. The loss of 1500 lives made the word "Titanic" a synonym for tragedy. The *Telegraph* reported that "Twitter users thought 'Titanic' disaster was just a film plot." More than a few posts on Twitter proclaimed ignorance of the historical disaster as those posting revealed that they thought "Titanic" was simply a movie starring Leonardo DiCaprio and Kate Winslet. The 1997 film was re-released in a 3-D version for the hundredth anniversary of the Titanic's sinking in 2012. Those unfamiliar with the historical facts could hear more about them by going to Belfast, where the ship was built and launched, to attend a three- week festival highlighted by, not surprisingly, another staple of pop culture, an MTV rock concert. For too many people today, the movie based on an historical event is more important than the event itself, if they have even heard of it.

We have developed a strange notion that history is irrelevant to the modern age and that the only things that matter are new and contemporary. Along with this flawed concept is an equally false idea that since our culture can only evolve, the music, books, art, theater, dance, and films of today are *by definition* superior to those of yesterday.

What are we to make of the high school student who appeared on an ABC television special, admitting he had no idea when the Civil War had been fought, and then snickering, "Who cares?" What should we think of students at South Puget State Community College, featured on *Sixty Minutes,* who identified Senator Joseph McCarthy as "a communist"? Another student, failing to recognize the name of Irving Berlin, composer and lyricist of "God Bless America," "White Christmas," "Easter Parade," and hundreds of classic songs, admitted she had been busy studying "blanket crocheting" in high school. Nor is this a case of one or two badly managed colleges. In 1989, the National Endowment for the Humanities commissioned the Gallup polling organization to conduct a survey of college students. The Director of the Endowment, Lynne Cheney, reported, "Twenty-five percent of the nation's college seniors were unable to locate Columbus's voyage within the correct half-century. About the same percentage could not distinguish Churchill's words from Stalin's, or Karl Marx's thoughts from the ideas of the U.S. Constitution. More than 40 percent could not identify when the Civil War occurred. Most could not identify *Magna Carta*, the Missouri Compromise, or Reconstruction. Most could not link major works by Plato, Dante, Shakespeare, and Milton with their authors. To the majority of college seniors, Jane Austen's *Pride and Prejudice*, Dostoyevsky's *Crime and Punishment*, and Martin Luther King, Jr.'s *Letter from a Birmingham Jail* were clearly unfamiliar." Former Assistant Secretary of Education Chester E. Finn, Jr. observed that many colleges were busy marketing amenities rather than quality education to prospective students. He said, "Today's college admissions game also saps some of what I'm rashly going to term the dignity of higher education, as marketing strategies for a number of institutions come to resemble those of resort hotels." A housing administrator at a Florida university explained that today's demanding students required cable television in their dorm rooms. Lack of MTV would apparently render the rooms impossible to rent.

One place in which students might be expected to learn something about history is the college classroom. Unfortunately, too many students have turned out like those in a YouTube prank video released by "Whatever." The video's narrator went to Isla Vista, a community heavily populated by Santa Barbara, California college students and asked them a few questions to which one would think they had learned the answers in first or second grade. Three young women were embarrassed that they didn't know from which country the U.S. won its independence, although one volunteered "France" as her answer. Other students suggested British Columbia. One simply said, "Who knows?" The students didn't know how many stars or stripes there were on the American flag or why they were there. They didn't know when the U.S. became an independent nation. (One offered "1700" as his answer.) When asked to explain the difference between July 4 and Independence Day, one student thought he had the answer. "Independence Day was the day we declared independence and the 4th of July was when we won the Civil War," he said. Not to be outdone, another said, "Independence Day is a movie and July 4 is today." As to why they were all celebrating the Fourth of July, one student declared that after abusing the Indians, Christopher Columbus "like, said it was a good day to, like, be alive in America." Eric Owens, education editor of *The Daily Caller*, reported this story with a headline proclaiming, "Wasted College Students Show Deplorable, Hideous Ignorance of American History."

Nor is this only a California phenomenon. Dan Joseph, a videographer and reporter for the Media Research Center, quizzed college students enrolled at George Mason University in Virginia. When asked to identify U.S. Secretary of State John Kerry or Russian President Vladimir Putin, the students appeared confused or puzzled. But their puzzled expressions quickly disappeared when Joseph asked them about "twerking," a sexually provocative dance fad in the news after pop star Miley Cyrus shocked her fans with an exceptionally vulgar performance during the Video Music Awards. Reporter Robby Soave described a female student questioned by Dan Joseph who had never heard of John Kerry, but explained, "It's more of a talent here. It's praised if you can twerk." These students are attending a university named after George Mason, the man responsible for creating the first declaration of rights and the first state constitution in the American colonies. Mason, a friend and neighbor of George Washington, was a delegate to the Constitutional Convention. He did not sign the proposed document because it did not contain a bill of rights. Together with James Madison, he is widely credited for the ultimate adoption of the U. S. Bill of Rights. Do the college students questioned by Dan Joseph know anything about the man after whom their university is named? One can only hope.

How many students are emerging from college as allegedly educated men and women, blissfully ignorant of how little they have learned? In a few years, the students who are oblivious to their own lack of knowledge will be choosing America's leaders, deciding which books, music, films, art, and plays will be successful, and ready to give society the benefit of all that they do not know.

We have no reason to assume that college graduates are familiar with most basic facts of American history. The American Council of Trustees and Alumni commissioned the Roper Organization, The Center for Survey Research and Analysis at the University of Connecticut, to test seniors at fifty-five elite colleges. A study by the American Council of Trustees and Alumni reports that 55 percent of top U.S. colleges grant degrees to students without requiring an American history course and often without offering any instruction in history at all. Students were asked questions to determine their familiarity with America's history and founding principles. The study concluded, "As we move forward into the 21st century, our future leaders are graduating with an alarming ignorance of their heritage— a kind of collective amnesia— which bodes ill for the future of the republic." Less than half of the students could identify George Washington as "first in war, first in peace, and first in the hearts of his countrymen." Less than a quarter could identify James Madison as the father of the Constitution or Lincoln's celebrated quote from "The Gettysburg Address," "government of the people, by the people, and for the people." But 99 percent could identify the cartoon characters Beavis and Butthead and 98 percent were familiar with the rap singer Snoop Doggy Dog. Most of the students, if asked, wouldn't have been able to identify the remarks of Thomas Jefferson who said, "If a nation expects to be ignorant and free, it expects what never was and what never will be." With 81 percent of the students receiving grades of "D" or "F" on the test, Jefferson's words may prove sadly prophetic. These results are shocking.

They suggest that our country has a vast population ignorant of our history, our language, our culture, and even our location in the world. But many of these same people are totally familiar with the transient names and faces that make up the panoply of celebrities who appear in the tabloids and on the Internet. If students are emerging from school unfamiliar with the leading figures and events of American history, can we be surprised that they also have little or no familiarity with the arts or their impact on our culture?

Nor does this situation seem to be improving. The Intercollegiate Studies Institute, led by President T. Kenneth Cribb, Jr. established a National Civic Literacy Board, chaired by Lt. Gen. Josiah Bunting, III. The Board espoused Benjamin Franklin's view that colleges should nurture civic leaders by teaching them their country's history and institutions, and subsequently encourage them to think critically and participate effectively in public affairs. But 71 percent of Americans failed ISI's Civic Literacy test. Just 49 percent could even name the three branches of government.

More than twenty years after the National Endowment for the Humanities found that college students didn't know the difference between Churchill and Stalin, the problem remains. Consider a 2010 Marist Poll in which participants were asked the question "From where do the latter think the U.S. achieved its independence?" Only 76 percent of respondents gave the correct answer. Twenty percent were unsure, while 6 percent actually believed that the United States won its independence from France, China, Japan, Mexico, or Spain.

The Constitution of the United States did not fare better in a 2010 survey conducted for the Center for the Constitution at James Madison's Montpelier. Only 28 percent of those surveyed, a random selection of adults over eighteen questioned by telephone, acknowledged having read the entire U.S. Constitution. Only 35 percent believed that the Constitution limits the power of government, suggesting that a significant number believe that the government's powers are unlimited. Only 68 percent believe that their rights are "natural rights," while the remainder said they believe that rights are granted in whole or in part by the government. This is in spite of the fact that the Founding Fathers clearly believed that freedom of speech and religion were among natural human rights. The Declaration of Independence uses the famous phrase "endowed by our Creator" to define the origin of human rights, specifically establishing the principle that rights are not merely granted by a monarch or by the state. Only 48 percent expressed the view that government's powers are derived from the people, while 50 percent said that government powers are derived from elected officials. But ignorance of our founding principles doesn't stop there.

In December of 2010, Harris Interactive conducted a national survey on behalf of the Bill of Rights Institute. The survey reported that 42 percent of Americans attribute the quotation, "From each according to his ability, to each according to his needs," to America's founding documents. Nearly one-fifth of Americans think the phrase comes from the Bill of Rights. They would be embarrassed to learn that the quote is actually the essence of communism, as articulated by Karl Marx. Thirty percent of those polled thought that Marx's most famous political utterance was extracted from the Declaration of Independence, the U.S. Constitution, or the *Federalist Papers*. The same survey also reported that 60 percent of Americans do not realize that the principle that government's powers are derived from the people is a principle unique to America's history.

In 2011, *Newsweek* reported the results of a citizenship test given to 1000 Americans. The results were discouraging. Twenty-nine percent couldn't correctly name the Vice President. Seventy-three percent couldn't explain why we fought the Cold War. Forty-four percent were unable to define the Bill of Rights. A shocking 6 percent couldn't identify Independence Day as July 4 on a calendar. Add to this the results of an experiment conducted by the European Journal of Communications. Questions of international affairs were posed to citizens of the U.S., Britain, Denmark, and Finland. Only 58 percent of Americans correctly identified the Taliban, despite the events of September 11, 2001— al-Qaeda's terrorist assault on the New York World Trade Center—and our military response in Afghanistan. In contrast, 68 percent of Danes, 75 percent of the British, and 76 percent of Finns responded to the same question correctly.

Ignorance regarding the past does not occur by accident; ironically, it is often the product of misguided attempts at education. A Pennsylvania high school band performed a halftime show, "St. Petersburg 1917," commemorating the Bolshevik Revolution. Incredibly, the performance included hammers and sickles, military uniforms, and the red flag of the communists who followed Lenin and ruled the Soviet Union. The Superintendent of schools responded to outraged parents by describing the performance as "a representation of the time period in history called St. Petersburg 1917." She went on to apologize if anyone was offended by the celebration of the music since it "wasn't just looked at as a history lesson." Students receiving instruction from instructors with this type of attitude are likely to emerge from school ignorant of the millions of deaths caused by communism. (*The Black Book of Communism* published by Harvard University Press cites seventy-million slaughtered by Mao Tse-tung and sixty-million executed by Stalin.) Nor will these students understand the true facts of the induced famine in Ukraine, Stalin's pact with Hitler, the millions who perished in Mao's "Cultural Revolution," or the Berlin Wall. Paul Kengor, professor of political science at Grove City College, concludes, "We now have an entire generation of Americans born after the collapse of the Berlin Wall and USSR. They didn't live through the mass repression and carnage that was Soviet communism. They need to learn about it, just as my generation learned the evils of Nazism. Unfortunately, they are not. And so, we shouldn't be surprised when they merrily march to the triumphal sounds of the Bolshevik Revolution."

Why then would educators jettison the study of our own history from the curriculum and replace it with a list of vague topics subject to the whims of the moment? In 2010, North Carolina unveiled a proposal to radically redesign its high school curriculum, replacing "World History" with something called

"Global Studies." The Greeks, the Romans, and the French Revolution would be replaced by "environmental modification," "quality of life," and "effectiveness of organizations to maintain peace and security." In effect, students would be led into discussions of contemporary and often highly political issues without the background or knowledge of history to understand the origin of today's problems. Worse, North Carolina also proposed limiting high school studies in American history to events beginning in 1877. That's right, no more Founding Fathers, Declaration of Independence, U.S. Constitution, American Revolution, or Civil War. No more study of the Bill of Rights or the conflict over slavery. No more Washington, Adams, Jefferson, Madison, or Lincoln. Instead, this new and thoroughly modern history instruction would begin with the presidency of Rutherford B. Hayes and give students the chance to learn about "struggles for power and human rights," "changes in the physical environment and technology," and "changes in lifestyles." The result of this absurd proposal is easy to predict: students heading into college ignorant of the history of their nation or the world around them, but able to mouth politically correct slogans regarding current debates about the environment and economic policy according to the agendas of those designing the curriculum.

When many citizens are ignorant of even the most basic facts of history, how can we expect them to make mature or responsible decisions about the future of our country? How can we expect them to understand the events of the present if they do not understand the basic principles on which the United States of America was founded? Dr. Larry P. Arnn, President of Hillsdale College, writes, "There is only one way to return to living under the principles of the Declaration of Independence and the institutions of the Constitution. We must come to love those things again. And if we love them, then we will serve them. But we cannot love them until we understand them. And we cannot understand them until we know them. So the first step is to study them and teach them." We should be able to explain to our friends why the past matters. Historian Kenneth Stampp said, "With the historian it is an article of faith that knowledge of the past is a key to understanding the present." Novelist Pearl Buck expressed similar sentiments when she said, "If you want to understand today, you have to search yesterday."

Former Supreme Court Justice Sandra Day O'Connor lamented an increasing public ignorance of subjects that relate to citizenship. She maintained that learning the facts of citizenship are just as significant as learning multiplication tables or how to read. Justice O'Connor saw the problem beginning with the education provided to small children and believes that it only gets worse as a child grows and attends high school and college. In an address at Boise State University, she observed that two-thirds of Americans cannot correctly identify the three branches of government or provide the name of a single Supreme Court Justice. Justice O'Connor went on to explain, "Less than one-third of eighth-graders can identify the historical purpose of the Declaration of Independence, and it's right there in the name." She concluded, "The more I read and the more I listen, the more apparent it is that our society suffers from an alarming degree of public ignorance."

Unfortunately, Canadian history is vanishing too, also displaced by the celebrity culture. Dick Pound is former Vice- President of the International Olympic Committee and Chairman of the Canada's History Society. He was dismayed that when a CBC reporter asked passersby to identify a picture of Sir John A. Macdonald. Few recognized Canada's first Prime Minister, but many could easily recognize teen pop star Justin Bieber. An Ipso Reid survey of young adult Canadians revealed that only about a third received a passing grade when asked questions about their country's history. Pound asked his fellow Canadians, "Can you understand present day western alienation, Quebec separatism, our native people's aspirations, our vibrant musical recording industry, Canada's love of hockey, and our relationship with the United States or the monarchy, without knowing the history--the background--of all these issues? "

Nor are the benefits of understanding the past limited to politics and diplomacy. Dr. Ernst Toch was a distinguished 20th century composer and a renowned teacher. Toch was primarily self-taught, and when pupils asked him technical questions about the most contemporary music, he said he could find the answers to any musical question in the works of Mozart. Yet today it has become fashionable to dismiss history as unimportant and irrelevant to the modern age, a study that belongs in dusty libraries, ivory-towered classrooms, and faded museums. Ernst Toch's respect for the legacy of history is applicable not only to music. It is relevant to every discipline and endeavor.

No one has made the case for the study and appreciation of history more eloquently than David McCullough, whose books have won prizes and plaudits throughout the nation. In an interview with Brian Bolduc, published in the *Wall Street Journal*, McCullough said, "We're raising young people who are, by and large, historically illiterate . . . I know how much these young people—even at the most esteemed institutions of higher learning—don't know . . . It's shocking." McCullough identified the origins of the problem: teachers of history who only have degrees in education and lack a passion for the subject. He explained, "The great teachers love what they're teaching, and you can't love something you don't know any more than you can love someone you don't know." McCullough was also critical of fads and political correctness used to distort history. He says, "History is often taught in categories—women's history, African-American history, environmental history—so that many of the students have no sense of chronology. They have no idea what followed what." As for textbooks, he describes them as "so politically correct as to be comic." He says, "Very minor characters that are currently fashionable are given considerable space whereas people of major consequence farther back, such as, say Thomas Edison, are given very little space at all." McCullough was also realistic about some of his colleagues, historians who only write to please each other, with boring books as a result.

The solution, of course, is to forcefully address the problems and challenges McCullough raised: history teachers should be schooled in and devoted to history, not educational methodology and jargon. History should focus upon great figures and events of all time, not an effort to promote minor individuals or achievements as misguided attempt to make our past relevant. We should not confine our studies to the achievements of people who are arbitrarily classified in groups. We should be familiar with the true chronology of history. Writers of history should follow David McCullough's lead and realize that a bored reader or listener will quickly turn his attention elsewhere.

As for the relevance of history, consider an observation by author and scholar, Lt. Gen. Josiah Bunting III. He says that the Founding Fathers deserve to be placed alongside the classical generation found in Athens. He observes, "What they read was the classics and the classics populated their minds and their memories with heroes. The whole idea was that by studying history you can fill your mind with models of not only behavior, but models of intellectual achievement." In effect, we learn from the best of the past to inspire the best of the present.

HISTORY ACCORDING TO PINOCCHIO

While George Bernard Shaw's quip in his play, *The Devil's Disciple*, was said facetiously—"History will tell lies as usual"—many of today's historians have proven that they are pursuing a vigorous path to make Shaw's witticism a reality. Pinocchio, the beloved puppet in the classic children's story by Carlo Collodi, wants desperately to become a real boy. But he has to contend with a tendency to lie and when he does, his nose grows. Quite a number of academicians and writers, who should pursue truth, have become real-life Pinocchios. They want to be taken seriously as historians, but they are often more devoted to ideology.

Millions of students today do not absorb the lessons of history out of ignorance and the disappearance of true history from the curricula of schools and colleges. But the substitution of ideology for facts poses an even greater threat to future generations than even the ignorance of students who know little and think they know much.

Students are emerging from secondary schools, colleges, and universities not just ignorant of their country's history but hating their country and all for which it has stood for over two centuries. How did this happen? Unfortunately, not by accident but by design.

There are many influences on the way American history is taught today, but none more important than two: the late radical Marxist historian Howard Zinn, author of *The People's History of the United States,* the most widely used and acclaimed textbook in America, and Nikole Hannah-Hones, a journalist-architect of *The 1619 Project,* a collection of revisionist articles suggesting that the entire history of the United States was defined by the introduction of slavery.

Howard Zinn was a professor who taught for twenty-four years at Boston University. He was the author of twenty books, but it was his book, *The People's History of the United States*, that made him a legend. Zinn's book has transcended mere academic recognition.

What did Zinn teach? He wrote and taught that the United States was an evil, exploitative country responsible for most of the world's faults. When he was interviewed on radio by author and broadcaster Dennis Prager, Prager asked him if the United States had done more good than bad throughout the world. "Probably more bad than good," said Zinn.

Zinn's approach to history was simple. He took selectively all of the negative episodes of American history, some accurate and some not, and essentially mixed them into an ideological salad which portrays the country's entire story through the eyes of various groups of victims. The nation's achievements which drew immigrants from around the world are casually dismissed or ignored.

Zinn's version of American history isn't one most parents and grandparents of today's schoolchildren would recognize: he depicted the American Revolution as a class struggle led by rich property owners eager to seize the colonies from the British Empire.

He discounted Lincoln and the Civil War because capitalism was not overthrown. Instead of crediting the U.S. and its allies with victory over Nazi Germany and militarist Japan, Zinn implied moral equivalence between the U.S. and the Nazis, and portrays the Japanese as victims. The post-war Marshall plan is rejected as an effort to support capitalist Western Europe against the true "people's democracies"—the Soviet Union and their Eastern European satellites under Soviet domination. Zinn supported pro-communist causes all of his life, including the potential for a communist victory in Vietnam and the retention of Soviet missiles aimed at the United States from Castro's communist Cuba.

He remained an apologist for the Soviet Union and ignored the havoc caused by Soviet spies and militarism around the world. Zinn was no cheerleader for the victory of the U.S., the U.K., and the western nations in the Cold War. Perhaps he believed that the wrong side had won.

Mary Grabar produced the most detailed critique to date in her book, *Debunking Howard Zinn*. Writing in *The Federalist*, Grabar characterizes Zinn's life as "a progression from being a budding teenage communist to Pied Piper professor and globe-trotting anti-American agitator." She described him as violating all the rules for writing history as established by the American Historical Association.

Roger Kimball, editor of *The New Criterion,* responds to Zinn by observing, "In any normal world, Zinn would have stolen away in the middle of the night, fled to a mountain fastness in Peru, and taken up llama ranching. In this world, however, he went on to fame and fortune."[45]

And what fame and what fortune! Actor Matt Damon, who spent his childhood as Zinn's next-door neighbor, starred in and co-wrote a film, *Good Will Hunting,* in which he promoted Zinn's book. Later, he appeared in a star-studded movie made for television, *The People Speak,* based entirely on Zinn's history. Zinn remains revered as an icon by a host of Hollywood power brokers and celebrities, including actress Jane Fonda. Public officials have actually taken their oaths of office substituting Zinn's book for The Bible during the swearing-in ceremony.

These may seem like isolated incidents; they are not. Zinn's magnum opus has sold over 2.6 million copies. The College Board, highly influential in textbook purchases, supports his work. Even the U.S. government gets into the act, with the American Embassy in Moscow ironically arranging for publication of *The People's History of the United States* in Russia. So American taxpayers are paying for Russians to learn the old Soviet view that the United States is an illegitimate country.

Today, polls abound that suggest college students and young adults are perfectly willing to consider communism as an alternative system of government. Generations of students are being taught the worst, not the best, about the United States. They haven't spoken to anyone who fled the Soviet Union, Communist China, Cuba, Venezuela, or North Korea; but they have read Howard Zinn. Nor are they likely to have studied the writings of the distinguished economist, author, and educator Thomas Sowell. Said Sowell, "One of the most important reasons for studying history is that virtually every stupid idea in vogue today has been tried before and proved disastrous before, time and again."

In 2019, nearly four decades after Zinn's textbook made its debut, the *New York Times* launched *The 1619 Project.* The project which appeared in conjunction with the *New York Times Magazine,* was a series of essays that, in the words of editor Jake Silverstein, intended to "reframe" American history.

In *The 1619 Project,* America had a new birthday, the "true" day of the nation's founding, 1619, when a pirate ship landed in Jonestown, Virginia with a group of captive Africans. According to this new narrative, America's entire culture, history, and prosperity was the result of the exploitation of black Americans.

Nikole Hannah-Jones was the lead author of this document for which she was awarded the coveted Pulitzer Prize. What of America's traditional birthday, July 4, 1776, and the signing of our founding document, the Declaration of Independence? The project was a bold effort by the nation's so-called "paper of record" to portray the United States of America as the product of systemic racist oppression and the result of four centuries of exploitation. School systems all over the country have adopted this version of American history. So it should surprise no one that many of today's students loathe their own country. They have been taught to do so in classrooms for which their parents have paid!

The *New York Times* did not provide footnotes, a bibliography, or the sources that would normally appear in a major work of history. Not surprisingly, a number of prominent historians were quick to criticize the project.

The project ignores the fact that slavery was widespread in Africa, Central America, the Spanish colonies, and other parts of the world and had existed for centuries; it falsely suggests that the American Revolution—the War for Independence—was merely an effort to preserve slavery if it were abolished by Great Britain; Abraham Lincoln, who freed the slaves with his Emancipation Proclamation, is dismissed as a racist; it implies that black people fought against slavery alone, ignoring the sacrifice and efforts of white abolitionists and thousands of soldiers who lost their lives during the Civil War; it implies that capitalism only thrived because of slavery and that the history of the United States was basically a struggle against advocates of white supremacy.

Fortunately, accomplished and distinguished historians were quick to criticize the inaccuracies and conclusions of *The 1619 Project*. Mary Grabar (in *Debunking the 1619 Project: Exposing the Plan to Divide America*) and Peter W. Wood (in *1620: A Critical Response to the 1619 Project*) meticulously dissect the project from beginning to end.[46]

Peter W. Wood, President of the National Association of Scholars, concludes, "We are in a cultural Marxist, radical anti-American end of the pool, where the goal is to indoctrinate American children with a hatred of their country."[47] Nor should it surprise anyone that in an interview with Ezra Klein for a *Vox* podcast, Nikole Hannah-Jones revealed which western nation she thought had made the greatest strides in diversity and equity, communist Cuba under the dictatorship of Fidel Castro, declaring "Cuba has the least inequality between black and white people anywhere in the hemisphere."

Was the preservation of slavery in the United States really the reason for the American Revolution? If so, why did a group of prominent and well-to-do white men in New York, including Alexander Hamilton and John Jay, form the New York Manumission Society? Its purpose was the abolition of slavery and "manumission" or freeing of slaves of African descent by their owners. Thomas Jefferson, though a slaveholder, included abolition of slavery in his first draft of the Declaration of Independence. Because the southern, slaveholding states, wouldn't agree to a union without the anti-slavery clause being excised, Jefferson reluctantly agreed. A devil's bargain admittedly, but the Declaration and its principles set up the philosophical basis for the eventual abolition of slavery. Similarly, James Madison, although also a slaveholder and widely acknowledged to be "the Father of the Constitution," saw that there were no references to slavery in that remarkable document.

The great black abolitionist and former slave, Frederick Douglass, used the values proclaimed in the Declaration as the basis for abolition of slavery and the American Civil Rights movement. Douglass, who spoke passionately against slavery, said something very different than the notions promoted by *The 1619 Project* regarding the Founding Fathers. He said, "Fellow Citizens, I am not wanting in respect for the fathers of this republic. The signers of the Declaration of Independence were brave men. They were great men too—great enough to give fame to a great age. It does not often happen to a nation to raise, at one time, such a number of truly great men. The point from which I am compelled to view them is not, certainly, the most favorable; and yet I cannot contemplate their great deeds with less than admiration. They were statesmen, patriots and heroes, and for the good they did, and the principles they contended for, I will unite with you to honor their memory."

As for Rev. Dr. Martin Luther King, Jr., a century later, he proclaimed, "When the architects of our republic wrote the magnificent words of the Constitution and the Declaration of Independence, they were signing a promissory note to which every American was to fall heir. This note was a promise that all men, yes, black men and well as white men, would be guaranteed the unalienable rights to life, liberty, and the pursuit of happiness." And consider the words of Lincoln, included in the text of Aaron Copland's stirring musical setting, *A Lincoln Portrait*: "As I would not be a slave, so I would not be a master. This expresses my idea of democracy. Whatever differs from this, to the extent of the difference, is no democracy."

Certainly children in the United States and abroad should learn the facts of national and world history, including the shameful history of slavery, but also the sacrifice, energy, and efforts that led to its abolition. To take but one element in the remarkable patchwork quilt of history and make it into the whole story is not history at all, but incredible distortion. If this distortion is successful, the history of the United States will indeed vanish, supplanted by a fiction the purpose of which is to create a new and entirely different country based on principles that have already been tested, failed, and devolved into many of the worst tyrannies the world has ever known.

In contrast to *The 1619 Project* is *The 1776 Report*, the official report of the President's 1776 Commission. Released in 2021, the report explains the core principles of the American founding, how they shaped American history, and considered challenges to this history at home and abroad. The Commission was led by Dr. Larry Arnn, President of Hillsdale College, Vice-Chairman Dr. Carol Swain, former professor of political science at Princeton and Vanderbilt, with Matthew Spaulding, Dean of the Van Andel School of Government at Hillsdale College.

The report advises, "Rather than learning to hate one's country or the world for its inevitable wrongs, the well-educated student learns to appreciate and cherish the oases of civilization: solid family structures and local communities; effective, representative, and limited government; the rule of law and the security of civil rights and private property; a love of the natural world and the arts; good character and religious faith."

To learn the true history of the United States, students must learn about mistakes that were made during the nation's formative years; but it is far more important that they learn of the struggles and sacrifices made by generations of Americans to right the wrongs, to always build "a more perfect union." These include, of course, the Civil War in which thousands of citizens regardless of race, died in a war that ended with the abolition of slavery, the victories in two World Wars, the defeat of the Fascists, Nazis, and imperial Japanese militarists in the second of those two wars, the original civil rights movement, and the victory over communism in the Cold War.

They must further learn about the unique American experiment in a republican form of government in which rights were proclaimed as coming "from our Creator" at the nation's birth, and the rights and freedoms which have made the United States of America a beacon of liberty around the world.

American education cannot survive if students are literally taught to despise their own country. Yeonmi Park, a young woman who fled unspeakable horrors in communist North Korea, was surprised by strident anti-Americanism and race-based elements throughout her studies at Columbia University. She told the New *York Post*, "I thought North Koreans were the only people who hated Americans, but turns out there are a lot of people hating this country in this country."

In the original Collodi book, Pinocchio does not remain a puppet; he becomes a real boy. But in the real world, we, too, have our Pinocchios: a number have Ph.D. degrees like Howard Zinn or, like Nikole Hannah-Jones, win Pulitzer Prizes. What a tragedy it would be if the modern day Pinocchios pose an even greater threat to the survival of liberty and knowledge than the innocent child who believes every word said in class or the slothful teenager who glories in ignorance after failing to learn the true lessons of history.

ILLITERACY INTERNATIONAL

The problem of cultural illiteracy is not exclusively American. In fact, this disturbing phenomenon can be found in cities as culturally diverse and geographically distant as Mexico City and London.

Consider a survey of 1800 schoolchildren conducted by the Mexican National Consumer Institute. The survey compared what the Institute called "national reality" vs. "television reality." Not surprisingly, "television reality" won. It seems that the Mexican children who were surveyed spend 1460 hours each year in front of the television set, while devoting only 960 hours annually to school. Ninety-two percent knew that a duckling selling chocolate cakes on television said, "Remember me"; but only 64 percent were aware that a national historical figure, Father Miguel Hidalgo said "Viva La Independencia!" Ninety-six percent of the children knew the names of popular cartoon characters, but only 19 percent recognized the names of Aztec emperors. Ninety-eight percent were familiar with Superman, though only 33 percent could identify the Mexican revolutionary Emiliano Zapata. Only 74 percent of the children knew the name of José Lopez-Portillo, former President of Mexico, though 97 percent identified a character that appeared on local television. Mexico's "Monument to the Revolution" was known to only 17 percent of the students surveyed, but 77 percent of these same students correctly named the trademark of Adams Chiclets chewing gum. More children knew the times of television programs than the dates of religious festivals, including Christmas.

The Guardian, a British newspaper, discovered equally disturbing information in a survey of young eighteen to twenty-four-year-old British adults. The paper reported the distressing results. Even the most significant events of British history and the names of its greatest heroes have faded into oblivion. Only 10 percent of these Britons knew that the Battle of Waterloo occurred in 1815. A mere 23 percent could identify Magna Carta. Two of Britain's best-known Prime Ministers were little known by those surveyed. Some may realize that Munich is a city in Germany, but only 8 percent could recognize the name of Neville Chamberlain, despite the fact that Chamberlain's disastrous attempts to appease Hitler in Munich led to World War II. Even fewer, 6 percent knew that the welfare state in Britain was launched by David Lloyd George, Prime Minister during World War I. Most shocking of all was the revelation that less than a third even identified Winston Churchill as the Prime Minister who served before 1945. If British schools are not teaching students about Winston Churchill, the country's heroic leader during World War II (regarded by many as the "man of the century"), what are they teaching? Jacqui Smith, Britain's Schools Minister at the time, admitted, "There are worrying gaps in the education of too many young adults." What is most telling about *The Guardian's* survey, however, is information regarding the names and places that the future leaders of Britain do recognize.

In England, Katharine Birbalsingh sharply criticized historical illiteracy as a by-product of failed teaching methods, which consider facts, figures, and basic knowledge to be "old-fashioned." Birbalsingh spoke of fourteen-year-olds who think "Churchill" is an animated dog of the same name appearing in a television advertisement for an insurance company. She also talked about students who don't think there is a difference between Paris and France. Birbalsingh explained, "Teaching historical facts or lists of vocab which rely on memory skills is considered old-fashioned. Instead, we think it better to inspire children to be creative through group discussion and project work. But background knowledge is absolutely essential to enable children to absorb new ideas." She went on to criticize an emphasis on "soft skills," making sure children can work in teams or make presentations, instead of consuming facts, and relegating the role of a teacher to that of a spectator watching student socialization. Birbalsingh's reward for her candor was the loss of her job. She was forced to resign from her position as deputy head of a comprehensive school in South London. Will the teenagers who think "Churchill" is a dog ever learn about the great achievements of the man who guided their nation through its greatest crisis? It is anyone's guess. Chris Smith, Britain's Culture Secretary, said, "I fear it may represent a slipping of knowledge. They do clearly know about other things such as Internet search engines and rock music. But the fundamentals of what I would call cultural literacy are sadly missing for too many of them. I hope the trend can be reversed." In both Mexico and England, the trends are the same.

Schoolchildren and young adults alike are blissfully ignorant of the most basic facts and important figures of their own heritage. Should we be surprised that a young Englishman who has never heard of Winston Churchill will not recognize the names of Sir Edward Elgar, Sir Ralph Vaughan Williams, Frederic Delius, or Sir Thomas Beecham? Or that a young Englishwoman who thinks *Magna Carta* is a pop singing group will know nothing of lighter music from Gilbert and Sullivan to Noël Coward? The Mexican schoolchildren who are learning about chewing gum commercials are unlikely to develop a familiarity with the music of Carlos Chávez or Silvestre Revueltas, let alone the popular melodies of Agustin Lara.

What is clear from these surveys is that the problem of cultural illiteracy transcends nationality and geography. The Mexican children are familiar with the things they see on television. The young British adults recognize the names of rock groups and Internet search engines. It is the media, old and new, that are driving the agenda, which determines what captures the attention of societies around the world. If the television and film industries regarding something as important, mass audiences will regard it as important too. If the entertainment industries think something should be headed for oblivion, it will be forgotten. The Internet has sparked a revolution in the dissemination of information. However, the Internet is only a tool. Like television before it, the Internet provides a means for sending information around the world. But who chooses the information to be sent? It is possible for someone to be highly skilled in the use of computers, facile in the use of high tech equipment, and to be a cultural ignoramus? The cultural ignoramus is likely to be an individual full of self-esteem. He knows what is important, because he knows what his friends consider to be important. He does not realize that he is a pawn on a media chessboard.

We may well coin a word to describe the society, which produces thousands of mediocre and uninformed students like those in the United States, England, and Mexico: a "mediocracy," a society in which priorities are set by the media. Unfortunately, the entertainment industry thrives on marketing something new each day. Therefore, its priorities are always skewed in favor of instant gratification, instant sales, and instant promotion. "Now" is the only thing that matters. Yesterday is regarded as irrelevant, tomorrow as insignificant. It is a sad truth that a "mediocracy" produces mediocrity. The cultural ignoramus who knows all about the latest rock groups and the "hottest Internet search engines" thinks he is well-informed. The problem is that when he uses a search engine, he doesn't know for what he should be searching. His curiosity is limited by his ignorance. His enthusiasm is limited by his narrow range of ideas. What is to become of such an individual? If we are speaking of children, we can only hope that they will one day be taught an awareness of people and ideas who are not necessarily regarded as "hot properties" by the media. If we are speaking of high school and college graduates, the problem becomes more serious. These are the people, who in a few years will be making decisions about music, books, art, and language. Will books be read by cultural illiterates? Will good music or art find an audience among those whose view of the world is limited by the listings in *TV Guide* or their experiences in an online chat room? That such persons become ignorant voters and incompetent citizens is obvious. But they also become arbiters of a culture, a role for which they are decidedly ill-equipped and unqualified. In a few years, the fate of good music, books, art, and language will be entirely dependent on these people, and the prospects for their survival are dismal unless we take action today.

A STAR SPANGLED DILEMMA

Music often collides with history and unfortunately with politics. If we are ignorant of our own history, how can we expect to address issues, which require familiarity with the past? Consider our national anthem, "The Star Spangled Banner," which someone, somewhere, somehow, is always trying to replace.

Talk show-host Bill Press created a firestorm by declaring the song "an abomination" that embarrasses him. Press explained his crusade by saying, "Bombs bursting in air, rocket's red glare it all kinds of, you know a lot of national anthems are that way, all kinds of military jargon and the land there's only one phrase 'the land of the free' which is kind of nice and 'the home of the brave?' I don't know," Press wasn't finished. He went on to proclaim, "Are we the only ones who are brave on the planet? I mean all the brave people live here. I mean it's just stupid I think," Press concluded. "I'm embarrassed; I'm embarrassed every time I hear it." His self-proclaimed crusade to eliminate it is neither new nor unique; someone sounds this off-key trumpet every few years. ESPN analyst Kevin Blackistone displayed a similar misunderstanding of "The Star Spangled Banner," when he protested the performance of what he termed a "war anthem" before football games.

Michael Kinsley joined the fray in the *Washington Post*, asking "Oh Say Can You Sing It?" Kinsley wants to do away with "The Star Spangled Banner" and replace it with something else. He offers two arguments to advance his position. First, the anthem is hard to sing. This is true, but no reason to discard the anthem. Most good music is harder to sing or play than bad music. Even deceptively simple pieces may seem easy on the piano or violin, but you can always tell when they are being performed by a brilliant master or an inept amateur. It is also true that "The Star Spangled Banner" is often performed badly, especially by celebrity entertainers who see fit to change the melody (or even the words) by adding their own personal stamp or style. At its worst, such performances result in the ghastly and embarrassing spectacle of Roseanne Barr massacring the anthem before a baseball game or Christina Aguilera, confusing the words while performing at the Super Bowl.

There is a simple reason why there have been so many outrageous performances of our National Anthem. Most of the vocalists who perform it at major public events are pop singers who cannot sing on pitch. They are used to singing in a style, which allows them to cover their off-key voices with vocal mannerisms that represent their individual personalities. Often they perform with special effects, light shows, and massive amplification. They are typically unable to project their voices without microphones and are surrounded by gyrating back up groups of singers and dancers. Listen to any major pop star attempting to sing real music, including the songs of classic Broadway musicals. These vocalists and their publicists will insist that their efforts project star quality, not a lack of musicianship; presumably, they are improvising and changing the melody out of inspiration, but this is simply untrue. They sing in this manner because they are mediocre singers whose real talent is self-promotion. Compare their voices to the intonation and pitch control of the best jazz vocalists. Ella Fitzgerald and Sarah Vaughan for instance, changed melodies, improvised on them, and expressed themselves creatively with an ability to sing on pitch! When legitimate singers perform "The Star Spangled Banner" without trying to turn it into a pop hit reflecting their personal style, it is an inspiring and moving piece of music. When a non-celebrity soloist, a member of the military, sings it accompanied by the U.S. Marine Band, we hear the song as it should be sung. If we suddenly replaced "The Star Spangled Banner" with another, simpler melody, there is no guarantee that untalented singers would sing the new anthem with more skill than they exhibit singing the former one.

But Michael Kinsley's real problem with our national anthem is its lyric, especially the part about all those nasty "bombs bursting in air." For the peaceable Mr. Kinsley, all this talk about bombs and war is downright distasteful. While Kinsley tries to frame his argument in musical terms, the essence of his view clearly reflects his politics. He writes, "In the first verse—the one we generally sing—there is only one reference to any value commonly associated with America: 'land of the free.' By contrast, 'home of the brave' is empty bravado. There is nothing in the American myth (let alone reality) to suggest that we are braver than anyone else." Kinsley, who once studied at Oxford, needs to go back and read his history books again. It shouldn't take long to find out that American exceptionalism is not a myth, that military and political bravery and sacrifice by Americans dispatched tyrannies around the world, saving the lives and freedom of millions of people. Michael Kinsley concludes, "Anything would be better than those bombs bursting in air." Kinsley forgets that without those bombs bursting in air, he might be singing "God Save the King" today, if he were lucky. Were it not for the exceptional bravery of Americans, our national anthem today might also be "Horst-Wessel Lied" as sung by goose-stepping Nazis in Berlin or the Communist "Internationale" accompanying a parade of missiles in the now defunct Soviet Union.

Kinsley goes on to discuss the alternatives, dismissing "My Country 'Tis of Thee," " America the Beautiful," "The Battle Hymn of the Republic," and "God Bless America." He worries and frets about "The Battle Hymn of the Republic" being a bit martial, and about references to God (presumably the Creator by whom our unalienable rights are endowed in the Declaration of Independence). He goes so far as to speculate about a song by rock star Bruce Springsteen. The song he seems to like best is Woody Guthrie's "This Land Is Your Land." Consider what Kinsley has to say about this potential replacement for "The Star Spangled Banner." He writes, "Woody Guthrie wrote "This Land Is Your Land" out of annoyance at the popularity of "God Bless America." The melody has a range of just seven notes, which is hard to beat. The lyrics can be treated as either a generalized appreciation of the American landscape or a more pointed political claim for equality ('This land was made for you and me'). There's no question which one Guthrie had in mind. He was a communist fellow-traveler. But the song has been absorbed into our culture and is loved even by Republicans who have no idea about its origins."

Guthrie's original version of "This Land is Your Land" included two stanzas expressing his political protest. In one stanza, Guthrie wrote about the experience of seeing a two-sided sign that warned against trespassing on one side and said nothing on the reverse side. The side that said "nothing," declared Guthrie was "made for you and me." Guthrie wasn't finished. He also devoted a stanza to seeing "his people" by the relief office, standing hungry, as he stood there asking, "Is this land made for you and me?" This is hardly the view of a writer whose words should be transformed into our national anthem.

There you have it; Michael Kinsley wants to replace "The Star Spangled Banner" with a song written by a folk singer who wrote a column for the communist newspaper *The Daily Worker*, because it's easy to sing ("only a seven note range") and can mean whatever the singer wants it to mean. Every time our anthem is badly sung, someone wants to replace it with something else.

While Guthrie's song was originally filled with criticism of America, consider the contrast in the attitude of Irving Berlin. As for the lyrics of "God Bless America," the song that annoyed Woody Guthrie, the composer (and immigrant) Irving Berlin was eternally grateful to his country as a land of opportunity. This is clear is the words of the verse, not always sung today, but made famous by Kate Smith in her many performances on radio and on record. Berlin wrote,

> *While the storm clouds gather far across the sea, Let us*
> *swear allegiance to a land that's free,*
> *Let us all be grateful for a land so fair,*
> *As we raise our voices in a solemn prayer.*[48]

Some critics of "The Star Spangled Banner" have suggested replacing it with the song "America," which begins with the line, "My country 'tis of Thee." However, the music for this song is identical with that of Great Britain's "God Save the Queen" (or King, depending on who is the monarch of the day.) "America the Beautiful" has also been proposed as an alternative to our present national anthem. The lyrics for "America the Beautiful" were written by Katharine Lee Bates as a poem, "Pike's Peak," and published in 1895 under the title, "America." She was inspired by the magnificent American landscape. In 1910, her words were published under the title, "America the Beautiful," and combined with music composed in 1882 by organist-choirmaster Samuel A. Ward. "America the Beautiful" is justifiably one of the most beloved patriotic songs, but its older ancestor, "The Star Spangled

Banner," represents elements of our history which its critics choose to ignore.

Let's look at the history of our national anthem. It is only through understanding history that we can engage in an intelligent debate on this subject. When we are aware of its history, we can understand why this song's fate is important. The melody of "The Star Spangled Banner" is usually credited to John Stafford Smith, who was a prominent British composer during the 18th century, although some historians suggested that the melody, originally written as an English drinking song, "To Anacreon in Heaven," was actually composed by Dr. Samuel Arnold. The melody was transformed into a patriotic song in Boston, when a man named Thomas Paine (not to be confused with the famous American revolutionary pamphleteer) wrote the words for "Adams and Liberty" and used the music of "To Anacreon in Heaven" for his lyric.

In 1814, the United States was an independent nation fighting for survival against the British in a war that had started two years earlier. The Royal Navy dominated the seas, and British troops had attacked Washington, DC, burning the White House and the Capitol Building. Then the British turned their attention to Baltimore. Francis Scott Key was a lawyer practicing in Georgetown in Washington, DC, and an amateur poet. The British Fleet was anchored in Chesapeake Bay, and the British detained a non-combatant American, Dr. William Beames. Key, who served as a special envoy from President James Madison, appealed to the British to release his friend. But the British were planning on bombarding Ft. McHenry, below Baltimore. They were afraid that Key might discover their plans, so they detained him too. On September 13, 1814, the Royal Navy began shelling the American fort. The British forces bombarded Ft. McHenry continuously for twenty-five hours. Key was helpless to do anything about the situation, but when he saw the American flag still flying over Ft. McHenry, he wrote the first verse of what became "The Star Spangled Banner". The lyrics were set to the tune of "Adams and Liberty" and Key's words became part of our history. The section about the "the rockets' red glare, the bombs bursting in air" reflected Key's pride that the American flag was still flying. In effect, he was giving us a timeless message that the American dream has survived bombardment from enemies before and it can survive the assault of our enemies again.

Today, the British are our closest allies, but America has faced new and deadly enemies throughout history. Key's message, that the land of the free and the home of the brave can survive, is a very different one than that suggested by those who would simply have us sing "This land is your land, this land is my land." Would the world collapse if "The Star Spangled Banner" were replaced as our national anthem? Of course not. But a treasured element of our history and our heritage would disappear. A nation and its culture are made up of hundreds of such elements, and if they are allowed to disappear, not in a violent revolutionary coup, but through ignorance and neglect, one day that culture and heritage will be gone.

Those who are ignorant of our history, however, will be easily persuaded by those with a political agenda, which encourages the belief that changes are always good. There is a reason to study history. "The Star Spangled Banner" may be hard to sing, but there's a reason why it has endured as our national anthem. The song is not a celebration of our beautiful landscape, though it certainly merits celebrating. "The Star Spangled Banner" addresses the sacrifices made by those from whom we inherited an exceptional country. When our country's survival has been threatened, the message of "The Star Spangled Banner" rings true. During the Civil War, John Knowles Paine, the first professor of music at Harvard, wrote a series of variations on "The Star Spangled Banner" which he performed on the organ to great acclaim.

The actual flag that inspired Francis Scott Key is now a national treasure. Robert K. Wittman was the founder of the FBI Art Crime Team and its leading expert on art. In his memoir *Priceless*,[49] Wittman writes, "Flags hoisted by the soldiers at Fort McHenry, the marines at Iwo Jima, and the firefighters at the World Trade

Center are symbols of American resolve. The legend of the Fort McHenry battle flag inspired our National Anthem. Today, the tattered Star-Spangled Banner is the most visited artifact displayed at the Smithsonian Institution's National Museum of American History, viewed by some six million tourists annually. That flag, hand-stitched with 42-foot reams of wool, is the most valuable artifact in the entire Smithsonian collection—worth more than the Hope Diamond, Charles Lindbergh's Spirit of Saint Louis, or the Apollo 11 lunar module." Talking about "everybody coming together" may superficially sound more appealing than singing about "bombs bursting in air," even though the bombs in question were being targeted against and not by Americans. By studying the history of our national anthem, we learn an important lesson: if America had not been the home of the brave, it would not today be the land of the free.

Perhaps the most improbable challenge to "The Star Spangled Banner" came from an unlikely source, the YMCA, which co-hosted a 2021 contest dubbed "Kitizenship." The platform's founder was Amanda Little, a journalism professor at Vanderbilt University. While paying lip-service to the National Anthem and acknowledging such unofficial anthems as "The Stars and Stripes Forever," "America the Beautiful," and "God Bless the USA," the efforts by Little and co-author Emily Lordi clearly are geared to promoting a very different type of anthem, those that provide "empowerment and beauty." While the organizers talk about unity, their examples are clearly divisive along the lines of race and gender. Included are Lady Gaga's "Born This Way," described as a song that "has been embraced as an anthem by the LGBTQ community," and "Allright," described as "the unofficial anthem" of Black Lives Matter, a Marxist organization, and composed by rapper Kendrick Lamar. The organizers asked children from 8-18, "What is your song for America or for your community?" They proudly announced that the judges would include folk-rock guitarist Jason Isbell and "hip-hop artist and activist Genesis Be." Their language speaks of unity, but their examples preach division, group identities, and of course, as ALWAYS in such efforts, the opportunity for stars of the rock-pop-rap industry to promote themselves and their products.

The real message coming from such a contest is that children mistakenly think that our National Anthem is all about *them*. The real National Anthem, "The Star Spangled Banner" is about the triumph of liberty and the survival of our flag (and the values for which it stands) over adversity and great odds. Many of those wanting to jettison "The Star Spangled Banner" would like it replaced for the same reason that they dislike our national motto *E Pluribus Unum*. ("Out of many, one.") They would replace it with symbolism, musical and otherwise, that implies a notion of "Out of one, many." In other words, the great American melting pot (with people of many races, religions, and national origins) uniting to share common values, we are offered a salad bowl, a jumbled mix of individual and group identities with little in common as parts struggling for control of the whole.

In recent years, campaigns to attack the National Anthem have become downright toxic. The reasons offered are the usual ones, that Francis Scott Key was a slaveholder and that the third verse of "The Star Spangled Banner" contains a reference to "hireling or slave." But there is debate as to what the phrase means and the third verse is almost never sung. The reasons for singing "The Star Spangled Banner" haven't changed, the values of patriotism, sacrifice, resilience, and liberty are as valid today as they were during the War of 1812.

Perhaps the worst was a proposal by a historian named Daniel E. Walker and a writer named Kevin Powell. These two and their admirers proposed as the new National Anthem, "Imagine" by John Lennon, one of the Beatles. Powell positively gushed in describing the song as " the most beautiful, unifying, all-people, all-backgrounds-together kind of song you could have." Really?

Apart from the fact that Lennon was British and with due respect to our longtime ally Great Britain, "The Star Spangled Banner" was written during the War of 1812 in which Ft. McHenry was being shelled by the British Navy. What are the "unifying" elements of "Imagine?" The lyrics include the lines, "Imagine there's no countries, it isn't hard to do, nothing to kill or die for, and no religion too." Are Walker and Powell suggesting a new "National Anthem" celebrating the absence, decline, and disappearance of our country? "No religion?" Are Walker and Powell suggesting a "National Anthem" celebrating atheism? (Perhaps they are. Another line in "Imagine," the first one, in fact, suggests, "Imagine there's no heaven.") Perhaps Walker and Powell, like Lennon before them, find this appealing, but it would not appeal to the millions of Americans who believe, as stated in our Declaration of Independence that our rights come from our Creator. From where do Walker and Powell think their rights come from? King George III? A recording company in Hollywood or New York? Or perhaps a British media conglomerate? Facebook, Google, and Twitter? A committee of college professors?

Walker is chairman of a consulting firm that "uses history, faith, education, and the arts to bring progressive change to the world." it should surprise no one that one of his areas of interest is hip-hop. Powell was the curator for the first exhibit on the history of hip-hop in America at the Rock and Roll Hall of Fame in Cleveland, Ohio. He has written extensively about the rapper Tupac Shakur. Behind every effort to jettison "The Star Spangled Banner," one can usually find an advocate of the rock-rap-pop repertoire.

In case "Imagine" doesn't catch on, the sages of Twitter, dutifully reported by the *New York Post,* have suggested such patriotic classics as "Ribs" by Lorde or Miley Cyrus's "Party in the USA."

Although "God Bless America" has been suggested as a substitute for "The Star Spangled Banner," it too, has been targeted with the wrath of those who are offended by faith or patriotism. Gersh Kuntzman, a sportswriter for *The New York Daily News,* demanded that attendees at baseball games stop singing what he called "the song that offends everyone." Kuntzman, who once said that he "didn't know the difference between an aria and an enema" described the performance of "God Bless America" by Kate Smith as "as much a symbol of post-war patriotism as the flag, the space program, and all the white people moving to the suburbs." Kuntzman, who dislikes expressions of faith in the public square, also objects to "In God We Trust" appearing on American money as the national motto.

He says that the song is offensive to foreigners, that the song implies that America is an exceptional nation, and dismisses patriotism as self-righteous and fascistic. If visitors to the United States don't like American citizens expressing their love of country, perhaps they should visit some other nation instead; China, Cuba, Iran, and North Korea are countries in which they would never hear "God Bless America," although many of the permanent residents of those countries would certainly like to hear it. The best response, of course, is found in the writing of Mary Ellin Barrett, daughter of Irving Berlin, the composer of "God Bless America" and his biographer. She spoke of Berlin singing the song and says, "He meant every word. He meant it then. He meant it thirty years later. It was the land he loved. It was his home sweet home. He, the immigrant who had made good, was saying thank you."

Protestors have not only targeted Berlin's classic song but Kate Smith, whose performances of "God Bless America" made her an American icon during World War II. Following the 9/11 attacks, the New York Yankees played her recording of Irving Berlin's best-known composition for eighteen years; the Philadelphia Flyers hockey team regarded Smith as a "good luck charm" and a statue of her was erected outside the Wells Fargo Center. The Flyers had been using her recording since 1969, beginning three years after her death. But in 2019, protestors called attention to Smith's having performed songs containing what would today be regarded as racially insensitive lyrics. The Yankees and Flyers immediately stopped using her recordings and the Flyers even covered the statue of Kate Smith so no one would be "offended" by a recording she made eight decades earlier and dismissed her entire career by labeling her a "racist."

The Yankees and Flyers could have ignored the demands of those seeking to malign Kate Smith's memory and they had ample evidence to do so. On October 26, 1982, President Ronald Reagan awarded the nation's highest civilian award, the Medal of Freedom, to Kate Smith. He did so while praising her by declaring, "The voice of Kate Smith is known and loved by millions of Americans, young and old. In war and peace, it has been an inspiration. Those simple, but deeply moving words, 'God Bless America,' have taken on added meaning for all of us because of the way Kate Smith sang them. Thanks to her, they have become a cherished part of all of our lives, an undying reminder of the beauty, the courage, and the heart of this great land of ours. In giving us a magnificent, selfless talent like Kate Smith, God has truly blessed America."

The assault on patriotic music hasn't been limited to one side of the Atlantic. The Proms are a series of concerts in London founded by conductor Sir Henry Wood in the 1890s and supported by the BBC since 1927. But in 2020, a huge row erupted over "Last Night at the Proms," which traditionally features performances of British patriotic music including "Rule Britannia," based on a poem by James Thomson and set to music by Thomas Arne in 1740, and "Land of Hope and Glory," with music adapted by Sir Edward Elgar in 1901 from his *Pomp and Circumstance March No.1* and lyrics by the poet A.C. Benson. The audience typically waves British flags and members join in the singing if they so choose.

Accusations were hurled suggesting that these musical pieces, so identified with Great Britain were relics of colonialism and of course, therefore, "racist" and associated with the slave trade. John O'Sullivan responded, citing the movement to abolish slavery led by the British. He wrote, "So the Brits delivered more than "Rule Britannia" promised: It wasn't only Brits who never would be slaves but anyone living under British rule or on the high seas. It was, moreover, a peculiarly *national* achievement. In order to buy the slaves their freedom peacefully, the British government raised 20 million pounds sterling in a loan on the money markets. That's 2.4 billion in today's money. The British taxpayer finally paid off the last installment of the loan on February 1st, 2015."[50]

In any given year, those seeking to destroy Americans' sense of patriotism are always trying to find a way to get rid of our symbols, musical ones included. They will be supported by those ignorant of history and willing to accept what they are told. Of course, they will be encouraged ALWAYS by the craven and predatory promoters in the music business, those whose interest is neither politics or history, but cash pure and simple. Their motive is what is always has been, to sell anything and everything they can regardless of its complete lack of musical worth or societal consequences. John Lennon's lyric for "Imagine" also suggests "Imagine no possessions." Do you know of any rock, pop, or rap stars or their managers and promoters who eschew material wealth? They are fine with attacking capitalism as long as they are permitted to keep their off-shore bank accounts, multiple mansions, luxury estates, and expensive cars. If they can take credit for getting rid of the National Anthem, they will be pleased to do so.

The assault on patriotic music, of course, is only part of the attack on patriotism in general. If love of country can be diminished, then a country's music, books, art, and culture can be eliminated and replaced by those who have appointed themselves to do the replacing.

It should come as no surprise to anyone that in recent years, the flag itself, along with all symbols of patriotism, is under assault, often by the least-informed among us. In June of 2021, a singer named Macy Gray wrote an op-ed blasting the flag as "tattered, dated, divisive, and incorrect." Incredibly, she demanded a new race-based flag incorporating colors from the sixty-four count Crayola crayon box. "Colors of ALL of us—your skin tone and mine," demanded Gray, apparently unaware that the red, white and blue colors of the flag have nothing to do with skin color. Gray urges a flag with "off-white bars" and stars with black and brown hues. She would permit the red and blue colors to remain. There would also be fifty-two instead of fifty stars; although the stars represent the number of states in the U.S., Gray thinks apparently that she should bypass Congress and add two stars for the District of Columbia and Puerto Rico since she supports their campaign for statehood and dismisses anyone opposing D.C. statehood as racist. Charles Thomson, secretary of the Continental Congress, knew more about the reason for the color scheme than Gray. Thomson, who signed the Declaration of Independence, explained, "White signifies purity and innocence, Red, hardiness and valour, and Blue . . . signifies vigilance, perseverance & justice."

HYSTERICAL HISTORY: TRIVIALIZING HEROES

Hollywood has always been notorious for portraying historical events inaccurately, often with comic results. The best directors, writers, composers, costume and set designers, however, worked meticulously to present history as it actually took place. Miklós Rózsa, the eminent film composer, for instance, spent hours in research to insure that musical instruments heard in the historical epics he scored actually fit the appropriate historical period. Some motion picture adaptations of classics, especially those produced in England, have presented such works accurately. However, when motion picture and television producers wade into history, the results, more often than not, are disastrous. Movies and television programs are not history classes, however, and a little artistic license can be excused. But in recent years, Hollywood has played fast and loose with historical facts in the extreme. The result is not just bad entertainment. It's also bad education, because unfortunately, movies, television, and recordings have become instructors in the popular culture. Students who fail to identify major historical figures are all too familiar with the icons of pop culture. So Hollywood's version of history is often far more influential than traditional teaching tools. The Hollywood version doesn't always tell us what we need to know about history, but it usually tells us a great deal about Hollywood.

A case in point is the Warner Brothers animated series for children, *Histeria*. The premise of *Histeria* would seem to be highly original: an animated cartoon series featuring the great events and characters of history. Humor and history are not mutually exclusive. W.C. Sellar and R.J. Yeatman were British humorists who wrote for the celebrated humor magazine, *Punch*. Their 1930 classic, *1066 and All That*, was a light-hearted plunge into English history that left readers laughing for years. The prolific humorist Richard Armour wrote volumes of historical and literary satires, playfully retelling the history of nations, literature, and great art. He had great fun writing a hilarious version of American history, dedicated to Sellar and Yeatman, called *It All Started with Columbus*.[51] It was the first of his many books proving that history can not only be fun but funny. However, Dr. Armour was also a scholar who made certain that his facts were unquestionably accurate before putting pen to paper. As a dedicated professor, he was delighted when students told him they found it easier to remember historical facts from his satires than their real textbooks.

The same cannot be said for the *Histeria* television series that has unfortunately turned the great figures of history into buffoons, mixing fact and fiction from the past and present in a psychedelic smorgasbord of utter confusion. *Histeria* presented the assorted adventures of a series of characters, usually children, as they encounter the giants of history. *Histeria* wasn't produced by amateurs. Producer Tom Ruegger is a veteran of the multi- Emmy award winning *Animaniacs* series. He is also a parent, whose three sons all recorded voices for the series. Promotional materials described the show as "historical subject matter in an exciting, original and hysterically amusing way, taking viewers on a fast-paced ride through well-known and not-so-well-known events and people of the past." An advertisement for the show declares enthusiastically, "Add heaps of history to lots of laughter and oodles of education. Mix together, well sprinkle with comedy, animate and, voilà, endless entertainment!" "Oodles of education?" One principal character in *Histeria* is Pepper Mills, who is described by an enthusiastic fan as "hyperactive, loud, and sometimes annoying fan of celebs." Pepper asks historical figures for their autographs, only to find that she has mistaken them for someone else. She is, therefore, disappointed to find that Abraham Lincoln isn't "Lurch" a character from *The Addams Family* cartoons, that Confucius isn't martial arts movie star Jackie Chan; that Gen. Dwight D. Eisenhower isn't Bugs Bunny's nemesis, Elmer Fudd, and that Joan of Arc isn't *Sabrina the Teenage Witch*. When animated boys and girls actually participate in historical events, the figures they meet behave like clowns . . . or worse. The colloquial slang and music of the moment are tossed into history like an improbable salad. Mahatma Gandhi doesn't impress a young interviewer, who calls him, "Gandhi-dude." Atomic scientist J. Robert Oppenheimer is given a chance to impress a young listener who impertinently asks him, "Why should I care?" Oppenheimer then catapults to oblivion. Thomas Edison may have been our most important inventor, but he fails to appreciate rock music. World War II is depicted as a contest between the maniacal Hitler, Mussolini and Tojo, and two caped superheroes, Winston Churchill and Franklin Roosevelt. Roosevelt, who refused to be limited by his confinement in a wheelchair, is shown flying through the air like a latter-day Superman. Joseph Stalin, who sent millions to their deaths on a whim, appears to be a heavyweight wrestler. When Hitler appears to vanquish the heroes and orders them tied and lowered in a vat of boiling oil, Roosevelt sends his dog Fala to the rescue. Fala returns with a version of Wonder Woman, Eleanor Roosevelt, who smashes Hitler and company and saves the day. The lesson to be learned from all this silliness has nothing to do with the blood, toil, tears, and sweat of millions that won World War II, but it is politically correct. If you want to win a war, you need a woman in charge.

Not all women are portrayed sympathetically. A meeting between Joan of Arc, Golda Meir, Margaret Thatcher, and Evita Perón ends in a virtual four-way wrestling match. (Evita, for good measure, is depicted with the voice and mannerisms of the entertainer, Charo.) Historical figures from different periods often end up in slapstick sequences worthy of Barnum and Bailey's best circus clowns. The *Histeria* version of the post-war peace conference at Yalta begins when Froggo, another juvenile character, uses food to depict a map of Europe, and ends with Roosevelt, Churchill, and Stalin in a pre-adolescent food fight. Stalin also acts as an enforcer for Froggo.

Does any of this matter? Is *Histeria* just a harmless cartoon? Those knowledgeable about history may regard *Histeria* as silly, offensive, or both. The producers of this program would undoubtedly declare that serious critics of their show are humorless academics who can't take a joke. The official web-site for *Histeria* tells young Web-surfers, "If you think that Quetzalcoatl is the Backstreet Boys' drummer or that the French Revolution is some kind of gymnastics routine involving croissants and smelly cheese, then *Histeria*'s the place for you. Get the 411 on everything that happened before you were born by taking a magical history tour with swingin' dudes like George Washington and Alexander the Not So Great. You don't need Nostradamus to tell you this is the real poop, but hey, he's on the show, too, if you feel like asking."

Children watching this program may be seeing these historical characters and learning their names for the first time. High school and college students who are ignorant of the rudiments of history frequently confuse the past and present. An animated history program is a wonderful idea, but not when historical names, places, and faces, are simply used as substitutes for Tom and Jerry. It isn't hard to imagine boys and girls watching *Histeria* today remembering what they've learned tomorrow: that history is a playground for ill-mannered juveniles and a sideshow of buffoons who aren't nearly as important as the icons of pop culture. The real lesson of *Histeria* is that too many people in the entertainment industry believe that "truth" and "facts" are outdated and irrelevant. Historical figures and faces are no different from Daffy Duck or Elmer Fudd. Sadly, this is what members of the audience may think too. Children watching such shows have time to learn otherwise. But chances are, they won't. It will be far easier for them to accede to the notion that the past was dominated mostly by "boring old dudes" who really aren't "with it" today.

CANCELLING HEROES, ERASING HISTORY

On both sides of the Atlantic, historical figures and the statues that represent them are under assault. Initially, demands that statues be torn down were directed at figures and monuments associated with the Confederacy and at Confederate leaders during the Civil War. Soon, however, the wrath of those against maintaining the statues and historical monuments expanded to include many other historical figures of other eras. Nor were their demands simply peaceful protests; angry crowds pulled statues off their pedestals, smashed them with hammers in some cases, beheaded them and even tossed them into nearby waterways.

Vandals began to widely deface, decapitate, and topple statues following the death of a black man, George Floyd, in Minneapolis, Minnesota, after a white police officer Derek Chauvin, knelt on his neck for a prolonged period of time. Chauvin was subsequently convicted of his murder, but riots occurred all over the United States and protests, often led by the Marxist organization, Black Lives Matter, spread across the Atlantic to the United Kingdom.

A brief look at which figures have been chosen for cancellation by the crowd reveals that this assault on historical images is not always what it seems. Objections to Confederate monuments were based on the declaration that Confederate soldiers fought to defend the secessionist states that supported slavery. Activists choosing targets quickly pivoted to America's Founding Fathers, denouncing them indiscriminately as merely slaveholders: George Washington and Thomas Jefferson were especially targeted. The list expanded quickly. A close examination of the more than a hundred statues vandalized, destroyed, or removed in the United States makes it clear that this is an effort to target all of American history; vandals defaced statues of both Union and Confederate soldiers and people who had nothing whatsoever to do with slavery or racism. In Richmond, Virginia, rioters pulled down a statue of Christopher Columbus that was erected in 1927 and tossed it into the river before placing a burning American flag on it. In Chicago's Washington Park, vandals spray-painted red graffiti on a statue of America's First President, George Washington, placing a white Ku Klux Klan hood on his head accompanied by the message "God Bless Amerikkka." In San Francisco's Golden Gate Park, a mob attacked and pulled down a statue of the Spanish missionary and Catholic priest, St. Junipero Serra. In the same park, rioters also toppled a bust of Ulysses S. Grant, the commanding general who led the Union forces against slaveholding states before his election as President of the United States. Police stood passively by and watched.

In Boston, the city's Art Commission voted to remove a statue of Abraham Lincoln, "The Great Emancipator" holding the Emancipation Proclamation while a slave rose from a kneeling position with broken shackles on his wrists. In perhaps the most bizarre episode, a vandal celebrated the 168th anniversary of a speech in Rochester, New York by famed black abolitionist and heroic orator Frederick Douglass by ripping the statue from its base and seriously damaging it. Ronald Reagan lived in Dixon, Illinois from the age of nine to the age of twenty-two, so there is a statue of him in his home town; two women vandalized the Reagan statue.

In Britain, vandals attacked statues of Winston Churchill, Mahatma Gandhi, and Abraham Lincoln. The British government decided to literally cover the statue of Churchill to protect it from protestors, none of whom understood that without Churchill's leadership, England might have fallen to the Nazis and they would have grown up under a totalitarian regime that would have quickly executed them for protesting anything.

London's Mayor, Sadiq Khan, announced that a new commission would make a list of statues to be torn down that didn't reflect the city's diversity. Among the statues targeted were those of Charles Gray, the Prime Minister whose government led the efforts to abolish slavery in 1833, Oliver Cromwell, Horatio Nelson, Sir Francis Drake, and even Nancy Astor, the first woman elected to Parliament. Italian journalist, Giulio Meotti, editor of *Il Foglio,* wrote, "The statue in London of Churchill—who stood against the Nazis during the Second World War and saved Europe from barbarism—was covered up by the city authorities during recent protests. Its visual erasure reminds one of the nude statues in Rome covered up by authorities to please Iranian President Hassan Rouhani, or the 'disappearance' of portraits in the former Soviet Union, of people whom the Politburo decided had fallen out of favor. There is a falsity in erasing one's history. One may not have a perfect history, but it is one's history, nevertheless. As the historian Victor Davis Hanson wrote, a country 'does not have to be perfect to be good.' Excising the distasteful parts does not change what happened; they may even be replaced with parts that are more distasteful."[52]

Rejection of historical figures by those who know only ideology, not history, did not impress Garry Kasparov, legendary world chess champion and longtime advocate for liberty in Russia. Said Kasparov, "I was shocked to see the rush to debunk historical figures judged by our current criteria. The West should be proud of them instead of hating itself."

Historical figures are all imperfect, even the greatest heroes. Historical assessments of men and women change over the years and with the passage of time. But there are reasons why certain individuals were honored in the past and should be honored and have their memories respected today. George Washington could have easily been crowned King George I of the United States; instead, he gladly gave up power granted him by the people and went home to Mt. Vernon. He was the Father of His Country who led the American forces to victory and independence. Washington freed his slaves and those of his wife Martha upon his death. Washington was also a great champion of religious liberty, writing that "the Government of the United States, which gives to bigotry no sanction, to persecution no assistance, requires only that they who live under its protection should demean themselves as good citizens, in giving it on all occasions their effectual support."

Thomas Jefferson was the principal author of the Declaration of Independence. Despite being a slaveholder, Jefferson tried to include the abolition of slavery in the Declaration. In speaking of slavery, Jefferson declared emphatically, "I tremble for my country when I reflect that God is just; that His justice cannot sleep forever."

Abraham Lincoln opposed slavery, freed the slaves through the Emancipation Proclamation, and led America through its most divisive war in a successful effort to save the Union. Are we to expect efforts to tear down the Washington Monument and the Jefferson and Lincoln memorials?

It is interesting to note that there is a statue in the Fremont section of Seattle, Washington that has not been torn down. In 1981, the Communist Party of Czechoslovakia, commissioned a Bulgarian sculptor, Emil Venkov to create a statue of Soviet communist icon Vladimir Lenin. The statue was installed just a year before communism in Czechoslovakia fell during the Velvet Revolution. Later, an American teacher, Lewis Carpenter, who had befriended Venkov, found the statue abandoned and eventually transported it to his home in Issaquah, Washington. For some reason, the rioters, vandals, and mobs who want to erase the memories of most American and British historical figures have no problems with a statue of the man most identified with the creation of the Soviet Union.

What is actually taking place here is an effort to *erase* history, to destroy a nation's memories and with them, the nation itself. This is a longtime tenet of cultural Marxism; before the Marxist utopia can be established, history and all the institutions it supports must be eliminated. Following the communist revolution in Russia and the establishment of the Soviet Union, there were revolutionaries who wanted to burn down all the museums. Mao's Cultural Revolution in China pursued a similar communist goal. In the Soviet Union, it was easy to determine which historical figures had fallen out of favor; their images disappeared from pictures in which they were previously visible. Their names were no longer mentioned in print. It was as if they had ceased to exist. As Rich Lowry has written, it's pointlessly destructive to tear down what deserves to be honored and to forget what should be remembered.

While militant ideologues expand their lists of heroes to be cancelled, there are those whose lives are defined by the celebrity culture who have their own idea. In Tennessee, Alex Parsons started a petition to replace all Confederate statues with statues of singer Dolly Parton. A website called *Tylt* published an article by Jennifer Boeder in 2017 asking if Confederate monuments should be replaced by statues of celebrities. An online survey on the site produced support for the celebrities from forty percent of those responding; not a majority yet, but "yet" is the operative word.

How long will it be before a majority supports replacing all historical figures with statues of the people they most admire: rock, pop, and rap stars, professional athletes, and celebrities who are famous for just being famous?

Examples of foolish and ignorant commentaries abound. A writer named Matt Stopera, writing for *Buzzfeed*, applauded efforts to replace Confederate monuments in Louisiana with statues of Britney Spears. Says Stopera, "A genius and humanitarian is petitioning the governor of Louisiana to replace those old Confederate statues with ones of Louisiana native, living legend, and vocalist Britney Spears." In perhaps the most telling example of the literacy and cultural awareness of the pop culturists, Stopera goes on to opine, "Who would want a statue of this stupid racist horse and some dusty old dude . . . when you could have a statue of someone with two diamond albums, a successful Las Vegas residency, and 287 perfumes?" Who indeed? Stopera's casual question is actually quite revealing. He has no real knowledge of the statues in Louisiana he wants taken down, no arguments in favor of doing so because of history, no recognition of even the identity of historical figures, for good or ill. Like all acolytes of the ubiquitous pop culture, he just doesn't have any use for "dusty old dudes." After all, who needs historical figures when we can worship at the altar of pop stars? Anything or anyone old or dusty needs to be jettisoned for someone young, new, and exciting. The Founding Fathers, along with Shakespeare, Beethoven, Mozart, and Rembrandt, have all had their day. There are plenty of new stars to replace the old ones.

Stopera, a senior editor at *Buzzfeed*, attended college at New York University (NYU) where he clearly didn't learn much about American history or the "dusty old dudes" who fought and died for the freedoms that enable him to exercise his First Amendment rights. According to Wikipedia, Stopera explained, "I originally wanted to go to school for journalism because I thought it was cool or something. I took the intro class and HATED it, so I decided to do Comm [Communications] because there were a bunch of classes about pop culture, which is what I really like. I quickly learned you didn't have to go to school for journalism to write." Stopera's interest in pop culture began early. When he was only fourteen, he appeared on MTV in an episode of Fanography to talk about his favorite celebrity—Britney Spears.

But Stopera is hardly alone. In Portsmouth, Virginia, a man named Nathan Coflin launched a petition to replace a Confederate monument with "Grammy award-winning rapper, dancer, record producer" Missy Elliott. The petition gave the reason for choosing Elliott, claiming she expressed the real spirit of Portsmouth, advising those ignorant of her accomplishments that she was a platinum recording artist with over thirty million albums sold and without once even owning a slave." The petition was endorsed by its 35,000 signers.

If this effort is successful, consider the children who will grow up familiar only with the names and images of celebrities. They will know little of history or the men and women who made it, their ideas, virtues, and even flaws; they will only know the names of celebrities for whom fame itself is their only achievement.

Opposing the celebrity culture with its false idols and undeserving plastic heroes is hazardous; the fans and idolaters who worship celebrities don't want to see them taken off their pedestals; they're too busy trying to replace historical figures about whom they know little more than popular slogans. The media have a vested interest in celebrities, one reason why so many television shows, radio programs, and podcasts are devoted to their every minute, their every move.

It is interesting to note that there are no major publicized efforts to put up statues of accomplished classical and jazz musicians, great writers, gifted artists; the pop culture, glorying as always in its own ignorance, wants statues of its only heroes, celebrities.

But we must begin by looking at the achievements of true heroes, often not people that are famous and more often than not, neglected. Heroes, like all men and women, may have their flaws. But they have done something in their lives that sets them apart, something that merits our admiration and attention and the capacity to see that their accomplishments remain in our collective memory and are not forgotten.

Heroism is not determined by a popularity contest but by history. Unfortunately, in a pop culture plagued by permanent attention deficit disorder, we don't have time to wait for the judgment of history, especially when historians of today may be likelier to reflect contemporary bias rather than historical truth. So we must take action to defend those historical figures worthy of defense and oppose the erection of false idols whether foisted upon us because of ideology or celebrity. It does not mean that we regard every historical figure in precisely the same way as he or she was regarded a century ago. But it does mean that we should pursue truth, not ideology or celebrity in a culture which increasingly places a much greater emphasis on the latter.

SLOGANS AND SUBSTANCE

It is not enough for us to remember a few isolated names or slogans in history. We need to recall the substance of important events and the reasons those events took place. For many years, February 22 was a national holiday, "George Washington's Birthday." But in 1968, Congress passed a law mandating the celebration of Washington's Birthday on the third Monday in February. Presumably, this would allow us to enjoy a three-day weekend since the holiday would always come after a leisurely Saturday and Sunday. Primary supporters of the legislation were business groups who saw another three-day weekend as an opportunity to promote sales and marketing campaigns. As Abraham Lincoln was born on February 12, the idea of celebrating the two great Presidents' birthdays together was discussed. Congress specifically rejected the idea of "President's Day." Thirty years later, a dozen U.S. Senators again tried to advance the notion of changing "George Washington's Birthday" to the vague and confusing "President's Day," but the idea was rejected again. Yet advertisers, politicians and members of the press alike constantly refer to "President's Day." For all practical purposes, the celebration of this vague holiday has replaced the day on which we honor the man known as "The Father of His Country." Which presidents are honored on "President's Day"? Millard Fillmore, Andrew Johnson, Jimmy Carter, Bill Clinton, or just whoever happens to be the current occupant of the White House? Do we know? Do we care? In 1968, Rep. Dan Kuykendall of Tennessee predicted that if we no longer celebrated Washington's Birthday on Feb. 22, in a decade children in school would have no idea why the holiday was celebrated at all. He said, "They will not know or care when George Washington was born. They will know that in the middle of February they will have a three-day weekend for some reason. This will come." In 1999, John Fonte, Senior Fellow and Director of Hudson's Center for American Common Culture, argued persuasively that Kuykendall's prediction had come true. Fonte wrote, "Sometimes more wisdom is found among the losers of congressional debates than among the winners. Thirty-one years ago in opposing the legislation to change the February 22 date of Washington's Birthday, Congressman Joe Waggonner of Louisiana told the bill's sponsors: 'You have further commercialized and made further meaningless something that has the respect of the people of this country.' Surely, it is time, on the 200th anniversary of George Washington's death, to bury President's Day and to resurrect and celebrate the birthday of the Father of our country." More than a decade after Fonte's conclusions, the vaguely amorphous "President's Day" has somehow still supplanted Washington's Birthday in the popular culture, even though the federal holiday is legally "Washington's Birthday."

There are many reasons to honor George Washington. During the American Revolution, he held the tiny Continental Army together against all odds and led it to victory. He served as President of the Constitutional Convention and as first President of the United States. By voluntarily retiring and giving up both military and political power, he established the precedent that our country would exist under the rule of law, not the rule of man. Other leaders who seized power with military force, including Caesar, Oliver Cromwell, Napoleon, and Lenin, became dictators who fought to retain their power. Washington could have been

America's first king, but he walked away after the Revolutionary War and again after two terms as President. King George III asked the American painter Benjamin West what Washington would do after winning America's independence. West told the British monarch that Washington would simply return to his farm, Mt. Vernon. The astonished George III said, "If he does that, he will be the greatest man in the world."

So it matters that children in school know why we celebrate the birthday of George Washington. Otherwise, they will think that Washington was simply "an old dude in a funny wig" whose face appears on dollar bills. Washington's courage, sacrifice, and devotion to his country set a standard to which most of us could only aspire. The principles he espoused, especially vesting power in the people, not in the government or in kings, caudillos, theocrats, or tyrants, establish the values and freedoms we must guard so zealously today. Similarly, Abraham Lincoln's Birthday, February 12, should be a reason to study Lincoln's life and his achievements. It isn't enough to know that Lincoln's "Gettysburg Address" contained the phrase, "government of the people, by the people, and for the people." We need to know why Lincoln is regarded as one of our greatest presidents. It isn't enough to know that Martin Luther King, Jr. made a speech using the phrase "I have a dream." We need to remember the ideas he expressed in his *Letter from a Birmingham Jail*. In this document he explained the entire rationale for the Civil Rights Movement in America. It isn't enough to know that Ronald Reagan made a speech in Berlin and said, "Mr. Gorbachev, open this gate! Mr. Gorbachev, tear down this wall!" We need to understand what prompted President Reagan's use of these words, especially over the objections of many of his advisors. Those who are too young to remember the Berlin Wall will have no idea of its significance. The Wall was a symbol of tyranny and a terrible reminder of the lives of those who were shot trying to escape the Iron Curtain. Today, too many Americans barely recognize the Nazi swastika or the Communist hammer and sickle and do not understand the ghastly consequences that occurred when the ideas behind those symbols were put into place.

William F. Buckley. Jr. summed up this problem eloquently in a 1980 speech before the Heritage Foundation. He said, "Abraham Lincoln told a biographer that his worst fear for America was that the revolutionary experience would dilute as the country grew older. His parents remembered the revolution as part of their own experience. His own generation, he said, remember it as a vivid part of the experience of their parents. But what of future generations, to whom the struggle of the Founding Fathers would become an abstract reminiscence, of no great personal concern than the struggles of the ancient Romans, or of the medieval Englishmen, for their liberties?" Ronald Reagan said that freedom is never more than a generation away from extinction. In order to appreciate our freedom, it is mandatory that we understand our past as well as our present.

LOOKING BACK TO LOOK AHEAD

Writers and artists have been fascinated by memory. The gastronome James Beard possessed a "taste-memory" that enabled him to recall every minute detail of the foods he enjoyed. He could describe every dish served on a dinner that delighted him three or four decades earlier. Beard referred to Marcel Proust recounting the flood of emotions and memories that overcame him when tasting petites madeleines, the biscuits of his youth. In *Swann in Love,* Proust introduced a fictional sonata supposedly written by Vinteuil, a composer he invented, that also brought forth a sense of the past. Proust's most famous book is usually listed with its English title, *Remembrance of Things Past,* but the French title translates literally as *In Search of Lost Time.*

Rod Serling, creator of the popular television series, *The Twilight Zone,* expressed similar longings for the innocence of childhood and the serenity of a bygone era in his masterful teleplays. Nostalgia was a major theme in the television plays of the great writer, especially in his scripts for the legendary series. In episodes like *Walking Distance* and *A Stop at Willoughby,* Serling created characters who were big city men, middle-aged and disillusioned, yearning for the calm serenity of life in a small town in which people moved more slowly and took the time to take life "full-measure." Serling wrote these scripts decades before the digital revolution, but his prescient observation was quite accurate. In his final narration for *Walking Distance*, he wrote of a "little errant wish, that a man might never have to become old, never outgrow the merry-go-rounds of his youth." He concluded, "We too can smile," knowing as he did that "it is just an errant wish across some wisp of memory, not too important, really, some laughing ghosts that cross a man's mind."

In discussing the past, it is easy to slide into pure nostalgia for an idealized world that never existed. Those who actually remember "the good old days" may have selective memories, remembering the good and conveniently forgetting everything else. George Ball called nostalgia "a seductive liar." Then there are those who are nostalgic for a time they are too young to remember. Carson McCullers said that as often as not, we are homesick most for the places we have never known. It is easy enough to assume that if you don't like things that are happening today, yesterday was undoubtedly much better.

But in criticizing those who speak well of the past, through memory or history, it is important not to make the opposite mistake, to automatically accept the notion that "new and improved" is infused with an intrinsic truth. The worst ideas in history, often those with disastrous consequences, have invariably been sold to a willing public under the label of progress. We often want to feel that we are receptive to "new progressive ideas," even if they prove to be neither new nor progressive. Jeffrey Hart addressed the nature of change in his book, *When the Going Was Good*,[53] a reexamination of the 1950s. He observed, "The historical past is constantly changing before our eyes. Details that were once important fade like the inscriptions on old tombstones. As Eliot wrote in *Little Gidding*, his masterly reflection on time: 'See now they vanish, the faces and places.'" Thus as we look back, there are some things we need to remember.

Let us concede that science and technology have been responsible for incredible improvements in our lives. The refrigerator, the automobile, and air-conditioning have made life easier. Medical discoveries have lengthened our lives. Travel by air, land, and sea is faster than ever before. The telephone (and now the cell phone), radio, television, motion pictures, and now the Internet have revolutionized communications and the distribution of information. The poorest among us enjoy things our richest ancestors might never have imagined. But there is more to life than science and technology. In the arts and humanities, the inexorable march of progress is far less predictable.

Even the most nostalgic among us would probably not want to give up modern conveniences to recapture the culture and ideals of the past. (There have been exceptions. Tasha Tudor, a popular 20th century contemporary New England author and illustrator, lived a 19th century life on a farm filled with working antiques and spinning wheels, serving milk from the goats she raised.) But while we can applaud technological progress, we cannot blind ourselves to the realities of contemporary culture. To see where we are today, we must first remember (or discover) where we have been. Leszek Kolakowski was a distinguished Polish scholar and historian of ideas. In 1986, he was selected for the U.S. government's highest honor for achievement in the humanities, an invitation to deliver the Jefferson Lecture. Kolakowski used the occasion to remind us, "We learn history not in order to know how to behave or how to succeed, but to know who we are." We should well recall the words of Margaret Fairless Barber who said, "To look backward for a while is to refresh the eye, to restore it, and to render it the more fit for its prime function of looking forward."

A TALE OF TWO CULTURES

HIGH ART (SAVANTS OF THE AVANT, INTELLECTUAL SNOBS, ELITE EGGHEADS) AND POP CULTURE (HUCKSTERS, HUSTLERS, SINGERS WHO CAN'T SING, PAINTERS WHO CAN'T PAINT, AND WRITERS WHO CAN'T WRITE)

IN 1965, THE THREE-MEMBER MUSIC JURY responsible for awarding the prestigious Pulitzer Prize in Music recommended unanimously that a special prize be given to Duke Ellington for his four decades of composition and performance. Ellington was often identified as a jazz icon, but his music transcended labels. He often described the greatest musicians as "beyond category"; his biographer John Edward Haase concluded that no one deserved the description more than Ellington himself. The fourteen member Pulitzer advisory board rejected the recommendation of the jury, setting off a public debate. While the reason given by the board was that the prize was supposed to be awarded for a single work, not an entire career, there was reason for skepticism. *Washington Post* critic Jonathan Yardley dubbed the act the "cultural establishment's hostility to the new and the different and the unsanctioned." Yardley went on to praise Ellington's contribution to American music as "A total body of work that was neither jazz nor classical but something that drew strength from both, and emerged triumphantly, sui generis." Ellington himself was gracious, declaring at sixty-seven, "Fate is being kind to me. Fate doesn't want me to be famous too young."

Duke Ellington was not the only musician or the only creative artist to be plagued by the need of critics and commentators to apply labels to the objects of their affection or disdain. In 1935, George Gershwin's opera, *Porgy and Bess*, premiered, beginning a legend of worldwide praise and controversy. Gershwin's identity as a leading composer of popular music and his inspiration drawn from African-American and jazz sources didn't please some operatic purists. Critic Lawrence Gilman, writing in the *New York Herald Tribune,* dismissed Gershwin's arias as "song hits" and therefore, a blemish on the work's integrity. "Surefire rubbish," said Gilman. Nor was Gilman alone. Gershwin's *An American in Paris* throbbed with the rhythms of the big city, complete with honking taxi horns. But some years earlier, critic Oscar Thompson, in the *New York Post,* dismissed Gershwin's *An American in Paris* as "blunt banality" and "ballyhoo vulgarity," and concluded, "The Honks Have It."

Two decades later, another titan of Broadway's musical theater, Frank Loesser, wrote *The Most Happy Fella,* an extraordinary work that combined tunes with forms usually associated with opera. Loesser's daughter Susan wrote a biographical profile of her father, observing, "He used classical forms, including them in his dramatic aims. He wrote arias, recitatives, duets, trios, two-part inventions, choral numbers purely orchestral sections, and scattered pop tunes among them like candy flowers on the cake." *The Most Happy Fella* was one of the most creative and innovative works in American musical theater, but it had its critics. Henry Hewes, writing in the *Saturday Review,* announced, "When a musical comedy composer turns to opera he is apt to seem a child on a man's errand. So it is with Frank Loesser, whose *The Most Happy Fella* is a dull, poorly blended mixture of musical trifles."

What do all three of these episodes have in common? They reflect the cultural confusion that results when a work of art and the collected works of an artist cannot be neatly classified. Through our history, societies—and American society in particular—have tried to classify and label elements of our culture. Usually, this results in a war between those who advocated "high culture" or "high art," written for an elite audience of connoisseurs and those who champion "popular culture," which is often driven by the marketplace and which elicits the support of large audiences that lack pretensions. But this battle has led us to an unlikely place in the 21st century. Consider an individual, casually dressed in blue jeans, listening to country western music or the latest rock group, who has a framed work of art on the wall depicting a can of Campbell's soup. Is he a rural farmer with a pickup truck in the driveway, unfamiliar with fashionable dress and unlikely to be reading reviews in the *New York Times*? Or is he a tweedy professor finely tuned to the trends of the day and likely to be writing reviews in the *New York Times*? He could be either, but the second description is likely to be the more accurate of the two. In a time of cultural confusion, nothing should surprise us.

A significant number of cultural commentators are oblivious to this problem, but as usual, there are notable exceptions. John Simon was an early observer of the situation. In *Paradigms Lost*[54] he wrote, "What creates this confusion bordering on chaos is the loss of boundaries. Intellectuals or at least potential intellectuals haunt rock concerts and body-building exhibitions, stock-car races, and porn movie houses, while hoi polloi hang out at museums and art galleries, classy restaurants, and ballet and opera houses." For Simon, the blurring of the differences between high and pop culture can be traced to "pop, camp, dropping out, turning on, various kinds of inverse snobbery," and what he terms the "ubiquitous braying, screeching, howling of rock." Simon maintained that the only way to tell the difference between those who are followers of pop culture and those who are not is through their language.

The arbiters of elite culture today profess that popularity implies inferiority, but they remain obsessed with trends and fashions. The arbiters of popular culture insist that quality engenders unpopularity and they celebrate the lowest common denominator in creativity. Books, films, and pop lyrics filled with four-letter words are inevitably defended as art. A painting consisting of a blank canvas or a sculpture created with human excrement will be the subject of graduate dissertations and critical analysis. A brilliant portrait will be dismissed as dated realistic art. Singers who can't carry a tune or articulate a recognizable lyric will be heralded as "superstars," and if they are British, probably receive a knighthood. Gifted vocalists who offer sensitive interpretations of sophisticated lyrics and well-crafted melodies may be perpetually unemployed. A piano composition in which the pianist doesn't play a single note is considered a milestone in 20th century music, while scores of music reflecting musical values that inspired us for centuries remained unperformed. How did high art and popular culture collide and produce a curious stew of cultural confusion? Let's start at the beginning.

THE ARTIST: SUPERSTAR OR PANHANDLER?

Throughout our history, Americans have always been ambivalent about the importance of the arts in society. While individual musicians, artists, and actors have been given the status of celebrities, many people often regard the arts as non- essential to our daily lives.

Plato advocated training in music for the ancient Greeks. He regarded the study of rhythm and harmony as essential to human development. For centuries, musicians were regarded as no better than servants, expected to serve the whims and caprices of patrons throughout their lives. Even such figures as Haydn and Mozart were relegated to the status of servants in the royal courts of 18th century Europe. Beethoven, as a belligerent, bellicose genius, found such treatment offensive. When instructed to use the servant's entrance to a palace where he was supposed to play, Beethoven barked at the startled doorman, "If I am good enough to play for your master, I am good enough to enter by the same door." Were the arts essential to elevate the culture of a large population or were they a luxury for the few? This question has been debated throughout the ages.

This ambivalence has been present since the earliest days of the United States. Francis Hopkinson, a signer of the Declaration of Independence, was also one of America's first composers. Thomas Jefferson, the Declaration's principal author, played the violin and was an avid collector of musical instruments. But outside of church, performing musicians in America had no more respectability than their European counterparts. Actors, opera singers, and dancers were regarded as even worse than musicians. In colonial times, theatrical troupes were banned in Boston and Philadelphia. One New York audience rioted when it became convinced that an itinerant troupe of actors was nothing more than an ensemble of pickpockets, thieves, and scoundrels hiding under theatrical make-up.

Nor did the academic establishment regard the arts as respectable. Twentieth-century composer Jack Beeson wrote, "A thousand years ago, more *and* less, music, together with its then-related subjects astronomy, arithmetic, and geometry, formed the quadrivium, that part of the medieval curriculum that led to the Master of Arts. Music has long since had no such honorable place in universities, and in the American university had no place at all until well into the nineteenth century."

The journey of music into the groves of academe was anything but harmonious. When Lowell Mason, the father of public school music instruction in the U.S., tried to persuade the Boston school board to include music classes in its curriculum, he met intense resistance. In 1837, after years of struggle, Mason finally was accepted as a teacher in the Boston public schools, after agreeing to serve without salary. In 1870, New England composer John Knowles Paine persuaded the new President of Harvard, Charles W. Eliot, to establish a music department and to grant college credits for courses in music history. Paine did not exactly receive a warm welcome from faculty colleagues. For good measure, Paine's critics also insisted that, since music was not academically respectable, he should not be paid for his services. However, three years later, Paine was put on salary and he spent three decades training future generations of composers and professors at Harvard. It is ironic that throughout history there are those who always find a way for good musicians not to be paid, while today the most unbelievably incompetent musicians are richer than King Midas. In the years following Paine's appointment at Harvard, the prevailing view of music in academia was that the history of music could be mildly respectable. Its performance, however, remained highly suspect.

Academicians also fostered an attitude that Americans could only be accomplished in the arts if they emulated their cultural superiors, Europeans, particularly those with training in Germany. Consequently, the overall view of music in the schools was condescending and patronizing at best. Academicians of the day believed that music or art teachers should be paid as little as possible because their disciplines were simply not as legitimate as mathematics, history, or literature. When the arts were allowed a small level of academic respectability, they needed to be judged by European standards. Local influences indigenous to the United States had to be avoided at all costs.

Critics and historians promulgated the notion that superior art was "serious" and inferior art was "popular." However, this idea was flawed from the beginning. In Europe, for instance, composers of operas wanted to appeal to the largest possible audiences. Italians in every walk of life could whistle the melodies of Puccini just as Americans today can sing the words of music of the latest popular songs. A composer who announced that he wanted to write an opera that would appeal to a small group of professors and critics would have been subjected to ridicule, and likely would have seen his work unproduced. A host of composers began absorbing the influences of popular music, everything from ragtime to military marches, folksongs, and jazz. In the 1920s, American and British musical theater began to evolve as a genre featuring the sophisticated lyrics of Cole Porter, Ira Gershwin, Lorenz Hart, and Noël Coward, among others. Although popular music by definition appealed to a large audience, its creators were constantly developing their craft by elevating the level of material they offered their audiences. Not every creator of popular entertainment directed his output at the lowest common denominator of taste.

WHICH BROW ARE YOU?

In the 20th century, arguments about high art and popular culture were often related to social status. Certain types of art have been considered respectable, while others have been regarded as highly suspect. The state of the American eyebrow has fascinated several generations of culture warriors. What is the position and perspective of your brow? The answer may reveal the extent to which you may be a snob, and what kind. The British satirical magazine *Punch* used the term "middlebrow" as far back as 1925. Virginia Woolf ridiculed middlebrows in an unsent letter published posthumously in a book of essays, *The Death of the Moth*.[55] Woolf said that middlebrows read the books they were told to read, basing their decisions on a desire to appear cultured rather than because of their own taste. In contrast, Woolf saw both highbrows and lowbrows as choosing books, art, music, and general behavior according to their own likes and dislikes, not how those tastes appear to others.

In 1949, Russell Lynes, editor of *Harper's Magazine*, had some fun with Virginia Woolf's thesis. Lynes wrote an article suggesting that American culture could be divided into three categories: "highbrow," "middlebrow," and "lowbrow." For good measure, "middlebrows" could be divided into "highs" and "lows." Then *Life* magazine picked up the discussion, inviting Lynes to prepare a chart so readers could find out where their personal brows were positioned. Lynes took a satirical, tongue-in-cheek approach to the subject, having fun with the cultural pretensions of those who considered themselves sophisticates, elitists, and "highbrows." But when *Life* announced that Lynes had declared that "true prestige now belongs only to scientists, writers, critics, commentators, and thinkers of global thoughts," people took him seriously. For status seekers in the 1950s, the "Chart of the Brows" was a quick way to determine who and what were "in" and "out" on the cultural scale.

Lynes suggested that the true "highbrow" wasn't always what people expected. He wasn't just someone who'd made or inherited a lot of money. The true "highbrow" was "a shaggy sophisticate found on liberal arts faculties in college towns." Lynes' "highbrow" was "a cultural snob of the worst sort" who "cherishes obscure trends in thought and art and fights to keep them pure, noncommercial and within his own limited circle, especially out of the hands of the hated middlebrows, who he considers culturemongers." *Life* went on to explain that the "highbrow" "feels an affinity with lowbrows and even envies the uncritical enjoyment of the things they like."

According to Lynes, the "highbrow" of the 1950s liked ballet, music written by Bach or before or by Charles Ives and after, and read obscure "little magazines" devoted to avant-garde literature. "Upper middlebrows" preferred the theater, operas and symphonies, and quality books and magazines. "Lower middlebrows" watched movie musicals, enjoyed musical comedies, and read books chosen by book clubs. The lowly "lowbrows" liked westerns, listened to pop music played on jukeboxes, and read comic books. *Life* also ran a light-hearted defense of "highbrows" by Winthrop Sargeant. Sargeant described himself as taking his culture with a capital "C," a man who liked the ballet and was bored by sports. Sargeant made an interesting observation. He said, "Highbrows are apt to assume that widespread commercial success is a sure sign of inferiority." He added that "Ninety percent of the time they are right. Highbrows therefore devote themselves to fostering a type of culture that is not commercially successful. It is lucky they do. Without them this type of culture would probably not exist." Sargeant expressed clearly a view that is most fashionable today in academic circles. Popularity is considered evidence of inferiority; unpopularity is considered a manifestation of quality. However, if the creative product in question is identified with youth and progress (i.e., rock music or rap) or it proves that the academician is "with it," these concerns are cast aside.

Writers, musicians, artists, and creative people of all kinds have always been faced with a dilemma. Do you create to please yourself or your audience? If you create to please your audience, does this improve or diminish your creative output? During and following World War II, intellectuals took such questions quite seriously. Dwight Macdonald suggested that high art should be created for connoisseurs, while "lowbrow" culture was based on products created for specific communities filled with those lacking artistic taste. Macdonald took a dim view of mainstream American culture. In his influential essay, "A Theory of Mass Culture,"[56] he emerged as a champion of the avant-garde, creators who were divorced from and in opposition to the marketplace. Later, he coined the term "Masscult" for mass produced items for an unthinking, mass audience of consumers. Macdonald didn't like "middlebrows" either, accusing them of adulterating and vulgarizing high culture, which could only be defended by the avant-garde "highbrow." He dubbed the "middlebrow" culture "Midcult."

Like Macdonald, the great poet T.S. Eliot was also a champion of high art, but he called for a more cultivated audience of cultural connoisseurs, not for artists, writers, and musicians to divorce themselves from an audience and only write for themselves. However, not everyone agreed that writers and artists should be creating primarily to please themselves. The writer and humorist Anita Loos was especially dismissive of this view when she advised writers, "Don't just write for yourself, think of your reader." Times have changed. On the 100th anniversary of Macdonald's birth, James Wolcott, writing in the *New York Times*, said, "Today, he and many of his concerns could hardly seem more dead. Masscult, midcult — who cares anymore?" One element of the debate remains quite contemporary in the twenty-first century. Those who consider themselves sophisticates still equate popularity with inferiority. Those who consider themselves populists still equate unpopularity with inferiority.

Why should anyone care about this? Because we can learn something very important from a lighthearted view of the American eyebrow, raised or lowered as the case may be. A significant number of Americans cared about "culture," not because they really found the arts or literature interesting, but because it was a status symbol. Those who cared about cultural status (Russell Lynes' "middlebrows") were disliked by the elite "highbrows," who thought they were corrupting and commercializing true music, art, and literature, and by the "lowbrows," who didn't care what anyone thought of their taste and considered "highbrows" to be unrepentant snobs.

SNOBS: RIGHT SIDE UP AND UPSIDE DOWN

If any single individual typifies the problem with contemporary culture, it is the snob. Snobs come in all shapes, sizes, and attitudes. We have all met snobs during our lives. The classic image of a snob is someone who goes to a concert expecting a refined performance of obscure 18th century French art songs and is horrified when a vocalist bursts into a spirited performance of *Who Threw the Overalls in Mrs. Murphy's Chowder?* There are, however, two types of snobs that are a particular problem in the modern age. The first is an intellectual snob who is utterly dazzled by his own intelligence and erudition, often without possessing very much of either. The second, usually ignored in discussions about snobbery, is the "inverse, upside down" snob. This is the individual who thinks of himself as ordinary and bitterly resents anyone who isn't. The two types of snobs have a lot in common, although they would be horrified and surprised to realize that fact.

The word "snob" has been with us for a long time, but it was popularized by the 19th century British writer, William Makepeace Thackeray, in *The Book of Snobs*.[57] In 1848, Thackeray wrote a series of satirical sketches that were published in *Punch*, the popular magazine of English humor. Thackeray described the snob as someone who "meanly admires mean things"; but he also characterized as snobs those who "boast of their wealth or are ashamed of their poverty and blush for the calling."

The typical snob considers himself superior to everyone else for a variety of reasons. He may think he has more distinguished ancestors, is better looking, has more money, or is simply smarter than everyone else. Russell Lynes was quite correct when he said, "The true snob never rests; there is always a higher goal to attain, and there are, by the same token, always more and more people to look down upon." Intellectual snobs abound on college campuses and in a literary and artistic milieu. Intellectual snobs may be professors, but they may also be college students, convinced of their superiority to everyone else by virtue of admission to a prestigious school. Brander Matthews described the academic snob as someone educated beyond his intelligence. They are frequently found in the news and entertainment media. Dan Rather once characterized an intellectual snob as "someone who hears the *William Tell Overture* and doesn't think of *The Lone Ranger*." (Rossini's very Italian overture became the musical theme for the heroic character of the iconic radio western and the countless television shows, films, comic books, and elements of popular culture it inspired.) This is not entirely accurate, since it is possible to know Rossini's opera backwards and forwards and still be reminded of *The Lone Ranger* the minute the music starts playing. For some devotees of classical music, Rossini's music can immediately conjure images of the masked Texas Ranger pursuing villains in the old American west. The true intellectual snob may never have heard of *The Lone Ranger* in the first place. Yet the same intellectual snob who looks puzzled or outraged when people link the *William Tell Overture* to *The Lone Ranger* is likely familiar with Minnie, owner of the Polka Saloon, Dick Johnson, secretly the bandit Ramerez, and Sheriff Jack Rance, all residents of a Gold Rush mining camp in California. They are all characters in Puccini's opera *La Fanciulla del West* (*The Girl of the Golden West*). In this opera, Puccini's very romantic Italian arias are improbably sung by characters that might seem more at home in a movie starring John Wayne. Is this combination of great Italian music and the folklore of the Wild West any more incongruous than Rossini's very Italian overture being inexorably linked to *The Lone Ranger*?

People can be snobs about all kinds of subjects. In Boston, people are more apt to talk about their ancestors, in New York, about their wealth, in Washington, DC, about their political power, and in Los Angeles, about the size of their homes and the brands of their cars. Food snobs may insist that it is pointless to compare Kobe beef from Japan to beef from Argentina, let alone from Kansas City. Film snobs may be convinced that the only good films come from anywhere outside the United States, and are only artistically valid if they are shown with subtitles and leave the audience puzzled as to the meaning of the film after two hours of confusion. Nevertheless, snobs are often incredibly insecure. Their snobbery and sense of superiority is reinforced by the assurances of others who also consider themselves superior. Rudyard Kipling once described this attitude as thinking that "everyone like us are 'We' and everyone else is 'They.'"

No one played a snob in the movies better than George Sanders, who won an Oscar for his performance as the acerbic and cynical Addison DeWitt in the film *All About Eve*. But Sanders expressed the credo of the snob best in another film, *That Certain Feeling*, opposite Bob Hope. Hope and Sanders are rivals for the attentions of "Dunreith Henry," a character portrayed by Eva Marie Saint. Sanders is shocked to learn that Dunreith, his chic, sophisticated fiancée, seemingly so comfortable in Manhattan society, isn't really from New York, but is actually Ethel Jankowski, "plain, proud, Polish, and Port Huron." Sanders responds incredulously, in a voice overflowing with hauteur, "Port Huron, Michigan? *Nobody* comes from Port Huron." This attitude doesn't just occur on screen. Off screen, in real life, entertainment industry executives refer to territory between the New York and Hollywood coasts as "fly-over" country. The world of cultural and intellectual snobs is filled with people who really do think that nobody comes from Port Huron.

The world of self-proclaimed intellectuals is full of people like the character played by George Sanders. They are convinced that intelligence and sophistication belong only to them and to their friends. In fact, they are utterly provincial in their belief that nothing of consequence happens outside their own neighborhood. Sometimes the neighborhood is Manhattan, or Hollywood or a major college campus. When confronted with anything that seems out of fashion or socially maladroit, they respond (in the words of P.G. Wodehouse) with "a look of furtive shame, the shifty hangdog look which announces that an Englishman is about to speak French." Snobs like to congregate together, to share knowing smiles that they are collectively following the latest fashions. But the problem is always the same. Louis Kronenberger was quite correct when he said, "True individualists tend to be quite unobservant; it is the snob, the would-be-sophisticate, the frightened conformist, who keeps a fascinated or worried eye on what is in the wind."

We must be aware of the psychology of the snob to understand why so much incredibly bad music, art, books, plays, and films are welcomed with open arms by people who consider themselves cultured. Paul Johnson, the British historian, writes that a novelist has "achieved aesthetic dominance when those who cannot understand what he is doing or why he is doing it are inclined to apologize for their own lack of comprehension rather than blame his failure to convey his meaning." Dr. Thomas Sowell, in his intriguing and provocative book, *Intellectuals and Society*[58] has declared, "Somewhat related to the undermining of the idea of objective truth has been the undermining of standards in various fields, including music, art, and literature." Sowell concludes, "The same inevitably self-serving result has likewise been achieved by painters, sculptors, poets, and musical composers, among others, many of whom draw financial support from taxpayers whom they have no need to please, nor even to make their work comprehensible to them." In some cases, the "artistic" products of these subsidized artists are clearly intended to mock, shock, or insult the public, and may even be questionable as art. But, as the great Oklahoma humorist Will Rogers said long ago, "When you ain't nothing else, you can claim to be an artist, and nobody can prove you ain't."

Snobbery is unfashionable in egalitarian America. John Simon wrote, "There is no creature more detested anywhere—unless it be the elitist or the intellectual—than the snob, who cannot even enjoy the semi-favorable publicity accorded bank robbers, necrophiliacs, and starters of forest fires." As the creators of classical music and art, serious books, films, and plays became increasingly elitist, their retreat from a relationship with real people benefited another group of people who don't think of themselves as snobs at all. The "inverse" or "upside down snob" doesn't receive the public attention of his elitist counterpart. But inverse snobs permeate and often direct our popular culture, and they are, in their own way, just as narrow and closed-minded as their "highbrow" counterparts. The "inverse snob" resents anything and anyone who believes in traditional values or standards, especially in the arts. Inverse snobs pride themselves on appreciating the culture "of the streets." They are quick to dismiss the past and celebrate the present, for no reason other than their assumption that new is automatically better than old.

Several important developments provided inverse snobs with energy and power, and ultimately, control over America's popular culture. The first of these developments was initially benign and provided an opportunity unmatched in the history of western civilization: the development of mass communications media. Inventions like the telephone, the radio, the television set, the motion picture camera, and more recently, the personal computer and access to the Internet, have revolutionized the world in which we live. Mass media changed the nature of the marketplace and the identity of the consumers of our culture. Popular culture is defined by the mass media, because the media provide access to the marketplace. Changes in technology offered an opportunity for the best of our past and present culture to reach a large audience, and the danger that such access could be abused.

With the dawn of the 21st century, John Simon's view of snobbery as unfashionable in America has been challenged. The pandemic beginning in 2020 indicated a new and disturbing trend in American society. Like all social and cultural trends found the U.S., this advent of a two-tier society can be found in other countries that were always far more class conscious than the United States. James Pinkerton identified this development with a series of questions. Asked Pinkerton, "Which side of the velvet rope are you on? Are you one of the cool kids? Were you born on the right side of the tracks? Did your ancestors come over on the Mayflower? Are you on the Forbes 400 list of the richest Americans? And now another question to test your social standing: *Do you have a high enough status so that you don't have to wear a face mask?*"

Pinkerton goes on to consider the mandates requiring the wearing of masks in the midst of a serious public health crisis, the spread of Covid-19. Beginning in 2020 and throughout 2021, there were numerous episodes in which celebrities or members of social elites went maskless at events at which others (including "servants") were required to wear masks. Discussing the 2020 Emmy Awards, Pinkerton observes, "The Hollywood glitterati, performers, and guests did not wear masks, while the help *did*." Onlookers were treated to a similar scene at New York's posh Metropolitan Museum of Art Gala. Masked waiters and waitresses served drinks and hors d'ouevres to the rich and famous who paid $35,000 a ticket to attend presumably *sans* mask.

While corporations, government agencies, and academic institutions enforced mandates requiring the wearing of masks at all times on employees, students, and ordinary people, these rules did not seem to apply to government officials, those politically well-connected, and the usual corps of bi-coastal celebrities, especially those from Manhattan, Hollywood, and Silicon Valley. We should be aware that we are not considering the validity of mask mandates or the efficacy of wearing masks. But it should be clear that a virus, bacteria, or germs are not respecters of persons. A virus doesn't know if a person it infects is eating truffles and caviar or serving them.

Clearly, if there is a reason for everyone to be masked all the time, then the elite attendees at these events should have been masked too; if there isn't a reason for everyone to be masked all the time, then those waiting hand and foot upon the elites should have been permitted to do their jobs without being masked. The image of masked helpers kneeling while fixing the long train of a gowned celebrity at the Met Gala doesn't exactly suggest an egalitarian society. Neither does the image of high-powered politicians partying in tony nightclubs or dining in the world's most expensive restaurants without masks while college students in their states are forbidden to even eat indoors, avoid talking to others, and wear masks at all times.

Status symbols are as old as time immemorial. But the reasons for status change. While rulers (unelected or elected depending on the period of history) and the very rich have always ignored the rules and diktats they oppose on others, a new and curious group has emerged as an essential component of today's elites: celebrities. These are individuals who may be famous for a reason or none at all; but in either case, they are made famous by the media, both the old and traditional media and the new social media. In either case, a two-tiered society is undesirable and the establishment of such tiers usually sows the seeds of its own destruction.

THE FIRST GREAT CHANGE: THE MEDIA TAKE CHARGE

Whenever there is a vacuum, someone always steps in to fill it. In the case of an artistic vacuum, that "someone" turned out to be the television set. Joined by its ubiquitous cousin, the computer, television provides easy access to thousands of musical and visual images, all the products of pop culture. The entertainment industry has been quick to provide musical and artistic products that can be easily understood. They are not limited by the tastes of an elite critical movement. Hence, while a small artistic elite presided over the decline and disappearance of accessible art and music, pop culture thrived. One must be tempted to wonder what might have happened to music and art if the advocates of "the painted word" and their musical counterpart hadn't triumphed. Today there is a reaction to the dominance of artistic theories. The revival and new recognition of realistic art is a positive step. Composers of serious intent have also started to write music in styles, which suggest that accessibility to an audience is not an automatic disqualification of value. Nor is a verbal explanation of these works necessary for an audience to enjoy them, as the audience for classical music and legitimate art has declined. If there is a revival of artistic realism and music reflecting a new lyricism, will there be an audience for it?

There was a time when broadcast media were not completely hostile to good music or drama. Even the mass media—radio and television—which by definition were directed at a large public audience, offered programs of culture and intellect. While radio and television networks were in business to make a profit, they managed to broadcast programs that introduced outstanding musicians to a mass audience. While today there are a number of public broadcasting stations and cable channels featuring classical music or jazz, these outlets are designed to attract much smaller, niche audiences. Broadcast historians and critics regard the 1930s and '40s as the "golden age of radio." During this period, it was possible to hear a virtual cornucopia of concert music on the air. In

1928, *The Voice of Firestone* became the first commercial radio program to blend classical and light classical music successfully. The program became a national favorite for audiences every Monday night. In 1942, conductor Howard Barlow began a long association with the show. He recalled that at the height of its popularity, over a fifth of the total radio audience listened to the show regularly; over a third listened occasionally. In 1949, *The Voice of Firestone* also began airing on the new medium of television, the first program to be broadcast simultaneously on radio and TV.

In 1931, the Metropolitan Opera decided to permit its performances to be broadcast on radio. Sponsored by Texaco and hosted by Milton Cross, a former singer with a deep, resonant voice, the programs are still airing today, although Texaco terminated its sponsorship in 2004, after sixty-three years of support. (Cross's voice was described by radio historian Gerald Nachman as a "burnished announcer-profundo sound.") He hosted over 800 broadcasts during his 43-year career with NBC. In the 1930s and 1940s, radio audiences could actually hear symphony concerts on network broadcasts. In 1937, the legendary Arturo Toscanini came to the airwaves as conductor of an orchestra designed especially for him, the NBC Symphony. He led it with distinction for seventeen years. Yehudi Menuhin was a celebrated child prodigy and violin virtuoso of the time. He recalled the impact of concerts led by the indomitable Toscanini. He said, "In those days, more cultivated days, the New York Philharmonic was broadcast every Sunday, throughout the nation, Toscanini conducting. There was no television in those days. That was the great cultural event that fashioned the musical audiences of that time. The whole of the United States. I remember listening to a broadcast of his with my father somewhere on tour in Colorado. We were in a car, and that unmistakable Toscanini sound was on. It had natural pace, precision, incision, everything was as sharply defined as you could imagine. That was his greatness."

Rival network CBS broadcast performances led by Toscanini's main rivals, Serge Koussevitzky, who conducted the Boston

Symphony, and Leopold Stokowski, who directed the Philadelphia Orchestra. CBS also had its own symphony orchestra. Bernard Herrmann is best remembered by the public as the legendary film composer who scored *Citizen Kane* and many of the best films of Alfred Hitchcock. However, Herrmann was also a renowned symphony conductor; in 1935, he persuaded CBS boss William Paley to give him free reign to introduce an eclectic variety of concert music to his audience. (Herrmann seized the opportunity to present new works that otherwise might have waited years for exposure to a large audience. He didn't believe in pandering to the public or to CBS executives. Herrmann told Paley, "You think everyone is as ignorant of music as you are.") Herrmann launched the show, *Exploring Music*. For fifteen years, Herrmann led the orchestra through nationally broadcast performances of works ranging from compositions by unfamiliar Baroque and romantic composers to the latest contemporary pieces. Herrmann was an Anglophile and introduced many British composers to American audiences. In 1943, he began welcoming guest conductors and soloists to his show, *Invitation to Music*. The program featured such eminent guests as composers, Béla Bartók, Igor Stravinsky, Heitor Villa-Lobos, Darius Milhaud, Erich Wolfgang Korngold, and Paul Hindemith, soloists Wanda Landowska, Lotte Lehmann, Claudio Arrau, and Gregor Piatigorsky, and conductor Sir Thomas Beecham. Other radio programs featuring the classics included *The Bell Telephone Hour* and *The Railroad Hour*.

Former Interior Secretary Stewart Udall recalled the 1930s in a letter to his grandchildren:

> *Optimism had a brief surge in the 1930s with the advent of radio and talking pictures. Radio had a positive influence on national culture. It gave a president the power to tell the country what he was trying to accomplish. It also enabled families to sit in a circle to hear news reports—and be entertained. It was a welcome advance because it used so little electricity that it was essentially free in a society that was struggling to make ends meet. Movies, likewise, had a positive impact on culture. Like radio, Hollywood's stunning*

> *visuals did not make a dent in the depressed economy, but their appeal was educational and proffered solace. Going to a movie, too, was usually a family activity. Life values taught, say, by a Spencer Tracy, a Katherine Hepburn, or a Bette Davis, resonated with meaning. Whether one liked comedies (Chaplin, W.C. Fields, etc.), fantasies ("The Wizard of Oz"), nostalgia for "the good old days" (Thornton Wilder's "Our Town"), or social tragedies ("The Grapes of Wrath"), filmgoers went home feeling that tenacious individuals could make a difference. Besides, the admission fee was minimal. The first film that came to my hometown, in 1934, was "Small Town Girl," with Janet Gaynor. A ticket cost just 25 cents. Those technologies made families more cohesive and created a "we're all in this together" spirit that encouraged positive thinking at a time when there was no national "safety net." Governments only got involved, in those days, if there was an epidemic or a local disaster.*[59]

Original plays and adaptations of classics were also broadcast over the networks, highlighting the creative talents of such figures as Orson Welles and Norman Corwin. Corwin's writing elevated radio drama to an art form that continues today, but only for selective audiences. In radio's golden age, such dramas were enjoyed by millions. In the early days of television, this tradition continued with dramatic series such as *Playhouse 90.* While television hardly welcomed opera, ballet, or symphony orchestras, in its early days the box in everyone's living room did provide unique avenues for performers. *The Voice of Firestone* and *The Bell Telephone Hour* both successfully made the transition from radio to TV. In 1952, the Ford Foundation underwrote its first television series, *Omnibus*, and then offered it to commercial advertisers. *Omnibus*, hosted by Alistair Cooke, ran for seven years, carried at various times by CBS, ABC, and NBC. The series presented an impressive array of operas, musicals, plays (by Shakespeare, Shaw, and Chekhov), and documentaries. In 1953, Orson Welles, radio's leading dramatic star (and the creator of the legendary film, *Citizen Kane*), made his dramatic debut on *Omnibus*. The following year, conductor Leonard Bernstein was given an opportunity to explain *Beethoven's Fifth Symphony* to an audience. Bernstein used some of Beethoven's nearly illegible sketches to demonstrate how many revisions the composer had made before arriving at his "perfect" result. Bernstein was such a success that he began a whole series of such broadcasts and eventually also launched a series of Young People's Concerts designed to introduce classical music to children.

Even comedy in the early days of television could attract an audience that was familiar with classical music, Broadway shows, films, and classic books. One of the most popular television programs of the 1950s, *Your Show of Shows*, starred Sid Caesar and Imogene Coca. The program featured incredibly funny parodies of movies and even operas, brilliantly executed by Caesar and Coca. After several years, Caesar had his own program called *Caesar's Hour*. His new program featured the comedic talents of Caesar opposite Nanette Fabray. *Caesar's Hour* continued the tradition of hilarious parodies of well-known films, plays, and operas. (The classical music parodies were skillfully composed and arranged by concert pianist Earl Wild.) The writers assumed that the audience would be familiar enough with the original material so that it would understand what was being satirized. Caesar and an ensemble of talented performers and writers were not addressing their satires to an audience of college professors. A live audience spontaneously and constantly laughed at their comedic antics. In later years, television would depend on "laugh tracks," recorded sounds of audiences laughing, to persuade living room audiences that shows were supposed to be funny. Caesar and Coca needed no "canned laughter" to produce real laughter in their audiences, in the theater studio where they performed or at home.

Larry Gelbart, known as the creator of *M*A*S*H**, one of the most successful television series, began his career as one of the team of writers working on Caesar's television shows. At a panel of writers, many years later, Gelbart observed that the proliferation of television sets resulted in the decline of opportunities for such writing. A mass audience meant that writers would be required to appeal to the lowest common denominator within that audience. Viewers unfamiliar with books, movies, and operas couldn't be expected to appreciate parodies of those works. Imagine how this problem has been exacerbated over the years by the cultural revolution of the 1960s and its gradual absorption into the mainstream of our culture.

Television programs like *Omnibus* always had to struggle in competition with situation comedies and sports events. But it was the advent of rock music that made it least likely for classical performers (and accomplished jazz musicians) to have an outlet on television. Soprano Roberta Peters celebrated the fiftieth anniversary of her Metropolitan Opera Debut in 2000; she recalled that she was able to make sixty-five appearances singing opera on *The Ed Sullivan Show,* a variety program watched by huge audiences in the 1950s and '60s. It is unthinkable today to imagine an operatic soprano, even one of the caliber of Roberta Peters, getting this type of television exposure on a network in prime time. *The Ed Sullivan Show* eventually became a leading launching pad for rock groups and network television turned away from such classical programs. Howard Barlow, longtime conductor of *The Voice of Firestone,* had no reservations about expressing his view of the changes taking place in music. Barlow saw the value in music and the message it delivered to its audience. He said, "Music, good music, is the vitamin of the soul. It can be a solace, a refuge, a tranquilizer. It contains joy, even rapture—it reflects sorrow, even pain. It services a universal need, in a universal language." Barlow once expressed his enthusiasm for all good music, but added, "I do not like cheap, vapid lyrics." One can only guess what Barlow's reaction would be to the language (and messages) contained in much of today's rock and rap music.

It is true that public broadcasting does present outstanding programs featuring operas, symphonies, ballets, musicals, and jazz concerts. But in the golden age of radio and television broadcasting, there were only three dominant networks. These networks were the primary source of entertainment for most listeners and viewers. Today, a television viewer is faced with an apparently infinite number of choices, including hundreds of cable channels and the Internet. There is far less likelihood that such programs will reach a mass audience.

Radio and television programs that featured good music were useful in another way. They opened the doors for many performers who toured the country. Audiences that listened to them on radio or saw them on television would be eager to attend a concert and see them in person. A network executive who suggested inviting opera singers to appear on a prime time television broadcast would likely find himself looking for work elsewhere. A television producer who proposed broadcasting a concert (other than a rock concert) on a commercial network's prime time schedule would find herself collecting unemployment benefits. The proliferation of outstanding musical performers in broadcasting sets a standard by which others may be judged. The problem, of course, is that there are those who insist that there are no objective standards by which performers may be judged.

Changes in technology offered an opportunity for the best of our past and present culture to reach a large audience, and the danger that such access could be abused. But then, the second key development leading to our current cultural confusion was no such mixed blessing. Contemporary society has devolved from the cultural revolution of the 1960s, in which many of our traditional values, attitudes, and standards were turned upside down. The '60s gave us the "youth cult" in which many in our society assumed that "young" or "new" is by definition better than old, that change always implies progress, and youth is not a time of life but a virtue to be pursued at all costs by persons of all ages. Economic purchasing power suddenly passed to buyers barely out of their teens. The coveted "youth demographic" became the defining standard of success in marketing, advertising, and promotion. The key question in the production of films, television programs, and all mass media became, "Will it sell to a younger and younger audience?"

THE SECOND GREAT CHANGE: THE TRIUMPH OF THE TALENTLESS

The 1960s brought a revolution in music. The advent of rock music sent pop music promoters and television producers in a mad dash toward the lowest common denominator. Composers unwilling to direct their creative efforts to teenage audiences were simply declared unemployable. Some experienced musicians protested and found themselves out of work, their careers over. Others declared themselves advocates of "the new sound" and continued to work. The days of elegant, sophisticated lyrics were gone, replaced by the frequently violent, obscene words of rock and rap. Radio and television, which had once given us programs capable of elevating and educating an audience, instead offered the vulgarians Howard Stern and Jerry Springer. Today, pop culture has a simple rule: "it's all about the money," and there are no rules or restrictions. Most figures in the film industry and tabloid television pontificate about "pushing the envelope" and "carrying things to the next level." When people speak of "pushing the envelope," they talk about challenging rules and breaking barriers. Inevitably, this is assumed to be a positive development, synonymous with progress and desirable change. However people who boast about pushing the envelope are assuming that the rules they challenge are bad and that the barriers they break should be shattered. Unfortunately, this is not always the case; in fact, quite the opposite may be true.

There are occasional bursts of honesty. Sally Jessy Raphael was one of Jerry Springer's principal rivals, hosting her own highly rated television talk show. As Springer and his competitor Maury Povich began dealing with increasingly bizarre and abnormal people and topics on their shows, Raphael followed suit. Subsequently, her show was cancelled. In a rare example of complete honesty in the entertainment industry, Raphael says she is now ashamed of her program and admits that she did it for the money. She also offers her opinion that despite protestations, Springer, whom she terms "very bright," had the same motive. Producers of tabloid and reality television have turned dysfunctional families, people dependent on alcohol and drugs, foul-mouthed ignoramuses, and potentially violent misfits into entertainment. People tune in to see a train wreck and they are seldom disappointed. Such programs not only debase their subjects and guests, who imagine exposure through the media will make them famous, they also debase the viewer, because they drive down the definition of our standards. Even the most staid and conservative among us cannot help but lose our capacity to be shocked. If everything is shocking, then nothing is shocking. Nevertheless, every producer and promoter, every huckster and charlatan pursuing a fast dollar, markets his wares with a declaration that he is "pushing the envelope."

Steve Allen was correct to identify "pushing the envelope" as one of today's worst clichés in *Vulgarians at the Gate*.[35] Allen wrote, "Our modern society is the most cliché-ridden in history. The problem with clichés is not that they so quickly become tiresome, but they eventually become used as substitutes for thought. A good example of recent vintage is 'pushing the envelope.' In the context of the present problem, the most unfortunate thing about the phrase is that it seems invariably to apply to going beyond the boundaries imposed by simple common sense and even tolerant good taste. The harm is compounded by the fact that the language of social critics and others who comment upon the culture of the moment, pushing the envelope seems never to involve a clear reference to reprehensible and sometimes truly revolting conduct or language." Allen bravely criticized the lack of ethical or moral comment by those who should be outraged by such behavior.

SAVANTS AND HUCKSTERS

Perhaps the most bizarre trend in our culture has been a union between many of the self-proclaimed arbiters of high art and the hard-driving hucksters of pop culture. Both groups benefit from this odd alliance. The museums and theaters that present the works of charlatans can portray themselves as "cutting edge" and appeal to the larger audience of pop culture. The authors who write books in praise of mountebanks and poseurs can be recognized as "in" and therefore insure themselves that their efforts won't be "out." The universities offering seminars in the deep meaning of rock and rap can be assured that their music departments will thrive in the new marketplace. They see themselves as "Savants," those who have deep insight into cultural trends. ("Savant" is derived from the French word "savoir, meaning, "to know.") But what do these self-styled savants really know? The creators and promoters of the worst of our pop culture, meanwhile, can achieve academic, social, and cultural respectability, all the while making a mint of money. Neglected are the true artists working in both classical and popular media who are rejected by the pop promoters as non-commercial, and the pseudo-intellectuals as old fashioned.

None of this would have surprised Jonathan Swift, whose book, *Gulliver's Travels*,[60] is a classic satire that is often mistakenly imagined to be a book for children. Swift, in fact, savagely turned his pen to portray the folly associated with human behavior in general and the British government in particular. Many people who haven't read *Gulliver* are familiar with only the first two books, depicting Lemuel Gulliver's encounter with the tiny people of Lilliput and the giants of Brobdingnang. But there are additional travels and in the fourth book, Gulliver finds himself torn between crude, uncouth creatures who look like humans, the Yahoos, and a group of wise and cultured beings who look like horses, the Houyhnhnms. In Swift's version, Gulliver returns home, but his life has been changed forever by his dialogues and encounters with the rational horses. In 1969, satirist Matthew Hodgart produced a satire, *A New Voyage to the Country of the Houyhnhnms*,[61] purportedly from a long, lost Swiftian manuscript in Dublin, but actually penned with tongue-in-cheek by the skillful Mr. Hodgart. On the new voyage, Gulliver has returned to the land of the Houyhnhnms to find severe changes. The once cultured horses are now emulating the worst elements of the human Yahoos. Suddenly, the Houyhnhnms have discovered qualities in the Yahoos never before recognized, including artistic abilities to produce "little Piles of Earth" and "Dung-smeared Slates" that are declared great works of art. Obscenities are cheered and applauded by the crowd. Hodgart was highly perceptive, since works made of human excrement have received honored places in modern museums, and so-called rock stars and rap stars have been idolized and lionized for their puerile lyrics filled with four letter words. The point of this new voyage, of course, is that when the most cultured and literate members of a society begin applauding and honoring the least cultured and most illiterate, that society is in decline. Today, sadly, the academic and critical establishment is filled with cultural arbiters who would feel right at home as the Yahoos oust the Houyhnhnms, unfortunately with their own aid and comfort. The merger of the worst elements of pseudo-artistic and pop culture derives from a counterculture that is all "counter" and no "culture." The advocates of the 1960s counterculture are no longer rioting in the streets or tearing down barriers. They have joined the faculty, have been elected to office, taken charge of influential publications, and presided over the abandonment and rejection of the best our culture has to offer.

In 1999, the Pulitzer Prize committee that had failed to award the prize to Duke Ellington gave him a posthumous citation on the occasion of his centennial year. The committee has also announced that it would now consider composers of jazz, film scores, and musical theater for the prize. Composer Gunther Schuller called this development a "welcome sea change," opening the prize to differences in styles, not differences in quality. However, composer John Harbison termed the changes "a horrible development," while composer Lewis Spratlan said, "The Pulitzer is one of the very few prizes that award artistic distinction in front-edge, risk-taking music. To dilute this objective by inviting the likes of musicals and movie scores, no matter how excellent, is to undermine the distinctiveness and capability for artistic advancement." The highbrows and lowbrows, the advocates of high art and popular culture, the self-proclaimed champions of cultural democracy and snobs (both right side up and upside down) are all ready to do battle. Thus, the debate goes on. But in the 21st century, does anyone care? Or are we preoccupied with the latest celebrity scandals on television?

The British historian Arnold J. Toynbee produced a twelve volume opus, *A Study of History*, in the 1930s. Toynbee maintained that civilizations would grow and prosper when led by "creative minorities," confident leaders noted for their style and virtue. They would be followed in their sense of purpose by an "uncreative minority." Toynbee maintained that with the passage of time, the "creative minority" would become no longer creative, simply dominant. The same groups of people would be in charge, but they would abandon their civic responsibilities and principles by accepting vulgarization of language, manners, and the arts.

Toynbee's description (and that of Charles Murray who invokes Toynbee's arguments) are a perfect analysis of what has happened to academicians, critics, and self-styled intellectuals. Like the Emperor Nero, who allegedly fiddled while Rome burned, these modern-day Neros are listening to post-1960s rock tunes while our culture is burning before our eyes. William Tucker, writing in *The American Spectator,* provides an updated view of today's crisis in similar terms when he writes, "Perhaps the most notable trend in the arts over the last twenty years has been the rise of pointless vulgarity. We haven't quite gotten to the point of full frontal nudity or open sexual intercourse on daytime television yet, but we're getting awfully close. And if and when it happens, you can be sure there will arise a chorus from the liberal intelligentsia saying it's just 'freedom of speech' and anyone who is opposed to it is either 'prudish' at one extreme or 'fascist' at the other. I've heard things chanted on rap radio stations that I would be embarrassed to read on bathroom walls. And this is music that can be recited line-for-line by 13-year-olds."

In fact, there are observers who can be described as politically or culturally liberal, but their perspectives nearly always date back to a time before the countercultural revolution of the 1960s and 1970s. The post-1960s radicals who led the charge to jettison our cultural legacy are now college presidents, deans, and department chairmen. They are designing our curricula. They and their own legatees are gleefully setting the standards for our decline. They are also every bit as hidebound and inflexible as the "establishment" they imagined to be making a revolution necessary. In fact, it is the exponent of traditional values, standards, and culture that is the dissenter today, not the professional non-conformist who is, in fact, conforming blindly to the cheering mobs hastening our devolution and decline.

No one has summed up the problem better than Russell Kirk in his book, *America's British Culture.* Kirk asked quite rightly, "What happens to a talented musicologist, say, when ninety-five percent of the rising generation have been subjected in their formative years to acid rock, and have paid no attention whatsoever to the music elevation and order? What happens to the class of professors of literature, say, when the accustomed reading of most of their male students has been *Playboy* and *Penthouse*?" But Kirk goes further, with an exceptionally astute observation about the way in which those who should be the custodians and conservationists of our culture have instead become the enablers of its destroyers. He wrote, "A received culture may be betrayed by the talented individual or culturally schooled class of men and women, quite as fatally as by the crowd. A musicologist who casts aside the great composers of the eighteenth and nineteenth centuries out of his enthusiasm for electronic dissonance; a professor of humane letters who lectures obsessively on the perverse in literature--such persons are false to their duty of holding certain norms of culture." Kirk described the willing pupils of such persons as "hungry sheep." He concludes, "It will not suffice for us who enjoy the old received culture to seek refuge in the embrace of Common, or Popular Culture. For the Common Culture commonly decides to do tomorrow what the Uncommon Culture does today; or, worse, the Common Culture, bewildered, converts itself into the Common Counterculture."

If the assault of the vulgarians has shaken the pillars of our culture, other equally disturbing elements have also contributed to our state of confusion. We have already seen how the decline of language has engendered the rise of "the inarticulate American," badly trained in reading, spelling and writing, and ready to sneer and laugh at the elitist with big words and big ideas. Unfortunately, the elitist's big words may be meaningless and his big ideas may prove worthless. The mass media, meanwhile, compensate for our ignorance by promoting the celebrity culture in which the ignoramus is encouraged to believe he knows what is important, and unfortunately, it isn't any of the subjects we are discussing. Meanwhile, the arts have been governed and populated for too long by self-declared "savants of the avant," intellectual snobs, and eggheads. Pop culture is simultaneously dominated by hucksters, hustlers, singers who can't sing, painters who can't paint, and writers who can't write. So we are compelled to ask ourselves how we got into this situation and if anything can be done about it.

WHATEVER HAPPENED TO MUSIC?

DO YOU LIKE MODERN MUSIC? Today if you ask someone's opinion on music, he will almost invariably talk about the music heard on radio and television or downloaded off the Internet: rock, rap, and perhaps country music. There is still an audience for other types of music, but it is declining daily. Audiences at concerts of classical music are overwhelming older and classical music (except for piano lessons or attendance at a Christmas performance of *The Nutcracker)* does not play an important role in the lives of the young. Jazz maintains a devoted following, but it appeals to a selective group of followers. Composers of the scores of classic Broadway musicals and film scores, once considered icons, are gradually fading into oblivion. In the contemporary, high tech world of IPods and digital downloads, the world of music has been turned upside down.

How did this happen?

THE CRISIS IN CLASSICAL MUSIC

For many years, people spoke of "classical" and "popular" music. "Classical" was the term applied to music played by symphonies, performed by opera companies, and included in chamber music recitals. "Popular" was indiscriminately applied to almost everything else.

When scholars use the word "classical," they are talking about music written during the "classical" period, one era in music history, which included composers like Haydn and Mozart, that evolved after the late works of Beethoven, into the "romantic" period. Most 19th century composers of what we call "classical" music, including Chopin, Liszt, Verdi, Wagner, Brahms, and Tchaikovsky, actually fit into the "romantic" era. Composers themselves were never quite sure what to call their music. Some composers of symphonies and operas took to calling their work "serious music." But the world of "classical" music is full of pieces that are anything but serious. (Think of Richard Strauss's *Till Eulenspiegel* or Sergei Prokofiev's *Peter and the Wolf* for a start.) A number of composers of concert works prefer the term "art music." Unfortunately, there is an abundance of "classical" music that is anything but artistic. "Art music" represents an aspiration but not always a result. Many pieces of classical music are incredibly popular, but their composers wouldn't describe them as "popular" music; on the other hand, they wouldn't want their work to be described as "unpopular" either. Nor did jazz musicians help by occasionally referring to "classical" music as "legitimate music," unconsciously suggesting that their own music was somehow illegitimate.

During the 20th century, a revolution in styles occurred. Composers of symphonies, operas, ballets, and chamber music began abandoning or redesigning many elements of music, including melody, harmony, rhythm, and orchestration. The result was a huge schism. Those composers who moved in new and sometimes shocking directions began to lose their audience. Today, a significant portion of the audience for "classical" music dislikes much modern concert music and avoids it altogether. Those composers who didn't move along with the revolution earned the disdain and rejection of critics and academics. Their works were often dismissed or ignored. Some years ago, a music critic named Henry Pleasants created a huge controversy when he wrote a book called *The Agony of Modern Music.*[62] Pleasants attacked and ridiculed much of the music written by 20th century symphonic composers. He meticulously made the case that much modern music wasn't modern and wasn't music. Was Pleasants right?

WHERE'S THE MELODY?

Music is composed of several elements: melody, rhythm, and harmony. Melody and rhythm are easier to explain to non-musicians. Everyone loves a good melody and even the most unmusical person may like to sing his favorite tune at the top of his lungs while in the shower. Rhythm refers to the pulse of music; for the non-musician, it is the element of music that makes you want to clap your hands or snap your fingers or perhaps even dance. "Harmony" results when a group of notes are played together, and if you like the way they sound, you may consider such music "harmonious" rather than dissonant.

Until the late 19th and early 20th centuries, music was typically said to be written "in a particular key." Melodies might wander around from one key center to another, rather like a baseball player running around the bases. But the baseball player always tried to end his journey at home plate, and so did most melodies. However, gradually, composers found such notions restrictive, and began pushing the boundaries of melody and harmony. In German opera, Richard Wagner and his followers began stretching the boundaries of what composers call "tonality." In France, Claude Debussy and his followers began revolutionizing music in the manner of French impressionist painters who were depicting images through points of light.

MUSIC AS MATHEMATICS

By the 20th century, composers began exploring what music would be like without the traditionally accepted notions of melody, harmony, and rhythm. It was as if vast numbers of composers had agreed to turn their backs on the past, but disagreed violently as to where they should go in the future.

Arnold Schoenberg was an Austrian composer who decided that he had found the true path of 20th century music. Although critics dismissed his early works with ridicule, Schoenberg became one of the most influential composers of the 20th century, renowned as a teacher, and followed by several generations of disciples who regarded his theories with an almost religious devotion. His twelve-tone technique called for composers to create their own "serial" scales, never repeating one note until all others had been used. Schoenberg declared that the artist's aim to create beauty was a "delusion." In Schoenberg's new creative world, there were no true dissonances or consonances—all were relative. (The composer Miklós Rózsa described a performance in which Schoenberg visibly winced whenever he heard a consonant chord piercing the blanket of dissonance in a new piece of music.) Schoenberg's music gained a huge following in the world's colleges and universities, and among certain influential critics and historians. Schoenberg saw his music as an outgrowth of the past traditions of German and Austrian music. Young composers who became his pupils were surprised that he didn't begin by teaching his controversial approach to modern music, but through analysis of the works of composers such as Mozart and Beethoven. He once asked one of his American assistants, a brilliant pianist, to demonstrate a passage from a particular Beethoven sonata. When the assistant confessed that he had never learned the sonata in question, Schoenberg snapped, "You call yourself a pianist and you don't know all the Beethoven sonatas?"

Schoenberg never intended for his music to be disliked or unappreciated by the public at large, and once expressed hope that his melodies would be as popular as those of Tchaikovsky. Unfortunately, this did not happen. David Raksin, famous as the composer of many film scores, including *Laura*, for which he wrote one of the most popular melodies of all time, was one of many composers who studied with Schoenberg when he settled in California. Raksin admired his teacher, but he still quipped, "No one is going to publish a folio called *Twelve-Tone Tunes the Whole World Loves.*

Today, Schoenberg is regarded as an icon in universities and conservatories around the world. However, many of Schoenberg's current admirers forget that he required his students to pursue an intense study of traditional harmony and counterpoint before studying his own contemporary ideas about music. When Schoenberg moved from Europe to California, numerous composers went to study with him. Some undoubtedly did so because they wanted to learn his method; others simply wanted to pick up a few avant-garde tricks and tell people they were "pupils of Schoenberg." They were in for a shock. Schoenberg expected them to begin working on two-part counterpoint, the most traditional course of study, one pursued in the Baroque era. Schoenberg said there were still good pieces to be written in the key of C major. Nor can we doubt that many who now consider themselves followers of Schoenberg today would reject his own views on the subject. Furthermore, much of their music may be described in the words of composer Mario Castelnuovo-Tedesco: they look better on paper than they sound.

Schoenberg's two best-known pupils in Europe were Alban Berg and Anton Webern. The more radical followers of Schoenberg rejected the more conservative path of Berg and embraced the goal of "total serialism" espoused by Webern. Led by Karlheinz Stockhausen in Germany and Pierre Boulez in France, they gradually dispensed with most elements of music as we know it. They applied serial organization to every note on the page, allowing the "system" to determine not only the order of the notes, but also how long they were held, their pitch, density, rhythm, etc. Boulez, successor to Leonard Bernstein as conductor of the New York Philharmonic, declared all new music other than twelve-tone to be useless. For Boulez, the whole work of any composer who didn't accept the required ideology was "irrelevant to the needs of his epoch." He announced that after the past had been successfully rejected, "one need think only of one's self."

Not everyone subscribed to the theories advanced by Schoenberg. The Swiss conductor, Ernest Ansermet, renowned as an advocate for much new music, explained his opposition in a book, *Les fondements de la musique dans la conscience humaine*[63] (*The Fundamentals of Music in the Human Conscience*). Ansermet's research and study led him to conclude that true musical expression had to come from the classical musical harmonic vocabulary. He insisted that music should come from tones related by a single interval, not a random group of intervals, hence rejecting Schoenberg's twelve-tone technique. In effect, Ansermet was arguing that harmony and beauty in music were determined in part by the laws of acoustics, not by any theory developed by man. If you strike a note on the piano and hold down the sustaining pedal with your foot, you will actually hear a series of tones, a basic or "fundamental" tone, and a series of overtones. The American composer and conductor Joseph Wagner taught orchestration based on the musical spacing that occurs in the "overtone series." Mario Castelnuovo-Tedesco, the renowned Italian composer and teacher, taught his pupils that this "overtone series" established a natural relationship between musical tones that couldn't be altered capriciously by human taste. The result would be similar to a declaration by a chef that sugar really tasted sour rather than sweet. The overtone series is sometimes called "the chord of nature," and critics of the Schoenberg School insisted that extremely dissonant music would strike the ear as dissonant, regardless of what theory might explain otherwise.

Earl Wild was a piano virtuoso renowned for his emotionally inspiring performances that spanned much of the 20th century. He was known for his transcriptions and improvisations. Wild was also a gifted and versatile composer. He summed up a most valid reaction to much contemporary concert music. In his memoir, *A Walk on the Wild Side,*[64] he declared, "I find it boring when composers put pieces together mechanically—it's a Rubik's Cube approach to composition! How can anyone go forward musically without knowing the past?"

It is doubtful that Schoenberg, who insisted that his pupils be thoroughly grounded in the fundamentals of music, would have approved of all the theories and notions developed in his name. Music critic Robert Reilly wrote recently of the historic effect of abandoning tonality. Reilly, in his book, *Surprised by Beauty,*[65] explained, "Gutting music of tonality is like removing grapes from wine. You can go through all the motions of making wine without grapes, but there will be no wine at the end of the process. Similarly if you deliberately and systematically remove all overtone relationships from music, you can go through the process of composition, but the end product will not be comprehensible as music. This is not a change in technique; it is the replacement of art by ideology." For much of the 20th century, the academic-critical establishment rendered its musical judgments based on ideology, while many of the best composers were subjected to ridicule and neglect.

Not all musicians gravitated towards music in which every sound was organized with mathematical precision and intellectual certainty. Composers reacted to the challenge of "total serial organization" in different ways. Some, like Schoenberg's archrival,

Igor Stravinsky, opposed it bitterly. (Schoenberg and Stravinsky were once invited by Nathaniel Shilkret to join several other renowned international composers in contributing movements to a musical setting based on the Book of Genesis. The other composers, Mario Castelnuovo-Tedesco, Ernst Toch, Alexander Tansman, and Darius Milhaud, were all quite cordial. But efforts were made to keep Schoenberg and Stravinsky from showing up for the premiere rehearsal at the same time. Naturally, they arrived at exactly the same time, and stood at opposite ends of the stage, their respective disciples glaring at one another across the musical chasm.) Ironically, Stravinsky appeared to change his mind after Schoenberg's death. With the encouragement of his musical associate Robert Craft, Stravinsky began using Schoenberg's serial techniques in his own music.

Many of Stravinsky's followers espoused what they called "neo-classicism," an attempt to turn music away from emotional expression and emphasize its structural organization. Other composers rejected the Webern-Boulez-Stockhausen ideal of "total organization" as restrictive. But their alternative was even more extreme. They suggested dispensing with all organization of sounds, so that a musical work wouldn't be a "work" at all, but a free happening of unplanned sounds. The eminent American symphonic composer Roy Harris quipped, "First they abandoned melody, then harmony, then rhythm. What do they have left?"

SAVANTS OF THE AVANT

What was left in some academic and critical circles was the contribution of the "avant-garde." This term, derived from the French, literally means "advance guard," a vanguard of soldiers who would explore terrain ahead of the advancing army. In the arts, the "avant-garde" considered themselves to be ahead of the crowd, exploring new paths before anyone else discovered them. The notion of the avant-garde was popularized by a 19th century French banker and socialist, Olinde Rodrigues, in an essay, *L'artiste, le savant et l'industriel* (*The Artist, the Scientist and the Industrialist*). In the 20th century, composers learned quickly that being part of the avant-garde might bring ridicule and controversy. It would also attract attention.

Nobody proved better at attracting attention than John Cage. Cage, who invited audiences and colleagues to join him in creating musical chaos, had a flair for the theatrical. Cage used a "prepared piano" whose strings were altered by the insertion of paper clips, safety pins, clothespins, rubber wedges, pencil erasers, and screws of various shapes and sizes. He selected notes by rolling dice, created "music" through randomly played radios and tape recorders on stage, and produced his ultimate masterpiece in the musical theater of the absurd: *4:33,* a piece for solo piano in which the pianist plays nothing for four minutes and thirty-three seconds. The "music" consists of whatever sounds the audience hears during that time. The nervous coughing and laughter of the audience, the sounds of a barking dog, or an ambulance siren outside the theater were all part of this "music." In recent years, a group of composers called "minimalists" have become quite popular writing music in which small phrases and groups of notes are simply repeated over and over. Pianist and composer Earl Wild described these works as filled with boring repetitions and no melody, minimal music for minimal minds. He quipped that he would rather listen to Cage's infamously silent *4:33* than the work of the minimalists, because Cage's silence offered better melodies. Silence did not dominate *The Wolfman,* created in 1964 by composer Robert Ashley. Thom Holmes, writing in *Wire,*[66] described Ashley's work as an "avalanche of noise" so overpowering to the listener that no one ever understands how the sound is made." In fact, Ashley put his own mouth against a microphone to control the feedback and played back his own vocal sounds simultaneously with a taped composition. Avant- garde composer LaMonte Young achieved notoriety and shock value in a New York performance of the *Concert Suite* from *Dromenon* by Richard Maxfield. The composer allowed performers in the small orchestra great freedom and Young took full advantage of the opportunity. Unbeknownst to anyone but Maxfield, he stuffed his violin with matches and lighter fluid. The high point of the performance was when LaMonte Young set fire to his violin and burned it on stage. In concert music, as in modern art, the "artist" was free to do whatever he pleased, as long as his work was accompanied by an explanation rich in pseudo- intellectual hyperbole that demanded it be taken seriously. Most critics and academics were eager to comply.

Who Needs Classical Music?[67] is a provocative book by Julian Johnson. The title itself raises an important question about the issue of contemporary concert music. Johnson observes that much of this music strikes audiences as so modern that it reflects dissonance, alienation, anxiety, and the meaninglessness of modern life. He writes, "This paradox causes problems for both the lover of classical music and the listener who cares for no classical music at all. It claims a relation to the past that works both ways: something two hundred years old is related to the modern, and a contemporary work is shaped by the past. It forces us to acknowledge that we are bound up with our history and suggests that a modern culture wrestles with this acknowledgement, with trying to distinguish itself as new in relation to the old. Perhaps it is no exaggeration to suggest that the denial of the claims of classical music is a sign of a more general contemporary denial of the historical and a stubborn insistence on the one-dimensional surface of the present."

THE DISSENTERS

There were exceptions. Music critic Henry Pleasants turned the word of modern music upside down with his book, *The Agony of Modern Music*. Pleasants suggested that jazz and popular music communicated with audiences while composers of "serious" or "art" music were busy writing for each other. Pleasants suggested that much modern music was neither modern nor music. Not surprisingly, Pleasants' book was not given a warm welcome in some circles. (Mark Schubart, Dean of the Juilliard School of Music, dubbed it "scurrilous, unfair, negative, destructive, and specious.") But the battle lines were drawn. Gone were the days when Puccini was writing operas to please a large Italian public. Instead, today's composers of concert works were writing (according to theory) to please themselves. Composers or painters who did not subscribe to the theories or fashionable styles were dismissed out of hand. Those who pursued traditional ideas of melody, harmony, and rhythm paid the price in academic and critical circles as they were dubbed "old- fashioned" and "conservative." Joseph Machlis, a professor of music at Queens College of the City of New York, dismissed the compositions of Mario Castelnuovo-Tedesco, one of the most prolific and eminent composers of the 20th century, by declaring, "Their avoidance of contemporary problems has told heavily against them. The time has passed them by." Mario Castelnuovo- Tedesco was one of the most important teachers of composition in the 20th century. He was fluent in over a half-dozen languages, and wrote hundreds of compositions, including concertos for such virtuosos as Jascha Heifetz, Gregor Piatigorsky, and Andrés Segovia, as well as operas, chamber music, dozens of piano works, hundreds of songs, and enough music to require a whole volume catalogue. His works for the classical guitar alone earned him an important place in music history. Yet Machlis dismissed his life's work with a few lines because he was politically incorrect. (By the beginning of the 21st century, there were more than a hundred compact discs devoted to the music of Castelnuovo-Tedesco. But Machlis and those of similar viewpoints had their day. Composers had to address "contemporary problems" or be dismissed out of hand, regardless of how appealing their music might be to performers and listeners alike.)

In the 19th century, critics were usually conservative, insisting that the arts must reflect the academic standards of Europe. In the 20th century, an increasing number of critics demanded that the arts must reflect the revolutionary standards of Europe. Universities and conservatories adhered to the new theories about writing music, often with the zeal of political zealots. Academicians applied a type of "political correctness" to classical music. If a composer did not accept the notions of Boulez and the self-proclaimed followers of Schoenberg, his works had to be ignored for ideological reasons. Those who dissented would be dismissed by critics like the serial composer Charles Wuorinen, who wrote in 1979 that the tonal system still appeared in commercial or popular music in "atrophied or vestigial form," and occasionally in the works of "backward-looking serious composers." Wuorinen then echoed the sentiments Boulez had expressed twenty-seven years earlier, that tonality "is no longer employed by serious composers of the mainstream, having been replaced or succeeded by the twelve- tone system."

Milton Babbitt was a mathematician and composer who taught for many years at Princeton. He was a rugged individualist who followed his own creative path, writing music that was cerebral, complex, and hard for audiences to understand or appreciate. Babbitt discussed the relationship between composers and audiences in an essay titled, "The Composer as Specialist."[68] An editor at *High Fidelity* changed the title to the more provocative "Who Cares If You Listen?" Although Babbitt didn't select the title, the question was well stated. In the 20th century, many contemporary composers of concert music were more interested in their own creative theories than in audience reactions. Babbitt was suggesting that academia should become a haven for composers of music that didn't necessarily communicate with large audiences. There have been many composers writing such music. If you didn't choose to appreciate their works, they simply decided that it was your problem, not theirs. In some circles, lack of popularity became a musical virtue and an implication of quality. Unfortunately, many members of the audience for classical music have become convinced that modern composers don't care if they listen or not. Thus, when it comes to contemporary concert music, many choose not to listen.

Musicologist Walter Simmons has studied the work of composers who didn't march to the beat of the serial drummers. In *Voices in the Wilderness*,[69] he writes that musical dissenters have been dismissed as "shallow, inept, unimportant hangers-on, journeymen of limited talent or intelligence, panderers to commercial interests, or guilty of some other deficiency of character or artistry." Simmons declares, "This disparagement and suppression of tonal music amounted to a de facto blacklisting of composers who failed to conform to the approved version of music history."

This was a worldwide phenomenon. The noted American composer David Diamond spent many years in Europe. When he returned to the United States in 1965, he declared, "I lived in Italy for close to sixteen years and the entire Italian musical establishment was dominated by the advanced twelve-note avant-garde. Everywhere I submitted music it was turned down because it was considered old-fashioned." Steven Lowe, writing notes for a Seattle Symphony recording of Diamond's music, expressed it well. Lowe said, "For some thirty years following World War II, the apostles of post-Webernian serialism and its offshoots determined the course of contemporary classic music. Diamond, and other such neo-Romantic voices as Roy Harris, Samuel Barber, Howard Hanson, William Schuman, and Walter Piston, to name only American composers of that persuasion, was dismissed with an imperious wave of the academic hand and a curt 'irrelevant' from the lips or pen of the ideologically purist Pierre Boulez."

Lowe speaks with a broad brush when he classifies all these composers as "neo-Romantic." (Harris is usually described as a nationalist, Piston as a neo-classicist.) But let us not quibble. Lowe has hit the nail squarely on its musical head when he writes, "While in no way demeaning the many fine works that have come from Boulez and gifted composers who had trod the chaste path of serialism, time has proven them wrong in consigning Diamond and his gloriously unrepentant Romantics to the trash bin of music history. In music, as in life itself, there are many roads to truth, many different drums, whose rhythms attract some, and repel others. One thing is very clear: Many composers and audiences have either re-embraced the Romantic spirit or never left its enveloping warmth in the first place."

Robert R. Reilly writes eloquently in *Surprised by Beauty*[57] about the reasons so many modern composers have written incontestably ugly music and why some are seeking new paths. Reilly suggests that many composers have assumed that beauty is the opposite of truth, so to be "true," they must be sure that their works are never beautiful. Reilly writes, "Ugliness became a norm. In music, you can hear it in the wailing and screeching of a multitude of compositions that embrace the agony of the 20th century by making listeners suffer." For Reilly, it was the rejection of the spiritual dimension of music that led to confusion and only a recovery of the spiritual dimension can lead to a recovery of music. Consider the views of distinguished and until recently, neglected composers like Howard Hanson, who wrote, "The arts were put into the world for a purpose, to do good rather than harm, so that the artist has a responsibility to his fellow man to use that gift for what he thinks would be the benefit of his fellow man, which to me means giving up things that are salacious and cheap and demeaning." The eminent composer Paul Creston described music as a spiritual practice, as vital to his spiritual welfare as prayer and good deeds. Contrast these views with those of the avant-garde's Karlheinz Stockhausen, who praised the terrorist attack on September 11 as "the greatest work of art in the cosmos" and declared that "compared to that we composers are nothing." Stockhausen's remarks resulted in boycotts of his music and even his own daughter changed her name after her father's comments.

In recent times, a fascinating phenomenon has occurred. Some composers who were devoted to fashionable theories about how concert music must be written have started to have second thoughts. George Rochberg was among the leading practitioners of serial music and an exponent of theories developed by Schoenberg. After the death of his son, however, he sought a more personal and expressive approach to music, turning away from serialism and back to elements of tonality. Did the academic and musical establishment welcome Rochberg's move? Not at all. In 1972, Rochberg's *Ricordanza*, his homage to Beethoven, was performed in Darmstadt, Germany, before an audience that adhered scrupulously to all the avant-garde theories. Listeners were invited to guess the identity of the composer. Most believed it was a 19th century romantic like Brahms. When they learned it was actually by George Rochberg, they were outraged. Rochberg was considered a traitor to the cause. Rochberg, however, remained unrepentant about his own changes of style and he paved the way for other, younger composers to follow his lead.

While "serious" art appealed to a small, academic, intellectual elite, popular culture became obsessed with appealing to increasingly ignorant audiences of teenagers. Not all creative artists chose to follow these trends. But what happened to the works of these artists? The painter who chose to put images on a canvas that people could recognize; the composer who wrote rich, full orchestrations or expansive, lyrical melodies; the lyricist who still pursued elegance, wit, and style in his work. Who could these people depend on in an increasingly confusing time? Some would suggest that schools and universities, the government, and the entertainment industry could play a key role. Except, all of these entities proved to be part of the problem, not the solution.

Composers, academicians, and their critical champions behaved very much like their colleagues in the art world. Composers understood that to achieve success in the world of concert music, it was necessary to make a Faustian bargain. The price of success was simple: one had to adhere to fashionable theories about modern music. Abstraction, dissonance, and acceptable notions of style had to be acknowledged. Just as the artists discarded color, form, three-dimension, and realistic images, musicians were quick to toss melody, harmony, and rhythm out the proverbial window. What was left for the musicians, like their visual artist friends, was theory. In short, to be successful in art or music, you had to be, first and foremost, a good theorist.

One reason for this problem is clearly that critics, writers, and historians, eager to avoid premature condemnation of the next Wagner or Debussy, tend to assume that to be radical is to be brilliant, to be revolutionary is divine. So in the modern age, many composers try to establish their musical credentials by simply declaring themselves members of the forward looking "avant-garde." Yet a look at history tells us that such a perspective is fatally flawed. Sergei Rachmaninoff is the composer whose romantic and expressive music is wildly popular with the public, but always drawing criticism from critics and self-styled intellectuals for its emotional style. Rachmaninoff wrote, "I do not have much heart-felt sympathy with music that is experimental, your so-called 'modern music.' Yet though I myself could not learn to write or love such music, I can respect the artistic aims of the composer if he arrives at his so-called modern idiom after an intensive period of preparation. Too much radical music is sheer sham, because the composer has set about revolutionizing the laws of music before he has even mastered them himself."

Nevertheless, Rachmaninoff, the last of the great Russian Romantic composers, along with his musical ancestor Tchaikovsky, are easy targets of musicians today. Especially in academia, their popularity with a large public and the emotional appeal of their music renders them automatically suspect. In 1951, pianist Rudolf Serkin founded the Marlboro Music Festival in Vermont, an event in which master performers become mentors and collaborators with young performers pursuing the art of chamber music. After Serkin's death, the Festival continued. But co-Artistic Director Mitsuko Uchida declared proudly that audiences wouldn't hear a note of Tchaikovsky during her tenure at Marlboro. Presumably, only the works of academically serious or abstract modern composers seemed fit to be on the same programs with Bach, Mozart, Beethoven, and Brahms. Not everyone agrees with this viewpoint.

Dr. Donald Shirley, an accomplished pianist, organist, and composer, was one of Rachmaninoff's greatest admirers. Shirley was a child prodigy who exhibited brilliance in a variety of subjects, including art and languages. He especially excelled at music, becoming a master of an eclectic repertoire including the classics, but also absorbing the influence of spirituals, jazz, and the sounds and rhythms of his Jamaican heritage. His extraordinary approach to music can be found in his recordings of excerpts from George Gershwin's folk opera *Porgy and Bess*. Shirley adapted vocal lines sung by the character of Porgy for the piano, assigning the roles of Serena and Maria to the cello and bass, respectively, and adding the superb singing voice of soprano Martha Flowers, who had portrayed Bess extensively, including a stellar performance at La Scala in Milan. Melodies from the expansive folk opera were suddenly transformed and infused with the intimacy of chamber music. He was an unabashed champion of the music of Rachmaninoff and Tchaikovsky. Donald Shirley was critical of the pseudo-intellectuals who scorn the romantic ethos of Tchaikovsky. He said, "I really don't know if they are saying they don't like Tchaikovsky or if they don't like something that's so obvious they can understand it. They want to be fooled, I believe. It's like looking at some graphic painting. The less understandable it is, the more money it is going to cost, and the more money it is going to cost, the more likely it is that a person will place a value judgment on it as being better than something else." For Donald Shirley, too much modern music could be characterized as "organized noise." Today, the new composer who holds to these ideals is apt to be dismissed as "old-fashioned," the ultimate dismissal by those who follow fads and fashions, and who seek to become what Roy Harris, America's most eminent composer of symphonies, used to call "savants of the avant."

Maurice Ravel was a composer quite different from Rachmaninoff. Yet Ravel declared, "I am not a 'modern composer' in the strictest sense of the term, because my music, far from being 'revolution,' is rather 'evolution.' Although I have always been open-minded to new ideas in music (one of my violin sonatas contains a 'Blues' movement), I have never attempted in it to overthrow the accepted rules of harmony and composition. On the contrary, I have always drawn liberally from the masters for my inspiration (I have never ceased studying Mozart!) and my music, for the most part, is built upon the traditions of the past and is an outgrowth of it. "

When asked about his own work, the eminent composer Mario Castelnuovo-Tedesco wrote, "As far as theories are concerned, I do not believe in theories. I have never believed in modernism, or in neo-classicism, or in any other 'isms.' I believe music is a form of language capable of progress and renewal (and I myself believe that I have a feeling for the contemporary, and therefore, am sufficiently modern). Yet music should not discard what was contributed by preceding generations. Every means of expression can be useful and just, if it is used at the opportune moment (through inner necessity rather than through caprice or fashion)."

The Hungarian composer, Dr. Miklós Rózsa, led what he called a "double life," dividing his time between writing works for the concert hall and scoring motion pictures. Rózsa was exceptional in that he achieved great public recognition through his film scores while never sacrificing his ethical principles or his musical integrity. In his memoir, *Double Life*,[70] he explained, "I believe in music as a form of communication; for me it is more an expression of emotion than an intellectual or cerebral crossword-puzzle. Like Sir Thomas Beecham, I have no time for any music which does not stimulate pleasure in life, and, even more importantly, pride in life." Rózsa declared, "I am a traditionalist, but I believe tradition can be so recreated as to express the artist's own epoch, while preserving its relationship with the past. I am old-fashioned enough also to maintain that no art is worthy of name unless it contains some elements of beauty." For Miklós Rózsa, composing was "an act of expressing human feelings and asserting human values." The wise words of Castelnuovo-Tedesco and Rózsa have been echoed by others. But there is a multitude of individuals ranging from college professors to commercial music executives who are obsessed with the new, not the good, and it is quite apparent in their words and deeds.

A recent book on film music by an active composer of motion picture and television scores included an interview with a Hollywood agent who gave his opinion on what it takes to be successful. The agent, whose musical qualification to provide this advice was mysteriously ignored, declared, "You have to be able to write a 'now sound.'" As opposed to what, we might ask, a "then" sound? Of course, anyone with knowledge of contemporary music knows precisely what the agent is talking about. He is reminding us in a not particularly subtle way, that to be successful, as he sees the term, one must emulate whatever someone sold yesterday, usually pop, rock, and rap. A "good film score" is one that sells as many CDs or inspires as many downloads as possible, all directed at an audience of teenagers. Bernard Herrmann, the brilliant, uncompromising, irascible composer of the finest film scores, was a man of great musical integrity. He once said, "There are no new sounds, only old sounds put together in new ways." The question we should be asking about film scores (or operas or ballets) is not whether they are modern, but whether they are good.

Those who revere music of the past and criticize music of the present are invariably characterized as curators, collectors, museum pieces mired in a sentimental nostalgia, or Scarlett O'Haras yearning for the society that has gone with the Hollywood or Madison Avenue wind. In fact, composers today who seek to celebrate (rather than ignore) our musical heritage are apt to find their work unfunded by "peer panels" of arts agencies who regard such cultural standards as culturally (if not politically) incorrect.

The fate of classical music in the modern era is a cause for concern. Composers of operas, string quartets, and piano concertos are writing for an elite, aging audience that sees classical music as a museum of masterpieces and dislikes (often with good reason) contemporary works. Recording companies will continue to promote a few classical artists who are perceived to have star power. But dare we ask how relevant classical music is in the lives of most people? As schools strive to capture the attention of young audiences, even teachers of music turn to rock and current pop music as a way of seeing relevance. The ignoramus who neither knows nor cares about classical music will have no interest in the works of obscure avant-garde composers turning out indigestible chamber works for their student audiences. Nor will he care about the great classical masterpieces to which he receives minimum exposure and which have nothing to do with the culture that captures the fancy of his equally uninformed peers.

In *Doing Our Own Thing: The Degradation of Language and Music and Why We Should, Like, Care,* John McWhorter observes, "Today's cultured listeners would need no reminding that classical is not exactly at the top of most people's list when they think of music! Nor would most people cherishing their rock, R&B, hip-hop, country, and World Beat take kindly to a trained classical musician dismissing the music they love as mere 'scherzos.' In fact, no classical musician would venture such a gaffe, because now they are on the cultural defensive." On the defensive, indeed! McWhorter goes on to comment about the disappearance of classical music stations and the desire of most people to hear classical music only as background music. In 2002, the city of Santa Cruz, California, decided to drive away loiterers by playing classical music over a downtown public address system; so much for music appreciation.

McWhorter writes of "a culture busy getting down" that no longer requires real songs. He observes, quite correctly, that two generations have grown up with what he aptly describes as "a musical sensibility based on beat and shaggy vocal passion." McWhorter concludes, "Whatever residual response one has to the melody and harmony, take away the beat and the cool voice and we lose interest, while music based entirely on melody and harmony appeals only to the few. Enter spoken music as default: the rock era."

THE CRISIS IN POPULAR MUSIC

While the music we usually describe as "classical" (symphonies, operas, ballets, and chamber music) was increasingly being addressed to a small audience of academic elitists, other types of music were achieving huge audiences. America's original art form, jazz, emerged and triumphed, at least for a time. Jazz emerged as a fusion of many musical elements: complex rhythms from the African tradition, ragtime, the blues, marches, and popular songs. True jazz was invariably the result of two key elements: improvisation and swing. Improvisation is simultaneous composition and performance. Jazz musicians may play from a written score or use notated compositions as the basis for their performances. However, the performances change each time and no two performances, even by the same musicians playing the same music, are identical. The definition of swing is elusive. As for those searching for a scholarly explanation of the phenomenon, Louis Armstrong once said, "If you gotta ask, you'll never know!"

American jazz has traveled across the country and around the world, from New Orleans to Chicago and New York, and eventually to Tokyo, Stockholm, Paris, and Rio de Janeiro. Jazz styles evolved from the traditional New Orleans sound of the 1920s to the big band era of the 1930s, through development of bebop in the 1940s and the "cool school" of the 1950s. The finest jazz musicians displayed technical virtuosity comparable to their classical counterparts; the music itself often reflected great rhythmic and harmonic sophistication and complexity. Dizzy Gillespie, the great jazz trumpet soloist, along with his friends Charlie Parker, Bud Powell, and Thelonious Monk, was one of the prime movers of the bebop era. During this period, musicians began concentrating on exploring highly complex rhythms and harmonies. The result was music during which audiences were expected to listen, not dance as they had during the big band era. In his autobiography, *To Be or Not to Bop*,[71] Gillespie said that jazz never attracted the huge audiences that were later to be found at rock concerts, because jazz was an art form. In other words, jazz might be considered "popular music" in some circles, but it also deserved the respect given to other forms of art.

Jazz was not America's only contribution to the world of music. Composers began writing for the Broadway musical theater; together with a brilliant group of lyricists, they created what has become known as "The Great American Song Book." Like jazz, "The Great American Song Book" had interesting origins. Europeans brought operetta to the United States, but Americans had influences of their own, including ragtime and jazz. Musical plays produced on Broadway evolved into a remarkable American art form. Many of our finest popular songs came from stage musicals. Lyricist and librettist Oscar Hammerstein provided the words for the historically important shows *Show Boat* (with music by Jerome Kern) and *Oklahoma!* (with music by Richard Rodgers). These shows represented a new theatrical form in which music, lyrics, and a coherent and appealing plot were all united. The great figures of American musical theater established a tradition and a standard by which others are judged.

James Maher, in his introduction to Alec Wilder's *American Popular Song: The Great Innovators 1900-1950,*[72] observed quite correctly, "One writing in the theater lives with that tradition, with its freedom, and its penalties. Puccini, far off, Lehar, in the middle distance, and Jerome Kern, Irving Berlin, George Gershwin, Richard Rodgers, Arthur Schwartz, and Harold Arlen close at hand are listening. (So are P.G. Wodehouse, Lorenz Hart, Cole Porter, Oscar Hammerstein II, Ira Gershwin, Dorothy Fields, and John Mercer.) The newest song writer in the theater must answer to them, for they are the measure of what he does. Throughout his career he must stand up against the formidable witness of their best work. And he cannot wish them away for they have instructed the communal ear—their songs are part of the unconscious reflex of the common memory."

Much of the most lyrical music of the 20th century was written for films, often recorded under the batons of outstanding conductors such as Paramount's eminent musical director, Irvin Talbot. Composers from Europe, including Erich Korngold, Max Steiner, Miklós Rózsa, Franz Waxman, and Bronislaw Kaper, among others, joined Americans like Alfred Newman, Bernard Herrmann, David Raksin, Hugo Friedhofer, Jerome Moross, Alex North, and Elmer Bernstein, to write dramatic film scores that were poignant, funny, terrifying, passionate, and emotionally intense. These brilliant men created an extraordinary musical legacy. We typically have called jazz, "The Great American Song Book," and film scores "popular" music. Certainly, these genres of music were popular, but they also assumed a certain level of intelligence and appreciation on the part of their audience. Then something quite remarkable happened.

ROCK IS STILL A FOUR LETTER WORD

In the late 1950s and throughout the 1960s, the rock music revolution overthrew nearly all traditions in popular music. Composers and lyricists who didn't like the simplified lyrics, the overt and explicit vulgarity of the new music were, like their classical colleagues, abandoned and ignored. "Pop" music was intentionally directed at the lowest common denominator of the musical audience; "classical" music became increasingly targeted to an elite minority of admirers, because the public didn't understand or like much of what was being written. Meanwhile, the new pop music was taking no prisoners and driving America's musical traditions and history into an early oblivion. What Henry Pleasants said years ago about modern classical music can be said today about much of today's current popular music as well. It isn't modern and it isn't music. Pleasants thought that the answer to confusion in the world of classical music would be a thriving, creative, original music derived from America's best popular songs and jazz. But no one could have anticipated what would happen next.

Rock music has proven to be the greatest sacred cow of our modern day pop culture. This has occurred for a variety of reasons. Rock stars not only earn huge fortunes for themselves, but for those who promote them. There are talented, principled people who work in the music industry, but it is overrun by scoundrels and mountebanks. Many of these individuals are privately contemptuous of the public, which idolizes their untalented clients. They often boast that they can make stars of anyone, because the real talent in the industry is theirs, a cunning and clever instinct for promotion. People are reluctant to criticize anything that makes money, especially in the entertainment business.

Rock music has always been identified with the young, and many, in and out of the entertainment industry, are convinced that identifying with the rock subculture keeps them young too, in their own minds and in the minds of those they seek to impress. Many people are drawn to rock music because of a herd mentality. These individuals have no cultural compass of their own, and they are obsessed only by a desire to be "in" and to be "with it," whatever "it" happens to be at the moment.

Finally, as several generations have grown up listening almost entirely to rock music, the words and repetitive beat of rock are part of their collective memory. They associate events in their lives with rock, just as their parents and grandparents remembered songs with a far different style of music and lyrics. Today, the "rock and roll" of the 1950s seems staid and conservative when compared to the rock, pop, and rap of today. There is a Rock and Roll Hall of Fame and Museum in Cleveland, Ohio. Composers working in films and on Broadway know that rock scores are considered a guarantee of commercial success.

Even composers of concert music are lured by the desire to be fashionable by writing so-called "rock operas" or incorporating the amplified sounds of rock in their works. Many jazz musicians similarly play in an idiom described as jazz-rock, while traditional jazz seems headed for a dusty museum. In short, with the triumph of cable television outlets such as MTV and the Internet, rock has become ubiquitous. It has become all music; all music has become rock. Even those who are articulate advocates for a return to traditional social values, on all sides of the political spectrum, are perfectly happy with rock music. There are rock music critics who analyze every amplified squeal of performers as if they were virtuosos. The true critics, those who recognize the rock juggernaut for what it is, are dismissed as hopeless conservatives, mired in nostalgia, and longing for the politics of William McKinley and the music of Lawrence Welk. At best, they are simply ignored; at worst, they are subjected to an atrabilious tirade of ridicule and abuse. There are no advantages to telling the truth about rock music. Professional and financial inducements are all on the other side.

Many academics, eager to recapture their youth or to prove their affinity with the teenage subculture, were quick to sing the praises of the rock revolution. Charles Reich, in his apologetic advocacy of the 1960s' counterculture, *The Greening of America*, [73]sang the praises of a new consciousness exhibited by those who wore a nonconformist uniform of jeans, smoked marijuana, and expressed themselves through rock music. In what may be the most absurd statement ever written on the subject, Reich suggested that rock music didn't take money seriously. In fact, the rock revolution is and has always been driven by the desire for wealth by the people who promote it. Reich declared that it is no criticism of eighteenth-or nineteenth- century geniuses to say that today's music has found a world that they never knew. He went on to describe the over-amplified, ear-deafening sounds of today's rock stars as expressing "greater energy than Beethoven's Ninth."

Fortunately, not everyone agreed. One critic who wasn't shy about taking on the rock juggernaut was University of Chicago Professor Allan Bloom. Bloom included a devastating (and highly accurate) description of today's pop music and its influence in his best-selling book, *The Closing of the American Mind.*[74] Bloom observed, "Rock music is as unquestioned and unproblematic as the air the students breathe, and very few have any acquaintance with classical music." Bloom concludes that classical music is dead among the young, and that classical music is now a specialized taste like Greek language or pre-Columbian archeology. In the world of rock music, according to Bloom, there is only room for the intense, changing, crude, and immediate. Bloom observed that in the era of rock music, listeners can enjoy a premature ecstasy without talent, effort, or virtue. As for rock concerts and the video culture of MTV, he wrote, "Nothing noble, sublime, profound, delicate, tasteful, or even decent can find a place in such tableaux." Eventually, this state of affairs will pass, Bloom said, as students "slip off the Michael Jackson costume to reveal the Brooks Brothers suit underneath." But by then, it is already too late. Bloom declared, "As long as they have the Walkman on, they cannot hear what the great tradition has to say. And after its prolonged use, when they take it off, they find that they are deaf."

Bloom was concerned about the decline of classical music. He might have added that in the world of popular music, there have been similar effects. The best historians of Broadway's musical theater have described the exceptional songs of Irving Berlin, George Gershwin, Cole Porter, Richard Rodgers, Jerome Kern, and others as the American equivalent of lieder. The finest jazz musicians have a musical vocabulary, which easily equals that of classical virtuosos. Yet "The Great American Songbook" and the masterpieces of jazz are also in danger of disappearing, while the untalented musical frauds of rock and rap remain triumphant. Bloom's point is well taken. Those whose tastes are defined by rock music can hardly be expected suddenly to appreciate a cultural legacy of which they are oblivious. Some may make discoveries later in life, but most likely will not, and by then, the damage will have been done.

Allan Jeffreys spent many years as a Broadway theater critic, pioneering in delivering his reviews on television. In "Goodbye to the Music of Broadway,"[75] he asked, "Is this all gone? Does it even matter in an age when we face economic and social woes? I think it does. I have to believe that someday in the future there will be another glittering opening of a brand-new musical that will rival *Carousel* or *My Fair Lady* or *Guys and Dolls.* In some faraway attic, a young lyricist is scribbling away and searching for that rhyme within a rhyme that will tug at our heart. In another attic, a composer hovers over a piano, seeking the lost chord and the magic note that will get our toes tapping and our lips puckered in perfect whistle format." But if a composer were to write a new *Carousel* or *My Fair Lady* today, could it even be produced? Or would it be dismissed as "old-fashioned" by the producers of so-called rock operas?

While many musicians privately despise much of the commercial cacophony that passes for music, very few have the courage to express their views publicly. They don't want to be considered "old-fashioned," an apparently innocuous label that can actually destroy their careers. Nevertheless, a few musicians have spoken out regarding the decline and fall of popular music. The Eastman School of Music at the University of Rochester is one of the world's most famous schools of music. The director for many years was Howard Hanson, a distinguished composer, conductor, and champion of the finest traditions in American music. The reading room in the school's library is named for Alec Wilder, described as "composer, writer, sage, wit, standard- bearer, iconoclast, mentor, benefactor, and friend."

Wilder was all of these things; he was also a curmudgeon who had strong opinions about music. His book, *American Popular Song:*

The Great Innovators 1900-1950, is deservedly recognized as the definitive study of the best popular songs written during the first half of the 20th century. Wilder was an improbable man, a nomadic figure whose only home for years was a room at New York's Algonquin Hotel. He became a major writer of popular songs in the 1940s and was a prolific composer of chamber music. He rarely kept any of his own music and often gave away the only existing copies of his pieces to friends. His friend, fellow composer and sometime collaborator Loonis McGlohon, described him as witty, erudite, rude, warm, and cantankerous.

As perhaps America's foremost analyst of American popular song, Wilder's view of the rock revolution is telling. His biographer Desmond Stone writes, "In Wilder's view, the rock and roll movement of the 1950s and '60s was like a blight spreading across the landscape of American music, staining all it touched, turning traditional values inside out." Long after everyone seemed to have accepted rock as America's music, Wilder, according to Stone, "was still out there shaking his fist on a lonely promontory." Wilder said, "The rock group has just played something on a TV show that is a dreadful insult to music, with lyrics that virtually exhort the kids to turn on with some drug. Following the usual hysterical audience response, the smiling 'host' holds up his hands and says, 'Wasn't that really super? And would you believe that these boys started to play the guitar only three weeks ago?' Three weeks ago, and they're already earning $500. A week each! Well, it's a familiar story in an age that's been conditioned to instant everything." Wilder said these words many years ago, but the only thing that has changed is that the three untalented and untutored guitarists are probably still caterwauling today, but for $500,000 each, or perhaps $5 million. Desmond Stone quotes Wilder as asking for self-discipline, good taste, and professionalism, qualities he did not find in the rock revolution of the 1960s and 1970s. Wilder called for a revival of work, excellence, self- discipline, perspective, wit, fun, joy, and wonderment. Stone writes that Wilder would "always detest rock for the explosive noise that displaced music, for the manic superstars, the Nuremberg-type rallies, the beads, the hair, and the facelessness of the rock generation." Perhaps his strongest condemnation was reserved for the magazines and newspapers and television stations that concentrated on the hippie/rock culture of the 1960s and ignored so many talented other young musicians.[76]

One of Wilder's well-chosen targets was television host Ed Sullivan. Few people remember Sullivan in 21st century America, but in the 1950s and 1960s, he hosted one of the most widely watched television programs in the country. Sullivan was an improbable television star, a New York newspaper columnist described by rival columnist Harriet Van Horne as a man with no personality. *Time* compared him to a stone-faced monument just off Easter Island. *Time* added, "He moves like a sleepwalker; his smile is that of a man sucking a lemon; his speech is frequently lost in a thicket of syntax; his eyes pop from their sockets or sink so deep in their bags that they seem to be peering up at the camera from the bottom of twin wells." But *Time* concluded that Sullivan somehow "charmed the whole family." Sullivan's awkward mannerisms and garbled syntax were imitated by numerous comedians and impressionists. Nevertheless, appearances on his program could turn anonymous performers into instant stars. Elvis Presley, The Beatles, and the Jackson Five (with a very young Michael Jackson) were all effectively launched into stardom with Sullivan's blessing. Sullivan's endorsement put rock music into millions of American living rooms and gave it instant respectability. Wilder characterized television's Ed Sullivan as "a nice guy, but not very bright, who had no business showcasing immature talent." An appearance on Sullivan's show, like one on Oprah Winfrey's program decades later, meant instant mass exposure and popular approval. Sullivan, out of ignorance or a desire for commercial success, opened the door for rock groups and their promoters. They were quick to rush into America's cultural mainstream.

At the beginning of the rock music revolution, many traditionalists believed that rock would merely enjoy a fugacious lifespan as a teenage phenomenon. But by the end of the 20th century, rock stars who survived the lifestyle of their youth were regarded as elder statesmen. Their hippie admirers were now called "faculty members" of major universities, where courses in rock music and rock culture abound. It is not hard to imagine what Wilder's curmudgeonly view of so called "rock music scholarship" would be, especially in the age of MTV. It is also not hard to imagine a day when punk rock, rap, and amplified noise are the subject of musical experts, while the best of our popular musical heritage is long since forgotten.

Alec Wilder was regarded by many as a quixotic and somewhat eccentric fellow who was tilting at windmills. He was, in fact, a perceptive observer who recognized the decline and fall of America's popular music. What had evolved into a significant art form devolved into the ubiquitous non-music of the 21st century. Composers were suddenly challenged to appeal to a new type of audience, described by James Maher as a young consumer group "notorious for its short attention span and its insatiable hunger for the new (a word that has since given way to the word now), with its dreary implication of manipulated hysteria." The talented young musicians of Wilder's day faced a struggle. They could swallow hard, offer their talents to the untalented tycoons who controlled the recording industry, or face professional oblivion.

WHO SHOULD BE AMERICA'S IDOLS?

In the 21st century, reality television has persuaded a generation that anyone can become a star. Programs like *American Idol* and *Pop Idol* reinforce the notion. Singer Lesley Garrett said, "It worries me that young singers think you can shortcut the training and go straight to fame and fortune, and programs like *Pop Idol* have encouraged that." Garrett's concerns are well taken.

Discussions about American popular music are always conducted within certain parameters established by the recording industry. People argue and debate about American pop music, but almost never challenge accepted norms of the entertainment business. Consider the television program, *American Idol.* This hugely successful program was based, like many American programs, on a British model. *American Idol* was derived from *Pop*

Idol, a British program, essentially a contest for aspiring pop stars seeking fame and fortune. The public and the media spend an apparently endless amount of time debating the fate of the "good" and "talented" performers, the prospects of the "poor" or "untalented" singers, and especially, the interaction of the judges. Much attention was paid to the remarks of the caustic, acid-tongued British judge, Simon Cowell, who wielded power on both the American and British versions of the show. But no one bothered to inquire as to Mr. Cowell's qualifications or considered the standards of the entire program. Simon Cowell's background is primarily in the recording industry. He can judge what people are buying and selling, but on what basis does he criticize singers? Consider, for instance, his remark that he "didn't care much about Katharine McPhee," adding "I don't think she was a credible recording artist. Katharine will end up on Broadway!"

Now for most gifted popular singers, ending up on Broadway is a goal, not a symbol of failure. Broadway musicals tend to feature two types of vocalists. There are singing actors who may lack the pure vocal technique of their classically trained counterparts, but who can use acting skills to "put over" a song with the audience. They are often expected to "belt" lyrics, so that they can be heard in the last row of the theater. There are also acting singers, who have superb singing voices and deal with the technically demanding scores while delivering credible acting performances. Untalented performers do not turn in bad performances on Broadway unless they are starring in rock musicals, since rock music does not require singers to sing on pitch and carry a tune.

If the ability to perform material chosen from "The Great American Songbook" doesn't meet the ethos of *American Idol* or its judges, what about skill as a jazz performer? Tierney Sutton is an internationally respected jazz singer. With five musical colleagues, she formed The Tierney Sutton Band, an ensemble that has achieved wide recognition and praise in the jazz world. She has become particularly well-known for her ability to redesign familiar musical standards in original and highly creative arrangements. One of her signature songs is an unusual jazz version of *Ding, Dong, The Witch Is Dead*, originally in the classic film *The Wizard of Oz*. The Tierney Sutton version features considerable "scatting" (improvised melodies using wordless jazz syllables). It was recorded in 2002, but in 2010, Jennifer Hersch, trying out for *American Idol*, apparently inspired by Tierney Sutton, performed a scatting version of *Ding, Dong, The Witch Is Dead*. She was eliminated from the show by Simon Cowell who told her she would only become "a jazz singer in New York City." "Only" a jazz singer; as compared to whom? "Only" a jazz singer; like Ella Fitzgerald or Sarah Vaughan? Or Mel Tormé? Tierney Sutton, who is qualified to judge the performance of jazz vocalists, turned down an opportunity to perform such a role in a competition, after being told that the judging standards were based 40 percent on "marketability." (She has always emphasized flawless pitch and phrasing to her own students.) However, such scruples do not inhibit the judges who choose the next "American Idol." It is all about marketability. Those who are not perceived as appropriate for the music-marketing machine can "only" end up on Broadway, in jazz clubs, or as a candid Hollywood agent once put it, "They can get out of the business." This explains why the world of pop music is full of teen idols who cannot sing. Nevertheless, they can afford a battery of public relations agents and promoters who know that the ability to carry a tune is last on the list of qualifications for pop musical stardom.

One experienced vocalist who gave thought to "getting out of the business" was Bobby Short. Short was a veteran cabaret performer known for his elegant performances of music by Cole Porter and other creators of sophisticated melodies and lyrics. In the 1960s, Short proposed an album to his former record label, Atlantic, and was asked, "Who wants to listen to Cole Porter?" Short considered "getting out of the business" and going into men's haberdashery. Fortunately, a substitute performance at New York's Café Carlyle revived his career. He became an international icon in the world of cabaret and remained in demand for the rest of his life. But his career, like so many, could just as easily have ended prematurely, driven out of music by the rock-pop-rap promoters. How many fine musicians saw their careers go up in smoke? When the pop musical juggernaut arrived, no one's career was safe.

Mel Tormé was known worldwide for his performances on recordings, radio, television, and in films and concert halls. He was multitalented, respected as a composer, arranger, writer, and actor. Although he performed many different types of music, he was especially celebrated as a jazz vocalist. Yet after the rise of rock groups and the dominance of their promoters, Tormé found himself out of work and no longer in demand. Tormé had become a role model for many other singers, but the advent of rock music nearly drove him into early retirement. Under pressure to change his style and musical values, he considered giving up his storied career to become an airline pilot. Harry Anderson, star of the television program *Night Court*, was one of Tormé's lifelong fans. Coincidentally, the popular situation comedy developed a running joke about the main character's desire to meet Tormé. Constant attention on national television helped revive Tormé's career. Fortunately, he remained in music and he was eventually discovered by a new and enthusiastic public.

Tormé was hardly alone. Dozens of gifted performers, some quite famous and others unknown, were told that the times had passed them by. Tormé survived the rock revolution, but others were not so fortunate. Several generations of gifted composers, lyricists, and singers and instrumentalists who performed their work were consigned to oblivion, sometimes without ever having had the opportunity to make their mark or display the mastery of their craft.

In the new world of pop music, performers, often with no vocal or instrumental skills, also declared themselves to be composers, writing their own material. People assumed that there were no special requirements to sing popular music. Publicity and special effects were enough to make anyone a star. On the other hand, there were dissenters. Mel Tormé was also an articulate, outspoken advocate for the music he loved and performed for a lifetime. Tormé wrote an interesting book, *My Singing Teachers:*

Reflections on Singing Popular Music.[77] Tormé paid tribute to his "singing teachers," not people from whom he had taken lessons, but the singers, instrumentalists, composers, lyricists, and arrangers who had influenced him and provided guidance over a lifetime of striving toward perfection of his craft.

These included not only the singers well known to the public, but legendary composers, lyricists, and arrangers who created an incredible musical legacy that is in danger of being lost. Tormé wrote, "In recent times, the public has been lulled into a senseless round of three-chord tunes, plunked on a guitar or based away at with electronic gear and drum machines. The glorious music of the talented people mentioned herein, the wit, intellect, ingenuity, and craftsmanship of the writers of words practicing their trade in the Twenties, Thirties, and Forties, reached a pinnacle we will never see or hear again."

Tormé talked about interpretation of lyrics, breath control and everything from inspiration to technique. Neither is present in the caterwauling of many of today's "superstars." Without a group of back-up singers, special effects, and massive amplification, their tiny off-key voices couldn't fool the most gullible of audiences. Nevertheless, unfortunately, they do fool audiences all the time.

Some of Tormé's role models, like his early idols Bing Crosby and Frank Sinatra, were stars whose names are familiar. Others were famous in their day, but they are gradually being forgotten. Still others were widely recognized in the music business, but not familiar to the public. All influenced Tormé as he learned about performing, phrasing, breath control, singing in tune, enunciation, and what he called "all the elements essential in becoming a successful singer." Perhaps we should say the elements that used to be essential in becoming a successful singer: phrasing, breath control, singing in tune, and enunciation. Today's typical pop star would be unfamiliar with the very concepts of singing in tune. As for breath control and enunciation, neither are necessary to the superstar who screams, howls, and caterwauls into a microphone, all the while supported by a group of gyrating back-up singers, and surrounded by a constant array of special effects worthy of a Fourth of July fireworks display.

For the teenagers of the world, discussions of musical technique or skill would be confusing and puzzling. What is important in the world of the teenager is being familiar with and acknowledging everything his friends are discussing. There is no greater oxymoron than a non-conformist who speaks, dresses, and likes the same music as all of his non-conformist friends. They are proud of their rebellion and dissent from the staid, rigid conformists of society, and they demonstrate this by speaking and dressing alike, and of course, by liking the same music. Nothing illustrates this more clearly than an episode described by writer and professor Mark Bauerlein. In an appearance at the University of Maryland, Bauerlein told a large student audience that they were six times more likely to know the names of contestants on *American Idol* as the name of the Speaker of the U.S. House of Representatives. A voice from the audience thundered proudly, "But *American Idol* is more important." The outraged student was correct, in a manner of speaking. Knowing the name of the Speaker of the House isn't "cool," especially when celebrities are often eager to advertise their ignorance in public. As long as they continue to make money and remain famous, celebrities are given a permanent pass regarding knowledge and behavior. (After a trip to Greece, basketball star Shaquille O'Neal, a product of Louisiana State University, was asked if he had visited the Parthenon. O'Neal responded "I can't really remember the names of the clubs that we went to.") The boy or girl who does retain such information will probably be dismissed as a "nerd" or whatever term is being applied to bookworms this week. A high school student will not diminish himself in the eyes of his friends if he has never read *David Copperfield* or thinks that "David Copperfield" is only the popular magician of the same name. But his status will drop quickly if he doesn't know who appeared on *American Idol* the night before.

Many in such audiences have never heard of Mel Tormé. Nor have they heard of vocalist Jack Jones who endorsed Tormé's book with the comment, "Read this one, boys and girls, before you rock and roll." But they are rocking and rolling, and of course, watching *American Idol.* Tormé expressed admiration for the consistency, concentration, and credibility in the vocal styling of Frank Sinatra. No one was more familiar with Sinatra's views on popular music than Vincent Falcone. Vincent Falcone was one of the last pianist-conductors to work regularly with Frank Sinatra. He also played for Sammy Davis, Jr., Jerry Lewis, Robert Goulet, Steve Lawrence and Edye Gormé, Diahann Carroll, and Tony Bennett, among others. With his friend Bob Popyk, he co-authored a memoir, Frankly *Just Between Us: My Life Conducting Frank Sinatra's Music.*[78] Falcone courageously spoke the truth about much of today's pop music. He writes, "In my estimation, hip-hop, rap, and heavy metal have destroyed the tradition of great American music that depended on interesting melodies and sophisticated lyrics. When I was young, music depicted love, romance, or the longing for a lost love. Today what passes for music often depicts violence, hatred, and sex. I have found that young people need only to be exposed to great art in order for them to recognize it as such. The problem today is the lack of availability of fine art to youngsters in public schools. To make matters worse, funding for music education in public schools is on the decline." The performers that Falcone accompanied during his performing career depended on musical and dramatic talent, not special effects. As for many of today's self-styled superstars, Falcone says, "Much of the music today has gone from understandable lyrics and musically-correct content to loud unintelligible noise. Obscenities and crotch-grabbing seem to be a part of mainstream performances of a lot of today's music. MTV and VH-1 should come with a warning label. I think those channels have been detrimental to the morality of youth in this country."

Falcone also calls attention to the difference between music and entertainment. Music, he says is art, but not all entertainment is art. He is correct in observing, "Half the popular groups today could not play without four-hundred watt amps, strobe lights, confetti guns, and fog. If they showed up at a gig and the electricity was off, they wouldn't be able to play." Vincent Falcone is hardly alone in these observations. Many people in and out of the music industry would be shocked to find how many good musicians of all ages agree with him. But most musicians don't want to speak out on the subject, because they are frightened and insecure at the thought of not being considered contemporary.

Falcone's most important point is that children need to be exposed to great art. "The Great American Songbook," the canon of music and lyrics by Irving Berlin, George and Ira Gershwin, Jerome Kern, Richard Rodgers (writing with Lorenz Hart and Oscar Hammerstein), Cole Porter, Frederick Loewe, Alan Jay Lerner, Harold Arlen, and Frank Loesser, among others, must not be allowed to fade into oblivion. The great popular singers of the 20th century could interpret the lyrics of the songs they sang. They worked to master their musical craft and perfect their vocal technique. America's great popular music, like its great classical music, can stand on its own, but we can't count on future generations discovering it on its own.

Years earlier, before Michael Jackson's acquittal on charges of child abuse or his strange personal behavior became a mainstay of tabloid journalism, the curmudgeonly Andy Rooney offered his own assessment of Jackson. Rooney was commenting on the state of pop lyrics and obviously had grown up with the lyrics of the truly great masters of the art. The rumpled, cantankerous commentator read, verbatim, the lyrics of a Michael Jackson hit, *Bad.* The lyrics consisted of the word "bad" repeated over and over again, augmented occasionally by "I'm bad" and "so bad." The lyrics are hardly eloquent: "Because I'm Bad, I'm Bad-Come On (Bad Bad-Really, Really Bad) You Know I'm Bad, I'm Bad-You Know It (Bad Bad-Really, Really Bad)." After the stanza which concludes "And the whole world has to answer right now, just to tell you once again, who's bad," Rooney took a dramatic pause, and then straight into the camera, concluded, "Bad."

One suspects that Jackson's fans weren't watching *Sixty Minutes,* and if they were, that they didn't understand Rooney's point. Those who did weren't Michael Jackson fans in the first place.

Rooney, of course, would be dismissed by the media's chorus of crickets as old-fashioned, grumpy, unfashionable, and worst of all, the opposite of "cool." Nonetheless, Rooney was clearly aware of the difference in the quality of music and lyrics in the repertoire of Michael Jackson, Britney Spears, Madonna, Lady Gaga, and other highly marketed pop stars, and the classic melodies and lyrics of the "The Great American Songbook." Consider the way our best lyricists use words to express their thoughts. The finest lyricists mastered the art of the particular word, the specific phrase, and the inevitable analogy. Great lyricists, like great poets or great composers, write in such a way that to change a single word in a lyric would seem wrong.

Ira Gershwin, in *Love Is Here to Stay* (1936), the final poignant song he wrote with his brother George Gershwin, isn't vague or general. Consider the imagery of his lines, "In time the Rockies may crumble, Gibraltar may tumble, They're only made of Clay." So when he concludes with the phrase, "But—our love is here to stay," he is finding a new way to say something traditional.

Lorenz Hart, Richard Rodgers' first great lyricist-collaborator, managed to compress irony into just a few words in the song, "I Wish I Were in Love Again" (1937). Hart could have expressed the words of the title in a sentimental way. Instead, he wrote of "The furtive sigh, The blackened eye." Then he continued, "The words, 'I'll love you till the day I die,' The self-deception that believes the lie—I wish I were in love again."

Oscar Hammerstein II, Rodgers' second great lyricist- collaborator, was a sentimental optimist with a very different creative outlook than the caustically witty Lorenz Hart. In "It Might as Well Be Spring" (1945), he didn't just write a lyric saying "I'm happy" or "I'm confused" over and over again. He wrote "I'm as busy as a spider spinning daydreams, I'm as giddy as a baby on a swing . . ." In "Oh, What a Beautiful Morning," the song that opened *Oklahoma! (1943),* Hammerstein wrote, "The corn is as high as an elephant's eye." In *South Pacific* (1949), he wrote the lyrics for "I'm in Love with a Wonderful Guy." Included was the phrase, "I'm bromidic and bright as a daisy in May, a cliché coming true." Hammerstein was a master of finding new ways to express the thoughts of a singing character in a musical play. Another less gifted lyricist might just have written, "I'm happy," to which the audience might have responded: "Who cares?" or "So what?" No one ever did that in response to a Hammerstein lyric.

Cole Porter was the master of the double-entendre. His sly use of double-meanings made his lyrics perfect for both laughter and analysis. Nobody wrote more sophisticated lyrics than Cole Porter. In "You're the Top" (1934), he makes one of his dazzling and improbable lists as the singer declares, "You're the top! You're the Colosseum. You're the top! You're the Louvre Museum." Again, Porter is finding an incredibly clever way of saying, "You're the best." But Porter wasn't through. He added, "You're a melody from a symphony by Strauss, You're a Bendel bonnet, A Shakespeare sonnet, You're Mickey Mouse."

Johnny Mercer was a born Southerner, a native of Savannah, Georgia, who could turn poetic with a snap of his fingers. Other lyricists had failed to please David Raksin, the composer of the haunting and suddenly successful film theme that became *Laura.* Raksin asked for Mercer whom he compared to a great circus performer when he called him "The Flying Wallenda of Lyricists." Mercer understood that he needed to express the character of *Laura* who reflected both beauty and mystery. A less inspired lyricist might have written "Laura is beautiful" or "I love Laura." Mercer didn't disappoint when he wrote, "Laura is the face in the misty light. Footsteps that you hear down the hall." Mercer was typically on target when he added, "The laugh that floats on a summer night, That you can never quite recall."

Comparing the work of truly fine composers and lyricists to the output of today's clay-footed idols is embarrassing. Yet the fans of these idols will be unmoved. For them, the pop stars are embedded in their memories of teenage trials and tribulations, never to be challenged by harsh realities. The true geniuses of the saga, the marketers and promoters, who have persuaded generations that they can encounter true genius for the price of a recording, are laughing all the way to the bank. The foolish lyrics of their era of bubblegum rock in the 1950s gave way to the trivialities of the Beatles' "I Want to Hold Your Hand." Nor have things improved. The one-word wonders like Michael Jackson's "Bad" are now being replaced by the contributions of lyricists whose language would once have resulted in their being charged with public obscenity.

Much has been written and spoken regarding the overt vulgarity, sexuality, and frequent obscenity of today's pop music and lyrics. In *Of Thee I Zing*,[79] Laura Ingraham observes, "If music reveals the heart of a culture, ours is in cardiac arrest." Critics can expect to be tarred and feathered as prudes, prim and proper censors, bowdlerizers, bigots, narrow-minded paragons of intolerance, and religious zealots. Worst of all, they should be prepared for defenders of musical progress to invoke the ultimate fulmination, the dreaded "F" word, "fogey." To be old-fashioned in the 21st century remains the cardinal sin.

Not all critics, however, can be easily dismissed. Mike Stock, one of the most commercially successful pop music producers, told the *Daily Mail*, "The music industry has gone too far. It's not about me being old fashioned. It's about keeping values that are important in the modern world. These days you can't watch modern stars–like Britney Spears or Lady Gaga–with a two-year-old." Stock continued, "Kids are being forced to grow up too young. Look at the videos. I wouldn't necessarily want my young kids to watch them. I would certainly be embarrassed to sit there with my mum." Stock criticized the images bombarding young children before they are even enrolled in school, usually from pop music and video games.

But Stock's critique of today's popular music, though correct, is only part of the problem. Certainly, the dismal state of pop music and its devolution from a standard of creativity and quality is a legitimate concern. But of equal concern, and receiving far less attention, is the neglect of music and musicians who do not become popular because their work is neglected, forgotten, or undiscovered.

The Grammy awards are presented for outstanding musical achievement in the recording industry, with both classical and popular artists receiving recognition. In 2010, a "Best Recording" nomination was awarded to C-Lo Green for a recording the title of which could not be fully announced on the air. The title was *F*** You*. Radio host and film critic Michael Medved observed that the title song used the actual obscene language, "F-words," "S-words," and the "N-word racial epithet," all of which had to be bleeped out on mainstream radio. Medved remarked, "In the 1960s, when the Rolling Stones performed their song on TV, they had to change the words 'Let's Spend the Night Together' to 'Let's Spend Some Time Together.' Now the music industry's most prestigious award honors the 'F-Word.' Is that progress?" The lyrics of this honored masterpiece are hardly a threat to the legacy of Ira Gershwin, Lorenz Hart, Cole Porter, Oscar Hammerstein II, and Johnny Mercer. The soloist performing this example of the contemporary music industry's idea of outstanding lyric writing begins by declaring "I see you driving around town with the girl I love and I'm like F*** You. I guess the change in my pocket wasn't enough. I'm like F*** You and F*** Her Too."

The always incisive author and radio personality Dennis Prager observes that a civilization does not decline overnight. It is a gradual process, often an erosion of standards and values that happens silently and quietly. As a result, a significant portion of the population is often blissfully ignorant of what is taking place until the damage has been done. Prager sees the plethora of songs and art celebrating the worst excesses of humanity as an assault on our civilization. He says, "The difference between a great civilization and a failing civilization is not the absence of barbarians. Barbarians exist, barbarians will always exist. It is that civilization condemns the barbarian. When the civilization honors the barbarian, we have gone from toleration to condemnation to adoration. That's why we're in decline." Prager quite correctly concludes that the barbarians govern in the world of the elites, education, and elsewhere. Of course, we can hear the apologists crying crocodile tears on behalf of the rights of so-called artists to express themselves. But, the issue is not whether they have a right to express themselves, but the value of what they are expressing.

Of course, in a society that respects free speech, they have a right to make fools of themselves in public or to advertise their lack of talent and taste. But when the recording industry honors ubiquitous trash and makes a huge profit in the process, they are making fools of a gullible audience. What does this say not only about the recording industry but also about this rest of us?

MUSICA DELENDA EST

In the 21st century, a new and troubling movement has been launched. Springing from an unholy alliance between radical college professors and ruthless commercial music promoters, this movement threatens the survival of good music in a way not seen before.

In 1870, when composer John Knowles Paine became Harvard's first music professor, his arrival on campus was greeted in less than amiable fashion. At a meeting of the Harvard Board of Overseers, Francis Parkman, a prominent historian, referenced the hatred of ancient Rome for Carthage with his slogan "Musica delenda est." Parkman was paraphrasing what ancient Roman Senator Marcus Cato said about Carthage: "Music must be destroyed."

Music may have survived the onslaught of the 19th century faculty at Harvard, but there is considerable doubt whether it will survive a 21st century attack by those who seek to use race, gender, radical politics, and ruthless personal ambition to do to classical music what they have already achieved in the world of pop music: destruction, devolution, and decline.

On both sides of the Atlantic, everything and everyone associated with what is generally called "the canon" of Western music is under attack. Revered composers—Bach, Handel, Mozart, Beethoven, among them—are targeted as symbols of racism, along with most other audience favorites—Schubert, Mendelssohn, Schumann, Chopin, Liszt, Brahms, and Tchaikovsky. The subjects studied by most composers, especially music theory, harmony, counterpoint, and music history, are also under attack. Presumably, this attack will encourage those cowed by angry groups of students and incensed professors to simply get rid of most music regarded for centuries as great. The very idea of "great music," we are told, must be abandoned; then and only then can this offensive music and its equally offensive creators be replaced. By what and by whom? By music that is "inclusive" and with much of it being created (not remotely a surprise) by those who are objecting to great music in the first place.

No single article or essay can serve as a blatant manifesto for this movement more than "Beethoven Was An Above Average Composer—Let's Leave It At That" by Hunter College professor Philip Ewell. Obsessed with race, Ewell has produced a list of terms associated with what he calls "Music Theory's White Racial Frame." Among these shockingly offensive terms are "authentic, canonic, civilized, classic(s), conventional, core ("core" requirement), European, function ("functional" tonality), fundamental genius, German ("German" language requirement), great ("great" works), maestro, opus (magnum "opus"), piano ("piano" proficiency, skills), seminal, sophisticated, titan(ic), towering, traditional and western." Of course, words like "master" or "masterpiece" or "masterful" are obvious hat tips to masters brutalizing slaves.[80]

When not looking for racists using terms of "whiteness" under every bed, Ewell, turns to a more human target, poor Ludwig van Beethoven. Ewell, a cellist with a doctorate from Yale, admits that he derives pleasure from playing Beethoven's chamber music, but he then informs us that Beethoven's reputation has been propped up by whiteness and maleness for centuries. He informs us that "Beethoven's *Ninth Symphony* is no more a masterwork than Esperanza Spalding's *12 Little Spells*. To state that Beethoven was more than, say, above average as a composer is to state that you know all music written on planet earth 200 years ago when Beethoven was active as a composer, which no one does."

Responding to Professor Ewell is a little like having to present a detailed analysis explaining that the moon is not made of green cheese. It should be obvious to the least musically inclined among us, but it is still necessary. Esperanza Spalding is a jazz bassist and vocalist; her *12 Little Spells* is a collection of pieces related to human body parts. Beethoven's Ninth is based, in part, on the "Ode to Joy" by German playwright, poet, and historian Friedrich Schiller. Beethoven's music and Schiller's words have inspired men and women for generations. (Beethoven's "Ninth" was broadcast by Chinese students in Tiananmen Square during the protest that should never be forgotten and performed under the baton of Leonard Bernstein on Christmas Day following the fall of the Berlin Wall.) The renowned Australian conductor Patrick Thomas wrote, "Above all, perhaps it was Beethoven's faith in Man's inextinguishable brotherhood and his hatred of tyranny that remain the finest examples of this man's unique and lasting inspiration."

Is everyone who finds the sentiments of the "Ode to Joy" more inspiring than human body parts therefore a racist? Ewell also invokes an article by Amanda Hess suggesting that artists' personal behavior be used in evaluating their work. True, musical geniuses often behave badly in their personal lives, but is Ewell suggesting that we ban or regard as illegitimate the works of composers whose behavior regarding race, gender, or politics don't pass his personal test? If so, we would also have to take into consideration the appalling number of rock and rap stars who have been in trouble with the law, have committed crimes, and lived lives filled with appalling personal behavior in public and private; this is a perfect case of someone in a glass house trying to throw stones at others.

What is interesting about Ewell's attitude is what he doesn't discuss, what he clearly leaves out of the discussion. He doesn't address the fact that Beethoven's works have been regarded as masterpieces because of their musicality, because of the composer's masterful use of the elements of music, melody, harmony, and rhythm. Ewell doesn't want to discuss these things because he can't. The finest works in music history by all composers of all genders and races have been the result of inspiration in the use of musical elements. But musical elements don't explain the success of one of Ewell's specialties; he is considered a specialist in rap and hip-hop. He has written about

To Pimp a Butterfly by Kendrick Lamar, a rapper. If Ewell thinks there are works written in Beethoven's day or today that are superior to those of Beethoven, let him produce them. But since he can't win the argument on musical terms, on musical standards, he simply falls back on race. It's rather like saying if a mediocre contestant can't win the game, protest that the rules are unfair and rearrange them so the mediocre contestant is somehow superior.

Ewell is not alone. Bassoonist turned radio talk show host Garrett McQueen holds forth on a podcast called "Trilloquy." *The Minneapolis Star-Tribune* reports that McQueen's favorite targets are "old dead white men" and declares, "McQueen is as likely to profess his love for Beyoncé or Nas as Dmitri Shostakovich or William Grant Still." In McQueen's world, anyone singing "Alleluia" in a Christmas choir is evidently one step removed from membership in the Ku Klux Klan. "You are complicit in racism every time you listen to Handel's 'Messiah,'" McQueen informs his listeners, since Handel owned stock in a company engaged in the slave trade. It is revealing that McQueen is also a fan of rappers and pop singers. His looking at what we typically term classical music through a racial prism is not about composers like William Grant Still, the brilliant and still neglected black composer of concert music. For Still, who faced a true struggle during his long and distinguished career, wrote music that could be appreciated by those who perceive today's rap and pop as an assault on the ears, the mind, and the culture. Handel, you see, is an "old, dead white guy" while NWA, quoted by McQueen, was a group that popularized "gangsta rap" and used as its name an abbreviation for a racial slur.

Like Ewell, McQueen's perspective suggests, even demands, that we respect musical figures that fit his racial and political biases. Lest you think these attitudes are found only among those who populate the musical and political fringe, think again.

In the UK, students at venerable Oxford University, which granted music degrees all the way back in the 15th and 16th centuries, jettison the study of traditional musical notation. The students, presumably assuming they know more than the professors and tutors under whom they nominally study, demanded in 2020 a new emphasis on "non-Eurocentric" musical traditions such as Hip-Hop and Jazz, as well as "African and African Diasporic Musics" and "Global Musics." The students also demanded politicized courses in such serious topics as "Artists Demanding Trump Stop Using Their Songs" at campaign rallies and "Dua Lipa's Record-Breaking Livestream."

The finest jazz musicians created a new art form, a genre with tremendous spontaneity and energy. Jazz emerged as a fusion of African rhythms and a host of American influences over decades. The best jazz musicians are highly sophisticated improvisers and (horrors!) many have been classically trained, steeped in the very traditional musical notation so offensive to the students at Oxford. Like Garrett McQueen, who walked out of a concert including favorable references to George Washington, the Oxford students demand obeisance to the political and cultural diktats of the Marxist organization, Black Lives Matter. It should be clear to anyone with common sense that this is all about politics, not music or art or creativity.

Harvard University, an institution that once regarded the study of real music as inappropriate, established the Nasir Jones Hip-Hop Fellowship in 2013 to honor rapper Nasir Jones, known as "Nas" and one of the "artists" likely to be quoted by Garrett McQueen. "Nas" is not to be confused with Montero Lamar Hill, known as "Lil Nas X," whose "Montero (Call Me By Your Name)" shows the rapper descending into hell on a stripper pole and giving Satan a lap dance. Johann Sebastian Bach used to sign his works Bach wrote *S.D.G.—Soli Deo Gloria—-To God Alone the Glory*. In the new "woke world" of academics, presumably students and scholars need to forget about Bach and begin emulating Nas and Lil Nas X. Music can inspire through its messages; the distinguished 20th century composer Paul Creston said that music as a spiritual practice was as vital to his spiritual welfare as prayer and good deeds. What messages are sent by the music advocated by professors advancing their careers by advocating for rappers?

The ultimate effort to confer respectability on the hip-hoppers came in 2018 when the once-respected Pulitzer Prize for Music was awarded to rapper Kendrick Lamar for his recording "Damn." Beginning in 1943 when William Schuman was awarded the Pulitzer Prize for Music, many distinguished composers won the award, including Howard Hanson, Aaron Copland, Leo Sowerby, Charles Ives, Gian-Carlo Menotti, Douglas Moore, Ernst Toch, Samuel Barber, Roger Sessions, Morton Gould, and Leon Kirchner. In 1965, controversy erupted when the Pulitzer Prize was denied to Duke Ellington after decades of creativity leading the world's most honored jazz ensemble. But there is a great difference between jazz and rap.

When Lamar was given the Prize, Terrence Henderson, described in the *New York Times* as a record executive known as Punch from Top Dawg Entertainment, warned that from now on, no one should "speak with anything less than respect in your mouth for Kendrick Lamar." If the Terence Hendersons of the world are seeking respect, they had best not look in these pages. Rap lyrics are typically filled with profanities, racial slurs and bad rhymes; the non-musical accompaniment usually consists of pulsating, over-amplified noises that appeal to two different audiences; one consists primarily of the very young, ignorant of real music and influenced almost entirely by peer pressure; the second consists of people eager to establish their bona fides as "hip," "woke," "with it," "politically correct," or to advertise their devotion to "diversity and inclusion."

Since rap was created by black promoters, anyone criticizing rap is assured of being accused of racism. Ironically, the musicians least likely to receive honors or attention from a world that appreciates rap are the incredibly gifted black classical and jazz musicians who have worked a lifetime to excel at their art only to be dismissed as passé in many cases before their careers have even started to garner public attention. It does not require talent or skill to produce commercially viable hip-hop; it requires a certain cunning genius in the art of self-promotion. Consider the young musician, black or white, who wants to be the next William

Grant Still or Margaret Bonds or Oscar Peterson or Charlie Parker or Duke Ellington. Such a musician is being sent precisely the wrong message: mediocrity trumps skill, talent, and standards.

African-American trumpeter, composer, and Pulitzer-Prize winner Wynton Marsalis made this very point to podcaster Jonathan Capehart. Said Marsalis, "You can't have a pipeline of filth be your default position, and it's free. Now, the nation is entertained by that. It's not free. Just like the toll the minstrel show took on black folks and on white folks. Now all this "nigga" this, "bitch" that, "ho" that, it's just a fact at this point." Marsalis concluded, "Something is wrong with you, you need your head examined if you like this. It's almost like adults left the room or something."

The members of the Pulitzer Prize committee may imply in public that they have elevated the award by being inclusive; in fact, they have done quite the opposite; they have reduced and dishonored a once revered award, for a prize is known by the company it keeps.

As for the promoters demanding respect for rap, like rock promoters before them, they are undoubtedly laughing at the academics and scholars who are trying to preserve their own relevance by jumping aboard the speeding rock 'n' rap train. It is nice to become a billionaire even if respectability was elusive; now that it is being literally thrown at them, they can laugh instead of crying . . . but still, all the way to the bank.

As for those who should know better, congratulating themselves on successfully surviving the rock 'n' rap revolution, do they think themselves morally and culturally superior to the rest of us? Or are they simply relieved that they are "relevant" and "woke," "with it" or whatever term is currently *en vogue* among the not truly elite pseudo-intellectuals who lend respectability to the decline and fall of our culture? They would do well to remember the words of Charles Péguy. Péguy, a French poet and essayist, expressed an idea that is truly relevant today all the way back in 1905 in *Notre Patrie*. Said Péguy, "It will never be known what acts of cowardice have been committed for fear of not looking sufficiently progressive."

Judge Robert Bork, though not a musician, summed up the case regarding rap well. He wrote, in his book, *Slouching Toward Gomorrah*, "The difference between the music and Tin Pan Alley and rap is so stark that it is misleading to call them both music. Rock and rap are utterly impoverished by comparison with swing or jazz or any pre-World War II music, impoverished emotionally, aesthetically, and intellectually. Rap is simply unable to express tenderness, gentleness, or love." Judge Bork wisely concluded, "Neither rock nor rap can begin to approach the complicated melodies of George Gershwin, Irving Berlin, or Cole Porter. Nor do their lyrics display any of the wit of Ira Gershwin, Porter, Fats Waller, or Johnny Mercer. The bands that play this music lack even a trace of the musicianship of the bands led by Benny Goodman, Duke Ellington, and many others of that era."[81]

Natalie Jones, the daughter of immigrants and a teacher at London's remarkable Michaela Community School, assails the message of much of rap as idealizing violence, money, power, and crime, and usually the notion of black men killing other black men. She writes in *The Power of Culture*, "Most black families would hear these violent lyrics and feel they're disgusting and awful." She speaks from personal experience. Her father, she says, would be horrified by the presentation of such notions as "black culture." [82] But the rap promoters, academic charlatans, and racial ideologues don't care. They have an agenda far different from concern about the message of rap or its cultural impact.

Thus far in the assault on great music using charges of racism as a political and economic bludgeon, there have been few defenders or heroes. The always prescient Heather Mac Donald, writing in *City Journal*, has called this "the suicide of classical music." She says, "The canonical repertoire—the product of a centuries-long tradition of musical expression—is allegedly a function of white supremacy. Not one leader in the field has defended Western art music against these charges. Their silence is emblematic."[83]

The fate of all good music written by composers of all races hangs in the balance; the unholy alliance of ruthless music promoters, radical political ideologues, craven but weak academicians, and students combining rare degrees of arrogance and ignorance present an improbable but deadly threat. No one would ever have imagined that Francis Parkman's cry of "Musica delenda est" in the 19th century would potentially come true in the 21st. The battle is not over; the struggle is not lost; but if great music is to survive, those devoted to it must take action before it is too late.

Thus, in the worlds of both classical and popular music, the problem is the same. Classical music has rejected its potentially large audience to pursue the quixotic tastes of an elite more interested in the wrapping than in the contents of the package. Popular music has pursued a willing and gullible mass audience to such a degree that it is void of all standards, except the margin of profit, and specifically ignores the ghastly consequences. Despite what has happened, there is room for hope! In 2017, during a copyright dispute, Bulgaria's public radio station was suddenly limited to airing music recorded at least seventy years ago. With the current pop stars unavailable, the station began airing classical music and jazz recordings from a bygone era. Did listeners flee in droves? Hardly. The station reported a twenty percent increase in listenership. When real music is given a chance, it can flourish and survive in the modern age.

Bernard Herrmann eloquently observed, "I count myself an individual. I hate all cults, fads and circles. I believe that only music that spring out of genuine personal emotion and inspiration is alive and important." Herrmann concluded, "Music is a beautiful art—if not the greatest of all arts. It's the kind of beauty that lives in time and space, and in each performance over and over again.... Some people have got to preserve the beauty of the past. It's important to preserve the past, because you can't have a present and a future if you have no past." Unless something changes, the best classical and popular music which has been written will fade gradually into oblivion; those capable of writing it today will wrestle with constant rejection and neglect; those capable of creating it in the future will be undiscovered. Audiences of all ages today and tomorrow will, for the most part, be unaware of what has been lost.

WHATEVER HAPPENED TO ART?

DO YOU LIKE MODERN ART?

IN 2007, DAMIEN HIRST, OFTEN DESCRIBED AS BRITAIN'S wealthiest artist, placed a new work on the auction block. Hirst offered a platinum skull, studded with 8,601 diamonds. It sold for $100 million to a group of investors who paid cash. Two years later, a silk screen by pop artist Andy Warhol was auctioned for a mere forty-four million dollars. Modern art is big business, but is it art?

Discussions about modern art, like those about politics and religion, can become intense and fueled by controversy. There is even substantial disagreement over the term "modern art." Some skeptics insist that much modern art isn't modern and isn't art.

A number of influential museums and galleries feature the work of modern artists, some of which are reviewed with acclaim by art critics and academics. But a significant portion of the general public is singularly unenthusiastic about what is generally described as modern art. This segment of the public may still respect the work of the old masters; but they often regard modern art as, at best, incomprehensible, and at worst, a fraud. Advocates of modern art frequently dismiss their critics as ignorant and uninformed. Simultaneously, they dismiss realistic artists, those who paint or draw recognizable subjects such as portraits, landscapes, and seascapes, as outdated and irrelevant to the contemporary age. Therein lies the controversy and confusion over modern art.

Robert Johanningmeier, a gifted realistic artist from New Mexico, provided a provocative view of modern art in his book, *The "Art" of Investing While Collecting*.[84] Johanningmeier wrote, "In contrast to Traditional Art (where the artist is more interested in communicating a worthwhile statement than in making a show of how he presents such a statement), the modern artist will often shift his emphasis away from the meaning of his work, while he intentionally draws the public's attention to the techniques, or manner of presentation." Johanningmeier wisely sees parallels between the presentation of modern art and contemporary music. He says, "Modern singers can be seen to be making highly animated movements, falling into a trance or grimacing in pain at sounds we hardly hear. By displaying a labored and strained performance, such artists are trying to convince the audience that the substance of what is being conveyed is indeed quite extraordinary. Among visual artists, one frequently hears more talk about the significance of this or that new material or procedure, than about the actual message that has (or has not) been conveyed to the viewer. In Modern Art, the how can become more important than the what."

Johanningmeier contrasts traditional art, often inspired by things the artist sees—scenery, nature, people, or even the history of art itself—and modern art, with an emphasis on the individual expressing himself. The artist who paints realistically has to acquire a substantial degree of technique, because his work can be evaluated on technical grounds. One need not be an art expert to recognize that a picture representing an apple is badly drawn if the fruit looks more like a grapefruit. But in modern art, the artist typically sets his own standards; since his paintings don't represent anything specific, they cannot be criticized technically. If an artist wants to express himself and you don't happen to like what he is expressing, it's your problem, not his. Artists do not need to spend years studying technique simply to express themselves.

Because many modern artists do not produce works that inspire or elevate the viewer, their success often depends on the degree to which they become recognized as famous or important. Endorsements from major museums and galleries often based in large art markets like New York may be the difference between fame and failure for the modern artist. Influential art critics and academics associated with prestigious institutions form an elite clique that determines which artists will be taken seriously by collectors and by the public. A modern artist can become famous because of his publicity, not his technique. In the world of modern art, nearly anything can be defined as "art"; the elite of the art world will dismiss skeptics as uninformed and unsophisticated. Modern artists are often quite prolific, since their works frequently require neither the time nor the technique demanded by traditional art. Hilton Kramer, founder of the cultural journal *The New Criterion* and former art critic of the *New York Times*, says that the art world has its share of licensed jesters and tenured revolutionaries. These people often receive the lion's share of publicity in the media.

Robert Johanningmeier sums up his argument by declaring, "But what a travesty that our society should be teaching the young that even the ugly and distasteful are to be thought of as being appealing or worthy of praise. And what confusion this must be creating in the minds of our children."

How did this happen?

THE FOUNTAIN AND THE BRILLO BOX

When 19th century artists began to sow the seeds of revolution, there were dissenting voices. Lord Leighton was a prominent and widely respected British painter. (He was an acquaintance of George Bernard Shaw and rumored to be Shaw's model for the character of Henry Higgins in the play *Pygmalion.)* As far back as 1881, Lord Leighton delivered a famous speech to the British Academy in which he urged artists to remember, "The province of Art is to speak to the emotional sense, not to make vain exhibition of acquired knowledge, and the work which reveals in the workman no impulse warmer or higher than vanity."

In the years before World War I, Kenyon Cox, an American muralist, expressed his concern regarding the fate of artists who followed tradition and painted things people could recognize through representational art. In "Two Ways of Painting,"[85] he wrote, "The pressure to conformity is upon the other side and it is the older methods that need justification and explanation. The prejudices of the workers and the writers have gradually and naturally become the prejudices of at least a part of the public, and it has become necessary to show that the small minority of artists who still follow the old roads do so, not from ignorance or stupidity or a stolid conservatism, still less from willful caprice, but from necessity; because those roads are the only ones that can lead them where they wish to go." Cox insisted, "The scientific spirit, the contempt of tradition, the lack of discipline and the exaltation of the individual have very nearly made an end of art." World War I turned the old order upside down, and in both Europe and America, a new breed of professional art critics were quick to jump aboard a Roaring Twenties bandwagon of change for change's sake. The vanity which troubled Lord Leighton and the contempt for tradition that alarmed Cox were suddenly worn by artists like badges of honor. As 20th century art evolved, shock and surprise were the order of the day. The critics applauded and the public, not wanting to seem ignorant or unfashionable, marched along in lock step.

In the years following World War I, Paris became a haven for writers, musicians, and artists. This was the Paris that Ernest Hemingway described in his memoir, *A Movable Feast.* Hemingway, F. Scott Fitzgerald, and James Joyce were only a few of the writers who found that Paris offered personal and artistic freedom at an affordable price. A new generation of young American composers, including Aaron Copland, Roy Harris, Virgil Thomson, and Walter Piston, took the remarkable step at the time of studying composition with a woman, Nadia Boulanger. The group would be nicknamed the "Boulangerie," the French word for "bakery." But it was in the visual arts more than in any other field that Paris would have a lasting legacy. Paris was also the capital of the fashion industry, an industry that required not only beauty and style, but marketing and promotion. The British historian Paul Johnson has argued that much of the most commercially successful 20th century art was "fashion art" as opposed to "fine art." For Johnson, this art was the result of a desire for novelty enhanced by the needs of the marketplace. He believes that this combination of novelty and promotion was tailor-made to turn art away from the ideal of beauty to the ideal of ugliness.

Post-war Paris would produce a plethora of artists who came from around the world; the most celebrated of these artists differed in talent, attitudes, and styles. Some were allies; others became bitter enemies. Some had started experimenting with new and radical departures from traditional art before the First World War. But now, their moment in history had arrived. What they shared was an ability to shock and surprise people, a capacity to promote themselves, and invariably, a skill at explaining their art through a movement or philosophy. Post-war artists in Germany and Italy joined the club. These were artists who identified with a whole series of "isms." There was "cubism," developed by the Spaniard Pablo Picasso and the Frenchman Georges Braques. The two were close friends and called each other "Orville" and "Wilbur" after the aviation pioneers, Orville and Wilbur Wright. The cubists could chop up an image and shift the pieces around; a person might have one eye where it belongs and the other in the back of his head. "Futurism" thrived in Milan, where the artists practicing it insisted that museums should all be destroyed. "Surrealism" was supposed to depict the artist's impression of the subconscious mind, as practiced by Spaniards Salvador Dali and Joan Miró and the Belgian René Magritte. Dali would portray nightmares on canvas, with human limbs, animals, watches, and various objects of his choosing all thrown together. "Expressionism" was practiced by the Russian, Wassily Kandinsky, who turned to abstraction and away from realistic depiction of anything. The most outrageous movement, "Dada" referred to a French nickname for a hobbyhorse. The person selecting the word was blindfolded and inserted a pencil at random into a dictionary. "Dada" was intentionally outrageous; its founder was Tristan Tzara, a Romanian poet who once appeared on stage for a half hour barking like a dog as part of "Dada theater." If the public didn't understand what Tzara was doing, so much the better. He said that any work of art which could be understood was the product of a journalist. So art that confused people and would be misunderstood became the ideal. The artist who gained the most attention through Dada was Marcel Duchamp.

In 1917, the French artist Marcel Duchamp shocked the art world when he signed a white urinal, renamed it *Fountain* and put it on display. Years later in 1946, Duchamp admitted, "I threw the bottle rack and the urinal in their faces, and they now admire them for their aesthetic beauty." But Duchamp's urinal was still taken quite seriously as recently as 2004. Five hundred art experts were surveyed and asked to name the most influential modern artwork. Duchamp's *Fountain* was chosen. Simon Wilson, one of the art experts, expressed surprise that Duchamp's urinal outpolled works by Picasso and Matisse, but he added that it "reflects the dynamic nature of art today and the idea that the creative process that goes into a work of art is the most important thing—the work itself can be made of anything and can take any form." Roger Kimball, author and editor of *The New Criterion*, summarized the problem in his book, *Art's Progress: The Challenge of Tradition in an Age of Celebrity,*[86] when he addressed the critical standards of the art world in general and museums in particular. Kimball said, "Notoriety, not accomplishment, became the chief goal of art, even as terms like 'challenging' and 'transgressive' took precedence over 'beautiful' and other traditional commendations in the lexicon of critical praise." Throughout the 20th century, the trend continued. The names and styles changed, but the pattern was almost always the same: an ambitious, highly promoted artist, a style that would provoke shock and controversy, and an artistic, political, or philosophical theory that could be offered to the public to explain what was taking place.

THE WORDS ON THE CANVAS

As in the world of music, advocates of the avant-garde have made their statement in the world of art. Therefore, "classical" or "serious" art suffered a curious fate. The composers of operas, ballets, and symphonic and chamber music, as well as serious painters and playwrights, began to regard mass audiences as anathema. They gradually adopted theories and ideas that led them to pursue creative styles, which divorced their work from qualities the public found appealing. While the artistic elite argued about theories and abstractions, the general public simply lost interest in modern art and music. The elite dismissed the public as ignorant and quickly established their own criteria for evaluating culture. For the cultural elite, especially those in academia, the theory by which a work could be analyzed was more important than the work itself. Anyone with a theory about art could become an arbiter of taste; this applied to music, books, theater, and anything else worthy of commentary. Like many music critics, a host of self-proclaimed art "experts" has been quick to praise the geniuses of modern art. Art critics, like their colleagues in music and theater, usually take the position that anything labeled as "new" must be progressive; those who are critical are considered to be against change. The art critic Clement Greenberg said, "All profoundly original art looks ugly at first."

There have been dissenters, none more articulate or lethal than Tom Wolfe. Wolfe identified these trends with devastating satire in his scathing and brilliant books on art (*The Painted Word)*[87] and architecture *(From Bauhaus to Our House).*[88] The premise of *The Painted Word* is that in contemporary art, what is meaningful is not the painting, but the artist's verbal explanation of his work and the critics verbal reaction to it. *From Bauhaus to Our House* traces origins of modern architecture to German post- war worker housing, applied, for political and aesthetic reasons, to completely unrelated conditions in America. There were no sacred cows to be found grazing in Wolfe's architectural pasture. He asked, "O Beautiful, for spacious skies, for amber waves of grain, has there ever been another place on earth where so many people of wealth and power have paid for and put up with so much architecture they detested within thy blessed borders today?" Wolfe compared new school buildings to warehouses and expensive summer homes in the north woods of Michigan or on the shore of Long Island to insecticide refineries complete with pipe railings, sheets of industrial plate glass, and banks of tungsten-halogen lamps. Wolfe's thesis was that both art and architecture have suffered from highly flawed theories, which have simply been imposed on the public.

If the public had no interest in theories about art, it cared deeply about being fashionable. (These are the people who go to the opera to be seen, go to symphony concerts even though they don't especially like music, and support the local museum to get their names listed on plaques and in newspaper columns.) Some, who could afford to become serious collectors, invested astronomical sums in works of art based on the advice of critics and "experts." In contrast, critics and academicians came to regard theories about art as paramount. Artists were quick to discover that a marketable theory could make their work highly marketable as well.

Realistic artists, on the other hand, are those who paint things we can actually recognize. Tom Wolfe happened to read a review of an exhibition of realistic paintings declaring that realistic artists lacked something crucial to painting, a "persuasive theory." For Wolfe, this was an epiphany. He suddenly understood why he found many modern paintings unappealing. Wolfe's thesis was provocative: modern art had become dependent upon verbal explanations to justify its existence and establish its artistic worth. Many of us believe, as Wolfe did, that "seeing is believing." But Wolfe was stunned by the realization that in the world of modern art, "believing is seeing." The astonished Wolfe wrote, "Modern art has become completely literary. The paintings and other works exist only to illustrate the text."

In *The Painted Word*, Wolfe went on to portray an art world dominated by many social and economic forces, most of which have nothing to do with art. Using his pen like a rapier, he dissected the social milieu of publishers, writers, performers, and socialites who desire, above all else, to be fashionable, to be accepted, to be where "things happen." In the world of the social and critical elite, everybody's opinion counts. But "everybody" includes only members of the club; the public is definitely not invited. For Wolfe, the art world is a small town, which always looks to bohemia for the "new wave" of art. Bohemia consists of circles, cliques, schools, coteries, and small groups of artists known as "cenacles." One new wave in the 1950s came from the "Tenth Street School." For a controversial group of painters in New York, flatness was the ideal. If a picture didn't seem flat, it was definitely not worthwhile. Three-dimensional images need not apply.

The works of these highly influential artists were explained and analyzed at length by a pair of equally influential critics, Clement Greenberg and Harold Rosenberg. Jackson Pollock was declared the artistic master of creating paintings, which were flat. Rosenberg described Pollock's approach to painting as "action painting," in which art became not just a picture but "an event." However, the name that stuck to the work of Pollock and his followers was "abstract expressionism." Although Greenberg and Rosenberg were supportive of Pollock, others did not agree and controversy followed. *Time* magazine gave Pollock the unflattering nickname of "Jack the Dripper." He earned that label because of his technique of throwing large amounts of red paint on a canvas placed on the floor. Craig Brown, a British artist and critic, dismissed Pollock's work as "brainless wallpaper" that should never be placed on the same pedestal as works of the masters. Those who didn't like abstract painting hoped that art would again present recognizable images on canvas. They didn't have to wait long.

In 1960, a Hunter College professor, Leo Steinberg, espoused a new theory. In a series of influential lectures at the Museum of Modern Art in New York, Steinberg insisted that some objects were intrinsically flat and a painter could reproduce them by giving them a "higher synthesis." The result of this "higher synthesis" was the birth of the "pop art" movement, which had started attracting attention two years earlier. Jasper Johns, Robert Rauschenberg, Roy Lichtenstein, and Andy Warhol were its stars. For the masters of "pop art," all kinds of ordinary objects could be turned into big time art. "Pop art" was appealing to the young, could be mass-produced and mass marketed, didn't have a long shelf-life, and fit the new pop culture of the 1960s. Unlike abstractions, the subjects were easy to understand and easy to promote. Jasper Johns, for instance, painted archery targets and rows of numbers; he also produced "Painted Bronze," a sculpture of two beer cans. Not to be outdone, Robert Rauschenberg exhibited three real Coca Cola bottles with angel's wings. Pop artists produced paintings of the American flag, comic strips, and soup cans. Andy Warhol became famous for his paintings of celebrities of pop culture, including Marilyn Monroe and Elvis Presley. No artist had a greater instinct for generating publicity than Andy Warhol. He did paintings of Campbell's Soup Cans and actually sold autographed soup cans to an adoring public. Warhol participated in a 1964 exhibit called "The American Supermarket," featuring his painting of a Campbell's Soup Can, which sold for $1500, and autographed soup cans, which were priced at $6. Warhol suggested that commercial objects like Brillo boxes could be displayed as art. His silkscreened ink-on-wood replicas of the boxes that contain Brillo soap pads are considered his most important sculptures. Reactions to the new pop art were mixed, as people with common sense asked how displaying a cereal box or a soup can was comparable to great sculpture or painting. Warhol disarmed his critics, however, by embracing commercialism quite openly. When accused of being "plastic," he responded, "I love Los Angeles. I love Hollywood. They're so beautiful. Everything's plastic, but I love plastic. I want to be plastic." Warhol's profits were not plastic, however, nor are the two museums devoted to his work. One is in Pittsburgh where he grew up—the largest American art museum dedicated to a single artist; the other in Slovakia, where his family was born. Although established critics like Clement Greenberg denounced the pop artists, others like Leo Steinberg insisted that pop art was here to stay.

In 1964, *Time* magazine informed the public of the arrival of yet another new movement: art based on optical effects. In contrast to "pop art," "op art" presented geometric designs that made no pretense at representing actual objects. In 1965, The Museum of Modern Art presented "The Responsive Eye," an exhibition devoted entirely to "op art." These works depicted optical illusions, apparently in motion, but actually quite still. The new art was taken seriously by everyone, while more traditional art was dismissed as "old-fashioned." When skeptics asked "What is art?" advocates for modern art were quick to answer, "Anything."

By 1970, Tom Wolfe would find a new form of modern art in which nothing was demanded of the artist. The new art did not require an artist to possess skills using colors, creating visual images, or mastering proportion. The new art represented for Wolfe an "insouciant withering away," and when its metamorphosis was complete, it emerged as "art theory." The word, not the picture, had become the real picture.

THE ARTIST'S NEW CLOTHES

The classic tale of *The Emperor's New Clothes* is the story of an Emperor who is fooled by charlatans into believing that his splendid new suit of clothes can only be seen by those who are intelligent. Actually, there is no suit of clothing, but the Emperor and his subjects are afraid of appearing ignorant, so they all pretend that the Emperor is fashionably dressed. Eventually one person is unafraid to call out, "The Emperor wears no clothes at all." Those cheering the Emperor in his birthday suit do not welcome the truth about the Emperor's new clothes.

Today, a group of elite academics and critics have appointed themselves arbiters of taste and culture. Like the Emperor's subjects, many people are afraid of being characterized as yahoos and ignoramuses who aren't smart or sophisticated enough to understand what is being offered as "art." At concerts, art exhibits, and theatrical and film premieres, the audiences and the arbiters smile knowingly at one another, congratulating themselves on their intellectual superiority. At soirees for authors, literary critics and readers sip wine and enjoy Brie and hors d'oeuvres, confident that they are secure in their symbiotic superiority. The publishers, art dealers, producers, and music executives are all making money out of the arrangement, as are the composers, authors, and artists. For the consumer, it's an easy way to join an exclusive club. You simply accept the fact that if you don't appreciate whatever is fashionable in our culture, it's your own fault. If you want to be chic and in fashion, you simply express disdain for the ignorant and unsophisticated who don't appreciate *The Emperor's New*

Clothes. Eventually someone will shout that the Emperor wears no clothes at all. But he will be dismissed as an uneducated fool.

Occasionally, the critics, dealers, and arbiters of artistic taste have been "hoisted by their own petards." In 1924, critics were enthusiastic about a brilliant and revolutionary new Russian artist, Pavel Jerdanowitch. Jerdanowitch came to public attention with a painting called *Exaltation*, featuring a woman triumphantly waving a banana peel over her head. Jerdanowitch explained that the woman was making a feminist statement about her newfound freedom after taking a bite of the banana. Jerdanowitch was so well received that he began offering other paintings in the modern cubist style, including one, *Illumination*, which featured various lines and eyeballs. Admirers were hailing Jerdanowitch as the leader of his self-described "disumbrationist" school of art. There was, however, a small problem in this saga of artistic success. Jerdanowitch didn't exist. He was actually Paul Jordan Smith, a California writer and Latin scholar who painted *Exaltation* as a joke intended to ridicule what he regarded as absurd styles of modern art. Smith continued painting for a while and then revealed the truth to *The Los Angeles Times*. He had proven his point. Anyone with an exotic name and a pompous theory explaining his artwork could be taken seriously by the critics. Admirers of the bogus "disumbrationist" master were embarrassed, but then they promptly moved to applaud the genius of other painters with similar qualifications. If any of these painters were laughing in private like Paul Jordan Smith, they weren't talking. They were too busy selling paintings to willing galleries and eager collectors.

The "disumbrationist" episode wasn't unique. Four decades later, critics began singing the praises of an avant-garde painter, Pierre Brassau. They complimented his strong brush strokes and compared his artistic delicacy to that of a ballet dancer. Brassau's paintings were proudly hung in a gallery until his mentors revealed that the true artist was not Pierre, but Peter, a four-year-old chimpanzee in the Boras Zoo in Sweden.

In recent years, Dr. Katja Schneider, director of the State Art Museum in Moritzburg, Sweden, mistakenly identified a painting as the work of Ernst Wilhelm Nay. She observed the blotches of color identified with Nay's style. Unfortunately, the artist was not as well known as Nay. Banghi, a thirty-one-year-old female chimpanzee, had painted the work at a local zoo. It is doubtful that Banghi will leave a substantial artistic legacy. News reports say that she enjoys painting, but her mate, Satscho, apparently no fan of modern art, destroys most of her works before they can be exhibited; obviously a cause for feminist protesters, but a step backward for art historians. Dealers in search of potentially marketable modern art stars need not confine themselves to Greenwich Village, Soho, or the Left Bank. Congo, a chimpanzee born in 1954, turned out four hundred paintings between the ages of two and four. Congo died in 1964, but his works are now collector's items. In 2005, a London auction house sold one of his paintings, which outsold both Renoir and pop art icon Andy Warhol by $25,000.

Estelle Lovatt, an instructor at the Hampstead School of Art in England and a freelance art critic, was surprised that her eight-month-old son, Freddy Linsky, could hold a paintbrush and liked to dip his fingers in paint. Freddy was allowed to throw ketchup onto a canvas and by the time he was two, he had graduated to acrylics. His mother decided to post some of Freddy's paintings on an online gallery established by art collector Charles Saatchi. Freddy's mother also added some absurdly impressive captions to his paintings. One painting, called "Sunrise," was described as offering "a bold use of color, inspired by the 'plein air' habit of painting by Monet, drawing on the natural world that surrounds us all." For good measure, Freddie was described as having devoted his whole life to art. (This wasn't an exaggeration, since Freddie had been painting for more than half of his two years.) Estelle Lovatt described her son's technique as influenced by the "splotch and blotch" approach favored by the American expressionists of the 1950s. The art teacher was startled when one of Freddie's paintings, consisting of black scrawling on canvas, appealed to a collector who paid twenty-five pounds for it. The painting, captioned "The Best Loved Elephant," was described as featuring "the striking use of Oriental calligraphy" with "kanji-like characters stampeding from the page, showing the new ascent of the East." When a Berlin museum expressed interest in exhibiting Freddie's paintings, the toddler didn't offer comments to the press. But his mother explained that he was always very excited about the mess he gets to make when he paints.

Damien Hirst's works sell for considerably more than Freddy Linsky's and his works are actually owned by Charles Saatchi. Hirst's artistic genius may be debatable, but his genius as a promoter of his own work can hardly be challenged. One of Hirst's works, *The Golden Calf*, was sold for 10.3 million pounds in Britain. *The Golden Calf* was denounced as a gilded vulgarity by writer Christopher Hart, who responded to those who suggested that Michelangelo and Hirst both depended on wealthy art patrons to succeed. Hart writes, "Look at the Sistine Chapel, and then look at Hirst's works—his pickled animals, dead flies, and pill collections. The contrast would be laughable if it weren't such a terrible example of how our cultural values have collapsed. The truth is, Hirst is not an artist, he's a businessman who manufactures art for a carefully groomed, gullible and obedient clientele. His name is now a global brand, like Nike or Coca-Cola." Hirst himself acknowledges not painting all his works, once laughing that the best ones were done by his assistant. One of Hirst's masterpieces is *The Physical Impossibility of Death in the Mind of Someone Living,* a 14-foot tiger shark in a tank of formaldehyde. When the odor of the pickled shark became unbearable, a team of specialists in industrial jumpsuits had to drain the tank and re-pickle the shark with fresh solution. Hart reports that Hirst never laid a finger on his artwork. Hirst paid the Wallace Collection, known for exhibiting works by Rembrandt and Rubens, 250,000 pounds to allow him to cover the walls of two galleries with blue silk and to then hang twenty-five of his own paintings, all of which were entirely his own work. Canvases were painted blue and then decorated with assorted images of skulls, cigarettes, and ashtrays.

Hirst also opened a chain of outlets to sell his products directly to the public.

Not all critics and historians have been fooled. Roger Kimball wrote a devastating critique of the current art world in *The New Criterion*.[89] Summing up the journey from Duchamp to Warhol and Hirst, Kimball targets not only the pied pipers of promotion, but the gullible public marching in their parade. He writes, "The public had been thoroughly softened up. They were weary and punch drunk. Above all, they were pliable. Here's a huge stylized blowup of a comic strip. What do you think? A short intake of breath. A furtive look around. Then some brazen soul raises his hand and ventures: 'A work of genius?' The chorus soon trumpeted its affirmation, 'A work of genius!' General merriment, exeunt omnes."

Damien Hirst is hardly alone in his ability to combine self-promotion and an ability to shock with a successful art career. Tracey Emin is another of the self-proclaimed "Young British Artists," who gained notoriety in 1997 by exhibiting a tent appliquéd with names under the title, *Everyone I Have Ever Slept With 1963-1995*. (The list included sexual partners, family members, and her two aborted children.) Two years later she produced an installation called *My Bed*, exhibiting her own dirty bed, complete with used clothing and representations of body fluids, as a work of art. The Saatchi Gallery offered an explanation of Emin's artistry. It called her the consummate storyteller, engaging the viewer with "her candid exploration of universal emotions." The gallery goes on to rhapsodize over the presence of "empty booze bottles" and used underwear, and concludes, "By presenting her bed as art, Tracy Emin shares her most personal space, revealing she's as insecure and imperfect as the rest of the world." Emin's work is taken quite seriously by critics and academicians. (She was invited to become a Royal Academician at the Royal Academy of Arts and is considered an honored lecturer at prestigious institutions throughout Europe.) Emin began her career by opening her own art shop with fellow artist Sarah Lucas. In addition to art, they sold T-shirts and ashtrays with pictures of

Damien Hirst on the bottom. Emin has been prolific in producing all sorts of products which are declared works of art, ranging from sexually explicit paintings with four-letter word titles to installation pieces like one made of hospital gowns, wire, hanging frames, and a water bottle. Like Damien Hirst, Emin uses assistants during the creation of her work. When she exhibited at the 52nd International Art Exhibition in Venice Biennale, Emin described her work as "pretty and hard-core." It is also highly profitable and tells us something about the insecurities and imperfections of gallery owners, critics, and professors.

The legacy of Marcel Duchamp is alive and well in the modern age. Jonathan P. Bionstock, curator of contemporary art at the Corcoran Gallery of Art, has praised Italian artist Maurizio Cattelan as "one of the great post-Duchampian artists and a smart ass too." What has Cattelan done to deserve this dubious encomium? In 2010, Cattelan, one of Italy's most famous modern artists, unveiled L.O.V.E, popularly known as "The Middle Finger," in the Piazza d'Affari just outside the Milan stock exchange. The work is an enormous hand, sculpted from Carrara marble, the same material used by Michelangelo and Bernini. But Cattelan's hand is most notable for its upraised middle finger. His admirers describe him as a "provocateur," and with good reason. His most famous work is *La Nona Ora* (The Ninth Hour), which depicted Pope John Paul II hit by a meteorite. The work was exhibited in 1999 at the Royal Academy in London and then sold by Christie's prestigious auction house for $3 million. Cattelan wasn't finished. The following year, his gallerist Emmanuel Perrotin spent a month dressed as a giant pink phallus. In 2004, Christie's sold another Cattelan work, *Par Peur de l'Amour*, for $2.7 million, depicting an elephant dressed as a Ku Klux Klansman. Do the works of Cattelan inspire or elevate the viewer? Clearly, they do not, but they are highly profitable.

In 2010, the prestigious National Portrait Gallery, under the auspices of the Smithsonian Institution, presented an art exhibit during the Christmas season, *Hide/Seek*. Among the images present were those of Christ on the cross with ants crawling over his body and face, male genitals, naked brothers kissing, men in chains, and comedian Ellen DeGeneres grabbing her breasts. David C. Ward, co-curator of the exhibit and a National Portrait Gallery historian, described the works of art as "masterpieces of American portraiture." After considerable public outrage, the video depicting Christ covered by ants was withdrawn. While some were outraged that the Smithsonian Institution, which received taxpayer funds, would sponsor such an exhibit, there is another question, which is usually ignored in such discussions. The opportunities to exhibit art at the National Portrait Gallery are limited. When exhibits of such works of art are presented, other artists lose the chance for their work to be featured. Those whose messages are inspirational or whose techniques are traditional are simply neglected. On occasion, the ambivalent definition of modern art can cause confusion. In 2011, a cleaning woman at the Ostwall Museum in Dortmund, Germany saw a trough placed under a tower of wooden slats in an exhibit area. The trough appeared to be stained with dried rain water. The cleaner zealously scrubbed the trough until the stains had entirely disappeared, only to learn later that the stains were caused by a thin layer of paint deliberately added by artist Martin Kippenberger. The work was titled "When It Starts Dripping From the Ceiling." It was on loan from a private collector and insured for over a million dollars. This was not the first such episode. In 1986, a cleaner mopped up a "grease stain" which turned out to be a creation of artist Joseph Beuys. The "grease stain" was part of an art exhibit at the Academy of Fine Arts in Duesseldorf, Germany, this time insured for over a half- million dollars. When these incidents occur, the cognoscenti are quick to sneer at the ignorance of uncultured domestics who don't recognize true art. But if we truly think of the implications of drips and stains as elements of art, we may ask ourselves who is really confused about the true nature of artistic expression.

None of these episodes suggests that artists should not experiment or that the definition of art must be eternally static. But they do validate an uncomfortable truth about the art world. Critics, academicians, and dealers are all too eager to accept the pretentious (and sometimes outright fraudulent) in their pursuit of modernity. Segments of the public, which often cares and knows little about art, are gullible enough to pay serious attention to this foolishness. All the while, the best and brightest artists are likely to be told that their work is irrelevant. The British historian Paul Johnson is also a painter. In his book, *Art: A New History*,[90] he describes the modern art establishment as wielding immense power to both create and render invisible. He says, "They do not burn paintings, as Hitler did, or send artists to the Gulag, as was the wont of Stalin. Nor do they manipulate mobs of Red Guards to butcher sculptors and craftsmen in the streets. But they break the hearts and impoverish the lives of artists who do not conform to their meretricious criteria. Writers and editors who resist these establishments quickly find themselves without jobs or platforms."

What has happened to those artists who are rugged individualists and do not conform to the tyranny of the new?

THE CURIOUS FATE OF REALISTIC ART

Tom Wolfe wrote *The Painted Word* in 1975. When it returned to print at the end of the 20th century, Wolfe could point to an interesting trend: a revival of realistic art. Painters of realistic images—those we can recognize, those with three dimensions, proportion, color, and form—did not disappear. But many moved underground, ignored and neglected by condescending critics who echoed the party line of the elite art world. "Everybody" knew that realistic art was old-fashioned and out of date. "Everybody" knew which theories on visual art were fashionable at the moment, being marketed by the "best" galleries, taught in the "best" schools, appreciated by the "best" people. With a wink and a nod, the elite of the art world bowed and scraped before their chosen stars. Anyone challenging the status quo could be dismissed as ignorant and uneducated in the ways of art. Should such challenge come from someone highly educated, the offending party could still be dismissed as a hopeless dinosaur—a relic of the past opposed to progress, change, and worst of all, "out" in a world of people whose most passionate desire is to be "in."

Many of the most gifted representational artists continue to struggle. Some have justifiably built reputations on their talents; there are those specializing in particular genres of painting, like "cowboy art" for instance, who have found niche markets producing a good economic return for the artist. Despite these problems, courageous and creative artists today are challenging the modern art establishment. They are now the true non-conformists, the true dissenters from the convention of confusion. There is a revival of interest and respect for artists of tradition. Thomas Hoving was Director of the Metropolitan Museum in New York and editor of *Connoisseur* magazine. Hoving described a refreshing gradual disappearance of art criticism based on ideology. He said, "Critics and historians are beginning to recognize that styles are simply languages with no one inherently better than another." He praised the new "forgiving, permissive mood" in the art world. What is most intriguing about Hoving's observations, however, is that he made them by explaining that the professional art world could now "tolerate" and even praise the incredibly popular work of Norman Rockwell. Rockwell, Hoving explained, had been dismissed by critics as a mawkish sentimentalist, an illustrator who saw life through rose colored glasses and imagined a perfect and unrealistic America. We can only hope that Hoving's optimism will be justified. But isn't it interesting to note that this new tolerance is needed not for wild-eyed revolutionaries, but for those who simply uphold the traditional artistic values that are so appealing to audiences? It is the conservatives and traditionalists in art who are seeking tolerance; those who simply claim to be revolutionaries get what amounts to a free pass to do as they please. Which artist, the one who maintains classical standards or the one who rejects them, is the true non-conformist?

Howard David Johnson is a contemporary visual artist and photographer whose traditional realistic art has been exhibited in the British Museum. He works in a variety of media, including oil, acrylics, chalk, and oil pastels, photography, digital artistry, and mixed media. Johnson is internationally known as a commercial illustrator and for his involvement in imaging software. Johnson has sharp words for much of what passes today as great art. He says, "By my own definition of art, which is: 'anything that makes you feel or think,' most abstract paintings are not 'real art' to me personally, because abstract paintings usually neither make me feel or think, usually focusing obsessively on technique and avoiding any coherent content."

What Johnson says about modern art can be fairly said about much of modern music, poetry, drama, and literature. Those who focus on technique instead of emotion or thought are likely to win the plaudits of one group of highly influential individuals, the critics. Johnson has choice words for them. He writes, "But snobbish art critics favoring abstract art have declared that realistic paintings or illustrations are not art for a century. With so many representational paintings by so many immortal master artists hanging in the Louvre, the Hermitage, and the British Museum and others, I think the disrespect for realistic illustrators that dominated the 20th century is academically ridiculous as well as vain and intolerant, insisting theirs is the only valid opinion. What is your definition of Art? I believe almost any form of human expression can be raised to the level of 'high art' especially visual art and Realistic illustration." Nor is this view limited to art. *Time* magazine once described Aaron Copland as "too popular to be a great composer." The brilliant writer G.K. Chesterton summed up the problem with the critics when he said, "By a curious confusion, many modern critics have passed from the proposition that a masterpiece may be unpopular to the other proposition that unless it is unpopular it cannot be a masterpiece."

Academicians are likely to agree with the haughtiest of the art critics—the two groups overlap. Artists who follow the approved "artistically correct" path can be assured their work will be taken seriously, while those who choose to march to the beat of their own drummer will suffer an ignominious fate: at best they will be ignored, at worst they will ridiculed. The losers in this sad scenario are not only the artists, but students who are not taught to appreciate great art but to know who is fashionable and famous.

Again, Howard David Johnson is on target with his remarks on the schools. He says, "Art education has been almost completely removed from American Schools as a result of generations of this kind of fabulous nonsense contributing to America's cultural illiteracy crisis. Now, the works of Leonardo da Vinci, Michelangelo, and other notables are being removed from school libraries. After generations of this, most American college graduates today cannot name even one living visual artist, abstract or realistic. There is no way that mandating more math, requiring more reading, or scheduling more science will replace what we have lost as a culture."

Art dealers, the businessmen who make money out of the sale of art, also had a motive in promoting many modern artists whose fame was frequently the result of good marketing, not artistic skills. Fred Ross, an art educator, gallery owner, and chairman of the Art Renewal Center, has said, "For over 90 years, there has been a concerted and relentless effort to disparage, denigrate, and obliterate the reputations, names, and brilliance of the academic artistic masters of the late 19th Century. Fueled by a cooperative press, the ruling powers have held the global art establishment in an iron grip. Equally, there was a successful effort to remove from our institutions of higher learning all the methods, techniques and knowledge of how to train skilled artists. Five centuries of critical data was nearly thrown into the trash. It is incredible how close Modernist theory, backed by an enormous network of powerful and influential art dealers, came to acquiring complete control over thousands of museums, university art departments, and journalistic art criticism." Ross talks about artists, who trained as apprentices in ateliers, 24-hour-a-day academies run by master artists. The apprentices would begin by copying the drawings of old masters, study modeling from plaster casts, create drawings from live models, and then spend four to six years learning the techniques of painting. But with much of so-called modern art, rules and techniques went out the window. According to Ross, the dealers had a vested interest in promoting artists who could dash off a painting or two in a day. The technical masters were often great artists who required time to finish their works. The quick-draw artists meant quick profits for the dealers. Critics and professors could achieve status in the art world by aligning themselves with the masters of the latest fads. Fame for the artists and fortune for the dealers was easier to achieve if the public would accept almost anything as art.

Consider the lives and works of several realistic artists who have pursued the classical ideal. Frank Covino was born and raised in New York, and he graduated from Pratt Institute in Brooklyn, where he earned an M.S. in Art Education. Covino was a rugged individualist, a veteran of the Korean War, and fascinated by the traditional styles of classical masters. Some of his instructors tried to discourage him, insisting that only innovative, "avant-garde" artists had anything to contribute to the modern art world. Schools were quick to reject the past and embrace the future. In the new upside-down world of contemporary art and music, studying the classics seemed a waste of time. Why try to create music or art according to the standards of the old masters if we regard them not as "masters," but just as "old"? Students could follow the lead of many influential professors and critics, but to do so often meant rejecting their own desire not to abandon traditions. Frank Covino decided to follow his heart. He began a process of self-education, devoting hours of study to the techniques of Leonardo da Vinci, and became a modern master in the art and craft of realistic painting. Covino believed that the craft must precede creativity if the creativity is to be communicative. He became internationally known as a painter, teacher, and writer, establishing his own academy in Connecticut. Eventually, he embarked on a grueling schedule of master classes throughout the United States. In the process, he taught and inspired several thousand students. His own technique was so well developed that the French government worried that his copy of Leonardo's *Mona Lisa* might be mistaken for the original.

Covino eloquently identified the fallacy in much of contemporary art education. In *Controlled Painting,*[91] one of his several books on realistic painting, Covino observed, "The problem with most painting classrooms it that the teachers frequently put the cart before the horse, students are encouraged to be creative before they have learned how to handle the tools of their profession. We don't find this peculiarity in any discipline other than the visual arts. Can you imagine a music teacher asking your child, who has never seen a piano, 'Sit down and play something, Johnnie, and I'll tell you what you're doing wrong,' or a ballet teacher casting your daughter in a performance of *The Nutcracker Suite* before she has ever learned a pas de deux? One can't be expected to compose a symphony before learning to identify and reproduce notes and chords, nor can one create poetry before learning to speak and write." Artists who were ignorant of technique could simply declare that technique is unnecessary, that only a desire to express one's self in contemporary terms is relevant to modern times.

As for critics, they too were tripping over their own feet in a rush to be perceived as progressive. Frank Covino reminded us, "Few critics would appreciate the realistic aspects of a contemporary genre painting in a public review for fear of being labeled reactionary." Covino asked a perceptive question. When Michelangelo was a child, he saw a marble statue, *Laocoön* that affected him profoundly. Michelangelo was thus influenced by an unknown Greek artist who worked 2000 years before he was born. What would the world have lost if Michelangelo had dismissed the medium of *Laocoön* as merely "old-fashioned?" As for much of modern art's fashions and fads, Covino said, "I believe it's a gigantic hoax perpetrated upon the public. But few people have had the courage to stand up and shout that the emperor has no clothes."

Stanislav Rembski was a renowned painter of portraits. Born in Poland near the home town of Frederic Chopin, Rembski was trained at the finest art schools in Warsaw and Berlin. But he rejected the French post-Impressionist and German expressionist styles, and refused to follow the lead of modern artists of the day, including Matisse and Picasso. He was so discouraged that he very nearly abandoned his life as an artist. He changed his mind after viewing Raphael's Sistine Madonna in Dresden, which he spent three days copying. Rembski emerged from the experience determined to pursue the classical style of art in the very non-classical 20th century. He declared that he would rather be insane with Raphael than sane with the rest of the world. He was a devout Catholic who spent a lifetime expressing his spiritual values through art. Rembski established a reputation in Europe, but decided to bring the traditions of classical portraiture to America. He knew virtually no one in his new country and didn't speak English. But he settled in Brooklyn Heights, New York and began painting. His one-man show at Carnegie Hall established his national reputation, but he was disenchanted with the commercialism of the New York art world, and eventually settled in Baltimore where he became the city's leading portrait painter. He explained his move by declaring, "I would rather be Rembski of Baltimore on a visit to New York than Rembski of New York on a visit to Baltimore." Eleanor Roosevelt commissioned him to paint a portrait of her late husband, which now hangs at the Franklin D. Roosevelt Memorial Library and Museum in Hyde Park, New York. His portrait of Woodrow Wilson adorns the walls of Woodrow Wilson House, the former president's residence in Washington, DC, and his portrait of Babe Ruth can be found at the Babe Ruth Museum. Rembski said he sought to find the essence of his subjects, to express the human soul, not just the face. Only a little over five feet tall, with a white goatee, Rembski looked every inch the artist. He summed up his philosophy when he said. "Art is the process of taking dust from the earth—pigment—and transforming it into luminous light. That is the task of the artist, of giving life and spirit to the dust of the earth." Contrast this view with that of the artists who have become rich and famous painting soup cans or pursuing headlines by shocking a naïve audience. Stanislav Rembski lived to be 101 and produced at least 1500 works of art. He was widely respected and known as a master in his field. But you are not likely to read about him in the press today or learn about him in school. With his skill and imagination, he could have become one of the best-known artists of the 20th century by following the latest trends in Berlin, Paris, and New York. But he chose another path.

D. Jeffrey Mims also followed his own personal path in the art world. A native of North Carolina, he wanted to pursue training in a traditional atelier, a private art academy run by a master painter. He found that atelier training was very rare in the United States. He was relatively disappointed by his experience in art schools, so he traveled to Europe and spent twelve years copying the great masterpieces in the museums of London, Paris, Florence, and Rome. He writes in *Fine Art Connoisseur*, "Along the way, I was fortunate to meet other artists also pursuing a classical heritage that was in very real danger of becoming lost. When it seemed like tradition was being buried in the rubble of two world wars, we poured our youth and energy into learning the fundamentals of realism, based on a vision of the Old Masters. It has been rewarding to watch many of these same artists—including Charles Cecil, Daniel Graves, Benjamin Long, and Edward Schmidt—establish their own successful and distinguished schools of art in response to the swell of younger people seeking an education not available at universities. The past several decades have seen significant, even heroic, progress toward recapturing the ability to imitate nature and in particular the human figure." Mims eventually opened his own studio in Southern Pines, North Carolina, providing atelier training for numerous talented artists and guiding them along the path he followed, emphasizing classical techniques and studying works in the world's great museums. He explains, "What interests me is the preservation and study of traditional visual design, painting, sculpture and architecture, so that through our work, we might conduct some of the beauty and significance of that tradition into contemporary life." In his essay, *Distinguishing the Essential from the Accidental,*[92] Mims concludes, "One thing is certain: The art world is changing, and this time we can hope to witness a reversal of deterioration. When contemporary painting is once again truly connected with the classic spirit, its arrival will not be announced by the engaging essay, or the blue chip gallery, or even the museum exhibition.

This reincarnation will be evident in the work itself, and recognizable by a quality it has always shown, a quality that seems at once to be both effortless and unapproachable. It will have about it a certain unfailing resemblance to all that has been great in the past and at the same time exhibit unmistakable modern resolutions to visual questions that we do not even know how to ask." For Mims, our modern age of confusion is in part a longing for the ideals of beauty, order, and tradition, all of which have been abandoned by many and never known by others. Alexander Stoddart has been described as the leading neo- classical sculptor in Scotland. His sculptures of Adam Smith, David Hume, Robert Burns, and Robert Louis Stevenson have won him praise throughout Scotland and around the world. Nonetheless, sometimes a prophet is without honor in his own home. The Scottish Arts Council once criticized him as a "backward looking historicist" who didn't reflect contemporary trends. Stoddart has a vigorous response to such remarks. In an interview with Susan Mansfield, Stoddart took direct aim at many of the trends in modern art. She reports that he declared many modern art works to be "rubbish," describing them as "narcissistic, snobby, devoid of skill, ignorant of taste, gripped by nostalgia for the future." Stoddart told her that art has always been about "trying to alleviate the pain of existence," while modern art "collaborates with misery as opposed to trying to oppose it." Stoddart said that "a painting by Titian was like Leningrad holding out against the forces of the world, while the work of artists like Tracey Emin are a complete surrender to it."

What do the great realistic artists have in common? Nearly all achieved their successes outside the "modern art world"; those who rose to prominence did so without the support of many in the contemporary art establishment. They achieved much of their skill and knowledge through self-education and studying the techniques of the great masters of art throughout history. The majority passed that same knowledge on to generations of students outside the typical college or university art departments.

With a few exceptions, they receive little attention or publicity from the mainstream media.

The "no-rules, push the envelope" approach has infected countless institutions that once would have seemed certain to be immune. Lynne Munson illustrates how museums have fallen prey to tossing standards out the window in her book, *Exhibitionism: Art in an Era of Intolerance.*[93] Munson declares, "When standards become relative, everything becomes art, and politics (or any other non-art priority) is left free to guide the mission of the museums." Columnist John Leo, in the *Washington Times,* and critic Roberta Smith, in *the New York Times*, give Munson a ringing endorsement. Smith writes, "Today's museums are under attack from the art-world ideology on one side and commerce on the other." Leo sums up the situation brilliantly, when he says, "In many ways, the decline of today's museums parallels what happened to the colleges: an ideological loss of faith in the classics, accompanied by a loss of standards, and a consumer-oriented dumbing-down." What Munson, Smith, and Leo say about museums is true about all forms of art today, even including pop culture. Those who fund the arts, in both commercial and non-commercial situations, are faced with a dilemma. The need to be profitable and the desire for approval from those with an ideological agenda create pressure. Publishers, film and television producers, record companies, museum and gallery directors, among others, are all targeted. Too many take the easy way out. They reject the best of our past (and thus, the best of our present). They declare themselves in favor of change for the sake of change, abandon standards, and hope that no one notices that the Emperor wears no clothes. Sadly, too many people today haven't read *The Emperor's New Clothes*, and those who care about cultural conservation are told to shut up and stop standing in the way of progress. Of course, it is not enough to simply criticize advocates of the "no-rules, no standards" school of arts and entertainment. Nor should we assume that their deconstruction of the music, books, and art we have long admired is merely a rejection of the past. When they urge us to reject the past, they are also making an important, if subtle, statement about the present. Those young artists who seek to develop their own creative language, to find new avenues while guided by the values and standards of the classics, are being given a message: conform to the "no-rules" school or take a flying leap out the nearest window. The true non-conformists are told to get off the boat. The "no-rules" clique will go sailing along without them. Every time a museum treats the classics as "dusty, old museum pieces," it is also sending a message to today's artists. Every time a record company discontinues a label of classical music or jazz to make room for another pop-rock-rap promotion, it is sending a message to today's composers. Every time a publisher or television production company "dumbs down" its product to appeal to a semi-literate teenage audience, it is sending a message to today's writers. Rejecting the past isn't just about the past. It's very much about the present and by conserving the best of yesterday's culture, we are also sounding the trumpet regarding the culture we want to have today.

To recognize the chicanery and charlatans in modern art does not suggest that artists should not experiment, evolve, or explore. Art is never static; tastes and fashions change over time. But the work of artists should be evaluated according to standards that have stood the test of time. The specious notion that there are no valid standards has been used by promoters to persuade an often gullible audience that art can be anything, that anything can be art. Roger Scruton, in *Culture Counts,*[94] stated it well. He said, "If anything can count as art, then art ceases to have a point. All that is left is the curious but unfounded fact that some people like looking at some things, some like looking at others. As for the suggestion that there is an enterprise of criticism which searches for objective values and lasting monuments to human spirit, this is dismissed out of hand as depending on a conception of the artwork that was washed down the drain of Duchamp's '*Fountain*.'" It is of prime importance that artists, whose goal is the pursuit of beauty, not be neglected or ignored because of the demand for stylistic correctness.

Throughout history there has nearly always come a time when someone shouts, "The Emperor Has No Clothes." Charles Saatchi, known as one of the world's leading collectors and an early collector of works by Damien Hirst and Tracy Emin, shocked the art world with a scathing description of dealers and collectors alike. In a broadside published in *The Guardian* and entitled "The Hideousness of the Art World,"[95] Saatchi declared, "Being an art buyer these days is comprehensively and indisputably vulgar. It is the sport of the Eurotrashy, Hedge-fundy, Hamptonites; of trendy oligarchs and oiligarchs; and of art dealers with masturbatory levels of self-regard." He then posed an astounding question, demanding to know, "Do any of these people actually enjoy looking at art? Or do they simply enjoy having easily recognized, big-brand name pictures, bought ostentatiously in auction rooms at eye-catching prices, to decorate their several homes, floating and otherwise, in an instant demonstration of drop-dead coolth and wealth?" Saatchi went on to ridicule collectors, "reduced to jibbering gratitude by their art dealer or art adviser, who can help them appear refined, tasteful and hip, surrounded by their achingly cool masterpieces." Saatchi now suggests that many collectors, dealers, and critics can't tell the difference between good and bad art, and concludes that many do not remotely care about that fact.

THE ART THAT ISN'T THERE

Throughout the late 20th and early 21st centuries, critics and academicians have bolstered art dealers by providing their imprimatur and approval of even the most outlandish works of "art." The result has been a cascade of unprecedented high prices that set the minds of the incredulous and proverbial man in the street spinning. But there have been exceptions. British critic Brian Sewell declared bluntly, "When I look at almost all contemporary art, I see nothing, nothing." Hilton Kramer, art critic and co-founder of a publication on culture, *The New Criterion,* assessed the collectors who spend a fortune on such works. Kramer said, "Just the act of spending money on an object makes them feel that they are collaborating in creating the art history of their time."

Perhaps the most devastating view of contemporary art was presented by a 1993 episode on the television program, *60 Minutes*, with the wry and caustic understatement of veteran newsman Morley Safer. The program became one of legend and the artists, critics, academics, and dealers howled in outrage. Safer began by presenting several "objets d'art" along with the prices for which they had recently sold: a vacuum cleaner ($100,000), a sink ($120,000), and a pair of urinals ($140,000). Then he had the temerity to ask the question on every viewer's mind: is it art? "That's what the artists say," said Safer, "the dealers and, of course, the people who lay out good money." Then he concluded, "It all makes you believe in the wisdom of P.T. Barnum, that there is a sucker born every minute."

Safer went on to present examples of modern art that completely mystify anyone with common sense, but are found to have mysterious artistic and financial value in the modern art world. A painting by artist Cy Twombly brought a seven-figure price at prestigious auction house Sotheby's although it appeared to be a collection of scrawls created with the wrong end of a paintbrush. An artist named Christopher Wool, specializing in "text paintings," produced a canvass with the word RAT appearing three times, worth $30,000 to eager bidders. Collectors were eager to acquire the work of Robert Ryman, although those not among the cognoscenti would be puzzled since Ryman offered a blank canvass consisting entirely of white space. Perhaps the most daring claims to artistic profundity were made by Jeff Koons, a former commodities broker turned artist. Koons' approach might seem more reflective of Wall Street than the unheated garret of a struggling artist in Paris. He produced works he hadn't actually painted or sculpted, but simply commissioned. He would use craftsmen to produce the works he designed, such as a forty-foot puppy made entirely of flowers. Koons suggested that the simplest possible images might have deep meanings. For instance, he submerged three basketballs in a fish tank. Was this a promotional item for the National Basketball Association? Hardly. "This is the eternal," said Koons. "This is what life is like after death."

Many years after the first broadcast, Safer returned with another *60 Minutes* episode on art, this time a visit to *Art Basel,* Miami's celebrated art fair visited by the world's most sophisticated and well-heeled collectors. At the fair, Safer observed, you could find "the kitsch, the cute, the clumsy, the incomprehensible." Jeffrey Deitch, then director of the Museum of Contemporary Art in Los Angeles, was quick to remind Safer of his famous (or infamous) send-up of modern art years before. He reminded Safer that Jeff Koons' works, selling initially for merely hundreds of thousands of dollars, were now selling for as much as twenty-five million dollars. So the artists and dealers were having the last laugh.

In 2007, *Phaedrus,* a three-panel work by Cy Twombly, he of the scrawls with the wrong end of the paintbrush, was exhibited at the Museum of Contemporary Art in Avignon, France. One panel, all-white, was smudged with red lipstick, when it was kissed by French-Cambodian artist Rindy Sam. Though Sam defended her act as "a loving gesture," she was arrested and fined for "voluntary degradation of a work of art." Twombly's work was described as having a value of an estimated $2 million.

As the years that have passed since Morley Safer's *60 Minutes* broadsides on modern art, things have changed, but not for the better. The works of Jeff Koons and Damien Hirst are considered incredibly more valuable today than they were in Safer's day. But consider the most revolutionary figure in the art world of the 21st century.

The art world has justly celebrated the major figures of Italian art, Leonard da Vinci, Michelangelo, Raphael, Giotto, Botticelli, Titian, and Giorgione, among others. Today, however, the Italian art world is captivated by Salvatore Garau. Garau is an artist with an unusual background. After studying at the Accademia di Belle Arti di Firenze, he began his artistic career as the drummer in the "progressive rock group" Stormy Six. He turned to the visual arts after the group disbanded.

In 2021, Garau produced what will undoubtedly be regarded as his masterpieces; they cannot be compared to other works of art. They are invisible. *Buddha in Contemplation*, erected in the Piazza della Scala in Milan, is near the entrance to the Gallerie d'Italia. The "sculpture" is "displayed" in an area cordoned off by tape, but of course, since it is invisible, it cannot be actually seen. Garau released a video so we could all appreciate his work, explaining that "It will remain eternally in the space and is made of air and spirit."

Not content with one sculpture that cannot be seen, Garau was back with another profitable masterpiece, *Io Sono*, Italian for "I Am." The sculpture is perhaps the ultimate in modern art. Like his portrayal of the Buddha, it has been described as invisible, although Garau explains that it is actually a vacuum. "The vacuum is nothing more than a space full of energy," declared the proud artist, describing his work as having "energy that its condensed and transformed into particles, that is, into us."

Like John Cage's famous (or infamous) *4:33*, the piano composition in which a pianist sits silently at the piano for four minutes and thirty-three seconds, *Buddha in Contemplation* and *Io Sono* are taken seriously by art critics, but more importantly, by collectors. *Io Sono* sold for €14,820 to a private collector in the spring of 2021. Hans Christian Anderson wasn't an art critic, but when he penned *The Emperor's New Clothes*, he would have understood the art of Salvatore Garau. Do remember that Garau started as a member of a rock group. Never underestimate the ability of any rocker for self-promotion, whether appealing to your ears, your mind, or your unfortunate gullibility.

Are any of these creations truly "art"? As for the nature of the public to accept anything and everything as "art," we can turn again to a reminder from George Orwell. Although Orwell is best known for his portrayal of a dystopian tyranny in *1984* and his savagely accurate parody of communism in *Animal Farm*, he wrote on many subjects, including art. In a devastating review of the life and work of surrealist artist Salvador Dali, Orwell declared, "Just pronounce the magic word 'Art', and everything is O.K."

In Orwell's view, the otherwise morally unacceptable, the celebration of ugliness and even evil, would be tolerated and even acclaimed as long as its creator called it "art." As usual, he was quite on target.

Gifted realistic painters may endure neglect, ridicule, and frustration when they hear of these "works of art" and the profits they bring to a network of promoters who create and sell them. Those outside the community of academics and collectors may laugh in disbelief at what they regard as a giant fraud committed against human intelligence and enabled by the desire of the gullible to appear sophisticated and culturally aware. But the promoters, whether creating works or promoting them, are able to withstand the astonishment of those who aren't members of their club. To use an expression more apropos of Hollywood than the proper world of museums and galleries, they are crying all the way to the bank.

Consider *Comedian*, a work exhibited by Galerie Perrotin at Art Basel Miami in 2019. Maurizio Cattelan had exhibited a fully-functioning gold toilet at New York's Guggenheim Museum, calling the work, *America*. Cattelan's new work, *Comedian,* presented a single ripe banana affixed to a wall by duct tape. Two versions of Comedian sold for $120,000. each and the third was then listed for $140,000. As the banana would rot and have to be replaced, what were the buyers getting for their money?

Elise Taylor, writing in *Vogue*, explained, "The certificate of art. Essentially you bought the idea rather than the object." Then a "performance artist" named David Datuna stole Cattelan's thunder by pulling the banana off the wall and eating it. He told Elise Taylor, "The same thing with Duchamp 100 years ago. With my performance, I put my question mark after his question mark. This is just a game between two artists. Conceptually, I ate the concept of the banana." All of this validates Tom Wolfe's view that in the contemporary art world, we do indeed live in the age of the painted word. It's the theory, the explanation, the critique, that counts. Who is truly being fooled in the pretentious charade taking place in art galleries throughout the world? The dealers are making a fortune, the artists are gaining fame, and as for the buyers, their investment will undoubtedly appreciate in value at a much greater rate than a banana acquired at the local grocery store. Perhaps the most revealing commentary on contemporary art in the 21st century comes from Danish artist Jens Haaning. Haaning had framed Danish and Austrian currency to illustrate a comparison between income in Denmark and Austria. The Kunsten Museum of Modern Art in Aalborg then provided Haaning with a loan of $84,000 for a new version of this "art." Instead, Haaning supplied the museum with two blank canvasses but kept the cash. The museum wanted its money back and insisted that Haaning was contractually obligated to return it. The museum included the two blank canvasses in an exhibition which included such other "innovative art" as a work by by sculptor Josh Klein depicting reproductions of the several lower arms of FedEx delivery drivers. But Haaning explained, "The work is that I have taken their money." His title for the two blank canvasses? "Take The Money and Run." In a few words, this Danish artist neatly summed up the state of much contemporary art. More could not be better said in a three-volume critique.

Curiously, one of the most honest appraisals of much of modern art comes from one of its leading practitioners, Andy Warhol, the prince of pop art. Andy Warhol practiced what he preached, converted many, while the tendentious critics shouted "Amen." Warhol said simply, "Art is what you can get away with." The critics and academics, the gallery owners, and those seeking to be socially fashionable all benefit from the modern art business. The public at large may not take a day-to-day interest in art. Andy Warhol would be smiling, however, because the most commercially successful modern artists are getting away with a lot.

WHATEVER HAPPENED TO BOOKS?

ASK A NEWLY MINTED COLLEGE GRADUATE in search of a job, "When was the last time you read a book? What did you read?" Don't be surprised if he can't remember.

Americans, unfortunately, seem to be reading less and enjoying it more. The National Endowment for the Arts released a study, *To Read or Not to Read*, analyzing the reading habits of Americans. The results are disturbing. The NEA concluded that Americans are spending less time reading, that reading skills are eroding, and that these results have serious civic, social, cultural, and economic implications. The survey compared reading scores for thirty-one industrialized nations. Fifteen-year-olds from the United States finished only fifteenth, behind teenagers from Poland, Korea, France, and Canada. Not only has reading declined significantly among teenagers, but attendance at college doesn't guarantee consistent reading or even a development of reading skills. Sixty-five percent of college freshmen read for pleasureless than an hour per week or not at all. The percentage of these students has nearly doubled since they graduated from high school and by the time they are college seniors, a third do not read for pleasure at all. Studies indicate that students who read for pleasure are likelier to do well academically. But American families are spending less on books than at any time in recent history.

Employers list the inability to read and write well as the primary deficiency among newly hired employees. Literary readers are considered three times as likely to visit museums, attend concerts or plays, or create their own art works. Surprisingly, readers are also likelier to engage in sports and outdoor activities. Poor readers, however, are far likelier to be found among high school dropouts and in the prison population.

Does it matter? Caleb Crain, writing in *The New Yorker,* thinks it does matter indeed. Crain suggests that reading books for pleasure may be the province one day of a special "reading class" enjoying "an increasingly arcane hobby." Crain says, "If one person decides to watch *The Sopranos* rather than to read Leonardo

Sciascia's novella, *To Each His Own*, the culture goes on largely as before—both viewer and reader are entertaining themselves while learning something about the Mafia in the bargain." He writes, "If over time, many people choose television over books, then a nation's conversation with itself is likely to change." Crain suggests that readers and viewers acquire information and see the world differently. He predicts unanticipated consequences if our decisions are made and our priorities are set by people who don't read for pleasure.

How did this happen?

To find the answer, we must explore two key questions. First, we must ask, what happened to our nation's reading skills? Second, we must explore not only how much we are reading, but what we are reading. The answers are not encouraging.

WHY JOHNNY STILL CAN'T READ IN THE 21ST CENTURY

How did we reach this sorry state of affairs? The inarticulate not only speak poorly, they often can't read properly. More than two decades ago, the U.S. Department of Education, under the auspices of Secretary William J. Bennett and Assistant Secretary Chester Finn, released a report revealing that 40 percent of thirteen-year-olds and 16 percent of seventeen-year-olds attending high school had not acquired intermediate reading skills. The report urged an increased emphasis on phonics, study of the relationship between letters and sounds. Nevertheless, years later, schools are still instituting the "whole word" or "whole language" method, in which students are taught to memorize pictures of whole words instead of the alphabet and the sounds they represent.

This debate has been continuing for years. Dr. Rudolf Flesch wrote *Why Johnny Can't Read*[96] in 1955, denouncing the "look-say" approach to teaching reading. In 1981, Dr. Flesch returned with a new book, unfortunately and accurately titled, *Why Johnny STILL Can't Read*[97]. If a student in a "whole word" reading class makes a mistake, he is not corrected. Julia Palmer, President of the American Reading Council, declared that a girl who reads the word "house" for "home" or "pony" for "horse" isn't corrected. She offered the excuse that "It's not very serious, because she understands the meaning." Incredibly, Palmer added, "Accuracy is not the name of the game." But this isn't reading, it's guessing.

Critics of teaching phonics suggest that learning to read by mastering the sounds of the letters of the alphabet is boring and reduces reading to a rote exercise divorced from the meaning of words. But advocates of the "look-say" approach ignore the fact that students who substitute one word for another that has a similar meaning aren't learning to read at all. When they encounter new and unfamiliar words, as they will throughout their lives, they won't be able to pronounce the words correctly or determine their meaning.

Marva N. Collins, founding principal of the Westside Preparatory School in Chicago, said, "Dr. Flesch warned us years ago that Johnny wasn't learning how to read. We are all suffering today for our reluctance to act then, that is, those parents and educators among us who did not listen and who continued to put Band-aids on hemorrhages instead of using the commonsense phonics approach to reading. People throughout the United States visit one school and talk about it being a kind of 'miracle,' when it is only commonsense or phonics." Professor Kenneth Goodman, a leading advocate of the "whole word" method, calls mistakes "miscues." Goodman debated the concept of "miscues" with Dr. Jeanne Chall, whose study, *Learning to Read: The Great Debate,*[98] criticized researchers for being less interested in the results of reading instruction and more interested in who developed the best theory. Students who are taught to read using a method, which accepts "miscues" and encourages guessing, are being taught another lesson as well: that written words can mean whatever you want them to mean. An inability to read correctly produces people who may not think clearly. Dr. Samuel Blumenfeld addressed the results of poor reading instruction and fuzzy thinking. He asked, "Have you ever corrected a teenager on a bit of factual information, or a misspelling, or an incorrect usage of the language, and gotten the response, 'Whatever'? What this response means is that the correct fact, or spelling, or usage is not important or even necessary. 'If you're going to make a case of it,' the teenager says, 'it's whatever you say it is.'" Blumenfeld went on to state his case. "It was Sir Francis Bacon who wrote, 'Reading maketh a full man . . . and writing an exact man.'" In other words, an accurate reader becomes an accurate thinker, an accurate speller, and an accurate user of language. An inaccurate reader becomes an inaccurate thinker, an inaccurate speller, and an inaccurate user of language. Blumenfeld went further, recognizing the relationship between careless thought and careless behavior. He said, "The cult of inaccuracy can be seen in the way teenagers dress. The boys wear jeans that are about to fall off their behinds. The girls dress in the most tantalizing clothes, revealing their navels as an obvious focus of sexual attention. They all look brainless. 'Whatever' is their response to the serious things in life that require a logical brain, objective thinking, and intellectual rigor."

Blumenfeld's point is well taken. Not all of society's ills can be blamed on poor reading instruction. But what could be more foolish than a failure to teach students to read well? Reading, writing, and speaking skills can be taught, and a student from any social or economic background will have a great advantage in life if he does these things well. The most absurd argument in behalf of allowing students to make mistakes or "miscues" is that correcting them may cause a loss of self-esteem. If a teacher allows a student to read poorly, he is doing the student no favors. If a good reader receives scant praise, he is simply sent a message that achievement doesn't matter. Either way, good reading is essential to good thinking and to good job performance. Would you like your life to depend on a surgeon or an airline pilot who makes "miscues" when he reads?

The inability to read has disturbing consequences. James E. Courter spent twenty-five years teaching English composition to university freshmen. He observed, "One big problem is that so few students are readers. As an unfortunate result, they have erroneous, and sometimes hilarious, notions of how the written language represents what they hear." Courter's students supplied him with an abundance of hilarity over the years. A music student sadly reported on his difficulties in appreciating the popular "Pachelbel's Canon," composed by Johann Pachelbel, dubbing it "Taco Bell's Canon." Two students, hopefully not future lawyers, explained absence from class due to legal difficulties, one charged with a "mister meaner," the other with a "misdeminor." Fortunately, neither had been accused of a felony. Another pupil had no legal difficulties, but still was tardy or absent from class because he could not get into "the proper frame of mime." One of Courter's students justified missing class because of "inclimate weather." A young woman confided that her boyfriend "took her for granite," while another discovered that college had made an impact on her when she returned to her childhood house and found the life she formerly known to be "homedrum."

The errors described by James Courter are certainly amusing as are the verbal mistakes of Dogberry in Shakespeare's *Much Ado About Nothing* and Mrs. Malaprop in Richard Brinsley Sheridan's *The Rivals.* When Mrs. Malaprop wants to talk about an arrangement of epithets, the phrase emerges as "a derangement of epitaphs." Mrs. Malaprop converts "obliterate him from your memory" to "illiterate him from your memory." Nor are such examples confined to ancient dramatists and bewildered college students. Chicago Mayor Richard J. Daley once made reference to efforts by a group to thwart alcoholism; he called the group "Alcoholics Unanimous." James Courter treated his students with bemused tolerance and was careful to emphasize that he had encountered many bright and serious students during his many years of teaching. But his concern was thoroughly justified by the student who declared, "Life has too much realism," another who talked about getting away from it all to spend his time "sitting on a peer," and a pupil who lamented that "writhing gives me fits." What does an English professor do with students who tell him that they are looking forward to being done with English? Courter asks, quite rightly, what language will they use then?

The results of our reading crisis are now obvious for all to see. RiShawn Biddle, writing in *The American Spectator*, observes that two out of every five Atlanta students heading into high school are functionally illiterate, unable to comprehend a work as simple as *Anne of Green Gables* or even complete mathematical word problems. He concludes, "Twenty-six percent of America's eighth-graders and one in three fourth-graders are functionally illiterate. If you've wondered why 1.3 million students drop out every year, why six million students languish in the nation's special ed ghettos, or why girls outnumber boys on campus by as much as two-to-one, just take a look at America's abysmally low levels of literacy. Far too few children, no matter their socioeconomic background, can read well enough to function in an economy in which literacy is more important than ever. Boys are especially hit hard, often trailing their female peers in reading and falling far behind in other academic studies by the time they reach middle school."[99]

The legacy of poor instruction in reading, spelling, writing, and grammar is here for all to see. In March of 2013, City University of New York (CUNY) announced that nearly eighty percent of New York City high school graduates needed remedial instruction in basic skills before they could enter the City University's community college system. They had to learn the basic skills in reading, writing, and mathematics that they were supposed to have already learned in high school. The New York City Department of Education offered a forty percent increase in graduation rates over the last seven years as a defense. But this argument entirely misses the point: what good are increased graduation rates if the graduates can't read well enough to take first-year classes at a community college? Whether or not they attend college, if they still can't read, why should they be surprised when employers don't want to hire them? Of course, there is more to reading well than finding a job. Those who don't read, by choice or by inability, will miss the knowledge and inspiration they could acquire by simply opening a good book.

Sadly, this is not exclusively an American problem. Allison Pearson writes in *The Telegraph* of her experience as an apprentice teacher in London trying to teach a primary school student how to sound out the letters spelling "C-A-T." Thirty years have not dulled the memory of what followed. She recalls hearing a shout from across the classroom, "We don't do that here." She explains, "I looked up. It was the teacher, a short, squat woman wearing a zip-up jumpsuit that made her look like a badly lagged boiler. The Boiler explained the traditional method of sounding out letters, the way my mother had taught me to read, was now banned. Phonics was considered boring; it put children off reading. Instead, the school had a fantastic new scheme which encouraged kids to become 'active constructors of their own learning.' Magically, infants would discover the power of story by themselves, aided by teachers holding up flashcards. By the end of term, the Boiler said proudly, the class would know up to twenty-three new words."

Pearson believed that she could teach a chimpanzee to learn twenty-three new words in one term, and imagined herself leading a great phonics rebellion. But as a young apprentice, she dutifully followed orders. She continues, "It was just as I'd feared. The six-year-old could recognize simple words, which he had memorized from flashcards, but when it came to more difficult words, he grew frustrated and upset. Nice reading scheme, shame about the illiteracy." She rightfully concludes, "A boy denied the building blocks of his own language. A teacher in thrall to an ideology which saw pedagogy as a tedious imposition on a child rather than the key to liberation."

In Great Britain as in other English-speaking countries, advocates of the "look-say" methods often have good intentions. But we know where the road paved with good intentions often leads; in this case, to generations of students who can't read. When children read correctly, even enthusiastically, obstacles are often placed in their path. Nine-year old Tyler Weaver won reading contests conducted by the local public library in Hudson Falls, New York. He read sixty-three books in six weeks over the summer to emerge as the community's top reader. His seven- year old brother came in second two years in a row and appeared poised to assume his older brother's mantle one day. But library director Marie Gandron objected, insisting that Tyler "hogs the contest" and should "step aside" to make room for others. Gandron's idea was to award prizes based on her drawing names out of a hat, presumably so each child could feel good about himself. Her plan was derailed when the boys' mother reported what was taking place to the local newspaper. Gandron's thoroughly misguided attitude, though well-meaning, is an example of everything that is wrong in teaching not just reading, but everything else. If the rules of the reading competition had been changed, small children would have emerged from the library learning two very bad lessons. First, they would be taught they can achieve recognition and rewards in life not by working, but by just showing up. They would have been taught that success in life is not based on merit, but on luck. These children also would have learned that those who read less are just as successful as those who read more. Is this really what children should be learning in a library?

Charles J. Sykes is a prolific author and broadcaster, whose book, *Dumbing Down Our Kids*,[100] turns a discerning and critical eye on the state of education. Sykes bluntly declares, "American children feel good about themselves but can't read, write or add." He explains the shocking but accurate history of why illiteracy is rampant in 21st century America. Academic "experts" have simply changed the definition of literacy. Under the old definition, people who were illiterate might suffer a loss of self-esteem. Under the new definition, everyone can be considered literate even if he or she doesn't read well or absorb the knowledge found in great books.

In fact, it is those who suggest that these people are illiterate or uninformed who need to suffer the opprobrium of the experts. Sykes writes, "Another response of the educationists to the decline of literacy is simply change the definition of literacy. A literate person is no longer someone who has mastered the grammar, usage, and diction of language. In the early 1980s, a Minnesota school district defined the literate person as one who has developed a feeling of self-worth and importance, respect for and appreciation and understanding of other people and cultures, and a desire for learning. The literate person is one who continues to seek knowledge, to increase personal skills and the quality of relations with others, and to fulfill individual potential. As Richard Mitchell noted, this leaves out Aristotle (didn't appreciate barbarians); Kafka (not into self-worth and self-importance); T.S. Eliot (undemocratic); and Norman Mailer (poor quality of relations with others)." As evidence, Charles J. Sykes cites the experiences of parents who discovered that their children's teachers would not even correct mistakes in spelling and grammar in order for children to feel that their creativity is not being stifled by old-fashioned rules. Sykes concludes, "For several decades now, educationists have emphasized 'appreciation' rather than basic skills perhaps because while spelling and grammar can be measured, 'appreciation' and 'enjoyment' cannot."

LIBRARIES AND SCHOOLS, BUT WHITHER THE BOOK?

Libraries and schools would appear to be the timeless repositories of books and the wisdom of the printed word. But libraries and schools are changing, and not always for the better.

Generations of students have learned to quote John Donne's *No Man is an Island,* in which he makes the famous assertion, "Therefore, send not to know for whom the bell tolls, It tolls for thee." But the bell may have already tolled for John Donne, Ernest Hemingway, and the writers of many classic books. The *Washington Post* reported that a library in Fairfax, Virginia, a Washington, DC area suburb, was discarding books that hadn't been checked out in twenty-four months. The librarian in charge proudly declared that the liquidations were being executed "ruthlessly." A computer software program determines which books haven't been in circulation recently, and they are automatically discarded by the library. Among the writers whose books have already been abandoned are Charlotte Brontë, William Faulkner, Thomas Hardy, Marcel Proust, and Alexander Solzhenitsyn. What is replacing *Jane Eyre* on the shelves of the Fairfax library system? Current potboilers and best-sellers that are in demand.

John J. Miller, writing in the *Wall Street Journal*, raises an interesting question. Are libraries themselves becoming outmoded? And should a library be a cultural repository or just a store that doesn't charge its readers by the book? Miller observes that our culture would be so much richer if the contents of the ancient Library of Alexandria had survived. Andrew Carnegie, who made a fortune in business and gave away a substantial part of it creating libraries, credited his success to borrowing books when he was very young. Today, there are many ways to obtain books. There are countless online outlets for inexpensive used volumes, and new high tech forms of publishing and distributing, such as Kindle, the digital tablet that can download whole books and be easily carried anywhere. Much public domain material is distributed without charge online, and much more will become available in the future.

John J. Miller suggests that libraries shouldn't compete with commercial outlets in this environment, but should be active in preserving elements of our culture. Using the dictionary as a model, he says, "New words come in and old ones go out, but a reliable lexicon becomes a foundation of linguistic stability and coherence. Likewise, libraries should seek to shore up the culture against the eroding force of trends." For John J. Miller, the choice for libraries is the choice between conserving our culture or becoming a store serving tastes of the moment. Miller calls the latter choice a "Faustian" bargain, perhaps unfamiliar to readers who won't be checking out Christopher Marlowe's play, *Dr. Faustus,* about the temptation of a deal with the devil. *Dr. Faustus,* it seems, hadn't been checked out in twenty-four months.

University libraries, like public libraries, have also been affected. Christopher Conkey, writing in the *Wall Street Journal,* observes, "Libraries beckon, but stacks of books aren't part of the pitch." Conkey cites the sleek, impressive new library at Valparaiso University, a magnet for thousands of students who ignored the school's older brick library, jammed with books. The new building features a Steinway piano, black leather couches, and a high-tech center filled with computers. Conkey reports,". . . a side entrance takes students to a café and bustling technology center where semicircular, computer-equipped booths are favorites of amorous couples." The lion's share of books was left in the old library. Conkey says that many libraries are now moving books to out-of-the-way floors or storing them in compact shelves. The library has become a social networking center; for those seeking a quiet place to study or read a book, an option remains. They can go outside or find a library that isn't moving along with the times.

Clearly there is nothing wrong with libraries being appealing places to visit, with good lighting and access to online services. But as books are relegated to the status of second-class citizens in libraries, a profound change is taking place and many of those affected neither notice nor care. Writer Larry McMurtry told interviewer David Medina, "Young people, especially, do not read anymore. Children love to read and love to be read to, but when they reach twelve, they are hit by a tsunami of technology: iPod, iPhone, Blackberries, computers." McMurtry, who spent a lifetime as a bookseller as well as author, sadly concluded that libraries today want computers, not books. In a lecture at Rice University, McMurtry quoted a poem by Philip Larkin, *Going, Going*, about Larkin's sadness regarding irrevocable changes in England. McMurtry concluded by declaring that he once believed that the book culture would last forever, but that today, he believes it will never come back.

The school systems of the nation would be likely candidates to encourage reading, and especially encourage the preservation of the classics. Consider two very different approaches to books in the classroom, both represented by teachers from Chicago. Will Okun is a Chicago schoolteacher who teaches English and photography in an inner city school with many students from low-income and minority homes. Okun, writing in the *New York Times*, states the case for replacing traditional English and American literary classics with newer, contemporary titles. He says that his students were uninspired by books like *The Great Gatsby*, *The Old Man and the Sea*, and *1984*. Only when he began using books by and about people of similar backgrounds did his students develop an enthusiasm for reading. So Okun's solution is to conclude that for his student audience, the classics have had their day. He writes, "There are some high school literature teachers in Chicago so superbly talented, energetic and creative that they are able to engage their students in any and all writings. However, these miracle workers are the remarkably few and their students are incredibly fortunate." For teachers who do not fall in this category, however, he suggests that classics by "white men of yesteryear" don't speak to modern day students in a contemporary way, and that teachers should choose what he terms good books that are "more accessible." Okun's position is taken by many teachers and critics. It is, however, flawed.

What inner city students, minority students, and in fact, all students need is to be exposed to a world other than the familiar one they know. They need to have their eyes opened to great events of the past and present that they will not encounter by opening the front door of their homes or looking out the window at the house next door. Consider the viewpoint of an extraordinary teacher, Marva Collins. She insisted that elementary school teachers should have broad backgrounds in literature, art, music, science, and philosophy, not just training in abstract educational methodology. When she founded Westside Preparatory School in Chicago, Marva Collins required her inner city pupils to become familiar with the classics, including writings by the Greeks, Romans, and Shakespeare. At Westside Preparatory, Mrs. Collins offered a reading list for four-to-six- year-olds. It included *Lamb's Tales from Shakespeare*, Mark Twain's *The Prince and The Pauper*, *Fairy Tales and Fables* by Leo Tolstoy, and E.B. White's *Charlotte's Web*. Older children were assigned classics by Charles Dickens, Emily Brontë, Sir Walter Scott, and Thomas Hardy, among others. They were also expected to memorize poetry and read biographies of historical figures like Benjamin Franklin and Frederick Douglass. Parents and pundits alike were shocked to see inner city children enthusiastically absorbing and being inspired by books that took them far away from the world they knew. However, according to Marva Collins, that was the whole idea. She proved that if a teacher doesn't start with low expectations because of the background of her students, extraordinary results can be achieved.

You won't find most students reading classic books today, in or out of school. But you will find them reading the *Harry Potter* novels, which made author J.K. Rowling richer than the Queen of England. When Michael Shaughnessy, a professor at Eastern New Mexico University, interviewed Kenneth Goodman, he asked how students could be encouraged to move from the popular Harry Potter books into the classics of literature, including Dickens, Hemingway, Chaucer, and Shakespeare. Goodman responded, "My goodness, Dickens and Shakespeare? There's a wonderful world of contemporary literature beautifully written for children and young people of which Harry Potter is just one." So much for tradition.

The great classics of literature (or those of music or art) address eternal values that transcend time and place. Elizabeth Kantor, author of *The Politically Incorrect Guide to English and American Literature*,[101] states it well. She writes, "Think about the wide range of concerns that occupied the 'dead white males' who wrote the great literature in our language. Those concerns are entirely alien to the thought of today's politically correct English professors: truth, beauty, and goodness; sin and salvation; free will; individual genius; poetic creation; the powers of the human imagination. These are things too many English professors today see through, and almost literally can't see. (To give just one example, there's a professor of English at San Francisco State University who argues that Milton wrote great poetry 'in spite of, not because of Christianity'—which is like saying that the Declaration of Independence is a very impressive document, except for all that blather about inalienable rights.)"

Of course, students should be familiar with good books by writers of every ethnic and racial background. But the standard should be good books, not the classification or categorization of the author's race or gender. The notion that students can only relate to the books by authors who are members of their racial, ethnic, or gender group is specious nonsense. It also represents a profound insult to their intelligence. Can students learn about truth, beauty, goodness, and the other values Elizabeth Kantor cites by reading selected books by modern authors of various nationalities and ethnic backgrounds? Of course, but too often, the books chosen by professors do not reflect these timeless values, but the values, biases, and quirks of the professors themselves. Also, the classics which are discarded have played roles of incredible importance in our history. Our culture, our political development, our evolution as a people were shaped and molded by many of these classics. If you have no idea where we have been, how can you understand where we are today, or where we should be going tomorrow? Elizabeth Kantor says, "Culture is not genetic; it doesn't come to us in our DNA. Culture is learned. We learn civilization itself from other human beings. From our families, certainly. But also from what used to be called 'higher culture.' Americans didn't use to consider themselves educated people unless they'd been formed by Shakespeare, at least—among the great classics in our language. If we allow ourselves to be cut off from those elements of our traditional culture, how do we know that we'll still be educated Americans, or citizens of the West?"

Frank Miele, Managing Editor and columnist for the *Northwest Daily Inter Lake*, addresses the issue directly in a discussion of today's writers. He says, "Can you think of any writer as essential as Charles Dickens alive today? Or Tolstoy? Or Emily Dickinson? Or Hemingway? Or Joseph Conrad? Or Jane Austen? Or Voltaire? Or Mark Twain? For that matter, can you think of any writer alive today who is essential not to you personally, but to our mutual understanding of what it means to be human? The emphasis must be on mutual, because it is just such touchstones of common understanding which have provided the glue of culture and society for at least the entire era of civilized life." Miele succinctly expresses the true nature of the problem. He writes, "Critical thinking is in critically short supply these days, and perhaps the explanation is that our modern world has chosen to educate itself on a diet of Conan, Borat and Oprah instead of Emerson, Rousseau and Dickens. We are limited only by our aspirations, but doesn't that mean this current generation is stuck inside an incredibly small box called TV?"

Miele tips his hat to celebrated novelist William Faulkner accepting the Nobel Prize for Literature with a warning. Faulkner urged his colleagues not to forget "the old verities and truths of the heart, the old universal truths lacking which any story is ephemeral and doomed–love and honor and pity and pride and compassion and sacrifice." Faulkner was speaking of some of the writers of his time, but his remarks possess the ring of truth to an even greater degree today. He recoils from writers who write "not of love but of lust, of defeats in which nobody loses anything of value, of victories without hope, and worst of all, without pity or compassion." Faulkner did not want to be a writer whose "griefs grieve on no universal bones, leaving no scars" or who "writes not of the heart but of the glands." For Faulkner, these writers were writing as though they stood among and watched the end of man. Critics who dismiss the classics often do so with a certain attempt at wit or style. But an ability to turn a clever phrase only reveals the writer as clever, not wise or even truly witty. Brigid Brophy, Michael Levey, and Charles Osborne dismissed a significant part of the canon of English and American literature in their book, *Fifty Works of English Literature We Could Do Without.*[102] The authors began with *Beowulf,* and moved through *Hamlet, Pilgrim's Progress, The Pickwick Papers, Wuthering Heights, Jane Eyre, Moby Dick, Huckleberry Finn, Alice's Adventures in Wonderland,* and *Peter Pan,* and conclude with numerous modern books, including *The Forsyte Saga* and *A Farewell to Arms.* Missing from the list are classics, admired by Brigid Brophy, especially those of Jane Austen and George Bernard Shaw. The books so casually dismissed by Brophy, Levey, and Osborne have also inspired numerous films (such as Laurence Olivier's *Hamlet* with its celebrated musical score by Sir William Walton) plays, ballets, and musical compositions. Bernard Herrmann's opera, *Wuthering Heights,* is a masterpiece and he also composed an extraordinary cantata based on *Moby Dick.* Think of how many children and adults have been delighted by Alice's misadventures and Peter Pan's determination to remain a boy forever. Anthony Burgess responded to Brophy, Levey, and Osborne by rejecting critics who mistake "the parade of prejudice for objective appraisal." Dismissing the classics of English and American literature has become fashionable on college campuses and in elite critical circles, often so that the classics can be replaced by newer works lacking in moral compass, and reflecting the political and social views of the people writing the criticism.

SHOULD ENGLISH TEACHERS READ SHAKESPEARE?

Even the most celebrated authors are not immune from neglect, from dismissal, and from the ghastly political correctness, that renders them irrelevant to the modern age. "To be or not to be? That is the question." For centuries, audiences have been listening to Hamlets on stage pondering their survival. But now, the author of Hamlet's famed soliloquy could well ask that question of himself. William Shakespeare, considered the mainstay of college English courses, may soon be heading for oblivion. In 2007, ACTA, the American Council of Teachers and Alumni, surveyed twenty-five of the top liberal arts colleges and twenty-five of the top national universities, as selected by *U.S. News and World Report*. Only one Ivy League School required a course in Shakespeare, as did four of the top universities and three of the liberal arts colleges. Students at many of the other schools can elect to take a course in Shakespeare, but these elective courses do not count for greater credit than classes in "Renaissance Food" (Swarthmore), "Renaissance Things" (University of Chicago), and medieval writing about flogging, stabbing, and rape (University of Pennsylvania). The Chairman of the English Department at the University of Pennsylvania said that the curriculum should reflect the makeup of the faculty. Schools with this point of view are designing courses without regard to a set of great works in the English language that every student (including future English teachers) should study. Some schools that do not require English majors to study Shakespeare do require them to study courses reflecting "other cultures" or classes in theory. One such institution, Duke University, offers a course in "Cool Theory," in which students explore the concept of "cool" by engaging with a variety of media, including fiction, memoir, music, television, fashion, and film. Duke University English majors who don't want to hear Marc Antony's call to "Friends, Romans, Countrymen" can sample "Creepy Kids in Fiction and Film," encountering "weirdoes, creeps, freaks and geeks of the truly evil variety." Princeton's theory classes explore new words each week, including language, ideology, performativity, sexuality, ethics, media, trauma, AIDS, globalization, and war. Undoubtedly, the most popular view of history can be found at Georgetown University, where students can enroll in a course called "Sexing the Past."

The ACTA report on Shakespeare lists numerous courses for English majors that cover everything except great literature. Included are such sources of intellectual stimulation as courses on adoption (Yale University), animals, cannibals, and vegetables (Emory University), radical vegetarian manifestos or, presumably for those uninterested in turnips and squash, "Madonna" (University of Pennsylvania), rock and roll (University of California at San Diego), and Hollywood in the 1970s (American University). Northwestern University offers perhaps the prize elective, a class on *Baywatch*, the popular television series featuring lifeguards who romp around the beach, sometimes saving lives, but always wearing provocative bathing suits. Presumably, students enrolled in the class are required to watch and analyze numerous episodes of the series. This provides an opportunity for male students to not only compare notes on pretty girls, but also to receive academic credit for doing so.

In effect, the ACTA survey on Shakespeare reveals that future English teachers at several of America's presumably best schools can meet their requirements by not only avoiding the Bard, but by participating in classes reflecting the political and cultural biases of their professors. Invariably, this means classes exploring radical politics and rock or rap music. The future English teachers may find themselves asked to teach courses on Shakespeare, a subject they haven't studied, later in life. Or they may teach at schools that regard such studies as unnecessary.

The problem, by the way, is not confined to the study of Shakespeare or even the teaching of English literature. Andrew Ferguson chronicles the problems of a parent trying to help his son get a good education in his book, *Crazy U: One Dad's Crash Course in Getting His Kid into College.*[103] Ferguson describes his son's school as a campus where history majors can fulfill a European requirement by taking a class in "Witchcraft." When Ferguson's son registered too late to enroll in a class in English composition, he was told he could substitute such grimly serious courses as "The 1960s," "AMC's *Mad Men* and American Life," and "Intro to Queer Theory." Ferguson describes colleges that actually recruit students by implying that they can spend their precious college time and their parents' hard-earned money "doing whatever they want." It should then come as no surprise that once on campus, they will see to it that schools live up to their advance billing.

John Zmirak correctly identifies much of the problem as the result of changes made during the tumultuous 1960s. In "The Top 5 Lamest Core Courses," an article in *The Intercollegiate Review,* Zmirak cites the abandonment of "course courses," which used to be required of all students at the best colleges and universities.[104] But after the countercultural revolution of the 1960s, students could choose the courses that interested them from a menu of dubious choices. Zmirak says, "The results of such changes are colleges like the one you're probably paying $40–$50K per year to attend. History majors can graduate without knowing how or why the United States became independent. English majors can finish without reading a single line of Shakespeare. Political science students can go on to grad school having never read the U.S. Constitution. And students from different majors have very little overlapping knowledge in common, so when they argue over ideas, they're pretty much speaking in different languages." Zmirak cites five key disciplines and the courses students can use to satisfy their requirements. At Harvard, the "Literature and Arts B" requirement can be met with a course called "Race, Gender, and Ethnicity in Martin Scorsese and Spike Lee." If you're not mathematically inclined and attending Stanford, you can satisfy the math requirement by enrolling in "The Mathematics of Sports." The Humanities and Arts requirement at Yale doesn't mean that you have to study the Federalist papers or the U.S. Constitution. Students can substitute "U.S. Lesbian and Gay History." The University of Texas at Austin requires students to enroll in three science classes in the same discipline. But one acceptable class is devoted to "Animal Sexuality." The College of the Holy Cross requires students to enroll in a class devoted to religion. Should a student be afraid that such a course might include reading thick books on religion or philosophy by long- dead theologians, he can substitute "Gardens and the World's Religions." Students who graduate from these and other prestigious schools will have a diploma and an impressive credential for those who take such things seriously. But what will they actually have learned?

There is a temptation to blame students for their own ignorance, but students cannot be blamed for what they have never been taught. Hugh Hewitt is an attorney and teacher who hosts a popular national radio talk show. Those who criticize talk radio for superficiality have undoubtedly not listened to Hewitt discussing the great books with such leading Constitutional scholars as Hillsdale College President Larry P. Arnn and Claremont Graduate University Professor Harry Jaffa. On one program, he was joined by guests John Mark Reynolds of Biola University and David Allen White of the U.S. Naval Academy. They quickly turned their attention to the problems of college students confronting the literary canon with little preparation. David Allen White provided a blunt assessment of the current attitudes in academia. He said, "They loathe Western civilization. They hate Western civilization, and they will do anything to destroy it, which means destroying the canon. If you don't teach the young where they came from, and the greatness of the past, you can do away with the whole thing." White identified the problem as a lack of shared knowledge. He concluded, "Now, no two students have ever read the same book, they barely read books at all. It is chaos in the classroom, and the price of these phony educations keep going up and up and up." But the situation isn't hopeless. John Mark Reynolds said, "We bring in freshmen students, none of whom have read the *Iliad* and the *Odyssey* in general, and we begin to work with them in trying to understand how to read great literature. We end up with waiting lists of people begging to get into this kind of thing. You know what? People eventually understand that they're being defrauded of their roots, they're being defrauded of a good education. And as you start to help them get a hold of the real thing, they become hungry for it, with a passion that passes anything you've ever seen. Our students aren't worse than they were 100 years ago. The teachers are worse. We're worse. And if we begin to man up, step up and begin to teach students these things with passion, they can be transformed and do well. I see it every single day."

Is there a lasting value in the study of Shakespeare and other writers of classics for the contemporary student? Dr. Larry P. Arnn reflects upon the approach to education that has been discarded by too many schools. In "The Crisis and Politics of Higher Education,"[105] he says, "In the older view, students should be invited to look, not to themselves and their own opinions, but rather outwards and upwards, beyond themselves to something against which they can judge the choices they must make. Shakespeare is beautiful and instructive, but not usually at first. He takes work. What justifies the work is the idea that some great thing awaits the one who does it successfully. Any recovery of excellence in education will entail a recovery of this older idea of the purpose of education."

HOW WE READ

Even if we do read, how well do we understand what we read? There is evidence that the answer to this question is "not very well." In 2005, the *Washington Post* reported the results of a survey conducted by The National Center for Education Statistics. Mark Schneider, Commissioner of Education Statistics, explained the depressing results of the study. He wrote, "The declining impact of education on our adult population was the biggest surprise for us, and we just don't have a good explanation. It may be that institutions have not yet figured out how to teach a whole generation of students who learned to read on the computer and who watch more TV. It's a different kind of literacy. What's disturbing is that the assessment is not designed to test your understanding of Proust, but to test your ability to read labels." The study evaluated the ability of adults to comprehend and compare two newspaper editorials or read prescription drug labels. The study concluded that while more Americans are graduating from college, fewer graduates have the skills necessary to understand what they read. Michael Gorman, a librarian at California State University at Fresno and President of the American Library Association, described the results as "appalling" and "really astounding." Gorman said, "Only 31 percent of college graduates can read a complex book and extrapolate from it. That's not saying much for the remainder."

The ability to think critically, to analyze, to understand the meaning of words, is essential to our cultural survival. People who lack these skills can be easily manipulated by political demagogues and persuaded to do all kinds of things that are not in their own best interests (or in those of society). Many of these college graduates undoubtedly leave college with a good sense of self-esteem. They don't realize how little they have to offer the world; many think that the world should have much to offer them. Publishers seeking to please these people will hardly publish the best books. As for art and music directed at this audience, the less said, the better.

Today, a fifth grade student can use a computer to zip and zoom around the Internet, grabbing huge chunks and volumes of information. He can do what scholars of old could only achieve through years of effort and yesterday's best students in days of research in a library. But access to a world of information doesn't mean that we know what do to with it. An oft-repeated joke asks, "What would a dog chasing a car do with it when he caught it?" If a speedy dachshund could actually jump in the front seat and drive, he would end up in the Guinness Book of World Records.

But if he simply had to look for another car to chase, what has he accomplished? Writer Nicholas Carr penned a provocative article, "Is Google Making Us Stupid?" in *The Atlantic.*[106] Carr probably didn't literally "pen" the article, a figure of speech, since he undoubtedly wrote it as nearly all of us do today, using a computer. He observes that while the use of "Google" and other online services make huge amounts of information available to us in an instant, there are consequences, and not all of them are positive. Carr suggests that if we become accustomed to reading everything in the way we surf the Internet, our capacity for concentration is affected. He says, "My mind now expects to take in information the way the Net distributes it: in a swiftly moving stream of particles. Once I was a scuba diver in the sea of words. Now I zip along the surface like a guy on a Jet Ski." Carr says, "Thanks to the ubiquity of text on the Internet, not to mention the popularity of text-messaging on cell phones, we may well be reading more today than we did in the 1970s or 1980s, when television was our medium of choice. But it's a different kind of reading, and behind it lies a different kind of thinking—perhaps even a new sense of the self." Carr cites the view expressed by Maryanne Wolf, a developmental psychologist at Tufts University and the author of *Proust and the Squid: The Story and Science of the Reading Brain,"* who says, "We are not only what we read, we are how we read." Wolf suggests that reading on the Internet encourages efficiency and immediacy, but weakens our ability to read seriously and absorb profound thoughts in print.

I once asked someone if he were a bibliophile, and he replied, "No, I don't do anything against the law." Bibliophiles—people who love books—don't engage in practices that are against the law; but in the modern age, they are often regarded as somewhat strange, peculiar, and more than a little eccentric. The book lover is seen as an odd introvert, rather like a Model-T Ford that showed up uninvited at a NASCAR event. Bibliophiles are captivated by the content of books, but also by the books themselves. Jeff Gomez, in *Print is Dead,*[107] talks about the many ways in which people love books. He says, "They love the way books look on their shelves, coffee tables and nightstands. People love the way books feel in their hands, and they even love the way books smell (well, the old ones yellowed with age and cured with dust). Booklovers the world over have spent countless hours caressing covers, fingering dust-jackets, and repeatedly running their hands up and down fabric spines. Homes everywhere house the collections of the hardback and the paperback covers of worn and dog-eared novels that bibliophiles have been amassing for years, moving them in near-bursting boxes from place to place over the span of their adult lives." Gomez then poses the question many are afraid to ask. Will the book, like the dodo, be extinct one day? He says, "Because of this level of devotion, and the fact that the people who love books love them in the way that patriotic people feel about flags or musicians feel about their instruments, how can books ever be replaced, let alone disappear?" Gomez sadly concludes that screens are already replacing books, and defers to George Landow, who observed in his essay, *The Future of the Book*, that sales of the volumes we once treasured are now fourth behind television, cinema, and video games. When video games are outselling books, the marketplace is telling us that something profound has changed in our society.

Sven Birkerts grew up as the child of Latvian parents who taught him to read at an early age. He became a devoted bibliophile, and views the advent of hundreds of television channels, audio books, and computer programs with concern. He expressed himself in *The Gutenberg Elegies*,[108] a series of essays in which he, like Jeff Gomez, speculates about the future of the book. Birkerts writes, "Words read from a screen or written onto a screen—words which appear and disappear, even if they can be retrieved and fixed into place with a keystroke—have a different status and affect us differently from words held immobile on the accessible space of a page." Birkerts observes that there is an important difference between hearing someone read an "audio book" aloud and reading it yourself. There is a difference between reading a book you hold in your hand and one that appears on screen and allows you to add comments or delete passages at will.

Not surprisingly, Birkerts and other bibliophiles have their critics, invariably dismissing them as champions of the quill pen, the manual typewriter, the printing press, and in effect, the horse and buggy in an age of lightning speed and vehicles that sail through outer space. These critics overlook the fact that the reader who "hears" rather than reads books, or reads them online is engaged in a totally different process than one who holds a book in his hand and reads it the old-fashioned way. The champions of progress are quick to suggest that "old-fashioned" is synonymous with "outdated." This is the old notion that change automatically implies progress. When questioned about what kind of change is taking place, the advocates for the future quickly demonstrate what kind of change they prefer: they change the subject.

THE ENTERTAINERS

Book publishers, like newscasters, have found themselves in what once would have been an improbable position. They are part of the entertainment industry. They may educate or inform their readers, but as publishing houses have increasingly fallen under the control of the same companies who dominate the production of movies, television, and pop music, entertainment profits have become the major goal. Obviously, good books can be entertaining. But the entertainment industry often becomes successful by emphasizing celebrities and superficial subjects that can be easily marketed to an uninformed public. It is the pop cultural values of the entertainment industry that have altered the publishing business.

This perspective is well-known in the worlds of both classical and popular music. Leonard Feather, a prominent British jazz critic, developed the "blindfold test," that became popular in *Down Beat* magazine, a leading jazz publication. In each test, an outstanding jazz musician was asked to listen to various jazz performances and comment about them without knowing the names of the performers. How many power brokers and decision makers in the entertainment industry today could survive such a test? Unfortunately, critics, academics, and the general public are often impressed by famous names and by publicity. Dr. Laurence

Peter, the distinguished author, satirist, and educator, was aware of this when he wryly observed, "a hamburger by any other name costs twice as much." Editors and publishers often try to set themselves apart, at least in public, from the entertainment industry. They pride themselves on judging work by its quality, not the name value of its authors. But does this usually happen?

The publishing world, like those of music and art, has increasingly become obsessed with name value, not quality. In 1975, an aspiring writer named Chuck Ross was selling cable television services. He was frustrated by the need to have an influential literary agent to gain access to major New York publishers. He decided to try an experiment. He copied twenty-one pages from *Steps*, a book by Jerzy Kosinski that had won the National Book Award. Random House, the book's publisher, promptly rejected it without recognizing it. So did three other publishers, Houghton Mifflin, Doubleday, and Harcourt, Brace, Jovanovich. Kosinski himself was critical of Ross's methods, insisting that the whole book should have been submitted. So four years later, Ross tried the experiment again, this time submitting a typed version of the whole book, but claiming to be the author, "Eric Demos." The original four publishers all rejected it again, along with ten additional publishers, Macmillan, William Morrow, the Atlantic Monthly Press, Farrar, Straus & Giroux, Alfred A. Knopf, Seymour Lawrence, David McKay, and Viking. Houghton Mifflin, publisher of another Kosinski book, rejected the typed version of *Steps* as "incomplete," while Harcourt, Brace, Jovanovich, which had also published Kosinski, said that work didn't inspire enough enthusiasm to be published. Ross then submitted the book to twenty-six literary agents. He didn't fare better with any of the agents; they all rejected it too.

However, Ross, again under the name "Eric Demos," wasn't finished. In 1985, he submitted a typed version of the film script of *Casablanca* to 117 motion picture agents. *Casablanca* had been based on a play, *Everybody Comes to Rick's*, so he used the play's title instead of *Casablanca*. Ross imagined that everyone was familiar with *Casablanca*, winner of the "Best Picture" Oscar in

1943, and selected by the American Film Institute as one of the three best films of all time. So he changed the name of "Sam," the musician who sings "As Time Goes By" in the film to "Dooley," in honor of Dooley Wilson, the actor who played "Sam" alongside Humphrey Bogart and Ingrid Bergman. Many of the agencies returned the script unread, while some scripts were lost in the mail. But the majority of agencies who claimed to have read the script rejected it, without realizing that it was *Casablanca.* To make matters worse, Ross was inundated with criticisms and suggestions for improvement to the classic script, which he submitted without changing a word. Agents suggested that he needed to study a textbook on screenwriting, to cut excessive dialogue, to polish the rambling plot, to improve the thin story line. One agent called him "talented," but said he would have to pay a professional writer to help him improve the script. Ross eventually became editor and publisher of a trade magazine for the television industry. Agents and publishers are undoubtedly still capable of rejecting successful works if submitted under the name of "Eric Demos" or any other non-name writer whose name they fail to recognize.

BOOKS ON SCREENS

Some would suggest that change is unimportant, that new inventions and technological innovations merely change the way in which we receive information. The phonograph, the radio, the motion picture camera, and the television set didn't result in the extinction of books or libraries. In fact, many films, radio programs, and television series were inspired by books. But none of these inventions actually replaced the book or the library. The computer, with its ability to deliver information on demand without reference to a permanent printed page, is another matter entirely.

Digital projects underway now make huge libraries of books available online often at little or no cost. But in order to access these "e-books," one must have access to a computer or a digital tablet, like the Kindle, designed to download books. In April 2011, Amazon, the largest seller of books online, reported that its sales of e-books in its Kindle format now exceed its sales of traditional printed books. The "book" only exists as a computer file. This is quite different from a book sitting on a shelf waiting to be discovered. The computer, like every other new invention, is a messenger. The nature of the message depends on its author and its reader. The fact that readers may be accessing information online is in itself meaningless. We must ask readers what kind of information they are accessing. Great literature, popular nonfiction, potboilers, and ubiquitous trash can all be found online. But the potential disappearance of the book as a messenger can have serious consequences.

Reading a book is active, not passive. You turn pages, you look up words, you think about what you are reading. But television has, for most of its history, been passive. You watch. You listen. But you don't do anything. This is not to say that you don't absorb messages and ideas. (Commercial advertisers spend billions on the assumption that you do.) Students have always found ways to avoid studying if they can. One popular technique is to use CliffsNotes, textual summaries of books that a student can read quickly instead of actually reading a book. Now AOL has produced short, humorous videos for students too impatient even to read the CliffsNotes. Ben Berger writes, "The newly proposed AOL videos offer shortcuts for shortcuts. Having stripped classic literature of all essential nutrients, the videos would add a comedic candy coating: a spoonful of sugar to help the sugar go down." Eliot Engel is a professor, writer, and speaker specializing in the works of Charles Dickens. He may have found the solution; Engel simply assigns his students the only Dickens novel never to be honored with a CliffsNotes summary.

The explosion of interest in digital readers raises an interesting question. Will hand-held digital devices with a screen replace books and libraries? Viv Groskop, writing in *The Telegraph,* confesses that the enthusiasm of her friends for the Kindle makes her feel surprisingly out of date. She writes, "Suddenly my favorite Christmas present—a weighty, unwieldy but beautiful hardback copy of Stephen Sondheim's *Finishing the Hat,* savored throughout January—makes me feel a complete Luddite." (The Luddites were

British workers who destroyed laborsaving machinery because they feared the loss of jobs. Today, the term "Luddite" describes someone opposed to technological change.) While the world is full of people who are ready to proclaim books and libraries ready to join the dinosaurs or the extinct passenger pigeon as relics of a bygone age, the triumph of the digital reader is not yet complete. Television producer Amanda Ross tells Groskop, "I'm passionate about the physical idea of books. There's no feeling quite like cracking open a new paperback. You can't read a Kindle in the bath. Curling up with a glass of wine in front of the fire with an electrical device is not conducive to relaxation. I spend my working day looking at a screen. Why would I want to spend my leisure time looking at one? It's an odd concept: a one-time download, for you personally, and that's it. You can't share them or pass them on; and what about the joy of growing a library of books?"

Are traditional books going to be as extinct as the dodo? John Steele Gordon, in his article, "The End of the Book,"[109] predicts that mass market paperbacks, as well as hardbacks for mysteries, thrillers, and "romance fiction," will probably only be available as e-books within a few years. Gordon observes that swords, which have no contemporary military function, are still carried by officers as a symbol of strength. Similarly, early steam ships continued to use sails until sailors were certain that they would no longer be needed. Despite new modern forms of heating, fireplaces are still popular for aesthetic reasons. Gordon concludes, "I think physical books will have a longer existence as a commercial product than some currently predict. Like swords, books have symbolic power. Like fireplaces, they induce a sense of comfort and warmth. And, perhaps, similar to sails, they make a useful backup for when the lights go out."

TO READ OR NOT TO READ, THAT IS THE QUESTION

The distinguished and prolific writer, Ray Bradbury, wrote *Fahrenheit 451,*[110] a tale set in a time of the future in which all books are burned. (Fahrenheit 451 is the temperature at which a book will burn. Scientists of every type were unable to provide

Bradbury with the correct temperature, but he got the correct answer from the fire department. He was initially concerned that the firemen might think him a potential arsonist rather than an eminent author, but they didn't, and the rest is history.) In Bradbury's world, the book is eventually saved by a group of dissidents and dissenters, each of whom memorizes the text of a book and saves man's literary heritage by "becoming" the book himself. Bradbury's book says much about the idea of censorship, but it also delivers a message about the importance of the survival of books. What will be lost if the extinction of books becomes a reality?

Some will point to the success of the Harry Potter books and films as evidence that books and reading will survive the modern age. But the Potter books and films have become part of pop culture, and to be ignorant of them in the teenage world is as unseemly as not knowing the latest pop hit or celebrity gossip. The bibliophobic teenager wants to be "cool," and reading books and going to libraries simply isn't cool any more. So the teenager graduates from high school, reading poorly, convinced that books are important if they are "relevant" and reinforce his opinions. A bright young college graduate enters the job market without having read books by people who are dead or old or from the wrong culture or are not politically correct. She doesn't know much, but she feels good about herself even though her disagreeable potential employers find her sadly lacking in preparation. The doctor or lawyer reads a lot, but typically on a computer screen or a hand-held digital device that enables him to make snap judgments about things, that pose no problem because he is so much smarter than everyone else. He knows this because he made the best grades in a school that cost a lot of money and has a famous name and glorious academic pedigree. All of these people are conscious of their own little cultures, always aware of what is "in," cool, hip, and trendy. Some will fail at most things they attempt, while others will make fortunes, run for public office, or become "superstars" in the pop culture. The ignoramus swaggers through life, convinced that he doesn't know of anything he needs that can be found between the covers of a book. That is the problem.

BOOKS ON FIRE

While high technology with its digital screens offers a serious challenge to the traditional book, there is another truly deadly threat to the survival of books in the modern era.

Book burning has a long and shameful history. Perhaps the most notorious episode in recent memory was the very public burning of books in Hitler's Germany, real bonfires filled with books (and ideas) the Nazis found unacceptable in their efforts to purge their country of authors whose very existence they wanted to eliminate. On May 10, 1933, a crowd of forty thousand people gathered in Berlin. Amidst a festive atmosphere, complete with singing and bands playing, members of the Hitler Youth, the paramilitary Brown Shirts, and infamous S.S. (The Gestapo) burned 25,000 books declared to be "un-German." Nazi Propaganda Minister Joseph Goebbels was smiling.

In the Soviet Union, books were expected to provide propaganda promoting socialism and communism. Both Lenin and Stalin used their regimes to control the books (and hence the ideas) available to the Russian people. Lenin's wife began a purge which instigated the banning of Plato, Descartes, Kant, Carlyle, Tolstoy, and William James, as well as the *Gospels*, the *Koran*, and the *Talmud*, among others. Books or authors that extolled the virtues of religious faith, free speech, free enterprise, or anything considered threatening to the communist state were especially targeted.

The purges of books continued throughout the 1930s as the contents of libraries were depleted; in one single year, over three quarters of a million books were destroyed and never reprinted. The Soviet Union continued to ban books throughout its history until it collapsed in the 1980s. Dissident writers such as Boris Pasternak and Alexander Solzhenitsyn were naturally on the "banned authors" list; not surprisingly, George Orwell's classic *Animal Farm* was banned. His fable about the corruption of a revolution by animals taking over a farm previously owned by humans was simply too close to the history of the communist revolution in the U.S.S.R. Even books or satire or humor weren't safe; Richard Armour, the eminent American humorist, penned a playful spoof of communism, *It All Started With Marx*. He made fun of Soviet icons; when his publisher naively sent a copy to the Soviet Embassy in Washington, D.C. thinking that Russians might enjoy it, the book was quickly banned in Moscow and Dr. Armour's Russian fans had to work hard to get a copy inside Soviet borders. Soviet satellite countries in Eastern Europe, and those around the world such as Cuba, quickly followed suit.

None of this would have surprised George Orwell, whose book about a dystopian tyranny, *1984*, described the type of mind control and censorship perfected in the Soviet Union. Orwell's fictional country in which every person was required to mindlessly love "Big Brother" was clearly a description of the communist revolution in Russia which he regarded with tragic disillusionment. Wrote Orwell, "Every record has been destroyed or falsified, every book rewritten, every picture has been repainted, every statue and street building has been renamed, every date has been altered. And the process is continuing day by day and minute by minute. History has stopped. Nothing exists except an endless present in which the Party is always right."

Orwell anticipated what has happened in the 21st century in the UK. The British Library has added Orwell's work to a "shame list" associated with "wealth obtained from enslaved people or colonial violence." Orwell's offense? The anti-authoritarian author's great-grandfather once owned slaves in the Caribbean. Clearly, *1984* delivers a message that must be suppressed. The University of Northampton offers an instructional module called "Identity Under Construction." Students enrolled at the university can now study literature and poetry through the lens of "feminism, postmodernism and postcolonialism" with an emphasis on "constructions of identity, around issues such as race, class, gender and sexuality." Not surprisingly, the English Department protects ultra-sensitive students from being warned about authoritarianism by Orwell's classic *1984* with a "trigger warning" that the volume contains explicit material that might upset or offend the fragile reader.

Book burning also has a long history in China. In 213 B.C., Chinese Emperor Quin Shi Huang ordered a bonfire of books he considered threatening. Communist dictator Mao Zedong, in the mid-twentieth century, ordered the total destruction of a vast portion of Chinese culture in his ghastly Cultural Revolution.

In 17th century England, "any seditious, scismaticall, or offensive Bookes or Pamphlets" were banned by the infamous "Star Chamber." In 1643, the British Parliament passed a "licensing law" which established prison sentences for authors, publishers, or printers of books violating the law. This led the celebrated poet John Milton to write his *Aeropagitica,* a pamphlet supporting freedom of the press and named for the Greek judges of Aeropagus. In it Milton declared, "He who kills a good book destroys reason itself."

Libraries have been perpetual targets of those who seek to destroy books and the ideas they contain. The British dispatched the Library of Congress during the War of 1812. In the face of such an onslaught, often unlikely heroes emerge. Consider a recent hero, Abel Kader Haidara, a librarian who oversaw the safety of 350,000 rare Arab manuscripts targeted by Al-Qaida Islamists who invaded Mali and Timbuktu.

What does any of this have to do with events taking place today? Surprisingly, a great deal. In the 21st century, we are witnesses to an international campaign to rid libraries, book stores, and private collections of all kinds of books. More often than not, this campaign is presented with a smiling face, a benevolent effort to rid the world of "hate speech" and "bigoted ideas." It is unfortunately also framed in terms of "fairness" and "equity" for writers based on their race or ethnicity. But a closer look at these efforts reveals that they reflect intolerance more often than tolerance and while their advocates may be clicking a mouse attached to a computer rather than lighting fires, the message is clear. Modern day book-burning is sadly alive and well and it needs to be addressed if the finest books written throughout the history of civilization will continue to be read. If this is not done, we may realize faster than we could imagine that the dystopian world of Ray Bradbury's *Fahrenheit 451* is indeed upon us.

First, we must recognize that the modern-day book burner isn't armed with an acetylene torch. He has his list of books to eliminate, but he can accomplish his nefarious deeds using modern tools of book-burning, a computer and a mouse.

Books (and their authors) are unfortunately being attacked using the incendiary issue of race. Race, like religion, has always been a controversial subject. But today, race, along with gender and ethnicity, is being used as a weapon to diminish or disqualify books, even those regarded as among the finest ever written. This action is taken in the name of virtue, of social justice, of fairness and equity. But are these really the values that are at play here?

In recent years, readers have been subjected to a campaign demanding that they "decolonize their bookshelves." Juan Vidal, writing on the National Public Radio website, classifies writers based on their race, nationality, and ethnicity. White readers, he declares, must "silence themselves" before reading books by people of color whose books should replace those of white authors on their bookshelves. "Have you considered that, if you identify as white and read only the work of white authors, you are in some ways listening to an extension of your own voice on repeat?" Vidal does what is fashionable in left-leaning literary circles today; he regards race as the defining characteristic of all writers and arbitrarily places them all together as members of a group rather than seeing them as individuals. This is a fatal error.

Consider short stories by Ernest Hemingway, F. Scott Fitzgerald, John Steinbeck, Noël Coward, and W. Somerset Maugham. Do all of these writers have the same viewpoint just because they are white? Or think of a list of writers from the American South: William Faulkner, Harper Lee, Truman Capote, Elizabeth Spencer, and Margaret Mitchell. Do their books reflect the same point of view or the same characters simply because they all grew up in the same region of the country?

The campaign to "decolonize your bookshelf" falls prey to the notions of cultural Marxism, that people are permanently divided into classes, in this case by race, that are eternally separated as "oppressors" and "oppressed."

In an article entitled "Why You Shouldn't 'Decolonize' Your Bookshelf," Ben R. Crenshaw reminds us, "Good literature teaches us that artificial identities that outsiders impose upon you do not define you. Your social location does not determine what you can know or the beliefs you choose to accept or reject. Your approximation to the righteousness or wickedness of others does not make you good or evil, for each person will be judged according to what he has done, not by what others who look like him have done."[111]

The battle regarding "decolonizing" is also being fought across the ocean in the United Kingdom and in Continental Europe. Katharine Birbalsingh, a prominent defender of high standards in teaching and known for inspiring students to achieve those standards at London's Michaela Community School, said, "Anyone who has ever overcome any obstacle in life knows that if you spend all your time worrying about how insurmountable it is, you will never overcome it. I am not going to spend my time begging the white man to undergo unconscious bias."

Advocates of the "decolonizing" movement assume, naively or deliberately, that slavery and imperialism are only associated with the cultures and nationalities of Europeans or Americans. But slavery and imperialism can be found throughout history as a careful study of the history of Asian, African, Latin-American, and Middle-Eastern nations reveals.

The basis for evaluating books should be merit; a book should be read if its author pursues legitimate truth using facts, evidence, logic, and reason. The authors of the great books of the civilized world came from many backgrounds and periods of history; yet ideas were able to survive and develop and display consistency whether formulated by the ancient Greeks or Romans, Renaissance Europeans, or America's Founding Fathers. It has been said that the concept of liberty treasured in the United States came from origins in Athens, Rome, Jerusalem, London, and Philadelphia, the latter city identified because of the Declaration of Independence and the United States Constitution.

A book should always be judged on its own merits. An author should be judged as an individual. There is no "fair" or "equitable" number of books by members of any group that justifies a book's inclusion on your bookshelf or, for that matter, its exclusion. Nor does owning or reading a book suggest that you automatically agree with or disagree with the views of its author.

The great books and great ideas have often been shared by writers and thinkers with totally different backgrounds; and the writers and thinkers of a single culture have often produced a multiplicity of viewpoints.

Does this mean that we should not read books by authors with Asian, African, Middle-Eastern, or Latin-American backgrounds? Of course not. But these books should be chosen by the same standards as the classics of Western Civilization, not because of the authors' race, religion, gender, or ethnicity.

Juan Vidal doesn't specifically say what should happen to the books removed from your bookshelf when it is decolonized, but we can guess. The "decolonizing" movement is actually an effort to replace one set of ideas with another. Curiously, none of the "decolonizers" ever suggest that the writings of Karl Marx (or others with similar points of view) be replaced. The reason for this should be obvious. Cultural Marxism, with its legacy of inspiring class struggle based on economics or race, is at the core of the attack on the great books.

Judging books and ideas based on the skin color of the writers responsible for their creation is also highly demeaning to the authors themselves. Implicit is an unstated judgment that there is one reason to read the author's book, that he or she is a member of the "correct group."

Writer Jarrett Stepman has declared, "A well-educated person should read deeply and broadly. The idea of combing through one's library and selecting books for right thoughts and wrong thoughts stands disturbingly in opposition to the fundamentals of a free society. If anything, we read too few of the classics in America, not too many."[112]

Today's book burners do not need to actually destroy books to destroy them; they can simply make it unfashionable and politically incorrect to read them. Books that suddenly disappear from a few high tech platforms where they can be purchased have effectively vanished. If one cannot find a book, it's capacity to elucidate the ideas of the author are eliminated with the same efficiency as those physically destroyed by the firemen in Ray Bradbury's *Fahrenheit 451.* The best books have survived the ages; but they may not survive our time if prejudice and ignorance, masquerading as tolerance and inclusion, are used to hasten their demise.

THE BEST OF THE PAST

CONSIDER THE FOLLOWING OBSERVATION: "I mean, they're gonna have to change sooner or later. Time is gonna make them change. I mean, they gotta stop doin' Tosca and all of that dead old classical (expletive deleted)."

Was the contemptuous view of dead classics expressed by a rebellious teenager or even an impudently obnoxious rap star, flushed with his own self-importance? Unfortunately, no. These words were extracted from *Spin* magazine and spoken by Miles Davis, the classically trained jazz trumpeter who once earned and deserved a place in music history. In the last years of his life, Davis tried to project the image of a rebel whose music, dress styles, and attitudes reflected youth and the culture of the streets. Davis was the son of a dentist, grew up in an affluent family, learned to ride horses on the family's ranch while still a child, and attended the Juilliard School of Music. But by accommodating the triumph of rock stars, Davis seemed desperate to be perceived as modern. His remarks did not go unchallenged. He was the subject of *On the Corner: The Sellout of Miles Davis,*[113] a devastating rebuke by the perceptive jazz critic and writer, Stanley Crouch. In blistering prose, Crouch declared, "The contemporary Miles Davis, when one hears his music or watches him perform, deserves the description that Nietzsche gave of Wagner, 'the greatest example of self- violation in the history of art.' Davis made much fine music for the first half of his professional life, and represented for many the uncompromising, Afro-American artist contemptuous of Uncle Tom, but he has fallen from grace, and has been celebrated for it. As usual, the fall from grace has been a form of success." For Stanley Crouch, Miles Davis was "desperate to maintain his position at the forefront of modern music, to sustain his financial position, to be admired for the hipness of his purported innovations." Davis chose, in Crouch's words, "to reject the beautiful in order to genuflect before the commercial." The world of music is full of Miles Davises, not great jazz trumpeters, but people willing to make the compromise Davis made: to trade their principles and common sense and taste for commercial approval. Ironically, Davis will be remembered for the musician he was, not the figure he became. Historians will write approvingly of Miles Davis's music, the music he himself rejected.

Contrast Davis's attitude toward musical tradition with that of trumpeter and composer Wynton Marsalis. As a young trumpet soloist, Marsalis was encouraged to take a serious look at the work of jazz icon Louis Armstrong by Stanley Crouch. Marsalis hadn't previously learned any of Armstrong's music, but he became such an admirer that when he became Artistic Director of Jazz at Lincoln Center, he paid tribute to the style and musical legacy of Louis Armstrong. Under Marsalis's direction and the baton of David Berger, the jazz repertory orchestra at Lincoln Center also presented an annual series of concerts devoted to the music of Duke Ellington. Marsalis has been outspoken in his view that young musicians should be aware of the traditions and accomplishments of the past giants of jazz, insisting that their music should not casually be discarded in the name of easy commercial success or historical ignorance. On *60 Minutes*, Morley Safer raised the problem of young people who don't recognize the names of such jazz legends as Duke Ellington and Charlie Parker. Marsalis said, "It saddens me that people my age may not know that. And it's a comment on the failure of our education system to deal with cultural education. Not just Duke Ellington. Walt Whitman. The list goes on and on. So, it saddens me for us as a nation. Because we have such a rich cultural heritage and we would be so much better for it and we would make such better decisions if we understood what brings us together." Marsalis also staunchly supported the importance of students learning about the best of the past. He maintained that the arts are our collective heritage and that familiarity with major creative geniuses makes you a better person. Marsalis explained, "If you know what Beethoven struggled with, if you know about Matisse. If you know what Louis Armstrong actually sang through his horn, you're better." While some students and even teachers dismiss the great musicians, writers, and artists of the past, Marsalis insists that learning about their lives and work is an opportunity literally to speak with the wisest people who ever lived.

A similar view was expressed by the great jazz pianist Sir George Shearing in his memoir, *Lullaby of Birdland.* Shearing said "I have to say that I observe a number of today's jazz musicians who are attempting to compose without much knowledge of jazz history. They don't know how it all started, and even some of those who do, don't really care. They take the attitude that, 'This is what I want to do, and there are the few chords that I want to play to do it.' My response is that if they took the trouble to listen to Teddy Wilson, Fats Waller, Art Tatum, and Coleman Hawkins, or to study wonderful orchestrators like Fletcher Henderson, Sy Oliver, and Bill Finegan, they'd have a much deeper grounding in music in general and jazz in particular."[114]

These two contrasting attitudes, one expressed by Miles Davis, the other by Wynton Marsalis and George Shearing, represent the cultural challenge of the 21st century. Do we reject it out of hand as a dated and vestigial legacy which should quickly be tossed overboard in the name of progress? Or do we conserve, preserve, and learn from the best of the past, which shouldn't be forgotten?

THE VALUE OF THE PAST

The argument about contemporary and classic writers and composers is not a new one. In eighteenth century France, Bernard le Bovier de Fontenelle, a prominent intellectual, vigorously defended the assertion that modern writers and philosophers of the day surpassed the ancient Greeks and Romans because the new 18th century commentators laid claim to the wisdom of science and reason. (Fontenelle was a colorful figure. He lived for a century, attributed his longevity to eating strawberries, and when introduced to a beautiful young woman late in his life, quipped, "If only I were eighty again.")

In contrast to Fontenelle, supporters of the Greek and Roman writers, known as "the ancients," insisted that writers and philosophers like Aristotle taught eternal truths that transcended time and were just as valid today as when they were first expressed. Sir William Temple was a prominent British diplomat who once served in the Irish Parliament. Temple responded to Fontenelle by insisting that the modernists must stand on the shoulders of the ancients who provided us with timeless wisdom. He said that modern writers reflect light, while the classic writers were the source of light. The most memorable comments on this debate came ironically from Temple's secretary, the brilliant satirist, Jonathan Swift, famous for writing *Gulliver's Travels.*[115] In 1704, Swift published *A Tale of a Tub*, a satire which incorporated "The Battle of the Books." Swift's satirical whimsy turns an imaginary library into a battlefield, as ancient and modern books come alive to do battle with each other. Swift allows the reader to determine which group of books would be the victor.

The history of music, literature, and art is full of colorful and controversial figures who have tried to throw tradition over the side of the boat and declare the triumph of the new age. In such arguments, those declaring themselves to be modern always have an advantage. The new and the young always seem more appealing than the past and the old. Nor is the debate limited to the arts. In 1996, when Bob Dole ran for President, he promised to be a link to the past, to the "greatest generation" that survived the Depression and won World War II. But Bill Clinton responded by offering "A Bridge to the Future," and in the public arena, a vaguely defined future always seems to trump the past, however grand and glorious it may have been. Of course, Clinton won the election.

It is only natural for some to suggest that the whole idea of cultural conservation belongs in a museum. The skeptics will quickly add, "There is already an abundance of good museums." If museums are preserving good art and there are still audiences for good music, is there really a problem? The answer is yes and the problem is two-fold. Great art and great music can exist entirely in an ivory-tower atmosphere. But they will have little or no impact on the public. The huge audiences that attend rock concerts and sports events dwarf the audiences for classical music and jazz. While there will always be academics, historians, and an elite audience for quality in the arts, there is a strong likelihood that quality will drown, sooner or later, in a flood of mass- produced mediocrity.

The arts have always depended on the kindness of strangers, to borrow a phrase from Blanche DuBois, the character created by Tennessee Williams in his play, *A Streetcar Named Desire.* Some of these strangers are people with money—wealthy patrons and corporate sponsors. What can we expect from new generations of patrons and corporate sponsors? An increasing number may be like the high-tech, Silicon Valley billionaire who decided to put his new money to work supporting music. He began promoting rock concerts. As for corporate sponsors, a survey of Fortune 1000 CEOs tells all. One-third of them were able to name more members of the cast of the television show "Survivor" than name members of the President's cabinet. More than three times as many watched "The Simpsons" than the 2000 Presidential debates. The corporate tycoons and patrons of the arts, who have been raised on rock music and who regard the animated under-achiever Bart Simpson as an icon, are part of the problem, not the solution.

CRITICS AND CRYSTAL BALLS

"Lighten up," sneer the skeptics. "Debates are boring; nobody cares about politicians. Mickey Mouse and Donald Duck became icons, and the world didn't collapse." This is a familiar argument and the first problem facing those who are dubious about any type of change. It portrays concerns about rampant cultural illiteracy as the foolish complaints of a group of intellectual snobs, old-fashioned old fogies in starched collars. In short, cultural conservationists are trivialized as out-of-date and, therefore, irrelevant to modern times. What these skeptics ignore is that in former times, there was still a large volume of information regarded as essential for everyone. We all knew who wrote the Declaration of Independence, who delivered "The Gettysburg Address," who said, "We have nothing to fear but fear itself." (How many students today would attribute the last quote to Franklin Roosevelt?) There was also general agreement that some books, works of art, and pieces of music were masterpieces that should be appreciated by everyone. (Yes, you could write a doctoral dissertation or a letter to the editor insisting that Beethoven couldn't compose, but you would be laughed out-of-town or ignored.) Today, the pendulum has swung so far that no book, work of art, or musical masterpiece is safe. In the age of Bart Simpson, the day may come when private and corporate patrons of the arts will still be proud of the art hanging on their walls. But the pictures on the walls will look like Bart Simpson.

The second problem, also ignored by skeptics, is that young writers, artists, and composers are given a message by those who evaluate their work: pursuing their craft along traditional lines is not the *Yellow Brick Road* to *Oz;* it is a rapid road to oblivion. People often assume there is an odd objectivity among critics, as if those who write and speak about the arts are dispassionate, fair-minded individuals who approach their subjects with a total lack of bias. But throughout history, critics have been notoriously biased and frequently mistaken. What are we to think, for instance, of critics like John Burroughs, who wrote in 1897 that Dickens' *A Tale of Two Cities* was "a sheer, dead pull from start to finish?" An editor at the *San Francisco Examiner* once rejected Rudyard Kipling by informing him that he didn't know how to use the English language. The *New York Herald Tribune* called F. Scott Fitzgerald's *The Great Gatsby* "a book of the season only," while *The Saturday Review of Literature* called it "an absurd story." Alan Dent called *The Cocktail Party* by T.S. Eliot "a finely acted piece of flapdoodle." *Commonweal* suggested that only 34 pages of *For Whom the Bell Tolls* were worthy of publication. Yet today, no one would raise an eyebrow by calling books by Dickens, Kipling, Fitzgerald, Eliot, and Hemingway "classics." (Some of their books would be denounced as politically incorrect, but this is another matter entirely.)

A similar situation existed in the world of art. In 1863, French avant-garde artists exhibited their paintings in the Salon de Refusés. This was a protest against the official (and very conservative) French Salon which rejected their works regularly. Today, these same paintings would be regarded as traditional and costly. French Impressionist painters were rejected in their day as dangerous revolutionaries, yet today, their works are among the most admired (and coincidentally, the most expensive) paintings in the world. The public did not respond instantly to the struggles of such masters as Monet, Manet, Renoir, Pissarro, and Degas. When a baker offered a painting by one Impressionist master as the prize in a local contest, the girl who won the picture asked if she could have a muffin instead. Today, the world's leading auction houses battle each other like pugilists in the ring for the privilege of selling paintings by the Impressionists for a king's ransom. Twenty years after the initial protests by Impressionists, Vincent van Gogh joined colleagues, including Georges Seurat and Henri Toulouse-Lautrec, in exhibiting works still banished by Salon. Vincent van Gogh couldn't sell more than one painting in his lifetime. Today, only billionaires can afford to even bid for a Van Gogh.

Nicolas Slonimsky's *Lexicon of Musical Invective*[116] reveals music critics at their best (or worst) depending upon their point of view. In 1878, The *Boston Advertiser* dismissed a new symphony by declaring, "We venture to express a doubt that this work demonstrates the author's right to a place beside or near Beethoven." Today, admirers of Johannes Brahms' *First Symphony* would disagree. Brahms' rival, Wagner, fared worse with Eduard Hanslick, the powerful critic who compared the *Prelude to Tristan and Isolde* to "an old Italian painting of a martyr whose intestines are slowly unwound from his body on a reel." Other critics called Wagner a madman, a communist, a man born to feed spiders with flies. Russian composer César Cui disposed of Wagner as a man devoid of talent, whose melodies were "in worse taste than Verdi and Flotow and more sour than the stalest Mendelssohn." Edward Robinson, writing in *The American Mercury*, declared Maurice Ravel's *Bolero* "the most insolent monstrosity perpetrated in the history of music." Today, no one would be shocked by a symphony program featuring these works by Brahms, Wagner, and Ravel. Audiences would stand and cheer, while critics would praise these old chestnuts as "good, traditional conservative music," but not "adventurous or experimental" like the pieces produced recently by their avant-garde friends.

But herein lies the problem. Critics today don't want to make the mistakes made by their predecessors. Lynne Munson, in her book *Exhibitionism: Art in an Era of Intolerance*,[117] identifies the dilemma. She says, "One argument makes the rounds during every art war: the claim that it has always been the duty of avant-garde artists to shock the public and to challenge social norms. According to this theory, people find the most advanced art of their time offensive because great artists are uniquely gifted at sensing and articulating society's cultural frailties. This argument often receives the same reaction as a trump card. But does it accurately represent the avant-garde enterprise or is the equation of shock-value equals artistic merit a sleight of hand put forth to justify the academic art of our time?"

It is easy enough to praise new works in general terms and preserve enough ambivalence to protect one's self. If a work is "revolutionary," "experimental," or "new-wave," it can be praised to the skies, and if it falls into oblivion, who will remember the critic who sang its praises? On the other hand, music with memorable melodies and art that represents recognizable objects receive a different treatment. The unlucky creators of these works can be dismissed as passé without causing the critic any problems. Critics who want to be seen in the vanguard of open-minded, freethinking, and progressive champions of the future know what to do. They reverse the roles played by all those critics who feared the new and experimental works of years past. Revolution is in, tradition is out. In 1934, Cole Porter wrote, "Good authors too who once knew better words now only use four-letter words, Writing prose, Anything Goes!" But in Porter's day, a single four-letter word in *Gone with the Wind* sent critics into a spiral. Today, stand-up comedians, both men and women, will walk out on a stage and shower their audiences with four-letter words. Obscenities will freely pepper the dialogue of movies, uttered by all members of the cast, including children. What would Porter, hardly a prude or a cultural conservative, think today? Have things changed? Absolutely.

Today's self-styled revolutionaries are hardly greeted by the unwelcoming critiques that ridiculed the work of Debussy or Monet. In fact, they are frequently beneficiaries of praise from academics eager to be fashionable and publicity from a well-oiled commercial machine that portrays them as victims. If the revolutionary is also an incompetent, a charlatan, a fool, a con-artist, or just an untalented ignoramus, who cares? The skeptic will insist that nothing has changed, that people are always resistant to "progress" and to "contemporary ideas," and to people "pushing the envelope" and "using art to challenge convention." It takes a rugged individualist to see through the promotion and hyperbole of those who think that "spin," not truth, defines our values. Occasionally someone punctures the promotional balloon, but not often. The public is usually influenced by a desire to be in fashion.

But once in a while, someone declares that the Emperor has no clothes. Artist and master teacher Frank Covino reminded us that in Vienna, the public was asked to express a preference between two groups of paintings. One group had been created by several of Vienna's leading avant-garde artists, the other by patients at what was then known by the now politically incorrect term "insane asylum." The public selected the paintings by patients residing in a mental institution as superior. Consider a dialogue between stage and film star Tony Randall and sportscaster Bob Costas. Randall, an avid opera buff, remained unmoved by Costas's efforts to elicit positive words from Randall about most of today's pop music. When Costas suggested that a young man with a guitar could use today's pop music to "express his humanity," Randall remained unconvinced and refused to praise the work of many of today's self-styled geniuses. "Because it isn't any good," he said. But how many of today's stars will use their celebrity to endorse the view expressed by Randall? It is easier to confuse genius with sales figures.

So the critics of today have become predictable. An artist who throws paint at a canvas can be praised for his "boundless energy." A composer who creates deafening tidal waves of noise can be applauded for "taking sound to a new level." A writer who covers a page with graffiti can be cheered for her ability to "infuse four-letter words with new meaning." Unfortunately, a herd of thundering elephants also display boundless energy, testing a nuclear weapon can also take sound to a new level, and four-letter words mean what they've always meant. Nonetheless such realizations do not deter our critical friends. As for the young composer pursuing melody, the artist exploring color, the writer creating elegant prose, the future is doubtful. He can, of course, depend upon being discovered by patrons of the arts. But today they may be watching "Survivor" or "The Simpsons."

BEETHOVEN, MALE CHAUVINIST PIG?

While some try to consign the classics to the ash heap of history for commercial reasons, others have pursued a political or ideological agenda. In academic circles, one of the more fashionable ways of achieving this goal is through a trendy type of literary and artistic criticism known as "deconstruction." Professors and critics have attacked each other like charging rams in arguments on this subject. But it is obvious that the general public is blissfully unaware of the writings of Jacques Derrida, the influential French writer admired and emulated by so many deconstructionists. The idea behind "deconstruction" is simple: there is no one true interpretation of a book. It doesn't even mean what the author intended it to mean. A text means whatever you, the critic and deconstructionist, say, it means.

It should surprise no one that deconstructionists have barged into the field of music and like their literary colleagues, they are armed with a political and ideological agenda. Perhaps the silliest and most foolish example of such an agenda was advanced by Susan McClary, a "feminist-musicologist" who wrote that the music of Beethoven "subjugated the feminine to the masculine." Poor Ludwig, an obvious male chauvinist pig, is not around to defend himself. Susan McClary's lengthy analysis clearly had nothing to do with Beethoven; it had a great deal to do with her attempts to impose her own feminist agenda on a totally unrelated work of art. For McClary, Beethoven's celebrated Ninth Symphony expresses the "murderous rage of a rapist." She went so far as to suggest that bar for bar, Beethoven's music is more violent than the amplified noise produced by heavy-metal rock groups.

What was the response to McClary's assertion? She received a six-figure grant from the influential MacArthur Foundation. Bowdoin College actually created a course devoted to the question, "Is Beethoven's *Ninth Symphony* a marvel of abstract architecture, culminating in a gender-free hymn to human solidarity, or does it model the process of rape?" Nor was McClary satisfied to limit herself to speculations about Beethoven. She also attacked the music of Schubert and Bach. To be sure, some have heaped deserved ridicule on this verbal assault, rightly declaring it to be absurd and pretentious. The brilliant pianist and musical polemicist Samuel Lipman wrote in *The New Criterion* that McClary was "explaining away the achievement of Bach." Alex Ross in his article, "A Female Deer? Looking for Sex in the Sound of Music,"[118] asked, "Are we seriously to believe that Axl Rose is innocent of malevolent cultural influence while Ludwig van Beethoven, dead these many years, commits acts tantamount to rape?" Pulitzer Prize-winning composer and University of Pennsylvania Professor Richard Wernick dismissed McClary's notions as "crazy" and said he laughed at them, but then noted that the Guggenheim Memorial Foundation lists contained "a lot of gender stuff." Nor should we assume this foolishness is going to disappear. McClary and her assorted admirers have survived the ridicule and criticism, and continue to pursue their politicized agenda at the expense of good music and common sense.

Unfortunately, in the years since McClary offered her bizarre interpretation of Beethoven, things have become worse, not better, in the world of classical music. In 2022, Marin Alsop, conductor of the Baltimore Symphony, explained her decision to jettison Friedrich Schiller's *Ode to Joy*, the text selected by Beethoven for the choral section of his *Ninth Sym*phony. Beethoven regarded this work as a challenge, writing that for a composer, it is more difficult to set the writing of a great poet to than to set a poem by a merely good one. Beethoven declared that to meet this challenge, the composer must rise higher than the poet and then concluded, "Who can do that with Schiller?" Historians and generations of music-lovers have felt that Beethoven was more than up to the challenge and regarded the *Ninth Symphony* with awe and inspiration.

Marin Alsop, however, has other ideas. She chose to posit the assertion that Schiller was no longer relevant to contemporary audiences. So in Baltimore, she found another "poet" to replace Schiller, her friend Anthony Carter, best known as the rapper "Wordsmith." Alsop wasn't finished "reimagining" the work to make it relevant to audiences in Baltimore. She opined, "I tried to insert music that was culturally relevant to the location where I'm doing it. Here in Baltimore, between the first and second movements, I have African drumming. Just three minutes. But it takes the motif and it evolves it. Because I think that's what Beethoven was thinking."

Of course, Marin Alsop has no idea what Beethoven was thinking, but why bother with trivial details? African drums and a jazz ensemble have no more business being interpolated into a Beethoven symphony than the *Moonlight Sonata* has being inserted into a jazz concert work written by Duke Ellington. True, as composer conductor Bernard Herrmann observed, Beethoven saw himself as a poet through music; would he truly approve of Wordsmith's mixture of bad rhymes and socially "woke" slogans? This matters not to Alsop as this establishes her credentials and those of the orchestra she conducts as "woke" and therefore immune from the wrath of the Twittermob.

What is actually happening here is that the deconstructionists, originally French intellectuals who persuaded academia that a literary work means whatever they choose to say it means, have come at last for music in general and classical music in particular. The best response to this nonsense comes not from a professional music critic, but from author and public intellectual Heather Mac Donald. Writing in "Making Beethoven Woke" in *City Journal*, she declares forthrightly, "In revising works to match contemporary sensibilities, we diminish, not expand, our human possibilities. No one would write Schiller's "Ode to Joy" today. That is precisely why it should be performed intact. Its elevated rhetoric belongs to a lost aesthetic universe of romantic idealism, classical allusion, and exacting formal craft. It speaks to a now-alien way of being in the world that we can nevertheless dimly sense through close engagement with its language."[119]

The capricious "reimagining" of the classics is actually the product of an alliance between two groups both lacking in principles: the first group is comprised of the ideologues whose end game is to do away with all of western culture so that it can be swept into oblivion and replaced with "art" that expresses their political and social agenda; the second group are the promoters, hustlers, and hucksters of Hollywood and Manhattan who could not care less about ideology. If they think they can make barrels of cash through socially woke "cultural Marxism," they are perfectly happy to do so.

So it continues with no end in sight. Marin Alsop announced that "Wordsmith" would now be applying his rapper's brilliance to *L'histoire du soldat*, a work by Igor Stravinsky, a tale about a soldier tempted by the devil in exchange for promises of a fortune. With "Wordsmith" supplying a new text, however, Stravinsky's "story of a soldier" is converted into an expression of a black American soldier fighting in Vietnam.

Nor is the Baltimore Symphony and its "woke" female conductor the only advocate of such revisions. The Metropolitan Museum hosted a performance of Beethoven's opera *Fidelio;* while the German text remained, the plot and dialogue were rewritten by Heartbeat Opera to insert speeches about the suppression of immigrants and persons of color in the U.S. prison system. Whatever this is, it's not Beethoven.

The emerging pattern is clear. Classical works, declare the "woke" among us, must become vehicles for political and social propaganda; those who agree are welcome in the new world to take their marching orders from the ideologues. Those who do not can be denounced as racists or antiquated purists and ultimately cancelled and consigned to a lifetime of cultural oblivion. In the minds and plans of these people, the classics can be used, desecrated, and ultimately destroyed, all in the name of their revolutionary cultural agenda.

Of course, it is easy enough for any would-be academician or critic to make up a plot, story, or explanation of musical sounds. Musicologists have often purported to hear the flowing of the brook or the wind whistling through the trees every time they hear a musical arpeggio. But often, they are interpreting sounds in ways the composer himself never heard or imagined. For example, Aaron Copland was often told by admirers that they could imagine the outdoor Appalachian scenes that inspired him to write the ballet *Appalachian Spring*. They could almost feel the gentle breezes and hear the twittering birds. Copland appreciated the compliments, but confessed that he had been inspired by no such scenes. He learned of choreographer Martha Graham's choice of a new title for her ballet after returning from a trip to Mexico. Graham confided to him that she had chosen the title from a line in a poem by Hart Crane. It had nothing to do with the ballet, she admitted, but she told Copland, "I liked it!" One shudders to imagine the theories that Susan McClary and her followers can concoct to explain the true meaning of *Appalachian Spring.*

In his article, "The Inside Story,"[120] the composer Ernest Kanitz observed a tendency of radio announcers to "discover" stories in music that were never intended by the person who wrote the music. He said, "This in my opinion is bad in all cases where music is played which has not been clearly linked with extra-musical ideas by the composer himself." He added, "Music's foremost task is bringing messages to its listeners which cannot be expressed in words, in stone or marble, or on canvas. Only pure music can do that, music in which no thought associations of a material nature are forced upon the listener's mind, but on whose immaterialized waves his soul can escape to regions of spiritual beauty." Dr. Kanitz was talking about people who tried to make abstract music more appealing to an audience by interpreting the emotions or a plot they could distill from a performance. Now we have academically respectable scholars using this approach to deconstruct the classics, usually based entirely on their own personal tastes or ideological biases.

Those who reject the past for commercial reasons, like Miles Davis, or for political and ideological reasons, like Susan McClary, are both making the same mistake. They are denigrating our musical heritage so that we will take them more seriously. There is a fitting response to their efforts. They should not be taken seriously at all.

SHOULD WE BE OPTIMISTIC?

When we raise the question of a cultural crisis in America, some would call us pessimists. Nothing is perfect, we are told, but we only see the half-empty glass, when in reality, the glass is half-full. To be sure, there are many dedicated college music departments and conservatories. Audiences still line up for performances of operas, symphonies, and ballets. Jazz bands have enjoyed a revival. Tickets to highly promoted museum exhibitions are very much in demand. So, our critics will scoff, is there really a problem? Why next summer, the nation will feature music festivals from coast to coast.

All this is true, but none of these facts mean that the problem occurs only in our imagination. There always have been and probably always will be a small minority of people who care about the arts. These people have worked for years to support the arts financially and work tirelessly to see that various arts institutions don't disappear. But in the environment of today's cultural crisis, true arts supporters may be an endangered species. First, these people do not appear by accident. They don't simply materialize on the scene out of nowhere and begin urging the rest of society to value the arts. In an environment dependent upon today's television industry, with pop-rock-video promoters, and a pervasive cultural illiteracy, it is likely that there will be fewer and fewer of these people in the future. Secondly, even if a small minority of arts supporters remains loyal and true to their cause, present trends suggest that the large, influential public is becoming increasingly detached from the arts. If only a small elite group increasingly appreciates good music, art, theater, books, and dance, these arts face a bleak future indeed. Not only will financial support of the arts be in jeopardy, but artists will also find themselves without the large, appreciative audience necessary for the arts to thrive. For art to succeed, it must find an audience. While much is said and written about the decline of art, little discussion is raised regarding the decline of the audience.

We can encourage continued enthusiasm for the arts in those institutions, museums, schools, and festivals that thrive. But we must remember that institutions alone do not protect the arts. They must be valued and treasured by a large, engaged, responsive audience; and the nature of the audience, both in quantity and quality, is threatened today. The arts may not be able to compete with every element of pop culture for the attention of the public, but it is essential that a large public value the arts and recognize their importance in the overall fabric of society. Otherwise, the arts will come to be regarded as exotic and esoteric, appealing only to a small audience. This trend bodes ill for both the arts in general and artists in particular. Those who respond to our present cultural crisis as cockeyed optimists or apathetic bystanders represent a serious challenge. These people mean well, but they will dismiss our legitimate concerns as the pessimistic concerns of a few misguided worriers. If they are proven wrong, it will be far too late to remedy the situation.

CHANGE AND PROGRESS

The mistake made by commercial apologists and academic ideologues is the same: they confuse change with progress.

Change is not synonymous with progress. Is change always good? Edmund Burke, the great British conservative of the 18th century, drew a distinction between "change" and "reformation." Burke said that change is a novelty that may eliminate the good as well as the evil in the object being changed. In contrast, the reformer seeks a remedy for a problem without changing the substance of an institution. In 1930, Gilbert Keith Chesterton observed, "Fallacies do not cease to be fallacies because they become fashions." Nearly two centuries after the era of Edmund Burke, his 20th century advocate, Dr. Russell Kirk, echoed his sentiments. In *The Conservative Mind,*[121] Kirk wisely declared that "Change may not be salutary reform: hasty innovation may be a devouring conflagration rather than a torch of progress." Kirk urged recognition of the principle of prescription; that we stand on the shoulders of giants, able to see farther than our ancestors only because of the great stature of those who have preceded us in time.

But today, we often are tempted to jump up and applaud furiously when told that something represents change. We assume that the change will be positive, and that the new is always better than the old. "New and improved" is a favorite advertising slogan. But too often, "new and improved" means a larger cereal box and fewer corn flakes. Politicians are ambivalent about change. If they are incumbents, they like the status quo, but if they are trying to get into office, change seems like a good idea. Some political slogans can backfire. In 1928, Republican businessmen, advocating the candidacy of Herbert Hoover, ran an advertisement in the *New York World* promising "A chicken for every pot and a car in every back yard to boot." It was a highly specific promise, and unless you were a vegetarian or a chicken, the consequences seemed entirely harmless. After the stock market crashed, voters were understandably angry that many pots not only didn't contain chickens, they were empty. Hoover had to insist that the widely quoted promise was one he'd never personally made.

In his 2008 campaign for the presidency, Barack Obama was singularly unspecific in promising "Change" and "Hope." When presented with vague promises of change, voters, like consumers, often assume that the changes implied will all be good. "Change" can mean more money, a marriage proposal, a rewarding new job, or your favorite team finally winning the Super Bowl or World Series. Of course, change can also mean loss of money, divorce, being fired by an unpleasant boss, or your favorite team ending up in last place . . . again.

It is human nature just to assume that change is always good. Unfortunately, it isn't. Sometimes it is nothing short of disastrous. In the arts, publishers, owners of art galleries, film and television producers, and executives of recording companies all have a vested interest in persuading you that "new" is synonymous with "better." If you're pleased with what you purchased yesterday, you might not be tempted to buy a newer product today. Part of promoting whatever is new today is persuading potential audiences (and possible customers) that whatever they bought yesterday is old-fashioned and out-of- date. Granted, the automobile rendered the horse and buggy obsolete, and the computer sounded the death knell for the traditional typewriter. However, some devices made today are crafted with planned obsolescence, so they don't work as well as items manufactured years ago. Ideas, however, do not necessarily wear out like equipment. Principles and values may be timeless. While some principles and values should be scrutinized, true principles and values are likely to be just as true today as yesterday. They may not be as fashionable today, or appeal to those who are obsessed with being "trendy" and being "with it."

Lyricist Dave Frishberg and composer Bob Dorough had fun with what Frishberg characterized as "those terminally trendy types" in their song, "I'm Hip." Frishberg's lyric declares, "I'm hip, I'm no square, I'm alert, I'm awake, I'm aware. I am always on the scene, makin' the rounds, diggin' the sounds, I read *People* magazine 'cause I'm hip." Later, Frishberg's imaginary hipster is immersed in macrobiotics and enthusiastically ready to start using narcotics. We all know people whose greatest mission in life is to be "with it." Unfortunately, most of them have no idea what "it" is, but they want to be thought by everyone as worldly, sophisticated, and modern. Ironically, much of the subculture they embrace is anything but sophisticated. It is frequently simplistic, vulgar, and appallingly unintelligent. Their attempts at non- conformity would be amusing if they didn't have such a devastating effect on society as a whole. You can always recognize the non-conformists in pop culture; they look, talk, dress, and sound exactly alike.

C.S. Lewis could not have been more accurate or more eloquent when he said, "We all want progress, but if you're on the wrong road, progress means doing an about-turn and walking back to the right road; in that case, the man who turns back soonest is the most progressive."

CLASSICS IN THE 21ST CENTURY - ROAD MAPS OR DINOSAURS?

If we accept the idea that the best of our past—music, books, art, plays, and films—should not be abandoned, how do we determine what is best? A classic book, painting, or piece of music (whether it be "classical," jazz, or part of the "The Great American Song Book") should be timeless. Are classics in the 21st century roadmaps or dinosaurs?

Whenever anyone suggests that certain works of art are "classics," someone else is certain to raise objections. Although these objections are stated in many ways, the fundamental attitudes behind these arguments are nearly always the same. Here are the major myths you will frequently encounter.

1. *There is no such thing as a classic.* It's all a matter of opinion. As the leader of a rock group once put it, "You do your thing, man, and I'll do mine." The implication is that your "thing" and my "thing" are equal: entitled to equal opportunity, equal standing, and equal critical attention. To speak against equality sounds downright un-American, rather like declaring publicly that you don't believe in the principles of the Declaration of Independence. The problem is a comparison of apples and oranges. The Declaration of Independence is expressing the fundamental rights of man. Works of art, music, plays, novels, and poems do not qualify. All men may be created equal, but are all works of art? Hardly. Would anyone rationally suggest that there is no difference in quality between Beethoven's Fifth Symphony and the fifth hit recording of any rock or rap singer selected at random? That there is a difference in quality between the complex jazz improvisation of Art Tatum or Charlie Parker, and the equally spontaneous ramblings of a cat strolling across a piano keyboard or a hound howling at the moon? There are undoubtedly those who would suggest that the answer is "yes." But these individuals are so illogical, so confused, that their absurd arguments do not

even merit a response. In fact, the sounds made by the cat or the hound may have more merit than some of today's successful pop music, but that is more a reflection on today's audiences than on the innate musicality of canines and felines.

It is true that wise men and women have disagreed throughout the ages regarding the quality of art. But should we accept such disagreements as an assumption that all judgments about the arts are simply relative? Philosopher Mortimer Adler addresses this question when he says, "There is no point in arguing about how things look, but there is good reason to argue about what things are." Adler declares, "To recognize excellence in a piece of music, one must have some knowledge of the art of composing music. If a man lacks such knowledge, of course, all he can say is that he likes or dislikes the music. The man who insists that is all he can say is simply confessing his own ignorance about music. He can go on expressing his likes and dislikes about music, but he should not, in his ignorance, deny others the right to make objective judgments based on knowledge he does not have."

Does this mean that only experts should be allowed to have or express opinions about music, art, or books? Of course not.

Experts can declare a work of art to be a masterpiece and yet, the same work may communicate nothing to an audience. Adler's point, however, is that there is a difference between subjective opinions and objective facts. Two people can argue, for example, over the recordings of their favorite singers. One likes opera and praises Luciano Pavarotti, the other likes popular music and praises Frank Sinatra. There is no "correct" answer in such an argument. These individuals simply have different tastes. One can argue, quite clearly however, over the relative merits of two pianists, one who hits wrong notes all the time and the other who plays the right notes. Even the pianist who plays all the wrong notes will undoubtedly have a defense in this day and age. While André Previn was conductor of the London Symphony Orchestra, he appeared in a memorable comedy sketch on a television program with the British comedy team of Morecambe and Wise. Previn, with a straight face, though dubbed "Andrew Preview" by the comedians, began conducting the orchestral accompaniment while comedian Eric Morecambe proceeded to massacre the opening movement of Grieg's *Piano Concerto.* When Previn, with superb comic timing and a look of incredulity on his face, walked over to the piano to confront Morecambe, the comedian protested without cracking a smile that he was simply playing "the right notes, but not necessarily in the right order."

Similarly, one can argue quite persuasively for superiority of the lyrics of Cole Porter, Ira Gershwin, Lorenz Hart, and Oscar Hammerstein II, over those of rock lyricists who repeat the same phrase over and over again to an amplified beat. The argument is not about who likes a particular lyricist, but which lyrics are better written. We can evaluate the quality of a melodic line, a brush stroke, a brilliant phrase of theatrical dialogue. Mortimer Adler cites the example of a well-made table. We may argue over which table we like best. But if a table falls apart because its legs are attached incorrectly, there is no argument. The table has been poorly made. This is especially clear in an area far removed from the arts: athletic competition. We may argue over which player should be the member of a team's starting line-up, but if a basketball player shoots a free throw, he either scores or misses his shot. The same can be said for evaluating the arts. Do not fall prey to a common misconception. Art can be judged by objective standards.

2. *Classics do not speak to us today.* Mortimer Adler again responds. He says, "The poets bear witness that ancient man, too, saw the sun rise and set, felt the wind on his cheek, was possessed by love and desire, experienced ecstasy and elation, as well as frustration and disillusion, and knew good and evil. The ancient poets speak across the centuries to us, sometimes more vividly than our contemporary writers." The emotions and profound ideas found in the music and paintings of great masters do not go out of date. Deal Hudson, in *How to Keep From Losing Your Mind,* a book dedicated to Adler's memory, observed, "Classics are classics because they've brought joy and understanding to generations over centuries." [122]

We may smile at Mark Twain's definition of a classic book, one that people praise and don't read. But Os Guinness writes of great books. "Despite the deadening effect of our modern preoccupation with success, and the 'bottom line,' we can be assured that the classics have an intrinsic human, cultural and spiritual worth." Scholars often use the term "classics" in reference to studies in Latin and Greek. But in time, lists of great books have come to be known as classics, in part because of the messages and values they transmit, transcending the passage of time. Louise Cowan, former Chairman of the English Department and Dean of the Graduate School at the University of Dallas, expresses this view in "The Necessity of the Classics."[123] A strong advocate for classic books, Cowan observes, "This body of writing, until recently considered the very center of European and American education, has stood guard over the march of Western civilization, preserving its ideals of truth and justice, whatever its lapses may have been. And the later writers included in this remarkable group of texts have continued the unsparing examination of conscience that the Greeks inaugurated three thousand years ago." She goes on to conclude, "Shakespeare's *Henry V,* Melville's *Moby Dick,* Conrad's *Lord Jim,* Crane's *The Red Badge of Courage,* Faulkner's *The Unvanquished,* Hemingway's *The Sun Also Rises,* these and other works enter into a dialogue with the Greek and Roman classics to kindle the age of the hero within the individual soul. The heroic thus becomes not a set of rules but a living idea, incarnated in the lives of us all." Great music and great paintings have inspired generations of listeners and viewers, not because they are old, but because they are great. A pernicious, but popular, notion today suggests that all of today's problems are contemporary, solved only by contemporary solutions. In fact, many of today's moral and cultural quandaries involve new technology. But the ideas, the fundamental principles and challenges of daily living, remain the same. Consider the story of Romeo and Juliet. The conflict between two feuding families provokes a familiar question: can love triumph over hate? Shakespeare's play has inspired many musicians: from Berlioz to Tchaikovsky, Prokofiev to Leonard

Bernstein. Opera, ballet, orchestral pieces, and Broadway musicals have all moved audiences emotionally. Musical styles differed, but Shakespeare's characters remain compelling in any age. A classic is a work of lasting value and should speak to us today with the same impact as in earlier times.

3. *Classics are old, and therefore, "old-hat."* This is foolishness. The 20th century is now over, and there are many 20th century paintings, musical compositions, and plays that qualify as classics. We should learn about our finest works of art because of their quality, not their age. History (like Hollywood's fabled cutting room floor) is full of bad art. But there are also neglected masterpieces to be found. Numerous celebrities and stars are highly over-rated. Consider two composers, Sir Edward Elgar and Samuel Barber. Elgar was a man of the 19th century, as British as could be, the creator of *Pomp and Circumstance*. Elgar's world, which he held dear, was swept away in the torrential cataclysm of World War I. Elgar anticipated the horror of the approaching war in his grieving 1914 work, *Sospiri.* Samuel Barber, a 20th century American composer, led a very different life than Elgar. In 1936, he adapted a movement of his string quartet and created his popular *Adagio for Strings.* The mood he expressed is one of grief and pathos. Elgar and Barber, each in his own way, managed to express a similar mood. Their pieces, both eloquent and expressive, arouse a sense of tragedy and regret in the audiences who hear them. We can find other pieces of music written by composers who lived and wrote hundreds of years before Elgar or Barber. These pieces of music last because the emotions expressed were contemporary at the time they were created, and they are still contemporary today.

4. *The best artists think only of today and reject the past.* The idea of the artist as an angry revolutionary is popular, but inaccurate. Some artists have earned a reputation by smashing past traditions. but others have not. Johann Sebastian Bach, for example, has been described by music historians as a composer so profound as to sum up all that had preceded him. A coherent and meaningful bond with the past is not limited to classical music.

Tap dancer Gregory Hines recalled Mohammed Ali telling his opponents, "You know, you're not just fighting me. You're fighting Joe Louis, Sugar Ray Robinson, Jack Johnson, and all the great champions that came before me." Hines said, "Sometimes, that's how I feel, when I tap dance for people, they're not just seeing me. They're seeing Bunny Briggs, Harold and Fayard Nicholas, Gene Kelly, Sandman Sims, Baby Lawrence, Steve Condos, and of course, Henry LeTang, my teacher." An artist (or audience) unfamiliar with the classics, with our artistic heritage, is ignorant. How can we evaluate what is done today if we have nothing to which we can compare it?

5. *Culture should only reflect the identity of selected groups within our culture.* There is no need for a common set of artistic values shared by all. This myth is especially destructive. Sadly, in recent times, individuals have begun to identify themselves primarily as members of groups rather than as individual citizens that share values. If race, gender, politics, age, and other divisive labels become a definitive standard, we all become more conscious of our differences rather than our similarities. There was a time when it was safe to assume that there were certain facts, historical details, books, stories, music, and art that were known by everyone, regardless of background, regardless of group identity. But no more. However, consider the observations of Ben Stein describing what he calls "the cheerful ignorance" of Los Angeles teenagers. Stein said he had never met a single high school or college student who knew when World Wars I and II were fought. Students were ignorant of Thomas Jefferson and the Bill of Rights, unable to find major cities in the world on a map. Since the publication of Stein's article, there have been dozens of reports, equally appalling, about the phenomenon of cultural illiteracy.

Can citizens be persuaded to support the local symphony if they think Beethoven is the St. Bernard who carried the composer's name in a successful Hollywood film? Can you expect the arts to survive when dependent upon the financial and moral support of those who have been educated by MTV? Clearly, there should be people, places, and facts that everyone knows. While history, geography, and government studies have received much attention, the arts have been neglected. Until we again share common familiarity with artists and their achievements, a serious discussion of this problem will be futile.

6. *Conserving the classics is unnecessary.* Future generations will discover classics on their own. This is an especially dangerous myth. Writers, artists, and musicians regarded today as great masters were often ignored during their lifetime. While their works have indeed been discovered and acknowledged, such discoveries have often been accidental or the result of a single dedicated individual. We may assume that the music of Johann Sebastian Bach was so magnificent as to ultimately achieve recognition. Today's world is unlike the world encountered by those who made their cultural choices before the advent of high technology and the entertainment media. It is possible for young people to grow up without exposure to the arts and still discover them later in life. But can we gamble that they will do so?

Discovery of the arts at any age requires a certain intellectual curiosity, a yearning of the spirit, a need for fulfillment not answered elsewhere. Now, it is perfectly feasible for huge numbers of people to go through their lives, to make money and pursue their careers, blissfully ignorant of anything not heavily promoted on television. If boys and girls are introduced to the arts early in life and they develop an enthusiasm for music, books, and art, they may indeed discover new pathways (and old classics) as adults. But if they regard the world of the concert hall, the library, or the museum as "foreign territory," such discovery is unlikely. Consider a modern-day ignoramus, convinced that he already knows about "good music" and "good books." When confronted with the name of any of our greatest composers, this self-satisfied person is likely to respond with a blank stare and ask, "Who's he?" Therefore, conserving the classics cannot be left to chance. A typical teenager is faced with dozens of competitors for his time: school, dates, sports, the ubiquitous computer, and the television set. Do we really expect the arts to compete for attention without more than a little help?

7. *Classics are only for an elite public and belong in a museum.* We live in an age of popular culture and classics are only created for an audience of intellectual snobs. This is another dangerous assumption. Many of the works we now admire as classics were originally created for large audiences. It is true that in the 18th and 19th centuries, composers and painters created works for wealthy patrons and a small aristocratic audience. But many works of art were intended to communicate with the general public. We think of operas as written only for a small audience. But in Europe, many of the greatest operas have been known and loved by audiences in the same way that Americans respond to Broadway musicals. It is true that individuals who consider themselves custodians of "high art" often act like intellectual snobs. But creative artists themselves are always seeking a large public reaction—the larger the better. In fact, the best classics set standards by which other works can be judged. What composer would not want to achieve the melodic spontaneity of Tchaikovsky or the harmonic colors of Debussy and Ravel? (Or for that matter, what dancer wouldn't like to be compared favorably with Fred Astaire's performances on screen?) Classics are not dated, and works that achieve the same standards as classics should not be considered "dated" or "old-fashioned." Yet too often, composers and artists who pursue the elegance, emotional expression, communication, and energy of the classics may be dismissed for stylistic reasons. A classic can emerge from popular culture. (Consider the greatest Broadway musicals, motion picture scores, or jazz improvisations.) The best of works in these genres may easily surpass a long-winded symphony, a dull opera, or a badly-written string quartet. But the creator of today's classics may face the same problems as the masters of former times: an apathetic and ignorant public, this time schooled by television to appreciate the trivial, superficial, vulgar, talentless star of the moment. The latter, needless to say, may be lacking talent, but the

beneficiary of a million-dollar marketing campaign that makes up for singing off key or throwing paint at a canvas.

8. *No one can agree on what is truly a "classic."* Nonsense. Classics stand the test of time. Classics are capable of speaking to many generations. There is a reason why audiences today are thrilled by the sound of jazz bands of the 1930s, by string quartets written in the 18th century, by a piano concerto composed a century ago. Fashions and trends change constantly, but classics speak in a language that is timeless and eternal. Because tastes change, we may look critically at works that were once regarded as classics. Other works, long neglected, may be justifiably discovered and elevated to the status of classics. But such judgments should be based on familiarity and understanding, not ignorance. It has become fashionable to dismiss many classics as "irrelevant" to the modern age. But too often, this argument is offered by those conveniently seeking to replace the classics (or the values they represent) with works of their own. A composer once declared confidently that even the most complex works of Richard Strauss were based on four-part harmony. He then boasted that his own pieces were crafted using two or three times as many "voices" or musical lines. Upon hearing this remark, composer Bernard Herrmann snapped, "Then let me see you write pieces as good as those by Strauss!" We may debate the list of classics in music, art, or literature, but the debate can be legitimately conducted by those who take the time and effort to become familiar with the candidates. Or, as is commonly said in sports, you can't tell the players without a scorecard.

9. *Classics are dull.* Of course not. They wouldn't become classics by boring an audience. But as our attention spans have shortened, it has become increasingly difficult to concentrate. In an age of sound bites, the philosopher isn't king. (Nor is the composer of three-hour operas or writer of thousand page novels.) Classics require greater concentration and attention than television situation comedies or videos on MTV. Handing *The Complete Works of William Shakespeare, War and Peace,* or *Moby Dick* to a small child probably isn't going to win an instant admirer.

But by introducing children to classics gradually, a parent, teacher, or friend can begin to inspire the curiosity that ultimately leads to artistic exploration and discovery. A child will be less likely to fall asleep listening to classical music upon learning of the "surprise" in Haydn's *"Surprise" Symphony* that kept the composer's patrons wide-awake at concerts. A work like Prokofiev's *Peter and the Wolf* may be the gateway to more complex and substantial works. Classics often require more study and concentration than more superficial works. But they also offer many more rewards.

10. *Classics don't matter at all, because everything important is going to be produced on computers or high-tech devices.* Computers (like television sets) are simply messengers. Their messages are dependent entirely upon the content that is created for them by (thankfully) human beings. The notion that art is rendered "out-of-date" by technology is simply absurd. Today, musicians depend heavily upon computers and an assortment of electronic equipment. But unless that equipment is used to create melodies, harmonies, rhythms, and orchestrations of great consequence and profound meaning, who cares? Richard Rodgers and Oscar Hammerstein wrote the score for *Carousel* without a computer. Art Tatum turned "Tea for Two" into an improvised jazz classic that intimidated the most technically brilliant classical pianists and his jazz colleagues alike. He did it without ever hearing or seeing an electronic keyboard. (Tatum, who was almost totally blind, couldn't see the acoustic keyboard of his day either.) A genius is a genius, at a computer or with a quill-pen. A fool is a fool, with or without a million-dollar multimedia studio. If he sings or plays badly, he is also an untalented fool.

11. *Respect for classical standards inhibits innovation and stifles progressive and experimental musicians, artists, and writers.* This argument is one of the most popular ones used to dismiss the best of our past. But there is always room in the world for new ideas and original approaches to creativity. Too often, those who abandon classical standards do so because they know in their hearts that they cannot be judged on the same basis as the best and brightest creators of the past. If we forget about the values of

melody, artistic beauty, or eloquent language, it's easy to produce music, art, and literature which are much easier to create and unfortunately, much easier to sell. The true innovator draws upon the best of the past as a springboard to launch his own creative efforts and appreciates the legacy that should inspire him.

12. *New works can't become classics.* Every product of a creative imagination was considered contemporary at the time. Chopin wasn't writing "classical piano music" during his lifetime; he was writing contemporary music. Today, we regard it as classic. Pioneers in jazz certainly didn't think they were creating a classical art form. Today, we look back at jazz history and marvel at those who developed the sounds that some call "America's classical music." The composers and lyricists who created the songs that make up the scores of our best musical theater or who scored motion pictures didn't think of themselves as classicists; they were busy earning a living, coping with difficult producers and directors, or trying to create a hit show.

A work created today may be regarded as a classic tomorrow. But today, we tend to regard every instant commercial hit as a work of genius. We do this by accepting the fallacy that yesterday's standards don't matter. So it's easy for a work or its creator to be declared "classic" today if it made money last year. The test of time may produce a different perspective and persuade us, contrary to the popular view, that today's lemonade is really just sour lemon juice.

These myths about classics are untrue. But they are widely held and we must respond to them vigorously if we expect to see our culture conserved.

PURGING THE CLASSICS

In the last decade, a new and disturbing campaign has started to purge classics from the curricula of schools and colleges. Howard University, perhaps the nation's most noted historically black university, has dissolved its classics department. Princeton University has jettisoned requirements for classics majors to study Latin and Greek. Even in innocuous ways, publishers of academic tests have denigrated the worth of classics. Daniel Buck, a secondary school English teacher, recalls, "A student turned to me during their standardized test to point out a question on the screen. It asked about a sentence that read: 'Shakespeare's works are outdated with themes that are irrelevant to today's students.' I do not remember what the question then asked, but likely it was something about how to improve the sentence, in which case I hope there was a fifth option: Delete it."[124]

The trend is ubiquitous; it pops up everywhere, even in GQ, the magazine formerly known as *Gentlemen's Quarterly,* with an article titled "21 Books You Don't Have to Read."[125] Among the writers and editors choosing a book we don't need any more is Jesse Ball, a faculty member of the School of the Art Institute of Chicago. He suggests that we stop reading *The Holy Bible.* While conceding that it contains some good parts, Ball goes on to declare, "It is repetitive, self-contradictory, sententious, foolish, and even at times ill-intentioned." Ball, who teaches classes on "lying, ambiguity, dreaming, and walking," recommends reading instead *The Notebook,* a novel by Agota Kristof which relates the tale of two brothers who "boggle at nothing: not theft, sodomy or murder, which last, when necessary, they manage with insouciance."

It shouldn't be necessary to defend *The Holy Bible* here, but it would do well to remind ourselves that scholar Michael Macrone wrote that *The Bible* is "the most important influence on our language, written and spoken," and that it was venerated by America's Founding Fathers, including Patrick Henry who called it "worth all the other books which have ever been printed."

The Gospel According to *GQ* dispenses with numerous classics, old and modern alike, including Swift's *Gulliver's Travels, The Lord of the Rings* by J.R.R. Tolkien, and both *The Old Man and the Sea* and *A Farewell to Arms* by Ernest Hemingway.

Why is this happening? One reason, unfortunately the answer to many questions about dubious changes in academia, is that politically-minded activists have started "cleansing" the curriculum and deleting writers because of their race. Daniel Padilla Peralta says that the ancient Greeks and Romans should be dethroned from their pedestals in order to save the field from "whiteness." Padilla Peralta teaches at Princeton, one of the universities downgrading its classics curriculum.

Advocates of such attitudes do not realize that understanding the classics is part of being able to lucidly comprehend our own history. As Cameron Hilditch has written, "The Jacobins are pushing for the cancellation of the classics because their project—a revolutionary impulse toward resetting the clock of history to Year Zero—has little to gain from mature historical understanding. But if it's the position of some of our friends on the left that ignorance of history—including classical history—makes us less likely to repeat the crimes and mistakes of the past, they really ought to reexamine their premises."[126]

Jeremy Tate, founder of the Classic Learning Test, echoes similar sentiments when he says, "The Western canon by itself cannot unite and give life to diverse and divided groups of people. But great books have always inspired and formed the great souls who can."

The failure of many academicians to defend the classics does not bode well for the their future; but while academics in the United States, Canada, and the UK are turning their backs on the classics, the Greeks, the Romans, and the icons of western culture in general, including classical music, are being preserved in an unlikely place: China.

Numerous Chinese universities offer courses in Latin and Greek. Peking University, the country's most prestigious school of higher learning, offers multiple courses on Plato, Aristotle, Kant, Hegel, Nietzche, and numerous classes in philosophy and logic. (Not surprisingly, in a country run by the Communist Party of China, there are plenty of classes studying Marxism.)

The National Association of Music Merchants reported that in 1909, 364,500 pianos were sold in the United States; by 2005, that number had dropped to 95,518; by 2017, it had fallen to 31,530. But there are approximately a million Chinese children studying piano and classical music thrives in Japan and South Korea. David P. Goldman, who writes for the *Asia Times*, observes with considerable irony, "As we burn down our own culture, China may become the last refuge of classical philology, Western philosophy, and classical music."

While assigning blame is not always necessary, it is extremely important to recognize that those most responsible for this severe cultural decline are not those ideologues pressuring the schools and colleges to meet their demands, but the weak, ineffectual, feckless administrators and professors who should know better but have surrendered anyway, out of fear for their careers of ambition to advance their careers by joining what they believe to be the winning side in a cultural struggle.

Victor Davis Hanson, author and former classics professor, has written, "So now some Americans quietly still revere Jefferson, Lincoln, and Washington, as if they are Christians reading their gospels in secret under Diocletian. They pray their neighborhood school will not be renamed. They think their school's or corporation's 'diversity training' is not much different from what they saw in 'The Manchurian Candidate,' or popular stories of 'brainwashing' from North Korea. So they prep for it, and are ready to nod, smile, parrot 'yes' and 'of course' but have pre-programmed themselves to have the edicts and commands of the 'facilitator' or 'trainer' and 'educator' go in one ear, pass unnoticed, and zoom out the other."[127]

With the passage of time, however, those who appear to passively accept the disappearance of the classics will give way to those who have never experienced the finest music, literature, art, or the ideas, aesthetics, and philosophical principles that inspired them. Instead, new generations will be familiar only with the latest fad of the moment. The very word "classic" will be gone from our vocabulary, replaced by the word "trending." Of course, what is trending may be absolute twaddle, complete codswallop, pure poppycock. Sadly, those obsessed with whatever is "trending" will have no idea what those words even mean; nor will they have anything to which they can compare what they are now mindlessly cheering.

None of this has to happen, but this trend will not go away by itself!

NEW AND IMPROVED

Is life truly changing for the best? Human nature suggests that the answer must be "yes." We want to believe that change is progress, that "new" means "improved," that "young" is always better than "old." But are these assumptions true?

Throughout human history, men and women have applauded the present by rejecting the past. Nowhere has this been truer than in the arts. Yesterday's culture, whatever it may be, is often assumed to have the value of yesterday's bread: stale and past its time. What seems more futile to the writer, painter, or musician than to see that his art is declared passé in his lifetime? Frequently, history reverses its judgment, but this typically occurs long after the artist in question can reap the rewards of his labor. It is not difficult to understand why the present has more appeal than the past. A plethora of factors, ranging from psychological to financial, all motivate us to assume that what is produced today is better than yesterday. These factors are related not just to popular culture, but also to politics, business, and every form of human endeavor.

There are several reasons for this well-meaning, but seriously mistaken, assumption.

1. *Time:* With the passage of time, there are fewer people who remember the past. Events like World War II and the Depression once shook the world to its foundations. But generations of students too young to personally remember such events have no reason to identify with them. People identify first and foremost with what is taking place in their immediate lives. This is especially true in the case of popular culture. The music, television shows, and movies that appeal to most people are the ones they discuss with their friends, the ones that relate to their immediate activities.

2. *Money:* Madison Avenue and Silicon Valley always want you to believe that something you bought last week isn't as good as the item you can purchase today. So it is only natural to suggest that the latest compact disc is best, that the newest star shines the brightest. There is no particular reason to accept this notion, but

most people do. The latest singing star may sound like a frog when he opens his mouth, but his recording company must convince the public that his musical message is more exciting than anything they bought yesterday.

3. *Groupthink:* Some people are unhappy unless they are part of a group, preferably one in which they receive the regular approval of others. "Groupthink" is the concept of like-minded people who talk only to each other; read each other's writings and absorb each other's thoughts. Then they draw conclusions based on the assumption that "everyone" agrees with them. Of course, not "everyone" can be found inside the narrow box in which they confine themselves, but this fact seems to escape them. Teenagers are especially subject to "peer pressure" in their desire to be "popular." Being popular for teenagers frequently means singing the song of non-conformity, while marching in lockstep to a rigid, group conformity of their own.

4. *Confusing Technology with Content:* Are today's motion pictures better than those of yesterday? Certainly, the equipment used by film production companies is much better. No one would suggest that the creaky, squeaky sound systems of the early days of film could challenge today's digital sound effects. But there is a profound difference between technology and content. A computer may be a far more sophisticated and improved tool for writers than a typewriter. But does the use of a computer mean that the output of today's writers will be superior to that produced by Shakespeare? Jefferson wrote with a quill-pen, as did Bach, Mozart, and Beethoven. But what writer today can draft words more eloquent than those in the Declaration of Independence? What composer can extract so much from a C-sharp minor chord as did Beethoven in the *Moonlight Sonata*? Would anyone suggest that the painstaking craftsmanship of yesterday's artisans has been surpassed by the slipshod work of some of today's manufacturers? This does not mean that someone using a computer will not produce work equal to that of Mozart. It just means that his work is not necessarily an improvement over that of someone who used pen and ink a century ago. Havelock Ellis once defined progress as

"exchanging one nuisance for another." Today, we too often assume that a technological endorsement is an endorsement of content. Did you hear an idea on television or on the Internet? Whether or not it is a good idea depends on its content, not its origin. Louis Gerstner, former Chairman and CEO of IBM, said, "Computers are magnificent tools for the realization of our dreams, but no machine can replace the human spark of spirit, compassion, love, and understanding." Wisdom is true even if written on a banana peel; foolishness would be nonsensical even if cast in bronze.

5. *Confusing Quality with Success:* Almost everyone wants to be successful. In our society, we often assume that everyone's definition of "success" is the same. Usually, "success" is measured in financial terms. If an artist paints a picture, a composer writes an opera, a writer creates a novel, people ask, "Was the work a success?" Usually, this means "did the work make money?" Which composer is truly successful — one who creates a neglected masterpiece and endures oblivion, or one who revels in the financial rewards of mediocrity and public acclaim? How often do we assume that the best works of art are those that make the most money? If a new movie made ten times as much money as last year's hit, does it follow that that the new picture is ten times better?

6. *Being Practical:* Try persuading students that the arts are important. Those who are not already interested in careers in the arts will likely say, "Will studying this help me make money?" "Will it help me get a job?" There is a curious view among some people that if a subject will not relate to one's future employment, it is a waste of time. Students do not always know what subjects will help them in their work. More often than not, the subjects they think may be least valuable will have the most profound effect upon their lives and careers. For instance, there are values communicated through the arts that may be very important in their lives, but these values may seem esoteric and unrelated to their challenges of the moment.

7. *Attention Span:* People are in a hurry. They scoot about, racing from one appointment to another. They are armed with cell phones, portable computers, devices designed to make everything faster. Many of them approach life with an attitude inspired less by philosophy than by the invention of the remote control. If something appears too challenging, they simply click the remote control and move on. People who are in such a hurry are not going to pay attention to the past. They may not even pay attention to where they are going, and as a result, may trip over their own impatience into a dubious and unsettling future.

8. *Assuming the Past Is Unrelated to the Present:* George Santayana said it best: "Those who do not learn the lessons of history are doomed to repeat them." In the arts, we might try a variation on Santayana's observation. "Those who do learn the lessons of past artists will be better artists today." We are bombarded today by experts who make judgments about the present while completely ignorant of how we got here.

9. *Confusing Change with Progress:* Change is seen differently by different people. The optimist assumes things are getting better, the pessimist that things are getting worse. There are pessimists who oppose all change, remaining convinced that changes are almost always bad. In contrast, the optimist says, "We must keep our minds open to new things, because we don't want to be opposed to progress." True, but we also want to be sure that change IS progress. We have witnessed many changes that have been disastrous for society. In the arts, throwing yesterday's work over the side of the boat is fashionable, but frequently unwise.

10. *A Desire to Avoid Being Judgmental:* Of all the trends in recent years, the one most responsible for mindless rejection of past standards in favor of present confusion is an absurd but understandable desire to avoid making judgments. "We must not be judgmental" is an assumption repeated like a mantra by those who assume that there are no standards or values by which a culture can be judged. "You do your thing, man, and I'll do mine" is a slogan right out of a 1960s protest. There are some things in life about which we cannot argue. There is no question as to which

major league baseball player hit the most home-runs in a given season. It is determined with mathematical certainty. But in the arts, in areas in which judgment comes into play, we are told we are dealing with intangibles. You may prefer Mozart or swing dance bands; someone else may like noise. But both the musician and the noisemaker are given equal deference. Otherwise, we would be making a judgment, implying that our taste, our cultural inclinations are superior to those of someone else. A desire to avoid hurting someone's feelings is fine, but not when one's common sense is checked at the door.

How then, should we regard our cultural past? It is essential that we achieve positive change and progress without rejecting the best of the past. Nor should we forget that the most accomplished men and women of our time recognize that we stand on the shoulders of those who came before us. Steven W. Semes is a distinguished architect and author who teaches at Notre Dame. He addresses a crucial issue in his book, *The Future of the Past.*[128] Semes believes that new additions to historical works of architecture should be designed in a classical, traditional style. Semes studied architecture at the University of Virginia. His instructors praised the "Bauhaus" style of architecture developed by Walter Gropius in Germany during the 1920s. Semes says, "Even though the explicit curriculum was thoroughly modern, there was no way to avoid falling in love with Thomas Jefferson's work. So, my architectural education happened on two contrary levels. On one level, my professors were telling me what I was supposed to do according to the Bauhaus; on another, more subliminal level, Thomas Jefferson's example was telling me what architecture was all about. Ultimately the latter won."

He writes of three alternative views of what we have inherited from the past. He describes the first as "something we can understand in part and sometimes restore to an approximate wholeness," the second as "a collection of broken fragments we can piece together to some degree but never make whole," and the third "merely as debris that we can appreciate as isolated objects from a vanished culture but can never fully understand or incorporate into our world." Semes concludes, "Of these three views of the past, only the second and third carry the official sanction of academic and critical thinking, and the last represents the most 'progressive' approach among some curators and museum directors. The first is highly controversial, suggesting as it does, that the past in not only knowable but may actually teach us something."

Semes' point is that there are values in architecture that are timeless. He could have just as easily been talking about music, painting, sculpture, or literature. His challenge is clear: do we dismiss the past or learn from it? Do we pursue the new to replace the old for its own sake or with good reason? Do we draw upon the best of the past to create a dynamic future?

Unfortunately, efforts to conserve, to preserve, and to sustain the best in our culture often run into a stone wall: today's media-driven pop culture. There is nothing inherently wrong with popular culture. Contrary to a belief maintained by elite pundits, many significant advances in our language, the arts, and society have originated in popular culture. (Jazz is a good example. Many of our most important political movements have started through grass roots activity.) However, today's popular culture is unique for several reasons. Modern day technology makes it ubiquitous. Pop culture is everywhere, working its way into every aspect of our daily lives. Today's popular culture is also unusually hostile to the idea of tradition. Its advocates have rather cleverly advanced the notion that traditions are old, stuffy, boring, and irrelevant.

In contrast, "new ideas," "progress," and "change" are always portrayed as positive, young, energetic, and looking to the future. Alicia Colon, writing in the *Irish Examiner*,[129] addresses the subject of celebrating the New Year, a pop cultural tradition for years. Colon compares celebrations of elegant past New Year's Eves (and the sentimental music of bandleader Guy Lombardo) with today's spectacles. She writes, "Somewhere in the city, possibly the Waldorf or the Roosevelt Hotel, celebrants were enjoying ballroom dancing, champagne toasts and a big band orchestra playing "Auld Lang Syne" like Lombardo did but it's unlikely we'll ever catch this type of programming on the networks' holiday presentations. Why not? Because today's viewers are more likely to demand reality starlets wearing skanky clothing, foul-mouthed comediennes and hip hop, tone deaf musical acts." But Colon isn't finished. She targets the source of the problem. She continues, "Back in the sixties, a new phrase came into vogue—generation. It meant that my generation was so far removed from the previous one of our parents that there remained only a large fissure in our cultural styles. What it has actually come to mean is that my generation has a deficit of elegance and class and we've spawned a generation with lowbrow tastes." Colon recalls that at age eleven, she admired the same glamorous stars as her mother. She writes, "I have the same connection with my daughters who join me whenever I watch an old film on TCM or AMC. One day I asked my daughter Danielle why she liked them and she said, 'They're clean. No bad language and no nudity.'" Colon compares these stars with those of yesterday. Browsing through the pages of today's tabloids, she finds them filled with near naked pictures of what she terms "exhibitionist movie stars who routinely complain about their lack of privacy."

There are many reasons for this situation, not the least of which is the triumph of the "youth cult," a notion popularized in the 1960s, that "new" and "young" always trump tradition. Middle-aged adolescents, parents, and teachers who should have known better, began literally aping the dress styles, language, and musical tastes of their children, grandchildren, and students. Today, the hippies and drop-outs of the 1960s have dropped back in; we now call them faculty members. The once revolutionary rejection of the past has now become a mainstream idea. We now reap the dubious rewards of this movement and must face the consequences.

Those who simply dismiss or reject the finest of our cultural traditions often do so simply as a matter of self-aggrandizement. At best, they are composers, writers, and artists whose work is likelier to receive praise if it escapes comparison with the legacy of great masters. At worst, they are charlatans whose redefinitions of music, art, and literature are designed to advance their own notoriety and prosperity, while making fools of their adoring crowds. In either case, the best composers, artists, and writers of today are neglected while the mediocrities and charlatans march forward. We, the consumers in our culture, are the big losers in this sorry charade. If these trends continue, future generations will inherit a radically diminished culture with no idea of what has been sadly lost along the way.

THE PRESENT: PROFESSORS, POLITICIANS, AND PRODUCERS

WHEN WE TRY TO SOLVE OUR CULTURAL CRISIS, we often turn to three groups of people who are seen as part of the solution: educators, government officials, and leaders in the entertainment industry. However, a close look reveals that many of these individuals are not going to be part of the solution, because they are already part of the problem.

SCHOOL DAZE: CONFUSION IN THE CLASSROOM

Simple logic would suggest that our schools would be likely champions of the arts. Yet frequently, our schools have proven to be anything but custodians of our culture. Nor have colleges and universities always been helpful. On the contrary, there are attitudes found throughout the educational world that merely exacerbate the problem.

1. Do the arts matter? Strangely, many academicians would respond with a definitive "no" if not an ambivalent "maybe." Historically, numerous academics have always regarded subjects like music, art, and dance as only peripheral to real education. These academics believe that the essence of a subject is not the activity itself, but what they say about it; therefore, music or art history becomes more respectable than playing an instrument or painting. Musicology, the analysis of music, becomes more significant than actual composing. Theory is more important than practice, self-proclaimed scholarship more important than professionalism. The arts have frequently been regarded as decorative to the curriculum. So when budgets have been cut, bands and orchestras have been silenced. A few academics have eliminated the arts reluctantly, sincerely unhappy over the financial need to jettison an important part of the curriculum. However, others believed that the arts could be cheerfully neglected in the groves of academe because they were convinced that the arts didn't belong there in the first place. Unfortunately,

they didn't heed the words of William J. Bennett, former Secretary of Education, who said quite correctly, "The arts are an essential element of education, just like reading, writing, and arithmetic, music, dance, painting and theater are all keys that unlock profound human understanding and accomplishment." Another Secretary of Education, Rod Paige, joined Arkansas Governor Mike Huckabee to declare, "To put it simply, we need to keep the arts in education because they instill in students the habits of mind that last a lifetime: critical analysis skills, the ability to deal with ambiguity and to solve problems, perseverance and a drive for excellence. Moreover, the creative skills children develop through the arts carry them toward new ideas, new experiences, and new challenges, not to mention personal satisfaction. This is the intrinsic value of the arts, and it cannot be overestimated." Our finest artists can create something new and wonderful. They can also preserve the best of the past. In the words of Evelyn Waugh, "Art is the symbol of the two noblest human efforts: to construct and to refrain from destruction."

2. *Do facts and standards matter?* The answer to this question would seem to be obvious. But in the topsy-turvy world of educational theory, nothing can be assumed. The obvious is sometimes first to be challenged. Even when schools have "taught the arts," what does this phrase mean? If students are merely provided with exposure to the arts, they are essentially being left to their own devices. Students may be taught to "appreciate" music, art, dance, or drama, but what most students have appreciated is approval by their peers. Students become popular by sharing values with their peers. In recent decades, students have acquired their attitudes about the arts from two sources: their friends and major entertainment media: the television, motion pictures, and recording industries. Since their friends depend on the same media for their values, there is really only one puppeteer pulling the strings—the entertainment industry. This is analogous to a joke told by Yakov Smirnoff, a Russian comedian, about the choices available to television audiences in the Soviet Union. "There were two channels," he explained, "Channel One

and Channel Two. Channel One was propaganda and Channel Two presented a man telling you to turn back to Channel One." In pop culture, "music appreciation" is a pale competitor when up against the mammoth budgets of entertainment conglomerates and peer pressure.

Unfortunately, many academics have mistakenly assumed that to teach the arts, we have to "communicate with the kids." This usually means that the teacher tries to use elements of pop culture, rock music, or television shows to capture the attention of a student audience, and then hope they will still be listening when the real curriculum is introduced. Nobody wants to listen to an uninspired teacher droning on about the glories of art. No one cares to be bored by dull and uninteresting talk masquerading as scholarship. But if teachers follow instead of leading, can we expect students to learn? Some teachers would suggest that it does not matter if students learn facts, only "how to think" and "how to approach problems." With this approach, a student in the arts is shortchanged. The teacher explains how to read a menu, but does not help the student understand why some items on the menu are more nutritious than others.

Students will always choose ice cream over spinach, but sometimes they need spinach in their academic diet. Too often, schools have tried to be fashionable, to welcome into the curricula those elements of popular culture that seek to undermine it. The teacher, instead of presenting an alternative to pop culture, simply reinforces it.

Instead of introducing children to the finest music at an early age, academicians and entertainment industry figures alike are quick to jump on the bandwagon of rock music. *The Wonder Pets*, a television series which aired on Nickelodeon, featured a guinea pig, duckling, and turtle that travel the world to save baby animals in distress. Music for the series was initially recorded by an orchestra and sung in operatic style. But in 2008, Josh Selig, the show's creator, proudly announced that the music would feature the music of the Beatles. The Associated Press trumpeted the use of the music by declaring, "It says something about the Beatles' continuing appeal that TV producers turned to a band that broke up nearly forty years ago as the best way to introduce children under five to 'rock 'n roll.'"

Why on earth do children under five (or over five for that matter) need to be "introduced" to rock music? They will be bombarded by it throughout their lives, and the purpose of the bombardment will be what it always has been: to make money for the people who market it. Small children should be introduced to music of quality that they may not discover on their own. Does a children's program using Beatles music mean the world is coming to an end? Of course not. But the mentality that adults in the field of educational television need to introduce small children to rock music is appalling. In fact, children will be "introduced" to rock music in the best as well as the worst of schools. It has become our music and they will be none the wiser of what has been lost along the way.

As children mature, they turn into teenagers and young adults. Are things different in high school or college? The schools are filled with instructors who think that the best way to "communicate with the kids" is to "give the kids what they like." Of course, they don't know what they like; they only like what they know. While classical music declines and jazz faces an uphill battle for recognition, rock music remains on the march. Colleges and universities now offer all kinds of courses in rock music. California State University at Los Angeles introduced a course called "Music Video 454." The class was popular, since students received credit for acting in rock videos on a Hollywood field trip. The class did have required work. Students still had to study their textbook thoroughly: *The Rolling Stone Book of Rock Video.* Philip Weiss, writing in *The New Republic,* recalled a course offered by the Ivy League's Brown University. Weiss quoted a student saying, "You don't have to go to class. I'd turn on the stereo and raise my hand in bed." The course title says it all: "Rock and Roll Is Here to Stay." The University of North Carolina at Greensboro offered a popular course called "Applied Social Theory and Qualitative Research Methodology." Despite the course's impressive name, the course materials consisted of recordings and reviews of The Grateful Dead and requirements that the students attend the group's rock concerts. Even the famed Juilliard School of Music is not immune. A student- initiated "Juilliard Rock Club" is thriving. Zach Villa, a drama student and member of the club, explains, "If you hear the music of AC/DC or the Stones blaring alongside Bach and Beethoven, the classical composers laid the groundwork for our musical tastes." Villa declares that Beethoven was the first "rock 'n' roll" star.

Consider The Ambitious Orchestra, a 20-piece ensemble, which according to *The Christian Science Monitor*, is "trying to draw a younger, hipper generation of music lovers, dyed hair, pierced tongues and all, to concert halls worldwide by experimenting with how an orchestra should look, sound, and relate to its listeners." Christina Couch, in an article headed "Roll Over Beethoven,"[130] writes that the group's appeal may be due to "the curse words, driving rhythms, and distinct lack of cummerbunds." The group's founder, Benjamin Ickies, says that he switched from writing classical music to rock songs in order to "make a connection with the audience." On the west coast, in Eugene, Oregon, The Everyone Orchestra dispenses with scores entirely, substituting "aleatory improvisational happenings." The audience is invited to join the orchestra in "improv games."

Everyone's a performer; everyone's a composer. Everyone is Beethoven and Beethoven is everyone. Special guests appearing with the orchestra come from bands, including The Grateful Dead, Phish, and the P-Funk Allstars. In Los Angeles, there is the daKAH Hip-Hop Orchestra which presents rap music spectacles combining a large orchestra with amplification and "human beat boxes." The notion of audience participation is carried to its ultimate level by the Vienna Vegetable Orchestra, an ensemble that makes its own instruments from produce. Scraps of vegetables left over from the organic instruments are mixed into a soup, which members of the audience eat.

"Why not?" say the compromisers, the middle-aged adolescents who think education is all about "communicating with the kids."

"Music has to change," declare the entertainment promoters, comparing the profits that can be earned by turning everything into a rock concert. The problem is that little by little, the rock/pop/hip-hop juggernaut becomes "music." Everything else becomes an exotic taste for a small group of antiquarians. Classical music won't disappear, nor will the melodies and lyrics from "The Great American Songbook," nor will jazz, nor will any type of true music. It simply won't matter anymore. The day will come when everything but the ghastly noise of the untalented superstars will be a source of amusement for those who assume they know what's happening. They will be eternally oblivious to the ghostly sounds of real music.

Many music teachers adopt the view that the only way to get students interested in music is to begin talking about the music they already know: pop, rock, and rap. Let them begin with MTV videos, the argument goes, and eventually they will graduate to more accomplished musical fare. However, this argument is also flawed. This approach primarily accomplished helping the teacher feel good about what he is doing. It makes a music teacher think that he or she is communicating with her students by making them feel good about themselves. On the contrary, teaching is not about making students feel good about themselves. It's about challenging them to encounter values, standards, and ideas that they will likely not encounter on their own. The student whose teacher talks about pop, rock, and rap is far likelier to emerge from class thinking he already is familiar with "good music." Such a teacher may be popular, but the students and teachers both lose something in this equation. The student doesn't learn what he needs to learn, and the teacher is losing the opportunity to help him do precisely what he should be doing in and out of class.

3. *Politics, unfortunately, entered the picture.* Some academics have suggested that the real purpose of education is for students to "feel good about themselves," to cultivate "self-esteem." The problem is that self-esteem results from achievement and the realization of one's potential. Every student should be encouraged to believe that such achievement is possible. But it should be

obvious that life (and culture) is competitive. If every football game were automatically a tie, those who play badly would feel good about themselves. Those who play well might not. Too often, curricula have become mired in political correctness and notions that no book, painting, play, or symphony is superior to another. This is ridiculous, but it has become perfectly acceptable in various teaching circles. Consider institutions like Monterey Peninsula College in California, which require every course in every subject to be taught with an emphasis on race, class, and gender issues. Even courses in subjects like Automobile Repair were not exempt. Race, class, and gender issues derived from the proper way to change a flat tire? When these attitudes of political correctness are applied to the arts, the results should be obvious. For example, students are subjected to a political or cultural agenda that has nothing to do with the subjects they are studying. An English professor developed an extensive analysis of motion picture music. Her approach was to use "poststructuralist, Marxist, feminist, and psychoanalytic criticism." The world of film scoring was populated by individuals who met deadlines, fought to please obnoxious and ignorant producers, and worried about whether the trombones were drowning out the piccolos. But are we seriously to believe that their achievements can be explained by reading Marx, Freud, and the writings of radical feminists?

Dr. Russell Kirk was a distinguished man of letters who wrote thirty books and hundreds of columns and articles on education. But as a young professor writing his very first essay on education, he expressed a viewpoint that holds up well to critical analysis a half-century later. Kirk said, "It is true that the average graduate of our colleges knows neither how to live nor how to think. His four years of membership in the academic body served chiefly to muddle his mind, to blur the sound prejudices in it. A liberally educated man has a great store of general knowledge and common sense; ignorant enthusiasm cannot remake the world."

Schools and colleges have unfortunately fallen into all of these traps in relation to the arts. Those who regard the arts as "unessential" have succeeded in using budget cuts as an excuse to eliminate the arts from the classroom. Even if the arts have been included, they have often been included in name only. Teachers, eager to appear fashionable, have given a pop culture designed by commercial promoters a dubious respectability. Agendas of political correctness have been applied to subjects that have nothing to do with political controversy. As a result, the schools, which should have been a guarantor of integrity and standards in the study of the arts, have frequently hastened its demise.

Of all groups looking at popular culture today, none goes through more confusion than intellectuals do. Many general audiences cheer what is on television or on social media simply because it is on television or social media. The assumption is, "If it's on the tube, it must be good." Concurrently, these same people assume that "If it's not on TV, it's probably not worthy of being on TV." Both propositions, of course, are hopelessly flawed and patently absurd. But there are serious, thoughtful people who spend time looking at today's popular culture and questioning not the value of the culture, but their own judgment. Typically, these people say, "Perhaps it's me. Perhaps I'm old-fashioned. Perhaps I'm not being open and receptive to change, to the new ideas, to creative energy of new and challenging artists." Now there is nothing wrong with being open-minded; too much open-mindedness can lead to ill-advised conclusions. Those who are concerned about such matters assume mistakenly that "change" and "new ideas" imply improvement. Those praising much of the amplified noise masquerading as today's music inevitably talk about "energy," but they can seldom talk about such elements as melody, harmony, and rhythm, the building blocks of our finest music. The director of an art museum who exhibited a painting, which was highly offensive to many religious people, justified his selection of the work by declaring, "The purpose of art is to irritate." Nevertheless, our museums and concert halls are full of works that inspire. The notion that irritation is a prerequisite of good art is specious.

Some intellectuals worry, however, about not being progressive and looking to the future instead of the past. In their zeal to be open-minded, they ignore key elements of cultural truth.

1. A pendulum can swing too far in either direction. We should keep the image of the swinging pendulum in mind when we use an expression that has become fashionable, "pushing the envelope." From its invention in 1656 by Christiaan Huygens until the arrival of quartz clocks in the 1930s, the pendulum was the key to keeping accurate time. A pendulum swings back and forth, but if it becomes stuck at either end of its arc or is broken off at either end, it ceases to function. Problems arise at the extremes. A chef who uses no seasoning in his food may produce dull cuisine, but a chef who uses far too much seasoning may serve food that is inedible. A nation that has no functioning government faces anarchy; but a country that suffocates under too much government is destroyed by tyranny. A composer who uses no dissonance may write dull and uninteresting music, but a composer who uses nothing but dissonance may produce nothing but noise. We do not live in a society that is overrun by cultural or social restrictions. While government regulations and bureaucracy seem to grow constantly, there are few restraints placed on personal or social behavior. The arts in the 21st century lean far closer to anarchy than tyranny. What rules are left to be broken? What barriers are left to be shattered?

Many of today's alleged artists (ranging from avant-garde painters to rock stars) substitute shock value for technique, inspiration, and true creative purpose. Those who recognize shock value for what it is are dismissed as "wanting to turn back the clock." The clock can obviously not be turned back. But while dissonance can be shocking, too much dissonance is like too much pepper. In the right amount, seasoning can be useful; when overdone, it leads to indigestion. Today, films contain dozens of four letter words, tossed off with abandon by women and children. Critics of such language will be dismissed as prudes or censors wanting to bowdlerize true art. But consider the swinging pendulum: when shock becomes the norm, it ceases to be shocking.

2. *Yesterday's radical may indeed seem like today's conservative.* In the 1920s, Stravinsky and Hemingway seemed revolutionary. Today they are regarded as mainstream legends. But this does not mean that anyone today identifying himself as a radical will automatically be tomorrow's mainstream legend. In 1920, artists were reacting to what they regarded as the conservative and traditional standards of the nineteenth century. To what traditional or conservative artistic standards does today's revolutionary react? In fact, those who pursue such standards are the true non-conformists of the 21st century, because it is they who are swimming upstream, moving against fashion.

3. *Younger writers, composers, and artists who do not produce creative work in line with styles and attitudes dictated within the entertainment industry are dismissed as irrelevant.* People are always asking, "Why don't we have composers and lyricists like those of the 1930s and 1940s?" Of course, that era was a unique time and it is unlikely that we will ever see another George Gershwin.. But the elements that made Gershwin's music great (or the lyrics of his brother Ira) can be found in the work of new, younger composers and lyricists. Unfortunately, anyone trying to write music like the Gershwins or Cole Porter or Richard Rodgers, for example, would be dismissed as "old hat." The same is true for painters, playwrights, novelists, or composers of string quartets. Those who control the entertainment industry (including publishing, now regarded as a form of entertainment) will define what is acceptable as "contemporary." It is a form of political correctness. Those who do not toe the line need not apply.

4. *Common sense may produce more intelligent evaluations of art than expertise.* William F. Buckley, Jr. once declared, "I am obliged to confess I should sooner live in a society governed by the first two thousand names in the Boston telephone directory than in a society governed by the two thousand faculty members of Harvard University." His point, of course, was that elite intellectuals may possess great erudition, theoretical skills, and

technical expertise, and still lack the common sense, humanity, and values to engender good judgment. The same is true in the arts. The thoughtful, serious member of the audience says, "Perhaps I just don't understand today's music" or "Perhaps I'm just more attracted to yesterday's art." This person may be giving the "artist" too much credit. The composer in question may have written an insipid piece of music; the artist under discussion may have produced an ugly painting; the vocalist singing off-key may simply have no talent.

5. *Every generation may reject the giants and triumphs of past generations. But such rejections may or may not be well advised.* What many in today's audience like best is the familiar: usually the result of exposure on television, through the Internet, pop magazines, or friends who get their information from these same sources. Ask yourself this question: do you believe that popular music, art, and literature have significantly improved from one generation to another? If you answer this question in the positive, can you base your answer upon a broad familiarity with yesterday's music, art, and literature? Can you reject what you do not know? If you do know the great classics of the past, can you seriously suggest that today's works are more technically accomplished or creatively inspired? This is not a suggestion that we should try to reproduce yesterday's works of art. They have already been produced and the originals are far better than today's pale copies. However, we should consider the standards that were used to evaluate these works and apply them to today's popular culture. For instance, singers today depend far more on staging, props, technical effects, and choreography than their voices. If we apply a vocal standard to many of these "artists," they will cease to be considered "artists" in a hurry.

6. *When you encounter singers who can't sing, painters who can't paint, or writers whose vocabulary is limited to four-letter words, don't always give them the benefit of the doubt.* Your initial instincts may be right. Intellectuals who are afraid of overlooking undiscovered genius may fail to recognize that there are far more charlatans and imposters making claims to greatness. It is

therefore easy for such intellectuals to dismiss or ignore those with true talent.

Why have we reached such a sorry state of affairs? One reason is that two groups of individuals have always regarded the arts with suspicion. Academicians have been willing, for a variety of reasons, to continue accepting the persistent notion that the arts are "frills," an unnecessary cherry on top of their scholarly sundae. Even those who should know better, frequently regard the arts only as icing on their academic cake, not the cake itself. Second, groups like entertainment industry executives are suspicious of genres of art, the very qualities of which make it difficult for them to make money. The assumption that "if it's really good, it will be profitable" can be dangerous. Many fine works of art prove unprofitable; many highly profitable entertainment products aren't the result of good art, just good promotion.

The National Commission on Music Education addressed the problem in a startling report on the state of arts education. The report was based on a series of nationwide forums, *America's Culture at Risk,* moderated by A. Graham Down, President of the Council on Basic Education. It stated bluntly, "From Plato to the present, no great teacher ever dreamed that the arts could become what many school districts have made of them in the last generation, an expendable frill, the first sacrificial lamb to fall under the budget axe when funds grow short." The Commission declared, "By our inattention to music and the other arts in our schools, we are dehumanizing our own people, and particularly our children, not by design, but by default." The Commission also challenged the notion that instruction in the arts represents "curricular icing," a diversion from acknowledged serious and essential subjects like history, science, mathematics, and reading. But advocacy for the arts is an uphill battle. "American Canvas," a report issued by the National Endowment for the Arts, makes this crystal clear. When the Endowment hosted a forum in California, Joan Boyett, Vice-President for Education at the Music Center of Los Angeles, summed up the grim news. "The statistics on the number of arts specialists are appalling," she said. "There are forty-five million students grades K-12 in the United States and more than fifteen thousand school districts. However, the responsibilities for reinforcing the teaching of the arts at the district level rests in the hands of only 114 music supervisors and fifty arts supervisors—nationwide. No separate figures are available for the number of theater or dance supervisors: is it possible that there are none? Do we wonder why the arts are a low priority in the curriculum?"

Advocates for the arts argue persuasively that many benefits flow to society from instruction in the arts. Dr. Madelyn Holmes has urged us to consider evidence that children who learn to read music on a musical staff do better on tests in spatial reasoning than those without musical instruction. Similarly, she observes that reading skills of grade school children improve when they also receive early instruction in drama. But it would be a mistake to regard the arts only as a teaching tool enabling instruction in other "necessary" subjects. Students who leave school ignorant of the arts stand a good chance of going through life ignorant of the arts. This is both their loss and ours. It is their loss because they miss the chance to appreciate works of art that have survived the test of time. They will not learn the lessons these works of art may teach. It is our loss because the arts do not survive by themselves. They must be nurtured, fostered, and promoted.

Historians may find legitimate interests in the events of the past. But is it surprising that while political and financial events of the past fade into memory, the music of Beethoven and the paintings of Rembrandt survive? More often than not, works of artistic genius survive while events of the moment are forgotten. We should not assume that the arts are, by definition, "non-commercial." Too often, commercial business interests make this assumption, deny our best artists any marketing or promotional financing, and allow predictions of commercial failure to become a self-fulfilling prophecy. We should, therefore, ask ourselves, what would society be like without any orchestras, dance or opera companies, theaters, libraries, and museums? Would we be better off as a people? We could certainly function, as mechanical beings, living economically profitable lives. But would the human spirit be elevated in the same way? Not very likely.

In the midst of this discussion, an interesting debate has arisen among educators. E.D. Hirsch, Kenan Professor of English at the University of Virginia and author of the best-selling book, *Cultural Literacy: What Every American Needs to Know* emerged as a leader in the "cultural literacy" movement. Hirsch placed blame upon the "cafeteria style curriculum," in which students were trained only in specific skills. Hirsch maintains that certain facts, historical figures, and ideas are so important that everyone should be familiar with them. He became interested in the subject when his son told him about students who thought that Homer had written an epic poem called *The Alamo* and that Latin-Americans spoke Latin. Hirsch is as concerned with history and geography as he is with the arts. He recalls a speech made by his father, in which a quotation from *Julius Caesar*, instantly recognized, moved an audience to resolution. Such a speech would not have the same effect today, because few would recognize the Shakespearean quotation. Hirsch's point is that we have always assumed the public's prior knowledge of events, people, and places. The assumption is that without a shared understanding and recognition of this information, people will be unable to communicate. For instance, let's assume that you hear a speaker refer to the Boston Tea Party. If you think the Tea Party is a rock group, a soccer team, or a group of Harvard professors debating the relative merits of Orange Pekoe vs. Earl Grey, you're going to miss the point about contemporary "Tea Party" protests against unfair taxes. The argument, found on these pages, that every student should be familiar with the giants of jazz, musical theater, the concert hall, etc., will fail if presented to those who are themselves blissfully ignorant of these musical titans.

One would think there are no good arguments against such a position, and that proponents of cultural literacy would have an easy time, rather like arguing against bank robbers, hurricanes, and the common cold. But wait! Hirsch's view has been challenged by no less than Roger Schank, an articulate professor formerly at

Yale and Northwestern. Schank always manages to turn dry, academic ideas into something exciting. (He once wrote a book analyzing the way both people and computers reason, based entirely on his experiences choosing gourmet cuisine in fine restaurants.) Nevertheless, Schank throws down the gauntlet to Hirsch and to those who believe in the whole idea of cultural literacy. Schank, author of *The Connoisseur's Guide to the Mind,*[131] declares, "The schools should reject Hirsch's ideas about literacy in favor of an opposing policy which we can dub the 'Unliteracy Policy.' The Unliteracy Policy states that there is no one fact or set of facts that everyone should know." Says Schank, "It makes little difference what children learn, it matters that they learn and that they want to continue to learn. Regardless of what they learn, certain things that we want them to know will come along for the ride anyway."

Really? Would Professor Schank, who knows more than a thing or two about food, substitute the word "eat" for the word "learn" in that sentence and think he is advancing a valid argument? Let's find out: "It makes little difference what children eat, it matters that they eat and that they want to continue to eat." Now offered the choice, no self-respecting child would choose fresh fruits and vegetables over an ice cream soda. Let spinach debate a hot fudge sundae and the sundae will win every time. But there are reasons why fruits and vegetables matter in one's diet, just as the reasons why certain facts, certain books, certain pieces of music are important. If we take Schank's "Unliteracy Policy" literally, it doesn't matter what music a child hears or learns about, it only matters that he or she develops a curiosity about music. The idea that no piece of music, no work of art, no book has a greater claim on our attention than another is absurd. Schank declares, "You can't make everyone the same by forcing them into one mold. Neither can we teach everyone something about everyone else." True enough. But we can make sure that everyone has the same opportunity to encounter the music, art, and literature that have earned their place in history as classics. We're not hurting students by ensuring that everyone knows that Brahms wrote four fine symphonies. This isn't "forcing everyone into a mold." If you decide that you like music composed by a computer better than the music of Brahms, so be it, but you should make this decision after you've encountered Brahms.

If we carry this viewpoint to its logical extension, it is theoretically possible for teachers to replace the classics with "rap music" on the grounds that teenagers will be more in tune with the sounds of the street than those of the drawing room. Well, it's not just a theory. Teachers in Worcester, Massachusetts encourage students to read a book of posthumously published poems by "gangster rapper" Tupac Shakur. In a column entitled "2 lazy 2 teach,"[132] Michelle Malkin describes Tupac Shakur as "the drug-dealing, baseball bat-wielding, cop hating, Black Panthers-worshipping, convicted sexual abuser who made a fortune extolling the "thug life" before he was gunned down in Las Vegas." Students presumably should identify with the characters of Romeo and Juliet, two teenagers who fell fatally in love despite the opposition and mutual hatred of their families. Romeo's impassioned speech was once thought unforgettable: "But soft, what light through yonder window breaks? It is the east, and Juliet is the sun. Arise, fair sun, and kill the envious moon, who is already sick and pale with grief that thou, her maid, art far more fair than she." In Worcester, however, the local Romeos and Juliets will be encouraged to read Shakur's tribute *2 Marilyn Monroe*, in which the poet declares, "They could never understand what u set out 2 do instead they chose 2 ridicule u." Presumably, Shakur saw himself, like Miss Monroe, as misunderstood by the media. His manager, Leila Steinberg, urged that Shakur be taken seriously as a "literary artist poet" and blames the press for neglecting him.

Deputy Superintendent Stephen E. Mills explained the school board's goal as "Reading counterculture in schools and to get kids to read anything that is not completely objectionable." Completely objectionable? In other words, encouraging "the kids" to read things that are partially objectionable is perfectly acceptable. Malkin, protesting this outrage, was told by Frances Arena, manager of curriculum and professional development of the

Worcester Public Schools that Shakur's book will remain on the reading list because it "heightens awareness of character education" and because "it's popular with the kids." Critics like Michelle Malkin will receive no applause for protesting the new academic respectability of Tupac Shakur. She will instead be denounced as an elitist and racist who doesn't want to "give the kids what they want." Malkin herself deals with her critics quite effectively. She concludes, "The presumption that children—and particularly inner-city children—can only be stimulated by the contemporary and familiar smacks of lazy elitism and latent racism. These educators, and I use that term as loosely as gangster rappers wear their pants, are clearly more interested in appearing cool than in inculcating a refined literary sense in students. Their aim is not enlightenment, but dumbed-down ghetto entertainment. The Western literary canon has been flushed down the cultural toilet in favor of shallow ramblings by celebrity thugs whose thoughts are best left on bathroom walls."

Why does this matter? Does one book on one reading list in Worcester, Massachusetts mean that the cultural sky is falling and that the civilized world is coming to an end? Of course not. But there are dozens of reading lists, hundreds of Worcesters, thousands of students whose misguided paths and lack of true education will add up to a sorry sum. The result is a mosaic, a patchwork quilt of cultural ignorance than can be truly threatening to those who care about real art, music, and literature. Many of those most eager to dismiss the literature of the past would not be troubled by students who can recite and sing all the latest rap lyrics from memory. But these same individuals would undoubtedly object to requirements that students memorize and recite great poems by celebrated poets, probably because they regard rote memorization as dull and boring. Columnist Suzanne Fields writes about poetry at least once a year. Fields defends the whole idea of rote memorization in a column celebrating the appointment of Ted Kooser, a retired Vice-President of the Benefit Life Insurance Company in Nebraska, as poet laureate of the United States. Fields declares, "It's out of fashion and that's a loss of considerable magnitude. Memorization encourages an appreciation for the sounds and rhythms of language. Youngsters are flooded with the idioms of rap, rock (hard and soft), and rock and roll, which represent their generation in slang, but they lack the discipline to understand their literary heritage as revealed in poetry." Fields shares the view of Michael Knox Beran, who writes in *City Journal*, "If there's one thing progressive educators don't like, it's rote learning. As educators have known for centuries, these exercises deliver unique cognitive benefits, benefits that are of special importance for kids who come from homes where books are scarce and the level of literacy low. In addition, such exercises etch the ideals of their civilization on children's minds and hearts." The child who learns to quote passages of Shakespeare, Whitman, Keats, Browning, or Frost may not remember these quotations all his life, but he will become comfortable with a new and expressive use of the language, which can only have a positive effect on the way he responds to words throughout the coming years. No one truly familiar with the finest writer's use of the English language will be as susceptible to the message of the rappers and rock and rollers. Similarly, anyone familiar with good music, classical and popular, will be far less likely to march in lockstep with teenage audiences who only know what they have heard on the Internet or seen recently on MTV.

Multiculturalism is also offered as a reason for dismissing the idea that we should share a familiarity with certain works of art. This argument suggests that members of various ethnic groups may find themselves learning the names and achievements of individuals of other ethnic groups. It suggests that if your ancestors came from one country or were a member of a specific group, you should find cultural gratification only in the accomplishments of your own group. This is political and cultural correctness run amok. It is true that discussions of symphonies may produce an unusually high percentage of German and Austrian works, that opera history may be dominated by the Italians, ballet by the Russians, and jazz by African Americans. These are simply facts of history. This does not imply that our idea of classics should be static and unchanging. A contemporary of Beethoven's once dismissed him as unworthy in comparison to the great musical trio of masters, Haydn, Mozart, and Cimarosa. Who, other than musicologists, remembers Cimarosa today? On the other hand, if you think Cimarosa has been unjustly neglected (or that your sister-in-law writes better symphonies than Beethoven), you're welcome to make your case and persuade the rest of us.

The conductor Sheldon Morgenstern made an eloquent plea for the arts in his book, *No Vivaldi in the Garage,*[133] a work with the gloomy subtitle, *A Requiem for Classical Music in North America.* Morgenstern wrote, "Children attending schools in which arts programs have been eliminated or drastically cut are, by the absence or paucity of such programs, taught that the arts are not worth funding. But athletic programs are, and the companies that advertise on mainstream television are fully aware that Michael Jordan and Joe Montana sell, Mozart and Picasso do not. We have become a continent of arts illiterates." Morgenstern wrote, "I strongly believe that art should define the culture of our people as it does in other nations. But today the entertainment industry, using its vast funds, has a disproportionate influence on our culture. Our culture is being defined only by Madonna, to the exclusion of Aaron Copland. Are we to continue to understand ourselves only as a nation of rock stars and soap operas?" When Morgenstern conducted in Poland, he was approached backstage by a shoe salesman seeking his autograph. He asked the man why he had such deep interest in classical music. His admirer responded, "Without music, there is no bread."

There are reasons why a common culture, like a common language, can unify us as a people. George Will makes a telling point in his column, "Readers' Block."[134] Will, like many writers and readers, has reason to be disturbed by "Reading at Risk," the National Endowment for the Arts report on the decline of reading. Literary reading declined 5 percent between 1982 and 1992, and 14 percent during the next decade. Only a little more than half of Americans say they read a book during the past year. Illiteracy is the problem posed by those who cannot read. Non-literacy is the problem posed by those who choose not to read. In both cases, the result is ignorance. Will turns to history to make his point. When Theodore Roosevelt was asked by the press in 1910 if he would run for President, he said, "Barkis is willin'" a reference to the wagon driver in Charles Dickens's *David Copperfield.* In 1940, a British officer on Dunkirk beach quoted a line from the Book of Daniel, "But if not" indicating the British believed in heavenly deliverance from Nazi tyranny, but that surrender was out of the question. The three-word message required no translation for all those Britons who were familiar with the Bible. George Will is concerned about the American non-readers who may not have heard the name *David Copperfield.* Many young non-readers today probably learned the name of Beethoven, the St. Bernard of movie fame, before they learned the name of the irascible composer. Will targets "professors, lusting after tenure and prestige," who "teach that the great works of the Western canon, properly deconstructed, are not explorations of the human spirit but mere reflections of power relations and social pathologies." Does it matter? Does it make any difference if we share a set of books read by everyone? The answer lies in the true meaning of books. Books represent ideas; they represent values. A shared understanding, a shared sense of values means that as a people, we can move together in a positive direction. Otherwise, our society is like a car with eight drivers, all trying to steer in different directions. If the treasure trove of ideas contained in good books is lost to non-readers, what will replace them in our cultural psyche? The likeliest candidate is the cultural anarchy promulgated by an entertainment industry devoid of taste, in pursuit of the fast buck and applauded by their academic acolytes eager to remain in fashion.

In fact, cultural conservationists need to answer Professor Schank and insist that what children learn is just as important as whether they learn. The assumption that enthusiasm, energy, and curiosity will automatically lead children (or adults) in the right direction is misguided. If you are wandering through a maze without a map, you may find your way out or still be lost amidst the trees. But you're likely to find your way with a map. Schank is correct when he declares that students are bored when they don't think what they are studying is relevant to their immediate lives. But it's up to a teacher to challenge them, to spark their imaginations, to make them understand that they won't always be leading their immediate lives. Schools are full of boring, uninspired teachers, and it shouldn't surprise anyone that their students are bored and uninspired. But the cure for such teaching is better teaching, not assuming that as long as students are listening to music, they will eventually find their way. They may or may not, but we shouldn't leave this to guesswork. That is a job for the committed cultural conservationist.

THE WAR ON MERIT

For as long as most of us can remember, the idea of rewarding merit and striving to be the best of whatever you are have been pillars of our society and our culture. The notion that other criteria should be substituted for merit and the pride of achievement seems improbable and absurd on its face; but in the 21st century, there is actually a movement designed to accomplish precisely this dubious goal. Its advocates posit the notion that the very idea of merit is subjective and discriminates against the disadvantaged.

Merit was never controversial on any side of the political spectrum. Jimmy Carter recalled admitting to the formidable Admiral Hyman G. Rickover that he hadn't always done his best at the U.S. Naval Academy at Annapolis and Rickover snapping, "Why not?" Legendary football coach Vince Lombardi used to tell his players, "If you're not fired with enthusiasm, you'll be fired with enthusiasm."

Today, education bureaucrats and ideologues are doing their best to eliminate standards and comparisons in the classroom. Oregon proudly jettisoned reading, writing, and mathematics requirements for high school graduates. The California Department of Education developed a program for "equitable, anti-racist" mathematics instructions suggesting that teaching math students that "there is one correct answer" is somehow racist. This is not only nonsense, it is based on the truly racist assumption that minority students can't achieve on the same level as those in the racial or ethnic majorities. A public school teacher in Virginia declared that expecting black students to behave well in class and treat their teachers with respect was an example of "whiteness" and therefore racist. Does this "teacher" realize he is demeaning his "students" by implying that bad behavior is a manifestation of African American culture?

Bill de Blasio, the Mayor of New York, proudly trumpeted the end of programs for gifted and talented children. Presumably, they discriminated against those children who are not talented or gifted. This is the world of participation trophies; everyone gets a trophy, deserving or not. This not only discriminates against those who are gifted or talented or who work harder, it teaches two disturbing lessons: (1) those who deserve rewards learn that hard work means nothing in a world of equal outcomes; (2) those who could work harder are taught that they needn't bother because results will always be the same.

Not surprisingly, the war on merit is taking an increasing toll in the arts. Anthony Tomassini, music critic for the *New York Times,* has suggested that "blind auditions" for positions in symphony orchestras be abandoned. A blind audition is one in which the conductor or orchestra officials hiring players can only hear, not see the players they are auditioning. So race, gender, and ethnicity cannot be held against any musician. But eliminating "blind auditions" would mean that choices would be made involving race and gender, the very elements that blind auditions were established to eliminate. Alan Dershowitz, longtime professor at Harvard Law School, characterized this move as one which favors diversity over musical talent. This is precisely the opposite of an effort to advance good musicianship. What it advances is the goal of critical race theorist Ibram X. Kendi, the notion of "equity." Although the word "equity" sounds similar to the instantly appealing and time-honored idea of "equality," it actually means the opposite. Equity calls not for equality of opportunity, but equality of outcome. Since everyone has different talents, potentials, and experiences, judging individuals only as members of groups isn't fair; it implies fairness, but is as unfair and discriminatory as the attitudes it pretends to eliminate.

Jordan Peterson, a clinical psychologist, author, and for many years professor at the University of Toronto, presents the world of the arts with a thoroughly serious and prescient challenge: "Musicians, artists, writers: stop bending your sacred and meritorious art to the demands of the propagandists before you fatally betray the spirit of your own intuition. Stop censoring your thought. Stop saying you will hire for your orchestral and theatrical productions for any reason other than talent and excellence. That's all you have. That's all any of us have. He who sows the wind will reap the whirlwind. And the wind is rising."[135]

Curiously, both institutions and individuals that regularly have become soldiers in the war on merit usually trumpet their credentials in the pursuit of tolerance and inclusivity. In a shocking move, the Smithsonian Museum of African American History released guidelines for discussions of race. Included were behaviors and ideas described as "whiteness." Listed were "hard work is the key to success," "work before play," "politeness," "rugged individualism," "respect for authority," "the nuclear family," and the notion that "if you didn't meet your goals, you didn't work hard enough."

What could be more insulting to African Americans (or members of any ethnic, racial, or gender-based group) than to imply that these aren't universal standards for everyone, including the most successful African Americans?

In the war on merit, the ideas of achievement, brilliance, inspiration, and even basic competence are suspect. Instead, the assault on meritocracy demands that people can only learn from or be inspired by others who "look like them." David Denby, writing in *Great Books* about his re-enrolling in the core curriculum at Columbia University, and cited again by the always incisive Heather Mac Donald, writing in the *Wall Street Journal*, spoke of a black student at Columbia angry and frustrated that she was expected to listen to the music of Mozart.[136]

"Who is this Mozart, this Haydn, these superior white men? There are no women, no people of color," thundered the outraged student. Said Heather Mac Donald, "These are not the idiosyncratic thoughts of one disgruntled student; they represent the dominant ideology in the humanities today."[137]

The student at Columbia, failing to realize that she is advertising her ignorance in public, does not understand that Haydn and Mozart are studied not because they are "superior white men," but because they are superior composers. And William Shakespeare has been a literary icon for decades because he was a superior writer, not because he was English or white or male. Yet students at the University of Pennsylvania successfully demanded that his portrait be removed from a prominent position in the building housing the English department and be replaced with a picture of Audre Lord, a black lesbian poet who checked the appropriate boxes on the intersectionality forms.

Fortunately, not every educator is cowering in fear, although those who are not seem far and few in between. Katharine Birbalsingh, an outspoken educator and head teacher at the Michaela Community School in Wembley, northwest London, criticized schools that chose to prioritize so-called grime rappers such as Michael Ebenezer Kwadjo Omari Owuo, known as "Stormzy," over Mozart. She said, "If you don't know who Mozart is, how are you meant to, later on in life, take your rich client out for dinner and hold a culturally literate conversation?" [138]

In *The Power of Culture,* a collection of essays edited by Katharine Birbalsingh and written by many of her colleagues at Michaela, Pritesh Raitchura, a form tutor at the school, describes his own cultural evolution after discovering classical music. Should pupils choose the music they study in school? Emphatically no, says Raitchura, "Pupils cannot choose to learn about composers they never heard of." Will students drawn to rap be unable to appreciate real music? Raitchura asks, "How can we be so presumptuous that a composer whom people around the world have admired for centuries would not speak to the souls of people in front of us today?" As for the notion that students can only relate to writers, musicians, or artists who "look like them," Raitchura is appropriately dismissive. "Shakespeare doesn't need to be Asian for Asian pupils to relate to the profound ideas about the human condition contained in his work. Mozart doesn't have to be black for black pupils' hearts to soar listening to his symphonies."[139]

Of course historically, the arts haven't been free of true racism, like most disciplines and institutions. But the very idea that merit discriminates is nonsense. meritocracy discriminates against the untalented and rewards the achievers. We must defeat the assault on merit to insure that the pride of achievement survives and prospers in years to come.

TRUTH AND TEACHING

What is education? How important are teachers? "Education is not the filling of a pail, but the lighting of a fire," said poet William Butler Yeats. "A teacher affects eternity; he can never tell where his influence stops," declared Henry Adams. William Arthur Ward stated emphatically, "The mediocre teacher tells. The good teacher explains. The superior teacher demonstrates. The great teacher inspires."

Yes, but what happens when a teacher lights a fire based not on facts but on ideology? What becomes of a generation of students who are influenced for an eternity in the wrong way? How is the student affected when a teacher "inspires" him to hate his country and his fellow students, and only embrace a destructive point of view?

Education and indoctrination are not synonymous. Education and fine teaching are based on facts, evidence, objectivity, and truth. The student is taught *how* to think, but not *what* to think. Indoctrination involves a teacher using his or her authority to present an unchallenged point of view, to repeat, propagandize, and demand fealty to ideas that are supported not by facts or evidence but by a chosen ideology.

Not all college professors and teachers are sympathetic to the rise of the indoctrinators. But those who object often find themselves without a home in academia. Peter Hoghossian, resigning his position as a professor at Portland State University in 2021, wrote that the university had been transformed from a bastion of free inquiry into a Social Justice factory whose only inputs were race, gender and victimhood, and whose only outputs were grievance and division." He concluded, "Students at Portland State are not being taught to think. Rather, they are being trained to mimic the moral certainty of ideologues."

How did this happen, not just at Portland State, but at universities, colleges, and secondary schools throughout the United States and in many other nations around the world?

In 1923, German Marxist intellectuals, a number of whom were associated with the German communist party, founded the Institute of Social Research at Frankfurt University. They became known as The Frankfurt School. In response to the failure of Marxism to incite communist revolutions in Western Europe or the United States, they developed "critical theory" or "cultural Marxism." They advocated destroying religion, nationalism, patriotism, and capitalism along with personal behavior, traditional morality, sexual restraint, and especially the nuclear family; with the collapse of society, a new secular Marxist utopia could be created.

They fled the Nazi takeover in Germany and settled in the United States, where, by the 1970s, one of the Frankfurt School, Herbert Marcuse, became the darling of youthful Maoist radicals on college campuses. By the 21st century, Marcuse's disciples, ex-hippies and campus protesters, were now faculty members, department chairmen, college deans, and university presidents.

What does an ideology, developed a century ago by a group of German intellectuals, have to do with your children and grandchildren today? Why should we care? In the 1970s and 1980s, an African American professor at Harvard Law School named Derek Bell injected the element of race into "Critical Theory," creating "Critical Race Theory" (CRT). In contrast to Rev.

Dr. Martin Luther King, Jr., Bell maintained that people should be judged not by the content of their character, but by an immutable characteristic, the color of their skin. *Bell's view that the system had to be made "unequal" to compensate for past grievances was adopted by Marxists who substituted "racial struggle" for "class struggle" in a way to divide society and foment a revolution.* Bell's disciples extended and developed his ideas. Kimberlé Williams Crenshaw, organized the Critical Race Theory Workshop at Harvard and pioneered the concept of "intersectionality." Essentially, this concept provides for different groups identified as victims of oppression, with greater advantages to be given to those who can check the box for being more than a single type of victim.

Cheryl Harris, a U.C.L.A. law professor, proposed suspending private property rights and seizing property to be redistributed along racial lines. Ibram X. Kendi, director of the Center for Antiracist Research and currently the most widely-quoted guru of the Cultural Marxists, has called for an unelected federal department of anti-racism that could nullify any law passed by elected representatives, and censor or limit the speech of public officials who fail his anti-racist test. If these two individuals were to see their proposals adopted, the U.S. Constitution, the Bill of Rights, including freedom of speech, religion, and the press, as well as private property rights, would all be gone. Marx, Lenin, Stalin, and Mao would be proud.

What does any of this have to do with classroom teachers? Why should this concern parents and grandparents? Simply because the colleges and universities, especially those that train teachers, have turned out a generation or more of teachers who have specifically brought Critical Race Theory into the classrooms not just in America's schools, but those all over the world.

When the first edition of *Mark! My Words* was published, the need for Cultural Conservation was impelled in part by the assault on the arts, language, and achievement in academia, typified by colleges replacing real education with silly and superficial "pop courses" and "academic fluff." However, in recent years, this effort has become far more intense, deliberate, and ultimately dangerous.

So indoctrination does not begin on college campuses; it begins on the first day a little boy or girl walks into a classroom. Children are never too young to be indoctrinated.

Exclusive private schools in New York have recommended that students over the age of eight read a children's book by author-illustrator Anastasia Higginbotham called *Not My Idea*. The villain of the book is a red-tailed, devil-like character who offers a Faustian bargain for a soul, a "whiteness contract" promising "stolen land," "stolen riches," and "special favors" and teaches little boys and girls that "Whiteness is a bad deal. It always was." In a public school in Philadelphia, fifth graders were assigned to simulate a "Black Power Rally" supporting 1960s radical and lifelong communist Angela Davis.

Not all teachers have submitted to the pressure to endorse CRT. Those who have refused have often been ostracized or labeled "racists" for objecting to students being taught that victimhood is the key to success. Students were already learning about slavery and racism, but the new CRT curricula often mean that great literature and art must be jettisoned to make room for the all pervasive "oppressor-oppressed" narrative.

Those who have experienced real oppression in communist countries are quick to see parallels between CRT and the malevolent chaos created by Chairman Mao Zedong beginning in 1966 with the Communist Chinese Cultural Revolution. In Virginia, Xi Van Fleet told the Loudon County School Board, "The Communist regime used the same critical theory to divide people. The only difference is they used class instead of race. This is indeed the American version of the Chinese Cultural Revolution." In North Carolina, Lei Zheng, a Chinese-born professor of physics at Winston-Salem State University, agreed when he encountered woke ideology, social justice curricula, and Critical Race Theory. He explained, "The ideology, the CRT, I thought this is very bad because it is the same as in China under Mao. The only difference is, in China's Cultural Revolution it is your status in community, your class, but CRT is your identity, your race."

Exaggeration? Hyperbole? Not at all. Consider the case of Gabriel Gipe, a teacher at Inderkum High School in Sacramento, California. Gipe hung a poster featuring Communist Chinese dictator Mao Zedong, the architect of the Cultural Revolution, along with a the flag of Antifa, a shadowy and violent network of far-left revolutionaries, combining the red flag of the 1917 Russian revolution and the black flag of 19th century anarchists. Gipe boasted that he had 180 days to turn students into revolutionaries; he would give them extra credit for participating in protests of which he approved. Gipe reportedly used stamps featuring Joseph Stalin and other communist leaders in class and posed for photos displaying a huge tattoo on his chest depicting a hammer and sickle, the emblem of the Communist Party appearing on the flags of both the Soviet Union and Communist China. Gipe was paid $190,000, ($100,000 after taxes) to quietly resign by the Natomas Unified School District, but how many Gabriel Gipes are in classrooms today, indoctrinating students instead of teaching them? No one knows for sure.

Attempts to label critics of CRT as "racist" run into an immediate brick wall when its advocates ignore the fact that many of the most eloquent critics of using the schools for indoctrination in general and CRT in particular are African Americans themselves. At a school board meeting in Colorado Springs, Colorado, Derrick Wilburn, a black parent, brought fellow parents to a standing ovation when he told the school board what he thought about what is currently taking place in classrooms across the country, their own laziness, and their own decision making." He said, "I can think of nothing more damaging to a society than to tell a baby born today that she has grievances against another baby born today simply because of what their ancestors may have done two centuries ago. There's simply no point in doing that to our children, and putting critical race theory into our classrooms in part does that."

But all school districts in Colorado (or many other states) are not interested in the views of parents such as Derrick Wilburn. Centennial Elementary School in Denver, for instance, announced in early 2022 its plans to participate in the Black Lives Matter "School Week of Action." The school's agenda calls for little kindergarteners and first graders to be indoctrinated through gender ideology (i.e., to be "queer affirming" and recognize that "heteronormative thinking no longer exists), globalism, and the disruption of Western nuclear family dynamics and a return to the 'collective village' that takes care of each other." Books and articles cited by the school are written by prominent CRT advocates. This pattern of political and ideological indoctrination can be found in schools all over the United States; it is directed at the youngest and most vulnerable among us, small children being turned against their parents, traditional values and standards, and their classmates.

Dr. Alveda King, niece of Rev. Dr. Martin Luther King, Jr., declared, "When I hear the term critical race theory, I say what's critical to know is that human beings share 99.5 percent of our DNA. That's what our students should hear from pre-school on. We are more alike than we are different. We are one blood. We are one human race."

When teachers become activists, they are no longer teachers. It is not the business of a classroom teacher to politicize instruction. Advocates of Critical Race Theory generally mount two defenses of their agenda; first, they insist that they're not really teaching CRT and second, they dismiss their critics as racists. But these defenses have been overcome by prominent African American writers including John McWhorter, a noted linguistics professor at Columbia University and Jason L. Riley of the *Wall Street Journal.* McWhorter observes that teachers don't have to invoke obscure academic articles on CRT to implement its goals, while Riley asks if the priority of teachers should be math and reading or turning elementary schools into social justice boot camps when a majority of American fourth and eighth-graders can read or do math at grade level.

Tony Kinnett, who wrote the science curriculum for 30,000 students in Indiana, concludes, "When we tell you schools aren't teaching critical race theory, that it's nowhere in our standards, that's misdirection. We don't have the quotes as state's standards *per se*, we do have critical race theory in how we teach. We tell our teachers to treat students differently based on color. We tell our students that every problem is the result of 'white men' and that everything western civilization built is racist. Capitalism is a tool of white supremacy. Those are straight out of Kimberlé Crenshaw's *Critical Race Theory: The Writings That Formed the Movement.* This is in math, science, English, the arts, and it's not slowing down . . . We call it "anti-racism" so you feel bad if you disagree with our segregationist pedagogy. It's taking advantage of kids' vulnerability and parents' inactivity to preen over social snake oil schemes designed to create division."

What may be the greatest shock for parents and grandparents is that many teachers are quite open in expressing their indoctrination agenda. Cecily Myart-Cruz, President of United Teachers of Los Angeles (UTLA) told *Los Angeles Magazine,* "It's OK that our babies may not have learned all their times tables," because they had learned words like 'coup,' 'insurrection,' 'riot,' and 'protest.'" The National Education Association in 2021 declared its intention to develop a study "that critiques empire, white supremacy, anti-Blackness, anti-Indigeneity, racism, patriarchy, cisheteropatriarchy, capitalism, ableism, anthropocentrism, and other forms of power and oppression at the intersections of our society." So don't be surprised if little Johnny or Mary can't read, write, add, or spell; they will be too busy learning whether they are victims or oppressors and which groups and categories of humanity they are expected to hate throughout their lives.

We may give the last word on this subject to the great Thomas Sowell, economist, social philosopher, author, and a wise observer of the human condition. Says Sowell, "Ours may become the first civilization destroyed not by the power of our enemies, but by the ignorance of our teachers and the dangerous nonsense that they are teaching our children. In an age of artificial intelligence, they are creating artificial stupidity."

THE ODD COUPLE: GOVERNMENT AND THE ARTS

The relationship between government and the arts has always been tenuous at best. Artists, frankly, see government as a source of money. Government is not supposed to be in the business of making a profit. So those artists, writers, musicians, and dancers who see their work as "non-commercial" look to government as an obvious means of funding. Government, however, by its very nature, is in the business of telling people what they can and cannot do. In dictatorships, government involvement in the arts has frequently been in the role of a censor. Nazi Germany banned and ultimately executed countless artists who displeased Hitler and his fanatical ideology. In the Soviet Union, writers like Boris Pasternak and Aleksandr Solzhenitsyn were persecuted by the government because of the views they expressed in their books. Pasternak's novel, *Dr. Zhivago,* was banned in the Soviet Union and he was forced to decline the 1958 Nobel Prize. Solzhenitsyn spent eight years in prison for merely writing a letter criticizing Joseph Stalin. His works were later seized by the KGB and his Nobel Prize was denounced by the government. Even the most distinguished Russian composers, including Sergei Prokofiev and Dmitri Shostakovich, were forced to pay homage to Stalin and to write music extolling the virtues of the Soviet police state. Dictatorships around the world, from Pyongyang to Tehran to Havana, have used the power of the state to silence artists whose works they find threatening. Even in more benign roles, government creates problems. In the United States and in other free countries, artists have frequently sought government help to survive financially. But the road has not been smooth. Even when government "helps" people, its help is usually in the form of regulations. Government money inevitably comes with government strings. In addition, government has no money of its own. It either prints money or takes it from taxpayers. When government spends taxpayers' money on the arts, the taxpayers in question often don't find the idea appealing.

There is a fundamental reason why government cannot be relied upon for cultural conservation. "Government" frequently means an alphabet soup of federal and state agencies run by bureaucrats. Since everyone agrees that bureaucrats make bad art critics, the alternative seems to be for artists to become bureaucrats. Decisions about how government money is spent are often turned over to so-called "peer panels." These are committees of individuals, invariably described as distinguished, who oversee the dispensation of federal dollars. The problem is that, despite public dithering about "the creative community," in fact, there is no "creative community." Artists, writers, and musicians thrive on disagreement. Literary feuds and musical rivalries are intense. Brahms and Tchaikovsky spoke ill of each other's music. In the 20th century, supporters of Schoenberg and Stravinsky became similarly hostile rivals. In short, there is no reason to assume that specific groups of artists are any more compatible than the Red Sox and Yankees, the Republicans and Democrats, the liberals and conservatives, or the Hatfields and McCoys. Members of peer panels who dispense government money do not spring from a vacuum. They come from the contentious world of the arts, with all the opinions, biases, energy, and preferences to be expected.

Should we expect such "peers" to be objective? In some ways, these individuals function like music or theater critics, making judgments about their colleagues. Ostensibly, they carry no biases as they walk into an auditorium or museum. Who are we kidding? Every artist is all too familiar with the biases of particular critics. While the critics insist their biases are only on the side of quality, in fact, their ostensibly "objective" views reflect two kinds of biases: ideological and personal. A critic may dislike an artist's style or he may just dislike the artist himself. One well-known critic in Los Angeles always gave good theater reviews to plays set in prison. A biography of a prominent symphony conductor received rave reviews, except in one very important newspaper: a close friend of the reviewer was writing a competitive biography of the same conductor. So when government appoints "distinguished peer panels" to dispense government money, there is a strong likelihood that such funds will go to the friends, colleagues, and ideological soul-mates of the peer panels. Typically, this means that artists who do not follow fashionable trends will be rejected. In contrast to what most people believe, it is the more conservative and traditional artists, not those representing themselves as the agents of change, who have encountered the greatest resistance in government circles. When rejections occur, they occur quietly, without the ballyhoo accorded to "artists" who are funded, to the consternation of offended taxpayers. Placing one's faith in the ability of government to make decisions about artists is a fool's errand indeed.

Much recent controversy has involved the National Endowment for the Arts making grants that set off a political firestorm. Just as in the schools, political agendas insure that government involvement in the arts will always generate fundamental problems. Some artists believe that government funds should be available to them without restriction. But if their work is sexually explicit, uses obscene language offensive to religious groups, or deals in political controversy, a problem is clear. Many taxpayers believe that government dollars, *their* money derived from *their* taxes, should not be used to fund art, which they find offensive. The fact that one director of the NEA described a controversial work of art as "tasteful" is beside the point. Tasteful to whom? Defenders of the NEA point out that only a small percentage of such grants are controversial. Artists quickly raise the specter of censorship. However, no artist has a right to taxpayer's money. It is not "censorship" for an artist to be denied government funds. When government agencies make choices, artists may not be selected because their work will offend taxpayers. More often than not, their work will not be chosen because their work doesn't appeal to members of the committee. Some artists are outraged that taxpayers (whom they regard as uneducated and culturally ignorant yahoos) have opinions about these subjects. They think that the taxpayers should go away quietly, after, of course, providing the money for artistic endeavors that may be difficult to fund privately. In any event, government involvement in the arts will always generate controversy. Some will insist that government should spend more money (with less regulation), while others demand that government spend less money (with more regulation). Either way, government involvement places an emphasis on what should be done with taxpayers' money, not the quality (or lack of it) found in specific artistic endeavors. Therefore, government, with its inevitable emphasis on politics and the biases of those who have artistic agendas of their own, is an unlikely candidate to save our culture.

Joseph Komonchak in his article, "The Separation of Art and State,"[140] declares, "If art is the quintessence of the free expression of private meanings—what artists do with their solitude—it should, of course, be free, not only from restrictions by government but also from what religion has long since known to be the suffocating embrace of its support. If art wishes to have public significance, let it earn it, as religions must. As it is not the business of government to choose among competing ultimate truths, it is not its business to choose among competing private meanings."

Government support inevitably means government supervision and supervision leads inexorably to government control. In the arts, whoever provides the money makes the decisions. This is true even when funds come from private rather than public sources. During a cold New York winter in 1933, the Rockefeller family commissioned the Mexican painter, Diego Rivera, to paint a mural that would adorn the new RCA Building at Rockefeller Center. Rivera, an avowed communist, included a flattering and provocative picture of Lenin in his mural. The Rockefellers would not tolerate a flattering portrait of the founder of the Soviet police state in their building. When Rivera refused to change the face of Lenin to a politically neutral image, the Rockefellers covered the mural for a year and eventually destroyed it. Rivera and his admirers insisted that his artistic independence and free speech had been violated. But Rivera had accepted money to do something, and had, in fact, done something entirely different. If you were to hire someone to paint the exterior of your house brown and he covered it instead with pink and purple polka dots, you would be outraged. Composers and writers in Hollywood have justifiably protested alterations and deletions in their work by hacks, bowdlerizers, and uncouth producers. But unfortunately, it is the uncouth producers and their bosses who control the money and therefore are legally entitled to control the artistic outcome. Artists and writers can do what they please in private, but when they sell their services, they are also surrendering their artistic independence. If private individuals provide funding for the arts, they will exercise control; if the government provides the funds, should we be surprised that the public expects its values and standards to be respected?

Government involvement offers little solace to those who see the taste of the public defined by mass commercial entertainment media. The problem of cultural conservation is, in short, one that may be helped or hurt by government. But it cannot be solved by government. If schools and government are not the answer then what about the entertainment industry? Clearly, it is motion picture and television producers, recording executives, and members of the media, who have a disproportionate influence over what we watch and hear. It is these people who define which artists are brought to public attention. But more than any other element, the entertainment industry is clearly part of the problem, so it cannot be part of the solution.

NO BUSINESS LIKE SHOW BUSINESS: THE MORALITY OF THE BOTTOM LINE

Hollywood! The very word inspires a myriad number of images, usually reflecting the mythical glamour and excitement of a dream factory. The entertainment industry is highly skilled at inventing images, especially its own. The mythical Hollywood is a delightful place fulfilling dreams of stardom for Cinderellas from Dubuque, and defining the standards of fame and fortune to which millions around the world aspire. The real Hollywood is, in some ways, more fascinating than its myth. But it is a place of hard realities, not dreams, of profit and cynicism, a land in which those with taste and talent must compete like gladiators in the ancient Roman arena with rivals consumed by blind ambition and unchecked greed. In a description variously attributed to comedian Ed Gardner, radio personality Henry Morgan, and pianist Oscar Levant, "In Hollywood, if you look underneath the tinsel, you'll find the real tinsel."

There are several reasons why the entertainment industry has exacerbated the problem rather than helped to facilitate a solution. Some are easy to understand, others more complex. What is the primary motive in the entertainment industry? Executives and self-appointed advocates for the industry will talk about the "creative community," about its message and aspirations to critical acclaim. Producers of television programs, motion pictures, and recordings will talk incessantly about their rights, but seldom about their responsibilities. Behind this façade, however, everyone familiar with the inner workings of the entertainment industry knows that since its inception, the driving force behind Hollywood has been money. One writer called this force "the morality of hard cash." It is not without reason that a leading trade magazine in the record industry is called *Cash Box*. Now no one expects entertainment companies to eschew an interest in profits. Entertainment executives are businessmen and businesswomen. If their companies don't make money, they won't remain in business for long. Margaret Thatcher said, "It is not the creation of wealth that is wrong, but the love of money for its own sake." There is a point at which money and morality conflict. In Hollywood and New York, the headquarters of the industry, there is little doubt as to whether money or morality will triumph. Herb Cohen is a professional negotiator who teaches the art of making deals. The deal is what really drives Hollywood, not glamour or fame, certainly not artistic achievement. Cohen expresses a view that is paramount in Hollywood. He describes a businessman who explains a rejection to a vanquished opponent. "It's not the money," says the victor to whom belong the spoils. *"It's the money."*

Decisions are made in the entertainment industry based on pure profit. If uninhibited trash will outsell products of quality, the latter are headed for the cutting room floor. Of course, there is a danger in painting the industry with too broad a brush. There are men and women of ideals and talent throughout the world of entertainment. But in most instances, decisions are made and orders are issued by those whose primary motive is, pure and simple: how much money did the company make yesterday? Most of these executives operate in an environment of perpetual insecurity. If their profits are not sufficient today, rivals will replace them tomorrow. A television mini-series about a movie studio of the 1930s reflected this well. In *The Lot*, written cleverly by Rick Mitz, a tycoon and munitions manufacturer—a thinly disguised parody of Howard Hughes—turns movie mogul and buys a studio. He finds himself being blackmailed by a ruthlessly ambitious publicist. "Do you mean you would do this to me just to get a job?" says the astonished executive. "Of course," says the blackmailer, "You're just in the war business. <u>This</u> is Hollywood!"

People who work in the entertainment industry often pontificate about "the creative community." The term belies the fact that the industry is viciously competitive, with powerful executives and producers at the top of the totem pole, and those with creativity often at the bottom. Writers and composers often keep their private opinions of Hollywood trends to themselves. They are aware that disagreeing with the opinions and attitudes of their bosses on anything from politics to taste in music or films can cause them problems. Worst of all is the possibility that they may be dubbed "old-fashioned" and "over the hill." This, by the way, has nothing to do with age. Hollywood is obsessed with immediate success, with the present, with everything that is happening now. In Hollywood, everyone lives in fear that one day the phone may stop ringing. Hollywood functions like a club, and personal contacts often determine how fortunes are made and lost. When a director, writer, or composer is told, "You'll never have lunch in this town again," Hollywood insiders understand the message. The offending individual is free to eat lunch wherever he pleases, but no one will be sitting at his table offering him a job or closing a deal. So those creative men and women with taste and talent are invariably faced with a hard choice: they can express their true opinions and render themselves potentially unemployable, or they can keep their opinions to themselves and smilingly march in lockstep with other sycophants who are willing to pay any price to stay in the club. The movie moguls who founded the studios were often uneducated and unpolished corporate bosses. Their successors today may be lawyers, accountants, or graduates of film schools, but beneath the expensive suits and oleaginous veneer, they are just as ruthless and crude as their predecessors, if not more so.

Occasionally, a Hollywood veteran speaks out about the system. Screenwriter Roger L. Simon did so in his book, *Blacklisting Myself*.[141] Simon writes, "Hollywood life is not secure even for the most famous. The powerful have had to claw their way to the top in a brutally competitive dog eat dog environment that has been well dramatized in such film classics as *All About Eve* and *Sunset Boulevard*." Simon observes, "Those who achieve in this atmosphere are quite often those who have learned to mistreat and step on others with impunity to succeed in the movie industry. Many are execrable in the way they treat associates, staff, and families in their private and business lives. Self-loathing lurks just below the surface. Also the fear of failure, of being 'found out.'" Simon explains, quite correctly, that to offset their appalling behavior, these Hollywood titans often develop an alternative persona that performs public acts of charity and is devoted to utopian, pseudo-idealistic causes. This enables the most ruthless executive to pride himself on his generosity and concern for humanity while cutting the throats of his rivals and even his friends in pursuit of his professional self-preservation. Such an individual can fool himself and a gullible public, at least for a little while. Almost any personal or professional behavior will be tolerated, as long as he continues to achieve financial success. But if anything he does is unsuccessful, he runs the risk of the dreaded sign of rejection. The phone may stop ringing and his Hollywood luncheon days may be over. Of course, there will always be a new and ruthlessly ambitious figure to step into his shoes and start the cycle all over again.

There are many extremely talented and nice people working in Hollywood. Unfortunately, those who control the industry are frequently untalented and usually not nice. In the words of Marilyn Monroe, "Hollywood is a place where they'll pay you a thousand dollars for a kiss and fifty cents for your soul." Comedian and wit Fred Allen put it another way. He said, "You can take all the sincerity in Hollywood, place it in the navel of a firefly and still have room enough for three caraway seeds and a producer's heart." Dana Wynter was an actress known for elegance on and off camera, the star of numerous films and television programs. She was also an accomplished writer. In her memoir, *Other People, Other Places*, she addressed an attitude dominant in Hollywood, the need for instant gratification. She said, "The word, 'Hollywood,' has become an anachronism representing a memory of the past; the capital of the film world, a mirage that was glamour success, and a lifestyle envied by the world. Now all that's left is a high wooden sign atop a hill with letters tilted and occasionally falling off. Perhaps the time has come to replace the sign and rename that place Instantville—for instant gratification, success, and failure." She concludes, quite correctly, "To out-shine and out- do is top priority here before that ultimate 'heave-ho' to make place for the next whiz-kid superstar . . . until then, bigger swimming-pool, blonder younger companion, better and newer everything."[142]

A second, equally powerful motive dominates the entertainment industry—an obsession with the present. Success is perceived as the property of the young, the new, and the fashionable. Trends are omnipotent. In the entertainment industry, everyone from the most senior executive to the lowliest employee understands that survival is predicated upon being "with it," whatever "it" happens to be. In an environment of intense competition, the present is everything, the past nothing.

In 1970, trucks pulled up and parked near a Southern California landfill. The trucks were filled with manuscripts and recordings from the legendary Hollywood studio Metro-Goldwyn-Mayer. MGM had been the home of some of the finest movie musicals, productions like *The Wizard of Oz, Easter Parade, An American in Paris, Singin' in the Rain*, and *Gigi*. Many MGM non-musical films had been scored by the world's finest film composers, including Miklós Rózsa, Bernard Herrmann, David Raksin, and Bronislaw Kaper, among others. The studio's music library was filled with a treasure trove of musical history, including the scores for films like the historical epic *Ben-Hur* and the suspense classic *North by Northwest*. The contents of the trucks were not on their way to a library. The scores, manuscripts, and recordings were dumped into the landfill. Eventually a section of the Golden State Freeway, north of Los Angeles, was constructed over the landfill, rendering the scores irretrievably lost forever. Gene Kelly's outtake of *I've Got a Crush on You*, cut from *An American in Paris*, and the original orchestral accompaniment for Judy Garland's *Somewhere Over the Rainbow* from *The Wizard of Oz* were among the items abandoned. The destruction of a significant piece of America's musical history was completed with full knowledge and approval of the studio. Presumably, MGM had no regard for anything but the films of the moment. A salvage crew was also hired to haul away items considered "waste material" from the studio back lot. Included was the original matte painting of "The Emerald City" used in *The Wizard of Oz*. The cartage company recognized the value of the painting, stored it, and the work eventually sold two decades later at an auction for $44,000. But many items were just abandoned. Barry M. Vilkin, president of a California auction house, told the *New York Times*, "With some items, people walked off with them without permission, but no one really cared because the studios saw no historical significance in any of what they had. Their attitude was: Let's get on to the next production."

While the MGM episode was perhaps the most infamous example of a Hollywood studio literally tossing its historical heritage into the trash, there are numerous other examples of the same type of neglect. In 1980, scores were thrown out by Columbia Pictures. The music library kept scores of films receiving three stars from a popular guidebook to old movies. Scores of films receiving fewer stars were discarded.

ARTISTS OF THE FAST BUCK

In the 1960s and '70s, motion picture studios sold off memorabilia of the past, threw away scripts, pictures, and motion picture scores. Irreplaceable music manuscripts were tossed into incinerators and thrown out with the trash. In recent years, the entertainment industry has rediscovered its past, but primarily because such items have monetary value. Writers, composers, directors, and creative people of every stripe are under intense pressure to succeed. To do so means following trends and conforming; the alternative is discovering unemployment. An industry obsessed with the present has had little motivation to preserve or value its past. What is most dreaded by the so-called "creative community"? To be dubbed "over-the-hill." In a mad rush to embrace the present, the industry has been quick to reject the words and music of the past. The psychology of the industry demands that what is being sold today is better than what was sold yesterday. In contrast to its image of freedom and creative expression, the pressures of the industry demand conformity and a lack of dissent.

While industry executives are always talking about freedom to express themselves, they have little toleration for criticism. Tipper Gore, wife of then Tennessee Senator Albert Gore, learned this the hard way. Shocked and dismayed by explicit language in records sold to teenagers and appealing to children, she campaigned for a rating system for recordings. Her views were outlined in a book, *Raising PG Rated Children in an X-Rated Society.*[143] Mrs. Gore expected the industry to respond to constructive criticism constructively. Instead, she and colleagues from the Parents Music Resource Center were vilified and ridiculed by industry executives and high profile entertainment stars. When Albert Gore began his quest for the Presidency, the Gores were forced to go to Hollywood and apologize for their indiscretion.

In a bipartisan attempt to hold recording companies accountable, Republican William Bennett, former Secretary of Education and drug czar, and Democrat C. Delores Tucker, director of the National Political Congress of Black Women, confronted Time-Warner executives over *Big Man with a Gun*, a hit for Nine Inch Nails, an "industrial rock project" founded by Trent Reznor, its primary producer, singer, songwriter, and instrumentalist. The executives were too embarrassed by the lyrics of their hit, filled with obscenities and threats of violence, to read them aloud. Bennett asked the executives if they were "morally disabled," and if there was "anything so low, so bad that you would not sell it." The executives were silent. According to *The Washington Post*, Warner Brothers Chairman, Danny Goldberg, described Nine Inch Nails as a critically acclaimed "artist," loved by millions of people and winners of the Grammy Award. He demanded, "Why should a corporation listen to a bunch of middle-aged people who don't like the music and don't listen to it, and ignore the people who do love it and who do buy it?" Time-Warner eventually sold Interscope, the division that marketed "gangsta rap." Goldberg's remarks were typical of what Hollywood executives do when they are challenged: they wrap themselves in the First Amendment, always stressing rights, not responsibilities. They also indulge in an ad hominem attack on their critics, always insisting that such critics are either stupid or mean-spirited censors who are intolerant of youth and progress. Profit, not progress, is the obvious origin of such a defense. No one with common sense or an awareness of what takes place in the real world of the recording industry can doubt for a moment that any producer or executive worthy of the name would toss all of his artists over the side of a boat the minute their sales numbers decline.

The most controversial aspect of Hollywood's role in our culture is what might be called the "Hollywood attitude." Writer Ben Stein characterized this attitude in his book, *The View from*

Sunset Boulevard.[144] Stein suggested with humor and irony that executives in Hollywood had a worldview, often different from a majority of Americans, and hostile to capitalism and business. This hostility, of course, did not prevent any of the executives or writers from enjoying the fruits of their labor. In the Hollywood attitude, it is usually objectionable for someone else to get rich. Getting rich yourself is not only desirable, but also the yardstick by which your value will be measured. Film critic Michael Medved expanded this subject with his book, *Hollywood vs. America: Popular Culture and the War on Traditional Values.*[145] Medved demonstrates that an insular group of executives and artists control the media. For Medved, these people are ideologically hostile to the family and religion, and believe in glorifying ugliness as the highest aesthetic ideal. He presents a highly persuasive argument that many of the trends in entertainment, including an increase in explicit sex, violence, and profane language, can be traced directly to these individuals. Why are there fewer films made about true heroes in society? Why do the new latest music and lyrics reflect a virtual assault on traditional American values, ideologically hostile to the family and religion, and believe in glorifying ugliness as the highest aesthetic ideal? Actress and talk radio personality Janine Turner developed an accurate perspective on Hollywood while starring in numerous films and television programs. She writes, "In Hollywood, they think America is inherently bad, a world embarrassment, even as they gorge themselves on the American dream. Hollywood is a surreal and pretend world whose way of life is actually ruthless free enterprise—it is called show *business*, after all. Hollywood is where stars, movie producers, writers and agents actively seek glamour, money, power and fame; where they covet fast cars and face-lifts and fly in private jets. They drink fine wines and insist on free spirits. They are the ultimate connoisseurs who insist on living liberty at large."

In Hollywood, executives and their creative minions often speak of "pushing the envelope" and "challenging boundaries." But the values that are acceptable to a society change. Like a swinging pendulum, standards and boundaries have been relaxed to a point at which there are no standards and boundaries. Entertainment companies may have the legal right to do as they please, but what about their responsibilities? They may be entitled to wage an assault on traditional values in entertainment; but does it mean that they should? Does this mean that such an assault is a good idea? By discussing their rights, not their responsibilities, those who control the industry reveal their true nature. They are concerned with themselves, not with their audience.

Pat Sajak is best known to the public as the host of the television game show, *Wheel of Fortune*. In a multifaceted broadcasting career, he has acquired a very accurate perspective on the attitudes that are prevalent in the entertainment industry. At a convocation for Hillsdale College, he spoke of the disconnect between Hollywood and America. Sajak stressed the fact that there is little diversity of thought in Hollywood. He asked, "How can you write about people fairly if they seem so out of touch with what you are used to in your everyday life?" He described Hollywood executives as clueless about this country and its people. Sajak explained, "It's not that they're evil people. They have kids and they care about them. But they see no connection between what they do and the results of what they do. And, besides, you're not really families and communities. You're ratings, demographics, and sales." Those with power in the entertainment industry socialize with each other; they join the same clubs, dine at the same restaurants, and participate in the same political causes. They live in a social and ideological bubble in which everyone seems to think alike. In their world, traditional values (especially those, which assume moral absolutes) are regarded with suspicion and skepticism. They see themselves as merely reflecting attitudes that are pervasive in the rest of the country. So they accept little or no responsibility for encouraging behavior that may have disastrous consequences for everyone else.

Some critics of Hollywood imagine a group of powerful movie studio bosses or television producers sitting around in a room scheming and plotting to corrupt public morals, destroy traditional values, and replace anything of quality with trash masquerading as entertainment. This is simply untrue. The truth is that most people in the entertainment industry tend to hire people who reflect the same perspectives and values that they hold. So people with the Hollywood attitude move up the ladder and acquire the power to hire more people with the exact same outlook. Of course, the industry is filled with those who disagree with such a viewpoint. Many hide their views for fear of not being hired. Others do speak out, often facing the consequences of their actions. In Hollywood, as in Washington, DC, it's always easier to go along in order to get along. The hero who challenges the system may still appear in the movies, but in real life, he is likely to find himself facing a choice between principles and employment.

The movie industry was founded by showmen and promoters. They were often immigrants, hardened by their quest for success, well aware that in entertainment, a thick skin was obligatory. They were often laughably ignorant of language and history, but appreciative of the country that had ultimately welcomed them and enabled their triumph. (Louis B. Mayer of Metro-Goldwyn-Mayer actually chose to celebrate his birthday on the Fourth of July.) Today's executives, often second and third generation descendants of Hollywood's pioneers, have been frequently raised in an environment of luxury, security, and prosperity. Yesterday's showmen made positive statements about society, because they believed they were commercial and because they believed in their message. Today's executives believe that negative statements about society are most easily sold, because they believe in no message at all. Those who challenge the way things are done are given a simple message: conform or get out of the business!

Consider the fate of Julia Phillips. Phillips, the first woman to win an Oscar for "Best Picture," was once considered one of Hollywood's best and brightest producers. She helped raise the funds for a whole generation of Hollywood's most successful directors. But Phillips had a drug problem, and when her career collapsed, she struck back at former friends and allies with a scathing book, *You'll Never Eat Lunch in This Town Again.*[146]

Phillips described Hollywood as "a place that attracts people with massive holes in their souls." She also provided a definition of "fun" in Tinseltown, "running someone around the room, preferably someone more talented and less powerful." When Julia Phillips died at fifty-seven, her passing was devoid of the usual tributes and plaudits of Hollywood's trend-setters. Nicholas Wapshott wrote that her death "was greeted with silence from colleagues who usually commemorate the loss of one of their number with conspicuous mourning and extravagant praise." Phillips had reflected on her ultimate banishment from Hollywood's inner circle. She said, "I wasn't a pariah because I was a drug-addicted, alcoholic, rotten person and not a good mother. I was a pariah because I lit them with a harsh fluorescent light and rendered them as contemptible as they truly are."

Can an industry with such motives preserve and conserve the best of our culture, values, and standards that have been reflected in the arts of the past? For an executive whose primary motive is making money, whose instinct is to conform to today's trends at the expense of yesterday's quality, and who regards traditional values as outdated and unsophisticated, the answer is an unqualified no! Like academics and government bureaucrats, entertainment executives have not been motivated to conserve our culture or preserve the arts. In fact, they are driven by motives and ambitions that virtually insure neglect and decline of arts that reflect traditional values, past or present.

Executives in the entertainment industry are not inclined to be passive in the face of criticism, however justified. In fact, they typically respond with a vigorous and clever defense of their behavior. Superficially, they seem to have all the answers directed at well-intentioned, but ill-advised, critics. On closer consideration, however, their arguments have more holes than Swiss cheese. Consider the arguments as stated by Hilary Rosen, President and Chief Executive Officer of the Recording Industry Association of America. In response to the assertion that the recording industry did little or nothing to curb the gratuitous sex, violence, and foul language in recordings and rock videos, Rosen testified before the

U.S. Senate Committee on Governmental Affairs. Rosen's testimony was delivered in 1997, but four years later, she confronted Fox television news anchor John Gibson with the same arguments. Her comments are revealing, because they represent the typical response of most entertainment executives facing criticism. Nearly all such executives present these same arguments in various forms.

1. *Parents always find their children's music shocking and a form of rebellion.* Parents in 1956 thought Elvis Presley was shocking, just as their parents thought the jitterbug was shocking. So nothing has really changed. This is a clever lawyer's argument, but it doesn't hold up under scrutiny. If we accept this argument, any change in our culture, however drastic, can be justified on the theory that it's just normal generational change. Apply this thinking to other activities and the flawed logic immediately becomes apparent. A police officer may be permitted to use acceptable levels of force to detain a suspect. But if succeeding generations of police are allowed to drastically increase the level of force used, "acceptable levels" may allow for change from democracy to a police state. A new generation of cooks may season their cuisine generously, while their teachers may have only used a pinch of spice. But if you empty the spice rack into a single dish, you're going to get indigestion, not a happy culinary memory. There is a difference between the violence and obscene language used in today's "art" and yesterday's. When today's rebels look around for something to shock the public, they have to go to extremes in "pushing the envelope," because the envelope has already been pushed off the planet. It's the difference between a slap in the face and being mugged by someone wielding a tire iron.

2. *Rock stars and music industry executives contribute money to socially responsible causes and are therefore not responsible for glamorizing violence or the use of drugs.* As for contributions to good causes, that's commendable. But it doesn't get Hilary Rosen's clientele off the hook regarding artistic or moral responsibility. We can debate whether such contributions are the result of true social

responsibility or a canny instinct for good public relations. But donating money to charity doesn't obviate accountability for the consequences of one's actions. All kinds of people donate money to good causes.

Philanthropy may be motivated by generosity. Still, the contributions of racketeers may be generated by guilt. Donations by billionaires may be in search of tax deductions. A well-known publisher of an X-rated magazine writes big checks to charities operated by his church, a church that thoroughly disapproves of the rest of his activities. A polluter can send baskets of money to the Committee for a Clean Environment, but he's still a polluter. This applies to moral and cultural polluters as well.

3. *Entertainers are merely playing "characters," and they (responsible family men and women devoted to the good, the true, and the beautiful) shouldn't be confused with "characters" they play.* (The "characters," by the way, blast messages filled with sex, violence, drugs, and obscene language into our consciousness.) This argument sounds good, but like the others, it's fatally flawed. Children emulate the on-camera behavior of their idols; when they hear about their idols' private behavior off-camera, it is usually because such behavior is appalling by objective standards, but appealing to those seeking to rebel. Teenagers growing up on a steady diet of rock videos aren't busy asking themselves what performers are doing after the concert is over, they're trying to be popular, to be "cool," to be "with it," even if being "cool" implies behaving in ways that tear our cultural and social fabric apart. Suggesting that these "characters" merely reflect what is taking place rather than defining cultural standards is entirely disingenuous.

4. *It's all about free speech.* The record industry wants all "artists" to express themselves, even if this expression is offensive or shocking to some people. After all, no one compels you to purchase certain recordings. So the industry merely provides a megaphone to artists and then insists that they alone are qualified to define what truly represents art. This is a neat argument, one that portrays record executives as civil libertarians, champions of

the First Amendment, and laughably, as patrons of "the arts." According to this argument, no one can define "art," so the industry can sell whatever it pleases and inoculate itself against criticism by labeling everything "art." Of course, if everything is "art," then nothing is "art," so this dodge is revealed to be an excuse quickly. The problem is that no one is challenging the right of the industry to do what it wants. We are challenging its judgment *and* its lack of responsibility. When the industry hands a megaphone to one such "artist," it simultaneously denies the megaphone to other competing voices. We should admonish executives daily: "Just because you have the right to do something, doesn't mean it is the right thing to do."

5. *There are far worse things to do than watch rock videos, engage in explicit dancing, or emulate the dress styles of people you see on television.* Of course there are. But this is one of the most deceptive arguments used by apologists for the entertainment industry. When critics suggest that very young teenagers should not emulate the extreme and often bizarre clothing of their on-screen idols, the editor of a teenage fashion magazine was outraged. After all, she said, there are far worse things than trying to look "cool" or "hip." When parents protested highly suggestive dances becoming popular with teenagers, a dancer from Las Vegas protested, "You're lucky if that's the worst thing your children do." On the surface, this argument seems to make sense. But upon closer examination, it becomes obvious that this attitude contributes substantially to our problems. No matter what happens in human behavior, it is usually possible to rationalize an activity by finding something worse. But as teachers of another era were fond of reminding us, "two wrongs don't make a right." (The brilliant humorist and hierarchiologist, Dr. Laurence Peter, parodied this advice with his own: "If two wrongs don't make a right, try three!") What the entertainment executives are trying to do is deflect criticism of whatever they may be selling by insisting that other alternatives are worse. Too much explicit sexuality in movies and pop music? "It's violence we need to worry about!" they say. Too much violence? "Watching violence is better than

being violent!" they insist. Blissfully ignorant students graduating from schools with diplomas and minimal cultural awareness? "Failing these students might lower their self-esteem!" we're told. "They might drop out of school and end up on the streets!"

This argument becomes a neat and casual way to constantly lower standards, lower the floor of acceptable behavior and knowledge, always by insisting that a worse alternative is around the corner. In fact, there should be positive reasons to behave in certain ways, and positive reasons to absorb elements of our culture. We shouldn't accept mediocre music, art, and theater because there are worse flaws than mediocrity. Our goal should be to seek the best, not the "less than the worst" standard. The phrase, "Everybody does it," has become a favorite excuse for downward definition of our standards. But there are two flaws in this argument. The first is the assumption, often untrue, that "everybody" does "it" whatever "it" happens to be. The second is that even if "everybody does it," everybody can be morally obtuse or singularly lacking in collective intelligence. In other words, "everybody" can be wrong or just plain stupid, neither condition of which is improved by quantity.

The entertainment industry thus sends a dual message to those easily deceived by a public relations campaign and to more skeptical industry critics. To those foolish enough to believe publicity, the industry says, "Appreciate what we sell because others will, and you don't want to be different, do you?" To its critics, the industry says, "What we're selling is popular and makes a lot of money. Those who make us rich could be spending their money on products far worse than what we're selling at the moment, so you should congratulate us for our contributions to society." This message would be laughable if it weren't so obviously riddled with inconsistency and hypocrisy. Mass conformity has never been a good reason to do anything. If a product, entertainment or otherwise, is good, there should be valid reasons for buying it besides a desire to be popular among one's peers. Just because there are worse products on the market is no reason to tolerate the excesses and flaws in today's pop culture.

Imagine the outrage if a manufacturer of automobiles or corn flakes said to parents, "You should be relieved that your children are using our products. They're poorly made cars and indigestible breakfast cereal, but at least they're not defective." These arguments are a form of intellectual "sleight of hand," designed to put critics on the defensive and enable the entertainment executives ostensibly to take the high road. There is no virtue in pursuing moderate ineptitude; there is no honor in defending limited incompetence. If we aim for the stars, we may not reach the stars, but we're certainly not going to reach the stars by aiming for a mud puddle.

Apologists for the entertainment industry speak the language of tolerance and moderation in public. But in private, they see a direct correlation between "pushing the envelope" and making more money. The best music, the best art, the best theater do not have to "push the envelope" to get attention. But industry spokesmen use their arguments in a slick and superficially appealing way. They insist that it is their critics who are antiquated, intolerant, unsophisticated, opposed to progress, elitist, extremist, and just plain narrow-minded.

Most commentators and industry critics are thrown off balance by these arguments. No one wants to be against free speech, art, or upstanding citizens who give money to charity. No one wants to appear old-fashioned, square, ultra-conservative, and worst of all, judgmental. But there are exceptions. After Hilary Rosen expressed her views on a Fox news television interview, John Gibson responded. Gibson started his career in the record business and he wasn't about to be fooled. Gibson advised his listeners, "You don't have to listen to stuff that tells you to beat your mom or stomp your girlfriend or shoot somebody. Believe it or not, life does not become worse if you don't listen to things that make you angry or make you hate somebody or make you run your car into a tree. It might make you feel better to know that your money isn't making some music business crook become rich.

I used to be in the record business; I know it from the inside." Gibson continued, striking at the heart of the industry's defense. "If they thought you would buy a piece of plastic with the sounds of pigs snorting, slick looking record producers would be crowding the hog farms of American signing new acts. They don't care about art, at least most of them. It's all about the money. Huge, big money. You don't have to give it to them." When confronted by an occasionally irate public or demands for self- restraint, representatives of the entertainment industry usually insist that imposing standards is a highly subjective act. To be judgmental, we are told is worse than the ills we seek to cure.

In a discussion about movie ratings, the industry had no more articulate defender than Jack Valenti, President and CEO of the Motion Picture Association of America. Valenti, who once declared that he slept a little better each night because Lyndon Johnson was his President, was essentially the chief spokesman for motion picture producers before Congress. In testimony before a Senate committee conducting hearings on movie ratings, Valenti declared, "What movie raters have to face is that they are not dealing with the purity of Euclid's geometric equations, the answers of which are always clear-shaped and precise. Movie raters, vexing though it is to social scientists and Wall Street analysts, are dealing with the ghostly form of subjectivity, which is barren of all Euclidean finality. Now where is the cyclopean eye, this all Seeing Eye, that's going to organize all of this and mold it into a harmonious whole? It can't be done!" To which Sen. Joseph Lieberman of Connecticut, the committee's chairman, responded, "I was hoping that you would be the one who would find the cyclopean eye and that you would do it with Euclidean finality!"

Valenti's point, rich as it was with references to the mathematics and mythology of ancient Greece, is that taste is simply too subjective and individual, judgments about the arts are too personal, for anyone to exercise restraint. Nevertheless, in the real world, the producers Valenti represented (or their counterparts in the television industry) make such judgments every day. Consider the television program, *South Park*, an animated program which shocked some members of the viewing public by using a single four-letter word 162 times during a thirty-minute television show. A small meter at the bottom of the screen actually tabulated the number of times the word was used. The show continues to attract large audiences of young viewers who regard such language as "hip" and "cool." The Parents Television Council reports that during an average week, one-half million children between the ages of two and seventeen watch this program. When asked, the show's producers insisted that they were startled that such words could be offensive. Presumably, they believe either that continuous, uninterrupted profanity is mainstream, or that they are successful and powerful enough within the industry to thumb their noses at the segment of the public that objects to what they are doing. One *South Park* producer declared that discussions about standards were moot, since few standards or restrictions remain.

Columnist L. Brent Bozell III discussed the role of advertisers and their responsibility for what appears on the air in a scathing column. Bozell wrote, "We mustn't forget the sponsors' vital role in this steady decline in standards. David Stanley, a producer of another raunchy Comedy Central series, *The Man Show*, told *The Los Angeles Times* last year that 'the line [regarding acceptable television program content] is being drawn almost exclusively by [advertisers]. If advertisers are willing to buy time on shows with more risqué content, [networks] will go ahead and sell it.' Sponsors of the *South Park* episode in question included Disney, Nike, Best Buy, and Reebok. They are directly responsible for turning 'taste' and 'decency' into dirty words."

When pressed for answers, spokesmen for the industry cite vagueness and confusion, and an inability of the industry to even agree on ratings for the products it sells. But in the real world, the industry is guided almost exclusively by a profit motive. No one expects the entertainment industry to be unprofitable, but not to the exclusion of decent standards of taste. "Decent by whose definition?" thunder the industry apologists. The answer, of course, is that someone's definition must be used, or else the producer of

South Park is right, and there are no standards. The entertainment industry's top executives seem to find nothing unsuitable for the marketplace, as long as they make as much money as possible. Should we therefore be surprised that a culture, which is packaged, managed, defined, and created by the entertainment industry, will target the lowest common denominator in public taste? For those who care about culture, the signals are clear.

How many of today's motion pictures truly elevate the human spirit? How many simply indulge the worst instincts of humanity? How many merely reflect the personal and bizarre outlooks of writers and directors with no relationship to reality? If old Hollywood presented an idealized version of our lives, today's Hollywood presents a view that is warped and distorted. It offers pathologies as reality, and with its huge budgets, marketing skills, and star power, persuades the gullible among us to accept its point of view. Anita Loos was a legendary writer of books and screenplays for decades. She was the author of the classic satire *Gentlemen Prefer Blondes* and countless screenplays for films such as *San Francisco*. No fan of many of the newer films, she recognized that the new Hollywood would turn even a fairy tale on its ear. She suggested that a modern day *Cinderella* would star Barbra Streisand and Dustin Hoffman; instead of an elegant gown and stunning coiffure, La Streisand would be rolled in cinders and don a fright wig, she would not end up living happily ever after with Prince Charming in a castle, but in an East Village pad of the hero, complete with cigar and chronic drug habit. She concluded, "I think life would be more sane and certainly less guilt-ridden if present day humanity were required to wash their mouths out with soap and practice a little good, old-fashioned mid-Victorian hypocrisy."[147] Philip Dunne was an accomplished screenwriter, director, and producer of many classic films. He was a man of principle and a master of elegant dialogue. Dunne said, "We say and show things on the screen we couldn't say or show before and probably shouldn't. Instead of meeting girl, boy now rapes girl and the hero's shining coat of mail has been replaced by a dirty undershirt." [148]

Nor is the problem exclusively American. June Dally-Watkins was an icon in the world of fashion, especially in her native Australia. Once the most photographed model in Australia, she became one of her country's most celebrated business women, establishing the first personal development school in the southern hemisphere. More than sixty years later, over 300,000 students have passed through her schools in Australia and Hong Kong; she remained a widely quoted expert on fashion, etiquette, and personal behavior. In her memoir, *Still Smiling,* she wrote bluntly of the trends in today's high tech celebrity pop culture, describing an increasing decline in speech and grammar, manners, etiquette, dress, and behavior. She said, "Today people seem less inclined to be the best, preferring to look as though they haven't made an effort." She observed correctly that "Advertisers battle for our minds. People increasingly find their gods in celebrities, violence, sex, and drugs. Fashion and young people follow these dubious role models." "Miss Dally," as she was widely known, was also concerned about the decline in manners and personal communication. As for the youngest among us, she wrote, "I have named them the 'me' generation — they seem only concerned with themselves. There is a lack of consideration for others. They are bereft of face-to-face connection. They are glued to their ears. They text message rather than talk. They watch too much television. There are so many bad influences out there promoting bad language, violence, sex and inappropriate dress. Young people are encouraged to believe this is the way to be accepted by their peers. I try to encourage our students not to be followers. They should decide themselves what is right and wrong, good or bad, beautiful or ugly." She concluded, "Many don't understand having good manners simply means being kind, thoughtful, and considerate to other human beings."

As for interest in real art, past or present, the perspective of the entertainment industry is laughable. As for interest in entertainment, the attitude of the industry is deficient. While the entertainment industry has its critics, and they are legion, few critics focus on a fundamental problem facing men and women of taste and talent within the industry today. What has happened to the audience for recordings, concerts, television programs, plays, and motion pictures? Alex Wainer, who teaches communication and media classes at Palm Beach Atlantic University, raised this issue effectively in an article, "No Singing, No Dancing."[149] Wainer provided an answer for his own question, "Whatever happened to the movie musical?" Wainer correctly observes, "The generation that had produced the films of Hollywood's "Golden Age" had lost its ability to reach the public with entertaining films of broad appeal—in part because the public itself had changed. In taking over, the new Hollywood generation turned the values of old Hollywood on its head—and that included the rejection of what was viewed as the phony, studio-bound unreality of traditional romance film." The moguls who founded the film industry were skilled in the ruthless tactics of their business, however, and often had the sixth sense of showmen who knew what the public wanted. Newer generations of filmmakers, often including the children and grandchildren of successful producers, grew up in a different environment. They did not share the gratitude their predecessors felt toward America for providing them a home and an opportunity to become successful beyond their wildest dreams. Instead, the newer and younger producers saw our society not as one to be admired, but one to be rejected and against which they sought to rebel. This sense of rebellion, of course, did not prevent them from zealously pursuing their profits.

Once there was a consensus that pervaded both the entertainment industry and our society as to what would be acceptable on the screen. Alex Wainer correctly concludes, "The cultural revolution of the last few decades, though, has ended the cultural consensus once reflected by the film musical. The restraint once imposed on studios is long shattered and filmmakers have reveled in their freedom to seek out and destroy, in the name of art, anything that could be considered a boundary. The audience, with few qualms, has relished the results like children let loose in a candy shop." What is the fate of the movie musical? Wainer declares, "If the classic movie musical is essentially restrained romance given flamboyant expression, its return must wait for someone who believes in it." That "someone," of course, is a new audience, and it will not appear by accident.

What Wainer has written about musicals and Hollywood's tycoons is true about all other forms of entertainment as well. It is not enough simply to aim well-deserved criticism at the bosses of the entertainment industry. If audiences didn't buy tickets to their productions, they would change their products in a hurry. If audiences didn't pitch tents to camp out on the parking lot of an auditorium to insure their admission to hear the caterwauling of today's talentless rock stars, the concert promoters would find something else to promote faster than you can say "Bring on the ear plugs!" In 1990, Steve Allen addressed the behavior of the industry in a newspaper column. Allen described much of today's popular entertainment as "vulgarians addressing barbarians." Allen said, "Marketplace factors are already largely responsible for having thoroughly debased popular music, a billion-dollar industry since the tastes of poorly educated teenagers with discretionary income dominate the field. Most of today's punk and heavy-metal lovers have yet to even hear such names as George Gershwin, Cole Porter, and Richard Rodgers. Forget Ludwig van Beethoven." This situation is far worse today, years after Allen sounded his warning trumpet.

So merely appealing for changes within the entertainment industry will not be enough. It will be necessary, through education, energy, and singular inspiration, to change the nature of the audience for their products. If an audience consists primarily of adolescents driven by a need to be popular with each other and adults trying to look, behave, and sound like adolescents, the result will be a predictable disaster. Any attempts to change the effect of the entertainment industry on our society will have to be twofold: fostering new creative efforts that thrive outside the Hollywood-New York entertainment axis, and building an audience receptive for entertainment that fosters excitement and imagination within traditional standards.

We shouldn't assume that such an audience does not exist. Many potential members of today's audiences have never seen anything but the entertainment products that are heavily promoted today. Building a new audience will take time, but it is well worth the effort. The industry is concerned with quantity, not with quality. They live in their own little world, superficially glamorous, but in reality, a cross between a gang street fight and the arenas of ancient Rome. Charles Vidor, a prominent film director, once sued Harry Cohn, the powerful boss of Columbia Pictures in the 1940s and 50s. Vidor tried to use Cohn's "profane, obscenely abusive language" to get out of his contract. The judge who ruled against Vidor decided that Hollywood had its own rules or lack of them, and that people who thrived in the industry essentially eschewed the values that govern the rest of us. He described the atmosphere as "a fictitious, fabulous, topsy-turvy, temperamental world that is peculiar to their way of life." He concluded, "Their standards are not my standards. Let them be judged by those people of decency who inhabit their world of fantasy and fiction." What the judge said all those years ago remains true today. Many fine and talented people toil in the Hollywood vineyards. But those in control in Hollywood are clearly part of the problem and unlikely to be part of the solution.

THE FUTURE: WHERE WE ARE GOING

ON FRIDAY JANUARY 12, 2007, a man entered the L'Enfant Plaza Metro Station in Washington, D.C. Thousands of people were hurrying through the station during morning rush hour on that cold January day. The man wore jeans, a T-shirt, and a baseball cap, and he carried a violin case. He positioned himself near an escalator, took out the violin, put a few dollars and some change into the hat to give the passing commuters a suggestion, and began to play. The violinist played rather challenging music, including Bach's demanding *Chaconne in D Minor*. He continued to play for almost forty-five minutes.

Gene Weingarten, writing about the episode in the *Washington Post*,[150] expressed the dilemma of those passing by. "Each passerby had a quick choice to make, one familiar to commuters in any urban area where the occasional street performer is part of the cityscape: Do you stop and listen? Do you hurry past with a blend of guilt and irritation, aware of your cupidity but annoyed by the unbidden demand on your time and your wallet? Do you throw in a buck, just to be polite? Does your decision change if he's really bad? What if he's really good? Do you have time for beauty? Shouldn't you? What's the moral mathematics of the moment?"

For most passersby, the answer was simple. They ignored the violinist. After four minutes, a woman threw money into the hat, but didn't stop to listen. Several small children were intrigued by the violinist and his music, but in each case, their parents turned their heads away and continued to move forward. Only a half dozen people stopped to listen for a moment and when he finished playing, the violinist had collected $32 from twenty-seven people who had tossed money into the hat, but didn't bother to stop or listen.

The incident wasn't as simple as it seemed. It had been planned by the *Washington Post*. The violinist, who left the station ignored and without applause, was Joshua Bell, an internationally recognized concert violinist. Two days earlier, audiences bought every seat in a Boston auditorium, paying up to $100 a ticket to hear Bell. His violin was a $3.5 million dollar instrument made by the legendary Antonio Stradivari. Years earlier, it had been twice stolen from a previous owner, the famed virtuoso Bronislaw Huberman. Over a thousand people, some of whom would have stood in line to buy tickets to one of Bell's concerts, ignored the violinist and his music.

Gene Weingarten won a Pulitzer Prize for his description of the episode, which raises a plethora of troubling questions. The incident was also described in an anonymous letter on the Internet, concluding: "If we do not have a moment to stop and listen to one of the best musicians in the world, playing some of the finest music ever written, with one of the most beautiful instruments ever made, how many other things are we missing as we rush through life?"

The Joshua Bell episode is not isolated. (Weingarten and Bell were surprised to learn that a similar experiment had produced similar results in 1930, with renowned violinist Jacques Gordon playing in front of a Chicago subway station.) But unlike commuters in the 1930s, today's audiences are faced with a far greater array of influences competing for public attention. Nor is the problem limited to just classical music. It resonates with all musicians, writers, and artists whose work requires patience and attention on the part of an audience. Randall Sandke is an internationally respected jazz trumpeter, composer, and historian. In his book, *Where the Dark and the Light Folks Meet,*[151] he poses an important and troubling question. Sandke writes, "The real question for the future of jazz is: will people accustomed to the kind of interactive recreation provided by the Internet be willing to sit long enough to take in and appreciate the intricacies of jazz? Will jazz go the route of the epic novel or poem, cultural remnants of a slower paced era that prized contemplative solitude? Today, most people experience music while multitasking: working, taking care of children, exercising, or serious engagement. Are people today as equipped to internalize further developments as they once were?"

In the 21st century, people are in a hurry. They're rushing around, scrambling about, tweeting, twittering, grabbing their cell phones, clutching their iPads, often doing three or four or twenty-four things at once. E-mails go anywhere in the world in seconds. A few years ago, only birds twittered. Google was once a comic strip character. Amazon was a river in South America. No one had ever heard of eBay, Wikipedia, Facebook, Instagram, or TikTok, and "The Web" was spun by a wise spider in E.B. White's famous children's book, *Charlotte's Web.* Now everyone twitters and tweets. The best of times and the worst of times are now on YouTube.

How did this happen?

A NATION OF HARES

We all know the story of the Hare and the Tortoise. The speedy hare and the slow, plodding tortoise, compete in a race. The hare quickly takes the lead. Confident of his blinding speed, he stops to take a nap. Meanwhile, the tortoise, patient and determined, keeps going and passes the sleeping hare. By the time the hare awakens, it is too late. This classic Aesop's fable teaches us "slow and steady wins the race."

In many ways, we have become a nation of hares, worshipping speed as the only laudable virtue. We do what we do in a perpetual hurry. "Multitasking" has become the norm. We assume that we can do several jobs at once and that each will be done with the same care and quality. We also minimize the importance of tasks that cannot be accomplished quickly. But where are we actually going and what are we actually accomplishing? Maggie Jackson offers an answer to these questions in her book, *Distraction.*[152] She presents disturbing evidence. The average information worker switches tasks every three minutes throughout a workday. One-third of high school and college students juggle five to eight media while studying. Maggie Jackson says, "We flip between people and tasks, layer the moment, keep one eye on the road." All of this occurs in what she terms a culture of mobility and portability.

We even eat in a hurry. The term "fast food" has become as American as apple pie. The American way of eating has unfortunately failed to follow the advice of Robert Louis Stevenson, who said, "He who sews hurry reaps indigestion." In 1986, Carlo Petrini, an Italian writer specializing in food and wine, founded "Slow Food" as a response to the opening of a fast food restaurant in Rome. In *Slow Food Nation,*[153] Petrini writes, "The increasing speed of the world, which imposes on us ever-accelerating rhythms of life, work, and thought, accentuates the existing distortions, and the complexity around us threatens to overwhelm us. Since speed has become the dogma of modern life, we are compelled for the sake of our survival not to think too much and to discard anything that seems to slow us down. Moreover, the consumer society merely justifies the creation of new 'garbage'; it justifies waste and the discarding of anything that seems unproductive or 'slow.' Anything that is of no use (people, cultures, countries) is rejected." Petrini urges gastronomes to pursue a quest for slowness, encountering the finer things of life, which are often discarded because they do not conform to the world's idea of pace and speed. Petrini makes observations about fast food that can also be applied to the fast life and fast culture.

The "slow food" movement did not go away. In 2021, Alice Waters, a prominent chef, restaurateur, and Vice-President of Slow Food International, wrote a new book with Bob Carrau and Cristina Mueller, *We Are What We Eat: A Slow Food Manifesto.*

Waters wrote that the fast food culture prioritizes cheapness, availability, and speed, ruining not only our health but also dehumanizing the way we live and relate to one another. She praised values such as beauty, simplicity, and value in work. "When we force ourselves to slow down," she says, "the world comes into focus."

Waters' views on food are equally applicable to the arts. She writes, "Beauty is expressed in myriad ways in our lives through art, poetry, music, architecture, and dance . . . It naturally deepens your awareness and inspires a sense of awe and joy." She likes keeping things simple. She says, "Valuing simplicity is about cherishing the elemental. It fosters clarity, helping us cut through the confusion of our world, weed out the extraneous and the false, in order to see and connect with what's basic, authentic, and true."

As we move forward in life with an increasing number of technological innovations, it is imperative that we remember to slow down and smell the roses; otherwise, we may wake up one day and find that there are no more roses to appreciate.

Unless you are entered in the Indianapolis 500, speed is not a virtue unto itself. In the process of doing everything faster or doing six things at once, something is lost along the way. Sometimes what is lost is more important than what is gained. Winston Churchill said, "Men occasionally stumble over the truth, but most of them pick themselves up and hurry off as if nothing had happened." Truth, accuracy, taste, style, beauty, logic, and just plain common sense can be most uncommon as we forget that the tortoise, not the hare, ultimately won the race.

One reason why we are so often in a hurry to form opinions, make judgments and decisions, and leap before we look is that our national attention span has declined. This didn't happen in a moment, but gradually, evolving (or perhaps devolving) through a series of changes in technology. These technological changes have always been a double-edged sword. They provide incredible blessings and fascinating challenges, but also unplanned and unanticipated consequences. The demise of travel by horse and buggy made it possible for people and information to travel at previously unimaginable speeds. But it also resulted in traffic jams, morning rush hour, drunk drivers, a dependence on gasoline, a plethora of unemployed horses, and perhaps worst of all, teenagers behind the wheel.

Radio brought a box into everyone's living room and suddenly voices from afar became as familiar as members of the family. Radio was an entertainment medium, but it turned the worlds of news and advertising upside down. It also changed history. Can we underestimate the impact on history of the reassuring words of Franklin Roosevelt (delivered in a voice that was made for radio) or the eloquent defiance of Winston Churchill promising "We will never surrender"?

Radio was an aural medium, not a visual one. Like readers, people who listened to the radio would use their mind's eye to see things. They would imagine how people looked, what they were doing or where they were doing it. Readers of a good book would see *The Three Musketeers* or *Sherlock Holmes* through their imagination. Sometimes their imagination would get the best of them. Thousands of people thought of Sherlock Holmes as a real person. (There is a well-known literary society, the Baker Street Irregulars, which is purportedly founded on the assumption that Holmes was real and that Doyle was merely his "literary agent." The Irregulars have great fun with this and it is likely that more than one will be sending the author of this book a letter in mock outrage, denouncing the implication that Holmes was a fictional character.) But there were admirers of Holmes around the world whose view of Holmes as real was not declared with whimsy. Sir Arthur Conan Doyle said that he received countless letters addressed to Sherlock Holmes, some containing marriage proposals. Listeners to popular radio programs during the 1930s and '40s would have been shocked to see that some of their favorite voices belonged to people who didn't look the way they imagined them. A demure, fragile young ingénue might actually be the grandmother of such a girl, while a muscular superhero or flint-eyed marshal with a fast gun might be a homely, ineffectual looking fellow wearing a tweed jacket, horn-rimmed glasses, and a bow tie. But in the last half of the 20th century, everything changed. The new technological innovations were visual media. Of greatest importance was not what we read or heard, but what we could see. As a result, we became a nation of screens. Let's look at how three technological innovations changed communications forever. For the better? Don't make a quick judgment.

THE TUBE: A WORLD ON SCREENS

Technology has driven the changes that affect us all. When silent films became talkies, actors were suddenly judged by their voices as well as their appearance. Radio journalists of the World

War II era often had memorable speaking voices. But television placed an emphasis on appearance. When televisions appeared in nearly every American household in the 1950s, everything from politics to purchasing habits, from the music we hear to the people we admire changed forever. The advent of 24-hour cable news channels changed the way news is covered. Cable television revolutionized the broadcasting industry, because whole channels could be dedicated to a specific market. If a viewer wanted to watch sports or programs on cooking all day long, his wish would be granted with a click of the remote control. As always, the cable revolution was a mixed blessing. Viewers were offered many choices. Not all were constructive. MTV emerged as a huge influence in pop music, and suddenly the sounds and values of Hollywood's rock-pop-rap music industry could be in every living room, with or without the approval of parents. In music, there are dozens of aspiring superstars who can't sing or play. Parents have placed enormous financial resources in the hands of their children. So broadcasters are frequently obsessed with appealing to a market dominated by teen and post-teen viewers. All changes are not bad. Technology (i.e., cable television) decentralized the television industry. No one is more nostalgic for a return to the days when three networks based in New York controlled television news than executives of the three networks. Competition is good, even if the networks don't like it.

People may be reading less, but they are clearly spending a significant amount of time in front of screens, especially television and computer screens. Television plays a key role in determining what we think is important and what we regard as insignificant. Television has its critics, like William J. Bennett, for instance, who wrote, "It makes an enormous difference, for example, whether children get messages from television telling them that honesty is the best policy, and to honor their fathers and mothers—or messages telling them that adultery is the norm, and that the breakup of a family is an expected thing." Nevertheless, television also has its defenders, like Jib Fowles, author of *Television Viewers vs. Media Snobs.*[154] Fowles holds a doctorate in "Media Ecology." In

Fowles' world, television is a constructive influence on society. He even includes a chapter in his book entitled, "Television is Good for Your Children." For Jib Fowles, critics of television are "media snobs" whose elite view of culture causes them to overlook the positive benefits of television (and presumably, the pop culture it dispenses). He declares, "The fears of Media Snobs are premised on the notion that television primarily shoots improprieties into young, uninformed minds." Clearly, television is a medium that can be used for good or ill. If children are watching Leonard Bernstein's "Young People's Concerts" or a good dramatization of a Dickens novel, television may indeed be good for them. But what examples does Fowles cite? He says, approvingly, "One thing they learn is some vocabulary. The toddler who says, 'frosted flakes,' 'rub-out,' 'Triple Crown' and 'Yabba-dabba-doo' has been an apt pupil." Indeed, and as this toddler grows up, he will undoubtedly continue to derive a sense of what is important and unimportant from the people who decide what we watch on television, whether broadcast, streamed, or delivered via cable. He may grow into an adult who is perceived by society as successful, but whose cultural frame of reference is woefully limited.

Ben Berger, an associate professor of political science at Swarthmore College, has written a book addressing many of these issues, *Attention Deficit Democracy: The Paradox of Civic Engagement.*[155] Berger argues that the decline in attention span, fostered and stimulated by television, produces citizens who are disinterested in the serious challenges that face us all. He writes, "Heavy TV viewing produces heavy TV viewers, not to mention ones who tend to be inattentive, lazy, gluttonous, and unpopular." As evidence, Berger offers studies like the 2010 report in *Archives of Pediatrics and Adolescent Medicine* which reports a direct correlation between time spent watching television and decreases in classroom engagement, math achievement, and physical activity. This change in attention span even affects the length of camera shots in motion pictures. Writing in *National Review,* Berger observes, "The average shot length of American movies stood at 27.9 seconds in 1953, just after TV began its ascent, fell to 7.3

seconds in 1986 as MTV gradually took hold, and was 2.5 seconds in 2007. TV programs have followed a similar path." Berger then asks, "Who among us, having once seen '*The Electric Company*' as a child, could go back to watching *Mister Rogers*?"

Consider the results of a poll conducted by Jericho Communications and reported in the *Washington Times*. Barely 6 percent of Fortune 1000 CEOs surveyed watched all three presidential debates between George W. Bush and Al Gore. Their decisions (and what they consider important) go far beyond the immediate day-to-day issues affecting their businesses. No, knowledge of current events or the arts isn't a requirement to be a successful executive. Most professional intellectuals (including many devoted to the arts) would be terrible executives. But a broad cultural perspective can hardly hurt one's judgment. And there is nothing more deadly in the culture than a commercially successful ignoramus, especially one who thinks he knows what is important.

Advocates for the television industry are quick to dismiss their critics as an elite group of "media snobs" who think entertainment shouldn't be fun and secretly want the television set to be used to dispense their own brand of intellectual amusement. They forget that the television industry is driven by ratings. Survival depends upon popular approval. So the industry is obsessed with giving the public "what it wants." Television producers are hired to anticipate the tastes and inclinations of the public. But while they insist that they are merely following the public's tastes, they are often determining and designing those tastes. Entertainment executives are often quick to insist that they merely reflect a public taste that is already established. But more often than not, they unleash a huge, highly skilled, and financially overwhelming marketing machine to persuade the public what it should want, and what it should like. The result is a symbiotic relationship. The television executive decides what the public should think is important; the public thinks something is important if it appears on television. The result may be a blissfully ignorant CEO of a media conglomerate, who may be determining which books are published, which movies are made, which music is recorded, and, of course, which television producers are hired to start the cycle all over again.

We constantly underestimate the power of television to determine what merits our attention. Suppose a television network executive decided to devote two hours per night, five nights a week, promoting the lieder of Franz Schubert (or the operettas of Gilbert and Sullivan or repeated performances of *Yes, We Have No Bananas.*) Can we doubt for a moment that large segments of the public would become enamored of these works? Or that these same audience members would be convinced that they had come to such conclusions entirely on their own? (Nor can we doubt that such an executive would be fired quickly and would be given a one-way ticket to oblivion by his bosses, whose parting words would be, "You'll never work in this town again.")

If works of quality are given exposure, they may achieve a widespread popularity. Would fans of Schubert overwhelm those of Cardi B? It is most unlikely. But when anything, from the sublime to the ridiculous, is placed upon the public stage, paraded about the public square, it achieves in the mind of the public an importance, a significance, that cannot be denied. This explains why people place videos of themselves engaged in the most outlandish behavior on the Internet.

When a video is said to go "viral," the subject, for better or worse, is turned into an instant celebrity. The point is that we live in a world in which a significant portion of the population equates quality with exposure. Many people also assume that lack of media exposure implies insignificance. But what about the corporate CEOs who are more familiar with the personality quirks of Bart Simpson and the cast of *Survivor* than those of the Secretary of State? Certainly, the President's cabinet doesn't suffer from lack of media exposure. The problem is that while the Secretary of State may get media exposure, our society truly values the icons of pop culture. Celebrity, not achievement, is the standard. While government officials (or truly gifted musicians) may appear on television, they are not the icons of pop culture, which begins with

Professor Fowles' toddlers learning their vocabulary from television. Ask a typical teenager which media "superstar" wore one glove, and he will likely know that the answer is "Michael Jackson." Ask a typical teenage girl about what reality television and social media pop star Kim Kardashian was wearing last week and she will probably know to the last detail. But ask them about the true "superstars" of our culture, those who contributed the most to the arts, and you will find yourself facing blank stares.

The defenders of the all-pervasive pop culture say, "What do you expect? They'll have plenty of time to learn about Duke Ellington or Benny Goodman later. They'll have years to learn to appreciate Chopin and Debussy. They're just teenagers and they'll outgrow their tastes of the moment." Really? Or will they turn into successful individuals who know about Bart Simpson and *Survivor*, but remain ignorant of anything not blessed by the entertainment industry? A T-shirt featuring the image of the cartoon character "Bart Simpson" also featured the words "under achiever and proud of it." It is sad that, in today's pop culture, the underachiever may be running the company and concurrently, defining the culture itself.

It is almost impossible to overestimate the influence of television in modern life. The television set has become a member of most families and in some cases, has replaced traditional family members as the primary influence in a household. The U.S. Bureau of Labor Statistics reports that Americans spend about half their leisure time watching television. The A.C. Nielsen Company, which measures the television ratings that govern the survival of commercial television programs, advises us that the average American watches more than four hours of television daily. That comes to two months of nonstop TV-watching per year, so a sixty-five-year-old man or woman will have spent nine years viewing television programs. Nor is this an exclusively American phenomenon. London's *The Daily Mail* reports in 2011 that Great Britain's "Mr. Average" spends eleven years of his entire life in front of the television screen.

The Washington, DC-based TV-Free America has also compiled statistics on the ubiquitous television set and its viewers. Ninety-nine percent of American homes have at least one television, and 66 percent have at least three. Fifty-six percent of Americans also pay for cable television service and Americans rent six million videos each year. Television affects every aspect of family life. For instance, in many homes, the idea of families sitting down to dinner together and talking over the events of the day is a thing of the past. Two-thirds of Americans watch television while having dinner. In a survey of four to six-year-olds, small children were asked to choose between watching television and spending time with their fathers. Fifty-four percent chose the television set. Meaningful conversation between parents and children is reported as 3.5 minutes per day, but meaningful television time is measured at 1680 minutes daily. Parents who place their children in day care may not realize that 70 percent of day care outlets offer television. Children do spend time in school, but consider the fact that the average American youth spends 900 hours in school, but 1500 hours in front of the television set annually.

Adults also spend many hours in front of the television set, as well as a variety of other screens, including computer monitors and cell phones. The Center for Media Design at Ball State University completed a study of adult time spent in front of screens, including televisions. According to this study, adult Americans spent as much as eight hours a day in front of screens, five hours of which is spent in front of a television set.

Statistics may be boring, but they, consistently demonstrate that television is incredibly influential. Now not all television programming represents a deleterious influence. There is a difference between watching Leonard Bernstein's "Young People's Concerts" and MTV. There is a difference between watching outstanding dramas, documentaries, or quality entertainment and trash. Television technology, like all forms of technology, depends upon the user and the creator. A gun isn't the same in the hands of a bank robber or a police officer, a terrorist or a U.S. Marine. A computer may be a tool for good in the hands of a teacher, but an instrument for ill in the hands of a predator. But how much of the television programs that children and adults of all ages watch are really constructive? Clearly, an hour spent watching educational television may be more constructive than an hour spent reading a tabloid newspaper delivering the latest gossip. But the sad truth is that the non-reader isn't likely to be spending his television or computer time constructively either. Of course, there is nothing wrong with being entertained, but we should be aware that entertainment delivers both messages and their consequences.

Television, which once broadcast classical and popular music of quality, now demands music that can be absorbed quickly, at high volume, and with little attention. The current rock-pop-rap charlatans are made to order: a loud amplified beat, puerile lyrics, and vocalists who all sound alike. As for news coverage, the sound bite too often replaces substance. Television has also totally altered the way political campaigns are conducted. In 1960, the first debate between John F. Kennedy and Richard M. Nixon profoundly affected the presidential election. Many observers believe to this day that Nixon won the debate in the ears of radio listeners, while Kennedy triumphed in the eyes of television viewers. Every four years we are given breathless coverage of so-called "great debates" among candidates for the presidency. But there is usually nothing great about these encounters, which are not true debates, but joint press conferences. Real debates, like those conducted by Abraham Lincoln and Stephen Douglas, would require both time and attention. Today, too many audiences possess neither, so should we be surprised that political candidates or television producers are willing and eager to address them in high-speed superficiality?

The ability to communicate well on television is now essential to political success. Just as radio was tailor-made for the voice of Franklin D. Roosevelt, television seemed to have been invented for Ronald Reagan. Could anyone have been a more effective communicator than President Reagan, who established a personal rapport with audiences that watched him on television? Reagan modestly said that it was not great communication, but great ideas that resonated with the American electorate. But in the years following the Reagan era, candidates must prove they can not only take valid political positions; they must successfully communicate them to audiences on television. Television once seemed not only ubiquitous, but likely to last in its traditional form forever. In the 21st century, digital platforms such as YouTube and various streaming services have challenged the traditional television industry. But the principle is the same and massive amounts of time spent in front of screens continue. Then came another revolution, led to some degree by a device that looked like a children's toy and was named after a rodent.

THE MOUSE IN THE HOUSE: THE PARADOX OF TECHNOLOGY

On November 17, 1970, inventor Douglas Engelbart received a patent for an invention called X-Y Indicator for a Display System. No one could have guessed at the time that this invention would change the world. Seven years earlier, Engelbart, working at the Stanford Research Institute, developed the prototype for his invention, which was built by his colleague Bill English. Early models, which detected two-dimensional motion for use in computing had cords attached to the rear portion of the device. The cords resembled the tail of a mouse, so Engelbart's invention became known as "the mouse."

Ironically, Engelbart's patent expired before he could reap the considerable rewards of his imagination. In the commercial world, the use of the mouse seemed improbable and revolutionary. It empowered the user to control a GUI, or Graphic User Interface, on a monitor screen connected to a computer. Although Xerox first marketed computers using the mouse, business marketing experts scoffed. Such a device might interest someone playing games, but one could hardly imagine people sitting in offices using something called "a mouse" that looked like a toy. In 1984, the new upstart company, Apple Computer, launched its Macintosh model, and the mouse took over the world.

PC columnist John Dvorak joined the ranks of those who had ridiculed Thomas Edison and Henry Ford when he declared, "There is no evidence that people want to use these things." In 21st century America, it is hard to find a house without a mouse.

Today, we live our lives under the direction of a chorus of beeps, squeaks, and digital noises. We use cell phones with ringtones, carry tiny video cameras around in our pockets, and many felt deprived without a high tech device named after a fruit (The Blackberry). iPods, iPads, iPhones and computers of every shape and size govern our every action. The telephone, once used only to make telephone calls, has become a constant companion with a staggering menu of services, entertainment, and storage capabilities. The ensemble of equipment upon which we depend has become a computerized orchestra playing a song to which everyone dances. (This is not just an indulgence in colorful phraseology. Traditional musical instruments and the musicians who play them are challenged daily by digital controllers that produce the sounds of everything from a symphony orchestra or jazz band to the deafening amplified cacophony that masquerades as pop music.) The high tech world and the mouse in the house have had a revolutionary impact on our culture. But has it been a constructive impact?

In the early years of the 20th century, one could imagine a high school student sitting on the front porch, reading his way through a six-hundred-page copy of *Moby Dick*, Herman Melville's saga of Captain Ahab's search for the great white whale. He might be imagining himself surviving in the cold, salty ocean air off the New England coast or merely feeling frustrated that his teacher hadn't assigned a nice short story instead of this vast literary tome. With each new invention of consequence, the way in which this student confronted *Moby Dick* would change. Radio brought him the voice of great actors like Orson Welles reading and portraying great literature over the air. Motion pictures and television added pictures, and he could experience *Moby Dick* through Ray Bradbury's adaptation of Melville's words brought to the screen by director John Huston. Today, he can sit in front of a computer and download the entire text of *Moby Dick* with a mouse click. But then what? That is precisely the question.

Matt Richtel addresses this issue in the *New York Times*, writing about those students who are "growing up digital, wired for distraction." He profiles Vishal Singh, a bright seventeen-year-old high school student who in two months has only read forty-three pages of his summer reading assignment, Kurt Vonnegut's *Cat's Cradle*. Vishal prefers Facebook, YouTube, and making digital videos. He has decided to pursue a career as a filmmaker because of his online experience. But as he approaches his senior year of high school, he has yet to finish the only book he has been assigned to read at home. Vishal explains, "On YouTube you can get a whole story in six minutes. A book takes so long. I prefer the immediate gratification." Richtel reminds us that researchers have suggested that as young brains become accustomed to quickly switching tasks, they are less able to sustain attention.

Matt Richtel also visited a school district which has invested a small fortune in equipment, all with the hope of improving student achievement. In the 21st century, we are often told that we can solve the problems of poor academic achievements simply by adding shiny new ensembles of high-tech equipment to the classroom. But consider the example of schools in the Kyrene School District in Arizona. Richtel reports on the high-tech gamble and its impact on a seventh-grade English class in the *New York Times*. He says, "In this technology-centric classroom, students are bent over laptops, some blogging or building Facebook pages from the perspective of Shakespeare's characters. One student compiles a song list from the Internet, picking a tune by the rapper Kanye West to express the emotions of Shakespeare's lovelorn Silvius."[156] For some reason, these experiments calling for students to express themselves always begin with the noble intentions of learning about Beethoven or Shakespeare, but they always seem to end with the student exploring rock music or playing video games.

Not everyone is impressed by this 21st century approach to *As You Like It*. Consider the words of David P. Goldman, an investment banker who also writes about and teaches music history and theory. He thunders, "What about trying to understand what Shakespeare actually said? At my kids' Waldorf school, the seventh-graders performed *Twelfth Night* in costume, alternating major roles so that all of them had to memorize a couple of hundred lines of the Bard. They learned about the characters by acting the roles, that is, reading the play through the eyes of its author." Goldman suggests that the Chinese show more interest in our cultural heritage than we do. He says, "They are embracing the best of our culture in vast numbers while we let it gather dust in the attic," and concludes, "If you want your kid to compete, throw out the video games, block the Internet, and start the music lessons."

In the Kyrene School District, the new approach to Shakespeare, music, and everything else is a by-product of a $33 million investment in a vast array of computers, screens, and high- tech wizardry expected to transform the way seventh- graders learn. Matt Richtel continues, "The digital push here aims to go far beyond gadgets to transform the very nature of the classroom, turning the teacher into a guide instead of a lecturer, wandering among students who learn at their own pace on Internet-connected devices." The teacher in this particular classroom, Amy Furman, is described as dedicated and bubbly, "devouring young adult novels to stay in touch with her students." Unfortunately, English and math scores have been stagnant in the district. Down the hall, Sharon Smith, a social studies teacher, engaged her students by asking them to answer a true or false question. Was Jefferson Davis a commander in the Union Army? The students were delighted when their answers popped up on a high-tech screen. But when 23 percent thought the Confederate President belonged in a blue uniform, the equipment didn't improve their answers. The classrooms are full of students interacting with technically impressive gadgets.

But are the results impressive? As students gain greater access to equipment, they are getting less access to teachers. Not everyone is enthusiastic about the new emphasis on students "engaged" with equipment. Randy Yerrick, Associate Dean of

Educational Technology at the University of Buffalo, says, "Engagement is a 'fluffy term' that can slide past critical analysis. Yerrik defers to Stanford University Professor Larry Cuban, who insists that an environment of constant novelty cannot be sustained, simply to keep children engaged. Computers and digital media may indeed capture the interest of students more easily than old-fashioned books, memorization, and writing on paper. But if they don't master the content of their lessons, their medium of study will be irrelevant. Too often, the new high-tech equipment becomes an excuse for the students to express themselves without having very much to express. After his visit to Arizona, Matt Richtel concludes, "There are times in Kyrene when the technology seems to allow students to disengage from learning: They are left at computers to perform a task but wind up playing around, suggesting, as some researchers have found, that computers can distract and not instruct." Instruction, not distraction, must be the goal.

If results are the true test of new teaching methods throughout the country, we do not have reason to be optimistic. In 2011, the College Board, the nonprofit organization that administers the Scholastic Aptitude Test, reported discouraging results of the college-entrance exam administered to 1.6 million students. The College Board sets a benchmark predicting the extent to which students taking the test will succeed in college. Only 43 percent of students posted a score suggesting a high degree of success in college. A student who scored 1550 on the test out of a possible 2400 would be expected to have a 65 percent chance of getting a B-average in his freshman year. The average reading and writing scores were the lowest ever recorded, hardly the result expected by those who have promised educational miracles through increased expenditures and high-tech equipment. Results of the 2011 ACT college-entrance exam were no less discouraging. Only 25 percent of high school graduates taking the test appear to be ready for higher education. *The Chronicle of Higher Education* reported that "A minority of high-school students who took the ACT college-entrance exam and graduated in 2011 met the ACT's minimum scores for college readiness in all four of these core areas: English, mathematics, reading, and science." Jim Montoya, a vice-president of the College Board, told *The Wall Street Journal*, "At the precise time the importance of a college degree is increasing, the ability of the U.S. to compete in a global economy is decreasing,"

Every new revolution in technology has brought blessings and problems. The triumph of the automobile over the horse-drawn buggy meant faster transportation and industrial growth, but also traffic jams at morning rush hour and skylines of smog. Television has made it possible for a viewer in his living room to move vicariously around the world and even watch scenes on the moon. The small screen can bring the news of the world as well as great music and drama into your home. It also can provide a gateway to some of the most puerile, obnoxious programs one could possibly imagine. The computer has provided a similar revolution. Changes in recording technology have been unpredictable and incredible. The long-playing record gave way to the CD and one can now carry around a small, boxed set of discs containing all nine symphonies of Beethoven. The advent of computer technology means that the Beethoven nine can be downloaded onto a device that can be carried anywhere in your pocket.

Vast amounts of information are available with the click of a mouse. The Internet, like television before it, offers of cornucopia of possibilities. Do you want to explore great works of art? You don't have to go to New York, Washington, DC, London, Paris, Amsterdam, or Madrid. Right from your home or office, you can take virtual tours of the Metropolitan Museum, the National Gallery, the British Museum, the Louvre, the Rijksmuseum, or the Prado. Do you want to listen to great music? You can download great performances of the complete piano works of Frederic Chopin and actual scores that you can study while you're listening. Do you prefer jazz? There are video clips of the greatest jazz artists, some of which have been rescued from oblivion, from early recordings and ancient black and white kinescopes from the early days of television, all yours for the asking. Great literature, anyone?

Thousands of classic books have been digitized and are available online. The contents of several of the world's great libraries are yours for the asking. Of course, the Internet has also enabled pornography, the hate speech of bigots, and the propositions of scoundrels who could sell the Brooklyn Bridge and probably have done so more than once. We all know technology itself is neither good nor bad. This is determined only in the way it is used. A weapon in the hands of a police officer is very different from a weapon in the hands of someone trying to rob a bank.

But the advent of the Internet has changed our lives in way far different from other technological revolutions. A child watching television or listening to the radio is essentially passive. But radio stirred the imagination in a way that television does not. The child listening to the radio would exercise his imagination in the same way he would if he were reading a book. But the computer offers interactive technology, so the child becomes not only a participant, but often the instigator of activity. In an age of modern confusion, life online can present children with an alarming array of choices. In Britain, a children's charity called "Kidscape" released a report called "Virtual Lives: It is more than a game, it is your life." The report was the result of a study of online activities of 2,300 British eleven to eighteen-year-olds. Kidscape discovered that 45 percent of those questioned said they found their lives online superior to their real lives. One eighth of those surveyed acknowledged lying about appearance, age, or background in communications online with complete strangers. What is the appeal of living much of one's life online? Teenagers suggested that it is the ease in which one can escape problems. They can do as they please online; if something isn't fun or proves troubling, they can simply click a mouse and escape. But in real life, there are no mouse-clicks that can simply make distressing situations just go away. How will these young people function as adults when they are forced to deal with the problems and challenges of real life? One doesn't usually associate the Spanish artist Pablo Picasso with computers and with good reason. He didn't like them and said they were useless because they only provide answers. Picasso's point was well taken.

Certainly, computers are not useless and in the decades following Picasso's life, they have revolutionized the world. But a child just obtaining answers from a computer isn't being educated. You must know the right questions to ask in order to get the right answers.

The speed with which information becomes available is breathtaking. It radically affects the way we receive information, the way we read, and the way we listen. The student reading *Moby Dick* online may abandon his efforts after a few moments (or a few mouse-clicks) and jump directly into something else. The mouse-clicker at a computer (like the channel surfer armed with a remote control and watching television) doesn't have to concentrate, think, or be patient. A single click can always take you on a journey somewhere else. The tortoise and the hare can both use the computer. But the hare, in a perpetual hurry, may be tempted to confuse fast information with good information, quick data with valid data, shock value with importance, and absurdity with profundity.

TEXTING: SPEAKING IN ABBREVIATIONS

In 1992, a twenty-two-year-old test engineer named Neil Papworth used his computer to send a text message, "Merry Christmas," directly to the phone of Richard Jarvis. Jarvis was at the headquarters of the British company, Vidaphone, in Newbury, England, attending a Christmas party. Papworth used his computer because the cell phones of the day had not been designed to type out text messages. It may have been the most momentous Christmas greeting in decades. For with this message, the world of text messaging was born. Today nearly two and a half-billion phone users send text messages around the world and the world has never been quite the same.

We are just beginning to cope with the realities of a wired world. Emily Listfield, in an article entitled "Generation Wired,"[157] writes, "The average teen sends more than fifty texts a day; younger children spend over ten hours a week playing video games; and the amount of time all kids spend online daily has tripled in the past ten years." *Parade* magazine commissioned a poll of parents regarding the effects of texting; 67 percent said texting was hurting their children's performance in school. Children from eleven to fourteen spend an average of seventy-three minutes a day texting, while teenagers spend nearly two hours. Sherry Turkel, director of the Initiative on Technology and Self, reports that children tell her they almost don't know what they are feeling until it is expressed in a text. According to Listfield, extensive texting between parents and children often results in the latter being reluctant to talk on the phone, even to members of their own family. In effect, texting becomes an abbreviated substitute for real conversation.

The consequences of texting have been extraordinary. Drivers, many of whom seem irrevocably attached to their cell phones, have caused and suffered the consequences of accidents because they were too busy texting to observe oncoming traffic. If a driver crashes into an oncoming vehicle because he was busy texting his girlfriend, the driver of the other vehicle will not be consoled by receiving a text message, which reads "I didn't CU." The dubious and sometimes shocking practice of "sexting" involves sending salacious and often explicit messages over the phone. Everyone from high school students to politicians to star athletes have seen their lives and careers turned upside down as a result. Texting has dramatically changed the way in which political candidates communicate with voters, both in delivering their own messages and in fundraising.

But the most profound effect of texting has been the change it has imposed on language, especially our capability to communicate with one another. The Computer and Technology Program at the University of Alabama posed the key question, "IYO TXTng = Gd 4 or NME of GMR?" or, if written in non-texted English, "In your opinion is texting good for or the enemy of grammar?" A case study issued by the program explains, "If you cannot understand the previous statement, then you most likely have not been exposed to the language of text messaging. Who are the creators of this language? The answer is today's teenagers."

But most teenagers are in the process of just learning to use the English language well. Their reading and writing skills are highly suspect. Sara Ring, writing on the Web site *Edutopia,* explains the issue.[158] She writes, "IYO txtng = NME or NBD?" Translation: 'In your opinion, is text messaging the enemy, or no big deal?' As more and more students immerse themselves in "Textspeak" over their cell phones and computers, educators worry that their writing skills are suffering. After all, the short-message format routinely sacrifices grammar, syntax, and punctuation for the sake of slang and brevity. There is concern that students who frequently express themselves in abbreviations and smiley faces may lose the capacity for more nuanced, grammatically correct writing. But other educators see little evidence that the language of texting is having a negative impact on students' schoolwork. In fact, some are even glad that students are communicating so frequently through writing and are creating their own language, albeit one with a nontraditional vocabulary. Is the prevalence of text messaging something to worry about? WDYT?"

A high school teacher posted a revealing comment in reply. The teacher advises us, "I teach ninth and eleventh grade English, and regardless of the age, my students' spelling is atrocious. Texting does not and has not helped. My students even speak to me in text. They do not see the relevance or value of using Standard English, though I have explained it many times. It's frustrating. My former students, who are seniors and have not passed the English portion of the exit exam and keep flunking the writing part, are beginning to understand the relevance."

Now there are those who insist that texting offers no threat to language. Advocates of this view usually offer two arguments. The first is that the abbreviations and shortcuts used in texting are simply another type of speech, like slang. Just because someone uses slang is no reason to assume that the same person could not write or speak traditional English. But if a writer, especially a teenager, hasn't learned the rules of grammar or is unable to write a simple declarative sentence, he is likely to just incorporate texting shortcuts into real writing. The second argument simply suggests that at least the texting teenager is writing something. But this is ludicrous. Substitute the word "eating" for the word "writing" and read the sentence again. Would anyone suggest, in our nutrition conscious world, that it doesn't matter what a teenager eats as long as he is "eating something"? Bad writing isn't somehow better than no writing.

This doesn't remotely suggest that there is anything wrong with shorthand abbreviations. But the teenager who writes that he didn't have time "2work4u cuz the dog 8 his homework" is not likely to make good grades or impress an employer after he graduates.

THE TWEET HEARD 'ROUND THE WORLD

In 2006, three computer programmers, Jack Dorsey, Evan Williams, and Biz Stone, were trying to inject energy into Odeo, Inc., a San Francisco podcasting company with an apparently dim future. "For good or ill?" is a question that may replace Hamlet's "To be or not to be?" as the question of our time. On March 21, Jack Dorsey sent the first tweet: "just setting up my twttr." But it was Tweet 38, sent by Dom Sagolla, who summed up the new platform by declaring, "Oh this is going to be addictive." The programmers considered calling their platform "Friendstalker" or "Dodgeball." The dictionary defines twitter as "a series of chirps from birds" and "a short burst of inconsequential information." The carrier limit was 160 characters, so Twitter limited its messages (or "tweets") to 140 characters.

Today, there are a billion tweets sent each week. Major celebrities can boast of thirty million people following their tweets. Even Queen Elizabeth II, Popes Benedict XVI and Francis I, and the Dalai Lama have used Twitter; the Church of England invited Twitter users to help choose the next archbishop of Canterbury. In 2013, the framed announcement of the birth of Prince George was placed on a wood and gold easel behind the gates of Buckingham Palace; but the news that the Duke and Duchess of Cambridge had a son was also revealed to the world through an official "tweet" from Clarence House. In effect, the Town Crier and Twitter were on the same world stage. The President of the United States is usually has one of the top five most popular Twitter accounts, but the President is rarely number one. Pop stars Lady Gaga, Justin Bieber, Katy Perry, Britney Spears, and Kim Kardashian are typically the most followed and they often outrank the President in followers. In other words, the icons of the celebrity culture are ubiquitous as usual. Political candidates declare and suspend their campaigns on Twitter; results of major athletic events and even events relating to war and peace are announced not through headlines, but through tweets.

Not everyone has jumped aboard the Twitter bandwagon. In *The Weekly Standard,* Matt Labash produced a scathing essay aimed at "The Twidiocracy," declaring it to represent "the decline of Western civilization, 140 characters at a time." For Labash, we have become a society with an abundance of "Twidiots." He says, "People used to write more intelligently than they speak. Now, a scary majority tend to speak more intelligently than they tweet." Labash recounts a conversation with Todd Butler, a digital strategist who has released an app for iPhone users which enables users to put all the important decisions in their life up for a vote among their social network. According to Butler, his application allows people to "have that layer of assurance that the world likes their decision." Butler also provided an interesting perspective on the values of the 'Twitterverse.' He explains, "People judge success in social media not necessarily by the quality of the work, but how many will follow. Which skews and diminishes the ability of people who actually want to put quality out there because they're like, 'Nobody cares if it's quality. They care if they get 'liked' 5,000 times.'"

Where does this leave us? The novelist E.M. Forster couldn't have imagined Twitter in 1909, but he wrote of an omnipotent, eternal, blessed machine through which we speak to each other, see one another, and in which we have our being. Matt Labash cites a plethora of university studies, from Michigan State, Oxford University, and Western Illinois University, linking excessive media use to everything from depression and anxiety, narcissism, and high tech addiction. Stanford University reported that seventy-five percent of iPhone users fall asleep with their phones. But the biggest problem caused by the high-tech chirping phenomenon is that it encourages us to assume that anything important can be said in 140 characters or less. Saying the least and getting the most attention becomes a goal. Does this mean that everyone who tweets is twittering life away? Of course not. But it does mean that a future generation may wake up one day and find that the ability to use our language requires more than 140 characters and that true expression has gone the way of the long-extinct Dodo.

IS FAST BEST?

When we speak of "information" online, we are making assumptions about truth and accuracy. Nowhere is this more of a challenge than in the lives of journalists who are in a perpetual hurry to deliver the news faster than their rivals. But is faster always better? Is doing something fast always the best way of doing it? The high tech world has changed the definition of "journalist." Reporters for traditional print and broadcast media zealously guard their identities as "professional journalists." But what about those who create web logs (popularly known as "blogs"), or those who post their own reports or pictures online?

There are four basic requirements for good journalism: accuracy, objectivity, linguistic proficiency, and historical literacy. Unfortunately, all of these requirements are in short supply today.

Accuracy: Jack Webb became famous for his tight-lipped, poker-faced delivery of lines when he starred in the television show *Dragnet.* Webb played Sgt. Joe Friday, a Los Angeles policeman who did everything by the book. Sgt. Friday always told crime victims and suspects alike that he sought "just the facts." For a time, everyone in America was familiar with his classic request, "Just the facts, ma'am." Accuracy was also a hallmark of good journalism. Sadly, the days of journalists concerned with simply gathering and reporting just the facts appears to be over. True journalists understand the importance of writing with a respect for facts and plain language. Mohsin Ali was the diplomatic editor for *Reuters* and later correspondent for *The Times of London,* covering every major summit meeting and diplomatic conference from the days of Atlee, Truman, Eisenhower, Churchill, and De Gaulle to the end of the Cold War in the age of Reagan. He declared, "Many of our news media do not check facts properly and report a lot of misinformation and, later do not even correct it." He recalled, "In my journalism days in London, we were taught that facts are sacred, comment is free." Donald Armour is a veteran journalist who spent four decades as a foreign correspondent for *Reuters* and the BBC. He sums up the demands of his profession eloquently, observing, "The art of the journalist is to fill in for the other members of the public, give them an immediate, easily understood outline of news events. He or she is not a professor. Your task is different, it is not to be obscure or learned, but to translate complicated facts and concepts into easily understood pros—without over-simplifying. A fine art." We can be struck by the degree to which we hear or read obvious mistakes on the air or in print. We are all imperfect, but the kinds of mistakes made today could be prevented by simple fact checking.

Objectivity: It is more difficult than it sounds. No one is totally objective, and often, people who are always talking about how objective and fair they are usually prove to be the opposite. Some are bothered by the proliferation of radio and television commentators who are really just the 21st century version of editorial writers. What is far more objectionable is the blurring of distinctions between the news and editorial content, between reportage and entertainment. In addition, there are some journalists who carry the notion of objectivity to extremes. For instance, the notion that in reporting, we must be equally fair to terrorists and their victims, is absurd on its face. A famous American journalist was once asked if he would warn American troops if he saw them in immediate danger while covering a war. He responded that he would have to think about his answer. Presumably, his loyalties were less to the country that guaranteed his free speech than to "the profession of journalism." Such journalists, if they had been tolerated in ancient Rome, would have pontificated about their objectivity in covering a conflict between the lions and the Christians in the Roman arena. They would proudly declare themselves objective in reporting from the perspective of both participants. At the same time, obvious bias can be found in much contemporary reportage. To be fair, it did not start with the Internet. It has been a problem for years—one reason why the public does not hold many journalists in high regard.

Linguistic proficiency: Loss of communications skills is a sad casualty of popular culture. Grammar and syntax are sadly neglected in today's schools, and reading is badly taught as well. If you listen to unscripted television interviews or reality programs, you will constantly hear people on television saying "Him and I" did this or "Her and me" did that, and no one blinks an eye. The advent of popular high tech communications has produced even more truncated communications. Is this E-Z 4U2 read? As we tweet on Twitter, fast is presumed to be best. Literary style and elegant prose are now rarities.

Historical literacy: For most of our history, we have assumed a certain level of popular historical references, a shared past with which everyone could identify. These were not obscure academic references. Not everyone has been expected to know the names of composers such as Cimarosa or Raff, but shouldn't everyone recognize the names of Beethoven and Chopin? Shouldn't those who write about world events or local politics be familiar with the great names and major events of our history? Some of those students who fail dismally in surveys and polls about knowledge of basic history and geography are attending schools of journalism. Journalists without knowledge of history are free to develop a perspective based entirely on a flawed popular culture. As for a solution, there is no magic formula. Good writing skills and knowledge of history are not learned in journalism schools, but they should be learned as a basic part of education. Objectivity and accuracy can be encouraged, but today they are often offset by the "Watergate syndrome." After Watergate, many students went into journalism to become rich and famous. They learned quickly that the fastest way to achieve notoriety is through attack journalism and they often do so without adequate preparation. There was a famous television personality (the self-proclaimed "king" of cable talk) who always boasted that he never read a book in advance of an interview. He said this enabled him to ask the questions of ordinary listeners. If we take him literally, he was suggesting that you could discuss something much more intelligently if you don't know what you're talking about.

We should remember, however, that the virtues of journalism, accuracy, objectivity, linguistic proficiency, and historical literacy are valid in both old and new media. An accurate and objective journalist will remain so whether working with an old-fashioned pen or with the fastest online connection. An incompetent dolt will be just as incompetent in the world of bits and bytes as in the world of pen and ink.

It has become fashionable to talk about "The Information Age" or "The Information Highway." Everyone assumes that more information is always a good thing, always a symbol of progress. But T.S. Eliot, the poet who died when today's commonly used high tech devices would have sounded like science fiction, raised the key questions. In *The Rock*,[114] Eliot asked, "Where is the life we have lost in living? Where is the wisdom we have lost in knowledge? Where is the knowledge we have lost in information?" He concluded, "The world turns and the world changes. But one thing does not change. In all of my years, one thing does not change, However you disguise it, this thing does not change: The perpetual struggle of Good and Evil." So even mere facts are not enough; wisdom is harder to achieve than facts and speeding along the information highway may lead us to wisdom, but it may also lead us to a head-on collision.

On one level, the solution is simple: a return to basic standards in which journalists learn their craft, perfect their skills, and do their homework. Leonard Bernstein reflected upon the deceptive ease with which George Gershwin produced his work. He asked the tongue-in-cheek question, "Why don't you run upstairs and write a nice Gershwin tune?" The answer, of course, is that it is not as easy as it sounds.

THE HIGH-TECH ROAD TO THE LOW LAND OF CULTURAL ILLITERACY

There are clear advantages to information traveling quickly. In 1799, it took a week for news of the death of George Washington to travel from Virginia to New York. By 1963, 70 percent of Americans learned of the assassination of John F. Kennedy within a half-hour. Today, courtesy of the Internet, news can travel around the planet, across oceans and to the most remote outposts on earth in real time.

The change was never more apparent than when a group of high-ranking Soviet officials launched an abortive coup against Mikhail Gorbachev. They approached the coup as if they were back in the 1950s; tanks ominously rolled through the streets while the Soviet propaganda machine on television began playing the music of Tchaikovsky. (The great Russian composer would have doubtlessly disapproved of the fact that the Soviet media always used classical music to cover governmental atrocities.) But in the age of high technology, people in Moscow were getting the news anyway, in faxes from Americans who were watching television and reporting back to the Russians what was actually taking place in the streets. We have become accustomed and almost blasé about calmly watching the events of the world in our living rooms. By 2011, coverage of protests in the streets of Cairo, Damascus, and Tripoli could stream over the Internet. The Sphinx might remain enigmatic, but people could draw their own conclusions sitting in front of their computers. By 2022, it was easy for people around the entire world to watch Canadian truckers in Ottawa protesting against Prime Minister Justin Trudeau's government vaccine mandates.

However, while information now travels faster, how is it being absorbed? One of the assumptions of people who don't concentrate on what they are doing is that they can still give proper attention when necessary. It takes a certain amount of time to listen to someone play a Chopin nocturne on the piano or to hear an orchestra play a pastoral exaltation of an English spring by Frederick Delius. You can study speed-reading, but even the fastest reader requires a minimum amount of time to read a good book. Furthermore, reading the words doesn't mean that you understand the meaning of the author. Scholars have been arguing about the precise meaning of the printed word for years, disagreeing about the interpretations of The Bible, the U.S. Constitution, the plays of Shakespeare, or even the true meaning of children's books. So the notion that everything can be quickly absorbed and processed by the casual reader is absurd.

The anfractuous path to cultural illiteracy takes many twists and turns. Some are the direct result of technological changes, which produce unintended consequences. First Ladies Barbara and Laura Bush both made major efforts to focus the public's attention on illiteracy. (The National Literacy Survey suggests that one in five Americans functions at the lowest level of literacy.) But the advent of television and especially computer technology has also produced thousands of people who do not read by choice. This is the new and little recognized problem of "aliteracy." These "aliterates" are not illiterate. They can read but simply choose not to do so. They decline to read in favor of visual media. Why read a book if you can obtain the same information on television or through a computer? Fewer people today read newspapers than ever before. As for books, the future is in doubt. Aldous Huxley said, "Every man who knows how to read has it in his power to magnify himself, to multiply the ways in which he exists, to make his life full, significant and interesting." Augustus Hare suggested that reading is a form of mental exercise. He wrote, "Reading is to the mind what exercise is to the body. It is wholesome and bracing for the mind to have its faculties kept on the stretch."

Too many consumers of information and entertainment are not keeping their minds "on the stretch." We may even paraphrase Huxley and suggest that those who do not read are (by necessity or choice) diminishing themselves, reducing the ways in which they exist. Audiovisual media (including the ubiquitous computer) can do many things that books can't. But when large segments of the public depend almost entirely upon audiovisual media, they allow executives in the entertainment industry the greatest possible control in determining our national priorities. What is lost if people stop reading? The capacity to discover all the treasures found between the pages of a book. The non-reader may lead a happy life, convinced that all is well, that television and computers are more interesting than the printed word. He will have no idea what has been missed.

We live in a time of instant gratification. We are used to watching television programs in which the problems of fictional characters (and sometimes the problems of the world) are tied up in neat packages by the time a thirty-minute or one-hour show comes to an end. The solution must come with enough time allowed for six to twelve minutes of commercials. Not surprisingly, audiences are impatient. While history buffs may be fascinated by The History Channel, a cable medium devoted entirely to the past, we live in a culture of the moment. People assume that if they haven't heard of something or someone, it's probably a person or an idea of no importance.

In the 1950s, audiences were treated to what is now called "the golden age of television drama." Not every television play was a masterpiece, and the small screen offered an abundance of superficial and commercialized ineptitude. But there were masterpieces—dramas in which dialogue was a key to understanding the characters. Today's most popular programs depend on action and fast movement. Cable networks like MTV have become successful through sound bites. It's a transformation best understood by Madison Avenue. If you can't get your message across in a few words, you can't get your message across! The problem is that not every thought, every idea, every message, can be translated into sound bites. Today's consumer of information is likely to think himself well-informed as he glances at a computer screen, flips and clicks his way through a few Web pages, all the while listening to music blaring from a hand-held device, and talking on his cell phone.

This behavior isn't limited to teenagers, but it carries over into the classroom. We are told that communicating in quick sound bites is the only way to reach students. Everyone is assumed to have some form of attention deficit disorder. Unfortunately, the assumption may be more correct than any of us would like to admit.

THE SMARTEST GENERATION?

Proponents of the notion that technological advances yield cultural progress are optimistic, even jubilant, over the prospects of young Americans growing up in the 21st century. Others are less enthusiastic. Mark Bauerlein was Director of Research and Analysis at the National Endowment for the Arts, where he oversaw studies about culture and American life. Now Professor Emeritus of English at Emory University in Atlanta, Bauerlein makes a compelling argument that the digital age actually stupefies young Americans and jeopardizes our future. In his 2009 book, *The Dumbest Generation: How the Digital Age Stupefies Young Americans and Jeopardizes Our Future,*[159] Bauerlein takes a realistic look at our modern age, one in which books are being replaced by video screens. A teenager today can reach friends around the world with a mouse-click, access a treasure trove of information without walking out of his room, and hear or watch an astonishing array of audio and video selections while still dressed in his pajamas.

But does this new digital world insure lively minds and creative imaginations? Not at all, says Bauerlein, who writes, "The mental equipment of the young falls short of their media, money, e-gadgets, and career plans. The eighteen-year-old may have a Visa card, cell phone, My Space page, part-time job, Play Station 2, and admission letter from State U, but ask this wired and on-the-go high school senior a few intellectual questions and the façade of the in-the-know-ness crumbles." For Bauerlein, the paradox of what he calls "The Dumbest Generation" is that a cornucopia of opportunities, diversions, and freedoms has yielded a paucity of mental achievement. The irony is that schools that have taught the teenager in question to "feel good about himself" have succeeded. He appreciates himself and is blissfully ignorant of what he doesn't know or hasn't learned, or more importantly, has yet to learn. He is well informed as to the details of pop culture, the latest stars on the silver screen or the football field; he can sing the latest recorded hits, probably as well as the untalented vocalist who recorded them; he knows his way around a computer; of paramount importance, he is eminently familiar with the tastes, attitudes, and choices of his friends and his peer group. Members of the group feel good about themselves too, and they regard anyone critical of their limited knowledge of anything outside their own little world as laughable, dated, and not worthy of their time.

Bauerlein's critics (and he has them) have a response and it is predictable. They could argue that young readers can absorb the same knowledge and acquire a rich vocabulary whether seated at a computer screen or roaming the stacks in a library. But more often, they simply argue that the things Bauerlein and other cultural critics say they are missing are simply worthless. They are what Bauerlein calls "the new bibliophobes." Mark Bauerlein offers a sagacious description of what happens when parents and teachers become "pals" rather than guides to knowledge. He writes, "When the mentors disavow their authority, when they let their discipline slacken, when they, in the language of the educators, slide from the 'sage on the stage' to the 'guide on the side', the kids wonder what goes. They don't consider the equalizing instructor a caring liberator, and they aren't motivated to learn on their own. They draw another, immobilizing lesson. If mentors are so keen to recant their expertise, why should students strain to acquire it on their own?" Bauerlein concludes, "If the guardians of tradition claim that the young, though ignorant, have a special perspective on the past, or if teachers prize the impulses of tenth-graders more than the thoughts of the wise and the works of the masters, learning loses its point."

Mark Bauerlein says, "It isn't funny anymore. 'The Dumbest Generation' cares little for history books, civic principles, foreign affairs, comparative religions, and serious media and art, and it knows less. Careening through their formative years, they don't catch the knowledge bug, and tradition might as well be a foreign word. Other things monopolize their attention: the allure of screens, peer absorption, career goals. They are latter day Rip Van Winkles, sleeping through the movements of culture and events of history, preferring the company of peers to great books and powerful ideas and momentous happenings." By 2022, Bauerlein offered proof of what had happened to this generation in a new book appropriately titled, *The Dumbest Generation Grows Up: From Stupefied Youth to Dangerous Adults.* Sadly, Bauerlein's past predictions and present analysis both proved right on target. He predicted that a generation of teenagers who didn't read books or magazines or newspapers, had no religion or awareness of civics, history, or great art, would become unsatisfied and confused adults. The passage of time has now rendered a verdict on the results of a formation that Bauerlein calls anti-intellectual, ahistorical, and vulgar: adults with short attention spans and extended adolescence, blissfully unaware of the great figures of history and culture, but confident in their ignorance of the past and a notion of what is paramount in life, the trends, celebrities, and slogans of the ubiquitous pop culture. Such adults know rock but not Bach, rap but not Chopin, Puccini, or Rachmaninoff or for that matter, George Gershwin or Duke Ellington; they know little of the Declaration of Independence, the Constitution, or the Bill of Rights, only that certain Founding Fathers were slaveholders; they have few opinions or ideas grounded in logic, facts, or faith, but they live their lives seeking approval on Twitter and Facebook. What is perhaps the most truly tragic aspect of all this is that they haven't the slightest idea what they've missed or what will fade into oblivion as they can't pass it on to succeeding generations.

Parents and grandparents of children, who are facile using computers, frequently make a serious error. They confuse the ability to retrieve information using high tech equipment with the taste and judgment to know which information merits attention. How often do we hear a proud mother or father boast that a son or daughter is "so much smarter than I am," because the child has been raised with computers?

The advent of the computer has also altered the way students learn and not always in ways that are positive. The "cut and paste" options available through basic word processing programs enable computer users to transfer huge blocks of text with a single mouse-click. Students can find it easy simply to download passages written by others and incorporate them without attribution in their own academic work. Authors traditionally quote others to support their own views and to criticize the work of others. But in academia and commercial publishing, literal quotations are supposed to be attributed and credited. Trip Gabriel, writing in the *New York Times*, concludes, "It is a disconnect that is growing in the Internet age as concepts of intellectual property, copyright and originality are under assault in the unbridled exchange of online information, say educators who study plagiarism." Students who have never known anything but the digital age are accustomed to downloading music and accessing free information online. The Internet makes it appear that written words or "texts" belong to no one and therefore belong to everyone. Such issues pose interesting legal issues for copyright lawyers and publishers. But students who think nothing of doing their school work using whole pages of material written by others are shortchanging themselves in the learning process. Students profiled in Gabriel's article were committing what has been traditionally regarded as plagiarism. But today, such behavior is regarded as standard operating procedure and the students see nothing wrong with it. The notion that "everything belongs to everyone" may sound appealing to students, but it has serious consequences. The documentary filmmaker Michael Moore has carried this notion to extremes by suggesting that vast amounts of cash in America are a national treasure also belonging to all of us. Presumably, Moore excludes his own funds and the copyrights to his own films from this imaginary national cherry pie ready to be served up to an audience of eager students.

THE TOOL ON YOUR DESK

A computer is a tool. Information derived from a computer depends on the intelligence of the person who placed it there. Computers, like radios and televisions before them, are capable of delivering all kinds of information. (Radio and television have broadcast the most sublime music and amplified noise. The choice of music is the key.) The same is true concerning computers. A child who spends hours playing video games at the computer is not spending his time in the same way as a child who is reading good books and articles or downloading good music. Computers offer an abundance of treasure and trash. In 1964, Marshall McLuhan wrote *Understanding Media: The Extensions of Man.*[160] The volume included his oft quoted declaration that "The medium is the message." McLuhan posited that the medium delivering information to a reader, listener, or viewer was more important than the content it carried.

Certainly different types of media are used and perceived in different ways. A book can provide all kinds of details on the page, but the dramatic effect of television, with potentially exciting pictures in motion, dramatic music, and memorable voices, is very different. The viewer seated at a computer screen becomes not only a participant, but also the editor of the content. If you're watching a video or reading a page on a computer screen, a split second mouse-click can take you to another Web site half way around the world. The computer caters to and encourages people with a short attention span. It's the ideal medium for people in a hurry. Unfortunately, not every great idea, picture, or musical masterpiece has been designed for people in a hurry. In music, for instance, true appreciation of the concord of sounds may require some concentration, some attention. People stroll through museums and spend hours standing in front of great works of art, insisting that they learn something new each time they view an outstanding painting. Many serious subjects cannot be reduced to sound bites, but computers, like fast moving television spots, encourage our lack of concentration.

The real problem with McLuhan's theory is that content does matter. It does make a difference if our rapid mouse-clicking takes us to a Web site featuring wisdom or poppycock. This is especially true because people are often gullible and assume that if something is said on radio or television (especially by a celebrity) or it appears on the screen of a computer, it must be so. In truth, the values, standards, and scrutiny to which ideas and artistic expression have been subjected for hundreds of years is perfectly valid. The medium is not the message; the message is the message. The technology of the 21st century may alter our perceptions or the speed with which we determine those perceptions. But two plus two still equals four, and the moon isn't made of green cheese, even if somebody on television or a digital video says so.

Alvin Toffler was a best-selling author and futurist. His books, *Future Shock* and *The Third Wave*, won him a worldwide audience. Toffler was a maverick intellectual who believed that scholarship shouldn't remain in an ivory tower. He worked in a variety of jobs in steel foundries and auto plants to learn about real people, and toiled for years as a freelance writer while pursuing his dream. While considering the concept of "culture shock," the idea that people could be geographically dislocated, Toffler hit upon the idea of people being dislocated in time. In effect, people could be surprised and dislocated by the future. After years of struggle, Toffler produced the phenomenally successful *Future Shock* and became recognized throughout the world as a highly influential independent thinker. Toffler's view of history was developed further in *The Third Wave*. For Toffler, civilization has undergone three principle changes, moving from agricultural and industrial ages to our present information era.

In *Third Wave* terms, information becomes the world's most valuable commodity. While we may have serious debates over the effect of the Internet and the World Wide Web, clearly the world will never be the same as it was before the revolution of computer technology.

BIG BROTHER AND THE TWITTERMOB

In the 21st century, it is hard to even imagine a world without the high tech devices or social media on which multitudes of men, women, and children have become dependent. The imaginary devices dreamed up by 20th century science fiction writers or the robots and computers predicted by futurists of the last century have been surpassed in a revolution that changes daily and by the minute.

It is easy to take the blessings of high technology for granted. An e-mail or text sent via a digital device can be seen or even heard halfway around the world in a minute; not so very long ago, such a message might take days or even weeks for delivery. But along with these innovations and opportunities, technology has brought us a new set of challenges. Technology has transformed the way we work, live, and relate to others; not all of these transformations are for the better. In fact, a number are destructive and even frightening.

Do you know someone who feels lost without an accessible cell phone or tablet? Someone whose every minute is devoted to thinking about posts on social media? It is likely that you do, especially if you are around children or teenagers. Dr. Jennifer Kaztenstein, Director of Psychology and Neuropsychology at Johns Hopkins Children's Hospital, says that people are so used to having an accessible cell phone that they may suffer anxiety even if they never had one growing up. Data suggests that this is especially the case among children and adolescents who spend a significant part of each day using one digital device or another—a cell phone, a tablet, a computer—or anything else that enables constant access to and involvement with social media.

Excessive use of such devices can lead not only to anxiety, but to depression, frustration, and an almost-addictive dependency on the device for reinforcement and approval.

Psychology Today reports that just forty percent of parents use parental controls available on YouTube. Ninety-three percent of children ages six to twelve have access to smart phones or tablets; two-thirds have a device of their own. Facebook has actually created an app for children over considerable objections from child advocates. Children can easily be exposed to the wrong influences through social media, especially if their use is unsupervised. Even if they avoid predators, social media can provide children with an incredibly distorted impression of what is important. Obsessive concern with celebrities or with whatever is "trending" can persuade impressionable children and adolescents that what matters is what appears on social media to the exclusion of everything else. It goes without saying that cyber bullies are a particular problem for young adults who may value approval from "the mob" more than the support of their own family and true friends or mentors.

The fame and adulation available to influencers on the Internet has had another profound effect on the career ambitions of boys and girls alike. In the 1940s and 1950s, children aspired to be soldiers, policemen, firemen, or even cowboys; with the advent of the space program, the most exciting and adventurous life suddenly became that of an astronaut. But no more. In conjunction with the anniversary of Apollo 11, at the behest of Lego, a Harris poll asked 3,000 children in the United States, the UK, and China about their knowledge of space flight. One of the questions asked the boys and girls, "What do you want to be when you grow up?" Nearly a third in both the U.S. and the U.K. responded, "A You Tuber or Vlogger"; "Professional Athlete" topped "Musician" on the list, with Astronaut scoring the much lower eleven percent response. In China, however, "Astronaut" was at the top of the list, with "Musician" coming in ahead of "Professional Athlete." We can suspect that this trend will continue, with more and more boys and girls dreaming of their childhood idea of success: fame and fortune as a celebrity on YouTube, Facebook, Twitter, and whatever new social media avenues become available by the time they are grown.

If addiction to digital devices is a problem, so is the challenge of "cancel culture." In today's world, a simple remark or photograph can be taken out of context, distorted, and sent literally around the world with a few mouse clicks or a tap on a touch screen. Adults and children alike have seen their worlds turned upside down with careers destroyed and lives ruined because of a casual remark made long ago or a simple comment made today that can be taken out of context. Lies and half-truths can be easily weaponized and disseminated quickly to destroy someone who is targeted. The Twittermob is relentless and unforgiving; an innocent remark or even a complete lie can capture the fancy of a few celebrities or "influencers" with millions of followers. The most innocent party can be verbally decimated and a reputation that has taken a lifetime to build can be torn to shreds. The virulent Twittermob is rather like those in the French Revolution who watched one person after another being marched to the guillotine. While someone's life may be in tatters after an assault, the mob simply moves on to attack someone else.

If addiction to technology and cancellation weren't enough, high tech companies themselves pose other dilemmas for us. They have demonstrated a distressing tendency to function as cyber-spies and self-appointed censors. These are developments that can turn the civil society upside down. Such assertions may seem melodramatic, but a careful look at the evidence reveals that the high tech behemoths have acquired vast power unequalled virtually in history.

First, we need to realize the extent to which tech giants both record and influence the purchasing and personal behavior of literally billions of people. Facebook's "newsfeeds" and "timelines" are based on personal information collected by the company. Many users of Facebook haven't a clue that they are providing marketing information to tech giants every time they log into their accounts. Tristan Harris, a former Google designer, described the goal of the tech companies to become as addictive as slot machines and then to put a slot machine in a billion pockets. Those who imagine Silicon Valley as the epitome of "hip" and "cool" behavior would be surprised to find that underneath sleek digital exteriors is the spirit not of the ivy covered walls of academe but the gaudy, gilded spirit of Las Vegas.

With the advent of the Internet, people have become accustomed to entering and storing all kinds of personal information on line: passwords, Social Security numbers, bank accounts—the list is endless. In addition, online shopping has mushroomed to become the dominant form of buying, not only in the United States, but all over the world. This has resulted in a veritable ocean of information that is incredibly valuable to marketers. It should surprise no one that marketers use this information in all kinds of ways, sometimes with your consent, but more often than not, without your knowledge.

In recent years, people all over the world have become accustomed to using digital "voice assistants," asking a friendly digital device to help with every type of task imaginable. In a startling article, "'Alexa, are you invading my privacy?'— the dark side of our voice assistants," Dorian Lynskey paints a disturbing picture of what happens when digital voice assistants can go wrong. He cites instances of the most personal information including medical data and intimate personal conversations being recorded "accidentally" and made available for marketing analysis or sent "by mistake" to third parties. He reminds us, "In 2015, Google's Eric Schmidt foresaw a day when the Internet will be 'part of your presence all the time,' making your real-life behavior as mappable as what you do on your laptop or phone. You will never be offline."

Does it seem impossible that a digital device might be keeping a record of who is in your house at any given time or what is being said? Dr. Jeremy Gillula, project director at the Electronic Frontier Foundation, has said that there are no technical obstacles to enabling dormant devices to track users' television viewing. The device could be triggered by the high-pitched signals that may be embedded in shows and advertisements. A voice assistant that is "always on" may be regarded by the user as merely a "virtual friend," but the "friend" may actually be spying and snooping and gathering data in a way that the secret police of past totalitarian states could never even have enjoyed in their dreams.

Finally, high tech companies have become censors. Facebook reportedly uses not just algorithms, but human beings with human failings and biases to access personal and private messages of users to censor comments, information, and ideas. If a user sends a private message to a friend, a parent, or spouse, why should this information be "evaluated" by an anonymous individual working for a high tech company? Groups of such individuals may become arbiters of public information with no qualifications to do so and a desire to impose their own political or personal agenda on others. How much do we know about platforms such as "Tasks" and "Centra" used within Facebook? How is information aggregated regarding users' activities on multiple platforms of social media?

By 2020, Twitter CEO Jack Dorsey was powerful enough to impact the presidential election by banning carriage of important news stories from Twitter. In 2021, Twitter's Jack Dorsey essentially banned President Donald J. Trump from the platform. The issue is not whether one agrees or disagrees with Donald Trump or approved of his administration. The issue is that the bearded boss of a high tech enterprise, Twitter, was proven functionally more powerful than the President of the United States. With Google as the dominant search engine in the world, people and businesses alike are dependent on Google to be found by like-minded individuals, consumers, and anyone interested in almost any subject. If a person or business enterprise "disappears" from Google, Facebook, and Twitter, that person may simply and functionally vanish.

Efforts by high tech companies to censor views or ideas they don't like or those eliciting disapproval of the companies' bosses are clear. In effect, a few corporations have acquired a veto power over ideas expressed in the public square. While the companies insist that these efforts at censorship are really benign, using terms like "content moderation" or describing efforts to stamp out "hate speech" or "misinformation," censorship is truly the accurate description of what is taking place. When an expert on any subject has to worry if his comments may offend a recent college graduate who happens to work for a high tech company armed with the power to censor his work, the marketplace of ideas is rapidly becoming not a marketplace at all but a mirror of the opinions of a small group of authoritarian technocrats overwhelmed by their own arrogance and power.

Renowned economist and educator, Dr. Thomas Sowell, has eloquently expressed the need for debates, exchanges of ideas, and intellectual and creative freedom. He has criticized those who have been taught to have views but not to know what you're talking about. He says, "It's important to hear the opposite viewpoint and more important to learn to distinguish why viewpoint A and viewpoint B are different and which one has the most evidence and logic behind it."

In their individual lives, parents and grandparents can set an example, limit their dependence on digital devices or see that their children and grandchildren learn to enjoy activities and resources away from the digital world. Good books, music, and art do not require WiFi; stimulating conversation, camaraderie, and human interaction with family and friends do not require text messages. The larger questions of surveillance and censorship cannot be easily settled by a single individual or family; but collectively, we need to work together to insure that we do not lose the blessings of high technology while surrendering simultaneously to entities that seek to compromise our privacy and limit our liberty and freedom.

HIGH TECH: FRIEND OR FOE?

The Internet offers incredible opportunities for self-education and for individuals to discover a cornucopia of music, art, and literature. For the first time, it is technically possible to distribute information (including recorded music and pictures) to a worldwide audience without the filter of commercial business interests. However, anyone interested in making such discoveries should be forewarned and forearmed. The Internet is not a panacea that will solve all of our problems. It offers one of many opportunities for us to encounter a great deal of information we might not encounter through television or the movies, or with the approval of the mainstream media executives.

Here are several things to keep in mind regarding technology:

1. *Information on the Web is only as good as its source.* The artistry of Pablo Casals or Art Tatum will be just as stunning in today's MP3 files as on old 78 rpm records. Musical junk will not turn into quality because it has been digitized and placed on a computer somewhere in the world. Too often, we conclude mistakenly that the revolutionary computer technology is a

substitute for carefully researched facts or just plain common sense. The phrase, "It's on my computer," tends to be a sorry attempt at self-justification. Whether or not a musician or artist is a genius will be determined by factors entirely divorced from whether or not his works appear on the Internet.

2. *Art doesn't become great art because it is on television or poor art because it is ignored on television.* The same is true for all the new multimedia of the Third Wave. Information available through the new media may be misinformation. Because it is so easy to obtain this information, it is incredibly easier to obtain misinformation as well. It is important to remember that the computer is simply a medium. The Declaration of Independence was written with a quill pen. Lincoln's "Gettysburg Address" wasn't created on a hard-drive. Today's composers may record their works in quadraphonic or digital sound, but how many have written an opera like *Carmen* or a musical the equal of *Show Boat?* Today's painters may use digital technology to record their works, but is their technique superior to Rembrandt? This in no way suggests that digital technology doesn't offer opportunities to today's creative men and women that were unimaginable centuries earlier. It only means that technology offers us techniques and media, but not substance. That must still be supplied by the human mind and divine inspiration.

3. *Technology offers opportunities which may augment or supplement traditional methods of learning without replacing them.* Just because you use a computer doesn't mean you shouldn't go to concerts, museums, or libraries. Just because you decide to pursue avenues of creativity or artistic exploration yourself doesn't mean you should ignore the opportunity to interact with (or learn from) others. Someone else will always have an idea that wouldn't occur to you. It may be a good or bad idea. (The composer Gerald Strang used to tell his students that one of a composer's best tools was a wastebasket.)

Technology offers opportunities for isolation and withdrawal, which may be hazardous to your intellectual health. On the other hand, technology also offers incredible opportunities for contact with people around the world that transcend geography. You may be sitting at a computer terminal in a small town in Alaska or New Mexico and access the artistic achievements and creative ideas of cultural conservationists in New York, London, Paris, or Vienna. Or (and this will come as a shock to the residents of those cities) you may be sitting at a computer terminal in one of those major cultural capitals and learn something from someone in a small town in Alaska or New Mexico. (Remember, there are more art galleries per capita in Santa Fe, New Mexico than in any other American city except New York.)

In any event, a combination of a personal enthusiasm for exploration and knowledge, combined with technology, offer tremendous opportunities for self-education. It would be ironic if the computer, promoted as the dominant technical tool of the 21st century, became, in fact, a primary tool of cultural conservation, preserving the best of our past and enabling a future that reflects traditional values and standards.

In the modern age, unlike in the age of *Aesop's Fables*, the hares have beaten the tortoises. Or, they think they have. No one expects us to go back to the 1880s or the 1930s, or to turn back the technological clock. In 19th century Britain, the Luddites tried to destroy looms that would displace human labor in weaving textiles. But technological progress could not be stopped. Certainly, many of us have had our fill of automated telephone answering systems with twenty menu options when all we want to do is make a simple phone call. A man who operated a bar in Colorado kept a shotgun mounted over his bar. One day, in full view of his patrons, he took down the shotgun and shot his laptop computer. The police objected to his discharging a firearm in a public place, but explained, "It's not against the law to shoot a computer." Later, he apologized, explaining that he knew he was wrong, but that at the time, "It seemed like the right thing to do." We all have such moments of frustration with our changing technological environment. However, technology can only move ahead. It is easy to blame problems on technology, but too often, it is the message and the messenger, not the medium, that is the problem. If readers read newspapers online instead of on paper, they can benefit from good reporting. If they read books using Kindle, they can benefit from good books or waste their time reading bad ones. If they watch television, they can learn about great music or audible trash. James Madison, Alexander Hamilton, and John Jay wrote the *Federalist Papers* without computers. Their messages still resonate today.

The technological revolution is not going away. We are going to live in a wired world forever, so we must prepare to meet these challenges presented by the high tech revolution. Friend or foe? Clearly, technology can be both.

In our zeal to enjoy the blessings of modern technology, we should not forget that old messages ring true through new media, and false messages are invalid whether delivered by a quill pen or the latest digital miracle. It is the message, not the medium, that counts.

THE ANSWER: WHAT WE CAN DO TOGETHER

IS THERE AN ANSWER OR WILL THE PAST ACHIEVEMENTS of our most accomplished artists fade into oblivion? What will happen to today's artists who seek to uphold the standards and ideals of the past in new ways? Will new voices be ignored and declared "old-fashioned" and "irrelevant" before they have a legitimate opportunity to be heard? Will our culture be drowned out by commercial mass media and the entertainment industry, while academicians and bureaucrats fiddle as Rome burns? Will our history simply fade into oblivion while our society focuses obsessively on celebrities? Will our ability to use language continue to decline to a point of no return? Will good music, art, and books be of interest only to small groups of specialists, while pop culture reigns supreme in an age of superficiality?

It is not too late for us to work together to conserve the best of the past, foster the best of the present, and see that the best of the future does not remain undiscovered. Just as we preserve our national parks, we must preserve our cultural treasures: the legacy of the greatest creative minds of the past and the efforts of those today who are following in the same traditions.

Clearly, there are conclusions we must accept.

The academic community does not provide the answer. Academicians are busy arguing over whether the arts matter. Assuming they conclude that the answer is "yes," too many are concerned with fashions, trends, politically correct attitudes, and their own hierarchy.

Government does not provide the answer. While government support of the arts enables certain institutions to survive financially, government efforts will always be hamstrung by political controversies and the dilemma of using taxpayers' funds in ways opposed by many taxpayers. In addition, government help often means government control and in the creative arts, control should be maintained by those who are doing the creating.

The entertainment industry does not provide the answer. Entertainment executives are entirely motivated by financial considerations. A majority foster a set of cultural attitudes, which are diametrically opposed to a substantial portion of our society. It is unlikely that they will change and highly probable that the industry will be the primary cause of the problem, not the solution.

If we cannot depend upon educators, the government, or the entertainment industry to address this problem, is there a solution?

The only credible answer is that there must be a solution. Good music, art, theater, and literature do not sustain themselves. They must be encouraged, fostered, supported. In a few years, decisions about which motion pictures are produced, which television programs are aired, which books are published, and which recordings are released will be made by today's students. These decisions are already being made by individuals who are frequently cultural illiterates. It may seem unkind to characterize them as such, but the hard truth is that many are familiar only with the culture of the moment. If this situation continues, much of our cultural heritage is destined for extinction, with its creators on the road to oblivion. Millard Fuller, founder of Habitat for Humanity, was appalled by the existence of sub-standard housing, both in the U.S. and around the world. He concluded that only action, not theories, could deal successfully with this problem. Fuller said that shacks without running water could not be eliminated until someone picked up a hammer. "Don't just focus on fighting the problem," he said, "find a solution." This is good advice, equally applicable to cultural dilemmas.

In planning this solution, we should keep in mind the principles we have observed on our journey.

1. *Change is not synonymous with progress.*
2. *Celebrity and notoriety are not synonymous with quality.*
3. *Technology is not synonymous with wisdom.*
4. *Cultural amnesia represents a serious threat to our society.*
5. *The media impose celebrity upon those who are famous, not accomplished.*
6. *The media will not tell you about the best of our culture.*

The answer can be found in a new approach to our culture, recapturing the joys of words and music and the pride of achievement, even in the era of trash talk and cultural chaos. The solution is Cultural Conservation! We can work together to foster positive change. Our greatest natural resources have not been preserved by accident. The preservation of our national parks, for example, was not predestined. We still have Yellowstone and the Grand Canyon because people cared enough to make their preservation important. Libraries and museums did not spring up throughout history without human effort and enthusiasm. Today, we need not only to conserve physical resources, but cultural resources, especially those of the mind and spirit. In some ways, this type of conservation is more difficult, because it is often invisible. It is easy to recognize a decaying parcel of land or a dilapidated building; it is far harder to notice the disappearance of good music over several generations. The decline of words and music, the tolerance and eventual approval of artistic absurdity, the triumph of vulgarians and charlatans, the rise of the celebrity culture, and the loss of our history come silently, "on little cat feet," as Carl Sandburg said in his poem, *Fog*. But unlike Sandburg's fog, which sits looking over harbor and city, the cultural decline grows and expands, hovering over our present and rendering our future dim and discouraging. It will not disappear in an instant. Eternal vigilance is not only the price of liberty, but the price of the bright, thriving cultural heritage that has been a gift to us. Those who care about the idea of cultural conservation must take immediate, positive action to develop creative solutions.

Action must be taken by individuals of energy, determination, and courage. If we recognize that the academic, government, and entertainment establishments will be of little help, we will not waste time expecting them to do their best (or worst) to eradicate the problem.

Entertainment media, so often a part of the problem, should become part of the solution. Music and art of quality can be delivered and introduced to the public through new communications media. The arrival of the Internet offers unparalleled opportunities to break the bottleneck created by middlemen in the arts. Works of art, which could thrive and earn wide public enthusiasm, frequently never reach their audience. The new media provide ways to reach the public directly, bypassing the intellectual and commercial doorkeepers who impose their own advance judgments on writers, artists, and musicians.

Education can be reformed. It will be a slow and difficult process, but we should insist that secondary schools and later, colleges and universities, match their words of inclusiveness with deeds. We must hold educators' feet to the fire and demand that the best of our cultural past not be dismissed and rejected as the work and ideas of people who no longer matter. Education reforms should include a new emphasis on the teaching of phonics and traditional instruction in reading, as well as in basic, objective, fact-driven courses in American history.

Government should generally stay out of the way, but should provide incentives for private support of the arts and culture. Government usually makes dubious choices when it supports the arts and even the good choices are then subject to the dubious art of politics.

Children should be introduced to the arts at an early age. We should not make the mistake of assuming the more ambitious music or art is "too difficult" for children. In particular, we should avoid the false assumption that children will only relate to that which seems immediately relevant to their daily lives. Children have imagination, often far greater than adults. A child who learns early in life to appreciate opera, ballet, chamber music, jazz, and the best musical theater and film scores will be fortunate. Otherwise, children are subjected to an onslaught of advertising media and pop culture. Worse, their standards will be determined by peer pressure, and this usually results in their assuming that "music" is what they hear on the radio or see performed on television.

We must make a concerted effort to discard the fatally flawed notion that change is progress, that "new" automatically means better. It is human nature to make these assumptions. Some new artists may be better painters than those who painted yesterday. Some new musicians may write better music than those who wrote yesterday, but not by definition. Just because something is new is no reason to assume it is automatically an improvement over works created yesterday. Paul Johnson characterizes the history of art as a struggle between the canonical and innovatory. This struggle is true in all creative endeavors, including music and literature. Johnson says, "Art is fundamentally about order, whether the canonical or the new currently has the upper hand. We must always look for the underlying order which runs beneath the surface of the battle, to see that it is healthy and intact, and strong enough to sustain the dynamics of change. For once art loses its fundamental order, it becomes disorderly and therefore ceases to sustain a moral society and may, in fact, become a menace to our happiness." So modern art, music, and books should first be good art, music and books; then we can worry about how modern they are.

We must develop a sense of respect for our rich cultural history. It is very easy to dismiss the work of artists or musicians as "old-fashioned." Knowing about the past never seems "cool" or "trendy." Knowing about the present always does. Though difficult, we must make clear that people whose awareness of the arts is limited to what they heard on television five minutes ago are ignorant. Ignorance, like smoking, must become something that was once fashionable and sophisticated and is now perceived to be distasteful and undesirable. As historian David McCullough observed, "The Gershwin side of American accomplishment is too seldom given credit."

We must begin to ask ourselves, "What values are encouraged and inspired by our culture?" Music, art, literature, theater, and film are all capable of sending messages beyond immediate gratification. When we look at much of today's art and music, we find a dearth of positive values and an abundance of negative ones. We should begin evaluating works of art based on the values they inspire, not just on the reputation of the artist or a desire to follow fads and fashions. A century ago, Gilbert Keith Chesterton wrote a book called *What's Wrong with the World?*[161] Chesterton made the case that we should ask what is right with the world, pursuing a social ideal to surmount society's ills. This same approach is applicable to the arts. Music and all the arts can express our best values and ideals. Who are the people in our culture who are doing this today?

Composers, writers, and artists should be able to express spiritual and patriotic values. They should have the freedom to pursue styles of elegance and beauty without automatically inviting ridicule and disdain. We must reject the assertions of self-styled experts who believe that such intentions automatically disqualify works of art and their creators from serious consideration.

We need to take positive action to encourage not only revivals of outstanding past works, but sponsorship of new ones in the same tradition. A national survey was once taken to determine why Broadway musicals were not being written with the same quality of music and lyrics that thrived from the 1930s through the 1960s. The conclusion was that we do not have composers and lyricists of talent comparable to George and Ira Gershwin. While the Gershwin brothers were indeed unique, we should be aware that a modern day George and Ira Gershwin would run the risk of being declared "old-hat" and ignored by the entertainment establishment, which might not produce their work. Could a new show like George and Ira Gershwin's *Of Thee I Sing* be produced on Broadway as an original musical today? Don't answer too quickly.

Concerted efforts must be undertaken to produce, publish, and distribute multimedia materials that present a positive view of our cultural past. It is hard to imagine that thousands of students are graduating from school wholly unfamiliar with much of our cultural heritage. This is not surprising, because many of their parents and teachers are equally unfamiliar with this heritage.

It is imperative that we persuade everyone willing to listen that cultural conservation is important. Some people can understand quite easily what will be lost if our streams are polluted and our national parks disappear. But these same well- meaning people may be apathetic if they are presented with the notion that music and other arts may disappear. They will assume the absurdity of this idea, because, after all, we have plenty of music, art, movies, plays, and books available. Some will dismiss the idea as a futile attempt to preserve the past at the expense of the present. Others will mistakenly assume that children, and especially teenagers, will outgrow their present influences and develop more mature tastes in later life. But we have to get the public to pay attention to a difficult proposition: that they are being culturally short-changed if they remain ignorant of the situation. We also have to persuade them that this cultural decline guarantees that something unique, precious, and irreplaceable will be lost from our society forever.

Cultural conservation would appear to be, at least on the surface, a non-controversial subject. Campaigning for better standards in our schools, a greater familiarity with the arts, should threaten no one. But in the age of the ignoramus, not all is as it seems. Today, nearly everything is politicized. Goals upon which nearly everyone would once have agreed become the basis for furious political donnybrooks. Most curious, however, is the fact that the pundits and alleged experts on all sides of the political fence can find reasons within their own ideology to oppose any change from the status quo.

Those who identify themselves politically as "conservative" might be expected to embrace cultural conservation with enthusiasm. The very word "conservative" suggests a desire to conserve that which ought to be preserved and valued. But conservatives are committed, first and foremost, to the marketplace. Certainly, a free market is best in providing economic opportunity and political freedom, but freedom means that people can behave irresponsibly if they choose. Among the ranks of many self-described conservative political pundits are a number of former rock music disc jockeys and columnists, admirers of much of today's vapid and inane pop music. These people are conservative in all of their political and social values. But when it comes to the arts, they are too often willing to accept the basic assumption that today's pop culture is fine as long as it doesn't ridicule the patriotic or religious values they deem important. In other words, musicians who can't sing or play a note in tune are acceptable if they are on the right side of the political fence. Try suggesting to many conservatives that widespread ignorance of music and art is a problem. Not a small number will reply, "You don't want to interfere with the marketplace, do you?" Those who identify themselves politically as "liberal" present a different problem. Just as conservatives worry about criticizing anything that is a product of the free market, liberals worry about being judgmental. Liberals again often look at art through their own political perspective. The first question conservatives ask about art is whether it reflects their patriotic and religious values. The first question liberals ask about art is whether it reflects their idea of "social justice." (This explains why so many liberals embraced music and art that grew out of the protests of the 1960s. What mattered was the political view being expressed, not the quality of the art in question.) For liberals, it is most important to appear open-minded, tolerant, and progressive. These individuals haven't learned that in such a quest, one may be devoid of judgment, lacking in all standards, and excessively permissive.

The conservatives cannot turn a blind eye to what is happening today on the grounds that the fruits of the marketplace are inviolate, especially if the fruits of today's entertainment marketplace are frequently rotten. It is not the business of the government to enforce artistic standards or impose the taste of bureaucrats on the public. But just because government has no business declaring that trios of caterwauling teenagers are talentless and uncouth adolescents, there is no reason why the rest of us shouldn't draw that conclusion. Liberals cannot pretend that the only vice or taboo in today's world is the act of being judgmental. To be tolerant of everything is to be blatantly intolerant of standards and values. The first question to be asked about artists is whether they are producing good art. This doesn't mean that they shouldn't be challenged on other grounds. A number of highly skilled composers, writers, and artists over the years have turned their talents to producing art that may be obnoxious, offensive, blasphemous, distasteful, and downright ugly. These are not virtues and these artists, whatever their talent, deserve the criticism they receive. But the mistake made by many conservatives and liberals alike today is simple: the first question they ask about art is whether it responds to their political and social agendas. If it does, they are willing to accept it, regardless of quality. It is the decline in quality that poses a severe threat to our culture.

Today, an artist is likely to be lauded if he makes more money than anyone else does. The conservatives accept the idea that he must be good because the marketplace says he is successful. Liberals accept the idea that this same artist must be good, because they don't want to appear judgmental in declaring him to be an incompetent nincompoop. The marketplace can produce bad art and frequently does so, to the critical acclaim of those who are afraid of seeming intolerant to their like-minded colleagues.

One of the most popular buzzwords of recent times is "relevant." Students find it easy to dismiss what they are taught in school because it isn't "relevant." It doesn't have any relationship to what they think they will need to cope in the modern world. Why bother learning about people who were important fifty years ago when there are plenty of celebrities today? This question, posed in a variety of ways, is one of the more challenging ones facing the cultural conservationist. You may be uttering words of distilled wisdom, but it does little good if nobody's listening. "Why should I listen?" says the typical student. "Who cares about a lot of forgotten composers, writers, and artists?" Who indeed?

If we don't know where we've been, we don't know where we're going. People wouldn't think about embarking on a journey as explorers without a map. Yet many are perfectly happy to go through their lives without the equivalent of a map: the knowledge of our past cultural journeys. Students will accept the idea of a sports star as "the best." But how do we know a particular athlete is best? Because we keep meticulous records and can compare today's performance to yesterday's best accomplishments. Henry Aaron was the first baseball player to break Babe Ruth's record of 714 home runs. Everyone knew Aaron had accomplished something, precisely because it had been so difficult for others to challenge Ruth's record. Can anyone make the case that today's composers, artists and writers are superior to the best and most creative figures of the '20s, '30s, and '40s. (Oddly enough, there are those who would make this dubious argument.) But why should people accept this argument if they are unfamiliar with our artistic heritage?

One reason for the problem is the silence of people who should know better. Steve Allen addressed this problem directly in *Vulgarians at the Gate.*[162] It is a problem of which many people in the arts are aware, but few acknowledge. Said Allen, "In the 1950s and 1960s there were hundreds of music critics in their middle years who had no doubt whatever that Cole Porter, let's say, was vastly superior at the song writing art than Mick Jagger, for instance. Why did they so rarely say as much? I submit that the reason was a sort of social cowardice. The critics thought they knew better, held their tongues, because they did not want to seem unhip." In a few words, Allen identified the essence of the problem. Seeming "unhip" has been deadly in a society, which values change for the sake of change. The "unhip" are expected to bid a fond farewell to their careers and go quietly out to pasture. If those who should know better remain silent, what happens to those who know little? Again, Steve Allen declared, "I make a distinction here between middle-aged, generally well-informed critics and the teenage fans then attending rock concerts. The young people could be forgiven on the classic grounds that they simply didn't know any better. They were not consciously rejecting Porter, Ellington, Gershwin, and the other representatives of the glorious Golden Age; they simply had never consciously heard them before." But the critics and academics who trip over their own feet jumping on the pop culture bandwagon are acting out of fear, not prescience or personal courage. They don't want to be left behind. They prefer, in the words of Leon Wieseltier writing in *The New Republic*, "to take one's instructions from the fickle world, to keep up. In our society, there is almost no greater apostasy than the refusal to keep up."

In the modern era, there is enormous pressure to go along with whatever the pop culture, as expressed by the Twittermob, accepts as fashionable. Many of those who do not live and work in complete fear of being cancelled; it's much easier to go along to get along. It takes courage to withstand pressure, be it financial, political, or social, along with an abundance of unpleasant and thoroughly vicious name calling.

Today, many of these blissfully ignorant and uninformed teenagers have become executives of music companies, television and film companies, Internet enterprises, publishers, and even teachers. Many are going through life blissfully unaware of the music they missed along the way. These conclusions regarding popular music can be applied equally to other arts as well. Books, theater, films, and the other visual arts have been subjected to similar circumstances. We cannot assume that today's students will discover the arts on their own. If they do, their perspective may be limited to the fads and fashions of today's pop culture. There are those who suggest that nothing can be done, that the battle is lost, and that the titans of our artistic past and those who seek to carry their torch in the present must surrender. Must we truly accept today's ubiquitous pop culture as the only one that can be understood or appreciated by a contemporary audience? Accepting this situation as inevitable and irreversible renders it an ineluctable, self-fulfilling prophecy.

In other words, the student who asks the question, "Why should I care about music, books, and art that were created yesterday" should be challenged. There is a temptation to accept apathy and ignorance as excuses, and we should avoid it at all costs. Otherwise, we will be fostering classes of students who only "like what they know" and unfortunately, they will not know very much.

SUMMING UP

Cultural Conservation does not provide an agenda of guarantees or promises. Cultural Conservation offers an abundance of challenges. The challenges for the Cultural Conservationist are many. The road will not be an easy one because it is always simpler to follow the lead of pop culture, or in today's vernacular, to "go with the flow." It is hard to be a contrarian, to watch the crowds marching confidently in one direction while you stride boldly on an opposite path. Even raising the questions we are asking is likely to result in criticism and ridicule.

Some of these issues are predictable. Here are the objections you will have to answer:

"You can't be opposed to progress." Our response must be, "Change and progress are not synonymous." Change may be progressive, or it may portend disaster.

"You can't impose your cultural standards on someone else." Our response must be, "No one is denying your right to choose your own art or music. If anyone is imposing cultural standards, it is those who dismiss a host of creative artists as "old-fashioned" and irrelevant, thereby eliminating serious competition.

"You must never be judgmental." Our response must be, "Just as you have a right to advertise your ignorance in public, we have a right to call it to public attention." Being judgmental in the arts doesn't imply that one is a prejudiced, narrow-minded, ill- informed cultural dinosaur. Being judgmental may imply that some works of art or music are better than others, and that debate is not whether or not to have standards, but which standards should apply.

"You're an elitist." Our response must be, "If you want to defend your views, you should do so by praising the positive virtues of the art you admire, not simply attacking those with dissenting ideas." The Cuban composer and educator Aurelio de la Vega provides an eloquent answer to this charge when he wrote that if being an elitist was a synonym for good tastes, esthetic and cultural refinement, and aspiration for knowledge and the defense of Western culture, he was happy to sustain the epithet. But he rejected it totally if the term was used negatively and pejoratively to indicate discrimination, lack of generosity, cultural egoism, and the closing of doors to the poorer classes.

"Today's children are the smartest generation because they use computers." Our response must be, "Technology is a tool. You can use the best tools and still come up with the wrong answers if you ask the wrong questions."

"Tastes change and it's only natural for one generation to reject the tastes of its predecessor." Our response must be, "It may be natural, but it's highly ill-advised for a generation to reject what it has not been taught and is unlikely to discover on its own." Today's students are tomorrow's television network executives, publishers, music moguls, and cable and Internet tycoons. They will determine what type of art we see, what music we hear, which books we read. Ignorance may be bliss, but it is still ignorance.

"It is unimportant whether we all share the same ideas of good books, art, and music. There is no need for shared knowledge or appreciation in the arts." Our response must be that classics become classics for a reason, and to neglect them is to turn our backs on our heritage in the name of fads and fashions. We must also make a positive case for the art and music created by those who did not (or do not) succumb to the trends and fads of today's pop culture. These artists include great masters of the past who must not be allowed to fade into oblivion and those of the present whose adherence to traditional artistic values should not be held against them.

Predicting the future can be a hazardous affair. The ash heap of history is littered with the predictions of experts who didn't know what they were talking about. From politics to financial matters to sports, gazing into a crystal ball can be downright embarrassing. A wise Wall Street pundit once said, "The stock market will go up. It will go down. As long as you don't try to predict when it will do either, you'll stay out of trouble." Sometimes predictions are nothing more than wishful thinking. Who can forget the premature 1948 election night headline, "Dewey Defeats Truman," displayed the next day by a beaming and victorious Harry Truman? (Nor are such episodes confined to history. Witness the behavior of the television networks in the 2000 presidential election, prematurely announcing the victories of both Al Gore and George

W. Bush in Florida, and then retracting both announcements.) A Broadway expert dismissed Rodgers & Hammerstein's musical, *Away We Go,* with the terse critique, "No girls, no gags, no chance." After changing the name of the show to *Oklahoma!,* the composer and lyricist celebrated their success with one of the biggest hits in the history of Broadway. Sometimes predictions have a boomerang effect. A Russian music critic named Leonid Sabaneev so detested the music of Sergei Prokofiev that he wrote a scathing review of the composer's *Scythian Suite* before he had ever heard it. The composer pulled the piece from a scheduled program at the last minute, but review of the unperformed work was still published, and the critic, not the composer, had to resign in disgrace.

Most efforts to predict where we are heading lead in two directions. Optimists assume that progress, usually spearheaded by technological advances, will solve most of our problems. They think world peace and prosperity are just around the corner. Pessimists see technology not as a dream, but as a nightmare. They imagine a world out of a science fiction novel, in which people are reduced to numbers. In such a society, the individual becomes only a cog in a well-designed wheel and only the fittest survive. One technological pundit declared, "In a few years, every function in your house will be performed by a computer. In fact, your home will be one giant computer." Optimists and pessimists might be willing to accept this statement, but would disagree furiously on whether it is cause to smile or recoil in horror.

Nevertheless, efforts to discuss the future in only technological terms ignore the spiritual and cultural dimensions of life. We may safely assume that technology will change our lives, in some ways for the better and in some ways for worse. But technology itself will not address the survival of our culture. What will happen if present trends continue, if we do not address the issue of cultural conservation? We may well find ourselves in a society that is technologically advanced, culturally ignorant, and spiritually deprived. In such a society, most people will derive their tastes from popular culture defined and controlled by the entertainment media. The publishers, film producers, recording executives, television tycoons, and corporate media barons will have been raised, groomed, and shaped by this same popular culture. They will exercise a disproportionate influence over our society, because one of these individuals makes daily decisions that affect the buying habits of millions of people. Since many people depend upon media approval to set their cultural and social values, these individuals will exercise far more real power than elected officials. Most of these media power brokers will be commercially successful, wise in the ways of the street and superficially sophisticated. They will know where to buy the most expensive pair of shoes or the most fashionable wristwatch. They will know a lot about gross profits and audience demographics. But they will be vaingloriously ignorant of music, art, and literature. They will be aware only of what sold yesterday and ignorant as to the consequences of their actions. Their tastes will be those of the crowd and the tastes of the crowd will be theirs. Few will heed the advice of Bishop Fulton J. Sheen, who once told a group of broadcasting executives, "You should realize that the community with which you deal is not the one of 42nd Street and Broadway or Hollywood and Vine. These are the crusts on the great American sandwich. The meat is in between."

What are the consequences of inaction? What can we expect if we do nothing? In 1919, Rudyard Kipling, disillusioned by World War I and the tragic loss of his son, wrote a poem, *The Gods of the Copybook Headings.* Copybooks were used by students at the time; they were blank except for quotations, proverbs, and sayings that the student was expected to copy onto the blank pages. In his poem, Kipling warned against following what he called "The Gods of the Market," the fashionable notions that seem temporarily appealing, but fail to hold up when compared to eternal truths and values. He wrote of these truths and values, and why they were abandoned:

With the Hopes that our World is built on they were utterly
out of touch,

They denied that the Moon was Stilton; they denied she was even Dutch;
They denied that Wishes were Horses; they denied that a Pig had Wings;
So we worshipped the Gods of the Market Who promised these beautiful things.

But in Kipling's view, values in society and in the arts represent truths that cannot be surmounted by fashion. Eventually, we can only expect to face the consequences of abandoning our past in pursuit of a superficial present. This does not mean that we should be against progress or change, only that change for its own sake is a false idol. The right kind of change represents progress; the wrong kind represents disaster. If we continue on our present path, pursuing fads and fashions to the exclusion of eternal truths, as Kipling warned us, we will indeed face the consequences.

The public will continue to confuse celebrity and achievement until the two become synonymous. In the end, corrupt and ignorant people will serve a grateful, but equally corrupt and ignorant audience. The protagonist in George Orwell's novel *1984* spends every chapter trying to escape the pervasive dominance of the all-powerful dictator, "Big Brother." In conclusion, Orwell's hero meets the only fate possible in such a society. He learns to love "Big Brother." The same fate may be in store for a society that allows the arts to slide slowly and quietly into oblivion. The public will celebrate the talents of the talentless and the mediocre, while the truly gifted achieve involuntary anonymity.

Winston Churchill said, "Without tradition, art is a flock of sheep without a shepherd. Without innovation, it is a corpse." This sad fate need not befall the arts. The entertainment industry, the schools, the government will not provide a solution. But we can. As individuals, we can commit ourselves to the goal of Cultural Conservation. Through self-education and vigorous efforts, we can see that the intangible values derived from the arts are not lost in society. Aaron Copland once said, "So long as the human spirit thrives on this planet, music in some living form will accompany and sustain it and give it expressive meaning." Through Cultural

Conservation, we can foster and encourage achievement that will provide inspiration to the soul, energy for the human spirit, enthusiasm for the heart. Tradition and innovation can thrive in the 21st century and beyond. The choice is ours.

A PERSONAL PLAN OF ACTION

THE OPPORTUNITY OF SELF-EDUCATION

AFTER READING THESE PAGES, do you feel you have missed the opportunity to discover the music, art, theater, and literature that are sadly neglected today? If our schools and entertainment media have "defined the arts down" to a point of no return, is the situation hopeless? Not at all. Can you rediscover the joys and words and music and the pride of achievement in the age of trash talk and cultural chaos? Do it yourself. You may be surprised at all the things you can teach yourself, if you become an informed and motivated learner.

Ray Bradbury, the iconic writer of novels, short stories, screenplays, and the most famous creator of works in every genre of science fiction, had the answer. Bradbury was a strong believer in self-education. This is because Bradbury acquired much of his extensive and eclectic knowledge of many subjects on his own. "Libraries raised me," he told the *New York Times*. "I don't believe in colleges and universities. I believe in libraries because most students don't have any money. When I graduated from high school, it was during the Depression and we had no money. I couldn't go to college, so I went to the library three days a week for ten years." Bradbury pursued an intensive program of self-education, but it was not designed for him by anyone else. He said, "I read everything in the library. I read everything. I took out ten books a week so I had a couple of hundred books a year I read, on literature, poetry, plays, and I read all the great short stories, hundreds of them. I graduated from the library when I was twenty-eight years old. That library educated me, not the college."

Like Bradbury, E.B. White, author of the beloved children's book, *Charlotte's Web*, appreciated libraries. He said, "A library is a good place to go when you feel unhappy, for there, in a book, you may find encouragement and comfort. A library is a good place to go when you feel bewildered or undecided, for there, in a book, you may have your question answered. Books are good company, in sad times and happy times, for books are people—people who have managed to stay alive by hiding between the cover of a book."

Of course, this doesn't mean that no one should go to college or that you can't learn very interesting things at colleges and universities. But Bradbury and others like him are proof that there are also other and sometimes better ways to learn. Ray Bradbury isn't the only example of a self-educated man who pursued knowledge on his own with spectacular results. History has been filled with successful people of great achievement who have not graduated from college. Some were entirely self-taught, others dropped out of high school or college to pursue their dreams.

George Washington and Benjamin Franklin didn't attend college. James Monroe dropped out of the College of William and Mary to fight in the revolutionary war. Andrew Jackson, Martin Van Buren, Zachary Taylor, Millard Fillmore, Abraham Lincoln, Andrew Johnson, Grover Cleveland, William McKinley, and Harry S. Truman all achieved the presidency without a college degree. Lincoln estimated that he had received about a year of formal education.

Many of the world's most successful businessmen were self-educated, including Henry Ford, Frederic Henry Royce (the Royce of Rolls-Royce automobiles,) Thomas Edison, George Westinghouse, George Eastman (founder of Kodak,) Milton Hershey (who gave us the Hershey Bar), James Cash Penney (J.C. Penney stores,) DeWitt Wallace (Founder and Publisher of *Reader's Digest,*) Henry J. Kaiser (Kaiser Aluminum,) Richard DeVos and Jay Van Andel (founders of Amway,) Ray Kroc (McDonald's), William Lear (The Lear Jet), Tom Monaghan (Domino's Pizza), and Walt Disney.

Some of the most accomplished figures in the arts were self-educated. People think of great composers as the products of great teachers and celebrated music schools. But that isn't always the case. Consider the career of Roy Harris, born in a log cabin on February 12, Lincoln's birthday, in Lincoln County, Oklahoma. Harris grew up on a farm in California. He was working as a truck driver, delivering milk and eggs, when he decided to pursue his ambition to become a great composer of symphonies. The University of California looked askance at his prospects, but Harris was undaunted. He pursued private studies, both in America and France, and eventually emerged as one of the most important American composers of the 20th century. He wrote thirteen symphonies, won worldwide acclaim, and taught at the most distinguished schools. The University of California eventually invited him to become head of their music department, a position which he turned down.

Paul Creston was born in New York to a poor but devoted and industrious family of Italian immigrants. He took lessons on the piano and organ in his youth, but as a composer, he was entirely self-taught. He worked to help support his family, all the while pursuing his interests in musical theory, composition, literature, and philosophy. He went on to compose five symphonies, concertos for piano and violin and for numerous less traditional instruments, including the saxophone, marimba, and accordion, and also wrote radio and television scores, and important books on the analysis of musical rhythm. Even after he became a nationally celebrated composer and teacher, he continued to pursue knowledge on his own, studying many foreign languages just for the joy of learning. Irving Berlin had no formal education of any kind, but he emerged as one of America's greatest songwriters, penning the music and lyrics for "God Bless America," "White Christmas," and "Easter Parade," among hundreds of classic melodies for musical shows and motion pictures.

The shelves of libraries are filled with books written by authors who didn't attend college and in some cases, were entirely self-educated. Abigail Adams, wife of John Adams and mother of John Quincy Adams, was educated at home and never went to school. Louisa May Alcott, author of *Little Women*, was taught at home, while Jane Austen wrote *Pride and Prejudice* with little formal schooling. Famed 19th century poets Robert and Elizabeth Barrett

Browning never graduated from college, nor did Scotland's most famous poet, Robert Burns. Herman Melville taught himself primarily by reading, but that fact didn't prevent him from writing *Moby Dick*. Mark Twain left school at thirteen to work and wander about the Mississippi River, while Charles Dickens left school at fifteen because his father was in debtor's prison. No one faced more obstacles than Frederick Douglass, born as a slave before the Civil War and forbidden by law to learn to read. An abolitionist taught him to read, however, and after extensive self-education, he emerged as one of the most important writers and orators of his generation.

Modern writers had similar experiences. William Faulkner and Scott Fitzgerald were college dropouts, as was the great New England poet, Robert Frost, who still managed to win Four Pulitzer Prizes. Frost's sometime rival Carl Sandburg also dropped out of school at thirteen and won two Pulitzer Prizes of his own. Ernest Hemingway skipped college entirely. Harold Ross was one of the most famous magazine editors of all time; as founding editor of *The New Yorker*, he edited the work of the most famous writers of the 1920s and '30s. He was also a high school dropout. Louis L'Amour was probably America's best-known writer of westerns and he left school at fifteen. Agatha Christie, the world's most famous mystery writer, was primarily educated at home. Eric Hoffer worked as a longshoreman. Despite little formal education, he became a prominent writer and philosopher.

History has also recognized artists, architects, and inventors who had little formal training. Buckminster Fuller was twice expelled from Harvard, but he pursued a unique and unconventional path, creating hundreds of inventions, including the geodesic dome. Frank Lloyd Wright became America's most celebrated architect before architecture was even regarded as an academic discipline. Ansel Adams explored photography on his own and became recognized as the nation's best-known landscape photographer. Newscasters like Walter Cronkite and Peter Jennings went to work rather than finish their formal education. A lack of formal studies didn't prevent Thomas Edison from becoming one of the world's greatest inventors or the Wright Brothers from developing the airplane.

You may say that you have no desire to pursue a career as a musician, artist, or writer, but this should not prevent you from learning about the achievements of people who do, even if their work is ignored or neglected by the formal academic establishment or the popular entertainment media.

DO IT YOURSELF!

Ronald Gross, a prolific author, editor, and educator, has written numerous books on self-education, including *Peak Learning*.[163] He has written eloquently of thousands of men and women who find that scholarship is their joy, not their job. The same could be said for those who see the arts (and the whole idea of Cultural Conservation) as a mission of pleasure, not just academic or intellectual pursuit. Gross advocates going beyond self-discovery to explore what is important or beautiful about the world, by becoming what he calls "risk takers of the spirit." Are you bold enough to take steps on your own to go wherever your intellectual curiosity takes you? What we learn from Gross is that such pursuits do not have to follow a straight line. You are never too young (or too old) to begin such journeys and they do not have to follow a path charted through traditional academic waters (or one defined by the media). He reminds us of a woman who published her first book, a history of her church, at eighty-four, and a sixteen-year-old student who translated an important scientific treatise from French to English. Neither the original author of the treatise nor a new publisher suspected his age. Nor is formal education essential to learning. Gross cites a leading scholar, critic, and conference organizer in the field of science fiction who is employed as a janitor. Gross says, "Many people have trouble at first with the idea of self-directed learning, because they have been trained to equate learning only with what is taught in educational institutions. They assume that the right way to learn is in a classroom from a teacher and textbooks, by listening to expert authorities, doing assigned readings, memorizing stale information for tests and getting grades."

Gross's own interest in pursuing knowledge independently was influenced by his mentor, Neil Hirschberg, who revealed to him the inner incentives for lifelong learning. Hirschberg said, "I have always lived, and always will live, my life as it can be lived at its best, with art, music, poetry, literature, science, philosophy, and thought. I shall know the keener people of this world, think the keener thoughts, and taste the keener pleasures, as long as I can and as much as I can. That's the real practical use of self- education and self-culture. It converts a world which is only a good world for those who can win at its ruthless game into a world good for all of us. Your education is the only thing that nothing can take from you in this life."[164]

Gross concentrates upon those of us who want to turn interest in any subject into expertise. But you do not have to become an "expert" on music, art, or literature to become an explorer. "Expertise" may happen incidentally. You may never compose a string quartet, paint a picture, or write a novel, but you can still discover and appreciate the achievements of those who do. Or you may find yourself drawn into an artistic realm you never thought possible. All you have to do is make a decision to become curious about what you don't know. Since learning is a lifelong experience, this shouldn't be difficult. You may want to begin by exploring music you've only heard superficially. Alternatively, you may want to discover art or books that are entirely new to you. There are many ways to accomplish this, but in recent years, the element of high technology has opened an incredible door to those of us who want to learn about the culture that we need actively to conserve.

Self-education offers both opportunities and hazards. The greatest opportunity is obvious. A self-educated individual is not subject to the conventional limitations of traditional academic thinking or the entertainment industry's notions regarding what is "old-fashioned." Highly educated people are often limited in their capacity for discovery by attitudes of a small pseudo- intellectual elite which tolerates certain writers, composers, and artists, and dismisses others. People with little formal education may be subjected to these same biases through their dependence on television and other media. Interestingly, both groups of people would be outraged at the suggestion that their outlooks are limited. They see themselves as "progressive" and up to date. They want to be "with it," although they would be hard pressed to explain exactly what "it" is. Yet their thinking is limited and confined as if contained in a sealed box. They allow the bias of others to determine what they think is important. A self-educated individual escapes these restrictions by thinking creatively, "outside the box" if you will. But moving "outside the box" also offers an obvious hazard. Just as the self-educated individual escapes the bias of others, this same individual can miss warning signs on the road. Someone trying to learn basic arithmetic needs to be corrected when operating on the assumption that 2+2=5. It is easier to avoid such mistakes in subjects that deal exclusively in facts. However, the arts are concerned more with expression than facts. One may draw all sorts of erroneous conclusions about music or art without the more obvious correction that 2+2=4.

Not every self-educated man or woman is going to become famous and not all will succeed. But not everyone with a prestigious degree or a background in formal studies will succeed either. Those who are self-educated learn differently, because there are no rules or requirements to their course of study. But how and where you study doesn't determine the end results of your education, and if you approach the never ending process of learning with enthusiasm, care, and energy, there is no telling what you can accomplish.

SELF-EDUCATION ISN'T SCHOOL

Self-education bears little relationship to how you performed in school. Exceptionally good students and those who did poorly during their school years both face different challenges in acquiring knowledge on their own. There are many outstanding students who make good grades because they are good at following rules, and especially in college, writing essays that regurgitate the tastes, biases, and prejudices of the teacher. But when pursuing self-education, with no one telling them what to do, they may feel lost without a map drawn by someone else. There are many people who have made poor grades because they were unmotivated, discouraged, and yes, sometimes lazy. Sometimes they had teachers with low expectations who convinced them that they had little talent. If someone tells you often enough that you have no ability or no future, you may begin to believe it. So the student with poor grades may doubt his capacity for self-education. But whether you made good grades, average grades, or poor grades in school, self-education depends on you. If you are determined, you can succeed.

It's not difficult to think you're the best at what you do if you only compare yourself to your next-door neighbor. Ask most students if they recognize the names of today's leading sports figures. How do we know these are true sports legends? By comparing their achievements to the great stars of the past. What would a student think of an instructor who said, "Let's talk about football, basketball, baseball, or golf, but skip the athletes who won the most championships and set the most records?" Yet today's world is full of individuals who don't recognize the names of our most accomplished figures in the arts, men and women whose achievements are easily equal to those of today's legendary sports figures.

As we study and learn, we cannot help but be struck by the vast amount of information left to absorb. Not only is there a vast storehouse of knowledge from the past, but a treasure trove of new information, techniques, and creativity awaiting discovery. The world's finest musicians continue to discover new aspects of compositions they have performed or studied all their lives. They consider the greatest musical works to be those from which they can always learn something new. The same can be said for great paintings or books. A teacher may spend a lifetime instructing students and never cease being a student himself.

Unfortunately, not everyone will encourage you to pursue learning on your own. In fact, some skeptics will say all kinds of things to discourage you.

TOO YOUNG TO LEARN, TOO OLD TO LEARN

One specious but popular argument offered by the skeptics is that you are either too young to learn or too old. Nonsense. The arts are ageless and timeless. The best art, music, and literature become classics because they speak to audiences of all ages. Regardless of your time of life, you can become a Cultural Conservationist. If you have little experience with the arts, a treat is in store. If you are a veteran, there is always more to learn. Children should be exposed to the arts at an early age. This is especially important because parents who do so will foster their children's appetite for quality before the entertainment industry begins offering its own alternatives. William J. Bennett, Chester E. Finn, Jr., and John T.E. Cribb, Jr. addressed this subject in their book, *The Educated Child.*[165] Among their key principles for parents of educated children is recognition that parents are the first and most important teachers, that their teaching must not stop when schooling starts. Learning about the arts encourages creativity and may boost general academic performance. Bennett and his colleagues have keen observations about the value of early arts education. They conclude, "When we hold up to students true masterpieces of art and music, we teach them to discriminate between what is fine and what is mediocre, between the sublime and the mundane. We cultivate in their hearts a love for beauty. With attention from adults, that capacity for delight will bloom. With nourishment it will flourish in the years beyond elementary school. As Wordsworth said, 'The music in my heart I bore, long after it was heard no more.'"

At an early age, children can begin looking at beautiful pictures, making discoveries about color and light. They can begin learning about scales and musical instruments. This should not be pedantic, but with a sense of discovery, adventure, and always a sense of humor. A child may have difficulty relating to a long, complex piece of music. But works like Haydn's *Surprise Symphony,* intended to wake up sleeping members of the audience, or Saint-Saens' wonderful depiction of birds and beasts in *Carnival of Animals* are another story entirely. Musical fairy tales like *Cinderella* or *Sleeping Beauty* have been adapted as operas and ballets. Children will also respond to jazz, especially if they realize that the performers are improvising, making up the music as they go along. What is essential is that children be introduced to good music and art early, and with enthusiasm. One mistake to be avoided at all costs is subjecting children to low expectations. Children from any social or economic background can still learn about the finest elements of culture.

The humorist Richard Armour once wrote a book about the teenage years, *Through Darkest Adolescence.*[166] He playfully described these years as a disease from which teenagers and their parents would emerge fully cured. Everyone knows that the teenage years are frequently highlighted by rebellion against everything associated with parents and teachers. Unfortunately, this usually includes tastes in music, art, television, books, and motion pictures. Especially during adolescence, teenagers are subjected to a battery of destructive influences coming from the ubiquitous entertainment media. If a teenager has already formed a sound sense of values regarding the arts, there should be no problem. But if not, peer pressure will quickly swamp any advice coming from authority figures and the result will be a budding ignoramus. It is fine for students to feel good about themselves and to cultivate self-esteem. But they also have to have something to feel good about, a sense of accomplishment and achievement. As for the teenagers who have never experienced good music or art, there is still no reason for this to be accepted. More often than not, young audiences don't know what they like, they like what everyone else in their social circle likes. They like what they are told to like, although they would be shocked to realize this fact. They think of themselves as non-conformists, often rebelling against the "establishment." But they are quick to conform to the behavior and tastes of their peers. Introducing good music and art to these audiences may be difficult, but don't assume that they won't respond. Too often, there are limited opportunities for them to encounter anything other than pop culture. Familiarity with popular culture is one way that teenagers can be popular, by sharing the same music, for instance. But rugged individualism, not "groupthink," is essential if our culture is to survive. "Groupthink" occurs when a group of like-minded people speaks only to each other and assumes that the world agrees with them. They need to be informed that the world does not rotate around an axis of teenage celebrities.

Busy and active professionals sometimes feel they haven't the time to pursue the arts. Those who have missed college, for instance, may mistakenly assume that they have lost any chance really to understand the arts. (They would be surprised to learn how many college students and their professors don't understand the arts either.) Nonetheless, there are endless opportunities for learning at local libraries, museums, and even the campus. Good music, art, and literature can also be explored through selective and all-too-rare television programs. Many people, busy with their responsibilities with families and careers, may regard the arts as a luxury. Some reject the arts because of boring or apathetic teachers during their student days. Some are too busy making money. However, being busy is no excuse. If we are all too busy to do anything about the arts, they will disappear. Just as we must preserve our natural resources, we must take the time to conserve our cultural resources. Otherwise, we will wake up one day and find them gone. Those ignorant of the problem will not even realize what they have missed.

Some of the greatest artistic works have been created by people long past the alleged age for retirement. Great musical virtuosos like Artur Rubinstein and Vladimir Horowitz were concertizing in their eighties. Pablo Casals, the legendary cellist, was playing and conducting into his nineties. Earl Wild was the first major concert pianist to appear on television and decades later, the first to play a recital over the Internet. He celebrated his 90th birthday with a recital at Carnegie Hall. The renowned pianist and pedagogue Mieczyslaw Horszowski gave his final recital at ninety-nine and his last piano lesson a week before his death at one hundred and one. Eleanor Sokoloff, his colleague at the Curtis Institute of Music, taught generations of pianists at the famed Philadelphia conservatory from 1936 until her passing in 2020 at 106. The distinguished pianist Ruth Slenczynska began her career heralded as one of the most astonishing child prodigies since Mozart, a pupil of the world's most acclaimed virtuosos, including Sergei Rachmaninoff, Artur Schnabel, Alfred Cortot, and Egon Petri. She has continued to play and teach to international acclaim for nine decades, most recently playing a recital in Japan for her greatest fan there, the Empress Michiko, and her 97th birthday was celebrated in 2022 by the release of a new recording she had completed during the previous year.

Giuseppe Verdi wrote one of his greatest masterpieces, the opera *Falstaff*, at the age of seventy-four. Ralph Vaughan Williams was actively composing until his death at eighty-six. And the nonagenarian Havergal Brian, Britain's most prolific symphonic composer, told a BBC interviewer that he had no intention of dying in the near future because he had just purchased a new pair of trousers. Nicolas Slonimsky was a composer, conductor, pianist, critic, and raconteur. But he is best remembered as a lexicographer. For years, Slonimsky edited *Baker's Biographical Dictionary*, an important musical reference book used around the world. He remained busily productive until his death at 101. Albert Hirschfeld was the legendary artist who was recognized throughout the world as the master of caricature. He spent eight decades exploring the creative opportunities of line, specializing in theatrical caricatures that appeared in the *New York Times*. He never retired, and when he passed away just short of his 100th birthday, he was still going to the theater and producing new caricatures to world acclaim.

If these creative geniuses can be productive throughout their lives, there is no reason why men and women of any age can't learn about music or the other arts at any time. Even if you have retired, there is no such thing as being too old to learn. Montaigne said, "There is nothing more remarkable in the life of Socrates than that he found time in his old age to learn to dance and play an instrument and thought it time well spent." Learning about the arts is the beginning of Cultural Conservation. You begin (at any age) to appreciate and discover our cultural legacy. Then you pass it on to others. One child tells another, one adolescent speaks to a friend, one parent encourages another, and one grandparent makes a discovery and passes it on. The arts are ageless and timeless for a reason. The best works of art can be studied at any age and they will yield new discoveries. Approach a work of art at any age and you will see it differently.

So put the skeptics behind you and prepare a plan of action. Have you decided to become a Cultural Conservationist? You can join others with the same set of interests, but there is much you can do all by yourself. Let's assume, for the moment, that these pages have persuaded you. What can you do?

LEARNING FOR A LIFETIME

Here are a few principles to remember.

1. *Learning is a never-ending process.* The more you know, the more you realize you don't know. We often make the mistake of assuming that learning is a finite process, with a definite beginning and ending. But this is untrue. Learning, unlike a baseball game, doesn't have nine innings and a final score. The world is full of educated ignoramuses, many of whom have degrees and certificates that ostensibly attest to their knowledge. They go through life pontificating on subjects both familiar and unfamiliar

to them, never for a moment realizing how little they know and how much more they have to learn. True learning today is challenged by two types of people: those who are aggressively ignorant and ridicule the value of learning, and those who think they have already learned everything and have nothing more to achieve. The legendary basketball coach John Wooden told players at UCLA that what you learn after you think you know it all is what is important.

Learning is a continuous process of discovery. You never stop learning. The most accomplished musicians and artists are humbled when they compare their works to great masters of the past. Often, it is those of few accomplishments who are convinced that they've "done it all." Their view of "all" is limited, their range restricted. Artur Schnabel was one of the most famous pianists in the world, and internationally recognized as a specialist in playing the sonatas of Beethoven. After decades of concerts, he told his son of the joy he felt when he finally felt he had played one passage in a single sonata the way Beethoven would have wanted it to be played. Often the most accomplished people are the first to recognize that learning never ends. Oscar Peterson was regarded as the world's preeminent jazz pianist and widely respected as a teacher. Yet he said, "With what I don't know about the piano, believe it or not, and have yet to learn, and what I don't know about music, I could live fifty lifetimes and still be learning, and would enjoy every minute of it. I'm a learner."

Similar sentiments were expressed by Rafael Méndez, the amazing trumpet virtuoso from Mexico. He had a phenomenal technique that simply dazzled audiences and displayed an ability to execute passages on the trumpet that were usually played only by the world's finest violinists. Yet Méndez was uncomfortable being billed as "the world's greatest trumpeter." He modestly told Jerry Russell, "There is no such thing as the best in the world. I don't feel that I've reached my peak, and if I'm not able to improve myself in future years, it won't be because I haven't tried. The greatest satisfaction I get from my work is to be able to improve myself with each performance and perhaps act as an inspiration to younger musicians."

Everyone, including the author of this book, should start each day conscious of how much more there is to learn. Learning shouldn't be boring, dull, or frustrating. It should be exciting, challenging, and filled with discovery. Not everyone learns best in the same way. But in the 21st century, the opportunities for self-education are unlimited. No one can learn everything about music, the arts, or any other subject worth exploring from a single book or a single course. But if you have the desire and the enthusiasm for adventures of the mind and heart, you're ready to begin. Your journey isn't ending, it is just starting. Mortimer Adler, who spent a lifetime exploring and advocating reading great books, said, "The purpose of learning is growth, and our minds, unlike our bodies, can continue growing as we continue to live."

2. *You never know what you may need to know in life.* Most students assume that they already know what they will need to know, but they couldn't be more wrong. Typically, teenage boys think they need to know things that make them popular with girls and may be useful in their careers. Teenage girls think they need to know things that make them popular with boys and may be useful in their careers. But life is full of twists and turns, and often we are tempted to assume that we need to know what is popular at the moment. In five, ten, or fifteen years, the issues of the moment may fade into memory, along with many of the heroes we admire, and especially today's celebrities, fads, and trends. Something (or someone) we may consider unimportant today may have a major impact on our lives in the future. Students can be forgiven for not understanding that what seems desperately important today may seem less significant in a few years. But if students miss the opportunity to discover the arts today, we shouldn't assume they will discover them on their own tomorrow.

3. *Often, we don't know what we like.* We like what we know. The actor Vincent Price was an enthusiastic art collector. He once

wrote a book about his lifelong devotion to the visual arts, *I Like What I Know*. How often do we hear someone say, "I don't like that!" and discover he is rejecting something with which he is totally unfamiliar?

Nevertheless, familiarity doesn't automatically justify or demand approval. Academic and critical elitists frequently dismiss public rejection of unpopular works by charging that the public is too ignorant or unsophisticated to appreciate anyone highly promoted as a genius. Such remarks are common among intellectual snobs sipping wine and contemplating brie at receptions. Pop culture advocates are similarly quick to dismiss criticism of the untalented charlatans who are dubbed "superstars." However, instead of dismissing critics as stupid and uncultured, they simply reject them as obsolete and prejudiced against anything new that overturns taboos. We mustn't assume that being familiar with something automatically results in approval. The multitalented composer-conductor-pianist, André Previn, once agreed to spend an afternoon listening to rock music with a neighbor, a famous rock star. Previn had spent a lifetime involved in jazz and high quality popular music as well as the classics. But he remained unconvinced about the merit of much of today's amplified pop music. The neighbor was convinced that if Previn only became familiar with today's pop music, he would be a converted fan. After spending several hours patiently listening to the music, Previn dismissed it as "the worst garbage I've heard." To be fair, you can draw your own conclusions. There is nothing wrong with saying "I didn't like this work of art and I didn't understand it. Now I understand it and I still don't like it." No one should object if you say, "I have listened to the voice of the latest amplified teen idol and I still think he can't sing." No one, perhaps, except the "superstar's" agent, and he is unfortunately crying all the way to the bank.

Today's students are often eager to learn the lyrics to the latest hits, but much of their enthusiasm comes from a desire to be familiar with what is "in" at the moment. Being "in" and not "out" in one's tastes is part of being popular. It is a phenomenon as familiar to followers of fads in fashionable art galleries as to a group of eighth-grade teenagers. There is a difference between rejecting something because you don't like it and because you don't know it. Students are often inclined to reject that which they don't know simply because it is unfamiliar. If it doesn't seem relevant to their lives now, they will be tempted to reject it as outdated without ever knowing it. A challenge to students should be, don't reject what you don't know or understand. Learn about it first, and then determine your own taste. While some will always reject the unfamiliar, others will learn that it is easy to "like what you know" and much harder to "know what you like."

4. *Light candles rather than curse the darkness.* The key to Cultural Conservation is not just to develop critiques of our problems, but to find solutions. "It is better to light one candle than to curse the darkness." This motto, adopted by the Christopher Society, was derived from an old Chinese saying. It can serve as very good advice in dealing with the cultural crisis that faces our society. There are many opportunities to light candles. For those without special skills or backgrounds in the arts, the challenges are not easy, but one person with energy and enthusiasm can still accomplish much.

Sometimes, a single person can change history through persistence and enthusiasm. Today, concert audiences are very familiar with the music of Antonio Vivaldi, the Italian composer who thrived in 18th century Venice. Vivaldi's work, *The Four Seasons*, has been recorded many times and is even used in films and television commercials. But in 1949, Vivaldi's music, known to scholars and musicologists, was not widely recorded or recognized by the general public. Louis Kaufman was an internationally recognized violin virtuoso, who had also spent many years providing violin solos for motion picture soundtracks. (His work is heard on the soundtracks of hundreds of films, including *Gone With the Wind* and *Casablanca*.) Kaufman was scheduled to perform a modern work with the CBS Symphony, the radio orchestra conducted by Bernard Herrmann. Kaufman learned that Alfredo Antonini, an Italian conductor, would substitute for Herrmann on one concert. Antonini had acquired copies of Antonio Vivaldi's *Four Seasons* concertos, and both Herrmann and Antonini urged Kaufman to learn the Vivaldi works and perform them. Kaufman was subsequently asked by Concert Hall Records to suggest solo concertos, accompanied by a small orchestra, for recording. Kaufman suggested *The Four Seasons* and the rest was history. He described these pieces by Vivaldi as possibly the first examples of solo concertos written as "program music," depicting something above and beyond an abstract musical idea. Vivaldi had written these works inspired by the year's seasons, with hunts, festivals, and dances. Louis Kaufman thus made the first recording of *The Four Seasons*, pieces that are adored around the world. Dr. Alfred Einstein, a noted music historian, told Kaufman that the four concertos were from a group of twelve. Kaufman became an expert on Vivaldi, aware that the Italian master had composed around 225 concertos, most of which were not published or recorded in America. Eventually Kaufman and his wife Annette, a distinguished pianist, traveled throughout Italy in search of Vivaldi's elusive scores. Their investigation could have been the plot of a detective novel, as they searched libraries and consulted obscure European scholars. They finally found the score of Vivaldi's *Opus 8* in Brussels. Kaufman introduced the work to audiences in a World Premiere in Paris. He subsequently introduced Vivaldi's music to American audiences. It is hard to believe that the music of Antonio Vivaldi, so popular today among lovers of classical music and the public, was largely forgotten. Thanks to the efforts of Louis Kaufman, Vivaldi's music achieved its rightful place in a contemporary view of music history.

Carnegie Hall is undoubtedly the most famous concert hall in the world. Pyotr Ilyich Tchaikovsky himself came to New York for its opening music festival in 1891. Since then, Carnegie Hall remained the symbol of musical achievement. The world's most celebrated artists performed there, including pianists Leopold Godowsky, Josef Hoffman, Ignacy Paderewski, Sergei Rachmaninoff, Artur Rubinstein, and Vladimir Horowitz; guitarist Andrés Segovia, violinists Fritz Kreisler, Eugène Ysaÿe, Jascha Heifetz, Efrem Zimbalist, Mischa Elman, Nathan Milstein; and tenor Enrico Caruso. The greatest orchestras appeared under the batons of the finest conductors, while jazz made its Carnegie Hall debut in 1912. But with the advent of New York's Lincoln Center complex, the unthinkable was about to happen. Carnegie Hall was to be torn down and replaced by a tall red office building. This was too much for Isaac Stern. At the time, Stern was recognized as one of the world's foremost concert violinists. In his memoir, *My First 79 Years,*[167] he explained, "I had always thought of Carnegie Hall as our country's affirmation of the human spirit. The great artists who had played in it since its opening in May 1891! The music that had resonated within its walls! When I played there that December, I knew that the edifice was to be torn down within the next few months. On the site would rise an office skyscraper with an exterior colored Chinese red." Stern continued, "For me, Carnegie Hall was the Holy Grail, the be-all and end-all of musical life in this country for all performing artists. No other place we played in had its unique history. The whole measure of American musical performance was created at Carnegie Hall. We were all its children. I could not see the one building that represented the American tradition of music internationally be torn down—I just could not bear it." Many concert artists would have simply walked away from the situation, but not Isaac Stern. In 1960, Stern organized a small gathering of civic leaders in his home. He turned to philanthropist Jacob Kaplan for financial support and sought a governmental ally in Mayor Robert Wagner. Through Stern's incredible efforts, including his successful enlistment of endorsements from the world's most prominent musical artists, Carnegie Hall was saved, restored, and designated as a National and New York City Historic Landmark.

In 1953, Elaine Lorillard was attending a classical music concert and found herself seated next to John Maxon, Director of the Rhode Island School of Design Museum. During intermission, Maxon turned to her and said, "It's too bad we can't do something like this for jazz. That's another music form that's worth a big-time festival." Elaine Lorillard took his suggestions seriously. Together with her husband Louis, she contacted George Wein for assistance. Though jazz had been performed in Carnegie Hall, many people still didn't think jazz was quite respectable. That attitude had to change when the Lorillards asked Wein to organize a jazz festival in Newport, Rhode Island. Wein proved to be exactly the right man for the job. As a young jazz pianist, George Wein had studied with legendary Boston jazz piano pedagogue Sam Saxe. He was running Storyville, his own jazz club in Boston. The Lorillards and Wein changed Newport forever. The fashionable waterfront community became host to the Newport Jazz Festival. In 1954, seven thousand jazz fans flocked to the grounds of the Newport Casino to hear the world's finest jazz musicians. Among the artists performing were the Modern Jazz Quartet, the Oscar Peterson Trio, the Dizzy Gillespie Quintet, the Gerry Mulligan Quartet, the George Shearing Quintet, the Erroll Garner Trio, the Gene Krupa Trio, and vocalists Ella Fitzgerald and Billie Holiday. The Newport Jazz Festival still continues each year to attract new fans for the improvisatory art.

Traditional New Orleans jazz is a unique musical treasure, a part of our musical history. Yet without the efforts of a few special people, both musicians and non-musicians, the highly individual sound of jazz from the Crescent City might have been lost forever. In the 1940s, many jazz musicians began experimenting with revolutionary changes in melody, rhythm, and especially harmony, resulting in the style of jazz known as "bop." Exploring the new can often lead to rejecting the traditional. As older musicians who were pioneers in the development of traditional New Orleans jazz died or retired, there was a danger that the traditional New Orleans sound might simply fade away. The advent of rock music in the '50s and '60s seemed to toll the bell for the style of jazz that once seemed to define New Orleans. But Larry Borenstein, a true believer in the authentic traditional sound, operated a small art gallery and began inviting the surviving masters of early jazz to a series of rehearsal sessions. Under the auspices of Barbara Reid, Ken Mills, and the Society for the Preservation of Traditional New Orleans Jazz, the building was converted to "Preservation Hall." As Reid and Mills lacked business experience, Borenstein turned to Allan and Sandra Jaffe, two newlyweds from Philadelphia who took an extended honeymoon in New Orleans and never left.

Initially, neither musicians nor critics expected the music to thrive or Preservation Hall to survive. A writer in the *Richmond Dispatch* described the music as "on its deathbed" and warned audiences, "You've got about ten years to catch its act." Trumpeter Kid Howard said, "It was good music then, it's good music now, this may be its swan song." Under the leadership of Allan and Sandra Jaffe, Preservation Hall did more than thrive. The Preservation Hall Jazz Band has performed in concert halls throughout the world, including Carnegie Hall, and for everyone from British royalty to the King of Thailand, himself a fine jazz musician. Ben Jaffe followed in his father's footsteps, playing bass and the tuba, and managing Preservation Hall as it celebrated its fiftieth anniversary. Today, young musicians in New Orleans are trained in the traditional style and repertoire, and the music will be passed from one generation to another.

Pinehurst is an internationally known resort in North Carolina, recognized around the world primarily for its renowned role in the history of golf. In 1986, Mal and Marge Owings decided to organize a benefit for the Arts Council of Moore County. Jazz vocalist Maxine Sullivan and the Loonis McGlohon Trio gave a stellar performance. Three years later, Jan and Ed Schnell took over the event, first called "Jazz 'n' January," and eventually renamed "Heart 'n' Soul of Jazz" when the concert dates were shifted to Valentine's Day weekend. The Schnells had moved from Ohio to Pinehurst, where Ed Schnell continued his practice as an ophthalmologist. For more than two decades, Jan Schnell has worked tirelessly to share her deep love of jazz with local audiences who flock to the elegant Pinehurst Resort to enjoy a uniquely American musical art. Normally, residents of a small town wouldn't have access to such legendary musicians as Marian McPartland, Dorothy Donegan, Toots Thielemans, Art Van Damme, and Milt Jackson. The Schnells also took special delight in discovering new and exciting jazz artists whose talents have often been applauded by thousands of jazz lovers in Pinehurst before achieving major success on the world stage. It is interesting to note that the great vibraphone virtuoso Milt Jackson was a member of the Modern Jazz Quartet that played during the first Newport Jazz Festival. More than four decades later, he entertained a Pinehurst audience. The continuity of jazz history could not be sustained without the support and enthusiasm of those who recognize its importance.

In the world of popular music, it takes courage and conviction to record and perform music and lyrics which have stood the test of time, but do not reflect the latest teenage trends in Hollywood. Robert Davi is internationally known as one of the busiest actors in the entertainment industry. He has appeared in 100 films, numerous television series, and has also turned his hand to directing. On screen, Davi typically portrays a "tough guy," in the tradition of Humphrey Bogart and Edward G. Robinson. (One of his best-known roles was his portrayal of Franz Sanchez, the nemesis of James Bond in *License to Kill.*) But Davi never forgot his initial ambition to make his mark as a singer. He had studied opera seriously with such renowned teachers as Samuel Margolis, who also trained legendary operatic baritone Robert Merrill, Daniel Ferro, long time master teacher at the Juilliard School of Music, and the celebrated opera star Tito Gobbi. But when he found himself in demand as a non-singing actor, he concentrated on that aspect of his career. Davi is a great admirer of Frank Sinatra, who personally selected him for a major role in the television drama *Contract on Cherry Street* early in his career. In 2011, Davi decided to record a tribute to his musical hero, *Davi Sings Sinatra—On The Road to Romance.* He says, "'The Great American Songbook' is America's Shakespeare, the golden age of American music. This collection of unforgettable masterpieces helped the world fall in love with our country. During my parents' time while our country faced many difficulties, this music helped it glow with promise and optimism. It reminded them that our country was a place where dreams came true, and inspired people from all over the world to find for themselves the magic that was America. And Frank Sinatra's voice was the soundtrack for their lives. Today, we find our country in extremely difficult circumstances. We are seeing erosion in culture and music. This music is as relevant today as it was when it was created. It was Romantic without being crude, the songs were poetic, and if there was heartbreak, it was sung with a delicate tenderness, not a resentful anger and toward women. Take a song that I sing on the album, 'All the Way,' which won the Oscar in 1958 and juxtapose it with a song that won the Oscar just a few years ago, 'It's Hard Out There For a Pimp.' And you can see why we have an erosion of values." Davi concludes, "My humble mission as a singer, and interpreter of this Songbook, is to help reinvigorate the spirit of America, the spirit that makes it the greatest country in the world."[168] No single concert or recording by a single artist will magically restore taste, talent, and sanity to the world of popular music. But a generation of artists following this example could indeed accomplish that goal.

Alfred Lunt and Lynne Fontanne were the most prominent acting team in American theater. From 1928 through 1960 when they retired, the Lunts never appeared on stage separately. During their storied careers, they were pioneers in theatrical realism, introducing overlapping dialogue, turning their backs to the audience, and physical contact on stage that changed the way audiences everywhere regarded the theater. The world's finest actors regarded them as mentors. Laurence Olivier, Britain's most honored Shakespearean actor said, "Everything I know about acting I learned from Alfred Lunt." Helen Hayes, known as "The First Lady of the American Theater," described the Lunts as "my idols, my teachers, my mentors."

When the Lunts were not performing, they spent much of their time at Ten Chimneys, an estate in Genesee Depot, Wisconsin, named after the number of chimneys on the Main House. The sixty acre estate became a haven for their guests and theatrical friends. But after the death of the Lunts, developers were casting an eye at the valuable property with condominiums, not preservation of a theatrical legacy, in mind. In 1996, Dr. Joseph W. Garton, a film and theater historian, arts advocate, and successful restaurateur, acquired Ten Chimneys and spearheaded the drive to create the Ten Chimneys Foundation. On May 26, 2003, Ten Chimneys, restored and revitalized, was opened to the public on what would have been the Lunts' eighty-first anniversary. The Lunts would have undoubtedly been delighted that their former home is now a museum, a center for historic preservation, and the location of conferences, lectures, play readings, concerts, and educational programs all devoted to the theater and the other arts to which they devoted their lives. Joseph Garton passed away in 2003, leaving a remarkable legacy which will impact the American theater for many years to come.

The need for preservation has never been more apparent than in recent years as more and more people regard our culture and the wisdom of the past as entirely disposable. In his 2022 memoir, *Taste: My Life Through Food,* actor Stanley Tucci writes, "I don't know why, but we Americans feel little obligation to preserve what once *was*, because we choose to see it as less than what *is* or what *could be*. Like children and adolescents, we have not yet learn that the present isn't the only thing. Obviously change is good, but there is absolutely no need for us to obliterate the past while creating the future."

Adult education and lifelong learning have a grand historic tradition in America. There was a time when many families learned together and regarded it as a source of pleasure, not a boring or irrelevant school assignment. In 1836, Josiah Holbrook, a traveling lecturer and educator, founded a platform to present lectures, classes, and debates. It's called a Lyceum. During the years prior to the Civil War, lyceums appeared throughout the country, as audiences were inspired by such speakers as Ralph Waldo Emerson and Henry David Thoreau, and even a young man named Abraham Lincoln. In 1874, John Heyl Vincent. a Methodist minister, and Lewis Miller, an Ohio businessman, organized the first Chautauqua Assembly in New York. At the height of its popularity, the Chautauqua movement inspired educational summer camps for whole families throughout the country, especially in rural areas. In the late 19th and early 20th centuries, the Chautauqua movement provided an opportunity to hear concerts and lectures delivered by celebrated national figures. There were around three hundred Chautauquas to be found from coast to coast. The advent of radio and motion pictures hastened the decline of most Chautauqua assemblies. Radio brought the voices of faraway orators into American living rooms, while motion pictures proved a competitive alternative to live theater and concerts. When television sets appeared in virtually every American household, families didn't feel the need to attend lectures or debates on political, spiritual, and cultural issues. But the spirit of adult education lives on.

The original Chautauqua Institution thrives today as a community on the shores of Chautauqua Lake in southwestern New York, drawing as many as ten thousand visitors in pursuit of fine arts, lectures, interfaith worship, recreational activities, and a variety of concerts. Lakeside Chautauqua, on the shores of Lake Erie, was the outgrowth of a series of camp revival meetings started in 1873. By 1877, Sunday school teachers were being trained at Lakeside; by the 1890s, the Ohio summer resort was providing visitors with opportunities to combine religious experience with cultural and educational programs and a host of recreational activities. On the same site that welcomed Presidents

(Ulysses S. Grant, Rutherford B. Hayes, and William McKinley), entrepreneurs (J.C. Penney), and pioneering women (Susan B. Anthony and Amelia Earhart), thousands of families are pursuing the Lakeside pillars of learning today. Colorado Chautauqua had its inception in an effort in the late 1890s by the Texas Board of Regents to establish a summer school to train teachers in a cooler climate. The result was a Chautauqua in Boulder, Colorado, now in its second century and attracting vast numbers of visitors a year. While only a few of the original Chautauquas survived the 20th century, their legacy can inspire new efforts, such as the Hilton Head Island Institute in South Carolina. The Hilton Head Institute was founded to bring people together to share, challenge, and engage with each other, stoking the fires of imagination for what is possible today and, more importantly, for tomorrow. There is no reason why the legacy of the Chautauqua movement cannot spread across the country and around the world. In the 21st century, attending meetings is only a computer screen and a mouse-click away.

Dr. Christopher Armitage is another example of how the energy and enthusiasm of a single person can make a difference. Armitage retired after more than fifty years as a distinguished professor of English at the University of North Carolina at Chapel Hill. He taught Shakespeare for over four decades and he has been compared to James Hilton's legendary fictional teacher, "Mr. Chips," for his devotion to his students. In 1969, Armitage, a native of Manchester, England, and a graduate of Oxford, combined his love of country and Shakespeare. He started a summer program in England. Participating students not only receive an intensive exposure to Shakespeare, but a chance to learn about other major writers, including Oscar Wilde, T.S. Eliot, Evelyn Waugh, Dorothy Sayers, C.S. Lewis, and J.R.R. Tolkien. Armitage had his own personal encounters with Lewis and Tolkien; he faced them on his examination board during his own student days. Armitage also introduced his American students to the tutorial style of teaching long established at Oxford and Cambridge. He says, "The tutorial system is based on a personal exchange of ideas. You come in small numbers to your tutor with prepared work and present it orally to one or a few other students, and then you are engaged in a conversation in which you are challenged. You must defend your ideas. This increases mental agility. I think it encourages students to be much more 'participatory' than they are sitting in large classes with the professor lecturing at them. It obliges you to engage in a discussion that allows you to defend or modify your views. For some students, it's a process which enables them to develop confidence, much more than in the settings they are accustomed to. It's a mind-opening and confidence-building process." Thanks to Christopher Armitage, thousands of students of all ages have learned to appreciate Shakespeare.

You don't have to be a Shakespeare scholar to make a difference in preserving the delight of the English language. You can become active in an organization devoted to that very goal. In 1918, Sir Evelyn Wrench founded The English Speaking Union in the British Commonwealth. Two years later, the United States branch of the ESU was organized "to draw together in the bonds of comradeship the English-speaking peoples of the world." Today, chapters of the organization exist throughout the United States. Through the ESU, volunteer tutors help newcomers to the U.S. build their confidence and skills in conversational English. After World War II, the ESU established a program to send books across the sea to replace those lost in Britain during the war. That program still exists today. The ESU sponsors a variety of lectures and seminars devoted to the English language, and provides scholarships for enabling faculty members and students to broaden their knowledge and debating skills. It organizes workshops, competitions, and dialogues so that students and their teachers can celebrate the beauty and power of the writings of William Shakespeare. Therefore, students who may have missed the opportunity to learn about Shakespeare in school (or were bored by ineffective teaching) can have a second chance through the English Speaking Union. In more recent times, under the leadership of Lord Alan Watson, the ESU expanded its message internationally. In fifty-three countries, the ESU promotes "Global Understanding Through English," working with thousands of young people around the world, many of whom now speak English as a second language.

When Lt. Gen. Josiah Bunting III became Chairman of the ESU of the United States, nearly a 100 years after its founding, he said, "The aim then was to strengthen and celebrate the bonds of common cultural and linguistic heritage, bonds tested in the stern arbitrament of war. Almost a century later we strive to make that heritage, in its riches of culture, literature, language, and the arts, a heritage to be shared with all others, towards a common understanding of the aspirations of all nations and peoples."

One of the most frustrating battles facing cultural conservationists is the struggle against gobbledygook and legalese. In Great Britain, this battle has been led by an unlikely warrior, Chrissie Maher. Chrissie grew up in post-war Britain and didn't learn to read and write until she was in her teens. She said, "I thought that compensation was what made wallpaper peel off." Harry Deverell, her first employer, paid for her to go to night school. In 1971, she was a married mother of four living in Liverpool and was outraged by the struggles of friends and neighbors who couldn't obtain the financial aid they needed because they had such difficulties in filling in government forms. When newspapers refused to cover the problem, she started the *Truebrook Bugle,* the first community newspaper in the UK and three years later, she established "The Impact Foundation" to pass on what she had learned to others. She went on to launch the *Liverpool News*, a newspaper designed for people with reading difficulties. By 1975, she organized the Salford Form Market in Greater Manchester to assist people with government forms. Chrissie Maher knew how to get public attention. She and her followers shredded hundreds of government forms in Parliament Square and Chrissie appeared at 10 Downing Street dressed as the "the Gobbledygook Monster" intent on presenting her campaign's magazine, *Plain English,* to Britain's new Prime Minister, Margaret Thatcher. Eventually her efforts led to The Plain English Campaign, training thousands of people who worked for banks, insurance companies, businesses, and government agencies to write in plain English. The Plain English Campaign presents awards for the use of plain, simple English and the notorious "Golden Bull" award for the year's most outrageous example of gobbledygook. Chrissie Maher brought her campaign to the United States, with major events in New York and Washington, D.C. She won enthusiastic praise and endorsements from Prince Philip, Prince Charles, and Princess Anne, and in 1994, she received the OBE (Order of the British Empire) from Queen Elizabeth.

Prime Minister Margaret Thatcher said, "Human relationships depend on communication. Bad writing is a barrier to communication. When a large organization such as the Government tries to communicate with the man and woman in the street, the scope for misunderstanding is enormous. Too often clarity and simplicity are overwhelmed by pompous words, long sentences and endless paragraphs." She concluded, "Some people think that flowery language and complicated writing is a sign of intellectual strength. They are wrong. Some of our greatest communicators were—and—are passionate believers in the simplicity of the written word. As Winston Churchill is often credited with describing a particularly tortured piece of 'officialese:' 'This is the sort of English up with which I will not put.'"

Chrissie Maher has not been content to rest on her laurels. She continues to lead the campaign to simplify the English language on both sides of the Atlantic. Millions of men in women speaking English around the world will find it easier to communicate simply because a wife and mother in Liverpool decided to take action.

In 1975, Marva Collins was a Chicago schoolteacher who had become dissatisfied with the quality of education being provided to her own children. Instead of being a passive observer or simply complaining, she decided to take action. As a result, she founded a small but extraordinary private school of her own in the inner city. Marva Collins had taught in the Chicago school system for fourteen years. She used the $5,000 balance in her high school pension fund and started the Westside Preparatory Academy on the second floor of her home. Her two children became her pupils, along with four other children from the neighborhood. During her first year, Marva Collins accepted children with learning disabilities, problem behavior, and one little girl who had been labeled "borderline retarded" by the Chicago public school "experts." Through her energy and demanding standards, her students in the primary grades became familiar with (and enthusiastic about) the works of Shakespeare and the Greek and Roman classics. Her curriculum was not based on low expectations. She expected much of them, so they began to expect much of themselves.

Evidently, Marva Collins knew something that the "experts" didn't. The child who was supposed to be "borderline retarded" eventually graduated "magna cum laude" from college. Other graduates of her school attended Harvard, Yale, and Stanford, and emerged as attorneys, doctors, engineers, and teachers. Her own daughter, Cynthia B. Collins, eventually succeeded her as director of the school. Marva Collins' accomplishments are well known. She was featured on the television program, *60 Minutes*, and her story was told in a popular movie that starred Cicely Tyson.

Marva Collins understood the meaning of determination. She had grown up in segregated Alabama, where black Americans were not allowed to use the public library. She attended a school that had no indoor plumbing and few books. Yet she graduated from college and eventually created a model for teaching that has proven extraordinary. After turning day-to-day operation of her school over to her daughter, she developed a series of seminars designed to train teachers. The curriculum she developed was based on classical literature and what she termed "ideas, lofty thoughts, and abstract concepts."

In 2014, Michaela Community School, one of the most successful and controversial state schools in England, opened its doors. The driving force behind the school was Katharine Birbalsingh, the daughter of a Jamaican mother and Indian Guyanese father who had emigrated to the UK. Under Birbalsingh's leadership, the school achieved incredible success with students who came from what would be described as disadvantaged backgrounds. As Marva Collins did in Chicago decades earlier, Birbalsingh and her talented colleagues swam upstream against all prevailing trends among educators. In two books, *Battle Hymn of the Tiger Teachers* and *The Power of Culture,* the teachers of Michaela explain in detail the ethos of the school.

The principles which reign at the school would once have been accepted by the great majority of parents and teachers on both sides of the Atlantic. But in today's 21st century "woke" culture, these ideas are often regarded as more of a battle cry than a call for consensus. At Michaela, students are taught that truth exists, knowledge matters, and beliefs are important. Teachers are expected to respect their pupils, but what is perhaps even more important today, students are taught to respect their teachers. Family values and personal responsibility are stressed. Patriotism is regarded as a virtue; love of country is not regarded as a curiosity. At Michaela, teachers love their students, but this love is expressed as "tough love." Teachers are not considered to be kind to their pupils by letting them get away with bad behavior in class or irresponsible behavior outside the classroom. High standards are expected and achieved. In particular, a student's economic background, race, ethnicity, gender, or personal problems are not regarded as an acceptable excuse for a lack of achievement.

Katharine Birbalsingh has written, "I now think that victimhood culture, lack of family support, inappropriate music choice and friend choice, refusal to take personal responsibility, inability to embrace one's duty, inability to be grateful for what one has (however little it is), peer pressure to conform to the 'ways of the street' over academic pursuit are devastating obstacles in children's lives."

Critics, of course, have been legion, predictably denouncing the teaching of classical literature, music, art, English grammar, science, mathematics, and a strict moral code. The school has been mis-characterized as a haven for the tyrannical schoolmasters portrayed in Charles Dickens' 19th century novels such as *Oliver Twist* and *Nicholas Nickleby.*

But the success of Michaela tells a far different story. Students not only adjust to standards, tough love, and an introduction to a world they would never have known otherwise; they embrace it with enthusiasm. The school is a perfect example of educators following the advice of C.S. Lewis, going back to basic principles in order to move ahead instead of relentless following a detour based on flawed notions and arrogant ideology.

The achievements of Michaela's student speak for themselves.

Do you read short stories? There was a time when millions of Americans did. But changes in tastes and in the publishing business have rendered the short story an endangered literary species. The short story flowered during 19th century America, with writers like Washington Irving, Louisa May Alcott, Nathaniel Hawthorne, Henry James, Mark Twain, Jack London, and Edgar Allen Poe. Children read stories by European authors like Hans Christian Andersen and the Brothers Grimm. Who can imagine a world without Charles Dickens' classic, *A Christmas Carol*? In the 20th century, Ernest Hemingway and F. Scott Fitzgerald wrote short stories, as did Ray Bradbury. But in recent years, the lines between fiction and non-fiction have been blurred by writers advocating what they have called "the new journalism." Collections of short stories have been regarded as "non-commercial" by many publishers, so new short story writers have been left to dream of selling a story to *The New Yorker* or seeing their work published in obscure literary journals.

Tim Johnston is a writer and former English teacher who served for over ten years as headmaster of Beaufort Academy in South Carolina. He followed in the footsteps of his father, Robert Johnston, also a teacher and headmaster of a preparatory school in Wisconsin. Johnston decided to establish *Short Story America,* a Web site providing a forum and showcase for short story writers. Not only have new writers submitted stories for online publication, but established writers have also offered new works.

During the first week of operation, members from thirty-seven U.S. States and thirteen countries signed up to participate. Johnston's plans include publication of a new short story every week, secondary school and college writing competitions, and a national convention featuring workshops for writers. In addition, a new anthology of short stories from Johnston's web site has been published. The short story is far less likely to achieve extinction because of Tim Johnston's efforts.

The real solutions may be found in the actions of individuals operating outside of large institutions. For example, technology has enabled the creation of many independent, "boutique" recording companies. These companies are able to record and market fine recordings of classical music, jazz, and musical theater. The same can be said for small, independent publishers as well as producers of documentary films and television programs. Web sites enable people from all over the world with similar interests to reach one another, while study groups, book clubs, and gatherings of friends can share mutual goals and learn together. It is only natural to feel discouraged when encountering problems. But each individual can make a difference when there are thousands of us who take action. Helen Keller said, "Keep your face toward the sunshine, and you cannot see the shadow."

5. *Develop a set of goals for self-education.* This should be fun as well as work. You can't fight to preserve what you don't know. But learning about good music, great art, and fine books should be a pleasure, not a burden. Don't use the media for guidelines about

what is important. Instead, be sure you are familiar with the best of our past and present culture.

Speaking of the extraordinary generation that produced America's Founding Fathers, Lt. Gen. Josiah Bunting III observed, "The founding generation thought of education as a means of populating the minds with estimable models, the kinds of things that would influence your own conduct, your own interests much later in life. Secondly, they were concerned with making you a self-educated person for the remainder of your life. John Adams said, "A man can always have a poet in his pocket." Gen. Bunting recalled first meeting the writer Louis Auchincloss in the back of a taxi, at the time reading a work of French history, constantly stimulating the mind. He reflected, "Nowadays, you receive a credential from a prestigious university and you go out with the ambition of running a hedge fund, and on the airplane you're reading *USA Today*. Most of our public people, people in business, people in politics, don't continue the lifelong process of self-education." But the rewards of self-education are available to all who seek to pursue them.

6. *Spread the word.* If you can, support the efforts of those independent foundations and organizations dedicated to preserving the best of our cultural past, and promoting the work of outstanding creative individuals exploring new avenues in the tradition of great artists of the past. Be especially attentive to the offerings of schools, public and private, and to local colleges and universities. Pay attention to content, not labels. An institution may have a famous name and a distinguished academic pedigree and still offer courses in "Feminist Rock Music" or "Junk Art." Schools *can* be persuaded to offer solid instruction in the arts and the struggle over what the schools are teaching will be a major battle for Cultural Conservationists. Band together with like-minded people to exchange ideas and generate collective energy. Remember that individual efforts may seem small, but together, the message of Cultural Conservation can multiply and prosper.

7. *Work to change existing institutions.* This may be a challenge ranging from difficult to futile at times. Institutions, by definition, don't like to be changed. In the case of government or the academic establishment, there are entrenched bureaucracies, which have a vested interest in their own self-preservation.

If you are a parent or grandparent, don't just assume that your children or grandchildren are getting a good education because they attend school. For example, take an interest in their ability to read. Don't assume that because they are being taught "reading" in school that they are really able to read well. Do they read and understand unfamiliar material easily? Have they been taught phonics and grammar? Don't assume that because they are enrolled in "social studies" classes that they have studied history. Are they familiar with the major figures and events of American history? There are many fine teachers in the public schools, but the system is badly in need of reform. Charter schools, private schools, and home schooling are alternatives. But a few intensely interested parents can make a difference, both in the community and at home.

Expecting the government to make constructive changes in areas affecting the arts is like hoping for good weather. You may be lucky on a particular day, but you're dependent almost entirely on circumstances over which you have no control.

Positive things can be accomplished within the entertainment industry. Most of the time this requires going outside the confines of major television networks, motion picture studios, and media conglomerates. Public broadcasting is capable of presenting fine cultural fare. But public broadcasting also tends to be dominated by small cliques of individuals who favor (and fund) the work of their friends. The commercial media will dismiss suggestions of cultural programs or publications as "non-commercial." When confronted with serious criticism, people in the entertainment business often feel threatened and respond accordingly. In the 1980s, the Parents' Music Resources Center led a campaign for voluntary labeling of recordings and videos containing material unsuitable for children. The recording industry responded by attacking its critics as censors and unsophisticated yahoos.

8. *Consider home schooling.* If you are a parent or grandparent, consider homeschooling as an option for your children or grandchildren. There are many reasons to home school children: the opportunity to help children who may have special needs or may gifted; the potential to avoid bullying, peer pressure, drugs, and other problems plaguing many schools today; flexibility to explore subjects and ideas that may not be taught in school; the opportunity to learn at one's individual pace; a way for parents to insure that a student receives religious instructions and values. But the single most important reason for home schooling today is that home schooled boys and girls will not be subject to the political and ideological indoctrination which has so outraged so many parents.

Yes, schools need to be reformed. But the odds are that in most public and even private schools, your children and grandchildren will be subject to a racial and gender based agenda that may be the antithesis of everything you believe. Often, by the time parents realize what is going on, the damage has been done. Instead of learning reading writing, arithmetic, mathematics, science, and history, and being taught about music, art, and literature, their children have been thoroughly indoctrinated through a divisive and politicized curriculum that is filled with deceptively benign buzzwords falsely implying tolerance and suggesting diversity, equity, and inclusion.

Reform takes time and if you want to do something immediately, homeschooling is the answer. There are co-ops offering home schooling outside the traditional public school systems. With technology and numerous resources both on and off line, you do not need to devote every single hour of your life to your children's home schooling. If you can devote much of your time at home to protecting your children's future, so much the better. But if not, there are still many ways to home school that can insure a positive and productive future for today's children and grandchildren on whom society will depend after they are grown.

9. *Develop a plan.* Learning is a never-ending process. Follow the guidelines of this book to develop a personal plan for self-education. The more you learn, the more you realize that you have to learn. The popular culture and the media will not provide you with guidelines, but once you are aware of the problem, you can act on your own and then eventually, act to help others explore new pathways in culture and the arts. Learn a new word each day. Only one new word can broaden your vocabulary and your fascination with language. Develop a reading list. A reading plan for a year or for a lifetime can set you on the path to discovering books, new and old, and ideas that you may never have imagined. Consider the classics, for they contain a lifetime of knowledge. You can take the same approach with music. Explore aspects of our musical traditions that may be new to you. Resources are available in libraries and online that can lead to new explorations in classical music, jazz, musical theater, and scores for motion pictures. The most important music for you to discover will probably have been written by people of whom you've heard little on radio and television in recent years. But developing a plan doesn't have to be boring or pedantic; it can (and should) be fun.

10. *Devote a specific amount of time each day to cultural enlightenment.* You'll be amazed at how much you can accomplish by simply scheduling a regular amount of time for personal study. Read one chapter of a book daily and in time, you'll be surprised how much information you can absorb. Schedule a specific amount of time to listen to music and after six months or a year, you'll find your outlook changing in a remarkable way. The key, of course, is not just spending time, but spending it the right way. If you already have a familiarity with music, books, and art that express the great traditions and values, there is still much to learn.

But if you have missed the opportunity to acquaint yourself with such works, it is never too late to begin.

The processes of learning and discovery can be a private delight enriching your life. Sometimes, however, it can totally change your life. In 1965, Bob Timberlake was twenty-eight years old, married with three children and a job in the family gas company in his hometown, Lexington, North Carolina. He had never studied art or frequented galleries of museums. But his life changed when he read an article on the painter Andrew Wyeth in *Life* magazine. He was so inspired by Wyeth's paintings that he suddenly felt he was meant to become an artist. In a few years, Timberlake was indeed looking at many paintings in art galleries and prestigious museums: his own. With the encouragement of Andrew Wyeth, he became internationally acclaimed as a realist painter. Although his work attracted the attention and praise of the rich and famous, he never forgot his North Carolina roots. He spent time with Presidents Jimmy Carter and Ronald Reagan, and was even invited to Buckingham Palace to give advice on art to Britain's Prince Charles, whom he described as someone who would fit right in at Whitley's Barbeque in Lexington. His work always reflected the values that meant the most to him: love, family, and home.

Richard Gill could have been voted the least likely person to become an opera star. He was a forty-year-old college professor who knew little about opera. Gill was an accomplished academic; he had studied at Oxford, he taught for many years at Harvard, and wrote highly respected books on economics. But the pressures and demands of these achievements resulted in a bad habit. He smoked two and a half packs of cigarettes daily. He decided to quit smoking and to be sure he didn't return to tobacco, he took singing lessons from Herbert Mayer, a prominent vocal coach in New York. The first lesson didn't start promisingly. Gill sang *Drink to Me Only with Thine Eyes*, and his teacher responded by shouting at him "Stop, I can't stand it!" But within a few years, while on sabbatical in England, he auditioned at Covent Garden and on his return to the United States, he became an acclaimed operatic bass. Gill's desire to quit smoking led him in a totally unexpected direction; he sang at the New York City Opera and later at the Metropolitan Opera. It was not unusual for Gill to discover characters in classic operas for the first time by singing the roles himself. He had never seen performances of some of the operas before. Yet he shared the stage with the world's most celebrated opera stars, including Plácido Domingo, Kiri Te Kanawa, Shirley Verrett, and Beverly Sills.

Of course, not everyone who tries a hand at music, writing, or painting becomes a famous musician or a best-selling novelist. But the desire to learn, to explore, to improve, can lead you in directions that you might never otherwise anticipate or imagine.

11. *Use the new media to discover the best of the past, present, and future, and explore the arts on your own.* The existence of the Internet and new technologies make it possible for anyone to access great books, music, and art. For minimum expense, you can become aware of the work created by men and women of our past and present who are likely to be ignored in today's celebrity culture.

You may not become a famous writer like Ray Bradbury, an artist like Bob Timberlake, a composer like Roy Harris, or a basso profundo like Richard Gill. You may not even want to write books, play an instrument, or paint. But like Ray Bradbury, you can go to the library, a school from which you may never want to graduate. Of course today, there are online libraries with access to incredible amounts of printed, audio, and video information. You may not want to start your own school or develop your own creative talents. But the very fact that you explore and help preserve our cultural heritage means you are not only doing yourself a favor, but helping others as well. You will be opening doors for yourself that you may never have thought existed and there is no telling where such open doors will lead when you walk through them. You will be helping others do the same thing. There is no single list of books, recordings, or works of art that represent an automatic solution. Your best opportunity for self-education may not be the same as the best opportunity for someone else. Each individual is different. But there is something new each of us can learn daily, regardless of whether we are beginning or simply continuing something we have done all of our lives.

For some readers, the whole idea of a cultural crisis and the need for solutions may be new and startling. For many others, the problem of losing the best of our past and the challenge of a solution may seem daunting. If our times seem discouraging to you, remember that you are not alone. There are legions of others who may not only share your concern, but also your enthusiasm, if you commit yourself to taking action. Finally, conserving our culture should never be perceived as only an act of preserving the past. The world is not merely a museum; there are countless creative men and women of all ages today whose imagination and talent will yield a rich cultural legacy for the years ahead, if only they are given the opportunity.

No one can conserve our culture for us; we must do it ourselves. This task will not be easy. There will be obstacles along the way. We shouldn't assume that we will win every battle or succeed at every task. Instead of being foolishly optimistic or wildly pessimistic, we can be, in the words of Richard Armour, "realists with dreams." No one can give you a perfect path to follow that will lead to an appreciation of our cultural heritage. This book is not intended as an end, but a beginning. Its purpose is not to provide you with all the necessary answers, for that would be impossible and pretentious. Its purpose is to inspire you to begin asking yourself and others the right questions. The best of the past, which shouldn't be forgotten, the best of the present, which shouldn't be ignored, and the best of the future, which shouldn't remain undiscovered, are all waiting for you. Mark! My Words.

INDEX

F

T

Y

Z

ENDNOTES

[1] Udall, Stewart L. *The Quiet Crisis.* New York: Holt, Rinehart, and Winston, 1963.

[2] Allen, Steve. *Dumbth.* Amherst, New York: Prometheus Books, 1998.

[3] Ellison, Harlan. "Harlan Ellison's Watching." *Sci-Fi Buzz.* The Kilimanjaro Corporation, 1996.

[4] Corwin, Norman. *Holes in a Stained Glass Window.* Secaucus, New Jersey: Lyle Stuart, 1978.

[5] Pearcey, Nancy. *Saving Leonardo.* Nashville, Tennessee: B&H Publishing Group, 2010.

[6] McCullough, David. "Knowing History and Knowing Who We Are." *Imprimis,* Vol. 34, Number 5, April 2005.

[7] Bennett, William J. *Our Sacred Honor.* New York: Simon and Schuster, 1997.

[8] Lewyn, Helena. "Must Music Be Edited?" *Music and Dance in California and the West.* Hollywood, California: Bureau of Musical Research, 1948.

[9] Thomas, Patrick. *Some Fine Music Composers - One Composer's Selection.* Wollongong, NSW, Australia: Wirripang, 2013

[10] Hendrickson, Robert. *Facts on File Encyclopedia of Words and Phrase Origins.* New York: Facts on File, 2008.

[11] Halpern, Jake. *Fame Junkies: The Hidden Truth Behind America's Favorite Addiction.* Boston: Houghton, Mifflin, 2007.

---

[12] Epstein, Joseph. "The Culture of Celebrity: Let Us Now Praise Famous Airheads." T*he Weekly Standard*, October 15, 2005.

[13] de la Vega, Aurelio. "The Age They Wanted to Erase." *Herencia Review, Vol. 9, No. 1, Spring 2003.*

[14] Kirk, Russell. *The Wise Men Know What Wicked Things Are Written in the Sky.* Washington, D.C. : Regnery Publishing, 1988.

[15] Johnson, Paul. *Heroes: From Alexander the Great and Julius Caesar to Churchill and De Gaulle.* New York: Harper Collins, 2007.

[16] Johnson, Paul. *Creators: From Chaucer and Dürer to Picasso and Disney.* New York: Harper, Collins 2006.

[17] Newman, Edwin. *Strictly Speaking, Will America be the Death of English?* Indianapolis, Indiana: Bobbs-Merrill, 1974.

[18] Lyall, Sarah. *The Anglo Files: A Field Guide to the British.* New York: W.W. Norton & Co., 2008.

[19] Florey, Kitty Burns. *Sister Bernadette's Barking Dog: The Quirky History and Lost Art of Diagramming Sentences.* New York: Houghton Mifflin Harcourt, 2007.

[20] Lutz, William. *Doublespeak.* New York: Harper & Row, 1989.

[21] Armour, Richard. *Educated Guesses.* Santa Barbara, California: Woodbridge Press, 1983

[22] Sokol, Alan, "Transgressing the Boundaries: Towards a Transformative Hermeneutics of Quantum Gravity." *Social Text* #46/47, pp. 217-252 (spring/summer 1996).

[23] Boren, James. *When in Doubt, Mumble.* New York: Van Nostrand Reinhold, 1972.

[24] Boren, James. *Fuzzify.* McLean, Virginia: EPM Publications, 1987.

[25] Nickles, Harry G. *The Dictionary of Do's and Don'ts.* New York: McGraw-Hill, 1974.

[26] Ehrlich, Eugene. *Amo, Amas, Amat and More: How to Use Latin to Your Own Advantage and to the Astonishment of Others.* New York: Harper & Row, 1985.

[27] Carroll, Lewis. *Alice in Wonderland.* London: Macmillan, 1865.

[28] Carroll, Lewis. *Through the Looking Glass and What Alice Found There.* London: Macmillan, 1871.

[29] Buckley, William F., Jr. *The Lexicon: A Cornucopia of Wonderful Words for the Inquisitive Word Lover.* San Diego, California: Harcourt, 1996.

[30] Buckley, William F., Jr. *Rumbles Left and Right.* New York: G.P. Putnam's Sons, 1963.

[31] Noonan, Peggy. *What I Saw at the Revolution.* New York: Random House, 1990.

[32] Ravitch, Diane. *The Language Police.* New York: Alfred A. Knopf, 2003.

[33] Allen, Steve. *Vulgarians at the Gate.* Amherst. New York: Prometheus Books, 2001.

[34] Hughes, Geoffrey. *Swearing: A Social History of Foul Language, Oaths and Profanity in English.* New York: Penguin, 1998.

[35] Twitchell, James B. *Carnival Culture: The Trashing of Taste in America.* New York: Columbia University Press, 1992.

[36] Jeffreys, Allan. "Adult Language Is Anything But." *The Pilot.* May 22, 2011.

[37] Buono, Victor. *It Could Be Verse.* Los Angeles: Nash Publishing, 1972.

[38] McWhorter, John. *Doing Our Own Thing: The Degradation of Language and Music and Why We Should, Like, Care.* New York: Gotham, 2003.

[39] Alamo, Hector Luis. "The X-Ing of Language: The Case AGAINST 'Latinx'." *Mano,* August 12, 2020.

[40] Furedi, Frank, "'English operated as a language of the coloniser,' students at top university that produced several world-renowned authors are told." *Daily Mail,* July 27, 2021

[41] Bukovsky, Vladimir, "Opting Out of All Utopias." Interview with Derek Turner. *Right Now Magazine.* January-March 2001.

[42] Krylov, Anna. "The Peril of Politicizing Science." *Journal of Physical Chemistry.* June 10,2021

[43] Bertman, Stephen. *Cultural Amnesia.* New York: Praeger Publishers, 2000.

[44] Hanson, Victor Davis. "Don't Know Much About Geography." *National Review,* August 15, 2013.

[45] Kimball, Roger. "Professor of Contempt." *National Review*, February 3, 2020

[46] Grabar, Mary. *Debunking the 1619 Project: Exposing the Plan to Divide America.* Washington, D.C.: Regnery Publishing, 2021

[47] Wood, Peter W. *1620: A Critical Response to the 1619 Project.* New York: Encounter Books, 2020.

[48] Berlin, Irving. "God Bless America" © renewed 1965, 1966 *The Complete Lyrics of Irving Berlin,* edited by Robert Kimball and Linda Berlin Emmet. New York: Alfred A. Knopf, 2001.

[49] Wittman, Robert K. *Priceless.* New York: Crown, 2010.

[50] O'Sullivan, John. "Musical Jingoism." *National Review,* August 29,2020.

[51] Armour, Richard. *It All Started with Columbus.* New York: Mc-Graw Hill, 1961.

[52] Meotti, Giulio. "When Everyone Kneels, Who Will Stand Up for Western History and Culture?" Gatestone Institute, June 21, 2020.

[53] Hart, Jeffrey. *When the Going Was Good.* New York: Better Books, 1983.

[54] Simon, John. *Paradigms Lost.* New York: Clarkson N. Potter, 1976.

[55] Woolf, Virginia. *The Death of the Moth and Other Essays.* New York: Harcourt, Inc., 1942.

[56] Macdonald, Dwight. "A Theory of Popular Culture." *Diogenes*, 1953.

[57] Thackeray, William Makepeace. *The Book of Snobs.* London: Punch, 1848.

[58] Sowell, Thomas. *Intellectuals and Society.* New York: Basic Books, 2009.

[59] Udall, Stewart L. "A Letter to My Grandchildren." *Santa Fe Conservation Trust.* www.sfct.org.

[60] Swift, Jonathan. *Gulliver's Travels. (Travels Into Several Remote Nations of the World).* London: Benjamin Motte, 1724.

[61] Hodgart, Matthew. *A New Voyage to the Country of the Houyhnhnms.* New York: G.P. Putnam's Sons, 1970.

[62] Pleasants, Henry. *The Agony of Modern Music.* New York: Simon and Schuster, 1955.

[63] Ansermet, Ernest. *Les fondements de la musique dans la conscience humaine.* Neuchâtel, Switzerland: La Baconnière, 1961.

[64] Wild, Earl. *A Walk on the Wild Side.* Palm Springs, California: Ivory Classics Foundation, 2011.

[65] Reilly, Robert. *Surprised by Beauty.* Washington, D.C.: Morley Books, 2002.

[66] Holmes, Thom. "Robert Ashley: Built for Speed." *Wire,* issue *234,* 2003.

[67] Johnson, Julian. *Who Needs Classical Music?: Cultural Choice and Musical Value.* New York: Oxford University Press, 2002.

[68] Babbitt, Milton. "Who Cares If You Listen?" *High Fidelity,* 1953.

[69] Simmons, Walter. *Voices in the Wilderness.* Lanham, Maryland: Scarecrow Press, 2004.

[70] Rózsa, Miklós. *Double Life.* New York: Hippocrene, 1982..

[71] Gillespie, John Birks "Dizzy," with Fraser, Al. *To Be or Not to Bop.* New York: Doubleday,1979.

[72] Wilder, Alec. *American Popular Song: The Great Innovators 1900-1950.* New York: Oxford University Press, 1972.

[73] Reich, Charles. *The Greening of America.* New York: Random House, 1970.

[74] Bloom, Allan. *The Closing of the American Mind.* New York: Simon and Schuster, 1987.

[75] Jeffreys, Allan. "Goodbye to the Music of Broadway." *The Pilot,* June 27, 2010.

[76] Stone, Desmond. *Alec Wilder in Spite of Himself, A Life of the Composer.* New York: Oxford University Press, 1996.

[77] Tormé, Mel. *My Singing Teachers: Reflections on Singing Popular Music.* New York: Oxford University Press, 1994.

[78] Falcone, Vincent, and Popyk, Bob. *Frankly Just Between Us: My Life Conducting Frank Sinatra's Music.* Milwaukee, Wisconsin: Hal Leonard, 2005.

[79] Ingraham, Laura. *Of Thee I Zing.* New York: Threshold Editions, 2011.

[80] Ewell, Philip. "Music Theory's White Racial Frame." *Music Theory On Line,* June 2020.

[81] Bork, Robert. *Slouching Towards Gomorrah.* New York: Regan Books, 1996.

[82] Jones, Natalie. *The Power of Culture: The Michaela Way.* (ed. Katharine Birbalsingh). Woodbridge, UK: John Catt Educational Ltd., 2020

[83] Mac Donald, Heather. "Classical Music's Suicide Pact." *City Journal,* Summer 2021

[84] Johanningmeier, Robert. *The 'Art' of Investing While Collecting.* Carlsbad, New Mexico: Art and Communication, 1992.

[85] Cox, Kenyon. "Two Ways of Painting." *Metropolitan Museum of Art Bulletin,* 1912.

[86] Kimball, Roger. *Art's Progress: The Challenge of Tradition in an Age of Celebrity.* Chicago: Ivan R. Dee, 2004.

[87] Wolfe, Tom. *The Painted Word.* New York: Farrar, Strauss & Giroux, 1975.

[88] Wolfe, Tom. *From Bauhaus to Our House.* New York: Bantam, 1999.

[89] Kimball, Roger. "The /Art World vs. the World of Art." *The New Criterion,* December 2, 2009.

[90] Johnson, Paul. *Art: A New History.* New York: Harper Collins, 2003.

[91] Covino, Frank. *Controlled Painting.* Cincinnati, Ohio: North Light Publishers, 1982.

[92] Mims, D. Jeffrey. "Distinguishing the Essential from the Accidental." *Slow Painting: A Deliberate Renaissance.* Atlanta, Georgia: Oglethorpe University Museum, 1995.

[93] Munson Lynne, *Exhibitionism: Art in an Era of Intolerance.* Chicago: Ivan R. Dee, 2000.

[94] Scruton, Roger. *Culture Counts.* New York: Encounter Books, 2007.

[95] Saatchi, Charles. "The Hideousness of the Art World." London: *The Guardian*, December 2, 2011.

[96] Flesch, Rudolf. *Why Johnny Can't Read.* New York: Harper & Brothers, 1955.

[97] Flesch, Rudolf. *Why Johnny STILL Can't Read: A New Look at the Scandal of Our Schools.* New York: Harper Collins, 1981.

[98] Chall, Jeanne. *Learning to Read: The Great Debate.* Ft.Worth, Texas: Harcourt Brace College Publishers, 1996.

[99] Biddle, RiShawn, "The Kids Can't Read." *The American Spectator,* June 21, 2010.

[100] Sykes, Charles J. *Dumbing Down Our Kids.* New York: St. Martin's Press, 1995.

[101] Kantor, Elizabeth. *The Politically Incorrect Guide to English and American Literature.* Washington, D.C.: Regnery Publishing, 2006.

[102] Brophy, Brigid, Levey, Michael, and Osborne, Charles. *Fifty Works of English Literature We Could Do Without.* New York: Stein & Day, 1968.

[103] Ferguson, Andrew. *Crazy U: One Dad's Crash Course in Getting His Kid into College.* New York: Simon and Schuster, 2011.

[104] Zmirak, John. "The Top 5 Lamest Core Courses," *Intercollegiate Review,* February 4, 2013.

[105] Arnn, Larry P. "The Crisis and Politics of Higher Education." *Imprimis,* Vol. 35, Number 11, November 2006.

[106] Carr, Nicholas. "Is Google Making Us Stupid?" *The Atlantic,* July-August 2008.

[107] Gomez, Jeff. *Print is Dead.* New York: Palgrave Macmillan, 2007.

[108] Birkerts, Sven. *The Gutenberg Elegies: The Fate of Reading in an Electronic Age.* New York: Faber & Faber, 2006.

[109] Gordon, John Steele. "The End of the Book." *The American (Journal of the American Enterprise Institute)* , May 21, 2011.

[110] Bradbury, Ray. *Fahrenheit 451.* New York: Simon and Schuster, 1950.

[111] Crenshaw, Ben R. "Why You Shouldn't 'Decolonize' Your Bookshelf." *The Federalist,* June 16, 2020.

[112] Stepman, Jarrett. "Instead of 'Decolonizing Your Bookshelf,' Let's Halt the Closing of the American Mind." *The Daily Signal,* June 22, 2020.

[113] Crouch, Stanley. "On the Corner: The Sellout of Miles Davis." *The All-American Skin Game.* New York: Pantheon, 1995.

[114] Shearing, George, with Shipton, Alyn. *Lullaby of Birdland.* New York: Continuum, 2004.

[115] Swift, Jonathan. *Gulliver's Travels (Travels Into Several Remote Nations of the World).* London: Benjamin Motte, 1724.

[116] Slonimsky, Nicolas. *The Lexicon of Musical Invective.* New York: Coleman-Ross Company, Inc., 1953.

[117] Munson, Lynne, *Exhibitionism: Art in an Era of Intolerance.* Chicago: Ivan R. Dee, 2000.

[118] Ross, Alex. "A Female Deer? Looking for Sex in the Sound of Music." *Lingua Franca, Vol. 4, No. 5,* July/August 1994.

[119] Mac Donald, Heather. "Making Beethoven Woke." *City Paper,* April 5, 2022.

[120] Kanitz, Ernest. "The Inside Story." *Music and Dance in Southern California and the West.* Hollywood, California: Bureau of Musical Research, 1948.

[121] Kirk, Russell. *The Conservative Mind: From Burke to Eliot.* Chicago: Regnery Publishing, 1953.

[122] Hudson, Deal W. *How to Keep From Losing Your Mind.* Charlotte, NC: TAN Books, 2019.

[123] Cowan, Louise. "The Necessity of the Classics." *Intercollegiate Review.* Fall 2003.

[124] Buck, Daniel, "How to Incentivize the Classics." *National Review,* June 6, 2021

[125] Editors of *GQ.* "21 Books You Don't Have to Read." *GQ,* April 19, 2018

[126] Hilditch, Cameron. "Without the Classics, Our History is Incomprehensible." *National Review,* June 4, 2021.

[127] Hanson, Victor Davis. "Tuning Out Wokeism." *American Greatness,* May 9, 2021.

[128] Semes, Steven W. *The Future of the Past: A Conservation Ethic for Architecture, Urbanism, and Historic Preservation.* New York: W.W. Norton, 2009.

[129] Colon, Alicia. "Pop Culture Killing Classic Traditions." *The Irish Examiner.* January 4, 2011.

[130] Couch, Christina. "Roll Over Beethoven." *The Christian Science Monitor.* October 5, 2006.

[131] Schank, Roger. *The Connoisseur's Guide to the Mind: How We Think, How We Learn, and What It Means to Be Intelligent.* New York: Summit Books, 1991.

[132] Malkin, Michelle. "2 lazy 2 teach." *Townhall.com,* June 30, 2004.

[133] Morgenstern, Sheldon. *No Vivaldi in the Garage: A Requiem for Classical Music in North America.* Boston: Northeastern University Press, 2001.

[134] Will, George. "Readers' Block." *The Washington Post.* July 24, 2004.

[135] Peterson, Jordan. "Why I am no longer a tenured professor at the University of Toronto." *National Post,* January 9, 2022.

[136] Denby, David. *Great Books.* New York: Simon and Schuster, 1996.

[137] Mac Donald, Heather. "The Humanities Have Forgotten Their Humanity." *Wall Street Journal,* January 3, 2014

[138] Ellery, Ben. "Black Lives protests are a distraction, says head teacher Katharine Birbalsingh." *The Times*, August 5, 2020

[139] Raitchura, Pritesh. *The Power of Culture. The Michaela Way* (ed. Katharine Birbalsingh) Woodbridge, UK: John Catt Educational Ltd. 2020

[140] Komonchak, Joseph. "The Separation of Art and State." New York: *dotCommonweal*, July 23, 2009.

[141] Simon, Roger L. *Blacklisting Myself.* New York: Encounter Books, 2008.

[142] Wynter, Dana, *Other People Other Places, memories of four continents.* Ojai, California: Caladrius Press Dublin, 2005.

[143] Gore, Tipper. *Raising PG Rated Children in an X-Rated Society.* Nashville, Tennessee: Abingdon Press, 1987.

[144] Stein, Ben. *The View from Sunset Boulevard.* New York: Doubleday Anchor, 1980.

[145] Medved, Michael. *Hollywood vs. America: Popular Culture and the War on Traditional Values.* New York: Harper Collins Zondervan, 1992.

[146] Phillips, Julia. *You'll Never Eat Lunch in This Town Again.* New York: Random House, 1991.

[147] Loos, Anita. *Fate Keeps On Happening*. New York: Dodd, Mead & Company, 1984.

[148] Dunne, Philip. *Take Two: A Life in Movies and Politics.* New York: McGraw Hill in association with the San Francisco Book Company, 1980.

[149] Wainer, Alex. "No Singing, No Dancing." *Breakpoint Online.* 2000.

[150] Weingarten, Gene. "Pearls Before Breakfast." Washington, D.C.: The *Washington Post.* April 4, 2007.

[151] Sandke, Randall. *Where the Dark and the Light Folks Meet.* Lanham, Maryland: Scarecrow Press, 2010.

[152] Jackson, Maggie. *Distraction.* Amherst, New York:Prometheus House, 2009.

[153] Petrini, Carlo. *Slow Food Nation.* New York: Rizzoli, 2005.

[154] Fowles, Jib. *Television Viewers vs. Media Snobs.* New York: Stein & Day, 1982.

[155] Berger, Ben. *Attention Deficit Democracy: The Paradox of Civic Engagement.* Princeton, New Jersey: Princeton University Press, 2011.

[156] Richtel, Matt. "Grading the Digital School: In Classroom of Future, Stagnant Scores." *The New York Times*, September 3, 2011.

[157] Listfield, Emily. "Generation Wired." New York: *Parade*, October 9, 2011.

[158] Ring, Sara. "The Edutopia Poll." *Edutopia,* March 24, 2008.

[159] Bauerlein, Mark. *The Dumbest Generation.* New York: Jeremy P. Tarcher/Penguin, 2008.

[160] McLuhan, Marshall. *Understanding Media: The Extensions of Man.* New York: New American Library, 1964.

[161] Chesterton, Gilbert Keith. *What's Wrong with the World?* New York: Dodd, Mead, 1910.

[162] Allen, Steve. *Vulgarians at the Gate.* Amherst, New York: Prometheus Books, 2001.

[163] Gross, Ronald. *Peak Learning.* Reading, Massachusetts: Addison-Wesley, 1982.

[164] Gross, Ronald. *The Independent Scholar's Handbook.* Reading, Massachusetts: Addison-Wesley, 1982.

[165] Bennett, William J., Finn, Chester E., Jr., and Cribb, John T.E., Jr. *The Educated Child.* New York: The Free Press, 1999.

[166] Armour, Richard. *Through Darkest Adolescence.* New York: McGraw-Hill, 1963.

[167] Stern, Isaac, with Potok, Chaim. *My First 79 Years.* New York: Alfred A. Knopf, 1999.

[168] Davi, Robert. *Davi Sings Sinatra—On the Road to Romance.* Sun Lion Records, 2011.

Printed in Great Britain
by Amazon

36707166R00330